The Complete Works of
WASHINGTON
IRVING

Richard Dilworth Rust

General Editor

VOYAGES AND DISCOVERIES
OF
THE COMPANIONS OF COLUMBUS

Washington Irving

WASHINGTON IRVING

VOYAGES AND DISCOVERIES
OF THE
COMPANIONS OF COLUMBUS

Edited by
James W. Tuttleton

Twayne Publishers
Boston
1986

Published by Twayne Publishers

A Division of G. K. Hall & Co.

Copyright © 1986 by

G. K. Hall & Co.

The Complete Works of Washington Irving
Volume XII

CENTER FOR EDITIONS OF
AMERICAN AUTHORS

AN APPROVED TEXT

MODERN LANGUAGE
ASSOCIATION OF AMERICA

®

Library of Congress Cataloging in Publication Data

Irving, Washington, 1783–1859.
Voyages and discoveries of the companions of Columbus.

(The Complete works of Washington Irving; v. 12)
. America—Discovery and exploration—Spanish.
I. Tuttleton, James W.   II. Title.   III. Series:
Irving, Washington, 1783–1859.   Works.   1976; v. 12.
E123.I728   1986   970.01'6   85–28813
ISBN 0–8057–8517–5

In memory of

Henry A. Pochmann

ACKNOWLEDGMENTS

I wish to record here my gratitude for much valuable assistance I have received from many individuals and institutions. First, to Henry Pochmann for having conceived of and launched the editorial project that has resulted in *The Complete Works of Washington Irving*. Then to Hugh Holman, Lewis Leary, John McElroy, Richard Dilworth Rust, Herbert L. Kleinfield, and Edwin T. Bowden for their assistance with many questions about Irving's life, works, composition habits, texts, and contexts; to Andrew Myers and Saverio Procario of Sleepy Hollow Restorations and Sunnyside; to Jerry Stringer, Amy Tucker, Carole Rowe, Mary Tedeschi, Alice Theilheimer, and David DeVries for various assistance, including collating, typing, xeroxing, and manuscript crosschecking; and to the Research Council of the University of Wisconsin, the Research Council of New York University, and the American Philosophical Society, for financial assistance in the form of grants to microfilm, travel to manuscript collections, etc. I am particularly grateful to the National Endowment for the Humanities for an editorial grant made available to the Center for Editions of American Authors through the Modern Language Association. I wish also to thank Dean Norman F. Cantor of the Faculty of Arts and Science of New York University, as well as the research staffs of the Wisconsin Historical Society, the Humanities Research Center of the University of Texas, the Alderman Library and Clifton Waller Barrett Collections of the University of Virginia Library, the Elmer H. Bobst Library of New York University, the University of Wisconsin Library, the Fales Collection of New York University (especially the curator, Theodore Grieder), the Carl and Lily Pforzheimer Library (especially its curator, Donald Reiman), the New York Public Library (especially its Manuscripts and Rare Books Division and American History Division), the Berg Collection of the New York Public Library (especially the curator, Dr. Lola Szladits), and others who have given me innumerable helps and infinite patience and guidance in the preparation of this edition.

James W. Tuttleton
New York University

ILLUSTRATIONS

FRONTISPIECE

Washington Irving

From a drawing by David Wilkie, dated Seville, April 23, 1828, and engraved by H. H. Hall, reproduced in the *Life and Letters* by Pierre M. Irving.

MAP

Map Shewing the Discoveries made by the Companions of Columbus. Published as an illustration of *The Companions of Columbus* by John Murray, Albemarle Street, London, 1830, *page lvi–lvii.*

DEPOSITION

Testimony of Washington Irving about the composition, date, terms, and agreements touching *Companions of Columbus* in the Murray vs. Bohn lawsuit, dated September 22, 1850, *facing page liii.*

"Form of Requiring Entry of Proprietorship," John Murray's re-registration of copyright, October 29, 1850, *following page liv.*

CONTENTS

ALONZO DE OJEDA: HIS FIRST VOYAGE, IN WHICH HE WAS ACCOMPANIED BY AMERIGO VESPUCCI

ALONZO DE OJEDA: THIRD VOYAGE

DIEGO DE NICUESA

VASCO NUÑEZ DE BALBOA:
DISCOVERER OF THE PACIFIC OCEAN

EDITORIAL APPENDIX

INTRODUCTION

On January 30, 1826, at the age of forty-three, Irving was invited to Spain by Alexander Hill Everett of the American legation at Madrid. Everett's letter, offering Irving an appointment at the legation and a passport, also contained an important proposal: that Irving translate into English a recently published compilation of materials relating to Columbus's discovery of the New World. It was Fernandez de Navarrete's two-volume *Colección de los viages y descubrimientos, que hicieron por mar los españoles desde fines del siglo XV*.[1] Everett had read Navarrete's work on its publication in 1825 and had immediately recognized the importance of some of the records it contained—especially the journals of Columbus, abstracted by the Bishop de las Casas, as well as "a number of authentic documents connected with the same subject, many of which have never before been printed."[2]

Perhaps no one was better suited than Irving to present to the American people a translation in English of these significant records relating to the discovery and settlement of the New World. The task of translation, as well as the duties of the legation, offered no obstacle to Irving's acceptance, for he had undertaken the study of Spanish in 1824 in Paris and, in the following two years, had mastered the foreign language well enough to have accomplished an extensive survey of Spanish literature in the original. Moreover, Irving was at loose ends in 1826: he was

1. The full title of Navarrete's compilation may be translated "Collection of sea voyages and discoveries, made by the Spaniards, from towards the close of the 15th century—with various documents, hitherto unpublished, relating to the history of the Spanish marine, and the establishments of Spain in the Indies, arranged and illustrated by Don Martin Fernandez de Navarrete." Commissioned by the king and printed by the government, Navarrete's *Colección* appeared over an extended period in five volumes. Volumes 1 and 2 had appeared in 1825; they constitute the principal source for Irving's life of Columbus. Volume 3, published in 1829, contained additional documents relative to Columbus and accounts of the voyages of his companions; a minor source for *The Companions of Columbus*, this third volume also contained a discussion of Irving's life of Columbus, which had appeared in 1828. Volumes 4 and 5 appeared in 1837, long after Irving had concluded his Spanish writings of the first period and had returned to America.

2. A. H. Everett to Henry Clay, Madrid, March 25, 1826, United States Legation, Madrid, Official Papers, 1826 to 1827, no. 28, duplicate.

financially insecure, imaginatively depleted, melancholic, and in need of some peace and quiet—and rewarding but undemanding work. Yet serving on the staff of the legation and translating the new Spanish materials initiated an exhausting phase of Irving's career that would eventually cover a total of seven years in Spain and a number of books about the history, the myths, and the legends of her culture.

Reading Navarrete's two-volume collection, in the magnificent library of Obadiah Rich[3] in Madrid, Irving clearly saw that Navarrete's documents were too miscellaneous and disconnected to produce a translation which would enhance Irving's reputation. Nothing less than a full biography of Columbus, based on the raw materials in Navarrete's collection, but complemented by other sources, would do. This decision to write a full-scale biography, based on Navarrete's research, led Irving to other libraries and books relating to the life and times of Columbus. During the next three years, while he composed the biographies of Columbus and his companions, he was to exploit the manuscript and printed resources in Obadiah Rich's marvelous library of Spanish works in Madrid, in the library of the Jesuits' College of San Isidro, in the Archivo General de Indias at Seville, in the Biblioteca Colombina at Seville, and elsewhere. Nearly everywhere Irving went, however, the indefatigable Navarrete had preceded him, unearthing and exploiting documents descriptive of the maritime adventures of Columbus and his companions. The fruit of Irving's investigation into these Spanish manuscripts and books, some ninety in all, was *A History of the Life and Voyages of Christopher Columbus* (1828), published in four volumes in London by John Murray; *A Chronicle of the Conquest of Granada* (1829); *The Alhambra* (1832); *Mahomet and His Successors* (1850); a number of other miscellaneous Spanish writings; and, most important for our purposes, *Voyages and Discoveries of the Companions of Columbus* (1831), also first published by John Murray in London. Since Irving often shortened the title in his correspondence to *Companions of Columbus*, or *Companions*, these abbreviations will also be used throughout the Introduction and Textual Commentary.

The serious historical character of some of these books—particularly *Columbus* and *Companions*—represented a new literary departure for Irving, who was chiefly known in the 1820's for the whimsies of *The Sketch Book*; *Knickerbocker's History of New York*; *Letters of Jonathan*

---

3. Rich, the American consul at Madrid, provided Irving with an apartment in his home during the years 1826–1827. The value of his Spanish collection for Irving is suggested by the extensive catalogue "Manuscripts and Printed Books in Possession of Obadiah Rich, Esq.," printed by order of the House of Representatives of the U.S. Congress (20th Cong., 1st sess., Rept. 37, December 27, 1827, pp. 1–24).

Oldstyle, Gent; Bracebridge Hall; and *Tales of a Traveller.* In these Spanish histories Irving aspired to "weightier" productions which would identify him as a more "serious" man of letters. Suffering under the censure of some of his adverse critics, Irving nevertheless worried about the effect on his reputation of his new historical enterprises. Writing to Henry Brevoort on April 4, 1827, Irving observed: "I am now advancing towards the conclusion of my work [*Columbus*]. How it will please the public I cannot anticipate. I have lost confidence in the favorable disposition of my countrymen and look forward to cold scrutiny & stern criticism, and this is a line of writing in which I have not hitherto ascertained my own powers. Could I afford it I should like to write and to lay my writings aside when finished. There is an independent delight in study and in the creative exercise of the pen; we live in a world of dreams, but publication lets in the noisy rabble of the world and there is an end to our dreaming."[4]

But dream he did, extending his term in Spain beyond the date of the publication of *Columbus*, while he explored the manuscript and rare book riches of Madrid and Seville. As he awaited the British and American reaction to *Columbus*, Irving continued his studies for *Companions* in the libraries of Spain. His historical research, the patient work of reading, translating, collating texts, and composing *Companions*, all had the effect of calming and tranquillizing a writer who was often depressed and melancholic. In a letter to Prince Dolgorouki from Madrid, dated January 22, 1828, Irving writes:

As I live in the neighborhood of the library of the Jesuits College of St Isidro I pass most of my mornings there. You cannot think what a delight I feel in passing through its galleries filled with old parchment bound books. It is a perfect wilderness of curiosity to me. What a deep felt quiet luxury there is in delving into the rich ore of these old neglected volumes. How these hours of uninterrupted intellectual enjoyment, so tranquil and independent, repay one for the ennui and disappointment too often experienced in the intercourse of Society; how they serve to bring back the feelings into a harmonious tone, after being jarred and put all out of tune by the collisions with the world.[5]

Meanwhile, as he told Thomas W. Storrow in February, 1828, if *Columbus* "takes with the public its success will have a most favorable effect upon any thing I may afterwards produce."[6]

4. *Letters*, vol. 2, *1823–1838*, ed. Ralph M. Aderman, Herbert L. Kleinfield and Jenifer S. Banks (Boston: Twayne Publishers, 1979), p. 226.
5. Ibid., II, 266.
6. Ibid., II, 278.

In the course of more than three years, while Irving plumbed the old Spanish documents relative to Columbus, he assembled a vast quantity of material dealing with other exploratory voyages to the New World. Though much of it had an intrinsic interest of its own, these materials touching the voyages of the companions of Columbus had no direct pertinence to the *Columbus* volumes. What to do with them constituted a serious aesthetic and organizational problem. As he wrote *Columbus* the structure of the work became rapidly strained with the freight of sheer information about all of the other actors in the New World drama—King Ferdinand, Bishop Fonseca, Roldan, Ojeda, Nicuesa, and the others. Irving's literary method required several lines of narrative action inconvenient to interweave, and *Columbus* suffers from considerable doubling back and forth while Irving develops now one episode only to drop it so that the action may be advanced elsewhere by another.

The fortunes of Ojeda, Nicuesa, the Pinzons, Balboa, Valdivia, Ponce de Leon, and others constituted separate stories, interesting in their own right but peripheral to the story of Columbus, and in any event extending beyond the fate of the admiral, who died in 1506. Ever anxious to explore whatever might be turned to profit and literary applause—especially since *Columbus* appeared to be on its way to success—Irving wisely decided to write another book narrating the adventures and voyages of these companions of Columbus. Apparently the suggestion to exploit them in this way came from his brother, who was with him in Spain, for Pierre M. Irving calls *Companions* "a work to which he had been prompted by Peter."[7]

Columbus was published in 1828. As Irving awaited and then savored the reviews, he lingered in Spain in order to research and assemble the materials for *Companions* and some of his other Spanish works. The sheer volume of research to be accomplished was one of the problems delaying completion of *Companions* and his anticipated departure from Spain. More serious, however, was the government's suspicion of foreigners, particularly those interested in book trade and in libraries and research. Americans like Everett and Rich might open their rare book resource to Irving, but certain Spanish books were arbitrarily proscribed by the Inquisition and libraries were often closed to the foreign researcher. As he complained to Everett from Seville, on April 23, 1828: "I have visited the Archives of the Indias and presented a letter of introduction to the chief. . . . He tells me, however, that it is necessary to have an express order from the King before I can inspect the archives

---

7. Pierre M. Irving, *The Life and Letters of Washington Irving* (New York: G. P. Putnam, 1864), II, 447 (hereafter cited as PMI).

or make any extracts or copies. I wish very much to examine some documents prior to publishing the Second edition of my work. Can you, without inconvenience, in your intercourse at court, *proporcionar* me an order of the kind?"[8]

Getting royal permission to use the Archives of the Indias and assembling the materials for the story of his maritime explorers took longer than Irving anticipated. He was to spend a full year in Seville, working in the archives at the Biblioteca Colombina.[9] As he awaited the king's permission, he also assembled notes for *Granada, The Alhambra,* and *Mahomet.* But the completion of *Companions* and the revisions for the second edition of *Columbus* were impeded by another factor. In Madrid, Navarrete had announced the forthcoming publication of the third volume of his *Colección.* Irving had to see this third volume before he could conclude *Companions* or correct *Columbus,* which in the first edition was full of gross factual and typographical errors. And, more important to our purposes, Navarrete's third volume contained important documents relative to the companions of Columbus without which he could not complete this new work to which Peter had prompted him.

Throughout the year of 1828, Irving vacillated as to whether he should finish the volume of voyages or await Navarrete's publication. Writing to Everett from Seville, on May 7, 1828, Irving observes: "I fear the third volume of Mr. Navarrete will be as long in making its appearance as the Jewish Messiah." And he adds, probably referring to the former, "It is not, however, a matter of much moment." This last remark may be taken as an instance of Irving's continuing need to devalue the significance of Navarrete's research in the primary documents of New World discoveries. Irving concludes with his eye on his readers: "The documents are probably of greater importance in the eyes of Mr. Navarrete than they would be in the eyes of the public, and I believe I have already either ascertained or divined the substance of them."[10]

What he might be obliged to divine in the substance of this document not yet published plagued Irving for the next year. In the meantime, he sought to anticipate Navarrete's third volume by retracing the Spanish scholar's research in Seville. Irving had so many literary projects under way in 1828 that the vagueness of his letters is sometimes problematical. But the phrase "another work," in his letter to Storrow, dated June 20, 1828, may refer to *Companions*: "I am remaining at Seville correcting Columbus for a Second edition and preparing another work for the press. It is necessary for me to remain where I can have access

8. *Letters,* II, 306.
9. PMI, II, 310.
10. *Letters,* II, 309.

to the Spanish libraries, though the heat begins to grow extremely oppressive."[11]

The heat of the summer, as well as the delays in Navarrete's third volume and in the king's permission to use the archives, eventually drove Irving from Seville to the sea. Wishing to see the place where Columbus and his companions had taken ship for the New World, Irving journeyed down to the little port of Palos on August 11, 1828. There he met the descendants of the family of Martin Alonzo Pinzon, visited the convent of La Rabida, and gazed out over the much deteriorated little port from which such momentous discoveries had been launched more than three centuries before. A few days later, in a letter to Everett from Seville, dated August 20, 1828, Irving records:

Last week I made a journey to Palos, to visit the place from whence Columbus sailed on his first voyage of discovery. The journey was rather rough, and I had to put up with the usual evils of Spanish posadas, but I was extremely gratified. I had a letter to one of the descendants of the Pinzons, a most respectable and pleasant old gentleman, seventy-two years of age, healthful, cheerful, and active. He entertained me with great hospitality, made me acquainted with his family connection, and accompanied me to every place memorable in the history of the expedition. The Pinzon family is still numerous and apparently flourishing, and ever since the time of Columbus has continued in the neighborhood, principally at Moguer, where the best houses are occupied by members of the family, and they, for centuries, have filled the posts of trust and dignity of the little city. I visited Palos, the convent of La Rabida, the church at which Columbus read the order for the caravels, the church where he watched and prayed all night after his return, according to a vow which he had made in a storm at sea; in short, I sought everything that had any connection with him and his history.[12]

Back in Seville, Irving received a packet from Everett on Saturday, August 16, 1828, containing a letter from the secretary of state, "announcing the Kings permission for me to inspect the Archives of the Indias...."[13] Irving lost no time. On Monday he presented the letter to the archivist, Don Jose de Higuera y Lara, and commenced his long-delayed inspection of the Columbus papers there. In subsequent days,

11. Ibid., II, 318.
12. PMI, II, 339.
13. *Washington Irving Diary: Spain, 1828–1829,* ed. Clara Louisa Penney (New York: Hispanic Society of America, 1926), p. 59 (hereafter cited as Penney).

Irving's diary entries tell the story: "At Archives all morng."[14] And when he was not at the royal archives, he was at the cathedral library.

For the next few months Irving worked indefatigably in the Columbian archives verifying and correcting *Columbus* for a second edition and assembling notes and translations for the *Companions*. This research, exhausting in itself, was complemented by his extensive correspondence. One of his favorite correspondents was the young and lovely Mlle. Antoinette Bollvillier, niece of Mme. D'Oubril. To Antionette Irving began a letter in September describing, as in the earlier letter to Everett, his journey to Palos. Midway, the romantic possibilities of this pilgrimage to the source of New World exploration struck Irving. And he expanded the letter into a full-scale essay. His journal entry for Thursday, September 25, 1828, records: "All day writing acct of visit to Palos which I finish by Evg."[15] There is no evidence that Irving sought separate publication for this essay, which was eventually appended to *Companions of Columbus*. In any event, it is so charming and pleasantly written that a number of publishers later lifted it from the *Companions* and reprinted it with the appendixes to *Columbus*, where, perhaps, it more properly belongs.

Meanwhile, the journey and the writing of this little essay must have

14. Ibid., p. 60.
15. Ibid., p. 70. Irving's diary for 1828–1829 contains extracts descriptive of Irving's trip to Palos and his meeting with the Pinzon family. In view of the romantic picture of this experience recorded in "A Visit to Palos," these more prosaic entries have their interest: "Juan Fernandez Pinzon venerable man 72. Seated with family in little court with flowers, fresco. 5 brothers. One comes in who was in the navy, retired about 22 years since. Numerous family. Supper. Noise of closed doors. Maid servants demand[g] keys. Sons & daughters of him & his brothers. Send to church of St Clara to ask friar to be at La Rabida early in morning. Escribano of Palos dead who was very curious about Palos ec and had papers relative to its history. In the book of Pinzon he says that Columbus called consultation. The Pinzons determined to proceed. Columbus fired upon them." For Wednesday, August 13, 1828, Irving records: "Drove to Palos with Don Juan Fernandez. . . . Palos a wretched hamlet on hill distant from river, ruins of moorish castle & Village church, an arch of Mosque. When the Pinzons came to their estate have to bring every thing with them. Arms given to the Pinzones 3 armed caravels on the sea, from each a hand pointing out the first land discovered, & per orla of the said shield unas uncoras y unos corazones. . . . La Rabida, two internal cloisters, convent silent, cells of monks closed, solitary cat—scattered fig tree or two—olives, ec show where had been an orchard. The French destroyed it, which is enough to account for never repairing the garden. A few books piled in the corner of a room & covered with dust are all that remain of a once tolerable library—Church—Miraculous image of Virgin, before it was found this was called La Rabia from frequent madness of dogs & people, since it has been altered to Rabida—madness having disappeared" (ibid., pp. 50–54).

rekindled Irving's intention to complete the volume of minor voyages. His journal entry for Sunday, September 28, 1828, indicates the commencement of the story of Balboa: "Began MS. of Vasco Nuñez, write but little. . . ."[16] On Monday, September 29 and in successive days, he is "all day at Vasco Nuñez. . . . Work at Vasco Nuñez . . . Vasco Nuñez all day, write till 1 oclock at night . . . Vasco Nuñez all day." On Saturday, October 4, 1828, he records: "Vasco Nuñez, finish it towards evening."[17]

On Monday, October 6, he is back at work on the voyages: "Until 8 evg at Juan Ponce de Leon, call at John Shaws, resume writing until nearly 12 oclock at night." By Tuesday he is finished: "Write all day at Juan Ponce & finish it. Evg at home." The next morning he is back at work: "Wednesday 8. Write at Alonzo de Ojeda. . . . All day writing at Ojeda, at home all evg." On Friday, October 10: "All day at Ojeda, finish it & commence Nicuessa." On Saturday he is "occupied all day on Narrative of Nicuessa & until late in Evg."[18] Thus throughout September and October, Irving worked indefatigably on the voyages, assembling his material and drafting chapters on the individual explorers. On Tuesday, October 28, just before leaving for Cadiz, Irving records in his diary: "In Evg pack up trunks & burn papers."[19] These papers perhaps constituted his working translations, paraphrases, and early drafts of these mariners' biographies. But the accounts so concluded during this period were far from finished. Much revision yet remained to be accomplished, and further research was still required to verify his facts and suppositions. As he wrote to Henry Brevoort on December 20, 1828, "I am lingering here in Andalusia . . . and occupying myself with researches in the old Cathedral library and the archives of the Indias. All the Summer months have been passed by me in the country, first in a cottage about two miles from Seville & afterwards at a small country house near port St. Mary."[20]

Irving's final journal entry for the year 1828 indicates his sense of accomplishment during this extraordinary period of research and writing and his hopes for the future: "Thus ends the year—tranquilly. It has been one of much literary application, and generally speaking one of the most tranquil in spirit of my whole life, the literary success of the Hist of Columb has been greater that I anticipated and gives me hopes that I have executed something which may have greater duration than I

16. Ibid., pp. 70–71.
17. Ibid.
18. Ibid., p. 73.
19. Ibid., p. 76.
20. *Letters*, II, 367.

anticipate for my works of mere imagination. I look forward without any sanguine anticipations, but without the gloom that has sometimes oppressed me. The only future event from which I promise myself any extraordinary gratification is the return to my native country, which I trust will now soon take place."[21] This extraordinary gratification, however, was not soon to occur, for Navarrete's third volume had still not yet appeared; and, without it, *Companions* was still incomplete.

In his journal entry for November 12, 1828, Irving had noted that "Every one in Spain has his list of grievances to complain of."[22] Chief on Irving's list was Navarrete's delay. But another grievance soon presented itself. As a preparation for revising and correcting his completed biography of Vasco Nuñez de Balboa, which had been researched at the Biblioteca Colombina, Irving called at the Archives of the Indias to inspect documents relative to Balboa which he had not yet seen. His diary entry indicates his fate: "cannot examine the papers of Balboa without express order...."[23] The king's permission, earlier given, had stipulated only the documents relative to Columbus. And Jose de Higuera y Lara, the archivist, was adamant. Writing to Everett on February 14, 1829, from Seville, Irving expressed a disappointment which clearly implied how much such delays were costing him. "I have been disappointed in my hopes of being able to make researches in the archives of the Indias. I find the permission was confined to the papers relating to Columbus, and the keeper of the archives, though extremely civil and friendly, is rigorous in obeying the very letter of his instructions. I found it impossible, therefore, to obtain an inspection of other papers relative to the early discoveries, and have not thought it worth while to make further application."[24]

If the royal archives were closed to him, how much more important to Irving would be Navarrete's third volume—which reprinted those very papers to which he had been denied access. In the meantime, he was forced to rely on the resources of the Cathedral library in Seville. His journal entry for Tuesday, January 13, 1829, reads: "At the Library with Escribano making notes from Oviedo for Vasquo Nunez." Toward the end of the week he is still making "notes & alterations of Vasco Nunez."[25]

Irving's diary for the year 1829 indicates that on February 4 Irving

21. Penny, p. 90.
22. Ibid., p. 80.
23. Ibid., p. 92.
24. PMI, II, 370.
25. Penney, pp. 93–94.

wrote to Prince Dolgorouki and "recd parcel from him with book of Navarrete ec."[26] This must have been some book other than the third volume of the *Colección*. For Irving's letter observes: "What you mention of Mr Navarretes third volume is extremely tantalizing. It has been on the eve of publication for eighteen months; I am continually assured that there are matters in it important for me to know for the Second edition of my work, yet this third volume never makes its appearance, and my Second edition, I believe, has already gone to press in England, and perhaps is entirely printed. Cannot you procure me a sight of the work as it is, without the preface. I should shew it to no one, and make no use of it that could be unsatisfactory to Mr. Navarrete."[27]

At the end of March, 1829, Irving was still without the necessary third volume and ignorant of whether a revised second edition of *Columbus* had gone to press in London. Meanwhile, the manuscript of *Companions*, the first draft of which had been entirely finished on March 3, languished in his trunk for the vital verification that only Navarrete could provide. In a letter to John Murray II, Irving wrote from Seville on March 21: "The third volume of Sen Navarrete's collection of voyages is about coming out. In this I find there will be facts and documents concerning Columbus which it will be very important to notice in a new edition. I have tried, but in vain, to get a copy of the work from Mr. Navarrete (which is kept back until a preface can be written). His reply is that the work is printed at the order & expense of the King & that it would be a breach of loyalty to furnish any one else with a copy before it had been presented to his majesty. As soon as this important duty is complied with I am to have a copy."[28]

Irving's impatience at these delays—which prevented not only the completion of his *Companions* but his planned return to America—is suggested in his letter to Peter Irving from Seville, dated March 3, 1829: "I may never have a more favorable time to return home than the present year, when I shall have one work just launched and another launching, and materials in hand for easy arrangement. If I defer it, God knows what may arise to prevent me."[29] His nephew and biographer, Pierre M. Irving, suggests that "the work just launched" was *The Conquest of Granada* and that the other "launching" was "the Voyage of the Com-

---

26. Ibid., p. 98.

27. *Letters, II*, 377.

28. Ben Harris McClary, ed., *Washington Irving and the House of Murray: Geoffrey Crayon Charms the British, 1817–1856* (Knoxville: University of Tennessee Press, 1969), p. 119 (hereafter cited as McClary).

29. PMI, II, 373.

panions of Columbus, now in readiness."[30] *The Companions of Colum-bus*, however, was far from ready.

Navarrete's third volume was finally published in late March or early April of 1829, and by May 9 Irving was in a position to evaluate its use-fulness in revising the new edition of *Columbus* and in undertaking the laborious work of correcting and emending, revising and polishing, *Voyages and Discoveries of the Companions of Columbus*.[31]

The story of the composition and publication of *The Companions of Columbus* requires interruption here for fuller discussion of Irving's sources during this Spanish period. Clearly Navarrete's laborious re-search, conducted over a period of more than thirty years and published in his *Colección*, was the indispensable foundation upon which both *Columbus* and *Companions* were based. In the introduction to *Voyages and Discoveries of the Companions of Columbus*, Irving acknowledges his indebtedness to "the invaluable Historical Collection of Don Martin Fernandez de Navarrete," praising the Spanish historian's "usual industry, accuracy, and critical acumen" (5). Stanley T. Williams, Irving's biog-rapher, thought *Companions* to be merely "the leavings from *Columbus*" and *Columbus* itself little more than a rewrite of Navarrete.[32] But insofar as *Companions* is concerned, there are only nine footnotes to the text specifically acknowledging Navarrete's *Colección*, most of them specify-ing the third volume. In fact, as this account of the genesis and composi-tion of the text has sought to make clear, *Companions* was virtually complete, though in a preliminary draft, before Navarrete's third volume was published.

Navarrete was by no means the sole source of Irving's information about these Spanish explorers—though his debt in *Columbus* was great enough to bring him, later, under the charge of plagiarism. Irving also acknowledges, in his introduction, Gonzalo Fernandez de Oviedo's *His-toria general y natural de las Indias*, a manuscript copy of which Irving pored over in the Columbian Library of the Cathedral of Seville. In the Archives of the Indias in Seville Irving also studied those documents relative to the law case in 1508 between Don Diego Columbus and and the crown. Williams devalues Irving's originality in this work of

---

30. Ibid.

31. Irving's letter to Brevoort, dated May 23, 1829, mentions having just received Navarrete's third volume of documents (*Letters*, II, 425). A letter to Peter from Seville, dated April 29, 1829, mentions: "I have just received Navarrete's third volume, and will look over it to see what corrections it will be necessary for me to make in my History of Columbus" (PMI, II, 380).

32. Stanley T. Williams, *The Life of Washington Irving* (New York: Oxford Uni-versity Press, 1935), II, 24 (hereafter cited as STW).

research, but Irving deserves to be praised for his initiative and enterprise in gaining access to papers ordinarily closed to foreigners and in
fully exploiting more easily available sources when necessary.

Among the other sources for *Voyages and Discoveries of the Companions of Columbus*, cited by Irving in his introduction, was Antonio de
Herrera y Tordesillas's *Historia general de los hechos de los Castellanos,
en las Islas, y Tierra-Firme de el Mar Oceano*, which had been published
in Madrid in 1601. He also read the Bishop Bartolome de las Casas's
Historia de las Indias and the *Breuisima relacion de la destruycion de las
Indias*, which had been published in Seville in 1552. In addition, he
made extensive use of Francisco Lopez de Gomara's *La historia general
de las Indias*, which had been published at Anvers in 1554 and Pedro
Martir de Angleria's *De Orbe Nouo Petri Martyris* (1516), which Irving
read in the English translation by Lok. And, finally, Don Manuel Joseph
Quintana's *Vidas de españoles célebres* (the second volume of which,
appearing in 1830, contained a life of Vasco Nuñez) was useful to Irving in correcting his own narrative account, since he had been refused
permission to see the papers of Balboa in the Archives of the Indias. But
these are the sources merely cited in Irving's Introduction.

In addition to these authorities, Irving made use of other published
works acknowledged in his footnotes. These include F. Pizarro y Orellana's *Varones Ilustres*, Vespucci's letters and the *Viages de Vespucci*,
Pierre François Xavier Charlevoix's *Histoire de St. Domingo*, Martin
Fernandez de Enciso's *Suma de Geographia*, and Garcilaso de la Vega's
Historia de la Florida. These works were of course supplemented by
Irving's perusal of many other books touching the character of Spain
and her people, from the earliest times onward. Stanley T. Williams regarded this extensive research as "a vast fertilization for so puny an
egg."[33] But Irving's contemporaries were impressed with the depth of
his research and the range of his knowledge. As a reviewer in the
Athenaeum later noted, Irving was "better acquainted with the [Spanish]
people, their customs, habits, manners, and feelings, than the travelling
gentlemen who gallop over countries, and so often submit their impertinence in a quarto volume."[34]

Irving's method in handling these sources, both for *Columbus* and for
Companions, was to compare various narrative accounts ("collation"
was his term), to reconcile any contradictions or inaccuracies in the
particulars of an historical episode by choosing the most trustworthy
authority, and to translate, paraphrase, and in other ways to shape and

33. STW, II, 24.
34. Review of *Voyages and Discoveries of the Companions of Columbus*, in
Athenaeum, no. 169 (January 22, 1831), p. 52.

rewrite his multiple sources. Irving's episodes, always factually close to these sources, are sometimes conflations of the accounts of several sources, sometimes abbreviated summaries of the account of a single source. An instance of the latter is his narrative of Balboa's discovery of the Pacific Ocean, which is accomplished by the footnote: "Many of the foregoing particulars are from the unpublished volume of Oviedo's History of the Indias" (209.12–13). Such footnotes, however, are rarely an exact index of Irving's indebtedness, since, as he says of his sources in the introduction, "he has not thought proper to refer to them continually at the bottom of his page" (viii, 5–6).

This casual attitude toward Navarrete, Oviedo, Martyr, and other sources later brought Irving under severe criticism from nineteenth-century historians, Spanish and American, who charged him with virtual plagiarism. One anonymous critic, writing on "Navarrete on Spain" in the *Southern Literary Messenger* in 1841, complained that "Mr. Irving is not quite explicit enough, in acquainting the American public, with the full extent of his indebtedness."[35] His article is an extended condemnation of Irving and a celebration of Navarrete's prior scholarship. Referring largely to *Columbus*, the anonymous critic was devastating in describing Irving's vagueness about the true extent of his reliance on Navarette: "Above all, he saw as an author, how easy a thing it was, to take from Spanish literature all the materials that he needed, and to publish them as his own—knowing that very few would look behind him for the sources of his knowledge, and that, most probably, a neat paragraph of general compliments, very civil, though not very meaningful, would, with the immense majority of his readers, keep up his reputation for originality as well as liberality, and ... would hush the barking mouths of the Cerberus of criticism."[36]

Irving ignored this charge of plagiarism, which only provoked the Southern critic to conclude, in a later issue: "By all rules then, which govern in such cases, we are bound to infer that our distinguished countryman has preferred the quiet disparagement of a judgment by default, to the notoriety of a verdict, after a further contest."[37]

Whatever the accuracy of the critic's claim—and Irving defended himself warmly in the preface to the ARE *Columbus* in 1849—this view unduly disparages Irving's accomplishment. *Columbus* and *Companions* synthesize various narrative accounts which are only partly collected by Navarrete. The Spanish scholar himself recognized the importance

35. "Navarrete in Spain," *Southern Literary Messenger* 7 (March, 1841), 233.
36. Ibid., p. 238.
37. "Spain. Popular Errors—Their Causes—Travellers. No. III," *Southern Literary Messenger* 8 (May, 1842), 305.

of Irving's achievement for English readers. For, writing in the introduction to the third volume of his *Colección*, Navarrete observed:

A signal proof of the value of our collection has been afforded us by Mr.
Washington Irving, in the *History of the Life and Voyages of Christopher
Columbus*, which he has just published with a reception as generally favorable, as it is well merited. We stated, in our introduction, that we did not
propose to write the history of the admiral, but merely to publish notes and
material so that it might be written with truth and veracity; and it is fortunate that the first person who has availed himself of them is a literary man,
judicious and erudite, already well known in his own country and in Europe
by other works of merit. Living in Madrid, exempt from the rivalries which
have dominated some European natives with respect to Columbus and his
discoveries; with the opportunity to examine excellent books and precious
manuscripts; to converse with persons instructed in these matters, and
having always at hand the authentic documents which we have just published, he has been enabled to give his history that completeness, impartiality,
and exactness which make it much superior to those of the writers who
preceded him. To this he adds his regular method and convenient distribution; his style animated, pure, and elegant; the notice of various personages
who shared in the successes of Columbus; and the examination of various
questions in which always shine sane criticism, erudition, and good taste.[38]

38. "Insigne prueba de esto mismo acaba de darnos el señor Washington Irving
en la *Historia de la vida y de los viages de Christóbal Colon* que ha publicado con
una aceptacion tan general como bien merecida. Digimos en nuestra Introduccion
que no nos proponiamos escribir la historia de aquel Almirante, sino publicar noticias
y materiales para que se escribiese con veracidad, y es una fortuna que el primero
que se haya aprovechado de ellos sea un literato juicioso y erudito, conocido ya en
su patria y en Europa por otras obras apreciables. Colocado en Madrid, exento de
las rivalidades que han dominado entre algunas naciones europeas sobre Colon y sus
descubrimientos; con la proportion de examinar excelentes libros y preciosos manu-
scritos, de tratar á personas instruidas en estas materias, y teniendo siempre á la
mano los auténticos documentos que acabábamos de publicar, ha logrado dar á su
historia aquella extension, imparcialidad y exactitud que la hacen muy superior á
las de los escritores que le precedieron. Agrégase á esto su metódico arreglo y
conveniente distribucion; su estilo animado, puro y elegante; la noticia de varios
personages que intervinieron en los sucesos de Colon, y el exámen de varias cues-
tiones en que luce siempre la mas sana crítica, la erudicion y el buen gusto. Sin
embargo es de esperar que á la luz de los nuevos documentos que vamos publicando
y de las observaciones á que dan lugar, rectifique el señor Washington algunas
noticias ú opiniones, que tomadas de fuentes ménos puras carecen aun de aquella
certidumbre y puntualidad que se requiere para acercarse á la perfeccion." Perhaps
this final remark deserves translation, for it was the cause of Irving's anxiety during the more than eighteen months he waited for the publication of the book: Navarrete expresses the hope that Irving would "be induced, by the reflections conse-

Navarrete even sponsored Irving's election to the Academia de la Historia. And when he received a copy of *Companions* from Irving, he replied in terms of gracious acceptance, recognizing Irving and himself as co-laborers in the diffusion of exact information about Columbian affairs.

My dear friend: With great appreciation I received in due time the little book which you recently published on the voyages and discoveries of the companions of Columbus. Though less important than those of that great man, you make them interesting by your agreeable method and the gracious coloring with which you have described them. I congratulate myself that the documents and notices published in my collection about the first events in the history of America have fallen into hands so able to appreciate their authenticity, to examine them critically, to propagate them, and establish fundamental truths which have been adulterated by partial and prejudiced writers. I am preparing book 4 of the collection which contains the Voyages of Maluco, that is, those of Magallanes, Loaisa, &c. and an appendix of several documents supplementing the previous books.

Navarrete concluded by thanking Irving for his "repeated proofs of friendship" and for Irving's attention to him.[39] These are not the remarks of a man who felt that Irving had stolen from him or that

---

quent therefrom, to correct several of his views and opinions—which, having been derived from sources of less purity, are still wanting in that positive exactness, which is required to approach perfection" (Navarrete, *Colección* [Madrid, 1829], III, xiii–xiv).

39. Navarrete's letter, dated Madrid, April 1, 1831, and addressed to Sr. Washington Yrving, reads as follows:

Muy estimado señor mío: Con gran aprecio recíbí á su tiempo el tomito que Us. acababa de publicar sobre los viages y descubrimientos de los compañeros de Colon, que aunque menos importante que los de este gran hombre, adquieren mucho interes en la pluma de Us. por el buen metodo y gracioso colorido con que sabe describirlos. Yo me complazeo en que los documentos y noticias que publico en mi coleccion sobre los primeros acontecimientos de la historia de America, hayan recaido en manos tan hábiles para apreciar su autenticidad, para examinarlas con critica y propagarlas por todas partes echando los fundamentos de la verdad que hasta ahora há sido tan adulterada por los escritores parciales ó sistemáticos. Estoy preparando el tomo IV de la coleccion que contendrá los *Viages al Maluco*, esto es las de Magallanes, Loaisa, &c. y un Apendice, y suplemento de algunos documentos á los tomos anteriores.

Doy á Us. la mas espresivar gracias por sus repetidas preubas de amistad y por su atencion, [three words illegible] el sincero afecto y profunda gratitud con que es su amº y servʳ A.S.M.B.

Martin Fernᶻ de Navarrete

his life's work had been plundered illegitimately by an American plagiarist.

Columbus and *Companions* Navarrete understood for what they were—works of enormous labor and magnitude, attentive (wherever possible) to exact accuracy of historical fact (however well- or ill-acknowledged): yet works of the imagination, sometimes soaring beyond the known facts, sometimes sentimental; nevertheless highly readable "re-creations" or "inventions" of romantic history. If they are untrustworthy as scholarship, they nevertheless satisfied the public demand for a compelling, entertaining story which would, in the words of Fernan Caballero, "poetizar la realidad sin alterarla."[40]

Partly biography, partly history, partly poetry, *Voyages and Discoveries of the Companions of Columbus* was composed in Seville and Port St. Mary and completed, in a first draft, on March 3, 1829. We know nothing of the state of this first draft in manuscript, since the draft from which it evolved is no longer extant.[41] Its publication history, however, suggests that the first draft of *Companions* was much too imperfect to submit for publication in the spring of that year. Moreover, negotiations with John Murray over a second edition of Columbus, Irving's haste to abridge *Columbus* in order to forestall a threatened rival abridgment, composing the manuscripts of *The Alhambra* and *Mahomet*, as well as the task of seeing *The Conquest of Granada* through the press—all of these preoccupied Irving in the first six months of 1829, virtually preventing any serious effort at the revision of the incoherent manuscript of *Companions of Columbus*.

In addition, Irving worked fitfully, often in a state of depression, for which Murray was sometimes the cause. For Murray's reservations about the success of Irving's projects reached the author in the form of rumors, sometimes throwing him into a funk. Thus to Aspinwall Irving wrote from Seville on April 4, 1829: "A croaking paragraph from Murray's note . . . knocked my pen out of my hands for a day, but I resumed it and pursued my plans. It is better, however, not to communicate to me any more surmises and anticipations of the kind, which . . .

40. Fernán Caballero, "Carta a mi lector de las Batuecas," in *Clemencia: Obras Completas* (Madrid, 1898), III, 40.

41. Some of the materials from which Irving drafted *Companions* are extant, however. They include two long extracts certifying the Pinzon coat of arms, the principal events in the lives of the Pinzon brothers, the family's progress in the service of their Catholic majesties, &c. These documents, some ninety-one pages in all, were based on the accounts of Oviedo and Herrera and were certified by Don Felipe Lopez de la Huerta for Don Francisco Jose de la Rua y Astorga in Madrid on April 23, 1770. Copied in Spanish by a Madrid scribe, they were addressed to Irving at the Embassy.

may have a pernicious effect upon any literary undertaking in hand. Literary excitement is excessively precarious, and there is nothing an author is made more readily distrustful of than the picturings of his fancy. We are mere camelions, fed with air, and changing colour with every thing with which we come in contact. We are to be stirred up to almost any thing by encouragement and cheering, but the least whisper of doubt casts a chill upon the feelings & the invention."[42]

In July of 1829, moreover, Irving was preparing to leave Spain for London, where a secretaryship awaited him in the United States legation, under the new minister at the Court of St. James, Louis McLane. The responsibilities of his new post in London presented Irving with no anxieties as to the completion of *Companions* and his other incomplete Spanish manuscripts. Writing to Peter from the Alhambra on July 18, 1829, he observed: "My Spanish materials I can work up in England, where I can have all the necessary works, and where you will be within reach to consult with."[43]

Into his trunk, which was already crammed with materials of his other Spanish books, went this first manuscript draft of *Voyages and Discoveries of the Companions of Columbus*, to be put off until Irving was settled in at his lodgings—eventually 8 Argyll Street, and at the legation, where new duties awaited him. Negotiations with John Murray II, the "Prince of Booksellers," yet for Irving "the most difficult being on earth to please,"[44] began in the fall. While these negotiations proceeded, Irving periodically worked on the manuscript of *Companions*, expanded the growing draft of *Mahomet*, wrote an anonymous article for the *Quarterly Review* on his own *Granada* (the exposure of which would later embarrass him), and generally busied himself with what he hoped would be profitable literary projects.

Almost a year later, however, *Voyages and Discoveries of the Companions of Columbus* was still unfinished, doubtless owing to the chaotic state of the manuscript, if not to the precariousness of his literary excitement, which had spread itself too thin over other literary enterprises. On July 6, 1830, Irving wrote to John Murray:

I have been rather interrupted for some days past by the business of the office or should have had the volume of voyages ready for the press. In fact I could furnish copy to the printers immediately, but every day that I withhold it makes the work better. You spoke some time since of writing me a "Business Letter." I wish you would do so at once, and let me know what

42. *Letters,* II, 395–96.
43. PMI, II, 399.
44. *Letters,* II, 593.

you can offer for this work. It will form one volume and may be printed uniform with the Octavo edition of Columbus, and also in a smaller form as one of the Family Library. I cannot but think it will be found interesting & readable. The singular narrations of these voyages, have to me, even in the crude state in which I found them entangled in the old Spanish writers, all the charm of wild tales of romance; and I have endeavoured to set them off in the clearest and most striking manner.[45]

In view of Irving's completion of the first draft more than a full year before, and in view of his characteristic habit of using the printed proofsheets as a draft to be extensively rewritten, Irving's restraint in not furnishing this incomplete manuscript copy to the printer is remarkable. How inextricably "entangled" must have been the lines of his narrative, how disorderly must have been the state of his manuscript during the year and a half he worked over his "brief lives." Clearly the work was far from ready. Nevertheless, his intention to have it published in a one-volume octavo, uniform with the *Columbus*, suggests that Irving regarded *Voyages and Discoveries of the Companions of Columbus* as a matching work, if not an addendum, to the earlier four-volume biography of Columbus. Murray, however, had more modest plans for the *Companions*. The pervasive economic depression of that year, which had a disastrous effect on the book market; Murray's expensive litigations at the King's Bench; his ill health; and his growing irritability over the failure of Irving's books to produce profits—all of these factors inclined him to think that Irving's *Companions* was perhaps worth half of what Irving had asked and that it deserved publication, if at all, only in the "Family Library" series.[46]

Murray's "Family Library" had been conceived in 1828 as a venture in cheap literature. It was to be "a serial publication by means of which good literature and copyright works might be rendered cheaper and more accessible to a wider circle of readers than they had hitherto been."[47] The series was to appear as a pocket-size monthly volume, by contemporary authors, devoted to "a variety of subjects including His-

45. Ibid., II, 531.

46. Murray, in fact, had already officially registered the title for copyright at the Stationer's Hall. The entry for March 8, 1830, indicates that Murray had on that day deposited the title of a work to be called *Companions of Columbus*. No author was listed in the entry, but the title was designated as No. 18 of the Family Library. See McClary, pp. 220–21.

47. Samuel Smiles, *A Publisher and His Friends: Memoirs and Correspondence of the Late John Murray, with an Account of the Origin and Progress of the House, 1768–1843* (London: John Murray, 1891), II, 312.

tory, Science, and general literature. . . ."[48] Scott's *Life of Napoleon Bonaparte* and Irving's abridgment of *Columbus* had been previous choices and, before the series folded, volumes were to appear on Alexander the Great, the history of the Jews, the lives of various artists and physicians, a history of Venice, of India, of insects, even of demonology, and, of course, *Voyages and Discoveries of the Companions of Columbus*.

That this volume of voyages was not printed in the larger octavo, uniform with *Columbus*, was a severe disappointment to Irving. For Murray's characteristic doubt about Irving's literary production was a continual annoyance to the author, who wrongly believed himself to be one of the most profitable authors on Murray's list. This irritation possibly accounts in part for his delay in submitting *Companions* to the printer. "I have been annoyed too by your forebodings of ill success to this work," he had written Murray, about *Granada*, on May 9, 1829.

When you have the spirit to give a large price for a work, why have you not the spirit to go manfully through with it, until the public voice determine its fate. These croakings get to my ears, and dishearten and interrupt me for a time with other things which I may have in hand. Remember: you doubted the success and declined the publication of the Sketch book, when I offered you the materials for the first volume which had been already published in America, and it was only until after it had been published in London by another bookseller & had been well received that you ventured to take it in hand: remember too t[hat?] you lost heart about the success of Columbus, and dropt a th[ousand?] copies of the first edition after you had printed the first volume, and yet you see it continues to do well. I trust that you will be equally disappointed in your prognostications about the success of the Conquest of Granada, and that it will not eventually prove disadvantageous either to your purse or my reputation. At any rate, I should like hereafter to make our arrangements in such manner that you may be relieved from these apprehensions of loss and from the necessity of recurring to any management of the press to aid the publication of a work of mine.[49]

Under the sting of wounded pride, sometime in the summer of 1830, Irving therefore entertained a proposition from Dionysius Lardner to write a history of the United States for the *Cabinet Cyclopaedia*, a series of volumes on history to be published by Longmans. Irving eventually declined the offer. Whether Dr. Lardner expressed interest in *Companions of Columbus* cannot be shown. But the terms he offered

48. Ibid., II, 312.
49. *Letters*, II, 415.

for the projected history gave Irving a lever to use in bargaining with Murray. What Murray offered for *Companions* in the first round is not clear, but it was obviously not enough to satisfy Irving: "I am extremely sorry to say that the terms you mention as having given to others are much below what I had expected. I speak not from any reference to the value of my work, but to the offers mad[e] me by others, who may be supposed to have a knowledge of the literary market. When Dr Lardner applied to me to write for his series he offered me five hundred Guineas per Volume. On my declining it was intimated that I might have 700. I know that the latter sum per Volume is given by him to some of his authors, and that Moore is to receive 1000 Guineas for his Hist of Ireland in one Volume." Irving, who was about to leave London, concluded by saying, "Should you be disposed to give me five hundred guineas for my volume of voyages we may settle the matter at once, and a note sent to my lodgings any time before 5 oclock P M. will find me—I leave town in the Southampton coach at 6."[50]

Murray, whose generosity with Irving in previous negotiations had confounded Murray's advisors, unaccountably agreed to Irving's terms. (He was about to depart himself for Scotland on an extended vacation with the Scotts and Lockharts.) The issue of terms was settled that afternoon, before both men left London. Murray agreed to give Irving 525 guineas, payable in installments of £175 each at six, nine, and twelve months. The paperwork was left to be executed by John Murray III.[51] In agreeing to the terms, on the point of his departure, Irving thanked the elder Murray and noted: "I take the earlier part of the MS with me to Paris, to make some trivial corrections & will send it on to him [John Murray III] through the ambassadors bag, as I get it ready."[52]

Irving was in Paris for some three weeks. Whether he spent part of his time there revising *Voyages and Discoveries of the Companions of*

50. Ibid., II, 538.

51. The records of the House of Murray show these three promissory notes of £175 each, dated on December 17, 1830, and paid on June 20, September 20, and December 20, 1831. They were endorsed by Irving over to Henry Van Wart, who handled some of Irving's accounts (McClary, p. 216). This information is confirmed by Irving's letter to his brother Peter, dated December 21, 1830: "A few days since I sent the last page of the volume of Voyages to the printer, and have since received three notes of hand from Murray, dated Dec. 17, at six, nine, and twelve months, for £175, making five hundred guineas, or £525. I have endorsed them over and remitted them to H. Van Wart, with orders to pass them to your credit. They will form a fund, therefore, which you can draw against whenever you please" (PMI, II, 447).

52. *Letters*, II, 539.

Columbus cannot be shown. Nor can it be determined whether any "completed" portions of the manuscript were sent back to the younger Murray through the diplomatic pouch. None of the manuscript paper is apparently of French origin or watermark, and none of the leaves bears any stamp or seal that might indicate its passage through diplomatic channels. It is probable that Irving took the manuscript with him and revised it, however, for it was almost ready for the printer on August 28, 1830, the day Irving returned to London.

On the day of his return Irving announced to Murray the virtual completion of the work: " I send you the MS of the Voyages for the printer to make his estimate. Should I not furnish sufficient letter press I can readily furnish more in the appendix, from curious documents illustrative of the Voyages. I have retained in my hands for correction the introduction & some of the early part, making together about 110 pages similar to those sent. I shall be able to furnish the early part for the press on Monday Morng & then to continue the supply as wanted."[53] In the following days the much-revised manuscript of *Companions* was fed to the printer, C. Roworth of Bell Yard, Temple Bar, section by section, until the proofslips were completed, apparently about September 6, 1830. Pierre M. Irving implies that as each batch of proofsheets had come off the press, Irving had "been transmitting a duplicate copy of the Voyages of the Companions of Columbus for publication in America, simultaneously with its publication in England. . . ."[54] Irving's correspondence with Murray, however, suggests that a duplicate of 1E proofslips was mailed in a single shipment to America. For on September 6, 1830, Irving asked Murray to provide him with "a duplicate of the proof, to send off with this days dispatches to America—The lad who brings this note will go to the printers for the proof, if you will give him the requisite order & directions."[55]

This duplicate set of proofsheets was dispatched by Irving to his brother Ebenezer, who arranged for the publication of the first American edition (1A) in Philadelphia by Carey & Lea. The proof sent to America on September 6 indicates, however, that *Voyages and Discoveries of the Companions of Columbus* must still have been incomplete, for the first American edition lacks the table of contents, which Irving must have drawn up later, while he revised the 1E proofs, and while Murray's printer, Roworth, reset the corrected text. In early October Irving took a "diplomatic furlough" in order to visit the Van Warts in

53. Ibid., II, 541.
54. PMI, II, 442.
55. *Letters*, II, 546.

Birmingham, a vacation, according to Pierre M. Irving, which suspended "the printing of 'The Voyages of the Companions of Columbus,' then in progress. . . ."[56]

The process of revising the proofs extended from September through December, 1830, while Irving, as he wrote Peter, was "jogging on with the printing of the voyages."[57] That he continued to revise the 1E proofs, after duplicate proofsheets had been sent to America, is suggested by the number of substantive variations in the texts of the two works. These variations are discussed below in the Textual Commentary.

The problem of furnishing Murray "sufficient letter press" was solved by the addition to *Companions* of the two appendixes, "A Visit to Palos" and the "Manifesto of Alonzo de Ojeda," altogether some thirty additional pages in the printed text. The first appendix was an expanded and revised essay, begun as a letter to his friend, Mlle. Antoinette Bollvillier, while Irving was in Seville in 1828. In the headnote to the appendix, Irving observes: "He has been induced to insert it here from the idea that many will feel the same curiosity to know something of the present state of Palos and its inhabitants that led him to make the journey" (348). But the likelihood is that the necessity of expanding the letterpress, so as to fill in the final gathering, accounts for this appendage, as well as the "Manifesto of Alonzo de Ojeda."

Perhaps there was one additional reason for the slow progress through the press of *Voyages and Discoveries of the Companions of Columbus*— Irving's wish to illustrate the volume with a number of sketches descriptive of the scenes Irving had encountered at Palos. Unfortunately, however, he had left Spain without attending to this necessity and was obliged to seek the assistance of Mrs. Maria Hipkins in Seville. Toward the end of October, 1830, he finally received them. These drawings included a frontispiece sketch of "The Convent of La Rabida" at Palos, "at the gate of which Columbus asked bread & water for his child"; a view of Palos "from whence Columbus set sail for the discovery of America" (both opposite page 309 in 1E); and a title-page sketch of the Pinzon family coat of arms, featuring, on a shield (topped by a plumed visor) two men with muskets on a cliff overlooking three ships at sea under full sail. This whole prospect is surrounded by a decorative border within which appears a design of anchors and hearts, surmounted by a castle. In a letter from London, dated October 21, 1830, Irving thanked Mrs. Hipkins for obtaining these illustrations for his forthcoming work, which, he assured her, was partly printed and nearly ready

56. PMI, II, 437.
57. Ibid., II, 442.

for publication. The sketches were commissioned of the artist Ignacio Walker; they were engraved for the first English edition by E. Finden. Publication records indicate that Walker was paid for them in March of 1831. Writing to John Murray II on March 15, Irving encloses "a Bill exchange drawn on me for £10.11.8, which I paid a few days since, being for the expenses of the painter & the Sketches which he made at Palos, for the illustrations of 'The Companions of Columbus.' If you can pay the amount to the bearer of this note you will oblige."[58]

The business records of the House of Murray indicate that *Voyages and Discoveries of the Companions of Columbus* was published on December 31, 1830, as number 18 of the Family Library series. This first edition totaled 15,000 copies, of which only 10,000 were initially bound. In addition to the 525 guineas paid Irving, Murray paid £212.3.6 to Roworth for the printing; £433.4.6 for the paper; £8.14 to a workman named Williams for woodcuts; £5.5 for, apparently, the design of the wrappers; £35 to a workman named Parker for drawing the maps bound into the volume; £170 for the binding of 10,000 copies; £8 for 10,000 wrappers; £141.0.6 for advertising; £50.8 to a workman named McQueen for working plates and paper; two shillings for registry of the work at the Stationer's Hall; and £10.11.8 to Ignacio Walker for the sketches Irving had commissioned. The total cost to Murray in producing the volume was therefore £1,599.9.2. The purchase price of the work was five shillings.

At the end of the first year, 6,357 of the 15,000 copies had been sold, representing a return to Murray of £1017.3.4. Of the remaining 8,643, Murray deposited eleven in the Stationer's Hall and gave away 188,[59] leaving 8,444 on hand on December 31, 1831, a year after publication. The slow sale of *Voyages and Discoveries of the Companions of Columbus* meant that Murray had to carry over into 1833 a loss of £582.5.10. Murray made a halfhearted effort to continue advertising the work and commissioned a workman named Walker to redraw and engrave the maps, but between 1832 and 1834 the work sold only 498 additional copies. By 1832 the Family Library began to prove unprofitable, and Murray eventually sold the series "with minimal loss or marginal profit."[60] Before selling off the series, however, Murray disposed of the

---

58. *Letters*, II, 598.

59. One of these gifts was perhaps requested by Irving himself. On February 18, 1831, he asked the younger Murray for "a copy of the 'Companions of Columbus' neatly bound, to send to the Royal Academy of History at Madrid" (McClary, p. 146).

60. Scott Bennett, "The Family Library, 1825–1835: The Uses of Literacy in a Revolutionary Age" (Ph.D. diss., Indiana University, 1967), p. 222; McClary, p. 169.

remaining 7,946 unsold copies of *Companions* in the usual way: Thomas Tegg, the remainders man, carted them off to be sold for a shilling apiece. The last Murray ledger entry for *Companions*, dated December 31, 1834, indicates that Tegg's purchase left Murray a total profit during that four-year period of a paltry £58.11.[61]

Meanwhile, on Chestnut Street in Philadelphia, Carey & Lea published *Voyages and Discoveries of the Companions of Columbus* on March 7, 1831. It was advertised as "ready" on March 9. The work was printed from 1E proofsheets supplied by Ebenezer Irving, the writer's brother, who had received the duplicate 1E proofs sent from London in the diplomatic pouch on September 6, 1830. On the verso of the title page[62] the printer is identified as I. Ashmead & Company, one of eighty-odd printers employed by Carey & Lea.[63] A total of 3,000 copies were run off the press. Ebenezer Irving's financial arrangement for the publication of *Companions* differed from the terms he had arranged for the *Columbus* volume. According to Peter Irving, Ebenezer had offered *Columbus* "to Messrs. Carey in sheets, three volumes at $2 per volume, at 40 percent. discount, or in boards at 33½. They replied that they would wish to sell it to the trade at those discounts, and that the terms he proposed were out of all bounds, and would not permit them even to make him an offer. He showed the letter to

61. These figures are contained in the financial records of the Family Library in the House of Murray at 50 Albemarle Street, London. The editor gratefully acknowledges the assistance of Ben Harris McClary in making them available and thanks the Murray firm for permission to publish them.

62. Also printed on the title page verso is the following note subscribed by Fred J. Betts, Clerk of the Southern District of New York: "BE IT REMEMBERED, That on the 31st day of December, A.D. 1830, in the fifty-fifth year of the Independence of the United States of America, WASHINGTON IRVING, of the said district, hath deposited in this office the title of a book, the right whereof he claims as author, in the words following, to wit: 'VOYAGES AND DISCOVERIES OF THE COMPANIONS OF COLUMBUS. . . .' In conformity to the Act of the Congress of the United States intitled 'An act for the Encouragement of Learning, by securing the copies of maps, charts, and books, to the authors and proprietors of such copies, during the time therein mentioned.'—And also to an act, entitled, 'An act suplementary to an act, entitled, 'An act for the encouragement of learning, by securing the copies of maps, charts, and books, to the authors and proprietors of such copies during the times therein mentioned,' and extending the benefits thereof to the arts of designing, engraving, and etching historical and other prints."

63. Isaac Ashmead must have rendered faithful service to Carey, since he owned at least eight of the new "Treadwell Power Presses," which used "a live horse to supply the power, as steam engines were not easy to come by" in 1831. See Rollo G. Silver, *The American Printer, 1787–1825* (Charlottesville: University of Virginia Press, 1967), pp. 53, 56.

Brevoort, and on consultation they considered it necessary to seek another publisher. Brevoort applied to Messrs. Carvill, whom he knew, and who agreed to give "seven thousand dollars for the two thousand copies in sheets, one thousand dollars on delivery, the remainder in four, six, and nine months, giving you [Washington Irving] a profit on the edition of about three thousand dollars. Messrs. Carvill are the first booksellers in New York." According to Peter, "Mr. Carey came on to New York about the beginning of February, and after considerable conversation offered a profit of two thousand five hundred dollars, and when he found that it would not procure it manifested a disposition to augment the proffer, but was informed that it was too late."[64]

The loss of *Columbus* must have been a severe blow to Mathew Carey and a warning about future volumes. *Companions*, Carey determined, must not be allowed to escape. Rather than let Irving pay for the printing and then sell the sheets to another publisher for binding and distribution, Carey struck a new bargain with Ebenezer, described in Irving's letter to Peter, dated London, March 1, 1831: "I had a letter from E.I. lately. He had made a bargain with Carey and Lea of Philadelphia about the 'Voyages;' they are to give fifteen hundred dollars for the privilege of printing three thousand copies, and he binds himself to allow them three years to sell off the edition, though he trusts they will sell it in less than two. I observe they advertise it to be published in one octavo volume."[65]

The Cost Book of Carey & Lea, 1825–1838, while not satisfyingly complete, indicates that the publisher spent (in addition to the copyright payment to Irving of $1,500) the following: $330 for boards; $616 for paper (154 reams @ $4 each); $211.25 for printing expenses (528 tokens @ 40¢ each); $2 for 3,000 labels; 140.80 for composition (352 @ 40¢ each); and $2.10 for extras. The total cost to Carey & Lea was $2,802.15. It was to be recovered from the sales of the book—3,000 copies retailing @ $1.75 each, producing $5,250, leaving Carey & Lea

---

64. Pierre M. Irving observes that "In a letter to the author written about this time, Carey makes a proposition to him respecting any future publications; and about the last of March, 1828, put the question to his brother and agent, Ebenezer, what he would ask for the right of publishing the four previous works, History of New York, Sketch Book, Bracebridge Hall, and Tales of a Traveller, for seven or ten years." Pierre observes that "The result was an arrangement soon after with that house for a seven years' lease of the copyright of these works at six hundred dollars per annum, payable semi-annually, and to take the stock on hand at sixty-five cents per copy" (PMI, II, 279–80).

65. Ibid., II, 451.

66. *The Cost Book of Carey and Lea, 1825–1838*, ed. David Kaser (Philadelphia: University of Pennsylvania, Press, 1963), pp. 92–93.

a potential profit—less distribution costs, gifts, advertising, and discounts—of $2,447.85. How many copies were in fact sold, given away, or remaindered cannot be determined. But Irving had every reason to be satisfied with the terms which Ebenezer had concluded. "I think the arrangement a good one," Irving told Peter. "The 'Companions' seems to be very successful, and what is a good sign, are favorites with the publisher."[67]

Most of the reviewers also liked *Companions of Columbus*. The *Literary Gazette* thought *Companions* "a delightful volume" and Irving's name "a pledge how well their stories will be told." A week later the *Literary Gazette* noted that "The adventures, the disasters, and, generally, the melancholy fate of these daring bucaniers and their companions form a striking drama in the history of mankind. . . ." In fact, the reviewer thought that "Ojeda's whole career is beyond a romance," that Juan Ponce's adventures were "amusing," and that the pilgrimage to Palos "by so distinguished a citizen of the New World as Washington Irving,"[68] was most appropriate. A writer for the *Monthly Review*, noting that "the indefatigable labours of Navarrete have enabled Mr. Irving to trace the history of the followers of the admiral, in an authentic and satisfactory manner," observed that the narrative of Balboa's discovery of the Pacific was "described by Mr. Irving with his usual graphic power," in his "best style."[69] A Philadelphia reviewer reprinted this review.[70]

In a short piece in the *Athenaeum*, two days after the first English edition was published, a London reviewer noted that "Washington Irving has collected the scattered intelligence of many curious books and rare manuscripts into this volume, and has set forth the chequered fortunes of the intrepid followers of the great Columbus with equal elegance, spirit, and simplicity." Of the structure of the work—its movement from story to story—the reviewer remarked: "To drop naturally from one subject to another . . . seems easy till it is tried: this rare art is sufficiently visible in this book before us—we were scarcely prepared for one with an air so original. There is no bustle in the narrative—no wish to give strong light and shade: yet all that is necessary

67. PMI, II, 451.

68. Reviews of *Voyages and Discoveries of the Companions of Columbus*, in *Literary Gazette*, no. 728 (January 1, 1831), p. 8; no. 729 (January 8, 1831), p. 22; no. 731 (January 22, 1831), p. 56.

69. Review of *Companions of Columbus*, in *Monthly Review* 1 (February, 1831), 244, 246, 248.

70. Review of *Companions of Columbus*, in *Philadelphia Album and Ladies' Literary Port Folio* 5 (March 19, 1831), 90–91.

is done." The reviewer concluded by noting the melancholy effect of the book: "the careers of all end sadly and disastrously—in the great cause of discovery they suffered imprisonment, persecution, exile and death. This history of genius is the saddest of all histories. We shall enter more fully into the subject next week."[71]

In an extended review, three weeks later, the *Athenaeum* returned to the subject, calling *Companions* "a delightful book," "one of the very best accounts of the singular fortunes and adventures of the early conquerors of America." The writer praised Irving for having "consulted the best historians" and for having "selected from them the most important facts—and so judiciously, that his work is rich in all the glorious romance of the conquest, without offending against the plain sincerity and honesty of history." Nevertheless, on reflection, the *Athenaeum* reviewer raised "objections to the plan of his work: it is neither biographical nor historical"; and he observed that these unconnected narratives were "more like novels," and that for the well-informed, Irving's "historical knowledge" was "trifling." The *Anthenaeum* reviewer was right in complaining that "Mr. Irving's narratives want connexion" and that, in consequence, Irving was "frequently obliged to repeat what he has said before, although, historically, they are most intimately connected." This objection grew out of the reviewer's feeling that Irving ought to have undertaken a formal history of the period: "No man is better qualified either by genius, honesty, or enthusiasm, for the subject: and for materials, the old prosy Spanish historians, the modern writings of Navarrete and Quintana, and the unpublished works of Oviedo and others, with which Mr. Irving is intimately conversant, would have enabled him to add a standard work to our literature, and justly increased his own fame." Above all, the *Athenaeum* reviewer appreciated Irving's thesis about the redirection of the chivalric impulses to maritime exploration and was struck with the range and depth of Irving's knowledge of Spain, arguing that "Mr. Irving is somewhat better acquainted with the [Spanish] people, their customs, habits, manners, and feelings, than the travelling gentlemen who gallop over countries, and so often submit their impertinence in a quarto volume."[72]

The American writer for the *Southern Review*, however, took no satisfaction in Irving's theory of marine chivalry in the New World. "Without going out of our way, as we think Mr. Irving has done, to ascribe the ardour and fearlessness with which this field of dangerous dis-

71. Review of *Companions of Columbus*, in *Athenaeum*, no. 166 (January 1, 1831), p. 9.

72. Review of *Companions*, in *Athenaeum*, no. 169 (January 22, 1831), pp. 51–52.

tinction was occupied, to the fierce and long continued warfare between Spaniard and Moor, or to the more general influence of chivalry,
we can find, in the cupidity and ambition of human nature, motives
sufficiently strong to have tempted to their ruin, men less fitted, by their
nature and discipline, to encounter the hardships and dangers of an
unknown and unconquered world." This reviewer apparently felt that
Irving's implied definition denigrated the Southern idea of "chivalry":
"we are surprised that Mr. Irving should insist so strenuously upon the
influence which chivalry exerted over these Western discoveries. We
cannot, for the life of us, see any chivalry in the matter." For this writer,
the Spaniards were merely wild mercantile adventurers, whose evangelical Catholicism, far from humanizing them, condoned the genocide
they savagely practiced. Compared to Columbus, he wrote, "how inferior, nay almost contemptible, appear the characters of these companions. How unlike their great original!" He could find little basis for
Irving's belief that "the history of these Spanish discoveries abounds in
noble and generous traits of character."

Ideologies of history and chivalry aside, this Southern reviewer found
much to commend in Irving's style. The voyages, he observed, "are
told with just enough of detail to make them graphic, without degener-
ating into diffuseness or repetition. Mr. Irving has very wisely confined
himself closely to the matter in hand, and avoided those elaborate descriptions of scenery, real and fanciful, of which we had so much in his
life of Columbus. His style too, in this volume, is decidedly easier than
in his more laboured work: . . . there is a dash of carelessness about his
narration of the fortunes of these adventurers, for which he and they
are both better."[73] Stanley T. Williams observed that "Upon Irving's reputation this *addendum* [to *Columbus*] had no effect"[74] But the writer
for the *Southern Review* concluded that *Companions* added "to the
already well-deserved reputation of Mr. Irving. It has the merit, of
which so few American books can boast, of going to the bottom of its
subject." By his research into original and authentic documents, Irving
had "acquired a fulness and certainty of knowledge that give to his assertions and discussions, fearlessness and confidence, and to his commentary and illustrations, grace and vigour." The reviewer ended by
ranking Irving higher than all of his formidable contemporaries: "Mr.
Irving stands, as yet, unique in American literature. He is our only
writer, whose successive publications have added to his fame," and he

---

73. "Irving's *Voyages and Discoveries of the Companions of Columbus,*" *Southern
Review,* no. 13 (May, 1831), pp. 214, 217–18, 220, 226.

74. STW, II, 24.

concludes with the comment that "he alone continues to interest and instruct, to charm and improve us."[75]

This view was also shared by the anonymous author of the "Memoir of Washington Irving," which accompanied the pirated version of *Companions of Columbus* in the Paris Baudry one-volume edition of the *Complete Works of Washington Irving*. He felt that though *Columbus* was Irving's "most important work," *Companions* was necessary to complete it. *Companions*, he observed, "unites the marvellous of old romance with the sober charm of truth."[76]

Henry D. Gilpin, reviewing *Companions* in the *American Quarterly Review*, praised Irving for the "higher character" of his historical writing. He observed that although *Companions* was not as interesting as *Columbus*, it entitled Irving to "take his stand among those writers who have done more than amuse the fancy, or even gratify the heart. He is to be classed with the historians of great events...." Gilpin expressed the wish that Irving would do comparable volumes on the history of Mexico or Peru, and quoted extensively from the text in order to enable readers to "form a just estimate of the power and skill of the writer, and of the pleasure to be derived from the story he has recorded. We venture to say, that by none will that estimate be otherwise than favourable, either to the talents of the author, or the interest of the work."[77]

Stanley T. Williams complained that *Companions* bears "signs of Irving's haste and lacks the sweetness of diction of *Columbus* as well as its picturesque episodes."[78] But Irving's style, which was slowly refined during more than a year of revisions, was also celebrated by Henry Gilpin, who noted: "We find him adopting in the Life of Columbus, and in the volume before us, a different manner, but one equally well suited to the different nature of the subject he treats. Without losing the elegance and general purity by which it has been always characterized, it seems to us to have acquired more freshness, more vivacity; to convey to the reader that exquisite charm in historical writing—an unconscious-

75. "Irving's *Voyages* . . . ," *Southern Review*, p. 246.

76. "Memoir of Washington Irving," in *Complete Works of Washington Irving* (Paris: Baudry's European Library, 1843), p. xiii.

77. [Henry D. Gilpin,] "Irving's Spanish Voyages of Discovery," *American Quarterly Review* 9 (March, 1831), 163–65 (hereafter cited as Gilpin). The authorship of this review has been identified by Ralph Aderman in "Contributions to *The American Quarterly Review, 1827–1833*," *Studies in Bibliography* 14 (1961), 172. Gilpin (1801–1860) was editor of the *Atlantic Souvenir* and, later, attorney general of the United States (1840–1841).

78. STW, II, 24.

ness of any elaboration on the part of the writer, yet a quick and entire understanding of every sentiment he desires to convey." Gilpin commended Irving for his "lively perception of all those sentiments and incidents, which excite the finest and pleasantest emotions of the human breast" and he praised Irving for being, throughout, "the same undeviating, but beautiful moralist, gathering from all lessons to present, in striking language to reason and the heart."[79]

The undeviating but beautiful moralist—who recorded the tragic destruction of the native peoples of the Carribean, in the Spaniards' lust for gold, silver, and pearls—was understood differently, however, by the reviewer for the *Gentleman's Magazine, and Historical Chronicle*. Commenting on the abridgment of *Columbus*, this reviewer observed that the discovery and settlement of the New World offered

new illustrations of the history of man—especially on this point, that the gregarious principle cannot be acted upon so far as regards progressive improvement and solid happiness, except in a state of civilization. The history of America, in all other respects, lies in a nutshell. It is merely that of savages, from whom nothing could be learned, and of civilized Europeans labouring to overcome physical difficulties. It appears, too, that Providence does not permit population to increase in a state where land is not reduced to private property, and cultivated. In short, all the progressive conditions of man are exhibited in the history of America, as if it had been intended for a series of philosophical and political illustrations. And as to literature, the "Life of Columbus" is and can be no other than a Robinson Crusoe for philosophers, upon a scientific scale.[80]

Ten months later, turning to *Companions*, the reviewer for the *Gentleman's Magazine* lectured Irving's contemporaries in this vein:

now in the present day mob-principles are dominant. It is however utterly impossible that a civilized people can make a beneficial settlement in a barbarous country, or the latter be elevated in social happiness, unless the recruit submit to the drill of the serjeant, the schoolboy to that of the pedagogue. The liberty of civilized countries can no more be allowed to a savage, than fire-arms to an idiot. It is not that the mode of subjugation may be correct, but subordination there must be; or no good can be done to the people themselves. Could South America, or North America, ever have been what they now are, if the Indians of either country had been suffered to be triumphant? We speak only *en philosophe* in vindication of Providence,

79. Gilpin, pp. 184–85.

80. Review of the abridgment of *Columbus*, in *Gentleman's Magazine, and Historical Chronicle* 100 (April, 1830), 338–39.

which extracts only good out of evil; and openly manifests, that power cannot be entrusted to barbarians, without injury to the species.

These remarks, apparently directed against the romantic Rousseauvian primitivism of the early nineteenth century, appear equally to apply to the reform agitation, labor riots, and other current insubordinations threatening the British Establishment's attempts to effect "good . . . done to the people themselves." None of this attitudinizing is really relevant to *Companions.* But the *Gentleman's Magazine* reviewer concludes: "We have thus made a moral use of the work before us, because we thought it a good thesis, one that invited a commentary by way of lamp or candle, to exhibit its social character in certain main points. Mr. Washington Irving is a man who has many thousands in the consoles of public approbation, and therefore we need not say a word about his reputation in the stock-exchange of literature."[81]

All told, then, the reviews of *Companions* were highly laudatory, even if it was sometimes praised for the wrong reasons. Irving had every reason to think his literary stock was rising and that he could command his price with John Murray. Needing more income, Irving presented Murray with partial manuscripts of *Mahomet* and a "Spanish Sketch Book," urged immediate acceptance of them, and named a high figure for the pair—five hundred guineas for the first, a thousand for the second. Murray declined to proceed on the basis of the partial manuscripts Irving had shown him. At this, Irving threatened to "seek some other person or mode to publish it." Murray replied: "You told me upon our former negociations, and you repeated it recently, that you would not suffer me to be a loser by any of your works; and the state of matters in this respect, I am exceedingly unwilling because it is contrary to my nature to submit to you, and in doing so at length, you will I am sure do me the justice to believe that I have no other expectations than those which are founded upon your own good feelings. The publication of Columbus cost me. Paper—Print—Advertising—Author £5,700 and it has produced but £4,700—Grenada cost £3,073 and its sale has produced but £1,830, making my gross loss at £2,250.—I have thought it better to communicate with yourself direct, than through the medium of Mr. Aspinwall." Murray enclosed a copied extract of Irving's letter of May 9 in which the author stated his wish "to make our arrangements in such manner that you may be relieved from these apprehensions of loss, and from the necessity of recurring to any management

81. Review of *Voyages and Discoveries of the Companions of Columbus,* in *Gentleman's Magazine, and Historical Chronicle* 101 (February, 1831), 143–44.

of the press to aid the publication of a work of mine." The message was perfectly clear: Irving was not a profitable author for Murray and could not expect to impose his own terms. Still, Murray repeated his request to read the two new manuscripts, promising "and then we shall not differ I think about terms."[82]

Murray's implication that Irving's works were unprofitable is not completely accurate. As Irving observed of his copyright works, "you must not always expect to clear the price of a farm by the first year's crop."[83] The insignificant profit from works like *Companions* was partly the consequence of the piracy of the book in Paris by Anthony and William Galignani. The Galignanis pirated hundreds of English copyright works, offering them for sale "at a fifth of the price originally charged for each work," claiming accuracy, completeness, and compactness." Frequently the Galignanis were able to issue an English work within three or four days of its publication in London. The market for such pirated editions was actually England, rather than the Continent. Pirated French paperback editions were brought back into England so rapidly that the value of a London edition was rapidly lost both to publisher and author. Probably by early January of 1831 *Voyages and Discoveries of the Companions of Columbus* was available in Paris, for A. & W. Galignani rapidly pirated and printed it "at the English, French, Italian, German, and Spanish Library, No. 18, Rue Vivienne." The Galignanis' printer was Jules Didot, Sr., at No. 6, Rue du Pont de Lodi. Giles Barber observes that the Galignanis' "publishing programme settled down, from 1831, into a regular pattern. This consisted of the immediate republication of successful English writers in conjunction with Baudry's European Library...."[84] Louis Claude Baudry's 1831 piracy of *Companions*, in fact, was so successful that it was followed by reissues in 1834, 1836, and 1843 in *The Complete Works of Washington Irving* in *one* volume. Published at 3 Quai Malaquais, near the Pont des Arts, and printed by Stassin et Xavier of 9 Rue du Coq, this volume was offered for sale by Amyot, Rue de la Paix; Truchy, Boulevard des Italiens; Theophile Barrios, 13 Quai Voltaire; Brockhaus et Avenarius, Rue Richelieu; Leopold Michelsen of Leipzig; and by all the principal booksellers on the Continent. *Companions* took up only eighty-eight large, double-columned pages (943–1031) in the massive edition. Pirates all over the Continent were having their way with Irving's works. It is

82. McClary, p. 160.

83. *Letters*, II, 671.

84. Giles Barber, "Galignani's and the Publication of English Books in France from 1800 to 1852," *Library*, 5th ser., 16 (December, 1961), 272.

no wonder that Murray profited little from *Companions of Columbus* or that Irving, in unjustified high dudgeon, put his manuscripts of *Mahomet* and the Spanish tales into his trunk and announced to Leslie that "I am determined to have nothing more to do with him [Murray]."[85] The *Alhambra* went to the London publishers Colburn and Bentley, and Irving left for the United States in April of 1832.

The persistent problem of income, which dogged Irving in Spain and England, pursued him after his return to America. Periodically, Irving worked over these unfinished Spanish materials, while he completed "American" books like *Astoria* (1836) and *The Adventures of Captain Bonneville* (1837). Carey, Lea, and Blanchard reissued *Companions of Columbus* in 1835, but we may imagine that it did little to augment Irving's earnings. Machine collations reveal that the 1835 *Companions* is an impression of the original 1831 press run of Isaac Ashmead, with only the title page changed and brought up to date. How many of the original 3,000 were sold with the new title page date cannot be determined. But since Carey, Lea, and Blanchard were publishing other Irving titles in 1835, 1836, 1837, and 1840, it is likely that this 1835 date was a stratagem to make the work appear to be a new (and possibly revised) edition.

In 1842 Irving approached Lea and Blanchard with a proposal for a large, multivolume collected edition of his writings, "representing himself as tormented by profitable offers from publishing houses in New York and Boston."[86] But Lea and Blanchard were reluctant to enter into this scheme, apparently notifying Irving, according to George P. Putnam, that "in their judgment the demand for his writing had ceased and that there would be no profit to either author or publishers in making further attempts to keep the books in the market."[87] Whether Lea and Blanchard were this blunt is questionable, but in any event George Putnam approached Irving in 1845 and offered to publish any new works Irving might have on hand. Irving's reply was not completely negative: "I am preparing a complete edition of my works, with corrections, alterations, additions, and when in a sufficient state of forwardness, it is my idea to make an arrangement for the whole (and perhaps for any new writings I may have ready for the press), either by disposing of the copyrights, or by turning them out collectively for a term of years, at a yearly consideration. . . . If, hereafter, I can make a satisfactory

85. Letters, II, 679.
86. STW, II, 215.
87. George H. Putnam, *George Palmer Putnam: A Memoir* (New York: G. P. Putnam's Sons, 1912), p. 126.

arrangement of this kind with your House, I assure you there is none with which I would be more happy to deal."[88]

In July of 1848 Irving and George P. Putnam finally agreed to a re-issue of all of Irving's published works, together with a number of new volumes, like the never-completed *Mahomet* and *The Life of George Washington*. The terms of the Putnam proposal included, "in addition to the payment of royalty, for the first year of one thousand, for the second of two thousand, and for the third year of three thousand dollars." Irving was apparently so well pleased with Putnam's offer that he is said to have kicked over the office desk and to have told his nephew John Treat Irving II that there was no necessity for his "bothering further with the law": "Here is a fool of a publisher going to give me a thousand dollars a year for doing nothing."[89] In actuality, however, the terms of the contract did require a great deal of Irving—namely, to revise substantially all of his writings and to see this "Author's Revised Edition" through the press. Between mid-1848 and the close of 1850, Irving toiled endlessly at his work of revision.

Voyages and Discoveries of the Companions of Columbus was revised and published in February of 1848 by George Putnam at 155 Broadway in New York City. In this new fifteen-volume edition, however, it lost its name. It appears merely as the third of a three-volume subset called *The Life and Voyages of Christopher Columbus; To Which Are Added Those of His Companions*. This new amalgam of *Columbus* and *Companions* constitutes volumes 3–5 of the fifteen-volume "Author's Revised Edition." Each of the three volumes has its own volume number on its title page. In "Volume III" the text of *Companions* is printed, together with thirty-five appendixes originally published in *Columbus*, two new appendixes to *Columbus*, and an extensive index to all three volumes. Collation of the first English edition and the Author's Revised Edition indicates that printer's copy for the ARE was a revised and marked-up copy of IE. This marked-up printer's copy is no longer extant. Neither is the author-corrected ARE proof any longer available. But collation of these two editions reveals significant substantive evidence of Irving's revision and improvements, as well as extensive Putnam house styling of accidentals, including the Americanization of the spelling and the modernization of the punctuation. (These changes are fully discussed in the Textual Commentary.) Since most of the records of the Putnam firm have been destroyed, the editor cannot provide full information about the contracts, costs, and correspondence. It cannot

88. Ibid., pp. 85–86.
89. Ibid., p. 128.

be shown, for example, how many copies of *Companions* were printed
and bound in this ARE edition.[90] Nor can we determine Putnam's
expenses for printing, paper, maps, wrappers, advertisements, binding,
and the like. The printer, however, was John F. Trow, printer and
stereotyper, of 49 Ann Street, New York City. A duplicate set of plates
for *Companions* was sent by Irving in 1849 to John Murray, to be
reprinted by Bradbury and Evans of Whitefriars in London. The publication date for this, the second English edition by Murray, was December 10, 1849.[91] This "simultaneous" publication of the ARE in New
York and London occurred in the course of an extensive legal battle
between John Murray III and Henry Bohn and George Routledge. Both
Bohn and Routledge exploited the lack of an international copyright
law to reprint title after title of Irving's in cheap reprints like Bohn's
ten-volume popular library called the "Shilling Series" (London: Bohn,
1850) and the eight-volume shilling-apiece edition of Routledge (London: Routledge, 1850).[92] Though *Voyages and Discoveries of the Companions of Columbus* was owned and copyrighted by John Murray (as
the Copyright Registry Book, volume 4, entries and assignments, index
5795, makes clear), Bohn argued that Murray's copyrights were invalid
since Irving was an American and therefore not covered by British
copyright law. Murray's lawyers argued that foreign nationals were indeed covered by British copyright law. But in case the court should
find against him, Murray's lawyers investigated Irving's ancestry, eventually arguing that Irving was a British writer because his father had
been born in Scotland.[93]

Murray's copyright battle with Bohn had the effect of eliciting from

90. In all probability, however, the first printing of the ARE *Companions* ran to
2,500 copies. This was the number of first-run copies of the ARE *Goldsmith*, also
published in 1849. Since subsequent printings of *Goldsmith* were repeated in multi-
ples of 2,000, we may confidently assume that *Voyages and Discoveries of the
Companions of Columbus* was printed in comparable numbers.

91. This publication date is indicated by the "Form of Requiring Entry of Proprietorship," signed by John Murray III on January 4, 1850, and deposited in the
Public Record Office. The *Athenaeum* gives the first announcement of Murray's forthcoming edition of *Life and Voyages of Columbus, Together with the Voyages of
His Companions*, in three volumes octavo, as early as April 28, 1849 (p. 428). Subsequent advertisements appeared on November 3, 10, 17, and December 1. On December 8, 1849, it was listed as "Ready." The price for the three-volume set was
31s. 6d. The *Publisher's Circular* also advertises this set as "A New Edition" on
October 15 and December 15, 1849 (pp. 345, 423).

92. *Voyages and Discoveries of the Companions of Columbus* is advertised on
June 1, 1850, in the *Publisher's Circular* in Bohn's "Popular Library" series.

93. STW, II, 214.

Irving information which verifies the time and place of the composition of *Voyages and Discoveries of the Companions of Columbus*. In a letter to John Murray III, dated Sunnyside, August 8, 1850, Irving noted for the legal record that "Companions of Columbus" was written "partly in Spain partly in England," and that "the work entitled 'the Companions of Columbus' was purchased of me by the late Mr. John Murray of Albemarle Street London, and I am ready when called on to make a formal assignment of the same to his heirs."[94]

As the copyright war unfolded in London, Murray was moved to invite Irving to London to testify in his own behalf, as a British writer. Irving declined: "I am not disposed to enter litigation on my own account and wish no legal measures to be taken on my behalf—above all I have no idea of compromising my character as a native born and thoroughly loyal American citizen in seeking to promote my pecuniary interests, though I am willing to take all proper steps to protect yours."[95]

To protect Murray's interest, Irving prepared a memorandum which confirms Murray's proprietorship of the *Companions of Columbus*. This document also verifies other evidence, which has earlier been presented, as to the composition of the work. Writing from Sunnyside on September 22, 1850, Irving observed to John Murray III: "Part of the summer of 1828 I passed at a country house in the neighborhood of Port St Mary's opposite Cadiz, where I sketched out some of the voyages of the Companions of Columbus, from Notes and Memoranda taken in Madrid and Seville. The following winter was passed in Seville." He went on to note that in July of 1829, "I set out for England" and remained in London, "until the Spring of 1832 during which time I completed and published the Voyages of the Companions of Columbus (published in London 31st. Decr. 1830. In New York March 7th. 1831)."[96]

In preparing this memorandum, Irving was in fact replying to a series of specific questions Murray had asked him. The notes which Irving and his nephew Pierre assembled for this memorandum give other collateral evidence of the facts contained in the letters and jour-

---

94. *Letters*, vol. 4, *1846–1859*, ed. Ralph M. Aderman, Herbert L. Kleinfield, and Jenifer S. Banks (Boston: Twayne Publishers, 1982), p. 216.

95. Ibid., p. 222.

96. Ibid., pp. 224–25. Irving's reference to the publication of *Companions* in New York here does not conform with the known facts, since Isaac Ashmead (the printer) and Carey & Lea (the publisher) were Philadelphia firms. Perhaps Irving wrongly assumed that Ebenezer had had *Companions* printed by a New York printer and had sold it in sheets to the Philadelphia publisher, a kind of arrangement Ebenezer had made with previous Irving titles.

Irving's memorandum confirming John Murray's proprietorship of the *Companions of Columbus.* *Courtesy of the Beinecke Library, Yale University.*

nals between 1828 and 1832. His notes for *Companions*, housed at the Yale University Library, read as follows:

Companions of Columbus
1. Sketched out in Spain in 1827. & Finished in England 1830.
2. The revised edition corrected & completed in the United States in 1848. I residing there at the time.
3. Treated with Mr. Murray for the sale of work latter part of 1830.
4. Verbal agreement to sell it to him for 500 guineas. recd payt in notes.
5. Delivered MS. to Murray in London 1830 in pursuance of agreement.
6. I recd 500 guineas, in notes, do not recollect about a receipt.
7. Sent in sheets to E I in America [printers] to print an edition sold by him to Messrs Carey & Lea Philadelphia.
8. First published in Am. by Carey & Lea Phila March 7 1831.
9. First publd in England 31 Decr. 1830 by Mr. Murray.
10. Simultaneous publication intended in Engd and America.
11. Publication by Murray was on his own account.
12. I was residing in Engd at the time of its first publication there.[97]

In 1850 Irving's *Companions* was pirated by Bohn as part of his ten-volume reprint of the *Complete Works of Washington Irving. Columbus* and *Companions* are volumes 6–7. Moreover, the *Athenaeum* for June 29, 1850, lists Irving's *Companions* as available in the "Shilling Series" for ls. 6d.[98] The upshot of this thievery was that Murray re-registered, on October 29, 1850, a certification of his copyright proprietorship of *Companions* in the Register Book of the Stationer's Company. In May of 1851 he brought a suit against Bohn at the Queen's Bench. It was settled out of court with the purchase, by Bohn, of Murray's copyrights and the printed stock of all of Irving's works—including *Voyages and Discoveries of the Companions of Columbus*—for 2,000 guineas.

In addition to Murray's three-volume set of *Columbus* and *Companions* (1849) in the Library Edition, and the 1850 and 1852 Bohn reprints in the Standard Library and the "Cheap Series" (volumes 12–14, paged continuously), Putnam reissued the "Author's Revised Edition," including *Companions*, in 1850, 1851, 1859, 1860, 1868, and 1869, in complete sets called the "Kinderhook," the "Hudson," and the "Riverside" editions. After Irving's death and throughout the rest of the century, of course, Putnam continued to capitalize on this "Author's Revised Edi-

97. McClary, p. 218. In item 9, McClary, who publishes this memorandum, inadvertently omits the date "31"; it is here restored, as it appears in the original manuscript at the Beinecke Library, Yale University.
98. See F. G. M. Cordasco, *The Bohn Libraries* (New York: Burt Franklin, 1951), p. 48.

tion" of Irving's works. Bohn also reissued *Companions* in 1859, Routledge in 1860, and William Tegg reissued the whole of the Family
Library, including *Companions*, in 1861.[99] *Companions* was also reissued in scores of other reprints throughout the nineteenth century—
by Putnam, Lippincott, J. W. Lovell, Cassell & Company, F. F. Lovell,
David McKay, the Belford Company, Perkins, and J. B. Alden. None
of these reprints has any textual authority.

In addition to these English and American reprints, *Companions of
Columbus* was separately published, in pirated English editions, in
several foreign countries, including an 1835 and an 1837 Leipzig edition
by Baumgaertners Buchhandlung ("Mit Noten zur Erklaerung des
Textes und zur Erleichterung der Aussprache, nebst einem Woerter-
buche"); a Stockholm edition in 1837, published by H. G. Nordström
("Edited with accents and 1,000 notes"); two Renger editions in Leipzig (1840 and 1846)—"With a complete vocabulary compiled by Dr. E.
Amthor"; and editions by Baumgärtner in Leipzig and Kühtmann in
Dresden (both in 1885)—"Mit einer Einleitung und erklärenden Er-
läuterungen hrsg. von c. Th. Lion."

In addition to these reprints in English, *Voyages and Discoveries of
the Companions of Columbus* was translated into Dutch (Haarlem, A.
Loosjes, 1834), into French, by A.-J.-B. and C.-A Defauconpret (Paris:
C. Gosselin, 1833); by Henri Lebrun (Tours: A. Mame, 1839). (This
Lebrun translation went through sixteen editions by 1885.) *Companions*
was also translated by J. Girardin (Paris: Hachette et cie, 1880), which
achieved a third edition in 1893. It was translated into German by Ph.
A. G. von Meyer (Frankfurt: Sauerländer, 1831); into Italian by L. T.
(Milan: Dalla tip. de Paolo Andrea Molina, 1842); into Spanish
(Madrid: Gaspar y Roig, 1851, 1854); and into Swedish (Stockholm:
Wiborg & Co., 1832).

This summary of the printing history of *Voyages and Discoveries of
the Companions of Columbus* should not obscure the extent to which
the work was regarded in Irving's lifetime as an appendage to the
larger and more impressive life of Columbus. For this reason it is
usually passed over in the criticism of Irving's historical writing as
"an inconsequential affair," a "sturdy footnote" which "reached its

99. The *Athenaeum* for July 20, 1861 (no. 1760, p. 71), announces the "Reissue
of the Family Library" by William Tegg of Pancras Lane, Cheapside. *Columbus* (abridged) and *Companions* are offered in "Fcap. 8vo. cloth, gilt edges, illustrated, 3s.6d per volume." The *Publisher's Circular* also advertises an edition of
Companions in Tegg's "Cabinet Series" in 1866. It is a 32mo., cloth edition for
2s. (May 15, 1866).

FORM OF REQUIRING ENTRY OF PROPRIETORSHIP.

I, *John Murray* of *Albemarle Stock in the County of Middlesex Publisher*, do hereby certify, That I am the Proprietor of the Copyright of a Book, intituled *Voyages and Discoveries of the Companions of Columbus* ; and I hereby require you to make entry in the Register Book of the Stationers' Company of my Proprietorship of such Copyright, according to the particulars underwritten.

by Washington Irving

Title of Book.	Name of Publisher, and Place of Publication.	Name and Place of Abode of the Proprietor of the Copyright.	Date of First Publication.
Voyages and Discoveries of the Companions of Columbus — by Washington Irving.	John Murray 52 Albemarle Street London	John Murray No 50 Albemarle Street London in the County of Middlesex Publisher	31st December 1830

Dated this 29th day of October, 1850.

Witness, *W. Leith Field*

(Signed) *John Murray*

N.B. Office Hours from Ten to Four.

John Murray's re-registration of copyright, October 29, 1850.

proper mortuary in 'Murray's Family Library.' "[100] Stanley T. Williams called *Companions* "the sort of volume for which only John Murray could afford five hundred guineas and which only Washington Irving could write without being christened a common hack writer."[101] This judgment is unduly negative. Though *Companions* has its defects, the editor is more inclined to agree with Van Wyck Brooks, who praised "the glowing chapters" of *Companions of Columbus*, which "can hardly be excelled in human feeling and romantic enthusiasm." For Brooks, as for many other readers, "These chapters are chips from the workshop that produced the great *History*, but they are chips of the rarest material."[102]

100. STW, II, 23–24.
101. Ibid., II, 24.
102. Van Wyck Brooks, foreword to *Voyages and Discoveries of the Companions of Columbus*, by Washington Irving (New York: Rimington & Hooper, 1929), pp. xii, viii. These remarks are from the foreword to the most recently published edition of *Companions*—the "Savoy" edition of 374 copies, designed and printed by W. A. Kittredge at the Lakeside Press.

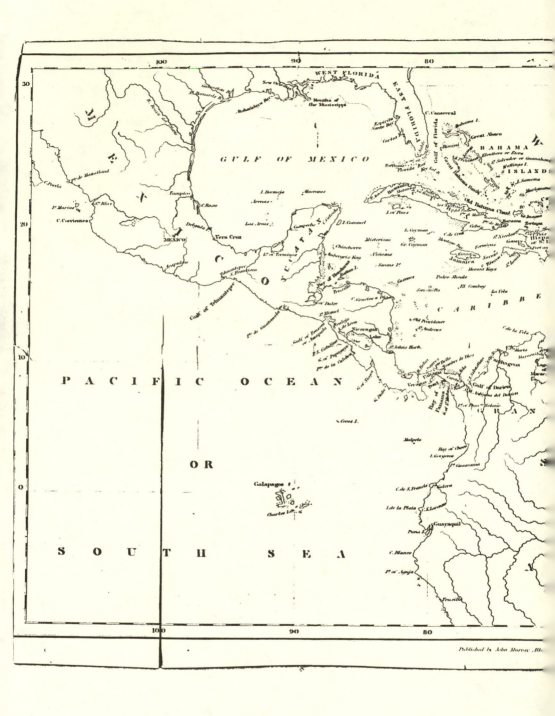

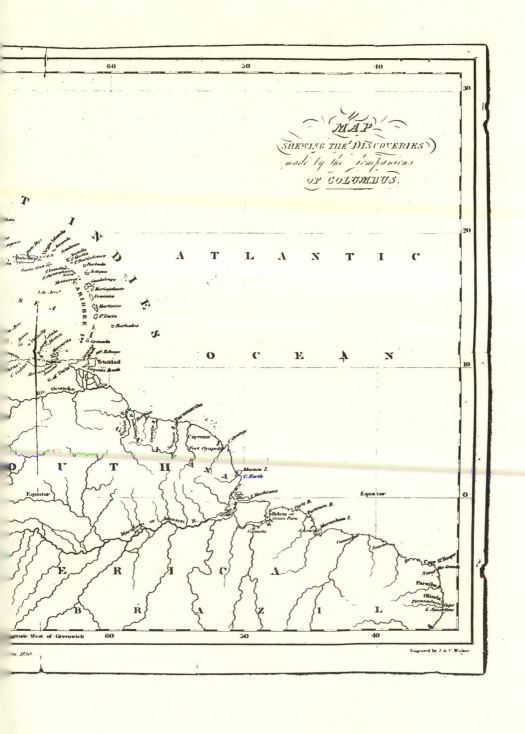

MAP
SHEWING THE DISCOVERIES
made by the Companions
OF COLUMBUS.

"To declare my opinion herein, whatsover hath heretofore been discovered by the famous travayles of Saturnus and Hercules, with such other whom the antiquitie for their heroical acts honoured as Gods, seemeth but little and obscure, if it be compared to the victorious labours of the Spanyards."

P. Martyr, decad. iii. c.4. Lok's translation.

VOYAGES AND DISCOVERIES
OF THE
COMPANIONS OF COLUMBUS

Venient annis
Sæcula seris, quibus, Oceanus
Vincula, rerum laxet, et ingens
Pateat tellus, Typhisque novos
Detegat Orbes, nec sit terris
Ultima Thule.

Seneca: *Medea.*

INTRODUCTION

The first discovery of the Western Hemisphere has already been related by the Author in his History of Columbus. It is proposed by him, in the present work, to narrate the enterprises of certain of the companions and disciples of the Admiral, who, enkindled by his zeal, and instructed by his example, sallied forth separately in the vast region of adventure to which he had led the way. Many of them sought merely to skirt the continent which he had partially visited; to secure the first fruits of the pearl fisheries of Paria and Cubaga; or to explore the coast of Veragua, which he had represented as the Aurea Chersonesus of the ancients. Others aspired to accomplish a grand discovery which he had meditated toward the close of his career. In the course of his expeditions along the coast of Terra Firma, Columbus had repeatedly received information of the existence of a vast sea to the south. He supposed it to be the great Indian Ocean, the region of the oriental spice islands, and that it must communicate by a strait with the Caribbean sea. His last and most dangerous voyage was made for the express purpose of discovering that imaginary strait, and making his way into this Southern Ocean. The illustrious navigator, however, was doomed to die, as it were, upon the threshold of his discoveries. It was reserved for one of his followers, Vasco Nuñez de Balboa, to obtain the first view of the promised ocean, from the lofty mountains of Darien, some years after the eyes of the venerable Admiral had been closed in death. The expeditions here narrated, therefore, may be considered as springing immediately out of the voyages of Columbus, and fulfilling some of his grand designs. They may be compared to the attempts of adventurous knights-errant to achieve the enterprise left unfinished by some illustrious predecessor. Neither is this comparison entirely fanciful: on the contrary, it is a curious fact, well worthy of notice, that the spirit of chivalry entered largely into the early expeditions of the Spanish discoverers, giving them a character wholly distinct from similar enterprises, undertaken by other nations. It will not, perhaps, be considered far-sought, if we trace the cause of this peculiarity to the domestic history of the Spaniards during the middle ages.

Eight centuries of incessant warfare with the Moorish usurpers of the Peninsula, produced a deep and lasting effect upon Spanish character and manners. The war being ever close at home, mingled itself with the domestic habits and concerns of the Spaniard. He was born a soldier. The wild and predatory nature of the war also made him a kind of chivalrous marauder. His horse and weapon were always ready for the field. His delight was in roving incursions and extravagant exploits; and no gain was so glorious in his eyes as the cavalgada of spoils and captives driven home in triumph from a plundered province. Religion, which has ever held great empire over the Spanish mind, lent its aid to sanctify these roving and ravaging propensities, and the Castilian cavalier, as he sacked the towns, and laid waste the fields of his Moslem neighbour, piously believed he was doing God service.

The conquest of Granada put an end to the peninsular wars between Christian and infidel: the spirit of Spanish chivalry was thus suddenly deprived of its wonted sphere of action; but it had been too long fostered and excited, to be as suddenly appeased. The youth of the nation, bred up to daring adventure and heroic achievement, could not brook the tranquil and regular pursuits of common life, but panted for some new field of romantic enterprise.

It was at this juncture that the grand project of Columbus was carried into effect. His treaty with the sovereigns was, in a manner, signed with the same pen that had subscribed the capitulation of the Moorish capital; and his first expedition may almost be said to have departed from beneath the walls of Granada. Many of the youthful cavaliers, who had fleshed their swords in that memorable war, crowded the ships of the discoverers, thinking a new career of arms was to be opened to them—a kind of crusade into splendid and unknown regions of infidels. The very weapons and armour that had been used against the Moors, were drawn from the arsenal to equip the heroes of these remoter adventures; and some of the most noted commanders in the New World, will be found to have made their first essay in arms, under the banner of Ferdinand and Isabella, in their romantic campaigns among the mountains of Andalusia.

To these circumstances may, in a great measure, be ascribed that swelling chivalrous spirit which will be found continually mingling, or rather warring, with the technical habits of the seaman and the sordid schemes of the mercenary adventurer, in these early Spanish discoveries. Chivalry had left the land and launched upon the deep. The Spanish cavalier had embarked in the caravel of the discoverer. He carried among the trackless wildernesses of the new world the same contempt of danger and fortitude under suffering; the same restless roaming spirit; the same passion for inroad and ravage and vain-glorious exploit; and the same fervent, and often bigoted, zeal for the propagation of his faith, that had distinguished him during his warfare with the Moors. Instances in point will be found in the extravagant career of the daring Ojeda, particularly in his adventures along the coast of Terra Firma and the wild shores of Cuba;—in the sad story of the "unfortunate Nicuesa," graced as it is with occasional touches of high-bred courtesy;—in the singular cruise of that brave but credulous old cavalier, Juan Ponce de Leon, who fell upon the flowery coast of Florida in his search after an imaginary fountain of youth;—and above all, in the chequered fortunes of Vasco Nuñez de Balboa, whose discovery of the Pacific Ocean forms one of the most beautiful and striking incidents in the history of the New World, and whose fate might furnish a theme of wonderful interest for a poem or a drama.

The extraordinary actions and adventures of these men, while they rival the exploits recorded in chivalric romance, have the additional interest of verity. They leave us in admiration of the bold and heroic qualities inherent in the Spanish character, which led that nation to so high a pitch of power and glory; and which are still discernible in the great mass of that gallant people, by those who have an opportunity of judging of them rightly.

Before concluding these prefatory remarks, the Author would acknowledge how much he has been indebted to the third volume of the invaluable Historical Collection of Don Martin Fernandez de Navarrete, wherein that author has exhibited his usual industry, accuracy, and critical acumen. He has likewise profited greatly by the second volume of Oviedo's General History, which only exists in manuscript, and a copy of which he found in the Columbian Library of the Cathedral of Seville.

He has had some assistance also from the documents of the law case between Don Diego Columbus and the crown, which exists in the Archives of the Indias, and for an inspection of which he is much indebted to the permission of the government and the kind attentions of Don Josef de la Higuera y Lara, the intelligent keeper of the Archives. These, with the historical works of Herrera, Las Casas, Gomara, and Peter Martyr, have been his authorities for the facts contained in the following work, though he has not thought proper to refer to them continually at the bottom of his page.

While his work was going through the press, he received a volume of Spanish Biography, written with great elegance and accuracy, by Don Manuel Josef Quintana, and containing a Life of Vasco Nuñez de Balboa. He was gratified to find that his own arrangement of facts was generally corroborated by this work; though he was enabled to correct his dates in several instances, and to make a few other emendations from the volume of Señor Quintana, whose position in Spain gave him the means of attaining superior exactness on these points.

ALONZO DE OJEDA,*
His First Voyage,
in which He was Accompanied by
AMERIGO VESPUCCI.†

Chapter I

Some account of Ojeda—of Juan de la Cosa—of Amerigo Vespucci—
Preparations for the voyage (1499)

Those who have read the History of Columbus will, doubtless, remember the character and exploits of Alonzo de Ojeda; as some of the readers of the following pages, however, may not have perused that work, and as it is proposed at present to trace the subsequent fortunes of this youthful adventurer, a brief sketch of him may not be deemed superfluous.

Alonzo de Ojeda was a native of Cuenca in New Castile, and of a respectable family. He was brought up as a page or esquire, in the service of Don Luis de Cerda, Duke of Medina Celi, one of the most powerful nobles of Spain, the same who for some time patronized Columbus during his application to the Spanish court.‡

In those warlike days, when the peninsula was distracted by contests between the Christian kingdoms, by feuds between the nobles and the crown, and by the incessant and marauding warfare with the Moors, the household of a Spanish nobleman was a complete School of Arms, where the youth of the country were sent to be trained up in all kinds of hardy exercises, and to be led to battle under an illustrious banner. Such was especially the case with the service of the Duke of Medina Celi, who possessed princely domains, whose household was a petty court, who led legions of armed retainers to the field and who appeared in splendid state and with an immense retinue, more as an ally of Ferdinand and Isabella, than as a subject. He engaged in many of the roughest expeditions of the memorable war of Granada, always insisting on leading his own troops in person, when the service was of peculiar difficulty and

*Ojeda is pronounced in Spanish Oheda, with a strong aspiration of the *h*.
†Vespucci—pronounced Vespuchy.
‡Varones Ilustres, por F. Pizarro y Orellana, p. 41. Las Casas, Hist. Ind. lib. i. cap. 82.

danger. Alonzo de Ojeda was formed to signalize himself in such a school. Though small of stature he was well made, and of wonderful force and activity, with a towering spirit that seemed to make up for deficiency of height. He was a bold and graceful horseman, an excellent footsoldier, dextrous with every weapon, and noted for his extraordinary skill and adroitness in all feats of strength and agility.

He must have been quite young when he followed the Duke of Medina Celi, as page, to the Moorish wars; for he was but about twenty one years of age when he accompanied Columbus in his Second Voyage; he had already, however, distinguished himself by his enterprizing spirit and headlong valour, and his exploits during that voyage contributed to enhance his reputation. He returned to Spain with Columbus, but did not accompany him in his third voyage, in the spring of 1498. He was probably impatient of subordination, and ambitious of a separate employment or command, which the influence of his connexions gave him a great chance of obtaining. He had a cousin german of his own name, the reverend Padre Alonzo de Ojeda, a Dominican friar, one of the first inquisitors of Spain, and a great favorite with the Catholic Sovereigns.*
This father inquisitor was, moreover, an intimate friend of the Bishop Don Juan Rodriguez Fonseca, who had the chief management of the affairs of the Indies, under which general name were comprehended all the countries discovered in the new world. Through the good offices of his cousin inquisitor, therefore, Ojeda had been introduced to the notice of the Bishop, who took him into his especial favour and patronage. Mention has already been made, in the History of Columbus, of a present made by the Bishop to Ojeda of a small Flemish painting of the Holy Virgin. This the young adventurer carried about with him as a protecting relique; invoking it at all times of peril, whether by sea or land; and to the especial care of the Virgin he attributed the remarkable circumstance that he had never been wounded in any of the innumerable brawls and battles into which he was continually betrayed by his rash and fiery temperament.

While Ojeda was lingering about the court, letters were received from Columbus giving an account of the events of his third voyage, especially of his discovery of the coast of Paria, which he described as abounding in drugs and spices, in gold and silver, and precious stones, and, above all, in oriental pearls, and which he supposed to be the borders of that vast and unknown region of the East, wherein, according to certain learned theorists, was situated the terrestrial paradise. Specimens of the

---

* Pizarro. Varones Ilustres.

pearls, procured in considerable quantities from the natives, accompanied his epistle, together with charts descriptive of his route. These tidings caused a great sensation among the maritime adventurers of Spain, but no one was more excited by them than Alonzo de Ojeda, who, from his intimacy with the Bishop, had full access to the charts and correspondence of Columbus. He immediately conceived the project of making a voyage in the route thus marked out by the admiral, and of seizing upon the first fruits of discovery which he had left ungathered. His scheme met with ready encouragement from Fonseca, who, as has heretofore been shown, was an implacable enemy to Columbus, and willing to promote any measure that might injure or molest him. The Bishop accordingly granted a commission to Ojeda, authorizing him to fit out an armament and proceed on a voyage of discovery, with the proviso merely that he should not visit any territories appertaining to Portugal, or any of the lands discovered in the name of Spain previous to the year 1495. The latter part of this provision appears to have been craftily worded by the Bishop so as to leave the coast of Paria and its pearl fisheries open to Ojeda, they having been recently discovered by Columbus in 1498.

The commission was signed by Fonseca alone, in virtue of general powers vested in him for such purposes, but the signature of the Sovereigns did not appear on the instrument, and it is doubtful whether their sanction was sought on the occasion. He knew that Columbus had recently remonstrated against a royal mandate issued in 1495, permitting voyages of discovery by private adventurers, and that the sovereigns had, in consequence, revoked their mandate wherever it might be deemed prejudicial to the stipulated privileges of the admiral.* It is probable, therefore, that the Bishop avoided raising any question that might impede the enterprize; being confident of the ultimate approbation of Ferdinand, who would be well pleased to have his dominions in the new world extended by the discoveries of private adventurers, undertaken at their own expense. It was stipulated in this, as well as in subsequent licences for private expeditions, that a certain proportion of the profits, generally a fourth or fifth, should be reserved for the crown.

Having thus obtained permission to make the voyage, the next consideration with Ojeda was to find the means. He was a young adventurer, a mere soldier of fortune, and destitute of wealth; but he had a high reputation for courage and enterprize, and with these, it was thought, would soon make his way to the richest parts of the newly discovered lands, and have the wealth of the Indies at his disposal. He had no diffi-

* Navarrete, tom. ii. Document cxiii.

culty, therefore, in finding monied associates among the rich merchants of Seville, who, in that age of discovery, were ever ready to stake their property upon the schemes of roving navigators. With such assistance he soon equipped a squadron of four vessels at Port St. Mary, opposite Cadiz. Among the seamen who engaged with him were several just returned from accompanying Columbus in his voyage to this very coast of Paria. The principal associate of Ojeda, and one on whom he placed great reliance, was Juan de la Cosa; who accompanied him as first mate, or, as it was termed, chief pilot. This was a bold Biscayan, who may be regarded as a disciple of Columbus, with whom he had sailed in his second voyage, when he coasted Cuba and Jamaica, and he had since accompanied Rodrigo de Bastides, in an expedition along the coast of Terra Firma. The hardy veteran was looked up to by his contemporaries as an oracle of the seas, and was pronounced one of the most able mariners of the day; he may be excused, therefore, if, in his harmless vanity, he considered himself on a par even with Columbus.*

Another conspicuous associate of Ojeda in this voyage was Amerigo Vespucci, a Florentine merchant, induced by broken fortunes and a rambling disposition to seek adventures in the new world. Whether he had any pecuniary interest in the expedition, and in what capacity he sailed, does not appear. His importance has entirely arisen from subsequent circumstances; from his having written and published a narrative of his voyages, and from his name having eventually been given to the new world.

Chapter II

Departure from Spain—Arrival on the coast of Paria—Customs of the natives

Ojeda sailed from Port St. Mary on the 20th of May 1499, and, having touched for supplies at the Canaries, took a departure from Gomara, pursuing the route of Columbus in his third voyage, being guided by the chart he had sent home, as well as by the mariners who had accompanied him on that occasion. At the end of twenty four days he reached

---

* Navarrete, Colec. Viag. tom. iii. p. 4.

the continent of the new world, about two hundred leagues farther south than the part discovered by Columbus, being, as it is supposed, the coast of Surinam.*

From hence he ran along the coast of the Gulph of Paria, passing the mouths of many rivers, but especially those of the Esquivo and the Oronoko. These, to the astonishment of the Spaniards, unaccustomed as yet to the mighty rivers of the new world, poured forth such a prodigious volume of water, as to freshen the sea for a great extent. They beheld none of the natives until they arrived at Trinidad, on which island they met with traces of the recent visit of Columbus.

Vespucci, in his letters, gives a long description of the people of this island and of the coast of Paria, who were of the Carib race, tall, well made, and vigorous, and expert with the bow, the lance and the buckler. His description in general resembles those which have frequently been given of the Aboriginals of the new world; there are two or three particulars, however, worthy of citation.

They appeared, he said, to believe in no religious creed, to have no place of worship and to make no prayers or sacrifices; but, he adds, from the voluptuousness of their lives, they might be considered Epicureans.†
Their habitations were built in the shape of bells; of the trunks of trees, thatched with palm leaves, and were proof against wind and weather. They appeared to be in common, and some of them were of such magnitude as to contain six hundred persons: in one place there were eight principal houses capable of sheltering nearly ten thousand inhabitants. Every seven or eight years the natives were obliged to change their residence, from the maladies engendered by the heat of the climate in their crowded habitations.

Their riches consisted in beads and ornaments made from the bones of fishes; in small white and green stones strung like rosaries, with which they adorned their persons, and in the beautiful plumes of various colours for which the tropical birds are noted.

The Spaniards smiled at their simplicity in attaching an extraordinary value to such worthless trifles; while the savages, in all probability, were equally surprized at beholding the strangers so eager after gold, and pearls and precious stones, which to themselves were objects of indifference.

Their manner of treating the dead was similar to that observed among the natives of some of the islands. Having deposited the corpse in a

* Navarrete, tom. iii. p. 5.
† Viages de Vespucci. Navarrete, tom. iii. p. 211.

cavern, or sepulchre, they placed a jar of water and a few eatables at its head, and then abandoned it without moan or lamentation. In some parts of the coast, when a person was considered near his end his nearest relatives bore him to the woods, and laid him in a hammac suspended to the trees. They then danced round him until evening when, having left within his reach sufficient meat and drink to sustain him for four days, they repaired to their habitations. If he recovered and returned home, he was received with much ceremony and rejoicing; if he died of his malady or of famine, nothing more was thought of him.

Their mode of treating a fever is also worthy of mention. In the height of the malady they plunged the patient in a bath of the coldest water, after which they obliged him to make many evolutions round a great fire, until he was in a violent heat, when they put him to bed, that he might sleep: a treatment, by which Amerigo Vespucci declares he saw many cured.

Chapter III

Coasting of Terra Firma—Military expedition of Ojeda

After touching at various parts of Trinidad and the Gulph of Paria, Ojeda passed through the Strait of the Boca del Drago, or Dragon's Mouth, which Columbus had found so formidable, and then steered his course along the coast of Terra Firma, landing occasionally until he arrived at Curiana, or the Gulf of Pearls. From hence he stood to the opposite island of Margarita, previously discovered by Columbus, and since renowned for its pearl fishery. This, as well as several adjacent islands, he visited and explored; after which he returned to the mainland, and touched at Cumana and Maracapana; where he found the rivers infested with alligators resembling the crocodiles of the Nile.

Finding a convenient harbour at Maracapana, he unloaded and careened his vessels there, and built a small brigantine. The natives came to him in great numbers, bringing abundance of venison, fish, and cassava bread, and aiding the seamen in their labours. Their hospitality was not entirely disinterested, for they sought to gain the protection of the Spaniards, whom they reverenced as superhuman beings. When they thought they had sufficiently secured their favour, they represented to Ojeda that their coast was subject to invasion from a distant island, the inhabitants of which were cannibals, and carried their people into captivity, to be devoured at their unnatural banquets. They besought Ojeda, therefore, to avenge them upon these ferocious enemies.

The request was gratifying to the fighting propensities of Ojeda and to his love of adventure and was readily granted. Taking seven of the natives on board of his vessels, as guides, he set sail in quest of the cannibals. After sailing for seven days he came to a chain of islands, some peopled, others uninhabited, supposed to have been the Carribee islands. One of these was pointed out by his guides as the habitation of their foes. On running near the shore he beheld it thronged with savages, decorated with coronets of gaudy plumes, their bodies painted with a variety of colours. They were armed with bows and arrows, with darts, lances and bucklers, and seemed prepared to defend their island from invasion.

The show of war was calculated to rouse the martial spirit of Ojeda. He brought his ships to anchor, ordered out his boats, and provided each with a paterero, or small cannon. Besides the oarsmen, each boat contained a number of soldiers, who were told to crouch out of sight in the bottom. The boats then pulled in steadily for the shore. As they approached the Indians let fly with a cloud of arrows, but without much effect. Seeing the boats continue to advance, the savages threw themselves into the sea, and brandished their lances to prevent their landing. Upon this, the soldiers sprang up and discharged the patereroes. At the sound and smoke the savages abandoned the water in affright while Ojeda and his men leaped on shore and pursued them. The Carib warriors rallied on the banks, and fought for a long time with a courage peculiar to their race, but were at length driven to the woods, at the edge of the sword, leaving many killed and wounded on the field of battle.

On the following day the savages were seen on the shore in still greater numbers, armed and painted, and decorated with war plumes; and sounding defiance with their conchs and drums. Ojeda again landed with fifty seven men, whom he separated into four companies and ordered to charge the enemy from different directions. The Caribs fought for a time hand to hand, displaying great dexterity in covering themselves with their bucklers, but were at length entirely routed and driven, with great slaughter, to the forests. The Spaniards had but one man killed and twenty one wounded in these combats—such superior advantage did their armour give them over the naked savages. Having plundered and set fire to the houses they returned triumphantly to their ships, with a number of Carib captives; and made sail for the main land. Ojeda bestowed a part of the spoil upon the seven Indians who had accompanied him as guides, and sent them exulting to their homes, to relate to their countrymen the signal vengeance wreaked upon their foes. He then anchored in a bay where he remained for twenty days until his men had recovered from their wounds.*

Chapter IV

Discovery of the Gulf of Venezuela—Transactions there—Ojeda explores the gulf—Penetrates to Maracaibo

His crew being refreshed and the wounded sufficiently recovered, Ojeda made sail and touched at the island of Curazao, which, according to the account of Vespucci, was inhabited by a race of giants, "every woman appearing a Penthesilea, and every man an Antæus."† As Vespucci was a scholar, and as he supposed himself exploring the regions of the extreme East, the ancient realm of fable, it is probable his imagination deceived him, and construed the formidable accounts given by the Indians of their cannibal neighbors of the islands, into something according with his recollections of classic fable. Certain it is that the reports of subsequent voyagers proved the inhabitants of the island to be of the ordinary size.

Proceeding along the coast, he arrived at a vast deep gulph resembling a tranquil lake, entering which, he beheld on the eastern side a village, the construction of which struck him with surprise. It consisted of twenty large houses, shaped like bells, and built on piles driven into the bottom of the lake, which, in this part, was limpid and of but little depth. Each house was provided with a draw bridge, and with canoes by which the communication was carried on. From these resemblances to the Italian city, Ojeda gave to the bay the name of the Gulph of Venice: and it is

---

* There is some discrepancy in the early accounts of this battle, as to the time and place of its occurrence. The author has collated the narratives of Vespucci, Las Casas, Herrera and Peter Martyr, and the evidence given in the law suit of Diego Columbus, and has endeavoured as much as possible to reconcile them.

† Vespucci—Letter to Lorenzo de Pier Francisco de Medicis.

called at the present day Venezuela, or little Venice: the Indian name was Coquibacoa.

When the inhabitants beheld the ships standing into the bay, looking like wonderful and unknown apparitions from the deep, they fled with terror to their houses, and raised the draw bridges. The Spaniards remained for a time gazing with admiration at this amphibious village, when a squadron of canoes entered the harbour from the sea. On beholding the ships they pauzed in mute amazement, and on the Spaniards' attempting to approach them, paddled swiftly to shore, and plunged into the forest. They soon returned with sixteen young girls, whom they conveyed in their canoes to the ships, distributing four on board of each, either as peace offerings or as tokens of amity and confidence. The best of understanding now seemed to be established; and the inhabitants of the village came swarming about the ships in their canoes, and others swimming in great numbers from the shores.

The friendship of the savages, however, was all delusive. On a sudden several old women at the doors of the houses uttered loud shrieks, tearing their hair in fury. It appeared to be a signal for hostility. The sixteen nymphs plunged into the sea and made for shore; the Indians in the canoes caught up their bows and discharged a flight of arrows, and even those who were swimming brandished darts and lances, which they had hitherto concealed beneath the water.

Ojeda was for a moment surprized at seeing war thus starting up on every side, and the very sea bristling with weapons. Manning his boats, he charged among the thickest of the enemy; shattered and sunk several of their canoes; killed twenty Indians and wounded many more, and spread such a panic among them, that most of the survivors flung themselves into the sea and swam to shore. Three of them were taken prisoner, and two of the fugitive girls, and were conveyed on board of the ships, where the men were put in irons. One of them, however, and the two girls succeeded in dexterously escaping the same night.

Ojeda had but five men wounded in the affray; all of whom recovered. He visited the houses but found them abandoned, and destitute of booty; notwithstanding the unprovoked hostility of the inhabitants, he spared the buildings, that he might not cause useless irritation along the coast.

Continuing to explore this gulf, Ojeda penetrated to a port or harbour to which he gave the name of St. Bartholomew, but which is supposed to be the same at present known by the original Indian name of Maracaibo. Here, in compliance with the entreaties of the natives, he sent a detachment of twenty seven Spaniards on a visit to the interior. For nine days they were conducted from town to town and feasted and almost idolized by the Indians, who regarded them as angelic beings, performing their natural dances and games, and chaunting their traditional ballads for their entertainment.

The natives of this part were distinguished for the symmetry of their forms; the females in particular appeared to the Spaniards to surpass all they had yet beheld in the new world for grace and beauty. Neither did the men display in the least degree that jealousy which prevailed in the other parts of the coast; but, on the contrary, permitted the most frank and intimate intercourse with their wives and daughters.

By the time the Spaniards set out on their return to the ship, the whole country was aroused, pouring forth its population, male and female, to do them honour. Some bore them in litters or hamacs that they might not be fatigued with the journey, and happy was the Indian who had the honour of bearing a Spaniard on his shoulders across a river. Others loaded themselves with the presents that had been bestowed on their guests, consisting of rich plumes, weapons of various kinds, and tropical birds and animals. In this way they returned in triumphant procession to the ships, the woods and shores resounding with their songs and shouts.

Many of the Indians crowded into the boats that took the detachment to the ships; other put off in canoes, or swam from shore, so that in a little while the vessels were thronged with upwards of a thousand wondering natives. While gazing and marvelling at the strange objects around them, Ojeda ordered the cannon to be discharged, at the sound of which, says Vespucci, the Indians "plunged into the water like so many frogs from a bank." Perceiving, however, that it was done in harmless mirth, they returned on board, and passed the rest of the day in great festivity. The Spaniards brought away with them several of the beautiful and hospitable females from this place, one of whom, named by them Isabel, was much prized by Ojeda, and accompanied him in a subsequent voyage.*

---

* Navarrete, tom. iii. p. 8. Idem., pp. 107, 108.

It is worthy of particular mention that Ojeda, in his report of his voyage to the Sovereigns, informed them of his having met with English voyagers in the vicinity of Coquibacoa, and that the Spanish government attached such importance to his information as to take measures to prevent any intrusion into those parts by the English. It is singular that no record should exist of this early and extensive expedition of English navigators. If it was undertaken in the service of the Crown, some document might be found concerning it among the archives of the reign of

Chapter V

Prosecution of the voyage—Return to Spain

Leaving the friendly port of Coquibacoa, Ojeda continued along the western shores of the Gulph of Venezuela, and standing out to sea and doubling Cape Maracaibo, he pursued his coasting voyage from port to port, and promontory to promontory, of this unknown continent, until he reached that long stretching headland called Cape de la Vela. There the state of his vessels, and perhaps the disappointment of his hopes at not meeting with abundant sources of immediate wealth, induced him to abandon all further voyaging along the coast, and changing his course, he stood across the Caribbean Sea for Hispaniola. The tenor of his commission forbade his visiting that island; but Ojeda was not a man to stand upon trifles when his interest or inclination prompted the contrary. He trusted to excuse the infraction of his orders by the alleged necessity of touching at the island to caulk and refit his vessels and to procure provisions. His true object, however, is supposed to have been to cut dye wood, which abounds in the western part of Hispaniola.

He accordingly anchored at Yaquimo in September, and landed with a large party of his men. Columbus at that time held command of the island, and, hearing of this unlicenced intrusion, despatched Francisco Roldan, the quondam rebel, to call Ojeda to account. The contest of stratagem and management that took place between these two adroit and daring adventurers has been already detailed in the History of Columbus. Roldan was eventually successful, and Ojeda, being obliged to leave Hispaniola, resumed his rambling voyage, visiting various islands, from whence he carried off numbers of the natives. He at length arrived at Cadiz in June 1500, with his ships crowded with captives, whom he sold as slaves. So meager, however, was the result of this expedition, that we are told, when all the expenses were deducted, but 500

Henry VII. The English had already discovered the continent of North America. This had been done in 1497, by John Cabot, a Venetian, accompanied by his son Sebastian, who was born in Bristol. They sailed under a license of Henry VII, who was to have a fifth of the profits of the voyage. On the 24th June they discovered Newfoundland and afterwards coasted the continent quite to Florida, bringing back to England a valuable cargo and several of the natives. This was the first discovery of the main land of America. The success of this expedition may have prompted the one which Ojeda encountered in the neighbourhood of Coquibacoa.

ducats remained to be divided between fifty five adventurers. What made this result the more mortifying was, that a petty armament, which had sailed some time after that of Ojeda, had returned two months before him, rich with the spoils of the new world. A brief account of this latter expedition is necessary to connect this series of minor discoveries, which will be found to lead to enterprises and transactions of more stirring interest and importance.

PEDRO ALONZO NIÑO*
and
CHRISTOVAL GUERRA (1499)

The permission granted by Bishop Fonseca to Alonzo de Ojeda to undertake a private expedition to the New World roused the emulation of others of the followers of Columbus. Among these was Pedro Alonzo Niño, a hardy seaman, native of Moguer, in the vicinity of Palos, who had sailed with Columbus, as a pilot, in his first voyage, and also in his cruizings along the coasts of Cuba and Paria.† He soon obtained from the Bishop a similar licence to that given to Ojeda, and like the latter, sought for some monied confederate among the rich merchants of Seville. One of these, named Luis Guerra, offered to fit out a caravel for the expedition; but on condition that his brother, Christoval Guerra, should have the command. The poverty of Niño compelled him to assent to the stipulations of the man of wealth, and he sailed as subaltern in his own enterprize; but his nautical skill and knowledge soon gained him the ascendancy, he became virtually the captain, and ultimately enjoyed the whole credit of the voyage.

The bark of these two adventurers was but of fifty tons burthen, and the crew thirty three souls, all told. With this slender armament they undertook to traverse unknown and dangerous seas, and to explore the barbarous shores of that vast continent recently discovered by Columbus. Such was the daring spirit of the Spanish voyagers of those days.

It was about the beginning of June 1499, and but a few days after the departure of Ojeda, that they put to sea. They sailed from the little port of Palos, the cradle of American discovery, whose brave and skillful mariners long continued foremost in all enterprizes to the New World. Being guided by the chart of Columbus, they followed his route, and reached the Southern Continent, a little beyond Paria, about fifteen days after the same coast had been visited by Ojeda.

---

* Pronounced Ninyo. The Ñ in Spanish is always pronounced as if followed by the letter *y*.

† Testimony of Bastides in the law suit of Diego Columbus.

They then proceeded to the Gulf of Paria, where they landed to cut dye wood, and were amicably entertained by the natives. Shortly afterwards, sallying from the gulf by the Boca del Drago, they encountered eighteen canoes of Caribs, the pirate rovers of these seas and the terror of the bordering lands. This savage armada, instead of being daunted, as usual, by the sight of a European ship, with swelling sails, resembling some winged monster of the deep, considered it only as an object of plunder or hostility, and assailed it with showers of arrows. The sudden burst of artillery, however, from the sides of the caravel, and the havoc made among the Caribs by this seeming thunder, struck them with dismay, and they fled in all directions. The Spaniards succeeded in capturing one of the canoes, with one of the warriors who had manned it. In the bottom of the canoe lay an Indian prisoner, bound hand and foot. On being liberated he informed the Spaniards by signs that these Caribs had been on a marauding expedition along the neighboring coasts, shutting themselves up at night in a stockade which they carried with them, and issuing forth by day, to plunder the villages and make captives. He had been one of seven prisoners; his companions had been devoured before his eyes at the cannibal banquets of these savages, and he had been awaiting the same miserable fate. Honest Niño and his confederates were so indignant at this recital, that, receiving it as established fact, they performed what they considered an act of equitable justice by abandoning the Carib to the discretion of his late captive. The latter fell upon the defenceless warrior with fist and foot and cudgel, nor did his rage subside even after the breath had been mauled out of his victim, but, tearing the grim head from the body, he placed it on a pole, as a trophy of his vengeance.

Niño and his fellow-adventurers now steered for the Island of Margarita, where they obtained a considerable quantity of pearls by barter. They afterwards skirted the opposite coast of Cumana, trading cautiously and shrewdly, from port to port; sometimes remaining on board of their little bark, and obliging the savages to come off to them, when the latter appeared too numerous, at other times venturing on shore and even into the interior. They were invariably treated with amity by the natives, who were perfectly naked, excepting that they were adorned with necklaces and bracelets of pearls. These they sometimes gave freely to the Spaniards, at other times they exchanged them for glass beads and other trinkets and smiled at the folly of the strangers in making such silly bargains.*

* Las Casas. Hist. Ind. lib. i. cap. 171.

The Spaniards were struck with the grandeur and density of the forests along this coast, for in these regions of heat and moisture, vegetation appears in its utmost magnificence. They heard also the cries and roarings of wild and unknown animals in the woodlands, which, however, appeared not to be very dangerous, as the Indians went about the forest armed solely with bows and arrows. From meeting with deer and rabbits they were convinced that that was a part of Terra Firma, not having found any animals of the kind on the islands.*

Niño and Guerra were so well pleased with the hospitality of the natives of Cumana, and with the profitable traffic for pearls, by which they obtained many of great size and beauty, that they remained upwards of three months on the coast.

They then proceeded westward to a country called Cauchieto, trading, as usual, for pearls, and for the inferior kind of gold called guanin. At length they arrived at a number of houses and gardens situated on a river and protected by a kind of fortress, the whole forming, to the eyes of the Spaniards, one of the most delicious abodes imaginable. They were about to land and enjoy the pleasures of this fancied paradise, when they beheld upwards of a thousand Indians, armed with bows and arrows and war clubs, preparing to give them a warm reception; having been probably incensed by the recent visit of Ojeda. As Niño and Guerra had not the fighting propensities of Ojeda, and were in quest of profit rather than renown, having moreover, in all probability, the fear of the rich merchant of Seville before their eyes, they prudently abstained from landing, and, abandoning this hostile coast, returned forthwith to Cumana, to resume their trade for pearls. They soon amassed a great number, many of which were equal in size and beauty to the most celebrated of the East, though they had been injured in boring, from a want of proper implements.

Satisfied with their success, they now set sail for Spain, and piloted their little bark safely to Bayonne in Gallicia, where they anchored about the middle of April 1500, nearly two months before the arrival of Ojeda and his associates La Cosa and Vespucci.†

The most successful voyagers to the New World were doomed to trouble from their very success. The ample amount of pearls paid to the treasury, as the royal portion of the profits of this expedition, drew suspicion instead of favour upon the two adventurers. They were accused

---

* Navarrete, tom. iii. p. 14.

† Peter Martyr. Other historians give a different date for their arrival. Herrera says Feb. 6.

of having concealed a great part of the pearls collected by them, thus defrauding their companions and the crown. Pedro Alonzo Niño was actually thrown into prison on this accusation, but, nothing being proved against him, he was eventually set free, and enjoyed the enviable reputation of having performed the richest voyage that had yet been made to the New World.*

VICENTE YAÑEZ PINZON (1499)

Among the maritime adventurers of renown, who were roused to action by the licences granted for private expeditions of discovery, we find conspicuous the name of Vicente Yañez Pinzon, of Palos, one of the three brave brothers who aided Columbus in his first voyage and risked life and fortune with him in his doubtful and perilous enterprize.

Of Martin Alonzo Pinzon, the eldest and most important of these three brothers, particular mention has been made in the History of Columbus, and of the unfortunate error in conduct which severed him from the admiral, brought on him the displeasure of the Sovereigns, and probably contributed to his premature and melancholy death.

Whatever cloud this may have thrown over his family it was but temporary. The death of Martin Alonzo, as usual, atoned for his faults and his good deeds lived after him. The merits and services of himself and his brothers were acknowledged, and the survivors of the family were restored to royal confidence. A feeling of jealous hostility prevented them from taking a part in the subsequent voyages of Columbus; but the moment the door was thrown open for individual enterprize, they pressed forward for permission to engage in it at their own risk and expense, and it was readily granted. In fact, their supposed hostility to Columbus was one of the surest recommendations to the favour of the Bishop Fonseca, by whom the licence was issued for their expedition.

Vicente Yañez Pinzon was the leader of this new enterprize, and he was accompanied by two nephews named Arias Perez and Diego Fernandez, sons of his late brother, Martin Alonzo Pinzon. Several of his sailors had sailed with Columbus in his recent voyage to Paria, as had also his three principal pilots, Juan Quintero, Juan de Umbria and Juan

* Navarrete, Colec. tom. iii. p. 11. Herrera, decad. i. lib. iv. cap. 5.

de Jerez. Thus these minor voyages seemed all to emanate from the great expeditions of Columbus, and to aim at realizing the ideas and speculations contained in the papers transmitted by him to Spain.

The armament consisted of four caravels and was fitted out at the port of Palos. The funds of Vicente Yañez were completely exhausted before he had fitted out his little squadron; he was obliged therefore to purchase on credit the sea stores and articles of traffic necessary for the enterprise. The merchants of Palos seem to have known how to profit by the careless nature of sailors and the sanguine spirit of discoverers. In their bargains they charged honest Pinzon eighty and a hundred per cent above the market value of their merchandize, and in the hurry and urgency of the moment he was obliged to submit to the imposition.*

The squadron put to sea in the beginning of December 1499, and after passing the Canary and Cape de Verde Islands stood to the southwest. Having sailed about seven hundred leagues, they crossed the Equator and lost sight of the North Star. They had scarcely passed the Equinoctial line when they encountered a terrible tempest which had well nigh swallowed up their slender barks. The storm passed away and the firmament was again serene, but the mariners remained tossing about in confusion, dismayed by the turbulence of the waves and the strange aspect of the heavens. They looked in vain to the south for some polar star by which to shape their course, and fancied that some swelling prominence of the globe concealed it from their view. They knew nothing as yet of the firmament of that hemisphere, nor of that beautiful constellation the Southern Cross, but expected to find a guiding star at the opposite pole, similar to the cynosure of the north.

Pinzon, however, who was of an intrepid spirit, pursued his course resolutely to the west, and after sailing about two hundred and forty leagues and being in the eighth degree of southern latitude, he beheld land afar off, on the 28th of January, to which he gave the name of *Santa Maria de la Consolacion*, from the sight of it having consoled him in the midst of doubts and perplexities. It is now called Cape St. Augustine and forms the most prominent part of the immense empire of Brazil.

The sea was turbid and discoloured as in rivers, and on sounding they had sixteen fathoms water. Pinzon landed, accompanied by a notary, and witnesses, and took formal possession of the territory for the

---

* Navarrete, vol. iii. See Doc. No. 7, where Vicente Yañez Pinzon petitions for redress.

Castilian Crown; no one appeared to dispute his pretensions, but he observed on the beach the print of footsteps, of gigantic size.

At night there were fires lighted upon a neighboring part of the coast, which induced Pinzon on the following morning to send forty men well armed to the spot. A band of Indians of about equal number sallied forth to encounter them, armed with bows and arrows, and seemingly of extraordinary stature. A still greater number were seen in the distance hastening to the support of their companions. The Indians arrayed themselves for combat, and the two parties remained for a short time eyeing each other with mutual curiosity and distrust. The Spaniards now displayed looking glasses, beads and other trinkets, and jingled strings of hawks bells, in general so captivating to an Indian ear; but the haughty savages treated all their overtures with contempt, regarding these offerings carelessly for a short time, and then stalking off with stoic gravity. They were ferocious of feature and apparently warlike in disposition, and are supposed to have been a wandering race, of unusual size, who roamed about in the night and were of the most fierce untractable nature. By nightfall there was not an Indian to be seen in the neighborhood.

Discouraged by the inhospitable character of the coast, Pinzon made sail and stood to the northwest, until he came to the mouth of a river too shallow to receive his ships. Here he sent his boats on shore, with a number of men well armed. They landed on the river banks, and beheld a multitude of naked Indians on a neighboring hill. A single Spaniard armed simply with sword and buckler, was sent to invite them to friendly intercourse. He approached them with signs of amity and threw to them a hawks bell. They replied to him with similar signs, and threw to him a small gilded wand. The soldier stooped to pick it up when suddenly a troop of savages rushed down to seize him. He threw himself immediately upon the defensive, with sword and target, and though but a small man, and far from robust, handled his weapons with such dexterity and fierceness, that he kept the savages at bay, making a clear circle round him, and wounding several who attempted to break it. His unlooked for prowess surprized and confounded his assailants, and gave time for his comrades to come to his assistance. The Indians then made a general assault, with such a galling discharge of darts and arrows that almost immediately eight or ten Spaniards were slain and many more wounded. The latter were compelled to retreat to their boats disputing every inch of ground. The Indians pursued them even into the water, surrounding the boats and seizing hold of the oars. The Spaniards made a desperate defence, thrusting many through with their lances and cutting down and ripping up others with their swords, but such was the ferocity of the survivors that they persisted in their attack until they overpowered the crew of one of the boats and bore it off in triumph. With this they retired from the combat and the Spaniards returned defeated and disheartened to their ships; having met with the roughest reception that the Europeans had yet experienced in the New World.

Pinzon now stood forty leagues to the northwest until he arrived in the neighborhood of the Equinoctial line. Here he found the water of the sea so fresh that he was enabled to replenish his casks with it. Astonished at so singular a phenomenon he stood in for the land and arrived among a number of fresh and verdant islands inhabited by a gentle and hospitable race of people, gaily painted, who came off to the ships with the most frank and fearless confidence. Pinzon soon found that these islands lay in the mouth of an immense river, more than thirty leagues in breadth, the water of which entered upwards of forty leagues into the sea before losing its sweetness. It was in fact the renowned Marañon, since known as the Orellana and the Amazon. While lying in the mouth of this river there was a sudden swelling of the stream, which, being opposed by the current of the sea, and strait-ened by the narow channels of the islands, rose more than five fathoms, with mountain waves, and a tremendous noise, threatening the destruc-tion of the ships. Pinzon extricated his little squadron with great difficulty, and finding there was but little gold, or any thing else of value to be found among the simple natives, he requited their hospitality in the mode too common among the early discoverers, by carrying off thirty six of them captive.

Having regained the sight of the Polar Star, Pinzon pursued his course along the coast, passing the mouths of the Oronoko and entering the Gulf of Paria, where he landed and cut Brasil wood. Sallying forth by the Boca del Drago, he reached the island of Hispaniola about the 23rd of June, from whence he sailed for the Bahamas. Here in the month of July while at anchor, there came such a tremendous hurricane that two of the caravels were swallowed up with all their crews in the sight of their terrified companions, a third parted her cables and was driven out to sea, while the fourth was so furiously beaten by the tempest that the crew threw themselves into the boats and made for shore. Here they found a few naked Indians who offered them no molestation, but, fearing that they might spread the tidings of a handful of shipwrecked Spaniards being upon the coast, and thus bring the savages of the neighboring islands upon them, a council of war was held whether it would not be a wise precaution to put these Indians to death. Fortunately for the latter, the vessel which had been driven from her anchors returned and put an end to the alarm and to the council of war. The other caravel also rode out the storm uninjured, and the sea subsiding, the Spaniards returned on board and made the best of their way to the Island of Hispaniola. Having repaired the damages sustained in the gale, they again made sail for Spain, and came to anchor in the river before Palos about the end of September.

Thus ended one of the most checquered and disastrous voyages yet made to the new world. Yañez Pinzon had lost two of his ships and many of his men. What made the loss of the latter more grievous was that they had been enlisted from among his neighbours, his friends and relatives. In fact the expeditions to the new world must have realized the terrors and apprehensions of the people of Palos by filling that little community with widows and orphans. When the rich merchants, who had sold goods to Pinzon at a hundred per cent advance, beheld him return in this sorry condition with two shattered barks and a handful of poor, tattered, weather beaten seamen, they began to tremble for their money. No sooner therefore had he and his nephews departed to Granada, to give an account of their discoveries to the Sovereigns, than the merchants seized upon their caravels and cargoes, and began to sell them to repay themselves. Honest Pinzon immediately addressed a petition to the government, stating the imposition practiced upon him and the danger he was in of imprisonment and utter ruin should his creditors be allowed to sacrifice his goods at a public sale. He petitioned that they might be compelled to return the property thus seized, and that he might be enabled to sell three hundred and fifty quintals of Brasil wood which he had brought back with him, and which would be sufficient to satisfy the demands of his creditors. The Sovereigns granted his prayer. They issued an order to the civil authorities of Palos to interfere in the matter with all possible promptness and brevity, allowing no vexatious delay, and administering justice so impartially that neither of the parties should have cause to complain.

Pinzon escaped from the fangs of his creditors, but of course must have suffered in purse from the expenses of the law, which, in Spain, is apt to bury even a successful client, under an overwhelming mountain of documents and writings. We infer this in respect to Pinzon from a royal order issued in the following year, allowing him to export a quantity of grain, in consideration of the heavy losses he had sustained in his voyage of discovery. He did but share the usual lot of the Spanish discoverers, whose golden anticipations too frequently ended in penury, but he is distinguished from among the crowd of them by being the first European who crossed the Equinoctial line, on the western ocean, and by discovering the great kingdom of Brasil.*

*On the 5th of September 1501, a royal permission was given to Vicente Yañez Pinzon to colonize and govern the lands he had discovered, beginning a little north of the river Amazon and extending to Cape St. Augustine. The object of the government in this permission was to establish an outpost and a resolute commander, on this southern frontier, that should check any intrusions the Portuguese might make in consequence of the accidental discovery of a part of the coast of Brasil by Pedro Alvarez Cabral in 1500. The subsequent arrangement of a partition line between the two countries prevented the necessity of this precaution, and it does not appear that Vicente Yañez Pinzon made any second voyage to those parts.

In 1506 he undertook an expedition in company with Juan Diaz de Solis, a native of Lebrija, the object of which was to endeavour to find the strait or passage supposed by Columbus to lead from the Atlantic to a Southern Ocean. It was necessarily without success, as was also another voyage made by them, for the same purpose, in 1508. As no such passage exists, no blame could attach to those able navigators for being foiled in the object of their search.

In consequence of the distinguished merits and services of the Pinzon family they were raised, by the Emperor Charles V, to the dignity of a Hidalguía, or nobility, without any express title, and a coat of arms was granted them, on which were emblazoned three caravels, with a hand at the stern pointing to an island covered with savages. This coat of arms is still maintained by the family, who have added to it the motto granted to Columbus, merely substituting the name of Pinzon for that of the admiral

A Castile y a Leon,
Nuevo Mundo dio Pinzon.

DIEGO DE LEPE
and
RODRIGO DE BASTIDES (1500)

Notwithstanding the hardships and disasters that had beset the voyagers to the New World, and the penury in which their golden anticipations had too frequently terminated, adventurers continued to press forward, excited by fresh reports of newly discovered regions, each in its turn represented as the real land of promise. Scarcely had Vicente Yañez Pinzon departed on the voyage recently narrated, when his townsman Diego de Lepe likewise set sail with two vessels from the busy little port of Palos, on a like expedition. No particulars of importance are known of this voyage, excepting that Lepe doubled Cape St. Augustine, and beheld the Southern Continent stretching far to the southwest. On returning to Spain he drew a chart of the coast for the Bishop Fonseca, and enjoyed the reputation, for upwards of ten years afterwards, of having extended his discoveries further south than any other voyager.

Another contemporary adventurer to the New World was Rodrigo de Bastides, a wealthy notary of Triana, the suburb of Seville inhabited by the maritime part of its population. Being sanctioned by the Sovereigns, to whom he engaged to yield a fourth of his profits, he fitted out two caravels in October 1500, to go in quest of gold and pearls.

Prudently distrusting his own judgement in nautical matters, this adventurous notary associated with him the veteran pilot Juan de la Cosa, the same hardy Biscayan who had sailed with Columbus and Ojeda. A general outline of their voyage has already been given in the life of Columbus; it extended the discoveries of the coast of Terra Firma from Cape de la Vela, where Ojeda had left off, quite to the port of Nombre de Dios.

Bastides distinguished himself from the mass of discoverers by his kind treatment of the natives, and Juan de la Cosa by his sound discretion and his able seamanship. Their voyage had been extremely successful and they had collected, by barter, a great amount of gold and pearls, when their prosperous career was checked by an unlooked for evil.

28

Their vessels to their surprize became leaky in every part, and they discovered, to their dismay, that the bottoms were pierced in innumerable places by the Broma, or worm, which abounds in the waters of the Torrid Zone, but of which they, as yet, had scarcely any knowledge. It was with great difficulty they could keep afloat until they reached a small islet on the coast of Hispaniola. Here they repaired their ships as well as they were able, and again put to sea to return to Cadiz. A succession of gales drove them back to port; the ravages of the worms continued, the leaks broke out afresh; they landed the most portable and precious part of their wealthy cargoes, and the vessels foundered with the remainder. Bastides lost moreover the arms and ammunition saved from the wreck, being obliged to destroy them lest they should fall into the hands of the Indians.

Distributing his men into three bands, two of them headed by La Cosa and himself, they set off for San Domingo by three several routes, as the country was not able to furnish provisions for so large a body. Each band was provided with a coffer stored with trinkets and other articles of Indian traffic, with which to buy provisions on the road.

Francisco de Bobadilla, the wrong headed oppressor and superseder of Columbus, was at that time Governor of San Domingo. The report reached him that a crew of adventurers had landed on the island and were marching through the country in three bands, each provided with a coffer of gold, and carrying on illicit trade with the natives. The moment Bastides made his appearance, therefore, he was seized and thrown into prison and an investigation commenced. In his defence he maintained that his only traffic with the natives was for the purpose of procuring provisions for his followers, or guides for his journey. It was determined, however, to send him to Spain for trial, with the written testimony and the other documents of his examination.

He was accordingly conveyed in the same fleet in which Bobadilla embarked for Spain, and which experienced such an awful shipwreck in the sight of Columbus. The ship of Rodrigo Bastides was one of the few that outlived the tempest; it arrived safe at Cadiz in September 1502. Bastides was ultimately acquitted of the charges advanced against him. So lucrative had been his voyage, that, notwithstanding the losses sustained by the foundering of his vessels, he was enabled to pay a large sum to the Crown as a fourth of his profits, and to retain a great amount for himself. In reward of his services and discoveries the Sovereigns granted him an annual revenue for life, to arise from the proceeds of the province of Uraba, which he had discovered. An equal pension

was likewise assigned to the hardy Juan de la Cosa, to result from the
same territory, of which he was appointed Alguazil Mayor.* Such was
the economical generosity of King Ferdinand, who rewarded the past
toils of his adventurous discoverers out of the expected produce of
their future labours.

* Navarrete. Colec. tom. iii.

SECOND VOYAGE

of

ALONZO DE OJEDA (1502)

The first voyage of Alonzo de Ojeda to the coast of Paria and its meagre termination in June 1500 has been related. He gained nothing in wealth by that expedition but he added to his celebrity as a bold and skillful adventurer. His youthful fire, his sanguine and swelling spirit, and the wonderful stories that were told of his activity and prowess made him extremely popular, so that his patron the Bishop Fonseca found it an easy matter to secure for him the royal favour. In consideration of his past services and of others expected from him a grant was made to him of six leagues of land on the southern part of Hispaniola, and the government of the province of Coquibacoa which he had discovered. He was furthermore authorized to fit out any number of ships, not exceeding ten, at his own expense, and to prosecute the discovery of the coast of Terra Firma. He was not to touch or traffic on the pearl coast of Paria; extending as far as a bay in the vicinity of the island of Margarita. Beyond this he had a right to trade in all kinds of merchandize, whether of pearls, jewels, metals, or precious stones; paying one fifth of the profits to the Crown, and abstaining from making slaves of the Indians without a special licence from the Sovereigns, He was to colonize Coquibacoa, and, as a recompense, was to enjoy one half of the proceeds of his territory, provided the half did not exceed 300,000 maravedies: all beyond that amount was to go to the Crown.

A principal reason, however, for granting this government and those privileges to Ojeda was that in his previous voyage he had met with English adventurers on a voyage of discovery in the neighborhood of Coquibacoa, at which the jealousy of the Sovereigns had taken the alarm. They were anxious, therefore, to establish a resolute and fighting commander like Ojeda upon this outpost, and they instructed him to set up the arms of Castile and Leon in every place he visited, as a signal of discovery and possession, and to put a stop to the intrusions of the English.*

* Navarrete, tom. iii. Document x.

With this commission in his pocket, and the government of an Indian territory in the perspective, Ojeda soon found associates to aid him in fitting out an armament. These were Juan de Vergara, a servant of a rich canon of the cathedral of Seville, and Garcia de Campos, commonly called Ocampo. They made a contract of partnership to last for two years, according to which the expenses and profits of the expedition, and the government of Coquibacoa, were to be shared equally between them. The purses of the confederates were not ample enough to afford ten ships, but they fitted out four. 1st, The Santa Maria de la Antigua commanded by Garcia del Campo; 2d, The Santa Maria de la Granada commanded by Juan de Vergara; 3d, The caravel Magdalena commanded by Pedro de Ojeda, nephew to Alonzo; and 4th, the caravel Santa Ana commanded by Hernando de Guevara. The whole was under the command of Alonzo de Ojeda.

The expedition set sail in 1502, touched at the Canaries according to custom to take in provisions, and then proceeded westward for the shores of the New World.

After traversing the Gulf of Paria, and before reaching the island of Margarita, the caravel Santa Ana, commanded by Hernando de Guevara, was separated from them, and for several days the ships were mutually seeking each other in these silent and trackless seas. After they were all reunited they found their provisions growing scanty, they landed therefore at a part of the coast called Cumana by the natives but to which from its beauty and fertility Ojeda gave the name of Valfermoso. While foraging here for their immediate supplies, the idea occurred to Ojeda that he should want furniture and utensils of all kinds for his proposed colony and that it would be better to pillage them from a country where he was a mere transient visitor, than to wrest them from his neighbors in the territory where he was to set up his government. His companions were struck with the policy if not the justice of this idea, and they all set to work to carry it into execution. Dispersing themselves therefore in ambush in various directions, they at a concerted signal rushed forth from their concealment, and set upon the natives. Ojeda had issued orders to do as little injury and damage as possible and on no account to destroy the habitations of the Indians. His followers however in their great zeal transcended his orders. Seven or eight Indians were killed and many wounded in the skirmish which took place and a number of their cabins were wrapped in flames. A great quantity of hamacs, of cotton, and of utensils of various kinds fell into the hands of the conquerors. They also captured several female Indians, some of whom were ransomed with the kind of gold called guanin, some were retained by Vergara for himself and his friend Ocampo, others were distributed among the crews, the rest, probably the old and ugly, were set at liberty. As to Ojeda, he reserved nothing for himself of the spoil excepting a single hamac.

The ransom paid by the poor Indians for some of their effects and some of their women yielded the Spaniards a trifling quantity of gold, but they found the place destitute of provisions, and Ojeda was obliged to despatch Vergara in a caravel to the island of Jamaica to forage for supplies, with instructions to rejoin him at Maracaibo or Cape de la Vela.

Ojeda at length arrived at Coquibacoa, at the port destined for his seat of government. He found the country however so poor and sterile, that he proceeded along the coast to a bay which he named Santa Cruz, but which is supposed to be the same at present called Bahia Honda: where he found a Spaniard who had been left in the province of Citarma by Bastides in his late voyage about thirteen months before, and had remained ever since among the Indians, so that he had acquired their language.

Ojeda determined to form his settlement at this place; but the natives seemed disposed to defend their territory, for, the moment a party landed to procure water, they were assailed by a galling shower of arrows and driven back to the ships. Upon this Ojeda landed with all his force, and struck such terror into the Indians, that they came forward with signs of amity, and brought a considerable quantity of gold as a peace offering, which was graciously accepted.

Ojeda, with the concurrence of his associates, now set to work to establish a settlement, cutting down trees, and commencing a fortress. They had scarce begun, when they were attacked by a neighboring cacique, but Ojeda sallied forth upon him with such intrepidity and effect as not merely to defeat but to drive him from the neighborhood. He then proceeded quietly to finish his fortress, which was defended by lombards, and contained the magazine of provisions and the treasure amassed in the expedition. The provisions were dealt out twice a day, under the inspection of proper officers; the treasure, gained by barter, by ransom, or by plunder, was deposited in a strong box, secured by two locks, one key being kept by the royal supervisor, the other by Ocampo.

In the mean time provisions became scarce. The Indians never appeared in the neighbourhood of the fortress, except to harass it with repeated though ineffectual assaults. Vergara did not appear with the expected supplies from Jamaica, and a caravel was despatched in search of him. The people, worn out with labour and privations of various kinds, and disgusted with the situation of the settlement, which was in a poor and unhealthy country, grew discontented and factious. They began to fear that they should lose the means of departing, as their vessels were in danger of being destroyed by the Broma, or worms. Ojeda led them forth repeatedly upon foraging parties about the adjacent country, and collected some provisions and booty in the Indian villages. The provisions he deposited in the magazine, part of the spoils he divided among his followers, and the gold he locked up in the strong box, the keys of which he took possession of, to the great displeasure of the supervisor and his associate Ocampo. The murmurs of the people grew loud as their sufferings increased. They insinuated that Ojeda had no authority over this part of the coast, having passed the boundaries of his government, and formed his settlement in the country discovered by Bastides. By the time Vergara arrived from Jamaica, the factions of this petty colony had risen to an alarming height. Ocampo had a personal enmity to the governor, arising probably from some feud about the strong box. Being a particular friend of Vergara he held a private conference with him, and laid a plan to entrap the doughty Ojeda. In pursuance of this the latter was invited on board of the caravel of Vergara to see the provisions he had brought from Jamaica, but no sooner was he on board than they charged him with having transgressed the limits of his government, with having provoked the hostility of the Indians and needlessly sacrificed the lives of his followers, and above all with having taken possession of the strong box in contempt of the authority of the royal supervisor and with the intention of appropriating to himself all the gains of the enterprize; they informed him, therefore, of their intention to convey him a prisoner to Hispaniola, to answer to the governor for his offences. Ojeda finding himself thus entrapped, proposed to Vergara and Ocampo that they should return to Spain with such of the crews as chose to accompany them, leaving him with the remainder to prosecute his enterprize. The two recreant partners at first consented, for they were disgusted with the enterprize which offered little profit and severe hardships. They agreed to leave Ojeda the smallest of the caravels with a third of the provisions and of their gains, and to build a row boat for him. They actually began to labour upon the boat. Before ten days had elapsed, however, they repented of the arrangement, the ship carpenters were ill, there were no caulkers, and moreover they recollected that as Ojeda according to their representations was a defaulter to the Crown, they would be liable as his sureties, should they return to Spain without him. They concluded, therefore, that the wisest plan was to give him nothing, but to carry him off prisoner.

When Ojeda learned the determination of his wary partners he attempted to make his escape and get off to San Domingo, but he was seized, thrown in irons and conveyed on board of the caravel. The two partners then set sail from Santa Cruz, bearing off the whole community, its captive governor, and the litigated strong box.

They put to sea about the beginning of September, and arrived at the western part of the island of Hispaniola. While at anchor within a stone's throw of the land, Ojeda, confident in his strength and skill as a swimmer, let himself quietly slide down the side of the ship into the water during the night and attempted to swim for the shore. His arms were free, but his feet were shackled, and the weight of his irons threatened to sink him. He was obliged to shout for help; a boat was sent from the vessel to his relief, and the unfortunate governor was brought back half drowned to his unrelenting partners.*

The latter now landed and delivered their prisoner into the hands of Gallego, the commander of the place, to be put at the disposal of the governor of the island. In the meantime, the strong box, which appears to have been at the bottom of all these feuds, remained in the possession of Vergara and Ocampo, who, Ojeda says, took from it whatever they thought proper, without regard to the royal dues, or the consent of the royal supervisor. They were all together, prisoner and accusers, in the city of San Domingo, about the end of September, 1502, when the chief judge of the island, after hearing both parties, gave a verdict against Ojeda that stripped him of all his effects, and brought him into debt to the Crown for the royal proportion of the profits of the voyage. Ojeda appealed to the Sovereign, and, after some time, was honourably acquitted, by the royal council, from all the charges, and a mandate was issued in 1503, ordering a restitution of his property. It appears, however, that the costs of justice, or rather of the law, consumed his share of the treasure of the strong box, and that a royal order was necessary to liberate him from the hands of the governor; so that like too many other litigants, he finally emerged from the labyrinths of the law a triumphant client, but a ruined man.

* Hist. Gen. de Viages. Herrera, Hist. Ind.

THIRD VOYAGE
of
ALONZO DE OJEDA

Chapter I

Ojeda applies for a command—Has a rival candidate in Diego de Nicuesa—His success

For several years after his ruinous, though successful lawsuit, we lose all traces of Alonzo de Ojeda, excepting that we are told he made another voyage to the vicinity of Coquibacoa in 1505. No record remains of this expedition, which seems to have been equally unprofitable with the preceding, for we find him in 1508, in the island of Hispaniola, as poor in purse, though as proud in spirit, as ever. In fact, however fortune might have favoured him, he had a heedless squandering disposition that would always have kept him poor.

About this time the cupidity of King Ferdinand was greatly excited by the accounts which had been given by Columbus of the gold mines of Veragua, in which the admiral fancied he had discovered the Aurea Chersonesus of the ancients, from whence King Solomon procured the gold, used in building the temple of Jerusalem. Subsequent voyagers had corroborated the opinion of Columbus as to the general riches of the coast of Terra Firma. King Ferdinand resolved, therefore, to found regular colonies along that coast and to place the whole under some capable commander. A project of the kind had been conceived by Columbus, when he discovered that region in the course of his last voyage, and the reader may remember the disasters experienced by his brother Don Bartholomew and himself, in endeavouring to establish a colony on the hostile shores of Veragua. The admiral being dead, the person who should naturally have presented himself to the mind of the Sovereign for this particular service was Don Bartholomew, but the wary and selfish monarch knew the Adelantado to be as lofty in his terms as his late brother, and preferred to accomplish his purposes by cheaper agents. He was unwilling, also, to increase the consequence of a family, whose vast, but just, claims were already a cause of repining to his sordid and jealous spirit. He looked round, therefore, among the crowd of adventurers, who had sprung up in the school of Columbus, for some individual ready to serve him on more accommodating terms. Among those, considered by their friends as most fitted for this purpose, was Alonzo de Ojeda, for his roving voyages and daring exploits had made him famous among the voyagers; and it was thought that an application on his part would be attended with success, as he possessed a stanch friend at Court in the Bishop Fonseca. Unfortunately he was too far distant to urge his suit to the Bishop, and what was worse, he was destitute of money. At this juncture there happened to be at Hispaniola the veteran navigator and pilot Juan de la Cosa, who was a kind of Nestor in all nautical affairs.* The hardy Biscayan had sailed with Ojeda and had conceived a great opinion of the courage and talents of the youthful adventurer. He had contrived, also, to fill his purse in the course of his cruisings, and now, in the generous spirit of a sailor, offered to aid Ojeda with it in the prosecution of his wishes.

His offer was gladly accepted; it was agreed that Juan de la Cosa should depart for Spain, to promote the appointment of Ojeda to the command of Terra Firma, and, in case of success, should fit out, with his own funds, the necessary armament.

La Cosa departed on his embassy; he called on the Bishop Fonseca, who, as had been expected, entered warmly into the views of his favorite Ojeda, and recommended him to the ambitious and bigot King, as a man well fitted to promote his empire in the wilderness, and to dispence the blessings of Christianity among the savages.

The recommendation of the bishop was usually effectual in the affairs of the new world, and the opinion of the veteran de la Cosa had great weight even with the Sovereign; but a rival candidate to Ojeda had presented himself, and one who had the advantage of higher connexions and greater pecuniary means. This was Diego de Nicuesa, an accomplished courtier, of noble birth, who had filled the post of grand carver to Don Enrique Enriquez, uncle of the king. Nature, education

---

* Peter Martyr gives the following weighty testimony to the knowledge and skill of this excellent seaman:—"Of the Spaniards, as many as thought themselves to have any knowledge of what pertained to measure the land and sea, drew cardes (charts) on parchment as concerning these navigations. Of all others they most esteem them which Juan de la Cosa, the companion of Ojeda, and another pilot, called Andres Morales, had set forth, and this, as well for the great experience which both had, (*to whom these tracks were as well known as the chambers of their own house,*) as also that they were thought to be cunninger in that part of cosmography which teacheth the description and measuring of the sea." P. Martyr, decad. ii. cap. 10.

and habit combined to form Nicuesa a complete rival of Ojeda. Like
him he was small of stature, but remarkable for symmetry and compactness of form and for bodily strength and activity. Like him he
was master at all kinds of weapons, and skilled, not merely in feats of
agility, but in those graceful and chivalrous exercises, which the Spanish cavaliers of those days inherited from the Moors; being noted for
his vigour and address in the jousts or tilting matches after the Moresco
fashion. Ojeda himself could not surpass him in feats of horsemanship
and particular mention is made of a favorite mare, which he could make
caper and caracole in strict cadence to the sound of a viol; besides all
this, he was versed in the legendary ballads or romances of his country,
and was renowned as a capital performer on the guitar! Such were
the qualifications of this candidate for a command in the wilderness,
as enumerated by the reverend Bishop Las Casas. It is probable, however, that he had given evidence of qualities more adapted to the desired post; having already been out to Hispaniola in the military train
of the late Governor Ovando.

Where merits were so singularly balanced as those of Ojeda and
Nicuesa, it might have been difficult to decide; King Ferdinand avoided
the dilemma by favouring both; not indeed by furnishing them with
ships and money, but by granting patents and dignities which cost
nothing, and might bring rich returns. He divided that part of the
continent which lies along the isthmus of Darien into two provinces,
the boundary line running through the Gulf of Uraba. The eastern part,
extending to Cape de la Vela, was called New Andalusia, and the government of it given to Ojeda. The other to the west, including Veragua,
and reaching to Cape Gracias á Dios, was assigned to Nicuesa. The
Island of Jamaica was given to the two governors in common, as a
place from whence to draw supplies of provisions. Each of the governors
was to erect two fortresses in his district, and to enjoy for ten years the
profits of all the mines he should discover, paying to the crown one
tenth part the first year, one ninth the second, one eighth the third,
one seventh the fourth, and one fifth part in each of the remaining
years.

Juan de la Cosa, who had been indefatigable in promoting the suit
of Ojeda, was appointed his lieutenant in the government, with the
post of Alguazil Mayor of the province. He immediately freighted a
ship and two brigantines, in which he embarked with about two hundred men. It was a slender armament, but the purse of the honest
voyager was not very deep, and that of Ojeda was empty. Nicuesa,
having ampler means, armed four large vessels and two brigantines,

furnished them with abundant munitions and supplies, both for the voyage and the projected colony, enlisted a much greater force, and set sail in gay and vaunting style, for the golden shores of Veragua, the Aurea Chersonesus of his imagination.

Chapter II

Feud between the rival governors Ojeda and Nicuesa—A challenge (1509)

The two rival armaments arrived at San Domingo about the same time. Nicuesa had experienced what was doubtless considered a pleasant little turn of fortune by the way. Touching at Santa Cruz, one of the Carribee islands, he had succeeded in capturing a hundred of the natives, whom he had borne off in his ships to be sold as slaves at Hispaniola. This was deemed justifiable in those days, even by the most scrupulous divines, from the belief that the Caribs were all anthropophagi, or man-eaters; fortunately the opinion of mankind, in this more enlightened age, makes but little difference in atrocity between the cannibal and the kidnapper.

Alonzo de Ojeda welcomed with joy the arrival of his nautical friend and future lieutenant in the government, the worthy Juan de la Cosa. Still he could not but feel some mortification at the inferiority of his armament to that of his rival Nicuesa, whose stately ships rode proudly at anchor in the harbour of San Domingo. He felt too that his means were inadequate to the establishment of his intended colony. Ojeda, however, was not long at a loss for pecuniary assistance. Like many free spirited men, who are careless and squandering of their own purses, he had a facility at commanding the purses of his neighbors. Among the motly population of San Domingo there was a lawyer of some abilities, the Bachelor Martin Fernandez de Enciso, who had made two thousand castellanos by his pleadings;* for it it would appear that the spirit of litigation was one of the first fruits of civilized life transplanted to the new world, and flourished surprizingly among the Spanish colonists.

Alonzo de Ojeda became acquainted with the Bachelor, and finding

---

* Equivalent to 10,650 Dollars of the present day.

him to be of a restless, and speculative character, soon succeeded in inspiring him with a contempt for the dull but secure and profitable routine of his office in San Domingo, and imbuing him with his own passion for adventure. Above all he dazzled him with the offer to make him Alcalde Mayor, or chief judge of the provincial government he was about to establish in the wilderness.

In an evil hour the aspiring Bachelor yielded to the temptation and agreed to invest all his money in the enterprize. It was arranged that Ojeda should depart with the armament which had arrived from Spain, while the Bachelor should remain at Hispaniola to beat up for recruits and provide supplies; with these he was to embark in a ship purchased by himself, and proceed to join his high mettled friend at the seat of his intended colony. Two rival governors, so well matched as Ojeda and Nicuesa, and both possessed of swelling spirits, pent up in small but active bodies, could not remain long in a little place like San Domingo without some collision. The Island of Jamaica, which had been assigned to them in common, furnished the first ground of contention: the province of Darien furnished another, each pretending to include it within the limits of his jurisdiction. Their disputes on these points ran so high that the whole place resounded with them. In talking, however, Nicuesa had the advantage; having been brought up in the court, he was more polished and ceremonious, had greater self command, and probably perplexed his rival governor in argument. Ojeda was no great casuist, but he was an excellent swordsman, and always ready to fight his way through any question of right or dignity which he could not clearly argue with the tongue; so he proposed to settle the dispute by single combat. Nicuesa, though equally brave, was more a man of the world, and saw the folly of such arbitrament. Secretly smiling at the heat of his antagonist, he proposed as a preliminary to the duel, and to furnish something worth fighting for, that each should deposit five thousand castellanos, to be the prize of the victor. This, as he foresaw, was a temporary check upon the fiery valour of his rival, who did not possess a pistole in his treasury; but probably was too proud to confess it.

It is not likely, however, that the impetuous spirit of Ojeda would long have remained in check, had not the discreet Juan de la Cosa interposed to calm it. It is interesting to notice the great ascendancy possessed by this veteran navigator over his fiery associate. Juan de la Cosa was a man whose strong natural good sense had been quickened by long and hard experience; whose courage was above all question, but tempered by time and trial. He seems to have been personally attached to Ojeda, as veterans who have outlived the rash impulse of

youthful valour, are apt to love the fiery quality in their younger associates. So long as he accompanied Ojeda in his enterprizes he stood
by him as a Mentor in council, and a devoted partizan in danger.

In the present instance the interference of this veteran of the seas
had the most salutary effect: he prevented the impending duel of the
rival governors and persuaded them to agree that the river Darien
should be the boundary line between their respective jurisdictions.

The dispute relative to Jamaica was settled by the Admiral, Don
Diego Columbus himself. He had already felt aggrieved by the distribution of these governments by the king without his consent or even
knowledge, being contrary to the privileges which he inherited from
his father the discoverer. It was in vain to contend, however, when the
matter was beyond his reach and involved in technical disputes. But
as to the Island of Jamaica, it in a manner lay at his own door, and he
could not brook its being made a matter of gift to these brawling
governors. Without waiting the slow and uncertain course of making
remonstrances to the king, he took the affair, as a matter of plain
right, into his own hands, and ordered a brave officer, Juan de Esquibel,
the same who had subjugated the province of Higuey, to take possession of that island, with seventy men, and to hold it subject to his command.

Ojeda did not hear of this arrangement until he was on the point
of embarking to make sail. In the heat of the moment he loudly defied
the power of the admiral, and swore that if he ever found Juan de
Esquibel on the island of Jamaica he would strike off his head. The
populace present heard this menace, and had too thorough an idea of
the fiery and daring character of Ojeda to doubt that he would carry
it into effect. Notwithstanding his bravado, however, Juan de Esquibel
proceeded according to his orders to take possession of the island of
Jamaica.

The squadron of Nicuesa lingered for some time after the sailing of
his rival. His courteous and engaging manners, aided by the rumour of
great riches in the province of Veragua, where he intended to found
his colony, had drawn numerous volunteers to his standard, insomuch
that he had to purchase another ship to convey them.

Nicuesa was more of the courtier and the cavalier, than the man of
business, and had no skill in managing his pecuniary affairs. He had
expended his funds with a free and lavish hand, and involved himself
in debts which he had not the immediate means of paying. Many of his
creditors knew that his expedition was regarded with an evil eye by
the Admiral Don Diego Columbus; to gain favour with the latter,
therefore, they threw all kinds of impediments in the way of Nicuesa.

Never was an unfortunate gentleman more harassed and distracted by duns and demands; one plucking at his skirts as soon as the other was satisfied. He succeeded, however, in getting all his forces embarked. He had seven hundred men, well chosen and well armed, together with six horses. He chose Lope de Olano to be his captain general, a seemingly impolitic appointment, as this Olano had been concerned with the notorious Roldan in his rebellion against Columbus.

The squadron sailed out of the harbour and put to sea, excepting one ship, which with anchor atrip and sails unfurled waited to receive Nicuesa, who was detained on shore until the last moment by the perplexities artfully multiplied around him.

Just as he was on the point of stepping into his boat he was arrested by the harpies of the law, and carried before the Alcalde Mayor to answer a demand for five hundred ducats, which he was ordered to pay on the spot, or prepare to go to prison.

This was a thunderstroke to the unfortunate cavalier. In vain he represented his utter incapacity to furnish such a sum at the moment; in vain he represented the ruin that would accrue to himself and the vast injury to the public service, should he be prevented from joining his expedition. The Alcalde Mayor was inflexible, and Nicuesa was reduced to despair. At this critical moment relief came from a most unexpected quarter. The heart of a public notary was melted by his distress! He stepped forward in court and declared that rather than see so gallant a gentleman reduced to extremity he himself would pay down the money. Nicuesa gazed at him with astonishment and could scarce believe his senses, but when he saw him actually pay off the debt and found himself suddenly released from this dreadful embarrassment, he embraced his deliverer with tears of gratitude, and hastened with all speed to embark lest some other legal spell should be laid upon his person.

Chapter III

Exploits and disasters of Ojeda on the coast of Carthagena—Fate of the veteran Juan de la Cosa (1509)

It was on the 10th of November 1509 that Alonzo de Ojeda set sail from San Domingo with two ships, two brigantines and three hundred men. He took with him also twelve brood mares. Among the remarkable adventurers who embarked with him was Francisco Pizarro, afterwards renowned as the conqueror of Peru.* Hernando Cortez had likewise intended to sail in the expedition, but was prevented by an inflammation in one of his knees.

The voyage was speedy and prosperous and they arrived late in the autumn in the harbour of Carthagena. The veteran Juan de la Cosa was well acquainted with this place, having sailed as pilot with Rodrigo de Bastides, at the time he discovered it in 1501. He warned Alonzo de Ojeda to be upon his guard, as the natives were a brave and warlike race of Carib origin, far different from the soft and gentle inhabitants of the islands. They wielded great swords of palm wood, defended themselves with osier targets and dipped their arrows in a subtle poison. The women as well as the men mingled in battle, being expert in drawing the bow and throwing a species of lance called the azagay. The warning was well timed for the Indians of these parts had been irritated by the misconduct of previous adventurers, and flew to arms on the first appearance of the ships.

Juan de la Cosa now feared for the safety of the enterprize in which he had person, fortune and official dignity at stake. He earnestly advised Ojeda to abandon this dangerous neighborhood, and to commence a settlement in the Gulf of Uraba, where the people were less ferocious, and did not use poisoned weapons. Ojeda was too proud of spirit to

---

* Francisco Pizarro was a native of Truxillo in Estremadura. He was the illegitimate fruit of an amour between Gonsalvo Pizarro, a veteran captain of infantry, and a damsel in low life. His childhood was passed in grovelling occupations incident to the humble condition of his mother, and he is said to have been a swineherd. When he had sufficiently increased in years and stature he enlisted as a soldier. His first campaigns may have been against the Moors in the war of Granada. He certainly served in Italy under the banner of the Great Captain, Gonsalvo of Cordova. His roving spirit then induced him to join the bands of adventurers to the New World. He was of ferocious courage, and, when engaged in any enterprize, possessed an obstinate perseverance that was neither to be deterred by danger, weakened by fatigue and hardship, or checked by repeated disappointment. After having conquered the great kingdom of Peru, he was assassinated, at an advanced age in 1541, defending himself bravely to the last.

alter his plans through fear of a naked foe. It is thought, too, that he
had no objection to a skirmish, being desirous of a pretext to make
slaves to be sent to Hispaniola in discharge of the debts he had left
unpaid.* He landed, therefore, with a considerable part of his force,
and a number of friars, who had been sent out to convert the Indians.
His faithful lieutenant, being unable to keep him out of danger, stood
by to second him.

Ojeda advanced towards the savages, and ordered the friars to read
aloud a certain formula recently digested by profound jurists and divines in Spain. It began in stately form. "I, Alonzo de Ojeda, servant of
the most high and mighty Sovereigns of Castile and Leon, conquerors
of barbarous nations, their messenger and captain, do notify unto you
and make you know, in the best way I can, that God our Lord, one and
eternal, created the heaven and the earth, and one man and one
woman, from whom you and we and all the people of the earth proceeded and are descendants, as well as all those who shall come hereafter." The formula then went on to declare the fundamental principles
of the Catholic faith; the supreme power given to St. Peter, over the
world and all the human race, and exercised by his representative the
Pope; the donation made by a late pope of all this part of the world,
and all its inhabitants to the Catholic Sovereigns of Castile; and the
ready obedience which had already been paid by many of its lands
and islands and people to the agents and representatives of those Sovereigns. It called upon those savages present, therefore, to do the same,
to acknowledge the truth of the Christian doctrines, the supremacy
of the Pope and the sovereignty of the Catholic King, but, in case of
refusal, it denounced upon them all the horrors of war, the desolation
of their dwellings, the seizure of their property, and the slavery of their
wives and children. Such was the extraordinary document, which, from
this time forward, was read by the Spanish discoverers to the wondering savages of any newly found country, as a prelude to sanctify the
violence about to be inflicted on them.†

When the friars had read this pious manifesto, Ojeda made signs
of amity to the natives and held up glittering presents. They had already suffered, however, from the cruelties of white men, and were
not to be won by kindness. On the contrary they brandished their
weapons, sounded their conchs and prepared to make battle.

Juan de la Cosa saw the rising choler of Ojeda, and knew his fiery
impatience. He again entreated him to abandon these hostile shores,

* Las Casas. Hist. Ind. lib. ii. cap. 57. MS.

† The reader will find the complete form of this curious manifesto in the Appendix.

and reminded him of the venomous weapons of the enemy. It was all in vain: Ojeda confided blindly in the protection of the Virgin. Putting up, as usual, a short prayer to his patroness, he drew his weapon, braced his buckler, and charged furiously upon the savages. Juan de la Cosa followed as heartily as if the battle had been of his own seeking. The Indians were soon routed, a number killed, and several taken prisoners; on their persons were found plates of gold, but of an inferior quality. Flushed by this triumph, Ojeda took several of the prisoners as guides, and pursued the flying enemy four leagues into the interior. He was followed, as usual, by his faithful lieutenant, the veteran La Cosa, continually remonstrating against his useless temerity, but hardily seconding him in the most hare brained perils. Having penetrated far into the forest, they came to a strong hold of the enemy, where a numerous force was ready to receive them, armed with clubs, lances, arrows and bucklers. Ojeda led his men to the charge with the old Castilian war cry, "Santiago!" The savages soon took to flight. Eight of their bravest warriors threw themselves into a cabin and plied their bows and arrows so vigorously that the Spaniards were kept at bay. Ojeda cried shame upon his followers to be daunted by eight naked men. Stung by this reproach, an old Castilian soldier rushed through a shower of arrows and forced the door of the cabin, but received a shaft through the heart and fell dead on the threshold. Ojeda, furious at the sight, ordered fire to be set to the combustible edifice; in a moment it was in a blaze, and the eight warriors perished in the flames.

Seventy Indians were made captive and sent to the ships, and Ojeda, regardless of the remonstrances of Juan de la Cosa, continued his rash pursuit of the fugitives through the forest. In the dusk of the evening they arrived at a village called Yurbaco; the inhabitants of which had fled to the mountains with their wives and children and principal effects. The Spaniards, imagining that the Indians were completely terrified and dispersed, now roved in quest of booty, among the deserted houses, which stood distant from each other, buried among the trees. While they were thus scattered, troops of savages rushed forth, with furious yells, from all parts of the forest. The Spaniards endeavoured to gather together and support each other, but every little party was surrounded by a host of foes. They fought with desperate bravery but for once their valour and their iron armour were of no avail; they were overwhelmed by numbers, and sank beneath war clubs and poisoned arrows.

Ojeda on the first alarm collected a few soldiers and ensconced himself within a small enclosure, surrounded by palisades. Here he was closely besieged and galled by flights of arrows. He threw himself on his knees, covered himself with his buckler, and being small and active, managed to protect himself from the deadly shower, but all his companions were slain by his side, some of them perishing in frightful agonies. At this fearful moment the veteran La Cosa, having heard of the peril of his commander, arrived, with a few followers, to his assistance. Stationing himself at the gate of the palisades, the brave Biscayan kept the savages at bay until most of his men were slain and he himself was severely wounded. Just then Ojeda sprang forth like a tiger into the midst of the enemy, dealing his blows on every side. La Cosa would have seconded him, but was crippled by his wounds. He took refuge with the remnant of his men in an Indian cabin; the straw roof of which he aided them to throw off, lest the enemy should set it on fire. Here he defended himself until all his comrades, but one, were destroyed. The subtle poison of his wounds at length overpowered him, and he sank to the ground. Feeling death at hand, he called to his only surviving companion. "Brother," said he, "since God hath protected thee from harm, sally forth and fly, and if ever thou shouldst see Alonzo de Ojeda, tell him of my fate!"

Thus fell the hardy Juan de la Cosa, faithful and devoted to the very last; nor can we refrain from pausing to pay a passing tribute to his memory. He was acknowledged by his contemporaries to be one of the ablest of those gallant Spanish navigators who first explored the way to the New World. But it is by the honest and kindly qualities of his heart that his memory is most endeared to us; it is, above all, by that loyalty in friendship displayed in this his last and fatal expedition. Warmed by his attachment for a more youthful and a hot-headed adventurer, we see this wary veteran of the seas forgetting his usual prudence and the lessons of his experience, and embarking heart and hand, purse and person, in the wild enterprises of his favourite. We behold him watching over him as a parent, remonstrating with him as a counsellor, but fighting by him as a partizan; following him, without hesitation, into known and needless danger, to certain death itself, and showing no other solicitude in his dying moments, but to be remembered by his friend.

The history of these Spanish discoverers abounds in noble and generous traits of character; but few have charmed us more than this instance of loyalty to the last gasp, in the death of the staunch Juan de la Cosa. The Spaniard who escaped to tell the story of his end was the only survivor of seventy that had followed Ojeda in this rash and headstrong inroad.

Chapter IV

Arrival of Nicuesa—Vengeance taken on the Indians

While these disastrous occurrences happened on shore, great alarm began to be felt on board of the ships. Days had elapsed since the party
had adventured so rashly into the wilderness; yet nothing had been
seen or heard of them, and the forest spread a mystery over their fate.
Some of the Spaniards ventured a little distance into the woods, but
were deterred by the distant shouts and yells of the savages and the
noise of their conchs and drums. Armed detachments then coasted the
shore in boats, landing occasionally, climbing the rocks and promontories, firing signal guns, and sounding trumpets. It was all in vain;
they heard nothing but the echoes of their own noises, or perhaps
the wild whoop of an Indian from the bosom of the forest. At length,
when they were about to give up the search in despair, they came to
a great thicket of mangrove trees on the margin of the sea. These trees
grow within the water, but their roots rise and are intertwined, above
the surface. In this entangled and almost impervious grove, they caught
a glimpse of a man in Spanish attire. They entered and to their astonishment found it to be Alonzo de Ojeda. He was lying on the matted
roots of the mangroves, his buckler on his shoulder and his sword in
his hand; but so wasted with hunger and fatigue that he could not
speak. They bore him to the firm land; made a fire on the shore to warm
him, for he was chilled with the damp and cold of his hiding place,
and when he was a little revived they gave him food and wine. In this
way he gradually recovered strength to tell his doleful story.*

He had succeeded in cutting his way through the host of savages
and attaining the woody skirts of the mountains; but when he found
himself alone, and that all his brave men had been cut off, he was
ready to yield up in despair. Bitterly did he reproach himself for having
disregarded the advice of the veteran La Cosa, and deeply did he de-
plore the loss of that loyal follower, who had fallen a victim to his

---

* The picture here given is so much like romance that the author quotes his
authority at length.—"Llegaron adonde havia, junto al agua de la mar, unos Man-
glares, que son arboles, que siempre nacen, i crecen i permanecen dentro del agua de
la mar, con grandes raices, asidas, i enmarañadas unas con otras, i alli metido, i
escondido hallaron à Alonso de Ojeda, con su espada en la mano, i la rodela en las
espaldas, i en ella sobre trecientas señales de flechazos. Estabo descaido de hambre,
que no podia hechar de si la habla; i si no fuera tan robusto, aunque chico de
cuerpo, fuera muerto."

Las Casas, lib. ii. cap. 58. MS. Herrera, Hist. Ind. d. l. lib. vii. cap. 15.

devotion. He scarce knew which way to bend his course, but continued on, in the darkness of the night and of the forest, until out of hearing of the yells of triumph uttered by the savages over the bodies of his men. When the day broke, he sought the rudest parts of the mountains and hid himself until the night; then struggling forward among rocks, and precipices and matted forests, he made his way to the sea side, but was too much exhausted to reach the ships. Indeed it was wonderful that one, so small of frame, should have been able to endure such great hardships; but he was of admirable strength and hardihood. His followers considered his escape from death as little less than miraculous, and he himself regarded it as another proof of the special protection of the Virgin, for, though he had, as usual, received no wound, yet it is said his buckler bore the dints of upwards of three hundred arrows.*

While the Spaniards were yet on the shore administering to the recovery of their commander, they beheld a squadron of ships standing towards the harbour of Carthagena and soon perceived them to be the ships of Nicuesa. Ojeda was troubled in mind at the sight, recollecting his late intemperate defiance of that cavalier; and, reflecting that, should he seek him in enmity, he was in no situation to maintain his challenge or defend himself. He ordered his men, therefore, to return on board the ships and leave him alone on the shore, and not to reveal the place of his retreat while Nicuesa should remain in the harbour.

As the squadron entered the harbour, the boats sallied forth to meet it. The first inquiry of Nicuesa was concerning Ojeda. The followers of the latter replied, mournfully, that their commander had gone on a warlike expedition into the country, but days had elapsed without his return, so that they feared some misfortune had befallen him. They entreated Nicuesa therefore to give his word, as a cavalier, that should Ojeda really be in distress, he would not take advantage of his misfortunes to revenge himself for their late disputes.

Nicuesa, who was a gentleman of noble and generous spirit, blushed with indignation at such a request. "Seek your commander instantly;" said he, "bring him to me if he be alive; and I pledge myself not merely to forget the past, but to aid him as if he were a brother."†

When they met, Nicuesa received his late foe with open arms. "It is not," said he, "for hidalgos, like men of vulgar souls, to remember past differences when they behold one another in distress. Henceforth, let all that has occurred between us be forgotten. Command me as a brother. Myself and my men are at yours orders, to follow you wherever

* Las Casas, lib. ii. cap. 58. MS. Herrera, Hist. Ind. decad 1. lib. vii. c. xv.

† Las Casas, *ubi sup.*

you please, until the deaths of Juan de la Cosa and his comrades are revenged."

The spirits of Ojeda were once more lifted up by this gallant and generous offer. The two governors, no longer rivals, landed four hundred of their men and several horses, and set off with all speed for the fatal village. They approached it in the night, and, dividing their forces into two parties, gave orders that not an Indian should be taken alive.

The village was buried in deep sleep, but the woods were filled with large parrots, which, being awakened, made a prodigious clamour. The Indians, however, thinking the Spaniards all destroyed, paid no attention to these noises. It was not until their houses were assailed and wrapped in flames that they took the alarm. They rushed forth, some with arms, some weaponless, but were received at their doors by the exasperated Spaniards and either slain on the spot, or driven back into the fire. Women fled wildly forth with children in their arms, but at sight of the Spaniards glittering in steel, and of the horses, which they supposed ravenous monsters, ran back, shrieking with horror, into their burning habitations. Great was the carnage, for no quarter was shown to age or sex. Many perished by the fire, and many by the sword.

When they had fully glutted their vengeance, the Spaniards ranged about for booty. While thus employed, they found the body of the unfortunate Juan de la Cosa. It was tied to a tree, but swoln and discoloured in a hideous manner by the poison of the arrows with which he had been slain. This dismal spectacle had such an effect upon the common men that not one would remain in that place during the night. Having sacked the village, therefore, they left it a smoking ruin, and returned in triumph to their ships. The spoil in gold and other articles of value must have been great, for the share of Nicuesa and his men amounted to the value of seven thousand castellanos.* The two governors, now faithful confederates, parted with many expressions of friendship, and with mutual admiration of each other's prowess, and Nicuesa continued his voyage for the coast of Veragua.

Equivalent to 37,281 Dollars of the present day.

Chapter V

Ojeda founds the colony of San Sebastian—Beleaguered by the Indians

Ojeda, now adopted, though tardily, the advice of his unfortunate lieutenant, Juan de la Cosa, and, giving up all thoughts of colonizing this disastrous part of the coast, steered his course for the Gulph of Uraba. He sought for some time the river Darien, famed among the Indians as abounding in gold, but not finding it, landed in various places, seeking a favorable site for his intended colony. His people were disheartened by the disasters they had already undergone, and the appearance of surrounding objects was not calculated to reassure them. The country, though fertile and covered with rich and beautiful vegetation, was in their eyes a land of cannibals and monsters. They began to dread the strength as well as fierceness of the savages, who could transfix a man with their arrows even when covered with armour, and whose shafts were tipped with deadly poison. They heard the howlings of tygers, panthers and, as they thought, lions in the forests, and encountered large and venomous serpents among the rocks and thickets. As they were passing along the banks of a river, one of their horses was seized by the leg by an enormous alligator, and dragged beneath the waves.*

At length Ojeda fixed upon a place for his town on a height at the east side of the Gulph. Here, landing all that could be spared from the ships, he began, with all diligence, to erect houses, giving this embryo capital of his province the name of San Sebastian, in honour of that sainted martyr, who was slain by arrows; hoping he might protect the inhabitants from the empoisoned shafts of the savages. As a further protection he erected a large wooden fortress, and surrounded the place with a stoccade. Feeling, however, the inadequacy of his handful of men to contend with the hostile tribes around him, he despatched a ship to Hispaniola, with a letter to the Bachelor Martin Fernandez de Enciso, his Alcalde Mayor, informing him of his having established his seat of government, and urging him to lose no time in joining him with all the recruits, arms and provisions he could command. By the same ship he transmitted to San Domingo all the captives and gold he had collected.

His capital being placed in a posture of defence, Ojeda now thought of making a progress through his wild territory; and set out, accordingly, with an armed band, to pay a friendly visit to a neighboring cacique, reputed as possessing great treasures of gold. The natives,

* Herrera, Hist. Ind. decad. 1. lib. vii. cap. xvi.

however, had by this time learnt the nature of these friendly visits and were prepared to resist them. Scarcely had the Spaniards entered into the defiles of the surrounding forest when they were assailed by flights of arrows from the close coverts of the thickets. Some were shot dead on the spot, others, less fortunate, expired raving with the torments of the poison; the survivors, filled with horror at the sight, and losing all presence of mind, retreated in confusion to the fortress.

It was some time before Ojeda could again persuade his men to take the field, so great was their dread of the poisoned weapons of the Indians. At length their provisions began to fail, and they were compelled to forage among the villages in search, not of gold, but of food.

In one of their expeditions they were surprized by an ambuscado of savages, in a gorge of the mountains, and attacked with such fury and effect that they were completely routed, and pursued with yells and howlings to the very gates of San Sebastian. Many died in excruciating agony of their wounds, and others recovered with extreme difficulty. Those who were well no longer dared to venture forth in search of food, for the whole forest teemed with lurking foes. They devoured such herbs and roots as they could find, without regard to their quality. The humours of their bodies became corrupted, and various diseases, combined with the ravages of famine, daily thinned their numbers. The centinel who feebly mounted guard at night, was often found dead at his post in the morning. Some stretched themselves on the ground and expired of mere famine and debility; nor was death any longer regarded as an evil, but rather as a welcome relief from a life of horror and despair.

Chapter VI

Alonzo de Ojeda supposed by the savages to have a charmed life— Their experiment to try the fact

In the mean time the Indians continued to harass the garrison, lying in wait to surprize the foraging parties, cutting off all stragglers and sometimes approaching the walls in open defiance. On such occasions Ojeda sallied forth at the head of his men and from his great agility was the first to overtake the retreating foe. He slew more of their warriors with his single arm than all his followers together. Though often exposed to showers of arrows none had ever wounded him, and the Indians began to think he had a charmed life. Perhaps they had heard from fugitive prisoners the idea entertained by himself and his followers of his being under supernatural protection. Determined to ascertain the fact, they placed four of their most dextrous archers in ambush with orders to single him out. A number of them advanced towards the fort sounding their conchs and drums and uttering yells of defiance. As they expected, the impetuous Ojeda sallied forth immediately, at the head of his men. The Indians fled towards the ambuscado, drawing him in heedless pursuit. The archers waited until he was full in front and then launched their deadly shafts. Three struck the buckler and glanced harmlessly off, but the fourth pierced his thigh. Satisfied that he was wounded beyond the possibility of cure, the savages retreated with shouts of triumph.

Ojeda was borne back to the fortress in great anguish of body and despondency of spirit. For the first time in his life he had lost blood in battle. The charm in which he had hitherto confided was broken; or rather, the Holy Virgin appeared to have withdrawn her protection. He had the horrible death of his followers before his eyes, who had perished of their wounds in raving frenzy.

One of the symptoms of the poison was to shoot a thrilling chill through the wounded part; from this circumstance, perhaps, a remedy suggested itself to the imagination of Ojeda, which few but himself could have had the courage to undergo. He caused two plates of iron to be made red hot and ordered a surgeon to apply them to each orifice of the wound. The surgeon shuddered and refused, saying he would not be the murderer of his general.* Upon this Ojeda made a solemn vow that he would hang him unless he obeyed. To avoid the gallows, the surgeon applied the glowing plates. Ojeda refused to be tied down, or that any one should hold him during this frightful operation. He endured it without shrinking or uttering a murmur, although it so inflamed his whole system, that they had to wrap him in sheets steeped in vinegar, to allay the burning heat which raged throughout his body; and we are assured that a barrel of vinegar was exhausted for the purpose. The desperate remedy succeeded: the cold poison, says Bishop Las Casas, was consumed by the vivid fire.† How far the venerable historian is correct in his postulate surgeons may decide, but many incredulous persons will be apt to account for the cure by surmising that the arrow was not envenomed.

* Charlevoix, ut sup. p. 293.
† Las Casas, Hist. Ind. lib. ii. cap. 59. MS.

Chapter VII

Arrival of a strange ship at San Sebastian

Alonzo de Ojeda, though pronounced out of danger, was still disabled by his wound; and his helpless situation completed the despair of his companions, for while he was in health and vigour his buoyant and mercurial spirit, his active, restless and enterprizing habits, imparted animation if not confidence to every one around him. The only hope of relief was from the sea, and that was nearly extinct, when one day to the unspeakable joy of the Spaniards a sail appeared on the horizon. It made for the port and dropped anchor at the foot of the height of San Sebastian, and there was no longer a doubt that it was the promised succour from San Domingo.

The ship came indeed from the island of Hispaniola, but it had not been fitted out by the Bachelor Enciso. The commander's name was Bernardino de Talavera. This man was one of the loose heedless adventurers who abounded in San Domingo. His carelessness and extravagance had involved him in debt and he was threatened with a prison. In the height of his difficulties the ship arrived which Ojeda had sent to San Domingo freighted with slaves and gold, an earnest of the riches to be found at San Sebastian. Bernardo de Talavera immediately conceived the project of giving his creditors the slip, and escaping to this new settlement. He understood that Ojeda was in need of recruits, and felt assured that, from his own reckless conduct in money matters, he would sympathize with any one harassed by debt. He drew into his schemes a number of desperate debtors like himself, nor was he scrupulous about filling up his ranks with recruits whose legal embarrassments arose from more criminal causes. Never did a more vagabond crew engage in a project of colonization.

How to provide themselves with a vessel was now the question. They had neither money nor credit; but then they had cunning and courage, and were troubled by no scruples of conscience; thus qualified, a knave will often succeed better for a time than an honest man; it is in the long run that he fails, as will be illustrated in the case of Talavera and his hopeful associates. While casting about for means to escape to San Sebastian, they heard of a vessel belonging to certain Genoese, which was at Cape Tiburon, at the western extremity of the island, taking in a cargo of bacon and cassava bread for San Domingo. Nothing could have happened more opportunely: here was a ship, amply stored with provisions, and ready to their hand. They had nothing to do but seize it and embark.

The gang, accordingly, seventy in number, made their way separately and secretly to Cape Tiburon, where, assembling at an appointed time and place, they boarded the vessel, overpowered the crew, weighed anchor and set sail. They were heedless haphazard mariners, and knew little of the management of a vessel; the historian Charlevoix thinks, therefore, that it was a special providence which guided them to San Sebastian. Whether or not the good father is right in his opinion, it is certain that the arrival of the ship rescued the garrison from the very brink of destruction.*

Talavera and his gang, though they had come lightly by their prize, were not disposed to part with it as frankly, but demanded to be paid down in gold, for the provisions furnished to the starving colonists. Ojeda agreed to their terms, and taking the supplies into his possession dealt them out sparingly to his companions. Several of his hungry followers were dissatisfied with their portions, and even accused Ojeda of unfairness in reserving an undue share for himself. Perhaps there may have been some ground for this charge, arising, not from any selfishness in the character of Ojeda, but from one of those superstitious fancies with which his mind was tinged; for we are told that, for many years, he had been haunted by a presentiment that he should eventually die of hunger.†

This lurking horror of the mind may have made him depart from his usual free and lavish spirit, in doling out these providential supplies, and may have induced him to set by an extra portion for himself, as a precaution against his anticipated fate; certain it is that great clamours rose among his people, some of whom threatened to return in the pirate vessel to Hispaniola. He succeeded, however, in pacifying them for the present by representing the necessity of husbanding their supplies, and by assuring them that the Bachelor Enciso could not fail soon to arrive, when there would be provisions in abundance.

* Hist. S. Domingo, lib. iv.
† Herrera, decad. 1. lib. viii. cap. 3.

Chapter VIII

Factions in the colony—A convention made

Days and days elapsed but no relief arrived at San Sebastian. The Spaniards kept a ceaseless watch upon the sea, but the promised ship failed to appear. With all the husbandry of Ojeda the stock of provisions was nearly consumed; famine again prevailed, and several of the garrison perished through their various sufferings and their lack of sufficient nourishment. The survivors now became factious in their misery, and a plot was formed among them to seize upon one of the vessels in the harbour and make sail for Hispaniola.

Ojeda discovered their intentions, and was reduced to great perplexity. He saw that to remain here without relief from abroad was certain destruction, yet he clung to his desperate enterprize. It was his only chance for fortune or command; for should this settlement be broken up he might try in vain with his exhausted means and broken credit to obtain another post or to set on foot another expedition. Ruin in fact would overwhelm him, should he return without success.

He exerted himself, therefore, to the utmost to pacify his men; representing the folly of abandoning a place where they had established a foot hold, and where they only needed a reinforcement to enable them to controul the surrounding country and to make themselves masters of its riches. Finding they still demurred, he offered, now that he was sufficiently recovered from his wound, to go himself to San Domingo in quest of reinforcements and supplies.

This offer had the desired effect. Such confidence had the people in the energy, ability, and influence of Ojeda, that they felt assured of relief should he seek it in person. They made a kind of convention with him, therefore, in which it was agreed that they should remain quietly at Sebastian's for the space of fifty days. At the end of this time, in case no tidings had been received of Ojeda, they were to be at liberty to abandon the settlement and return in the brigantines to Hispaniola. In the mean time Francisco Pizarro was to command the colony as Lieutenant of Ojeda, until the arrival of his Alcalde Mayor, the Bachelor Enciso. This convention being made, Ojeda embarked in the ship of Bernardino de Talavera. That cut purse of the ocean and his loose handed crew were effectually cured of their ambition to colonize. Disappointed in the hope of finding abundant wealth at San Sebastian, and dismayed at the perils and horrors of the surrounding wilderness, they preferred returning to Hispaniola, even at the risk of chains and dungeons. Doubtless they thought that the influence of Ojeda would

be sufficient to obtain their pardon, especially as their timely succour
had been the salvation of the colony.

Chapter IX

Disastrous voyage of Ojeda in the pirate ship

Ojeda had scarce put to sea in the ship of these freebooters when a
quarrel arose between him and Talavera. Accustomed to take the lead
among his companions, still feeling himself governor, and naturally of
a domineering spirit, Ojeda, on coming on board, had assumed the
command as a matter of course. Talavera, who claimed dominion over
the ship, by the right no doubt of trover and conversion, or, in other
words, of downright piracy, resisted this usurpation.

Ojeda, as usual, would speedily have settled the question by the
sword, but he had the whole vagabond crew against him, who overpowered him with numbers and threw him in irons. Still his swelling
spirit was unsubdued. He reviled Talavera and his gang as recreants,
traytors, pirates, and offered to fight the whole of them successively,
provided they would give him a clear deck, and come on two at a time.
Notwithstanding his diminutive size, they had too high an idea of his
prowess, and had heard too much of his exploits, to accept his challenge; so they kept him raging in his chains while they pursued their
voyage.

They had not proceeded far, however, when a violent storm arose.
Talavera and his crew knew little of navigation and were totally ignorant of those seas. The raging of the elements, the baffling winds and
currents, and the danger of unknown rocks and shoals filled them with
confusion and alarm. They knew not whither they were driving before
the storm or where to seek for shelter. In this hour of peril they called
to mind that Ojeda was a sailor as well as a soldier, and that he had
repeatedly navigated these seas. Making a truce, therefore, for the common safety, they took off his irons, on condition that he would pilot
the vessel during the remainder of the voyage.

Ojeda acquitted himself with his accustomed spirit and intrepidity;
but the vessel had already been swept so far to the westward that all
his skill was ineffectual in endeavouring to work up to Hispaniola
against storms and adverse currents. Borne away by the gulf stream,

and tempest tost for many days, until the shattered vessel was almost
in a foundering condition, he saw no alternative but to run it ashore
on the southern coast of Cuba.

Here then the crew of freebooters landed from their prize in more
desperate plight than when they first took possession of it. They were
on a wild and unfrequented coast, their vessel lay a wreck upon the
sands, and their only chance was to travel on foot to the eastern extremity of the island, and seek some means of crossing to Hispaniola,
where, after all their toils, they might perhaps only arrive to be thrown
into a dungeon. Such, however, is the yearning of civilized men after
the haunts of cultivated society, that they set out, at every risk, upon
their long and painful journey.

Chapter X

*Toilsome march of Ojeda and his companions through the morasses
of Cuba*

Notwithstanding the recent services of Ojeda, the crew of Talavera still
regarded him with hostility; but if they had felt the value of his skill
and courage at sea, they were no less sensible of their importance on
shore, and he soon acquired that ascendancy over them which belongs
to a master spirit in time of trouble.

Cuba was as yet uncolonized. It was a place of refuge to the unhappy natives of Hayti, who fled hither from the whips and chains of
their European taskmasters. The forests abounded with these wretched
fugitives, who often opposed themselves to the shipwrecked party, supposing them to be sent by their late masters to drag them back to
captivity.

Ojeda easily repulsed these attacks; but found that these fugitives
had likewise inspired the villages with hostility to all European strangers. Seeing that his companions were too feeble and disheartened to
fight their way through the populous parts of the island, or to climb
the rugged mountains of the interior, he avoided all towns and villages,
and led them through the close forests and broad green Savannahs
which extended between the mountains and the sea.

He had only made a choice of evils. The forests gradually retired
from the coast. The Savannahs, where the Spaniards at first had to

contend merely with long rank grass and creeping vines, soon ended
in salt marshes, where the oozy bottom yielded no firm foot hold, and
the mud and water reached to their knees. Still they pressed forward,
continually hoping in a little while to arrive at a firmer soil, and flattering themselves they beheld fresh meadow land before them; but continually deceived. The farther they proceeded the deeper grew the
mire, until, after they had been eight days on this dismal journey, they
found themselves in the center of a vast morass where the water
reached to their girdles. Though thus almost drowned, they were tormented with incessant thirst, for all the water around them was as
briny as the ocean. They suffered too the cravings of extreme hunger,
having but a scanty supply of cassava bread and cheese, and a few
potatoes and other roots, which they devoured raw. When they wished
to sleep, they had to climb among the twisted roots of mangrove trees,
which grew in clusters in the water. Still the dreary marsh widened and
deepened. In many places they had to cross rivers and inlets; where
some, who could not swim, were drowned, and others were smothered
in the mire.

Their situation became wild and desperate. Their cassava bread was
spoiled by the water, and their stock of roots nearly exhausted. The in-
terminable morass still extended before them, while, to return, after the
distance they had come, was hopeless. Ojeda alone kept up a resolute
spirit, and cheered and urged them forward. He had the little Flemish
painting of the Madonna, which had been given him by the Bishop
Fonseca, carefully stored among the provisions in his knapsack. Whenever he stopped to repose among the roots of the mangrove trees, he
took out this picture, placed it among the branches, and kneeling,
prayed devoutly to the Virgin for protection. This he did repeatedly
in the course of the day, and prevailed upon his companions to follow
his example. Nay, more, at a moment of great despondency, he made a
solemn vow to his patroness that if she conducted him alive through
this peril, he would erect a chapel in the first Indian village he should
arrive at; and leave her picture there, to remain an object of adoration
to the Gentiles.*

This frightful morass extended for the distance of thirty leagues, and
was so deep and difficult, so entangled by roots and creeping vines, so
cut up by creeks and rivers, and so beset by quagmires that they were
thirty days in traversing it. Out of the number of seventy men that
set out from the ship but thirty five remained. "Certain it is," observes
the venerable Las Casas, "the sufferings of the Spaniards in the New

---

* Las Casas, Hist. Ind. lib. ii. cap. 60. MS.

World, in search of wealth, have been more cruel and severe than ever nation in the world endured; but those experienced by Ojeda and his men have surpassed all others."

They were at length so overcome by hunger and fatigue that some lay down and yielded up the ghost, and others, seating themselves among the mangrove trees, waited in despair for death to put an end to their miseries. Ojeda with a few of the lightest and most vigorous continued to struggle forward and to their unutterable joy at length arrived to where the land was firm and dry. They soon descried a foot path and, following it, arrived at an Indian village commanded by a cacique called Cueybàs. No sooner did they reach the village than they sank to the earth exhausted.

The Indians gathered round and gazed at them with wonder; but when they learnt their story, they exhibited a humanity that would have done honour to the most professing Christians. They bore them to their dwellings, set meat and drink before them, and vied with each other in discharging the offices of the kindest humanity. Finding that a number of their companions were still in the morass, the cacique sent a large party of Indians with provisions for their relief; with orders to bring on their shoulders such as were too feeble to walk. "The Indians," says the Bishop Las Casas, "did more than they were ordered; for so they always do, when they are not exasperated by ill treatment. The Spaniards were brought to the village, succoured, cherished, consoled, and almost worshipped as if they had been angels."

Chapter XI

Ojeda performs his vow to the Virgin

Being recovered from his sufferings, Alonzo de Ojeda prepared to perform his vow concerning the picture of the Virgin, though sorely must it have grieved him to part with a relique to which he attributed his deliverance from so many perils. He built a little hermitage or oratory in the village, and furnished it with an altar, above which he placed the picture. He then summoned the benevolent cacique, and explained to him, as well as his limited knowledge of the language, or the aid of interpreters would permit, the main points of the Catholic faith, and especially the history of the Virgin, whom he represented as the mother of the deity that reigned in the skies, and the great advocate for mortal man.

The worthy cacique listened to him with mute attention, and though he might not clearly comprehend the doctrine, yet he conceived a profound veneration for the picture. The sentiment was shared by his subjects. They kept the little oratory always swept clean, and decorated it with cotton hangings, laboured by their own hands, and with various votive offerings. They composed couplets or areytos in honour of the Virgin, which they sang to the accompaniment of rude musical instruments, dancing to the sound under the groves which surrounded the hermitage.

A further anecdote concerning this relique may not be unacceptable. The venerable Las Casas, who records these facts, informs us that he arrived at the village of Cueybàs some time after the departure of Ojeda. He found the oratory preserved with the most religious care, as a sacred place, and the picture of the Virgin regarded with fond adoration. The poor Indians crowded to attend mass, which he performed at the altar; they listened attentively to his paternal instructions, and at his request brought their children to be baptised. The good Las Casas having heard much of this famous relique of Ojeda, was desirous of obtaining possession of it, and offered to give the cacique, in exchange, an image of the Virgin which he had brought with him. The chieftain made an evasive answer, and seemed much troubled in mind. The next morning he did not make his appearance.

Las Casas went to the oratory to perform mass, but found the altar stripped of its precious relique. On inquiring, he learnt that in the night the cacique had fled to the woods, bearing off with him his beloved picture of the Virgin. It was in vain that Las Casas sent messengers after him, assuring him that he should not be deprived of the relique, but, on the contrary, that the image should likewise be presented to him. The cacique refused to venture from the fastnesses of the forest, nor did he return to his village and replace the picture in the oratory until after the departure of the Spaniards.*

* Las Casas, Hist. Ind. cap. 61, MS.—Herrera, Hist. Ind. decad. i. lib. ix. cap. 15.

Chapter XII

Arrival of Ojeda at Jamaica—His reception by Juan de Esquibel

When the Spaniards were completely restored to health and strength, they resumed their journey. The cacique sent a large body of his subjects to carry their provisions and knapsacks, and to guide them across a desert tract of country to the province of Macaca, where Christopher Columbus had been hospitably entertained on his voyage along this coast. They experienced equal kindness from its cacique and his people, for such seems almost invariably the case with the natives of these islands, before they had held much intercourse with Europeans.

The province of Macaca was situated at Cape de la Cruz, the nearest point to the Island of Jamaica. Here Ojeda learnt that there were Spaniards settled on that island, being in fact the party commanded by the very Juan de Esquibel, whose head he had threatened to strike off, when departing in swelling style from San Domingo. It seemed to be the fortune of Ojeda to have his bravadoes visited on his head in times of trouble and humiliation. He found himself compelled to apply for succour to the very man he had so vaingloriously menaced. This was no time, however, to stand on points of pride; he procured a canoe and Indians from the cacique of Macaca, and one Pedro de Ordas undertook the perilous voyage of twenty leagues in the frail bark, and arrived safe at Jamaica.

No sooner did Esquibel receive the message of Ojeda, than, forgetting past menaces, he instantly despatched a caravel to bring to him the unfortunate discoverer and his companions. He received him with the utmost kindness, lodged him in his own house, and treated him in all things with the most delicate attention. He was a gentle man who had seen prosperous days, but had fallen into adversity and been buffeted about the world, and had learnt how to respect the feelings of a proud spirit in distress. Ojeda had the warm, touchy heart to feel such conduct; he remained several days with Esquibel in frank communion, and when he sailed for San Domingo they parted the best of friends.

And here we cannot but remark, the singular difference in character and conduct of these Spanish adventurers when dealing with each other, or with the unhappy natives. Nothing could be more chivalrous, urbane, and charitable, nothing more pregnant with noble sacrifices of passion and interest, with magnanimous instances of forgiveness of injuries and noble contests of generosity, than the transactions of the discoverers with each other; but the moment they turned to treat with the Indians, even with brave and high minded caciques, they were vindictive, bloodthirsty and implacable. The very Juan de Esquibel, who could requite the recent hostility of Ojeda with such humanity and friendship, was the same who under the government of Ovando laid desolate the province of Higuey in Hispaniola, and inflicted atrocious cruelties upon its inhabitants.

When Alonzo de Ojeda set sail for San Domingo, Bernaldino de Talavera and his rabble adherents remained at Jamaica. They feared to be brought to account for their piratical exploit in stealing the Genoese vessel, and that, in consequence of their recent violence to Ojeda, they would find in him an accuser rather than an advocate. The latter, however, in the opinion of Las Casas, who knew him well, was not a man to make accusations. With all his faults he did not harbour malice. He was quick and fiery, it is true, and his sword was too apt to leap from its scabbard on the least provocation; but after the first flash all was over, and, if he cooled upon an injury, he never sought for vengeance.

Chapter XIII

Arrival of Alonzo de Ojeda at San Domingo—Conclusion of his story

On arriving at San Domingo the first inquiry of Alonzo de Ojeda was after the Bachelor Enciso. He was told that he had departed long before, with abundant supplies for the colony, and that nothing had been heard of him since his departure. Ojeda waited for a time in hopes of hearing, by some return ship, of the safe arrival of the Bachelor at San Sebastian. No tidings, however, arrived, and he began to fear that he had been lost in those storms which had beset himself on his return voyage.

Anxious for the relief of his settlement, and fearing, that, by delay, his whole scheme of colonisation would be defeated, he now endeavoured to set on foot another armament, and to enlist a new set of adventurers. His efforts, however, were all ineffectual. The disasters of his colony were known, and his own circumstances were considered desperate. He was doomed to experience the fate that too often attends sanguine and brilliant projectors. The world is dazzled by them for a time, and hails them as heroes while successful, but misfortune dissipates the charm, and they become stigmatized with the appellation of adventurers. When Ojeda figured in San Domingo as the conqueror of Coanabo, as the commander of a squadron, as the governor of a province, his prowess and exploits were the theme of every tongue. When he set sail, in vaunting style, for his seat of government, setting the vice roy at defiance, and threatening the life of Esquibel, every one thought that fortune was at his beck, and he was about to accomplish wonders. A few months had elapsed, and he walked the streets of San Domingo a needy man, shipwrecked in hope and fortune. His former friends dreading some new demand upon their purses, looked coldly on him; his schemes, once so extolled, were now pronounced wild and chimerical, and he was subjected to all kinds of slights and humiliations in the very place which had been the scene of his greatest vainglory.

While Ojeda was thus lingering at San Domingo, the Admiral, Don Diego Columbus, sent a party of soldiers to Jamaica to arrest Talavera and his pirate crew. They were brought in chains to San Domingo, thrown into dungeons, and tried for the robbery of the Genoese vessel. Their crime was too notorious to admit of doubt, and being convicted, Talavera and several of his principal accomplices were hanged. Such was the end of their frightful journey by sea and land. Never had vagabonds traveled farther or toiled harder to arrive at a gallows!

In the course of the trial Ojeda had naturally been summoned as a witness, and his testimony must have tended greatly to the conviction of the culprits. This drew upon him the vengeance of the surviving comrades of Talavera, who still lurked about San Domingo. As he was returning home one night at a late hour, he was waylaid and set upon by a number of these miscreants. He displayed his usual spirit. Setting his back against a wall, and drawing his sword, he defended himself admirably against the whole gang; nor was he content with beating them off, but pursued them for some distance through the streets; and having thus put them to utter rout, returned tranquil and unharmed to his lodgings.

This is the last achievement recorded of the gallant but reckless Ojeda; for here his bustling career terminated, and he sank into the obscurity that gathers round a ruined man. His health was broken by the various hardships and by the lurking effects of the wound received at San Sebastian, which had been but imperfectly cured. Poverty and neglect, and the corroding sickness of the heart, contributed, no less than the maladies of the body, to quench that sanguine and fiery temper, which had hitherto been the secret of his success, and to render him the mere wreck of his former self; for there is no ruin so hopeless and complete, as that of a towering spirit humiliated and broken down. He appears to have lingered some time at San Domingo. Gomara, in his history of the Indies, affirms that he turned monk, and entered in the convent at San Francisco, where he died. Such a change would not have been surprising in a man who, in his wildest career, mingled the bigot with the soldier; nor was it unusual with military adventurers in those days, after passing their youth in the bustle and licentiousness of the camp, to end their days in the quiet and mortification of the cloister. Las Casas, however, who was at San Domingo at the time, makes no mention of the fact, as he certainly would have done, had it taken place. He confirms, however, all that has been said of the striking reverse in his character and circumstances; and he adds an affecting picture of his last moments, which may serve as a wholesome comment on his life. He died so poor that he did not leave money enough to provide for his interment; and so broken in spirit, that, with his last breath, he entreated that his body might be buried in the monastery of San Francisco, just at the portal, in humble expiation of his past pride, *"that every one who entered might tread upon his grave."**

Such was the fate of Alonzo de Ojeda,—and who does not forget his errors and his faults at the threshold of his humble and untimely grave! He was one of the most fearless and aspiring of that band of "Ocean chivalry," that followed the footsteps of Columbus. His story presents a lively picture of the daring enterprizes, the extravagant exploits, the thousand accidents by flood and field that chequered the life of a Spanish cavalier in that roving and romantic age.

"Never," says Charlevoix, "was man more suited for a coup-de-main, or to achieve and suffer great things under the direction of another: none had a heart more lofty, or ambition more aspiring; none ever took less heed of fortune, or shewed greater firmness of soul, or found more resources in his own courage; but none was less calculated to be commander in chief of a great enterprize. Good management and good fortune forever failed him."†

* Las Casas, ubi sup.
† Charlevoix, Hist. San Domingo.

THE VOYAGE
of
DIEGO DE NICUESA

Chapter I

Nicuesa sails to the westward—His shipwreck and subsequent disasters

We have now to recount the fortunes experienced by the gallant and generous Diego de Nicuesa, after his parting from Alonzo de Ojeda at Carthagena. On resuming his voyage, he embarked in a caravel, that he might be able to coast the land and reconnoitre; he ordered that the two brigantines, one of which was commanded by his Lieutenant Lope de Olano, should keep near to him, while the large vessels, which drew more water, should stand further out to sea. The squadron arrived upon the coast of Veragua in stormy weather, and, as Nicuesa could not find any safe harbour, and was apprehensive of rocks and shoals, he stood out to sea at the approach of night, supposing that Lope de Olano would follow him with the brigantines according to his orders. The night was boisterous, the caravel was much tossed and driven about, and when the morning dawned, not one of the squadron was in sight.

Nicuesa feared some accident had befallen the brigantines; he stood for the land and coasted along it in search of them until he came to a large river, into which he entered and came to anchor. He had not been here long when the stream suddenly subsided, having merely been swoln by the rains. Before he had time to extricate himself the caravel grounded and at length fell over on one side. The current rushing like a torrent strained the feeble bark to such a degree that her seams yawned and she appeared ready to go to pieces. In this moment of peril a hardy seaman threw himself into the water to carry the end of a rope on shore as a means of saving the crew. He was swept away by the furious current and perished in sight of his companions. Undismayed by his fate, another brave seaman plunged into the waves and succeeded in reaching the shore. He then fastened one end of a rope firmly to a tree, and the other being secured on board of the caravel, Nicuesa and his crew passed one by one along it, and reached the shore in safety.

Scarcely had they landed when the caravel went to pieces, and with it perished their provisions, clothing and all other necessaries. Nothing remained to them but the boat of the caravel, which was accidentally cast on shore. Here then they were, in helpless plight on a remote and savage coast, without food, without arms, and almost naked. What had become of the rest of the squadron they knew not. Some feared that the brigantines had been wrecked; others called to mind that Lope de Olano had been one of the loose lawless men confederated with Francisco Roldan in his rebellion against Columbus, and, judging him from the school in which he had served, hinted their apprehensions that he had deserted with the brigantines. Nicuesa partook of their suspicions and was anxious and sad at heart. He concealed his uneasiness, however, and endeavoured to cheer up his companions: proposing that they should proceed westward on foot in search of Veragua, the seat of his intended government, observing that, if the ships had survived the tempest, they would probably repair to that place. They accordingly set off along the sea shore, for the thickness of the forest prevented their traversing the interior. Four of the hardiest sailors put to sea in the boat and kept abreast of them, to help them across the bays and rivers.

Their sufferings were extreme. Most of them were destitute of shoes and many almost naked. They had to clamber over sharp and rugged rocks, and to struggle through dense forests beset with thorns and brambles. Often they had to wade across rank fens and morasses and drowned lands, or to traverse deep and rapid streams.

Their food consisted of herbs and roots and shellfish gathered along the shore. Had they even met with Indians they would have dreaded, in their unarmed state, to apply to them for provisions, lest they should take revenge for the outrages committed along this coast by other Europeans.

To render their sufferings more intolerable they were in doubt whether, in the storms which preceded their shipwreck, they had not been driven past Veragua, in which case each step would take them so much the farther from their desired haven.

Still they laboured feebly forward, encouraged by the words and the example of Nicuesa, who cheerfully partook of the toils and hardships of the meanest of his men.

They had slept one night at the foot of impending rocks and were about to resume their weary march in the morning when they were espied by some Indians from a neighboring height. Among the followers of Nicuesa was a favorite page whose tattered finery and white hat caught the quick eyes of the savages. One of them immediately singled him out and taking a deadly aim let fly an arrow that laid him expiring at the feet of his master. While the generous cavalier mourned over his slaughtered page, consternation prevailed among his companions, each fearing for his own life. The Indians, however, did not follow up this casual act of hostility, but suffered the Spaniards to pursue their painful journey unmolested.

Arriving one day at the point of a great bay that ran far inland, they were conveyed, a few at a time, in the boat, to what appeared to be the opposite point. Being all landed, and resuming their march, they found to their surprize that they were on an island, separated from the main land by a great arm of the sea. The sailors who managed the boat were too weary to take them to the opposite shore, they remained therefore all night upon the island.

In the morning they prepared to depart, but, to their consternation, the boat with the four mariners had disappeared. They ran anxiously from point to point, uttering shouts and cries, in hopes the boat might be in some inlet; they clambered the rocks and strained their eyes over the sea. It was all in vain. No boat was to be seen: no voice responded to their call; it was too evident the four mariners had either perished or had deserted them.

Chapter II

Nicuesa and his men on a desolate island

The situation of Nicuesa and his men was dreary and desperate in the extreme. They were on a desolate island, bordering upon a swampy coast, in a remote and lonely sea, where commerce never spread a sail. Their companions in the other ships, if still alive and true to them, had doubtless given them up for lost; and many years might elapse before the casual bark of a discoverer might venture along these shores. Long before that time their fate would be sealed, and their bones, bleaching on the sands, would alone tell their story.

In this hopeless state many abandoned themselves to frantic grief, wandering about the island, wringing their hands and uttering groans and lamentations; others called upon God for succour, and many sat down in silent and sullen despair.

The cravings of hunger and thirst at length roused them to exertion.

They found no food but a few shell fish scattered along the shore, and coarse herbs and roots, some of them of an unwholesome quality. The island had neither springs nor streams of fresh water, and they were fain to slake their thirst at the brackish pools of the marshes.

Niceusa endeavoured to animate his men with new hopes. He employed them in constructing a raft of drift wood and branches of trees, for the purpose of crossing the arm of the sea that separated them from the main land. It was a difficult task, for they were destitute of tools, and when the raft was finished they had no oars with which to manage it. Some of the most expert swimmers undertook to propel it, but they were too much enfeebled by their sufferings. On their first essay, the currents which sweep that coast bore the raft out to sea, and they swam back with difficulty to the island. Having no other chance of escape, and no other means of exercising and keeping up the spirits of his followers, Nicuesa repeatedly ordered new rafts to be constructed, but the result was always the same, and the men at length either grew too feeble to work or renounced the attempt in despair.

Thus day after day and week after week elapsed without any mitigation of suffering or any prospect of relief. Every day some one or other sunk under his miseries, a victim not so much to hunger and thirst as to grief and despondency. His death was envied by his wretched survivors, many of whom were reduced to such debility, that they had to crawl on hands and knees in search of the herbs and shell fish which formed their scanty food.

Chapter III

Arrival of a boat—Conduct of Lope de Olano

When the unfortunate Spaniards, without hope of succour, began to consider death as a desirable end to their miseries, they were roused to new life one day by beholding a sail gleaming on the horizon. Their exultation was checked, however, by the reflection how many chances there were against its approaching this wild and desolate island. Watching it with anxious eyes, they put up prayers to God to conduct it to their relief; and at length, to their great joy, they perceived that it was steering directly for the island. On a nearer approach it proved to be one of the brigantines that had been commanded by Lope de Olano. It came to anchor: a boat put off, and among the crew were the four sailors who had disappeared so mysteriously from the island.

These men accounted in a satisfactory manner for their desertion. They had been persuaded that the ships were in some harbour to the eastward and that they were daily leaving them further behind. Disheartened at the constant, and, in their opinion, fruitless toil which fell to their share in the struggle westward, they resolved to take their own counsel, without risking the opposition of Nicuesa. In the dead of the night, therefore, when their companions on the island were asleep, they had silently cast off their boat, and retraced their course along the coast. After several days' toil they found the brigantines under the command of Lope de Olano, in the river of Belen, the scene of the disasters of Columbus in his fourth voyage.

The conduct of Lope de Olano was regarded with suspicion by his contemporaries, and is still subject to doubt. He is supposed to have deserted Nicuesa designedly, intending to usurp the command of the expedition. Men, however, were prone to judge harshly of him from his having been concerned in the treason and rebellion of Francisco Roldan. On the stormy night when Nicuesa stood out to sea to avoid the dangers of the shore, Olano took shelter under the lee of an island. Seeing nothing of the caravel of his commander in the morning, he made no effort to seek for it, but proceeded with the brigantines to the river of Chagres, where he found the ships at anchor. They had landed all their cargoes, being almost in a sinking condition from the ravages of the worms. Olano perusaded the crews that Nicuesa had perished in the late storm, and, being his lieutenant, he assumed the command. Whether he had been perfidious or not in his motives, his command was but a succession of disasters. He sailed from Chagres for the river of Belen, where the ships were found so damaged that they had to be broken to pieces. Most of the people constructed wretched cabins on the shore, where, during a sudden storm, they were almost washed away by the swelling of the river, or swallowed up in the shifting sands. Several of his men were drowned in an expedition in quest of gold, and he himself merely escaped by superior swimming. Their provisions were exhausted, they suffered from hunger and from various maladies, and many perished in extreme misery. All were clamorous to abandon the coast and Olano set about constructing a caravel, out of the wreck of the ships, for the purpose, as he said, of returning to Hispaniola, though many suspected it was still his intention to persist in the enterprize. Such was the state in which the four seamen had found Olano and his party; most of them living in miserable cabins and destitute of the necessaries of life.

The tidings that Nicuesa was still alive put an end to the sway of
Olano. Whether he had acted with truth or perfidy, he now manifested
a zeal to relieve his commander and immediately despatched a brigantine in quest of him, which, guided by the four seamen, arrived at the
island in the way that has been mentioned.

Chapter IV

Nicuesa rejoins his crews

When the crew of the brigantine and the companions of Nicuesa met,
they embraced each other with tears, for the hearts even of the rough
mariners were subdued by the sorrows they had undergone, and men
are rendered kind to each other by a community of suffering. The
brigantine had brought a quantity of palm nuts and of such other
articles of food as they had been able to procure along the coast. These
the famished Spaniards devoured with such voracity that Nicuesa was
obliged to interfere, lest they should injure themselves. Nor was a
supply of fresh water less grateful to their parched and fevered palates.

When sufficiently revived, they all abandoned the desolate island and
set sail for the river Belen, exulting as joyfully as if their troubles were
at an end and they were bound to a haven of delight, instead of merely
changing the scene of suffering and encountering a new variety of horrors.

In the mean time Lope de Olano had been diligently preparing for
the approaching interview with his commander by persuading his fellow officers to intercede in his behalf, and to place his late conduct in
the most favorable light. He had need of their intercessions. Nicuesa
arrived, burning with indignation. He ordered him to be instantly
seized and punished as a traytor, attributing to his desertion the ruin
of the enterprize and the sufferings and death of so many of his brave
followers. The fellow captains of Olano spoke in his favour, but Nicuesa
turned indignantly upon them. "You do well," cried he, "to supplicate
mercy for him, you who yourselves have need of pardon! You have
participated in his crime; why else have you suffered so long a time
to elapse without compelling him to send one of the vessels in search
of me?"

The captains now vindicated themselves by assurances of their belief in his having foundered at sea. They reiterated their supplications for mercy to Olano, drawing the most affecting pictures of their past and present sufferings, and urging the impolicy of increasing the horrors of their situation by acts of severity. Nicuesa at length was prevailed upon to spare his victim, resolving to send him, by the first opportunity, a prisoner to Spain. It appeared, in truth, no time to add to the daily blows of fate that were thinning the number of his followers. Of the gallant armament of seven hundred resolute and effective men that had sailed with them from San Domingo, four hundred had already perished by various miseries, and, of the survivors, many could scarcely be said to live.

Chapter V

Sufferings of Nicuesa and his men on the coast of the isthmus

The first care of Nicuesa, on resuming the general command, was to take measures for the relief of his people, who were perishing with famine and disease. All those who were in health, or who had strength sufficient to bear the least fatigue, were sent on foraging parties among the fields and villages of the natives. It was a service of extreme peril, for the Indians of this part of the coast were fierce and warlike, and were the same who had proved so formidable to Columbus and his brother, when they attempted to found a settlement in this neighborhood.

Many of the Spaniards were slain in these expeditions. Even if they succeeded in collecting provisions, the toil of bringing them to the harbour was worse to men in their enfeebled condition than the task of fighting for them; for they were obliged to transport them on their backs, and, thus heavily laden, to scramble over rugged rocks, through almost impervious forests and across dismal swamps.

Harassed by these perils and fatigues, they broke forth into murmurs against their commander, accusing him, not merely of indifference to their sufferings, but of wantonly imposing severe and unnecessary tasks upon them out of revenge for their having neglected him.

The genial temper of Nicuesa had, in fact, been soured by disappointment; and a series of harassing cares and evils had rendered him irritable and impatient, but he was a cavalier of a generous and honourable nature, and does not appear to have enforced any services that were not indispensable to the common safety. In fact the famine had increased to such a degree, that, we are told, thirty Spaniards, having on one occasion found the dead body of an Indian in a state of decay, were driven by hunger to make a meal of it, and were so infected by the horrible repast, that not one of them survived.*

Disheartened by these miseries, Nicuesa determined to abandon a place which seemed destined to be the grave of Spaniards. Embarking the greater part of his men in the two brigantines, and the caravel which had been built by Olano, he set sail eastward in search of some more favorable situation for his settlement. A number of the men remained behind, to await the ripening of some maize and vegetables which they had sown. These he left under the command of Alonzo Nuñez, whom he nominated his Alcade Mayor.

When Nicuesa had coasted about four leagues to the east, a Genoese sailor, who had been with Columbus in his last voyage, informed him that there was a fine harbour somewhere in that neighborhood, which had pleased the old admiral so highly that he had given it the name of Puerto Bello. He added, that they might know the harbour by an anchor, half buried in the sand, which Columbus had left there; near to which was a fountain of remarkably cool and sweet water, springing up at the foot of a large tree. Nicuesa ordered search to be made along the coast, and at length they found the anchor, the fountain, and the tree. It was the same harbour which bears the name of Porto Bello at the present day. A number of the crew were sent on shore in search of provisions, but were assailed by the Indians; and, being too weak to wield their weapons with their usual prowess, were driven back to the vessels with the loss of several slain or wounded.

Dejected at these continual misfortunes, Nicuesa continued his voyage seven leagues further, until he came to the harbour to which Columbus had given the name of Puerto de Bastimientos; or, Port of Provisions. It presented an advantageous situation for a fortress, and was surrounded by a fruitful country. Nicuesa resolved to make it his abiding place. "Here," said he, "let us stop, *en el nombre de Dios!*" (in the name of God). His followers, with the superstitious feeling under which men in adversity are prone to interpret everything into omens, persuaded themselves that there was favourable augury in his words and called the harbour Nombre de Dios, which name it afterwards retained.

Nicuesa now landed and, drawing his sword, took solemn possession

* Herrera, Hist. Ind. decad. i. and viii. cap. 2.

in the name of the Catholic Sovereigns. He immediately began to erect a fortress to protect his people against the attacks of the savages. As this was a case of exigency, he exacted the labour of every one capable of exertion. The Spaniards, thus equally distressed by famine and toil, forgot their favourable omen, cursed the place as fated to be their grave, and called down imprecations on the head of their commander, who compelled them to labour when ready to sink with hunger and debility. Those murmured no less who were sent in quest of food, which was only to be gained by fatigue and bloodshed; for whatever they collected they had to transport from great distances, and they were frequently waylayed and assaulted by the Indians.

When he could spare men for the purpose, Nicuesa despatched the caravel for those whom he had left at the river Belen. Many of them had perished and the survivors had been reduced to such famine at times as to eat all kinds of reptiles until a part of an alligator was a banquet to them. On mustering all his forces when thus united, Nicuesa found that but one hundred emaciated and dejected wretches remained.

He despatched the caravel to Hispaniola, to bring a quantity of bacon which he had ordered to have prepared there, but it never returned. He ordered Gonzalo de Badajos, at the head of twenty men, to scour the country for provisions, but the Indians had ceased to cultivate: they could do with little food and could subsist on the roots and wild fruits of the forest; the Spaniards therefore found deserted villages and barren fields, but lurking enemies in every defile. So deplorably were they reduced by their sufferings that at length there were not left a sufficient number in health and strength to mount guard at night, and the fortress remained without centinels. Such was the desperate situation of this once gay and gallant cavalier, and of his brilliant armament, which but a few months before had sallied from San Domingo flushed with the consciousness of power, and the assurance that they had the means of compelling the favours of fortune.

It is necessary to leave them for a while, and turn our attention to other events which will ultimately be found to bear upon their destinies.

Chapter VI

*Expedition of the Bachelor Enciso in search of the seat of government
of Ojedo (1510)*

In calling to mind the narrative of the last expedition of Alonzo de
Ojeda, the reader will doubtless remember the Bachelor Martin Fernandez de Enciso, who was inspired by that adventurous cavalier with an
ill-starred passion for colonizing, and freighted a vessel at San Domingo with reinforcements and supplies for the settlement at San Sebastian.

When the Bachelor was on the eve of sailing, a number of the loose
hangers-on of the colony, and men encumbered with debt concerted
to join his ship from the coast and the outports. Their creditors, however, getting notice of their intention, kept a close watch upon everyone that went on board while in the harbour, and obtained an armed
vessel from the Admiral Don Diego Columbus, to escort the enterprizing Bachelor clear of the island. One man, however, contrived to elude
these precautions, and, as he afterwards rose to great importance, it is
proper to notice him particularly. His name was Vasco Nuñez de Balboa. He was a native of Xeres de los Caballeros, and of a noble though
impoverished family. He had been brought up in the service of Don
Pedro Puerto Carrero, Lord of Moguer, and he afterwards enlisted
among the adventurers who accompanied Rodrigo de Bastides in his
voyage of discovery. Peter Martyr, in his Latin decades, speaks of him
by the appellation of "egregius digladiator," which has been interpreted
by some as a skillful swordsman, by others, as an adroit fencing-master.
He intimates, also, that he was a mere soldier of fortune, of loose
prodigal habits; and the circumstances under which he is first introduced to us justify this character. He had fixed himself for a time in
Hispaniola and undertaken to cultivate a farm at the town of Salvatierra on the sea coast, but in a little time had completely involved
himself in debt. The expedition of Enciso presented him with an opportunity of escaping from his embarrassments, and of indulging his
adventurous habits. To elude the vigilance of his creditors and of the
armed escort, he concealed himself in a cask, which was conveyed from
his farm on the sea coast on board of the vessel, as if containing provisions for the voyage. When the vessel was fairly out at sea, and
abandoned by the escort, Vasco Nuñez emerged like an apparition from
his cask to the great surprize of Enciso, who had been totally ignorant
of the stratagem. The Bachelor was indignant at being thus outwitted,
even though he gained a recruit by the deception; and, in the first

ebullition of his wrath, gave the fugitive debtor a very rough reception, threatening to put him on shore on the first uninhabited island they should encounter. Vasco Nuñez however succeeded in pacifying him. "For God," says the venerable Las Casas, "reserved him for greater things." It is probable the Bachelor beheld in him a man well fitted for his expedition, for Vasco Nuñez was in the prime and vigour of his days, tall and muscular, seasoned to hardships, and of intrepid spirit.

Arriving at the main land, they touched at the fatal harbour of Carthagena, the scene of the sanguinary conflicts of Ojeda and Nicuesa with the natives, and of the death of the brave Juan de la Cosa. Enciso was ignorant of those events, having had no tidings from those adventurers since their departure from San Domingo; without any hesitation, therefore, he landed a number of his men to repair his boat, which was damaged, and to procure water. While the men were working upon the boat, a multitude of Indians gathered at a distance, well armed and with menacing aspect, sounding their shells and brandishing their weapons. The experience they had had of the tremendous powers of the strangers, however, rendered them cautious of attacking, and for three days they hovered in this manner about the Spaniards, the latter being obliged to keep continually on the alert. At length two of the Spaniards ventured one day from the main body to fill a water cask from the adjacent river. Scarcely had they reached the margin of the stream, when eleven savages sprang from the thickets and surrounded them bending their bows and pointing their arrows. In this way they stood for a moment or two in fearful suspense, the Indians refraining from discharging their shafts but keeping them constantly pointed at their breasts. One of the Spaniards attempted to escape to his comrades who were repairing the boat, but the other called him back, and, understanding something of the Indian tongue, addressed a few amicable words to the savages. The latter, astonished at being spoken to in their own language, now relaxed a little from their fierceness, and demanded of the strangers who they were, who were their leaders, and what they sought upon their shores. The Spaniard replied that they were harmless people, who came from other lands, and merely touched there through necessity, and he wondered that they should meet them with such hostility; he at the same time warned them to beware, as there would come many of his countrymen well armed, and would wreak terrible vengeance upon them for any mischief they might do. While they were thus parleying, the Bachelor Enciso, hearing that two of his men were surrounded by the savages, sallied instantly from his ship, and hastened with an armed force to their rescue. As he ap-

proached, however, the Spaniard who had held the parley made him
a signal that the natives were pacific. In fact the latter had supposed
that this was a new invasion of Ojeda and Nicuesa, and had thus arrayed themselves, if not to take vengeance for past outrages, at least
to defend their houses from a second desolation. When they were convinced, however, that these were a totally different band of strangers
and without hostile intentions, their animosity was at an end; they threw
by their weapons, and came forward with the most confiding frankness.
During the whole time that the Spaniards remained there, they treated
them with the greatest friendship, supplying them with bread made
from maize, with salted fish, and with the fermented and spirituous
beverages common along that coast. Such was the magnanimous conduct of men who were considered among the most ferocious and warlike of these savage nations; and who, but recently, had beheld their
shores invaded, their villages ravaged and burnt, and their friends and
relations butchered, without regard to age or sex, by the countrymen
of these very strangers. When we recall the bloody and indiscriminate
vengeance wreaked upon this people by Ojeda and his followers for
their justifiable resistance of invasion, and compare it with their placable
and considerate spirit when an opportunity for revenge presented itself, we confess we feel a momentary doubt whether the arbitrary appellation of savage is always applied to the right party.

Chapter VII

The Bachelor hears unwelcome tidings of his destined jurisdiction

Not long after the arrival of Enciso at this eventful harbour he was
surprised by the circumstance of a brigantine entering, and coming to
anchor. To encounter an European sail in these almost unknown seas
was always a singular and striking occurrence, but the astonishment of
the Bachelor was mingled with alarm when, on boarding the brigantine,
he found that it was manned by a number of the men who had embarked with Ojeda. His first idea was, that they had mutinied against
their commander, and deserted with the vessel. The feelings of the
magistrate were aroused within him by the suspicion, and he determined to take his first step as Alcalde Mayor, by seizing them and
inflicting on them the severity of the law. He altered his tone, how-

ever, on conversing with their resolute commander. This was no other than Francisco Pizarro, whom Ojeda had left as his locum tenens at San Sebastian, and who showed the Bachelor his letter patent, signed by that unfortunate governor. In fact, the little brigantine contained the sad remnant of the once vaunted colony. After the departure of Ojeda in the pirate ship, his followers, whom he had left behind under the command of Pizarro, continued in the fortress until the stipulated term of fifty days had expired. Receiving no succour, and hearing no tidings of Ojeda, they then determined to embark and sail for Hispaniola; but here an unthought of difficulty presented itself, they were seventy in number, and the two brigantines which had been left with them were incapable of taking so many. They came to the forlorn agreement, therefore, to remain until famine, sickness, and the poisoned arrows of the Indians should reduce their number to the capacity of the brigantines. A brief space of time was sufficient for the purpose. They then prepared for the voyage. Four mares which had been kept alive, as terrors to the Indians, were killed and salted for sea-stores. Then taking whatever other articles of provision remained, they embarked and made sail. One brigantine was commanded by Pizarro, the other by one Valenzuela.

They had not proceeded far when, in a storm, a sea struck the crazy vessel of Valenzuela with such violence as to cause it to founder with all its crew. The other brigantine was so near that the mariners witnessed the struggles of their drowning companions and heard their cries. Some of the sailors, with the common disposition to the marvellous, declared that they had beheld a great whale or some other monster of the deep strike the vessel with its tail and either stave in its sides or shatter the rudder, so as to cause the shipwreck.* The surviving brigantine then made the best of its way to the harbour of Carthagena, to seek provisions.

Such was the disastrous account rendered to the Bachelor by Pizarro, of his destined jurisdiction. Enciso, however, was of a confident mind and sanguine temperament, and trusted to restore all things to order and prosperity on his arrival.

* Herrera, Hist. Ind. decad. i. lib. vii. cap. 10.

Chapter VIII

Crusade of the Bachelor Enciso against the sepulchres of Zenu

The Bachelor Enciso, as has been shown, was a man of the sword as well as of the robe; having doubtless imbibed a passion for military exploit from his intimacy with the discoverers. Accordingly, while at Carthagena, he was visited by an impulse of the kind, and undertook an enterprize that would have been worthy of his friend Ojeda. He had been told by the Indians that about twenty five leagues to the west lay a province called Zenu, the mountains of which abounded with the finest gold. This was washed down by torrents during the rainy season, in such quantities, that the natives stretched nets across the rivers to catch the largest particles; some of which were said to be as large as eggs.

The idea of taking gold in nets captivated the imagination of the Bachelor, and his cupidity was still more excited by further accounts of this wealthy province. He was told that Zenu was the general place of sepulture of the Indian tribes throughout the country, whither they brought their dead, and buried them, according to their custom, decorated with their most precious ornaments.

It appeared to him a matter of course, therefore, that there must be an immense accumulation of riches in the Indian tombs, from the golden ornaments that had been buried with the dead through a long series of generations. Fired with the thought, he determined to make a foray into this province and to sack the sepulchres! Neither did he feel any compunction at the idea of plundering the dead, considering the deceased as pagans and infidels, who had forfeited even the sanctuary of the grave, by having been buried according to the rites and ceremonies of their idolatrous religion.

Enciso accordingly made sail from Carthagena and landed with his forces on the coast of Zenu. Here he was promptly opposed by two caciques, at the head of a large band of warriors. The Bachelor, though he had thus put on the soldier, retained sufficient of the spirit of his former calling not to enter into quarrel without taking care to have the law on his side; he proceeded regularly, therefore, according to the legal form recently enjoined by the crown. He caused to be read and interpreted to the caciques the same formula used by Ojeda, expounding the nature of the Deity, the supremacy of the pope, and the right of the Catholic Sovereigns to all these lands by virtue of a grant from his holiness. The caciques listened to the whole very attentively and without interruption, according to the laws of Indian courtesy. They then replied that, as to the assertion that there was but one God the Sovereign of heaven and earth, it seemed to them good, and that such must be the case; but as to the doctrine that the pope was regent of the world in place of God, and that he had made a grant of their country to the Spanish king, they observed that the pope must have been drunk to give away what was not his, and the king must have been somewhat mad to ask at his hands what belonged to others. They added that they were lords of those lands and needed no other Sovereign, and if this king should come to take possession, they would cut off his head and put it on a pole; that being their mode of dealing with their enemies.—As an illustration of this custom they pointed out to Enciso the very uncomfortable spectacle of a row of grizly heads impaled in the neighbourhood.

Nothing daunted either by the reply or the illustration, the Bachelor menaced them with war and slavery as the consequences of their refusal to believe and submit. They replied by threatening to put his head upon a pole as a representative of his Sovereign. The Bachelor, having furnished them with the law, now proceeded to the commentary. He attacked the Indians, routed them, and took one of the caciques prisoner, but in the skirmish two of his men were slightly wounded with poisoned arrows and died raving with torment.*

It does not appear, however, that his crusade against the sepulchres was attended with any lucrative advantage. Perhaps the experience he had received of the hostility of the natives, and of the fatal effects of their poisoned arrows, prevented his penetrating into the land, with his scanty force. Certain it is, the reputed wealth of Zenu, and the tale of its fishery for gold with nets, remained unascertained and uncontradicted, and were the cause of subsequent and disastrous enterprizes. The Bachelor contented himself with his victory and, returning to his ships, prepared to continue his voyage for the seat of government established by Ojeda in the Gulf of Uraba.

---

* The above anecdote is related by the Bachelor Enciso himself, in a Geographical Work entitled *Suma de Geographia*, which he published in Seville, in 1519. As the reply of the poor savages contains something of natural logic, we give a part of it as reported by the Bachelor. "Respondieron me: que en lo que dezie que no avia sino un dios, y que este governaba el cielo y la tierra, y que era señor de todo, que les parecia y que asi debia ser: pero que en lo que dezie que el papa era señor de todo el universo en lugar de dios, y que el avia fecho merced de aquella tierra al rey de Castilla; dixeron que el papa debiera estar boracho quando lo hizo, pues daba lo que no era suyo, y quel el rey que pedia y tomava tal merced debia ser algun loco pues pedia lo que era de otros," &c.

Chapter IX

*The Bachelor arrives at San Sebastian—His disasters there and sub-
sequent exploits at Darien*

It was not without extreme difficulty and the peremptory exercise of
his authority as Alcalde Mayor, that Enciso prevailed upon the crew of
Pizarro to return with him to the fated shores of San Sebastian. He at
length arrived in sight of the long wished for seat of his anticipated
power and authority, but here he was doomed like his principal, Ojeda,
to meet with nothing but misfortune. On entering the harbour his vessel struck on a rock on the eastern point. The rapid currents and tumultuous waves rent it to pieces; the crew escaped with great difficulty to
the brigantine of Pizarro; a little flour, cheese and biscuit, and a small
part of the arms were saved, but the horses, mares, swine and all other
colonial supplies were swept away, and the unfortunate Bachelor beheld the proceeds of several years of prosperous litigation swallowed
up in an instant.

His dream of place and dignity seemed equally on the point of
vanishing; for, on landing, he found the fortress and its adjacent houses
mere heaps of ruins, having been destroyed with fire by the Indians.

For a few days the Spaniards maintained themselves with palm nuts,
and with the flesh of a kind of wild swine, of which they met with
several herds. These supplies failing, the Bachelor sallied forth with a
hundred men to forage the country. They were waylayed by three
Indians who discharged all the arrows in their quivers with incredible
rapidity, wounded several Spaniards and then fled with a swiftness
that defied pursuit. The Spaniards returned to the harbour in dismay.
All their dread of the lurking savages and their poisoned weapons revived, and they insisted upon abandoning a place marked out for disaster.

The Bachelor Enciso was himself disheartened at the situation of
this boasted capital of San Sebastian, but whither could he go where
the same misfortunes might not attend him? In this moment of doubt
and despondency, Vasco Nuñez, the same absconding debtor who had
been smuggled on board in the cask, stepped forward to give counsel.
He informed the Bachelor that several years previous he had sailed
along that coast with Rodrigo de Bastides. They had explored the
whole Gulf of Uraba; and he well remembered an Indian village situated on the western side, on the banks of a river which the natives
called Darien. The country around was fertile and abundant and was
said to possess mines of gold, and the natives, though a warlike race,

never made use of poisoned weapons. He offered to guide the Bachelor
to this place where they might get a supply of provisions, and even
found their colony.

The Spaniards hailed the words of Vasco Nuñez as if revealing a
land of promise. The Bachelor adopted his advice, and, guided by him,
set sail for the village, determined to eject the inhabitants and take
possession of it as the seat of government. Arrived at the river, he
landed, put his men in martial array, and marched along the banks.
The place was governed by a brave cacique named Zemaco. He sent
off the women and children to a place of safety and, posting himself
with five hundred of his warriors on a height, prepared to give the intruders a warm reception. The Bachelor was a discoverer at all points,
pious, daring and rapacious. On beholding this martial array he recommended himself and his followers to God, making a vow in their name
to "Our Lady of Antigua," whose image is adored with great devotion
in Seville, that the first church and town which they built should be
dedicated to her, and that they would make a pilgrimage to Seville to
offer the spoils of the heathen at her shrine. Having thus endeavoured
to propitiate the favour of heaven, and to retain the holy Virgin in his
cause, he next proceeded to secure the fidelity of his followers. Doubting that they might have some lurking dread of poisoned arrows, he
exacted from them all an oath that they would not turn their backs
upon the foe, whatever might happen. Never did warrior enter into
battle with more preliminary forms and covenants than the Bachelor
Enciso. All these points being arranged, he assumed the soldier, and
attacked the enemy with such valour, that, though they made at first
a shew of fierce resistance, they were soon put to flight and many of
them slain. The Bachelor entered the village in triumph, took possession
of it by unquestionable right of conquest, and plundered all the hamlets and houses of the surrounding country; collecting great quantities
of food and cotton, with bracelets, anklets, plates and other ornaments
of gold, to the value of ten thousand castellanos.* His heart was wonderfully elated by his victory and his booty; his followers, also, after
so many hardships and disasters, gave themselves up to joy at this
turn of good fortune, and it was unanimously agreed that the seat of
government should be established in this village; to which, in fulfilment of his vow, Enciso gave the name of Santa Maria de la Antigua
del Darien.

* Equivalent to a present sum of 53,259 Dollars.

Chapter X

The Bachelor Enciso undertakes the command—His downfall

The Bachelor Enciso now entered upon the exercise of his civil functions as Alcade Mayor, and Lieutenant of the absent governor, Ojeda. His first edict was stern and peremptory: he forbade all trafficking with the natives for gold, on private account, under pain of death. This was in conformity to royal command, but it was little palatable to men who had engaged in the enterprize in the hopes of enjoying free trade, lawless liberty and golden gains. They murmured among themselves, and insinuated that Enciso intended to reserve all the profit to himself.

Vasco Nuñez was the first to take advantage of the general discontent. He had risen to consequence among his fellow adventurers, from having guided them to this place, and from his own intrinsic qualities, being hardy, bold and intelligent, and possessing the random spirit and open handed generosity common to a soldier of fortune, and calculated to dazzle and delight the multitude.

He bore no good will to the Bachelor, recollecting his threat of landing him on an uninhabited island, when he escaped in a cask from San Domingo. He sought, therefore, to make a party against him and to unseat him from his command. He attacked him in his own way, with legal weapons, questioning the legitimacy of his pretensions. The boundary line, he observed, which separated the jurisdictions of Ojeda and Nicuesa, ran through the centre of the Gulf of Uraba. The village of Darien lay on the western side, which had been allotted to Nicuesa. Enciso, therefore, as Alcalde Mayor and Lieutenant of Ojeda, could have no jurisdiction here, and his assumed authority was a sheer usurpation.

The Spaniards, already incensed at the fiscal regulations of Enciso, were easily convinced; so with one accord they refused allegiance to him, and the unfortunate Bachelor found the chair of authority to which he had so fondly and anxiously aspired, suddenly wrested from under him, before he had well time to take his seat.

Chapter XI

Perplexities at the colony—Arrival of Colmenares

To depose the Bachelor had been an easy matter, for most men are ready to assist in pulling down, but to choose a successor was a task of far more difficulty. The people at first agreed to elect mere civil magistrates, and accordingly appointed Vasco Nuñez and one Zemudio as alcaldes, together with a cavalier of some merit of the name of Valdivia, as regidor. They soon, however, became dissatisfied with this arrangement and it was generally considered advisable to vest the authority in one person. Who this person should be, was now the question. Some proposed Nicuesa, as they were within his province; others were strenuous for Vasco Nuñez. A violent dispute ensued which was carried on with such heat and obstinacy, that many, anxious for a quiet life, declared it would be better to reinstate Enciso, until the pleasure of the king should be known.

In the height of these factious altercations the Spaniards were aroused one day by the thundering of cannon from the opposite side of the gulf, and beheld columns of smoke rising from the hills. Astonished at signals of civilized man on these wild shores, they replied in the same manner, and in a short time two ships were seen standing across the gulf. They proved to be an armament commanded by one Rodrigo de Colmenares, and were in search of Nicuesa with supplies. They had met with the usual luck of adventurers on this disastrous coast, storms at sea, and savage foes on shore, and many of their number had fallen by poisoned arrows. Colmenares had touched at San Sebastian to learn tidings of Nicuesa, but, finding the fortress in ruins, had made signals in hopes of being heard by the Spaniards, should they be yet lingering in the neighborhood.

The arrival of Colmenares caused a temporary suspension of the feuds of the colonists. He distributed provisions amongst them and gained their hearts. Then, representing the legitimate right of Nicuesa to the command of all that part of the coast, as a governor appointed by the King, he persuaded the greater part of the people to acknowledge his authority. It was generally agreed, therefore, that he should cruise along the coast in search of Nicuesa, and that Diego de Albitez and an active member of the law, called the Bachelor Corral, should accompany him as ambassadors, to invite that cavalier to come and assume the government of Darien.

Chapter XII

Colmenares goes in quest of Nicuesa

Rodrigo de Colmenares proceeded along the coast to the westward, looking into every bay and harbour, but for a long time without success. At length one day he discovered a brigantine at a small island in the sea. It was part of the armament of Nicuesa, and had been sent out by him to forage for provisions. By this vessel he was piloted to the port of Nombre de Dios, the nominal capital of the unfortunate governor, but which was so surrounded and overshadowed by forests, that he might have passed by without noticing it.

The arrival of Colmenares was welcomed with transports and tears of joy. It was scarcely possible for him to recognise the once buoyant and brilliant Nicuesa in the squalid and dejected man before him. He was living in the most abject misery. Of all his once gallant and powerful band of followers but sixty men remained, and those so feeble, yellow, emaciated, and woebegone that it was piteous to behold them.*

Colmenares distributed food among them and told them that he had come to convey them to a plenteous country, and one rich in gold. When Nicuesa heard of the settlement at Darien, and that the inhabitants had sent for him to come and govern them, he was as a man suddenly revived from death. All the spirit and munificence of the cavalier again awakened in him. He gave a kind of banquet that very day to Colmenares and the ambassadors, from the provisions brought in the ship. He presided at his table with his former hilarity, and displayed a feat of his ancient office as royal carver, by holding up a fowl in the air and dissecting it with wonderful adroitness.

Well would it have been for Nicuesa had the sudden buoyancy of his feelings carried him no further, but adversity had not taught him prudence. In conversing with the envoys about the colony of Darien, he already assumed the tone of governor and began to disclose the

---

* The harbour of Nombre de Dios continued for a long time to present traces of the sufferings of the Spaniards. We are told by Herrera, that several years after the time here mentioned, a band of eighty Spanish soldiers, commanded by Gonzalo de Badajos, arrived at the harbour with an intention of penetrating into the interior. They found there the ruined fort of Nicuesa, together with sculls and bones, and crosses erected on heaps of stones, dismal mementos of his followers who had perished of hunger; the sight of which struck such horror and dismay into the hearts of the soldiers that they would have abandoned their enterprise, had not their intrepid captain immediately sent away the ships and thus deprived them of the means of retreating. Herrera, decad. xi. lib. i.

kind of policy with which he intended to rule. When he heard that great quantities of gold had been collected and retained by private individuals, his ire was kindled. He vowed to make them refund it, and even talked of punishing them for trespassing upon the privileges and monopolies of the crown. This was the very error that had unseated the Bachelor Enciso from his government, and it was a strong measure for one to threaten who as yet was governor but in expectation. The menace was not lost upon the watchful ambassadors Diego de Albitez and the Bachelor Corral. They were put still more on the alert by a conversation held that very evening with Lope de Olano, who was still detained a prisoner for his desertion, but who found means to commune with envoys, and to prejudice them against his unsuspecting commander. "Take warning," said he, "by my treatment. I sent relief to Nicuesa and rescued him from death when starving on a desert island. Behold my recompense. He repays me with imprisonment and chains. Such is the gratitude the people of Darien may look for at his hands!"

The subtle Bachelor Corral and his fellow envoy laid these matters to heart and took their measures accordingly. They hurried to depart before Nicuesa, and setting all sail on their caravel, hastened back to Darien. The moment they arrived they summoned a meeting of the principal inhabitants. "A blessed change we have made," said they, "in summoning this Diego de Nicuesa to the command. We have called in the stork to take the rule, who will not rest satisfied until he has devoured us." They then related, with the usual exaggeration, the unguarded threats that had fallen from Nicuesa, and instanced his treatment of Olano as a proof of a tyrannous and ungrateful disposition.

The words of the subtle Bachelor Corral and his associate produced a violent agitation among the people, especially among those who had amassed treasures which would have to be refunded. Nicuesa, too, by a transaction which almost destroys sympathy in his favour, gave time for their passions to ferment. On his way to Darien he stopped for several days among a groupe of small islands, for the purpose of capturing Indians to be sold as slaves. While committing these outrages against humanity, he sent forward Juan de Cayzedo in a boat to announce his coming. His messenger had a private pique against him and played him false. He assured the people of Darien that all they had been told by their envoys concerning the tyranny and ingratitude of Nicuesa was true. That he treated his followers with wanton severity; that he took from them all they won in battle, saying that the spoils were his rightful property, and that it was his intention to treat the people of Darien in the same manner. "What folly is it in you," added he, "being your own masters and in such free condition, to send for a tyrant to rule over you!"

The people of Darien were convinced by this concurring testimony, and confounded by the overwhelming evil they had thus invoked upon their heads. They had deposed Enciso for his severity and they had thrown themselves into the power of one who threatened to be ten times more severe! Vasco Nuñez de Balboa observed their perplexity and consternation. He drew them one by one apart and conversed with them in private. "You are cast down in heart," said he, "and so you might well be, were the evil beyond all cure. But do not despair; there is an effectual relief and you hold it in your hands. If you have committed an error in inviting Nicuesa to Darien, it is easily remedied by not receiving him when he comes!" The obviousness and simplicity of the remedy struck every mind and it was unanimously adopted.

Chapter XIII

Catastrophe of the unfortunate Nicuesa

While this hostile plot was maturing at Darien, the unsuspecting Nicuesa pursued his voyage leisurely and serenely, and arrived in safety at the mouth of the river. On approaching the shore he beheld a multitude headed by Vasco Nuñez, waiting, as he supposed, to receive him with all due honour. He was about to land when the public procurator or attorney called to him with a loud voice, warning him not to disembark, but advising him to return with all speed to his government at Nombre de Dios.

Nicuesa remained for a moment as if thunderstruck by so unlooked for a salutation. When he recovered his self possession he reminded them that he had come at their own request; he entreated, therefore, that he might be allowed to land and have an explanation, after which he would be ready to act as they should think proper. His entreaties only provoked insolent replies, and threats of violence should he venture to put foot on shore. Night coming on, he was obliged to stand out to sea, but returned the next morning, hoping to find this capricious people in a different mood.

There did, indeed, appear to be a favourable change, for he was now invited to land. It was a mere stratagem to get him in their power; for no sooner did he set foot on shore than the multitude rushed forward to seize him. Among his many bodily endowments, Nicuesa was noted for swiftness of foot. He now trusted to it for safety, and, throwing off the dignity of governor, fled for his life along the shore, pursued by the rabble. He soon distanced his pursuers, and took refuge in the woods.

Vasco Nuñez de Balboa, who was himself a man of birth, seeing this high-bred cavalier reduced to such extremity, and at the mercy of a violent rabble, repented of what he had done. He had not anticipated such popular fury, and endeavoured, though too late, to allay the tempest he had raised. He succeeded in preventing the people from pursuing Nicuesa into the forest; and then endeavoured to mollify the vindictive rage of his fellow alcalde Zamudio, whose hostility was quickened by the dread of losing his office should the new governor be received, and who was supported in his boisterous conduct by the natural love of the multitude for what are called "strong measures." Nicuesa now held a parley with the populace through the mediation of Vasco Nuñez. He begged that, if they would not acknowledge him as governor they would at least admit him as a companion. This they refused, saying that if they admitted him in one capacity he would end by attaining to the other. He then implored that if he could be admitted on no other terms they would treat him as a prisoner and put him in irons, for he would rather die among them than return to Nombre de Dios to perish of famine or by the arrows of the Indians.

It was in vain that Vasco Nuñez exerted his eloquence to obtain some grace for this unhappy cavalier. His voice was drowned by the vociferations of the multitude. Among these was a noisy swaggering fellow named Francisco Benitez, a great talker and jester, who took a vulgar triumph in the distresses of a cavalier, and answered every plea in his behalf with scoffs and jeers. He was an adherent of the Alcalde Zamudio, and under his patronage felt emboldened to bluster. His voice was uppermost in the general clamour, until, to the expostulations of Vasco Nuñez he replied by merely bawling, with great vociferation, "No—no—no! we will receive no such a fellow among us as Nicuesa!" The patience of Vasco Nuñez was exhausted; he availed himself of his authority as alcalde, and suddenly, before his fellow magistrate could interfere, ordered the brawling ruffian to be rewarded with a hundred lashes, which were taled out roundly to him upon the shoulders.*

Seeing that the fury of the populace was not to be pacified, he sent word to Nicuesa to retire to his brigantine, and not to venture on shore until advised by him to do so. The council was fruitless. Nicuesa, above

---

* Las Casas, Hist. Ind. lib. ii. cap. 68.

deceit himself, suspected it not in others. He retired to his brigantines, it is true, but suffered himself to be inveigled on shore by a deputation professing to come on the part of the public, with offers to reinstate him as governor. He had scarcely landed when he was set upon by an armed band headed by the base minded Zamudio, who seized him and compelled him, by menaces of death, to swear that he would immediately depart, and make no delay in any place, until he had presented himself before the King and council in Castile.

In vain that Nicuesa reminded them that he was governor of that territory and representative of the King, and that they were guilty of treason in thus opposing him; in vain that he appealed to their humanity, or protested before God against their cruelty and persecution. The people were in that state of tumult when they are apt to add cruelty to injustice. Not content with expelling the discarded governor from their shores, they allotted him the worst vessel in the harbour; an old crazy brigantine totally unfit to encounter the perils and labours of the sea.

Seventeen followers embarked with him, some being of his household and attached to his person; the rest were volunteers, who accompanied him out of respect and sympathy. The frail bark set sail on the first of March 1511, and steered across the Caribbean sea for the Island of Hispaniola, but was never seen or heard of more!

Various attempts have been made to penetrate the mystery that covers the fate of the brigantine and its crew. A rumour prevailed some years afterwards that several Spaniards, wandering along the shore of Cuba, found the following inscription carved on a tree:

Aqui feneciò el desdichado Nicuesa.*

Hence it was inferred that he and his followers had landed there, and been massacred by the Indians. Las Casas, however, discredits this story. He accompanied the first Spaniards who took possession of Cuba, and heard nothing of the fact, as he most probably would have done had it really occurred. He imagines rather that the crazy bark was swallowed up by the storms and currents of the Caribbean Sea, or that the crew perished with hunger and thirst, having been but scantily supplied with provisions. The good old Bishop adds, with the superstitious feeling prevalent in that age, that a short time before Nicuesa sailed from Spain on his expedition, an astrologer warned him not to depart on the day he had appointed, or under a certain sign; the cavalier replied, however, that he had less confidence in the stars than in God who made them. "I recollect, moreover," adds Las Casas, "that about

---

* Here perished the unfortunate Nicuesa.

this time a comet was seen over this island of Hispaniola, which, if I do not forget, was in the shape of a sword; and it was said that a monk warned several of those about to embark with Nicuesa to avoid that captain, for the heavens foretold he was destined to be lost. The same, however," he concludes, "might be said of Alonzo de Ojeda, who sailed at the same time, yet returned to San Domingo, and died in his bed."*

* Las Casas, *ut sup.* cap. 68.

VASCO NUÑEZ DE BALBOA, DISCOVERER OF THE PACIFIC OCEAN

Chapter I

Factions at Darien—Vasco Nuñez elevated to the command

We have traced the disastrous fortunes of Alonzo de Ojeda and Diego de Nicuesa; we have now to record the story of Vasco Nuñez de Balboa, an adventurer equally daring, far more renowned, and not less unfortunate, who in a manner rose upon their ruins.

When the bark disappeared from view which bore the ill starred Nicuesa from the shores of Darien, the community relapsed into factions as to who should have the rule. The Bachelor Enciso insisted upon his claims as paramount, but met with a powerful opponent in Vasco Nuñez, who had become a great favorite with the people from his frank and fearless character, and his winning affability. In fact he was peculiarly calculated to manage the fiery and factious, yet generous and susceptible, nature of his countrymen; for the Spaniards, though proud and resentful, and impatient of indignity or restraint, are easily dazzled by valour, and won by courtesy and kindness. Vasco Nuñez had the external requisites also to captivate the multitude. He was now about thirty five years of age; tall, well formed and vigorous, with reddish hair and an open prepossessing countenance. His office of alcalde, while it clothed him with influence and importance, tempered those irregular and dissolute habits he might have indulged while a mere soldier of fortune; and his superior talent soon gave him a complete ascendancy over his official colleague Zamudio. He was thus enabled to set on foot a vigorous opposition to Enciso. Still he proceeded according to the forms of law, and summoned the Bachelor to trial, on the charge of usurping the powers of Alcalde Mayor on the mere appointment of Alonzo de Ojeda, whose jurisdiction did not extend to this province.

Enciso was an able lawyer, and pleaded his cause skillfully; but his claims were, in fact, fallacious, and, had they not been so, he had to deal with men who cared little for law; who had been irritated by his legal exactions; and who were disposed to be governed by a man of the sword, rather than of the robe. He was readily found guilty, therefore, and thrown into prison, and all his property was confiscated. This was a violent verdict, and rashly executed; but justice seemed to grow fierce and wild when transplanted to the wilderness of the new world. Still there is no place where wrong can be committed with impunity: the oppression of the Bachelor Enciso, though exercised under the forms of law, and in a region remote from the pale of civilized life, redounded to the eventual injury of Vasco Nuñez, and contributed to blast the fruits of that ambition it was intended to promote.

The fortunes of the enterprizing Bachelor had indeed run strangely counter to the prospects with which he had embarked at San Domingo; he had become a culprit at the bar instead of a judge upon the bench; and now was left to ruminate in a prison on the failure of his late attempt at general command. His friends, however, interceded warmly in his behalf and at length obtained his release from confinement, and permission for him to return to Spain. Vasco Nuñez foresaw that the lawyer would be apt to plead his cause more effectually at the court of Castile, than he had done before the partial and prejudiced tribunal of Darien. He prevailed upon his fellow alcalde Zamudio, therefore, who was implicated with him in the late transactions, to return to Spain in the same vessel with the Bachelor, so as to be on the spot to answer his charges, and to give a favorable report of the case. He was also instructed to set forth the services of Vasco Nuñez, both in guiding the colonists to this place, and in managing the affairs of the settlement; and to dwell with emphasis on the symptoms of great riches in the surrounding country.

The Bachelor and the Alcalde embarked in a small caravel; and, as it was to touch at Hispaniola, Vasco Nuñez sent his confidential friend, the Regidor Valdivia, to that island to obtain provisions and recruits. He secretly put into his hands a round sum of gold as a present to Miguel de Pasamonte, the Royal Treasurer of Hispaniola, whom he knew to have great credit with the king, and to be invested with extensive powers, craving at the same time his protection in the new world and his influence at court.

Having taken these shrewd precautions, Vasco Nuñez saw the caravel depart without dismay, though bearing to Spain his most dangerous enemy: he consoled himself, moreover, with the reflection that it likewise bore off his fellow alcalde Zamudio, and thus left him in sole command of the colony.

Chapter II

*Expedition to Coyba—Vasco Nuñez receives the daughter of a cacique
as hostage*

Vasco Nuñez now exerted himself to prove his capacity for the government to which he had aspired; and as he knew that no proof was more convincing to King Ferdinand than ample remittances, and that gold covered all sins in the new world, his first object was to discover those parts of the country which most abounded in the precious metal. Hearing exaggerated reports of the riches of a province about thirty leagues distant, called Coyba, he sent Francisco Pizarro with six men, to explore it.

The cacique Zemaco, the native lord of Darien, who cherished a bitter hostility against the European intruders, and hovered with his warriors about the settlement, received notice of this detachment from his spies, and planted himself in ambush to waylay and destroy it. The Spaniards had scarcely proceeded three leagues along the course of the river, when a host of savages burst upon them from the surrounding thickets, uttering frightful yells, and discharging showers of stones and arrows. Pizarro and his men, though sorely bruised and wounded, rushed into the thickest of the foe, slew many, wounded more, and put the rest to flight; but, fearing another assault, made a precipitate retreat, leaving one of their companions, Francisco Hernan, disabled on the field. They arrived at the settlement, crippled and bleeding; but when Vasco Nuñez heard the particulars of the action, his anger was roused against Pizarro, and he ordered him, though wounded, to return immediately and recover the disabled man. "Let it not be said, for shame," said he, "that Spaniards fled before savages, and left a comrade in their hands!" Pizarro felt the rebuke, returned to the scene of combat and brought off Francisco Hernan in safety.

Nothing having been heard of Nicuesa since his departure, Vasco Nuñez despatched two brigantines for those followers of that unfortunate adventurer, who had remained at Nombre de Dios. They were overjoyed at being rescued from their forlorn situation, and conveyed to a settlement where there was some prospect of comfortable subsistence. The brigantines in coasting the shores of the Isthmus picked up two more Spaniards, clad in painted skins, and looking as wild as the native Indians. These men, to escape some punishment, had fled from the ship of Nicuesa, about a year and a half before, and had taken refuge with Careta, the cacique of Coyba. The savage chieftain had treated them with hospitable kindness, their first return for which, now that they found themselves safe among their countrymen, was to advise the latter to invade the cacique in his dwelling, where they assured them they would find immense booty. Finding their suggestion listened to, one of them proceeded to Darien to serve as a guide to any expedition that might be set on foot; the other returned to the cacique, to assist in betraying him.

Vasco Nuñez was elated by the intelligence received through these vagabonds of the wilderness. He chose a hundred and thirty well armed and resolute men, and set off for Coyba. The cacique received the Spaniards in his mansion with the accustomed hospitality of a savage, setting before them meat and drink, and whatever his house afforded; but when Vasco Nuñez asked for a large supply of provisions for the colony, he declared that he had none to spare, his people having been prevented from cultivating the soil by a war which he was waging with the neighboring cacique of Ponca. The Spanish outcast, who had remained to betray his benefactor, now took Vasco Nuñez aside, and assured him that the cacique had an abundant hoard of provisions in secret; he advised him, however, to seem to believe his words, and to make a pretended departure for Darien with his troops, but to return in the night to take the village by surprize. Vasco Nuñez adopted the advice of the traytor. He took a cordial leave of Careta, and set off for the settlement. In the dead of the night, however, when the savages were buried in deep sleep, Vasco Nuñez led his men into the midst of the village, and, before the inhabitants could rouse themselves to resistance, made captives of Careta, his wives and children, and many of his people. He discovered also the hoard of provisions, with which he loaded two brigantines, and returned with his booty and his captives to Darien.

When the unfortunate cacique beheld his family in chains, and in the hands of strangers, his heart was wrung with despair. "What have I done to thee," said he to Vasco Nuñez, "that thou shouldst treat me thus cruelly? None of thy people ever came to my land that were not fed and sheltered and treated with loving kindness. When thou camest to my dwelling, did I meet thee with a javelin in my hand? Did I not set meat and drink before thee, and welcome thee as a brother? Set me free, therefore, with my family and people, and we will remain thy friends. We will supply thee with provisions, and reveal to thee the riches of the land. Dost thou doubt my faith? Behold my daughter. I give her to thee as a pledge of friendship. Take her for thy wife, and be assured of the fidelity of her family and her people!"

Vasco Nuñez felt the force of these words, and knew the importance of forming a strong alliance among the natives. The captive maid, also, as she stood trembling and dejected before him, found great favour in his eyes, for she was young and beautiful. He granted, therefore, the prayer of the cacique, and accepted his daughter, engaging, moreover, to aid the father against his enemies on condition of his furnishing provisions to the colony.

Careta remained three days at Darien, during which time he was treated with the utmost kindness. Vasco Nuñez took him on board of his ships and shewed him every part of them. He displayed before him also the war horses, with their armour and rich caparisons, and astonished him with the thunder of artillery. Lest he should be too much daunted by these warlike spectacles, he caused the musicians to perform a harmonious concert on their instruments, at which the cacique was lost in admiration. Thus having impressed him with a wonderful idea of the power and endowments of his new allies, he loaded him with presents and permitted him to depart.*

Careta returned joyfully to his territories, and his daughter remained with Vasco Nuñez; willingly for his sake, giving up her family and native home. They were never married, but she considered herself his wife, as she really was, according to the usages of her own country, and he treated her with fondness, allowing her gradually to acquire great influence over him. To his affection for this damsel his ultimate ruin is in some measure to be ascribed.

Chapter III

Vasco Nuñez hears of a sea beyond the mountains

Vasco Nuñez kept his word with the father of his Indian beauty. Taking with him eighty men, and his companion in arms Rodrigo Enriquez de Colmenares, he repaired by sea to Coyba, the province of the cacique. Here landing, he invaded the territories of Ponca, the great adversary of Careta, and obliged him to take refuge in the mountains. He then ravaged his lands and sacked his villages, in which he found consider-

---

* P. Martyr, decad. 3. cap. vi.

able booty. Returning to Coyba, where he was joyfully entertained by Careta, he next made a friendly visit to the adjacent province of Comagre, which was under the sway of a cacique of the same name, who had three thousand fighting men at his command.

This province was situated at the foot of a lofty mountain in a beautiful plain twelve leagues in extent. On the approach of Vasco Nuñez the cacique came forth to meet him, attended by seven sons, all fine young men, the offspring of his various wives. He was followed by his principal chiefs and warriors, and by a multitude of his people. The Spaniards were conducted with great ceremony to the village, where quarters were assigned them, and they were furnished with abundance of provisions, and men and women were appointed to attend upon them.

The dwelling of the cacique surpassed any they had yet seen for magnitude, and for the skill and solidity of the architecture. It was one hundred and fifty paces in length, and eighty in breadth, founded upon great logs, surrounded with a stone wall; while the upper part was of wood work, curiously interwoven, and wrought with such beauty as to cause surprize and admiration. It contained many commodious apartments. There were store rooms also, one filled with bread, with venison and other provisions; another with various spirituous beverages, which the Indians made from maize, from a species of the palm, and from roots of different kinds. There was also a great hall in a retired and secret part of the building, wherein Comagre preserved the bodies of his ancestors and relatives. These had been dried by the fire, so as to free them from corruption, and afterwards wrapped in mantles of cotton, richly wrought and interwoven with pearls and jewels of gold, and with certain stones held precious by the natives. They were then hung about the hall with cords of cotton, and regarded with great reverence, if not with religious devotion.

The eldest son of the cacique was of a lofty and generous spirit, and distinguished above the rest by his superior intelligence and sagacity. Perceiving, says old Peter Martyr, that the Spaniards were a "wandering kind of men living only by shifts and spoil," he sought to gain favour for himself and family by gratifying their avarice. He gave Vasco Nuñez and Colmenares, therefore, four thousand ounces of gold, wrought into various ornaments, together with sixty slaves, captives taken in the wars. Vasco Nuñez ordered one fifth of the gold to be weighed out and set apart for the crown, and the rest to be shared among his followers.

The division of the gold took place in the porch of the dwelling of Comagre, in the presence of the youthful cacique who had made the gift. As the Spaniards were weighing it out, a violent quarrel arose

among them as to the size and value of the pieces which fell to their
respective shares. The high minded savage was disgusted at this sordid
brawl among beings whom he had regarded with such reverence. In
the first impulse of his disdain he struck the scales with his fist, and
scattered the glittering gold about the porch. "Why," said he, "should
you quarrel for such a trifle? If this gold is indeed so precious in your
eyes, that for it alone you abandon your homes, invade the peaceful
lands of others, and expose yourselves to such sufferings and perils, I
will tell you of a region where you may gratify your wishes to the
utmost. Behold those lofty mountains," continued he, pointing to the
south. "Beyond these lies a mighty sea, which may be discerned from
their summit. It is navigated by people who have vessels almost as
large as yours, and furnished, like them, with sails and oars. All the
streams which flow down the southern side of those mountains into
that sea abound in gold; and the Kings who reign upon its borders eat
and drink out of golden vessels. Gold in fact is as plentiful and common
among those people of the south as iron is among you Spaniards."

Vasco Nuñez enquired eagerly as to the means of penetrating to this
sea and to the opulent regions on its shores. "The task," replied the
prince, "is difficult and dangerous. You must pass through the territories
of many powerful caciques, who will oppose you with hosts of warriors.
Some parts of the mountains are infested by fierce and cruel cannibals,
a wandering lawless race; but above all you will have to encounter the
great cacique Tubanamá, whose territories are at the distance of six
days' journey, and more rich in gold than any other province; this
cacique will be sure to come forth against you with a mighty force. To
accomplish your enterprize, therefore, will require at least a thousand
men armed like those who follow you."

The youthful cacique gave him further information on the subject,
collected from various captives taken in battle, and from one of his own
nation, who had been for a long time in captivity to Tubanamá, the
powerful cacique of the golden realm. He moreover offered to prove the
sincerity of his words by accompanying Vasco Nuñez, in any expedition
to those parts, at the head of his father's warriors.

Such was the first intimation received by Vasco Nuñez of the Pacific
Ocean and its golden realms, and it had an immediate effect upon his
whole character and conduct. This hitherto wandering and desperate
man had now an enterprize opened to his ambition, which, if accomplished, would elevate him to fame and fortune, and entitle him to
rank among the great captains and discoverers of the earth. Henceforth
the discovery of the sea beyond the mountains was the great object of

his thoughts, and his whole spirit seemed roused and ennobled by the idea.

He hastened his return to Darien to make the necessary preparations for this splendid enterprize. Before departing from the province of Comagre he baptized that cacique by the name of Don Carlos, and performed the same ceremony upon his sons and several of his subjects; thus singularly did avarice and religion go hand in hand in the conduct of the Spanish discoverers.

Scarcely had Vasco Nuñez returned to Darien when the Regidor Valdivia arrived from Hispaniola, but with no more provisions than could be brought in his small caravel. These were soon consumed, and the general scarcity continued. It was heightened also by a violent tempest of thunder, lightning, and rain, which brought such torrents from the mountains that the river swelled and overflowed its banks, laying waste all the adjacent fields that had been cultivated. In this extremity, Vasco Nuñez despatched Valdivia a second time to Hispaniola for provisions. Animated also by the loftier views of his present ambition, he wrote to Don Diego Columbus, who governed at San Domingo, informing him of the intelligence he had received of a great sea and opulent realms beyond the mountains, and entreating him to use his influence with the king that one thousand men might be immediately furnished him for the prosecution of so grand a discovery. He sent him also the amount of fifteen thousand crowns in gold, to be remitted to the King, as the royal fifths of what had already been collected under his jurisdiction. Many of his followers, likewise, forwarded sums of gold to be remitted to their creditors in Spain. In the mean time, Vasco Nuñez prayed the admiral to yield him prompt succour to enable him to keep his footing in the land, representing the difficulty he had in maintaining, with a mere handful of men, so vast a country in a state of subjection.

Chapter IV

Expedition of Vasco Nuñez in quest of the Golden Temple of Dobayba (1512)

While Vasco Nuñez awaited the result of this mission of Valdivia, his active disposition prompted foraging excursions into the surrounding country.

Among various rumours of golden realms in the interior of this unknown land, was one concerning a province called Dobayba, situated about forty leagues distant, on the banks of a great river which emptied itself, by several mouths, into a corner of the Gulf of Uraba.

This province derived its name, according to Indian tradition, from a mighty female of the olden time, the mother of the god who created the sun and moon and all good things. She had power over the elements; sending thunder and lightning to lay waste the lands of those who displeased her, but showering down fertility and abundance upon the possessions of her faithful worshippers. Others described her as having been an Indian princess who once reigned amongst the mountains of Dobayba, and was renowned throughout the land for her supernatural power and wisdom. After her death, divine honours were paid her, and a great temple was erected for her worship. Hither the natives repaired from far and near, on a kind of pilgrimage, bearing offerings of their most valuable effects. The caciques who ruled over distant territories, also, sent golden tributes, at certain times of the year, to be deposited in this temple, and slaves to be sacrificed at its shrine. At one time, it was added, this worship fell into disuse, the pilgrimages were discontinued, and the caciques neglected to send their tributes; whereupon the Deity, as a punishment, inflicted a drought upon the country. The springs and fountains failed, the rivers were dried up; the inhabitants of the mountains were obliged to descend into the plains, where they digged pits and wells, but these likewise failing, a great part of the nations perished with thirst. The remainder hastened to propitiate the deity by tributes and sacrifices, and thus succeeded in averting her displeasure. In consequence of offerings of the kind, made for generations, from all parts of the country, the temple was said to be filled with treasure, and its walls to be covered with golden gifts.*
In addition to the tale of this temple, the Indians gave marvellous accounts of the general wealth of this province, declaring that it

---

* P. Martyr. decad. 3. cap. vi. Idem. decad. 7. cap. x.

abounded with mines of gold, the veins of which reached from the dwelling of the cacique to the borders of his dominions.

To penetrate to this territory, and above all to secure the treasures of the Golden Temple, was an enterprize suited to the adventurous spirit of the Spaniards. Vasco Nuñez chose one hundred and seventy of his hardiest men for the purpose. Embarking them in two brigantines and a number of canoes, he set sail from Darien, and, after standing about nine leagues to the east, came to the mouth of the Rio Grande de San Juan or the Great River of St. John, also called the Atrato; which is since ascertained to be one of the branches of the river Darien. Here he detached Rodrigo Enriquez de Colmenares with one third of his force, to explore the stream, while he himself proceeded with the residue to another branch of the river, which he was told flowed from the province of Dobayba and which he ascended, flushed with sanguine expectations.*

His old enemy Zemaco, the cacique of Darien, however, had discovered the object of his expedition and had taken measures to disappoint it. Repairing to the province of Dobayba, he had prevailed upon its cacique to retire at the approach of the Spaniards, leaving his country deserted.

Vasco Nuñez found a village situated in a marshy neighborhood, on the banks of the river, and mistook it for the residence of the cacique. It was silent and abandoned. There was not an Indian to be met with from whom he could obtain any information about the country, or who could guide him to the Golden Temple. He was disappointed also in his hopes of obtaining a supply of provisions; but he found weapons of various kinds, hanging in the deserted houses, and gathered jewels and pieces of gold to the value of seven thousand castellanos. Discouraged by the savage look of the surrounding wilderness, which was perplexed by deep morasses, and having no guides to aid him in exploring it, he put all the booty he had collected into two large canoes, and

---

* In recording this expedition, the author has followed the old Spanish narratives, written when the face of the country was but little known, and he was much perplexed to reconcile the accounts given of numerous streams with the rivers laid down on modern maps. By a clear and judicious explanation, given in the recent work of Don Manuel Josef Quintana, it appears that the different streams explored by Vasco Nuñez and Colmenares were all branches of one grand river, which, descending from the mountains of the interior, winds about in crystal streams among the plains and morasses bordering the bottom of the great gulf of Darien, and discharges itself by various mouths into the gulf. In fact, the stream which ran by the infant city of Santa Maria de la Antigua was but one of its branches, a fact entirely unknown to Vasco Nuñez and his companions.

made his way back to the Gulf of Uraba. Here he was assailed by a violent tempest, which nearly wrecked his two brigantines, and obliged him to throw a great part of their cargoes overboard. The two canoes containing the booty were swallowed up by the raging sea, and all their crews perished.

Thus baffled and tempest tost, Vasco Nuñez at length succeeded in getting into what is termed the Grand River, which he ascended, and rejoined Colmenares and his detachment. They now extended their excursions up a stream which emptied itself into the Grand River, and which, from the dark hue of its waters, they called Rio Negro, or the Black River. They also explored certain other tributary streams, branching from it, though not without occasional skirmishes with the natives.

Ascending one of these minor rivers, with a part of his men, Vasco Nuñez came to the territories of a cacique named Abibeyba, who reigned over a region of marshes and shallow lakes. The habitations of the natives were built amidst the branches of immense and lofty trees. They were large enough to contain whole family connexions, and were constructed partly of wood, partly of a kind of wicker work, combining strength and pliability, and yielding uninjured to the motion of the branches when agitated by the wind. The inhabitants ascended to them, with great agility, by light ladders, formed of great reeds, split through the middle, for the reeds on this coast grow to the thickness of a man's body. These ladders they drew up after them at night, or in case of attack. These habitations were well stocked with provisions; but the fermented beverages, of which these people had always a supply, were buried in vessels in the earth, at the foot of the tree, lest they should be rendered turbid by the rocking of the houses. Close by, also, were the canoes with which they navigated the rivers and ponds of their marshy country, and followed their main occupation of fishing.

On the approach of the Spaniards, the Indians took refuge in their tree built castles, and drew up the ladders. The former called upon them to descend and to fear nothing. Upon this the cacique replied, entreating that he might not be molested, seeing he had done them no injury. They threatened, unless he came down, to fell the trees, or to set fire to them, and burn him and his wives and children. The cacique was disposed to consent, but was prevented by the entreaties of his people. Upon this the Spaniards prepared to hew down the trees, but were assailed by showers of stones. They covered themselves however with their bucklers, assailed the trees vigorously with their hatchets, and soon compelled the inhabitants to capitulate. The cacique descended with his wife and two of his children. The first demand of the Spaniards was for gold. He assured them he had none; for, having no need of it, he had never made it an object of his search. Being importuned, however, he assured them that if he were permitted to repair to certain mountains at a distance he would in a few days return and bring them what they desired. They permitted him to depart, retaining his wife and children as hostages, but they saw no more of the cacique. After remaining here a few days, and regaling on the provisions which they found in abundance, they continued their foraging expeditions, often opposed by the bold and warlike natives, and suffering occasional loss, but inflicting great havoc on their opposers.

Having thus overrun a considerable extent of country, and no grand object presenting to lure him on to further enterprize, Vasco Nuñez at length returned to Darien with the spoils and captives he had taken, leaving Bartolome Hurtado with thirty men in an Indian village on the Rio Negro, or Black River, to hold the country in subjection. Thus terminated the first expedition in quest of the Golden Temple of Dobayba; which, for some time, continued to be a favorite object of enterprize among the adventurers of Darien.

Chapter V

Disaster on the Black River—Indian plot against Darien

Bartolome Hurtado, being left to his own discretion on the banks of the Black River, occupied himself occasionally in hunting the scattered natives who straggled about the surrounding forests. Having in this way picked up twenty four captives, he put them on board of a large canoe, like so much live stock, to be transported to Darien and sold as slaves. Twenty of his followers, who were infirm either from wounds or the diseases of the climate, embarked also in the canoe, so that only ten men remained with Hurtado.

The great canoe, thus heavily freighted, descended the Black River slowly, between banks overhung with forests. Zemaco, the indefatigable cacique of Darien, was on the watch, and waylayed the ark with four canoes filled with warriors, armed with war clubs, and lances hardened in the fire. The Spaniards, being sick, could make but feeble resistance; some were massacred, others leaped into the river and were drowned. Two only escaped, by clinging to two trunks of trees that were floating down the river, and covering themselves with the branches. Reaching the shore in safety, they returned to Bartolome Hurtado with the tragical tidings of the death of his followers. Hurtado was so disheartened by the news, and so dismayed at his own helpless situation, in the midst of a hostile country, that he resolved to abandon the fatal shores of the Black River and return to Darien. He was quickened in this resolution by receiving intimation of a conspiracy forming among the natives. The implacable Zemaco had drawn four other caciques into a secret plan to assemble their vassals and make a sudden attack upon Darien: Hurtado hastened with the remnant of his followers to carry tidings to the settlement of this conspiracy. Many of the inhabitants were alarmed at his intelligence; others treated it as a false rumour of the Indians, and no preparations were made against what might be a mere imaginary danger.

Fortunately for the Spaniards, among the female captives owned by Vasco Nuñez was an Indian damsel named Fulvia; to whom, in consequence of her beauty, he had shown great favour, and who had become strongly attached to him. She had a brother among the warriors of Zemaco who often visited her in secret. In one of his visits he informed her that on a certain night the settlement would be attacked and every Spaniard destroyed. He charged her, therefore, to hide herself that night in a certain place until he should come to her aid, lest she should be slain in the confusion of the massacre.

When her brother was gone, a violent struggle took place in the bosom of the Indian girl between her feeling for her family and her people and her affection for Vasco Nuñez. The latter at length prevailed, and she revealed all that had been told to her. The Spaniard prevailed on her to send for her brother under pretence of aiding her to escape. Having him in his power, he extorted from him all that he knew of the designs of the enemy. His confessions showed what imminent danger had been lurking round Vasco Nuñez in his most unsuspecting moments. The prisoner informed him that he had been one of forty Indians, sent some time before by the cacique Zemaco, to Vasco Nuñez, in seeming friendship, to be employed by him in cultivating the fields adjacent to the settlement. They had secret orders, however, to take an opportunity, when the Spaniard should come forth to inspect their work, to set upon him in an unguarded moment and destroy him. Fortunately, Vasco Nuñez always visited the fields mounted on his war horse and armed with lance and target. And the Indians were so awed by his martial appearance, and by the terrible animal he bestrode, that they dared not attack him.

Foiled in this and other attempts of the kind, Zemaco resorted to the conspiracy with which the settlement was now menaced. Five caciques had joined in the confederacy. They had prepared a hundred canoes;

had amassed provisions for an army, and concerted to assemble five thousand picked warriors at a certain time and place; with these they were to make an attack on the settlement by land and water, in the middle of the night, and to slaughter every Spaniard.

Having learnt where the confederate chiefs were to be found, and where they had deposited their provisions, Vasco Nuñez chose seventy of his best men, well armed, and made a circuit by land, while Colmenares, with sixty men, sallied forth secretly in four canoes, guided by the Indian prisoner. In this way they surprized the general of the Indian army and several of the principal confederates, and got possession of all their provisions, though they failed to capture the formidable Zemaco. The Indian general was shot to death with arrows, and the leaders of the conspiracy were hanged in presence of their captive followers. The defeat of this deeplaid plan, and the punishment of its devisers, spread terror throughout the neighboring provinces, and prevented any further attempt at hostilities. Vasco Nuñez, however, caused a strong fortress of wood to be immediately erected, to guard against any future assaults of the savages.

Chapter VI

Further factions in the colony—Arrogance of Alonzo Perez and the Bachelor Corral

A considerable time had now elapsed since the departure of Valdivia for Hispaniola, yet no tidings had been received from him. Many began to fear that some disaster had befallen him, while others insinuated that it was possible both he and Zamudio might have neglected the objects of their mission, and, having appropriated to their own use the gold with which they had been entrusted, abandoned the colony to its fate.

Vasco Nuñez himself was harassed by these surmises; and by the dread lest the Bachelor Enciso should succeed in prejudicing the mind of his Sovereign against him. Impatient of this state of anxious suspence, he determined to repair to Spain, to communicate in person all that he had heard concerning the Southern Sea, and to ask for the troops necessary for its discovery.

Every one, however, both friend and foe, exclaimed against such a measure, representing his presence as indispensable to the safety of

the colony, from his great talents as a commander, and the fear entertained of him by the Indians.

After much debate and contention, it was at length agreed that Juan
de Cayzedo and Rodrigo Enriquez de Colmenares should go in his place,
instructed to make all necessary representations to the King. Letters
were written also containing extravagant accounts of the riches of the
country, partly dictated by the sanguine hopes of the writers, and partly
by the fables of the natives. The rumoured wealth of the province of
Dobayba, and the treasures of its golden temple were not forgotten;
and an Indian was taken to Spain by the commissioners, a native of
the province of Zenu, where gold was said to be gathered in nets stretched
across the mountain streams. To give more weight to all these stories,
every one contributed some portion of gold from his private hoard, to
be presented to the King, in addition to the amount arising from his
fifths.

But little time had elapsed after the departure of the commissioners,
when new dissensions broke out in the colony. It was hardly to be
expected that a fortuitous assemblage of adventurers could remain long
tranquil, during a time of suffering, under rulers of questionable authority. Vasco Nuñez, it is true, had risen by his courage and abilities; but
he had risen from among their ranks; he was in a manner of their own
creation; and they had not become sufficiently accustomed to him as a
governor, to forget that he was recently but a mere soldier of fortune,
and an absconding debtor.

Their factious discontent, however, was directed at first against a
favorite of Vasco Nuñez, rather than against himself. He had invested
Bartolome Hurtado, the commander of the Black River, with considerable
authority in the colony, and the latter gave great offence by his oppressive conduct. Hurtado had particularly aggrieved by his arrogance one
Alonzo Perez de la Rua, a touchy cavalier, jealous of his honour, and
peculiarly gifted with the sensitive punctilio of a Spaniard. Firing at
some indignity, whether real or fancied, Alonzo Perez threw himself
into the ranks of the disaffected, and was immediately chosen as their
leader. Thus backed by a faction, he clamoured loudly for the punishment of Hurtado; and, finding his demands unattended to, threw out
threats of deposing Vasco Nuñez. The latter, with his usual spirit and
promptness, seized upon the testy Alonzo Perez, and threw him into
prison, to digest his indignities and cool his passions at leisure.

The conspirators flew to arms to liberate their leader. The friends
of Vasco Nuñez were equally on the alert. The two parties drew out
in battle array in the public square; and a sanginary conflict was on the
point of taking place. Fortunately there were some cool heads left in

the colony. These interfered at the critical moment, representing to the angry adversaries that, if they fought among themselves, and diminished their already scanty numbers, even the conquerors must eventually fall a prey to the Indians.

Their remonstrances had effect. A parley ensued, and, after much noisy debate, a kind of compromise was made. Alonzo Perez was liberated, and the mutineers dispersed quietly to their homes. The next day, however, they were again in arms, and seized upon Bartolome Hurtado; but after a little while were prevailed upon to set him free. Their factious views seemed turned to a higher object. They broke forth into loud murmurs against Vasco Nuñez, complaining that he had not made a fair division of the gold and slaves taken in the late expeditions, and threatening to arrest him and bring him to account. Above all, they clamoured for an immediate distribution of ten thousand castellanos in gold, yet unshared.

Vasco Nuñez understood too well the riotous nature of the people under him, and his own precarious hold on their obedience, to attempt to cope with them in this moment of turbulence. He shrewdly determined, therefore, to withdraw from the sight of the multitude, and to leave them to divide the spoil among themselves, trusting to their own strife for his security. That very night he sallied forth into the country, under pretence of going on a hunting expedition.

The next morning the mutineers found themselves in possession of the field. Alonzo Perez, the pragmatical ringleader, immediately assumed the command, seconded by the Bachelor Corral. Their first measure was to seize upon the ten thousand castellanos, and to divide them among the multitude, by way of securing their own popularity. The event proved the sagacity and forethought of Vasco Nuñez. Scarcely had these hot headed intermeddlers entered upon the partition of the gold, than a furious strife arose. Every one was dissatisfied with his share, considering his merits entitled to peculiar recompense. Every attempt to appease the rabble only augmented their violence, and in their rage they swore that Vasco Nuñez had always shewn more judgement and discrimination in his distributions to men of merit.

The adherents of the latter now ventured to lift up their voices; "Vasco Nuñez," said they, "won the gold by his enterprize and valour, and would have shared it with the brave and the deserving; but these men have seized upon it by factious means, and would squander it upon their minions." The multitude, who, in fact, admired the soldierlike qualities of Vasco Nuñez, displayed one of the customary reverses of popular feeling. The touchy Alonzo Perez, his coadjutor the Bachelor Corral, and several others of the ringleaders were seized, put into irons, and confined in the fortress, and Vasco Nuñez was recalled with loud acclamations to the settlement.

How long this pseudo-commander might have been able to manage the unsteady populace it is impossible to say, but just at this juncture two ships arrived from Hispaniola, freighted with supplies, and bringing a reinforcement of one hundred and fifty men. They brought also a commission to Vasco Nuñez, signed by Miguel de Pasamonte, the royal treasurer of Hispaniola (to whom he had sent a private present of gold), constituting him captain general of the colony. It is doubtful whether Pasamonte possessed the power to confer such a commission; though it is affirmed that the King had clothed him with it, as a kind of check upon the authority of the Admiral Don Diego Columbus, then Governor of Hispaniola, of whose extensive sway in the new world the monarch was secretly jealous. At any rate, the treasurer appears to have acted in full confidence of the ultimate approbation of his Sovereign.

Vasco Nuñez was rejoiced at receiving a commission which clothed him with at least the semblance of royal sanction. Feeling more assured in his situation, and being naturally of a generous and forgiving temper, he was easily prevailed upon, in his moment of exultation, to release and pardon Alonzo Perez, the Bachelor Corral, and the other ringleaders of the late commotions, and for a time the feuds and factions of this petty community were lulled to repose.

Chapter VII

Vasco Nuñez determines to seek the sea beyond the mountains (1513)

The temporary triumph of Vasco Nuñez was soon overcast by tidings received from Spain. His late colleague, the Alcalde Zamudio, wrote him word, that the Bachelor Enciso had carried his complaints to the foot of the throne, and succeeded in rousing the indignation of the King; and had obtained a sentence in his favour, condemning Vasco Nuñez in costs and damages. Zamudio informed him in addition, that he would be immediately summoned to repair to Spain and answer in person the criminal charges advanced against him on account of the harsh treatment and probable death of the unfortunate Nicuesa.

Vasco Nuñez was at first stunned by this intelligence, which seemed at one blow to annihilate all his hopes and fortunes. He was a man, however, of prompt decision and intrepid spirit. The information received from Spain was private and informal. No order had yet arrived from the King. He was still master of his actions, and had controul over the colony. One brilliant achievement might atone for all the past, and fix him in the favour of the monarch. Such an achievement was within his reach—the discovery of the Southern Sea. It is true a thousand soldiers had been required for the expedition, but were he to wait for their arrival from Spain his day of grace would be past. It was a desperate thing to undertake the task with the handful of men at his command, but the circumstances of the case were desperate. Fame, fortune, life itself depended upon the successful and the prompt execution of the enterprize. To linger was to be lost.

Vasco Nuñez looked round upon the crew of daring and reckless adventurers that formed the colony, and chose one hundred and ninety of the most resolute, vigorous, and devoted to his person. These he armed with swords, targets, cross bows and arquebusses. He did not conceal from them the danger of the enterprize into which he was about to lead them; but the spirit of these Spanish adventurers was always roused by the idea of perilous and extravagant exploit. To aid his slender forces, he took with him a number of bloodhounds, which had been found to be terrific allies in Indian warfare.

The Spanish writers make particular mention of one of those animals, named Leoncico, which was a constant companion, and, as it were, body guard of Vasco Nuñez, and describe him as minutely as they would a favorite warrior. He was of middle size, but immensely strong; of a dull yellow or reddish colour, with a black muzzle; and his body was scarred all over with wounds received in innumerable battles with the Indians. Vasco Nuñez always took him on his expeditions, and sometimes lent him to others, receiving for his services the same share of booty allotted to an armed man. In this way he gained by him, in the course of his campaigns, upwards of a thousand crowns. The Indians, it is said, had conceived such terror of this animal, that the very sight of him was sufficient to put a host of them to flight.*

In addition to these forces, Vasco Nuñez took with him a number of the Indians of Darien, whom he had won to him by kindness, and whose services were important, from their knowledge of the wilderness, and of the habits and resources of savage life. Such was the motley armament that set forth from the little colony of Darien, under the guidance of a daring, if not desperate, commander, in quest of the great Pacific Ocean.

* Oviedo, Hist. Indies, p. 2. cap. 3. MS.

Chapter VIII

Expedition in quest of the Southern Sea

It was on the first of September that Vasco Nuñez embarked with his followers in a brigantine and nine large canoes or pirogues, followed by the cheers and good wishes of those who remained at the settlement. Standing to the northwestward, he arrived without accident at Coyba, the dominion of the cacique Careta, whose daughter he had received as a pledge of amity. That Indian beauty had acquired a great influence over Vasco Nuñez, and appears to have cemented his friendship with her father and her people. He was received by the cacique with open arms, and furnished with guides and warriors to aid him in his enterprize.

Vasco Nuñez left about half of his men at Coyba to guard the brigantine and canoes, while he should penetrate the wilderness with the residue. The importance of his present expedition, not merely as affecting his own fortunes, but as it were unfolding a mighty secret of nature, seems to have impressed itself upon his spirit, and to have given correspondent solemnity to his conduct. Before setting out upon his march, he caused mass to be performed, and offered up prayers to God for the success of his perilous undertaking.

It was on the 6th of September that he struck off for the mountains. The march was difficult and toilsome. The Spaniards, encumbered with the weight of their armour and weapons, and oppressed by the heat of a tropical climate, were obliged to climb rocky precipices, and to struggle through close and tangled forests. Their Indian allies aided them by carrying their ammunition and provisions, and by guiding them to the most practicable paths.

On the 8th of September they arrived at the village of Ponca, the ancient enemy of Careta. The village was lifeless and abandoned; the cacique and his people had fled to the fastnesses of the mountains. The Spaniards remained here several days to recruit the health of some of their number who had fallen ill. It was necessary also to procure guides acquainted with the mountain wilderness they were approaching. The retreat of Ponca was at length discovered and he was prevailed upon, though reluctantly, to come to Vasco Nuñez. The later had a peculiar facility in winning the confidence and friendship of the natives. The cacique was soon so captivated by his kindness that he revealed to him in secret all that he knew of the natural riches of the country. He assured him of the truth of what had been told him about a great pechry or sea beyond the mountains, and gave him several ornaments ingeniously wrought of fine gold, which had been brought from the countries upon its borders. He told him, moreover, that when he had attained the summit of a lofty ridge, to which he pointed, and which seemed to rise up to the skies, he would behold that sea spread out far below him.

Animated by these accounts, Vasco Nuñez procured fresh guides from the cacique, and prepared to ascend the mountains. Numbers of his men having fallen ill from fatigue and the heat of the climate, he ordered them to return slowly to Coyba, taking with him none but such as were in robust and vigorous health.

On the 20th of September he again set forward through a broken rocky country, covered with a matted forest and intersected by deep and turbulent streams, many of which it was necessary to cross upon rafts.

So toilsome was the journey, that in four days they did not advance above ten leagues, and in the mean time they suffered excessively from hunger. At the end of this time they arrived at the province of a warlike cacique named Quaraquà, who was at war with Ponca.

Hearing that a band of strangers were entering his territories, guided by the subjects of his inveterate foe, the cacique took the field with a large number of warriors, some armed with bows and arrows, others with long spears, or with double handed maces of palm wood, almost as heavy and hard as iron. Seeing the inconsiderable number of the Spaniards, they set upon them with furious yells, thinking to overcome them in an instant. The first discharge of fire arms, however, struck them with dismay. They thought they were contending with demons who vomited forth thunder and lightning, especially when they saw their companions fall bleeding and dead beside them, without receiving any apparent blow. They took to headlong flight, and were hotly pursued by the Spaniards and their bloodhounds. Some were transfixed with lances, others hewn down with swords, and many were torn to pieces by the dogs, so that Quaraquà and six hundred of his warriors were left dead upon the field.

A brother of the cacique and several chiefs were taken prisoners. They were clad in robes of white cotton. Either from their effeminate dress, or from the accusations of their enemies, the Spaniards were induced to consider them guilty of unnatural crimes, and, in their abhorrence and disgust, gave them to be torn to pieces by the blood-hounds.*

It is also affirmed that among the prisoners were several negroes, who had been slaves to the cacique. The Spaniards, we are told, were informed by the other captives that these black men came from a region

* Herrera, Hist. Ind. decad. 1 lib. x, cap. 1.

at no great distance, where there was a people of that colour, with whom they were frequently at war. "These," adds the Spanish writer, "were the first negroes ever found in the new world and I believe no others have since been discovered."†

After this sanguinary triumph, the Spaniards marched to the village of Quaraquà, where they found considerable booty in gold and jewels. Of this Vasco Nuñez reserved one fifth for the crown, and shared the rest liberally among his followers. The village was at the foot of the last mountain that remained for them to climb; several of the Spaniards, however, were so disabled by the wounds received in battle, or so exhausted by the fatigue and hunger they had endured, that they were unable to proceed. They were obliged therefore reluctantly to remain in the village, within sight of the mountain top that commanded the long-sought prospect. Vasco Nuñez selected fresh guides from among his prisoners who were natives of the province and sent back the subjects of Ponca. Of the band of Spaniards who had set out with him in this enterprize, sixty seven alone remained in sufficient health and spirits for this last effort. These he ordered to retire early to repose, that they might be ready to set off at the cool and fresh hour of day break, so as to reach the summit of the mountain before the noon tide heat.

Chapter IX

Discovery of the Pacific Ocean

The day had scarce dawned when Vasco Nuñez and his followers set forth from the Indian village and began to climb the height. It was a severe and rugged toil for men so way worn; but they were filled with

---

† Peter Martyr, in his third Decade, makes mention of these negroes in the following words. "About two days' journey distant from Quaraquà is a region inhabited only by black moors, exceeding fierce and cruel. It is supposed that in time past certain black moors sailed thither out of Ethiopia to rob, and that by shipwreck, or some other chance, they were driven to these mountains." As Martyr lived and wrote at the time, he of course related the mere rumour of the day, which all subsequent accounts have disproved. The other historians who mentioned the circumstance have probably repeated it from him. It must have risen from some misrepresentation, and is not entitled to credit.

new ardour at the idea of the triumphant scene that was so soon to repay them for all their hardships.

About ten o'clock in the morning they emerged from the thick forests through which they had hitherto struggled, and arrived at a lofty and airy region of the mountain. The bald summit alone remained to be ascended, and their guides pointed to a moderate eminence from which they said the Southern Sea was visible.

Upon this Vasco Nuñez commanded his followers to halt, and that no man should stir from his place. Then, with a palpitating heart, he ascended alone the bare mountain top. On reaching the summit, the long-desired prospect burst upon his view. It was as if a new world were unfolded to him, separated from all hitherto known by this mighty barrier of mountains. Below him extended a vast chaos of rock and forest, and green Savannahs and wandering streams, while at a distance the waters of the promised ocean glittered in the morning sun.

At this glorious prospect Vasco Nuñez sank upon his knees, and poured out thanks to God for being the first European to whom it was given to make that great discovery. He then called his people to ascend. "Behold, my friends," said he, "that glorious sight which we have so much desired. Let us give thanks to God that he has granted us this great honour and advantage. Let us pray to him to guide and aid us to conquer the sea and land which we have discovered, and which Christian has never entered to preach the holy doctrine of the Evangelists. As to yourselves, be as you have hitherto been, faithful and true to me, and by the favour of Christ you will become the richest Spaniards that have ever come to the Indies; you will render the greatest services to your king that ever vassal rendered to his lord; and you will have the eternal glory and advantage of all that is here discovered, conquered, and converted to our holy Catholic faith."

The Spaniards answered this speech by embracing Vasco Nuñez and promising to follow him to death. Among them was a priest named Andres de Vara, who lifted up his voice and chaunted *Te Deum Lauda-mus*—the usual anthem of Spanish discoverers. The rest, kneeling down, joined in the strain with pious enthusiasm and tears of joy; and never did a more sincere oblation rise to the deity from a sanctified altar than from that mountain summit. It was indeed one of the most sublime discoveries that had yet been made in the new world, and must have opened a boundless field of conjecture to the wondering Spaniards. The imagination delights to picture forth the splendid confusion of their thoughts. Was this the great Indian Ocean, studded with precious islands, abounding in gold, in gems and spices, and bordered by the gorgeous cities and wealthy marts of the East? Or was it some lonely sea, locked up in the embraces of savage uncultivated continents, and never traversed by a bark, excepting the light pirogue of the savage? The latter could hardly be the case, for the natives had told the Spaniards of golden realms, and populous and powerful and luxurious nations upon its shores. Perhaps it might be bordered by various people, civilized in fact, though differing from Europe in their civilization; who might have peculiar laws and customs and arts and sciences; who might form, as it were, a world of their own, intercommuning by this mighty sea, and carrying on commerce between their own islands and continents; but who might exist in total ignorance and independence of the other hemisphere.

Such may naturally have been the ideas suggested by the sight of this unknown ocean. It was the prevalent belief of the Spaniards, however, that they were the first Christians who had made the discovery. Vasco Nuñez, therefore, called upon all present to witness that he took possession of that sea, its islands and surrounding lands, in the name of the Sovereigns of Castile; and the notary of the expedition made a testimonial of the same, to which all present, to the number of sixty seven men, signed their names. He then caused a fair and tall tree to be cut down and wrought into a cross, which was elevated on the spot from whence he had first beheld the sea. A mound of stones was likewise piled up to serve as a monument, and the names of the Castilian Sovereigns were carved on the neighboring trees. The Indians beheld all these ceremonials and rejoicings in silent wonder, and, while they aided to erect the cross, and pile up the mound of stones, marvelled exceedingly at the meaning of these monuments, little thinking that they marked the subjugation of their land.

The memorable event here recorded took place on the 26th of September 1513. So that the Spaniards had spent twenty days in performing the journey from the province of Careta to the summit of the mountain, a distance which at present, it is said, does not require more than six days' travel. Indeed the isthmus in this neighborhood is not more than eighteen leagues in breadth in its widest part, and in some places merely seven, but it consists of a ridge of extremely high and rugged mountains. When the discoverers traversed it they had no route but the Indian paths, and often had to force their way amidst all kinds of obstacles, both from the savage country and its savage inhabitants. In fact the details of this narrative sufficiently account for the slowness of their progress, and present an array of difficulties and perils, which, as has been well observed, none but those "men of iron" could have subdued and overcome.*

Chapter X

Vasco Nuñez marches to the shores of the South Sea (1513)

Having taken possession of the Pacific Ocean and all its realms from the summit of the mountain, Vasco Nuñez now descended with his little band, to seek the regions of reputed wealth upon its shores. He had not proceeded far, when he came to the province of a warlike cacique named Chiapes, who, issuing forth at the head of his warriors, looked with scorn upon the scanty number of straggling Spaniards, and forbade them to set foot within his territories. Vasco Nuñez depended for safety upon his power of striking terror into the ignorant savages. Ordering his arquebusiers to the front, he poured a volley into the enemy and then let loose the bloodhounds. The flash and noise of the fire arms, and the sulphurous smoke which was carried by the wind among the Indians, overwhelmed them with dismay. Some fell down in a panic as though they had been struck by thunderbolts, the rest betook themselves into headlong flight.

Vasco Nuñez commanded his men to refrain from needless slaughter. He made many prisoners, and on arriving at the village, sent some of them in search of their cacique, accompanied by several of his Indian guides. The latter informed Chiapes of the supernatural power of the Spaniards, assuring him that they exterminated with thunder and lightning all who dared to oppose them, but loaded all such as submitted to them with benefits. They advised him, therefore, to throw himself upon their mercy and seek their friendship.

The cacique listened to their advice, and came trembling to the Spaniards, bringing with him five hundred pounds' weight of wrought gold, as a peace offering, for he had already learnt the value they set upon that metal. Vasco Nuñez received him with great kindness, and graciously accepted his gold, for which he gave him beads, hawks bells,

* Vidas de Españoles Célebres, por Don Manuel Josef Quintana. Tom. ii. p. 40.

and looking glasses, making him in his own conceit the richest potentate on that side of the mountains.

Friendship being thus established between them, Vasco Nuñez remained at the village for a few days, sending back the guides who had accompanied him from Quaraquà, and ordering his people whom he had left at that place to rejoin him. In the mean time, he sent out three scouting parties of twelve men each, under Francisco Pizarro, Juan de Escaray, and Alonzo Martin de Don Benito, to explore the surrounding country and discover the best route to the sea. Alonzo Martin was the most successful. After two days' journey, he came to a beach, where he found two large canoes lying high and dry, without any water being in sight. While the Spaniards were regarding these canoes, and wondering why they should be so far on land, the tide, which rises to a great height on that coast, came rapidly in and set them afloat. Upon this, Alonzo Martin stepped into one of them and called his companions to bear witness that he was the first European that embarked upon that sea; his example was followed by one Blas de Etienza, who called them likewise to testify that he was the second. *

We mention minute particulars of the kind as being characteristic of these extraordinary enterprizes, and of the extraordinary people who undertook them. The humblest of these Spanish adventurers seemed actuated by a swelling and ambitious spirit, that rose superior at times to mere sordid considerations, and aspired to share the glory of these great discoveries. The scouting party having thus explored a direct route to the sea coast, returned to report their success to their commander.

Vasco Nuñez being rejoined by his men from Quaraquà, now left the greater part of his followers to repose and recover from their sickness and fatigues in the village of Chiapes, and, taking with him twenty six Spaniards, well armed, he set out on the twenty ninth of September, for the sea coast, accompanied by the cacique and a number of his warriors. The thick forests, which covered the mountains, descended to the very margin of the sea, surrounding and overshadowing the wide and beautiful bays that penetrated far into the land. The whole coast, as far as the eye could reach, was perfectly wild, the sea without a sail, and both seemed never to have been under the dominion of civilized man.

Vasco Nuñez arrived on the borders of one of those vast bays, to which he gave the name of Saint Michael, it being discovered on that saint's day. The tide was out, the water was above half a league distant, and the intervening beach was covered with mud; he seated himself, there-

* Herrera, Hist. Ind. decad. i. lib. x. cap. 2.

fore, under the shade of the forest trees until the tide should rise. After a while, the water came rushing in with great impetuosity, and soon reached nearly to the place where the Spaniards were reposing. Upon this Vasco Nuñez rose and took a banner on which were painted the Virgin and child, and under them the arms of Castile and Leon. Then drawing his sword, and throwing his buckler on his shoulder, he marched into the sea until the water reached above his knees, and waving his banner exclaimed with a loud voice: "Long live the high and mighty monarchs Don Ferdinand and Doña Juana, Sovereigns of Castile, of Leon, and of Arragon; in whose name, and for the royal crown of Castile, I take real and corporal and actual possession of these seas, and lands, and coasts, and ports, and islands of the south, and all thereunto annexed; and of the kingdoms and provinces, which do or may appertain to them, in whatever manner, or by whatever right or title, ancient or modern, in times past, present, or to come, without any contradiction. And if other prince or captain, Christian or infidel, or of any law, sect, or condition whatsoever, shall pretend any right to these lands and seas, I am ready and prepared to maintain and defend them, in the name of the Castilian Sovereigns, present and future, whose is the empire and dominion over these Indian islands and Terra Firma, northern and southern, with all their seas, both at the Arctic and Antarctic poles, on either side of the Equinoctial line, whether within or without the tropics of Cancer and Capricorn, both now and in all times, as long as the world endures, and until the final day of judgement of all mankind."

This swelling declaration and defiance being uttered with a loud voice, and no one appearing to dispute his pretensions, Vasco Nuñez called upon his companions to bear witness of the fact of his having duly taken possession. They all declared themselves ready to defend his claim to the uttermost, as became true and loyal vassals to the Castilian Sovereigns; and the notary having drawn up a document for the occasion, they subscribed it with their names.

This done, they advanced to the margin of the sea and, stooping down, tasted its waters. When they found that, though severed by intervening mountains and continents, they were salt, like the seas of the north, they felt assured that they had indeed discovered an ocean, and again returned thanks to God.

Having concluded all these ceremonies, Vasco Nuñez drew a dagger from his girdle and cut a cross on a tree which grew within the water, and made two other crosses on two adjacent trees, in honour of the Three Persons of the Trinity, and in token of possession. His followers likewise cut crosses on many of the trees of the adjacent forest, and lopped off branches with their swords, to bear away as trophies.*

Such was the singular medley of chivalrous and religious ceremonial, with which these Spanish adventurers took possession of the vast Pacific Ocean and all its lands—a scene strongly characteristic of the nation and the age.

Chapter XI

Adventures of Vasco Nuñez on the borders of the Pacific Ocean (1513)

While he made the village of Chiapes his head quarters, Vasco Nuñez foraged the adjacent country and obtained considerable quantity of gold from the natives. Encouraged by his success, he undertook to explore by sea the borders of a neighboring gulf of great extent, which penetrated far into the land. The cacique Chiapes warned him of the danger of venturing to sea in the stormy season, which comprizes the months of October, November, and December, assuring him that he had beheld many canoes swallowed up in the mighty waves and whirlpools, which at such time render the gulf almost unnavigable.

These remonstrances were unavailing. Vasco Nuñez expressed a confident belief that God would protect him, seeing that his voyage was to redound to the propagation of the faith, and the augmentation of the power of the Castilian monarchs over the infidels; and in truth this bigoted reliance on the immediate protection of heaven seems to have been in a great measure the cause of the extravagant daring of the Spaniards in their expeditions in those days, whether against Moors or Indians.

Finding his representations of no effect, Chiapes volunteered to take part in this perilous cruise, lest he should appear wanting in courage, or in good will to his guest. Accompanied by the cacique, therefore, Vasco Nuñez embarked on the 17th of October with sixty of his men in nine canoes, managed by Indians, leaving the residue of his followers to recruit their health and strength in the village of Chiapes.

Scarcely however had they put forth on the broad bosom of the gulf,

* Many of the foregoing particulars are from the unpublished volume of Oviedo's History of the Indias.

when the wisdom of the cacique's advice was made apparent. The wind began to blow freshly, raising a heavy and tumultuous sea, which broke in roaring and foaming surges on the rocks and reefs, and among the numerous islets with which the gulf was studded. The light canoes were deeply laden with men unskilled in their management. It was frightful to those in one canoe to behold their companions one instant tossed high on the breaking crest of a wave, the next plunging out of sight, in a watery abyss. The Indians, themselves, though almost amphibious in their habits, shewed signs of consternation, for amidst these rocks and breakers even the skill of the expert swimmer would be of little avail. At length the Indians succeeded in tying the canoes in pairs, side by side, to prevent their being overturned, and in this way they kept afloat, until towards evening they were enabled to reach a small island. Here they landed, and, fastening the canoes to the rocks, or to small trees that grew upon the shore, they sought an elevated dry place, and stretched themselves to take repose. They had but escaped from one danger to encounter another. Having been for a long time accustomed to the sea on the northern side of the isthmus, where there is little if any rise or fall of the tide, they had neglected to take any precaution against such an occurrence. In a little while, they were awakened from their sleep by the rapid rising of the water. They shifted their situation to a higher ground, but the waters continued to gain upon them, the breakers rushing and roaring and foaming upon the beach, like so many monsters of the deep seeking for their prey. Nothing, it is said, can be more dismal and appalling than the sullen bellowing of the sea among the islands of that gulf, at the rising and falling of the tide. By degrees, rock after rock, and one sandbank after another disappeared, until the sea covered the whole island, and rose almost to the girdles of the Spaniards. Their situation was now agonizing. A little more and the waters would overwhelm them: or, even as it was, the least surge might break over them and sweep them from their unsteady footing. Fortunately the wind had lulled, and the sea, having risen above the rocks which had fretted it, became calm. The tide had reached its height, and began to subside, and after a time they heard the retiring waves beating against the rocks below them.

When the day dawned, they sought their canoes, but here a sad spectacle met their eyes. Some were broken to pieces, others yawning open in many parts. The clothing and food left in them had been washed away, and replaced by sand and water. The Spaniards gazed on the scene in mute despair; they were faint and weary, and needed food and repose, but famine and labour awaited them, even if they should escape with their lives. Vasco Nuñez, however, rallied their spirits, and set them an example by his own cheerful exertions. Obeying his directions, they set to work to repair, in the best manner they were able, the damages of the canoes. Such as were not too much shattered, they bound and braced up with their girdles, with slips of the bark of trees, or with the tough long stalks of certain sea weeds. They then peeled off the bark from the small sea plants, pounded it between stones and mixed it with grass, and with this endeavoured to caulk the seams and stop the leaks. When re-embarked, their numbers weighed down the canoes almost to the water's edge, and as they rose and sank with the swelling waves there was danger of their being swallowed up. All day they laboured with the sea, suffering excessively from hunger and thirst and at night fall they landed in a corner of the gulf, near the abode of a cacique named Túmaco. Leaving a part of his men to guard the canoes, Vasco Nuñez set out with the residue for the Indian town. He arrived there about midnight, but the inhabitants were on the alert to defend their habitations. The fire arms and dogs soon put them to flight, and the Spaniards pursuing them with their swords, drove them howling into the woods. In the village were found provisions in abundance beside a considerable amount of gold and a great quantity of pearls, many of them of a large size. In the house of the cacique were several huge shells of mother of pearl, and four pearl oysters quite fresh, which shewed that there was a pearl fishery in the neighborhood. Eager to learn the sources of this wealth, Vasco Nuñez sent several of the Indians of Chiapes in search of the cacique, who traced him to a wild retreat among the rocks. By their persuasions Túmaco sent his son, a fine young savage, as a mediator. The latter returned to his father loaded with presents, and extolling the benignity of these superhuman beings, who had shewn themselves so terrible in battle. By these means, and by a mutual exchange of presents, a friendly intercourse was soon established. Among other things the cacique gave Vasco Nuñez jewels of gold weighing six hundred and fourteen crowns, and two hundred pearls of great size and beauty, excepting that they were somewhat discoloured, in consequence of the oysters having been opened by fire.

The cacique seeing the value which the Spaniards set upon the pearls, sent a number of his men to fish for them at a place about ten miles distant. Certain of the Indians were trained from their youth to this purpose, so as to become expert divers, and to acquire the power of remaining a long time beneath the water. The largest pearls are generally found in the deepest water, sometimes in three and four fathoms, and are only sought in calm weather; the smaller sort are found at the depth of two and three feet, and the oysters containing them are often driven in quantities on the beach during violent storms.

The party of pearl divers sent by the cacique consisted of thirty Indians, with whom Vasco Nuñez sent six Spaniards as eye-witnesses. The sea, however, was so furious at that stormy season that the divers dared not venture into the deep water. Such a number of the shellfish, however, had been driven on shore, that they collected enough to yield pearls to the value of twelve marks of gold. They were small, but exceedingly beautiful, being newly taken and uninjured by fire. A number of these shellfish and their pearls were selected to be sent to Spain as specimens.

In reply to the inquiries of Vasco Nuñez, the cacique informed him that the coast which he saw stretching to the west, continued onward without end, and that far to the south there was a country abounding in gold, where the inhabitants made use of certain quadrupeds to carry burthens. He moulded a figure of clay to represent these animals, which some of the Spaniards supposed to be a deer, others a camel, others a tapir, for as yet they knew nothing of the lama, the native beast of burthen of South America. This was the second intimation received by Vasco Nuñez of the great empire of Peru, and, while it confirmed all that had been told him by the son of Comagre, it awakened glowing anticipations of the glorious triumphs that awaited him.

Chapter XII

Further adventures and exploits of Vasco Nuñez on the borders of the Pacific Ocean (1513)

Lest any ceremonial should be wanting to secure this grand discovery to the crown of Spain, Vasco Nuñez determined to sally from the gulf and take possession of the main land beyond. The cacique Túmaco furnished him with a canoe of state formed from the trunk of an enormous tree and managed by a great number of Indians. The handles of the paddles were inlaid with small pearls, a circumstance which Vasco Nuñez caused his companions to testify before the notary, that it might be reported to the Sovereigns as a proof of the wealth of this newly discovered sea.*

Departing in the canoe on the twenty ninth of October, he was

* Oviedo, Hist. Gen. p. 2. MS.

piloted cautiously by the Indians along the borders of the gulf, over drowned lands where the sea was fringed by inundated forests and as still as a pool. Arrived at the point of the gulf, Vasco Nuñez landed on a smooth sandy beach, laved by the waters of the broad ocean, and, with buckler on arm, sword in hand, and banner displayed, again marched into the sea and took possession of it, with like ceremonials to those observed in the Gulf of St. Michael's.

The Indians now pointed to a line of land rising above the horizon about four or five leagues distant, which they described as being a great island, the principal one of an archipelago. The whole groupe abounded with pearls, but those taken on the coasts of this island were represented as being of immense size, many of them as large as a man's eye, and found in shellfish as big as bucklers. This island and the surrounding cluster of small ones, they added, were under the dominion of a tyrannical and puissant cacique, who often, during the calm seasons, made descents upon the main land with fleets of canoes, plundering and desolating the coasts, and carrying the people into captivity.

Vasco Nuñez gazed with an eager and wistful eye at this land of riches and would have immediately undertaken an expedition to it, had not the Indians represented the danger of venturing on such a voyage in that tempestuous season, in their frail canoes. His own recent experience convinced him of the wisdom of their remonstrances. He postponed his visit, therefore, to a future occasion, when, he assured his allies, he would avenge them upon this tyrant invader, and deliver their coasts from his maraudings. In the mean time he gave to this island the name of Isla Rica and the little archipelago surrounding it the general appellation of the Pearl Islands.

On the 3d of November he departed from the province of Túmaco, to visit other parts of the coast. He embarked with his men in the canoes, accompanied by Chiapes and his Indians, and guided by the son of Túmaco, who had become strongly attached to the Spaniards. The young man piloted them along an arm of the sea, wide in some places, but in others obstructed by groves of mangrove trees, which grew within the water and interlaced their branches from shore to shore, so that at times, the Spaniards were obliged to cut a passage with their swords.

At length they entered a great and turbulent river, which they ascended with difficulty, and, early the next morning surprized a village on its banks making the cacique Teaochan prisoner; who purchased their favour and kind treatment by a quantity of gold and pearls and an abundant supply of provisions. As it was the intention of Vasco Nuñez to abandon the shores of the Southern Ocean at this place, and to strike across the mountains for Darien, he took leave of Chiapes and of the youthful son of Túmaco, who were to return to their houses in the canoes. He sent at the same time a message to his men, whom he had left in the village of Chiapes, appointing a place in the mountains where they were to rejoin him on his way back to Darien.

The talent of Vasco Nuñez for conciliating and winning the goodwill of the savages is often mentioned, and to such degree had he exerted it in the present instance, that the two chieftains shed tears at parting. Their conduct had a favorable effect upon the cacique Teaochan; he entertained Vasco Nuñez with the most devoted hospitality during three days that he remained in his village. When about to depart he furnished him with a stock of provisions sufficient for several days, as his route would be over rocky and sterile mountains. He sent also a numerous band of his subjects to carry the burthens of the Spaniards. These he placed under the command of his son, whom he ordered never to separate from the strangers, nor to permit any of his men to return without the consent of Vasco Nuñez.

Chapter XIII

Vasco Nuñez sets out on his return across the mountains—His contests with the savages

Turning their backs upon the Southern Sea, the Spaniards now began painfully to clamber the rugged mountains, on their return to Darien.

In the early part of their route an unlooked for suffering awaited them. There was neither brook nor fountain nor standing pool. The burning heat, which produced intolerable thirst, had dried up all the mountain torrents; and they were tantalized by the sight of naked and dusty channels where water had once flowed in abundance. Their sufferings at length increased to such a height that many threw themselves fevered and panting upon the earth and were ready to give up the ghost. The Indians, however, encouraged them to proceed, by hopes of speedy relief, and, after a while, turning aside from the direct course, led them into a deep and narrow glen, refreshed and cooled by a fountain which bubbled out of a cleft of the rocks.

While refreshing themselves at the fountain and reposing in the little valley, they learnt from their guides that they were in the territories of a powerful chief named Poncra, famous for his riches. The Spaniards had already heard of the golden stores of this Crœsus of the mountains, and, being now refreshed and invigorated, pressed forward with eagerness for his village. The cacique and most of his people fled at their approach, but they found an earnest of his wealth in the deserted houses, amounting to the value of three thousand crowns in gold. Their avarice thus whetted, they despatched Indians in search of Poncra, who found him trembling in his secret retreat, and, partly by threats, partly by promises, prevailed upon him and three of his principal subjects to come to Vasco Nuñez. He was a savage, it is said, so hateful of aspect, so misshapen in body and deformed in all his members, that he was hideous to behold. The Spaniards endeavoured, by gentle means, to draw from him information of the places from whence he had procured his gold. He professed utter ignorance in the matter, declaring that the gold found in his village had been gathered by his predecessors, in times long past, and that as he himself set no value on the metal he had never troubled himself to seek it. The Spaniards resorted to menaces and even, it is said, to tortures to compel him to betray his reputed treasures, but with no better success. Disappointed in their expectations, and enraged at his supposed obstinacy, they listened too readily to charges advanced against him by certain caciques of the neighborhood, who represented him as a monster of cruelty and as guilty of crimes repugnant to nature;[*] whereupon in the heat of the moment they gave him and his three companions, who were said to be equally guilty, to be torn to pieces by the dogs. A rash and cruel sentence, issued on the evidence of avowed enemies, and which, however it may be palliated by the alleged horror and disgust of the Spaniards at the imputed crimes of the cacique, bears visibly the stamp of haste and passion and remains accordingly a foul blot on the character of Vasco Nuñez.

The Spaniards staid for thirty days reposing in the village of the unfortunate Poncra, during which time they were rejoined by their companions who had been left behind at the village of Chiapes. They were accompanied by a cacique of the mountains, who had lodged and fed them and made them presents of the value of two thousand crowns in gold. This hospitable savage approached Vasco Nuñez with a serene countenance, and taking him by the hand, "Behold," said he, "most valiant and powerful chief, I bring thee thy companions safe and well, as they entered under my roof. May he who made the thunder and lightning, and who gives us the fruits of the earth, preserve thee and

---

[*] P. Martyr, decad. iii. cap. 2.

thine in safety!" So saying, he raised his eyes to the sun, as if he worshipped that as his deity, and the dispenser of all temporal blessings.*

Departing from this village, and being still accompanied by the Indians of Teaochan, the Spaniards now bent their course along the banks of the river Comagre, which descends the northern side of the Isthmus, and flows through the territories of the cacique of the same name. This wild stream, which in the course of ages had worn a channel through the deep clefts and ravines of the mountains, was bordered by precipices, or overhung by shagged forests; they soon abandoned it, therefore, and wandered on without any path, but guided by the Indians. They had to climb terrible precipices and to descend into deep valleys, darkened by thick forests and beset by treacherous morasses, where, but for their guides, they might have been smothered in the mire.

In the course of this rugged journey they suffered excessively in consequence of their own avarice. They had been warned of the sterility of the country, and of the necessity of providing amply for the journey. When they came to lade the Indians, however, who bore their burdens, their only thought was how to convey the most treasure; and they grudged even a slender supply of provisions, as taking up the place of an equal weight of gold. The consequences were soon felt. The Indians could carry but small burthens, and at the same time assisted to consume the scanty stock of food which formed part of their load. Scarcity and famine ensued, and relief was rarely to be procured, for the villages on this elevated part of the mountains were scattered and poor, and nearly destitute of provisions. They held no communication with each other; each contenting itself with the scanty produce of its own fields and forest. Some were entirely deserted; at other places, the inhabitants, forced from their retreats, implored pardon, and declared they had hidden themselves through shame, not having the means of properly entertaining such celestial visitors. They brought peace offerings of gold, but no provisions. For once the Spaniards found that even their darling gold could fail to cheer their drooping spirits. Their sufferings from hunger became intense, and many of their Indian companions sank down and perished by the way. At length they reached a village, where they were enabled to obtain supplies, and where they remained thirty days, to recruit their wasted strength.

* Herrera, decad. i. lib. x. cap. 4.

Chapter XIV

Enterprize against Tubanamà, the warlike cacique of the mountains—
Return to Darien

The Spaniards had now to pass through the territories of Tubanamà, the most potent and warlike cacique of the mountains. This was the same chieftain of whom a formidable character had been given by the young Indian prince, who first informed Vasco Nuñez of the Southern Sea. He had erroneously represented the dominions of Tubanamà as lying beyond the mountains, and, while he dwelt upon the quantities of gold to be found in them, had magnified the dangers of any attempt to pass their borders. The name of this redoubtable cacique was in fact a terror throughout the country; and when Vasco Nuñez looked round upon his handful of pale and emaciated followers, he doubted whether even the superiority of their weapons, and their military skill, would enable them to cope with Tubanamà and his armies in open contest. He resolved, therefore, upon a perilous stratagem. When he made it known to his men, every one pressed forward to engage in it. Choosing seventy of the most vigorous, he ordered the rest to maintain their post in the village.

As soon as night had fallen he departed secretly with his chosen band, and made his way with such rapidity through the forests and defiles of the mountains that he arrived in the neighborhood of the residence of Tubanamà by the following evening, though at the distance of two regular days' journey.

There waiting until midnight he assailed the village suddenly, and captured the cacique and his whole family, in which were eighty females. Tubanamà lost all presence of mind and wept bitterly. The Indian allies beholding their once dreaded enemy, thus fallen and captive, urged that he should be put to death, accusing him of various crimes and cruelties. Vasco Nuñez pretended to listen to their prayers, and gave orders that his captive should be tied hand and foot and given to the dogs. The cacique approached him trembling, and laid his hand upon the pommel of his sword. "Who can pretend," said he, "to strive with one who bears this weapon, which can cleave a man asunder with a blow? Ever since thy fame has reached among these mountains have I reverenced thy valour. Spare my life and thou shalt have all the gold I can procure."

Vasco Nuñez, whose anger was assumed, was readily pacified. As soon as the day dawned, the cacique gave him armlets and other jewels of gold to the value of three thousand crowns, and sent messengers throughout his dominions ordering his subjects to aid in paying his ransom. The poor Indians, with their accustomed loyalty, hastened in crowds, bringing their golden ornaments, until in the course of three days they had produced an amount equal to six thousand crowns. This done, Vasco Nuñez set the cacique at liberty, bestowing on him several European trinkets, with which he considered himself richer than he had been with all his gold. Nothing would draw from him, however, the disclosure of the mines from whence this treasure was procured. He declared that it came from the territories of his neighbors, where gold and pearls were to be found in abundance, but that his lands produced nothing of the kind. Vasco Nuñez doubted his sincerity, and secretly caused the brooks and rivers in his dominions to be searched, where gold was found in such quantities that he determined, at a future time, to found two settlements in the neighborhood.

On parting with Tubanamà the cacique sent his son with the Spaniards to learn their language and religion. It is said, also, that the Spaniards carried off his eighty women, but of this particular fact Oviedo, who writes with the papers of Vasco Nuñez before him, says nothing. He affirms generally, however, that the Spaniards, throughout this expedition, were not scrupulous in their dealings with the wives and daughters of the Indians, and adds that in this their commander set them the example.*

Having returned to the village where he had left the greater part of his men, Vasco Nuñez resumed his homeward march. His people were feeble and exhausted and several of them sick so that some had to be carried and others led by the arms. He himself was part of the time afflicted by a fever, and had to be borne in a hamac on the shoulders of the Indians.

Proceeding thus slowly and toilfully, they at length arrived on the northern sea coast at the territories of their ally, Comagre. The old cacique was dead, and had been succeeded by his son, the same intelligent youth who had first given information of the Southern Sea and the Kingdom of Peru. The young chief, who had embraced Christianity, received them with great hospitality, making them presents of gold. Vasco Nuñez gave him trinkets in return, and a shirt and a soldier's cloak, with which, says Peter Martyr, he thought himself half a god among his naked countrymen. After having reposed for a few days, Vasco Nuñez proceeded to Ponca, where he heard that a ship and caravel had arrived at Darien from Hispaniola, with reinforcements and supplies. Hastening, therefore, to Coyba, the territories of his ally Careta, he embarked on the 18th of January 1514 with twenty of his men in

* Oviedo, Hist. Gen. Part II. cap. 4. MS.

the brigantine which he had left there, and arrived at Santa Maria de la Antigua, in the river of Darien, on the following day. All the inhabitants came forth to receive him, and when they heard the news of the great Southern Sea, and of his returning from its shores laden with pearls and gold there were no bounds to their joy. He immediately despatched the ship and caravel to Coyba for the companions left behind, who brought with them the remaining booty, consisting of gold and pearls, mantles, hamacs, and other articles of cotton, and a great number of captives of both sexes. A fifth of the spoil was set apart for the crown, the rest was shared in just proportions among those who had been in the expedition, and those who had remained at Darien. All were contented with their allotment, and elated with the prospect of still greater gain from future enterprizes.

Thus ended one of the most remarkable expeditions of the early discoverers. The intrepidity of Vasco Nuñez in penetrating with a handful of men far into the interior of a wild and mountainous country, peopled by warlike tribes; his skill in managing his band of rough adventurers, stimulating their valour, enforcing their obedience and attaching their affections, show him to have possessed great qualities as a general. We are told that he was always foremost in peril and the last to quit the field. He shared the toils and dangers of the meanest of his followers, treating them with frank affability; watching, fighting, fasting, and labouring with them; visiting and consoling such as were sick or infirm, and dividing all his gains with fairness and liberality. He was chargeable at times with acts of bloodshed and injustice, but it is probable that these were often called for as measures of safety and precaution; he certainly offended less against humanity than most of the early discoverers; and the unbounded amity and confidence reposed in him by the natives, when they became intimately acquainted with his character, speak strongly in favor of his kind of treatment of them.

The character of Vasco Nuñez had, in fact, risen with his circumstances and now assumed a nobleness and grandeur from the discovery he had made, and the important charge it had devolved upon him. He no longer felt himself a mere soldier of fortune, at the head of a band of adventurers, but a great commander conducting an immortal enterprize. "Behold," says old Peter Martyr, "Vasco Nuñez de Balboa, at once transformed from a rash royster to a politick and discreet captain:" and thus it is that men are often made by their fortunes; that is to say, their latent qualities are brought out, and shaped and strengthened by events, and by the necessity of every exertion to cope with the greatness of their destiny.

Chapter XV

Transactions in Spain—Pedrarias Davila appointed to the command of Darien—Tidings received in Spain of the discovery of the Pacific Ocean

Vasco Nuñez de Balboa now flattered himself that he had made a discovery calculated to silence all his enemies at court, and to elevate him to the highest favour with his Sovereign. He wrote letters to the King, giving a detail of his expedition, and setting forth all that he had seen or heard of this Southern Sea, and of the rich countries upon its borders. Beside the royal fifths of the profits of the expedition, he prepared a present for the Sovereign, in the name of himself and his companions, consisting of the largest and most precious pearls they had collected. As a trusty and intelligent envoy to bear these tidings, he chose Pedro de Arbolancha, an old and tried friend, who had accompanied him in his toils and dangers, and was well acquainted with all his transactions.

The fate of Vasco Nuñez furnishes a striking instance how prosperity and adversity, how even life and death hang balanced upon a point of time, and are affected by the improvement or neglect of moments. Unfortunately, the ship which was to convey the messenger to Spain lingered in port until the beginning of March, a delay which had a fatal influence on the fortunes of Vasco Nuñez. It is necessary here to cast an eye back upon the events which had taken place in Spain while he was employed in his conquests and discoveries.

The Bachelor Enciso had arrived in Castile full of his wrongs and indignities. He had friends at court, who aided him in gaining a ready hearing and he lost not a moment in availing himself of it. He declaimed eloquently upon the alleged usurpation of Vasco Nuñez, and represented him as governing the colony by force and fraud. It was in vain that the Alcalde Zamudio, the ancient colleague and the envoy of Vasco Nuñez, attempted to speak in his defence; he was unable to cope with the facts and arguments of the Bachelor, who was a pleader by profession, and now pleaded his own cause. The King determined to send a new governor to Darien, with power to inquire into and remedy all abuses. For this office he chose Don Pedro Arias Davila, commonly called Pedrarias.* He was a native of Segovia who had been brought up in the royal household, and had distinguished himself as a brave soldier, both in the war of Granada and at the taking of Oran and Bugia in Africa. He possessed those personal accomplishments which captivate

---

* By the English historians he has generally been called Davila.

the soldiery, and was called *el Galán*, for his gallant array and courtly demeanour, and *el Justador*, or *the Tilter*, for his dexterity in jousts and tournaments. These, it must be admitted, were not the qualifications most adapted for the government of rude and factious colonies in a wilderness; but he had an all powerful friend in the Bishop Fonesca. The bishop was as thoroughgoing in patronage as in persecution. He assured the King that Pedrarias had understanding equal to his valour; that he was as capable of managing the affairs of peace as of war, and that, having been brought up in the royal household, his loyalty might be implicitly relied on.

Scarcely had Don Pedrarias been appointed, when Cayzedo and Colmenares arrived on their mission from Darien, to communicate the intelligence received from the son of the cacique Comagre, of the Southern Sea beyond the mountains, and to ask one thousand men to enable Vasco Nuñez to make the discovery.

The avarice and ambition of Ferdinand were inflamed by the tidings. He rewarded the bearers of the intelligence, and, after consulting with Bishop Fonseca, resolved to despatch immediately a powerful armada, with twelve hundred men, under the command of Pedrarias, to accomplish the enterprize.

Just about this time the famous Gonsalvo Hernandez de Cordova, commonly called the Great Captain, was preparing to return to Naples, where the allies of Spain had experienced a signal defeat, and had craved the assistance of this renowned general, to retrieve their fortunes. The chivalry of Spain thronged to enlist under the banner of Gonsalvo. The Spanish nobles, with their accustomed prodigality, sold or mortgaged their estates to buy gorgeous armour, silks, brocades, and other articles of martial pomp and luxury, that they might figure, with becoming magnificence, in the campaigns of Italy. The armament was on the point of sailing for Naples, with this host of proud and gallant spirits, when the jealous mind of Ferdinand took offence at the enthusiasm thus shown towards his general, and he abruptly countermanded the expedition. The Spanish cavaliers were overwhelmed with disappointment at having their dreams of glory thus suddenly disspelled; when, as if to console them, the enterprize of Pedrarias was set on foot, and opened a different career of adventure. The very idea of an unknown sea and splendid empire, where never European ship had sailed, or foot had trodden, broke upon the imagination with the vague wonders of an Arabian tale. Even the countries already known, in the vicinity of the settlement of Darien, were described in the usual terms of exaggeration. Gold was said to lie on the surface of the ground, or to be gathered with nets out of the brooks and rivers; insomuch that the region hitherto called Terra Firma now received the pompous and delusive appellation of Castilla del Oro, or Golden Castile.

Excited by these reports, many of the youthful cavaliers who had prepared for the Italian campaign, now offered themselves as volunteers to Don Pedrarias. He accepted their services, and appointed Seville as the place of assemblage. The streets of that ancient city soon swarmed with young and noble cavaliers splendidly arrayed, full of spirits, and eager for the sailing of the Indian armada. Pedrarias, on his arrival at Seville, made a general review of his forces, and was embarrassed to find that the number amounted to three thousand. He had been limited in his first armament to twelve hundred; on representing the nature of the case, however, the number was extended to fifteen hundred; but through influence, entreaty and stratagem, upwards of two thousand eventually embarked.* Happy did he think himself who could in any manner, and by any means, get admitted on board of the squadron. Nor was this eagerness for the enterprise confined merely to young and buoyant and ambitious adventurers; we are told that there were many covetous old men, who offered to go at their own expense, without seeking any pay from the king. Thus every eye was turned with desire to this squadron of modern argonauts, as it lay anchored on the bosom of the Guadalquiver.

The pay and appointments of Don Pedrarias Davila were on the most liberal scale, and no expense was spared in fitting out the armament; for the objects of the expedition were both colonization and conquest. Artillery and powder were procured from Malaga. Beside the usual weapons, such as muskets, crossbows, swords, pikes, lances and Neapolitan targets, there was armour devised of quilted cotton, as being light and better adapted to the climate, and sufficiently proof against the weapons of the Indians; and wooden bucklers from the Canary Islands, to ward off the poisoned arrows of the Caribs.

Santa Maria de la Antigua was, by royal ordinance, elevated into the metropolitan city of Golden Castile, and a Franciscan friar, named Juan de Quevedo, was appointed as bishop, with powers to decide in all cases of conscience. A number of friars were nominated to accompany him, and he was provided with the necessary furniture and vessels for a chapel.

Among the various regulations made for the good of the infant colony, it was ordained that no lawyers should be admitted there, it having been found at Hispaniola and elsewhere, that they were detrimental to the welfare of the settlements, by fomenting disputes and litigations.

* Oviedo, lib. ii. cap. 7. MS.

The judicial affairs were to be entirely confided to the Licentiate Gaspar de Espinosa, who was to officiate as Alcalde Mayor or chief judge.

Don Pedrarias had intended to leave his wife in Spain. Her name was Doña Isabella de Bobadilla; she was the niece to the Marchioness de Moya, a great favourite of the late Queen Isabella, who had been instrumental in persuading her royal mistress to patronize Columbus.* Her niece partook of her high and generous nature. She refused to remain behind in selfish security, but declared that she would accompany her husband in every peril, whether by sea or land. This self-devotion is the more remarkable when it is considered that she was past the romantic period of youth; and that she left behind her in Spain, a family of four sons and four daughters.

Don Pedrarias was instructed to use great indulgence towards the people of Darien, who had been the followers of Nicuesa, and to remit the royal tithe of all the gold they might have collected previous to his arrival. Towards Vasco Nuñez de Balboa alone the royal countenance was stern and severe. Pedrarias was to depose him from his assumed authority, and to call him to strict account before the Alcalde Mayor, Gaspar de Espinosa, for his treatment of the Bachelor Enciso.

The splendid fleet, consisting of fifteen sail, weighed anchor at St. Lucar on the 12th of April, 1514, and swept proudly out of the Guadalquiver, thronged with the chivalrous adventurers for Golden Castile. But a short time had elapsed after its departure, when Pedro Arbolancho arrived with the tardy missions of Vasco Nuñez. Had he arrived a few days sooner how different might have been the fortunes of his friend!

He was immediately admitted to the royal presence, where he announced the adventurous and successful expedition of Vasco Nuñez, and laid before the king the pearls and golden ornaments which he had brought as the first fruits of the discovery. King Ferdinand listened with charmed attention to this tale of unknown seas and wealthy realms added to his empire. It filled, in fact, the imaginations of the most sage and learned with golden dreams, and anticipations of unbounded riches. Old Peter Martyr, who received letters from his friends in Darien, and communicated by word of mouth with those who came from thence, writes to Leo the Tenth in exulting terms of this event. "Spain," says he, "will hereafter be able to satisfy with pearls the greedy appetite of such as in wanton pleasures are like unto Cleopatra and Æsopus; so that henceforth we shall neither envy nor reverence the nice fruitfulness

---

* This was the same Marchioness de Moya, who during the war of Granada, while the court and royal army were encamped before Malaga, was mistaken for the queen by a Moorish fanatic, and had nearly fallen beneath his dagger.

of Trapoban or the Red Sea. The Spaniards will not need hereafter to mine and dig far into the earth, nor to cut asunder mountains in quest of gold, but will find it plentifully, in a manner, on the upper crust of the earth, or in the sands of rivers dried up by the heats of summer. Certainly the reverend antiquity obtained not so great a benefit of nature, nor even aspired to the knowledge thereof, since never man before, from the known world, penetrated to these unknown regions."*

The tidings of this discovery at once made all Spain resound with the praises of Vasco Nuñez; and, from being considered a lawless and desperate adventurer, he was lauded to the skies as a worthy successor to Columbus. The king repented of the harshness of his late measures towards him, and ordered the Bishop Fonseca to devise some mode of rewarding his transcendant services.

Chapter XVI

Arrival and grand entry of Don Pedrarias Davila into Darien

While honours and rewards were preparing in Europe for Vasco Nuñez, that indefatigable commander, inspired by his fortunes with redoubled zeal and loftier ambition, was exercising the paternal forethought and discretion of a patriotic governor over the country subjected to his rule. His most strenuous exertions were directed to bring the neighborhood of Darien into such a state of cultivation as might render the settlement independent of Europe for supplies. The town was situated on the banks of a river, and contained upwards of two hundred houses and cabins. Its population amounted to five hundred and fifteen Europeans, all men, and fifteen hundred Indians, male and female. Orchards and gardens had been laid out, where European as well as native fruits and vegetables were cultivated, and already gave promise of future abundance. Vasco Nuñez devised all kinds of means to keep up the spirits of his people. On holidays they had their favourite national sports and games, and particularly tilting matches, of which chivalrous amusement the Spaniards in those days were extravagantly fond. Sometimes he gratified their restless and roving habits by sending them in expeditions to various parts of the country, to acquire a knowledge of its

---

* P. Martyr, decad. 3. chap. iii. Lok's translation.

resources, and to strengthen his sway over the natives. He was so successful in securing the amity or exciting the awe of the Indian tribes, that a
Spaniard might go singly about the land in perfect safety; while his
own followers were zealous in their devotion to him, both from admiration of his past exploits and from hopes of soon being led by him to
new discoveries and conquests. Peter Martyr, in his letter to Leo the
Tenth, speaks in high terms of these "old soldiers of Darien," the
remnants of those well tried adventurers who had followed the fortunes
of Ojeda, Nicuesa, and Vasco Nuñez. "They were hardened," says he,
"to abide all sorrows, and were exceedingly tolerant of labour, heat,
hunger, and watching, insomuch that they merrily make their boast that
they have observed a longer and sharper Lent than ever your Holiness
enjoined, since, for the space of four years, their food has been herbs
and fruits, with now and then fish, and very seldom flesh."*

Such were the hardy and well seasoned veterans that were under
the sway of Vasco Nuñez; and the colony gave signs of rising in prosperity under his active and fostering management, when, in the month
of June, the fleet of Don Pedrarias Davila arrived in the Gulf of Uraba.

The Spanish cavaliers who accompanied the new governor were eager
to get on shore, and to behold the anticipated wonders of the land; but
Pedrarias, knowing the resolute character of Vasco Nuñez, and the
devotion of his followers, apprehended some difficulty in getting possession of the colony. Anchoring, therefore, about a league and a half from
the settlement, he sent a messenger on shore to announce his arrival.
The envoy, having heard so much in Spain of the prowess and exploits
of Vasco Nuñez and the riches of Golden Castile, expected, no doubt,
to find a blustering warrior, maintaining barbaric state in the government which he had usurped. Great was his astonishment therefore to
find this redoubtable hero a plain unassuming man, clad in a cotton
frock and drawers, and hempen sandals, directing and aiding the labour
of several Indians who were thatching a cottage in which he resided.

The messenger approached him respectfully, and announced the arrival
of Don Pedrarias Davila as governor of the country.

Whatever Vasco Nuñez may have felt at this intelligence, he suppressed
his emotions, and answered the messenger with great discretion; "Tell
Don Pedrarias Davila," said he, "that he is welcome, that I congratulate
him on his safe arrival, and am ready, with all who are here, to obey
his orders."

The little community of rough and daring adventurers was immediately
in an uproar when they found a new governor had arrived. Some of the

---

* P. Martyr, decad. 3. c. iii. Lok's translation.

most zealous adherents of Vasco Nuñez were disposed to sally forth, sword in hand, and repel the intruder; but they were restrained by their more considerate chieftain, who prepared to receive the new governor with all due submission.

Pedrarias disembarked on the thirtieth of June, accompanied by his heroic wife, Doña Isabella; who, according to old Peter Martyr, had sustained the roarings and rages of the ocean with no less stout courage than either her husband or even the mariners who had been brought up among the surges of the sea.

Pedrarias set out for the embryo city at the head of two thousand men, all well armed. He led his wife by the hand, and on the other side of him was the Bishop of Darien in his robes; while a brilliant train of youthful cavaliers, in glittering armour and brocade, formed a kind of body guard.

All this pomp and splendor formed a striking contrast with the humble state of Vasco Nuñez, who came forth unarmed, in simple attire, accompanied by his councillors and a handful of the "old soldiers of Darien," scarred and battered, and grown half wild in Indian warfare, but without weapons, and in garments much the worse for wear.

Vasco Nuñez saluted Don Pedrarias Davila with profound reverence and promised him implicit obedience, both in his own name and in the name of the community. Having entered the town he conducted his distinguished guests to his straw thatched habitation, where he had caused a repast to be prepared of such cheer as his means afforded, consisting of roots and fruits, maize and cassava bread, with no other beverage than water from the river. A sorry palace and a meager banquet in the eyes of the gay cavaliers, who had anticipated far other things from the usurper of Golden Castile. Vasco Nuñez, however, acquitted himself in his humble wigwam, with the courtesy and hospitality of a prince, and shewed that the dignity of an entertainment depends more upon the giver than the feast. In the mean time a plentiful supply of European provisions was landed from the fleet and a temporary abundance was diffused through the colony.

Chapter XVII

Perfidious conduct of Don Pedrarias towards Vasco Nuñez

On the day after his entrance into Darien Don Pedrarias held a private conference with Vasco Nuñez, in presence of the historian Oviedo, who had come out from Spain as public notary of the colony. The governor commenced by assuring him that he was instructed by the King to treat him with great favour and distinction, to consult him about the affairs of the colony, and to apply to him for information relative to the surrounding country. At the same time he professed the most amicable feelings on his own part, and an intention to be guided by his council in all public measures.

Vasco Nuñez was of a frank confiding nature, and was so captivated by this unexpected courtesy and kindness, that he threw off all caution and reserve, and opened his whole soul to the politic courtier. Pedrarias availed himself of this communicative mood to draw from him a minute and able statement in writing, detailing the circumstances of the colony and the information collected respecting various parts of the country; the route by which he had traversed the mountains; his discovery of the South Sea; the situation and reputed wealth of the Pearl Islands; the rivers and ravines most productive of gold; together with the names and territories of the various caciques with whom he had made treaties.

When Pedrarias had thus beguiled the unsuspecting soldier of all the information necessary for his purposes, he dropped the mask and within a few days proclaimed a judicial scrutiny into the conduct of Vasco Nuñez and his officers. It was to be conducted by the Licentiate Gaspar de Espinosa, who had come out as Alcalde Mayor, or chief judge. The Licentiate was an inexperienced lawyer, having but recently left the University of Salamanca. He appears to have been somewhat flexible in his opinions and prone to be guided or governed by others. At the outset of his career he was much under the influence of Quevedo, the Bishop of Darien. Now, as Vasco Nuñez knew the importance of this prelate in the colony, he had taken care to secure him to his interests by paying him the most profound deference and respect; and by giving him a share in his agricultural enterprizes and his schemes of traffic. In fact, the good Bishop looked upon him as one eminently calculated to promote his temporal prosperity, to which he was by no means insensible. Under the influence of the prelate, therefore, the Alcalde commenced his investigation in the most favorable manner. He went largely into an examination of the discoveries of Vasco Nuñez, and of the nature and extent of his various services. The governor was alarmed at the course which the inquiry was taking. If thus conducted, it would but serve to illustrate the merits and elevate the reputation of the man whom it was his interest and intent to ruin. To counteract it he immediately set on foot a secret and invidious course of interrogatories of the followers of Nicuesa and Ojeda, to draw from them testimony which might support the charge against Vasco Nuñez of usurpation and tyrannical abuse of power. The Bishop and the Alcalde received information of the inquisition, carried on thus secretly and without their sanction. They remonstrated warmly against it, as an infringement of their rights, being coadjutors in the government, and they spurned the testimony of the followers of Ojeda and Nicuesa, as being dictated and discoloured by ancient enmity. Vasco Nuñez was, therefore, acquitted by them of the criminal charges made against him, though he remained involved in difficulties from the suits brought against him by individuals for losses and damages occasioned by his measures.

Pedrarias was incensed at this acquittal, and insisted upon the guilt of Vasco Nuñez, which he pretended to have established to his conviction by his secret investigations; and he even determined to send him in chains to Spain, to be tried for the death of Nicuesa and for other imputed offences.

It was not the inclination or the interest of the Bishop that Vasco Nuñez should leave the colony. He, therefore, managed to awaken the jealous apprehension of the governor as to the effect of his proposed measure. He intimated that the arrival of Vasco Nuñez in Spain would be signalized by triumph rather than disgrace. By that time his grand discoveries would be blazoned to the world, and would atone for all his faults. He would be received with enthusiasm by the nation, with favour by the King, and would probably be sent back to the colony clothed with new dignity and power.

Pedrarias was placed in a perplexing dilemma by these suggestions; his violent proceedings against Vasco Nuñez were also in some measure restrained by the influence of his wife, Doña Isabella de Bobadilla, who felt a great respect and sympathy for the discoverer. In his perplexity the wily governor adopted a middle course. He resolved to detain Vasco Nuñez at Darien under a cloud of imputation which would gradually impair his popularity, while his patience and means would be silently consumed by protracted and expensive litigation. In the mean time, however, the property which had been sequestrated was restored to him.

While Pedrarias treated Vasco Nuñez with this severity, he failed not to avail himself of the plans of that able commander. The first of these was to establish a line of posts across the mountains between Darien and the South Sea. It was his eager desire to execute this before any order should arrive from the King in favour of his predecessor, in order that he might have the credit of having colonized the coast, and Vasco Nuñez merely that of having discovered and visited it.* Before he could complete these arrangements, however, unlooked for calamities fell upon the settlement, that for a time interrupted every project, and made every one turn his thoughts merely to his own security.

Chapter XVIII

Calamities of the Spanish cavaliers at Darien

The town of Darien was situated in a deep valley surrounded by lofty hills which, while they kept off the breezes so grateful in a sultry climate, reflected and concentrated the rays of the sun, insomuch that at noon tide the heat was insupportable. The river which passed it was shallow, with a muddy channel and bordered by marshes. Overhanging forests added to the general humidity, and the very soil on which the town was built was of such a nature that on digging to the depth of a foot there would ooze forth brackish water.†

It is not matter of surprize that a situation of this kind, in a tropical climate, should be fatal to the health of Europeans. Many of those who had recently arrived were swept off speedily; Pedrarias himself fell sick and was removed, with most of his people, to a healthier spot on the river Corobari. The malady, however, continued to increase. The provisions which had been brought out in the ships had been partly damaged by the sea, the residue grew scanty, and the people were put upon short allowance. The debility thus produced encreased the ravages of disease; at length the provisions were exhausted and the horrors of absolute famine ensued.

Every one was more or less affected by these calamities; even the veterans of the colony quailed beneath them; but to none were they more fatal than to the crowd of youthful cavaliers, who had once glittered so gaily about the streets of Seville, and had come out to the New World elated with the most sanguine expectations. From the very moment of their landing they had been disheartened at the savage scenes

* Oviedo, Hist. Ind. p. 2. cap. 8.
† P. Martyr, decad. 3, cap. vi.

around them and disgusted with the squalid life they were doomed to lead. They shrunk with disdain from the labors with which alone wealth was to be procured in this land of gold and pearls, and were impatient of the humble exertions necessary for the maintenance of existence. As the famine encreased their case became desperate; for they were unable to help themselves, and their rank and dignity commanded neither deference nor aid at a time when common misery made every one selfish. Many of them, who had mortgaged estates in Spain to fit themselves out sumptuously for their Italian campaign, now perished for lack of food. Some would be seen bartering a robe of crimson silk, or some garment of rich brocade, for a pound of Indian bread or European biscuit; others sought to satisfy the cravings of hunger with the herbs and roots of the field; and one of the principal cavaliers absolutely expired of hunger in the public streets.

In this wretched way, and in the short space of one month, perished seven hundred of the little army of youthful and buoyant spirits who had embarked with Pedrarias. The bodies of some remained for a day or two without sepulture, their friends not having sufficient strength to bury them. Unable to remedy the evil, Pedrarias gave permission for his men to flee from it. A ship load of starving adventurers departed for Cuba, where some of them joined the standard of Diego Velasquez, who was colonizing that island; others made their way back to Spain, where they arrived broken in health, in spirits and in fortune.

Chapter XIX

Fruitless expedition of Pedrarias

The departure of so many hungry mouths was some temporary relief to the colony, and Pedrarias, having recovered from his malady, bestirred himself to send expeditions in various directions for the purpose of foraging the country, and collecting the treasure.

These expeditions, however, were entrusted to his own favorites and partizans; while Vasco Nuñez, the man most competent to carry them into effect, remained idle and neglected. A judicial inquiry, tardily carried on, overshadowed him, and, though it substantiated nothing, served to embarrass his actions, to cool his friends and to give him the air of a public delinquent. Indeed to the other evils of the colony was now added that of excessive litigation, arising out of the disputes concerning the government of Vasco Nuñez, and which encreased to such a degree that, according to the report of the Alcalde Espinosa, if the law suits should be divided among the people, at least forty would fall to each man's share.* This too was in a colony into which the government had commanded that no lawyer should be admitted!

Wearied and irritated by the check given to his favorite enterprizes, and confident of the ultimate approbation of the King, Vasco Nuñez now determined to take his fortunes in his own hands, and to prosecute in secret his grand project of exploring the regions beyond the mountains. For this purpose he privately despatched one Andres Garabito to Cuba to enlist men, and make provisions for an expedition across the isthmus from Nombre de Dios, and for the founding of a colony on the shores of the Southern Ocean; from whence he proposed to extend his discoveries by sea and land.

While Vasco Nuñez awaited the return of Garabito, he had the mortification of beholding various of his colonizing plans pursued and marred by Pedrarias. Among other enterprizes the governor despatched his Lieutenant General Juan de Ayora, at the head of four hundred men, to visit the provinces of those caciques with whom Vasco Nuñez had sojourned and made treaties on his expedition to the Southern Sea. Ayora partook of the rash and domineering spirit of Pedrarias and harassed and devastated the countries which he pretended to explore. He was received with amity and confidence by various caciques who had formed treaties with Vasco Nuñez, but he repaid their hospitality with the basest ingratitude, seizing upon their property, taking from them their wives and daughters and often torturing them to make them reveal their hidden or supposed treasures. Among those treated with this perfidy we grieve to enumerate the youthful cacique who first gave Vasco Nuñez information of the sea beyond the mountains.

The enormities of Ayora and of other captains of Pedrarias produced the usual effect. The natives were roused to desperate resistance; caciques, who had been faithful friends, were converted into furious enemies, and the expeditions ended in disappointment and disaster.

The adherents of Vasco Nuñez did not fail to contrast these disastrous enterprizes with those which had been conducted with so much glory and advantage by their favorite commander; and their sneers and reproaches had such an effect upon the jealous and irritable disposition of Pedrarias, that he determined to employ their idol in a service likely to be attended with defeat and impair his popularity. None seemed more fitting for the

* Herrera, decad. 2. lib. i. cap. 1.

purpose than an expedition to Dobayba, where he had once already attempted in vain to penetrate, and where so many of his followers had fallen victims to the stratagems and assaults of the natives.

Chapter XX

Second expedition of Vasco Nuñez in quest of the Gold Temple of Dobayba

The rich mines of Dobayba, and the treasures of its golden temple, had continued a favorite theme with the Spanish adventurers. It was ascertained that Vasco Nuñez had stopped short of the wealthy region on his former expedition, and had mistaken a frontier village for the residence of the cacique. The enterprize of the temple was, therefore, still to be achieved, and it was solicited by several of the cavaliers in the train of Pedrarias, with all the chivalrous ardour of that romantic age. Indeed common report had invested the enterprize with difficulties and dangers sufficient to stimulate the ambition of the keenest seeker of adventure. The savages who inhabited that part of the country were courageous and adroit. They fought by water as well as by land, forming ambuscades with their canoes in the bays and rivers. The country was intersected by dreary fens and morasses, infested by all kinds of reptiles. Clouds of gnats and musquitoes filled the air; there were huge bats also, supposed to have the baneful properties of the vampire; alligators lurked in the waters, and the gloomy recesses of the fens were said to be the dens of dragons!*

Beside these objects of terror, both true and fabulous, the old historian Peter Martyr makes mention of another monstrous animal, said to infest this golden region, and which deserves to be cited, as showing the imaginary dangers with which the active minds of the discoverers peopled the unexplored wilderness around them.

According to the tales of the Indians, there had occurred, shortly before the arrival of the Spaniards, a violent tempest or rather hurricane in the neighborhood of Dobayba, which demolished houses, tore up trees by the roots, and laid waste whole forests. When the tempest had subsided and the affrighted inhabitants ventured to look abroad, they

* P. Martyr.

found that two monstrous animals had been brought into the country by the hurricane. According to their accounts they were not unlike the ancient harpies, and one being smaller than the other was supposed to be its young. They had the faces of women, with the claws and wings of eagles, and were of such prodigious size that the very boughs of the trees on which they alighted broke beneath them. They would swoop down and carry off a man as a hawk would bear off a chicken, flying with him to the tops of the mountains, where they would tear him in pieces and devour him. For some time they were the scourge and terror of the land until the Indians succeeded in killing the old one by stratagem and, hanging her on their long spears, bore her through all the towns to assuage the alarm of the inhabitants. The younger harpy, says the Indian tradition, was never seen afterwards. *

Such were some of the perils, true and fabulous, with which the land of Dobayba was said to abound, and in fact the very Indians had such a dread of its dark and dismal morasses, that in their journeyings they carefully avoided them, preferring the circuitous and rugged paths of the mountains.

Several of the youthful cavaliers, as has been observed, were stimulated rather than deterred by these dangers, and contended for the honour of the expedition, but Pedrarias selected his rival for the task, hoping, as has been hinted, that it would involve him in disgrace. Vasco Nuñez promptly accepted the enterprize, for his pride was concerned in its success. Two hundred resolute men were given to him for the purpose, but his satisfaction was diminished when he found that Luis Carillo, an officer of Pedrarias, who had failed in a previous enterprize, was associated with him in the command.

Few particulars remain to us of the events of this affair. They embarked in a fleet of canoes and, traversing the gulf, arrived at the river which flowed down from the region of Dobayba. They were not destined, however, to achieve the enterprize of the Golden Temple. As they were proceeding rather confidently and unguardedly up the river, they were suddenly surprized and surrounded by a swarm of canoes, filled with armed savages, which darted out from lurking places along the shores. Some of the Indians assailed them with lances, others with clouds of arrows; while some, plunging into the water, endeavoured to overturn their canoes. In this way one half of the Spaniards were killed or drowned. Among the number fell Luis Carillo, pierced through the breast by an Indian lance. Vasco Nuñez himself was wounded, and had great difficulty in escaping to the shore with the residue of his forces.

* P. Martyr, decad. 7, cap. 10.

The Indians pursued him and kept up a skirmishing attack but he beat them off until the night, when he silently abandoned the shore of the river, and directed his retreat towards Darien. It is easier to imagine than to describe the toils and dangers and horrors which beset him and the remnant of his men as they traversed rugged mountains, or struggled through the fearful morasses of which they had heard such terrific tales. At length they succeeded in reaching the settlement of Darien.

The partizans of Pedrarias exulted in seeing Vasco Nuñez return thus foiled and wounded, and taunted his adherents with their previous boastings. The latter, however, laid all the blame upon the unfortunate Carillo. "Vasco Nuñez," said they, "had always absolute command in his former enterprizes, but in this he has been embarrassed by an associate. Had the expedition been confided to him alone the event had been far different."

Chapter XXI

Letters from the King in favour of Vasco Nuñez—Arrival of Garabito—Arrest of Vasco Nuñez (1515)

About this time despatches arrived from Spain that promised to give a new turn to the fortunes of Vasco Nuñez and to the general affairs of the colony. They were written after the tidings of the discovery of the South Sea, and the subjugation of so many important provinces of the Isthmus. In a letter addressed to Vasco Nuñez the King expressed his high sense of his merits and services, and constituted him Adelantado of the South Sea and Governor of the provinces of Panama and Coyba; though subordinate to the general command of Pedrarias. A letter was likewise written by the King to Pedrarias, informing him of this appointment, and ordering him to consult Vasco Nuñez on all public affairs of importance. This was a humiliating blow to the pride and consequence of Pedrarias, but he hoped to parry it. In the mean time, as all letters from Spain were first delivered into his hands, he withheld that intended for Vasco Nuñez, until he should determine what course of conduct to adopt. The latter, however, heard of the circumstance, as did his friend the Bishop of Darien. The prelate made loud complaints of this interruption of the royal correspondence, which he denounced, even from the pulpit, as an outrage upon the rights of the subject and an act of disobedience to the Sovereign.

Upon this the governor called a council of his public officers, and, after imparting the contents of his letter, requested their opinion as to the propriety of investing Vasco Nuñez with the dignities thus granted to him. The Alcalde Mayor, Espinosa, had left the party of the Bishop and was now devoted to the governor. He insisted vehemently that the the offices ought in no wise to be given to Vasco Nuñez until the King should be informed of the result of the inquest still going on against him. In this he was warmly supported by the Treasurer and the Accountant. The Bishop replied, indignantly, that it was presumptuous and disloyal in them to dispute the commands of the King, and to interfere with the rewards conscientiously given by him to a meritorious subject. In this way, he added, they were defeating, by their passions, the grateful intentions of their Sovereign. The governor was overawed by the honest warmth of the Bishop and professed to accord with him in opinion. The council lasted until midnight and it was finally agreed that the titles and dignities should be conferred on Vasco Nuñez on the following day.*

Pedrarias and his officers reflected, however, that if the jurisdiction implied by these titles were absolutely vested in Vasco Nuñez, the government of Darien and Castilla del Oro would virtually be reduced to a trifling matter; they resolved, therefore, to adopt a middle course; to grant him the empty titles, but to make him give security not to enter upon the actual government of the territories in question, until Pedrarias should give him permission. The Bishop and Vasco Nuñez assented to this arrangement, satisfied, for the present, with securing the titles, and trusting to the course of events to get dominion over the territories.†

The new honours of Vasco Nuñez were now promulgated to the world, and he was every where addressed by the title of Adelantado. His old friends lifted up their heads with exultation, and new adherents flocked to his standard. Parties began to form for him and for Pedrarias, for it was deemed impossible they could continue long in harmony.

The jealousy of the Governor was excited by these circumstances, and he regarded the newly created Adelantado as a dangerous rival and an insidious foe. Just at this critical juncture, Andres Garabito, the agent

---

* Oviedo, part 2, cap. 9. MS. Oviedo, the historian, was present at this consultation and says that he wrote down the opinions given on the occasion, which the parties signed with their proper hands.

† Idem.

of Vasco Nuñez, arrived on the coast in a vessel which he had procured
at Cuba, and had freighted with arms and ammunition, and seventy
resolute men, for the secret expedition to the shores of the Pacific Ocean.
He anchored six leagues from the harbour, and sent word privately to
Vasco Nuñez of his arrival.

Information was immediately carried to Pedrarias that a mysterious
vessel, full of armed men, was hovering on the coast and holding secret
communication with his rival. The suspicious temper of the governor
immediately took the alarm. He fancied some treasonable plot against
his authority; his passions mingled with his fears, and, in the first burst
of his fury, he ordered that Vasco Nuñez should be seized and confined
in a wooden cage. The Bishop of Darien interposed in time to prevent
an indignity which it might have been impossible to expiate. He prevailed
upon the passionate governor, not merely to retract the order respecting
the cage, but to examine the whole matter with coolness and deliberation.
The result proved that his suspicions had been erroneous, and that the
armament had been set on foot without any treasonable intent. Vasco
Nuñez was therefore set at liberty, after having agreed to certain pre-
cautionary conditions; but he remained cast down in spirit and impoverished in fortune by the harassing measures of Pedrarias.

Chapter XXII

*Expedition of Morales and Pizarro to the shores of the Pacific Ocean—
Their visit to the Pearl Islands—Their disastrous return across the
mountains*

The Bishop of Darien, encouraged by the success of his intercession,
endeavoured to persuade the Governor to permit the departure of Vasco
Nuñez on his expedition to the South Sea. The jealousy of Pedrarias,
however, was too strong to permit him to listen to such council. He was
aware of the importance of the expedition, and was anxious that the
Pearl Islands should be explored, which promised such abundant treasures; but he feared to encrease the popularity of Vasco Nuñez, by
adding such an enterprize to the number of his achievements. Pedrarias,
therefore, set on foot an expedition consisting of sixty men, but gave the
command to one of his own relations named Gaspar Morales. The latter
was accompanied by Francisco Pizarro, who had already been to those

parts in the train of Vasco Nuñez, and who soon rose to importance in the present enterprize by his fierce courage and domineering genius.

A brief notice of the principal incidents of this expedition is all that is necessary for the present narration.

Morales and Pizarro traversed the mountains of the isthmus by a shorter and more expeditious route than that which had been taken by Vasco Nuñez; and arrived on the shores of the South Sea at the territories of a cacique named Tutibrà, by whom they were amicably entertained. Their great object was to visit the Pearl Islands; the cacique, however, had but four canoes, which were insufficient to contain their whole party. One half of their number, therefore, remained at the village of Tutibrà, under the command of a captain named Peñalosa; the residue embarked in the canoes with Morales and Pizarro. After a stormy and perilous voyage, they landed on one of the smaller islands, where they had some skirmishing with the natives, and thence made their way to the principal island of the archipelago, to which, from the report of its great pearl fishery, Vasco Nuñez had given the name of Isla Rica.

The cacique of this island had long been the terror of the neighboring coasts, invading the main land with fleets of canoes, and carrying off the inhabitants into captivity. His reception of the Spaniards was worthy of his fame. Four times did he sally forth to defend his territory, and as often was he repulsed with great slaughter. His warriors were overwhelmed with terror at the fire arms of the Spaniards, and at their ferocious bloodhounds. Finding all resistance unavailing, the cacique was at length compelled to sue for peace. His prayer being granted, he received the conquerors into his habitation, which was well built, and of immense size. Here he brought them as a peace offering a basket curiously wrought, and filled with pearls of great beauty. Among these were two of extraordinary size and value. One weighed twenty five carats; the other was of the size of a Muscadine pear, weighing upwards of three drachms, and of oriental colour and lustre. The cacique considered himself more than repaid by a present of hatchets, beads and hawks bells, and, on the Spaniards smiling at his joy, observed, "these things I can turn to useful purpose, but of what value are those pearls to me?"

Finding, however, that these baubles were precious in the eyes of the Spaniards, he took Morales and Pizarro to the summit of a wooden tower commanding an unbounded prospect. "Behold before you," said he, "the infinite sea which extends even beyond the sun beams. As to these islands which lie to the right and left, they are all subject to my sway. They possess but little gold, but the deep places of the sea around them are full of pearls. Continue to be my friends, and you shall have as many as you desire, for I value your friendship more than pearls, and as far as in me lies will never forfeit it."

He then pointed to the main land, where it stretched away towards the east, mountain beyond mountain, until the summit of the last faded in the distance and was scarcely seen above the watery horizon. In that direction, he said, there lay a vast country of inexhaustible riches, inhabited by a mighty nation. He went on to repeat the vague but wonderful rumours which the Spaniards had frequently heard about the great Kingdom of Peru. Pizarro listened greedily to his words, and while his eye followed the finger of the cacique, as it ranged along the line of shadowy coast, his daring mind kindled with the thought of seeking this golden empire beyond the waters.[*]

Before leaving the island, the two captains impressed the cacique with so great an idea of the power of the King of Castile, that he agreed to become his vassal and to render him an annual tribute of one hundred pounds' weight of pearls.

The party having returned in safety to the main land, though to a different place from that where they had embarked, Gaspar Morales sent his relation Bernardo Morales with ten men in quest of Peñalosa and his companions, who had remained in the village of Tutibrà.

Unfortunately for the Spaniards, during the absence of the commanders, this Peñalosa had so exasperated the natives by his misconduct, that a conspiracy had been formed by the caciques along the coast to massacre the whole of the strangers, when the party should return from the islands.

Bernardo Morales and his companions, on their way in quest of Peñalosa, put up for the night in the village of a cacique named Chuchama, who was one of the conspirators. They were entertained with pretended hospitality. In the dead of night, however, the house in which they were sleeping was wrapped in flames, and most of them were destroyed. Chuchama then prepared with his confederates to attack the main body of the Spaniards, who remained with Morales and Pizarro.

Fortunately for the latter, there was among the Indians who had accompanied them to the islands a cacique named Chirucà, who was in secret correspondence with the conspirators. Some circumstances in his conduct excited their suspicions; they put him to the torture, and drew from him a relation of the massacre of their companions, and of the attack with which they were menaced.

Morales and Pizarro were at first appalled by the overwhelming

---

[*] Herrera, decad. 2. lib. i. cap. iv. Peter Martyr, decad. 3. cap. x.

danger which surrounded them. Concealing their agitation, however, they compelled Chirucà to send a message to each of the confederate caciques, inviting him to a secret conference, under pretence of giving him important information. The caciques came at the summons: they were thus taken one by one to the number of eighteen, and put in chains. Just at this juncture, Peñalosa arrived with the thirty men who had remained with him at Tutibrà. Their arrival was hailed with joy by their comrades, who had given them up for lost. Encouraged by this unexpected reinforcement, the Spaniards now attacked by surprize the main body of confederate Indians, who, being ignorant of the discovery of their plot, and capture of their caciques, were awaiting the return of the latter in a state of negligent security.

Pizarro led the van, and set upon the enemy at day break with the old Spanish war-cry of *Santiago!* It was a slaughter rather than a battle, for the Indians were unprepared for resistance. Before sun rise, seven hundred lay dead upon the field. Returning from the massacre, the commanders doomed the caciques who were in chains to be torn in pieces by the bloodhounds; nor was even Chirucà spared from this sanguinary sentence. Notwithstanding this bloody revenge, the vindictive spirit of the commanders was still unappeased, and they set off to surprize the village of a cacique named Birù, who dwelt on the eastern side of the Gulf of St. Michael. He was famed for valour and for cruelty; his dwelling was surrounded by the weapons and other trophies of those whom he had vanquished, and he was said never to give quarter.

The Spaniards assailed his village before day break with fire and sword and made dreadful havoc. Birù escaped from his burning habitation, rallied his people, kept up a galling fight throughout the greater part of that day, and handled the Spaniards so roughly, that, when he drew off at night, they did not venture to pursue him, but retired right gladly from his territory. According to some of the Spanish writers, the Kingdom of Peru derived its name from this warlike cacique, through a blunder of the early discoverers; the assertion, however, is believed to be erroneous.

The Spaniards had pushed their bloody revenge to an extreme, and were now doomed to suffer from the recoil. In the fury of their passions, they had forgotten that they were but a handful of men surrounded by savage nations. Returning wearied and disheartened from the battle with Birù, they were waylayed and assaulted by a host of Indians led on by the son of Chirucà. A javelin from his hand pierced one of the Spaniards through the breast, and came out between the shoulders. Several others were wounded; and the remainder were harassed by a galling fire kept up from among rocks and bushes.

Dismayed at the implacable vengeance they had aroused, the Spaniards hastened to abandon these hostile shores and make the best of their way back to Darien. The Indians, however, were not to be appeased by the mere departure of the intruders. They followed them perseveringly for seven days, hanging on their skirts, and harassing them by continual alarms. Morales and Pizarro, seeing the obstinacy of their pursuit, endeavoured to gain a march upon them by stratagem. Making large fires as usual one night about the place of their encampment, they left them burning to deceive the enemy while they made a rapid retreat. Among their number was one poor fellow named Velasquez, who was so grievously wounded that he could not walk. Unable to accompany his countrymen in their flight, and dreading to fall into the merciless hands of the savages, he determined to hang himself, nor could the prayers or even tears of his comrades dissuade him from his purpose.

The stratagem of the Spaniards, however, was unavailing. Their retreat was perceived, and at day break, to their dismay, they found themselves surrounded by three squadrons of savages. Unable, in their haggard state, to make head against so many foes, they remained drawn up all day on the defensive, some watching while others reposed. At night they lit their fires and again attempted to make a secret retreat. The Indians, however, were as usual on their traces, and wounded several with arrows. Thus pressed and goaded, the Spaniards became desperate, and fought like mad men, rushing upon the very darts of the enemy.

Morales now resorted to an inhuman and fruitless expedient to retard his pursuers. He caused several Indian prisoners to be slain, hoping that their friends would stop to lament over them; but the sight of their mangled bodies only encreased the fury of the savages and the obstinacy of their pursuit.

For nine days were the Spaniards hunted in this manner about the woods and mountains, the swamps and fens; wandering they knew not whither, and returning upon their steps, until, to their dismay, they found themselves in the very place where, several days previously, they had been surrounded by the three squadrons.

Many now despaired of ever escaping with life from this trackless wilderness, thus teeming with deadly foes. It was with difficulty their commanders could rally their spirits and encourage them to persevere. Entering a thick forest they were again assailed by a band of Indians, but despair and fury gave them strength: they fought like wild beasts rather than like men, and routed the foe with dreadful carnage. They had hoped to gain a breathing time by this victory, but a new distress attended them. They got entangled in one of those deep and dismal marshes which abound on these coasts, and in which the wanderer is often drowned or suffocated. For a whole day they toiled through brake and bramble, and miry fen, with the water reaching to their girdles. At length they extricated themselves from the swamp, and arrived at the sea shore. The tide was out, but was about to return, and on this coast it rises rapidly to a great height. Fearing to be overwhelmed by the rising surf, they hastened to climb a rock out of reach of the swelling waters. Here they threw themselves on the earth panting with fatigue and abandoned to despair. A savage wilderness filled with still more savage foes was one one side, on the other the roaring sea. How were they to extricate themselves from these surrounding perils? While reflecting on their desperate situation, they heard the voices of Indians. On looking cautiously round, they beheld four canoes entering a neighboring creek. A party was immediately despatched who came upon the savages by surprize, drove them into the woods, and seized upon the canoes. In these frail barks the Spaniards escaped from their perilous neighborhood, and, traversing the Gulf of St. Michael, landed in a less hostile part, from whence they set out a second time, across the mountains.

It is needless to recount the other hardships they endured, and their further conflicts with the Indians; suffice it to say, after a series of almost incredible sufferings and disasters, they at length arrived in a battered and emaciated condition at Darien. Throughout all their toils and troubles, however, they had managed to preserve a part of the treasure they had gained in the islands; especially the pearls given them by the cacique of Isla Rica. These were objects of universal admiration. One of them was put up at auction and bought by Pedrarias, and was afterward presented by his wife Doña Isabella de Bobadilla to the Empress, who in return gave her four thousand ducats.*

Such was the cupidity of the colonists, that the sight of these pearls, and the reputed wealth of the islands of the Southern Sea, and the kingdoms on its borders, made far greater impression on the public mind, than the tale told by the adventurers of the horrors they had passed; and every one was eager to seek these wealthy regions beyond the mountains.

* Herrera, Hist. Ind. decad. 2, lib. i. cap. 4.

Chapter XXIII

Unfortunate enterprizes of the officers of Pedrarias—Matrimonial compact between the Governor and Vasco Nuñez

In narrating the preceding expedition of Morales and Pizarro, we have been tempted into what may almost be deemed an episode, though it serves to place in a proper light the lurking difficulties and dangers which beset the expeditions of Vasco Nuñez to the same regions, and his superior prudence and management in avoiding them. It is not the object of this narrative, however, to record the general events of the colony under the administration of Don Pedrarias Davila. We refrain, therefore, from detailing various expeditions set on foot by him to explore and subjugate the surrounding country, and which, being ignorantly or rashly conducted, too often ended in misfortune and disgrace. One of these was to the province of Zenu, where gold was supposed to be taken in the rivers in nets, and where the Bachelor Enciso once undertook to invade the sepulchres. A captain named Francisco Becerra penetrated into this country at the head of one hundred and eighty men, well armed, and equipped and provided with three pieces of artillery: but neither the commander nor any of his men returned. An Indian boy who accompanied them was the only one who escaped and told the dismal tale of their having fallen victims to the assaults and stratagems and poisoned arrows of the Indians.

Another band was defeated by Tubanamà, the ferocious cacique of the mountains, who bore as banners the bloody shirts of the Spaniards he had slain in former battles. In fine, the colony became so weakened by these repeated losses, and the savages so emboldened by success, that the latter beleaguered it with their forces, harassed it by assaults and ambuscades and reduced it to great extremity. Such was the alarm in Darien, says the Bishop Las Casas, that the people feared to be burnt in their houses. They kept a watchful eye upon the mountains, the plains, and the very branches of the trees. Their imaginations were infected by their fears. If they looked toward the land, the long waving grass of the Savannahs appeared to them to be moving hosts of Indians. If they looked towards the sea, they fancied they beheld fleets of canoes in the distance. Pedrarias endeavoured to prevent all rumours from abroad that might encrease this fevered state of alarm; at the same time he ordered the smelting house to be closed, which was never done but in time of war. This was done at the suggestion of the Bishop, who caused prayers to be put up and fasts proclaimed, to avert the impending calamities.

While Pedrarias was harassed and perplexed by these complicated evils, he was haunted by continual apprehensions of the ultimate ascendancy of Vasco Nuñez. He knew him to be beloved by the people, and befriended by the Bishop, and he had received proofs that his services were highly appreciated by the King. He knew also that representations had been sent home by him and his partizans, of the evils and abuses of the colony under the present rule, and of the necessity of a more active and efficient governor. He dreaded lest these representations should ultimately succeed, that he should be undermined in the royal favour and Vasco Nuñez be elevated upon his ruins.

The politic Bishop perceived the uneasy state of the Governor's mind, and endeavoured by means of his apprehensions, to effect that reconciliation which he had sought in vain to produce through more generous motives. He represented to him that his treatment of Vasco Nuñez was odious in the eyes of the people, and must eventually draw on him the displeasure of his Sovereign. "But why persist," added he, "in driving a man to become your deadliest enemy, whom you may grapple to your side as your firmest friend? You have several daughters. Give him one in marriage. You will then have for a son-in-law a man of merit and popularity, who is a hidalgo by birth, and a favourite of the King. You are advanced in life and infirm; he is in the prime and vigour of his days and possessed of great activity. You can make him your lieutenant; and, while you repose from your toils he can carry on the affairs of the colony with spirit and enterprize, and all his achievements will redound to the advancement of your family and the splendour of your administration."

The Governor and his lady were won by the eloquence of the Bishop and readily listened to his suggestion, and Vasco Nuñez was but too happy to effect a reconciliation on such flattering terms. Written articles were accordingly drawn up and exchanged, contracting a marriage between him and the eldest daughter of Pedrarias. The young lady was then in Spain, but was to be sent for, and the nuptials were to be celebrated on her arrival at Darien.

Having thus fulfilled his office of peace maker, and settled, as he supposed, all feuds and jealousies on the sure and permanent foundation of family alliance, the worthy Bishop departed shortly afterwards for Spain.

Chapter XXIV

Vasco Nuñez transports ships across the mountains to the Pacific Ocean (1516)

Behold Vasco Nuñez once more in the high career of prosperity! His most implacable enemy had suddenly been converted into his dearest friend; for the governor, now that he looked upon him as his son-in-law, loaded him with favours. Above all, he authorized him to build brigantines and make all the necessary preparations for his long desired expedition to explore the Southern Ocean. The place appointed for these purposes was the port of Careta, situated to the west of Darien; from whence there was supposed to be the most convenient route across the mountains. A town called Acla had been founded at this port, and the fortress was already erected, of which Lope de Olano was Alcalde; Vasco Nuñez was now empowered to continue the building of the town. Two hundred men were placed under his command to aid him in carrying his plans into execution, and a sum of money was advanced to him out of the royal treasury. His supply of funds, however, was not sufficient, but he received assistance from a private source. There was a notary at Darien, named Hernando de Arguello, a man of some consequence in the community and who had been one of the most furious opponents of the unfortunate Nicuesa. He had amassed considerable property, and now embarked a great part of it in the proposed enterprize, on condition, no doubt, of sharing largely in its anticipated profits.

On arriving at Acla, Vasco Nuñez set to work to prepare the materials of four brigantines that were to be launched into the South Sea. The timber was felled on the Atlantic seaboard; and was then, with the anchors and rigging, transported across the lofty ridge of mountains to the opposite shores of the Isthmus. Several Spaniards, thirty Negroes and a great number of Indians were employed for the purpose. They had no other roads but Indian paths, straggling through almost impervious forests, across torrents, and up rugged defiles broken by rocks and precipices. In this way they toiled like ants up the mountains, with their ponderous burthens, under the scorching rays of a tropical sun. Many of the poor Indians sank by the way and perished under this stupendous task. The Spaniards and Negroes, being of hardier constitutions, were better able to cope with the incredible hardships to which they were subjected. On the summit of the mountains a house had been provided for their temporary repose. After remaining here a little time to refresh themselves and gain new strength, they renewed their labours, descending the opposite side of the mountains until they reached the navigable part of a river, which they called the Balsas, and which flowed into the Pacific.

Much time and trouble, and many lives were expended on this arduous undertaking, before they had transported to the river sufficient timber for two brigantines; while the timber for the other two, and the rigging and munitions for the whole, yet remained to be brought. To add to their difficulties, they had scarcely begun to work upon the timber before they discovered that it was totally useless, being subject to the ravages of the worms from having been cut in the vicinity of salt water. They were obliged, therefore, to begin anew, and fell trees on the border of the river.

Vasco Nuñez maintained his patience and perseverance, and displayed admirable management under these delays and difficulties. Their supply of food being scanty, he divided his people, Spaniards, Negroes, and Indians, into three bands; one was to cut and saw the wood, another to bring the rigging and iron work from Acla, which was twenty-two leagues distant; and the third to forage the neighbouring country for provisions.

Scarcely was the timber felled and shaped for use when the rains set in, and the river swelled and overflowed its banks so suddenly, that the workmen barely escaped with their lives, by clambering into the trees; while the wood on which they had been working was either buried in sand or slime, or swept away by the raging torrent. Famine was soon added to their other distresses. The foraging party did not return with food; and the swelling of the river cut them off from that part of the country from whence they obtained their supplies. They were reduced, therefore, to such scarcity, as to be fain to assuage their hunger with roots gathered in the forests.

In this extremity the Indians bethought themselves of one of their rude and simple expedients. Plunging into the river they fastened a number of logs together with withes, and connected them with the opposite bank, so as to make a floating bridge. On this a party of the Spaniards crossed with great difficulty and peril, from the violence of the current, and the flexibility of the bridge, which often sank beneath them until the water rose above their girdles. On being safely landed they foraged the neighbourhood, and procured a supply of provisions sufficient for the present emergency.

When the river subsided the workmen again resumed their labours; a number of recruits arrived from Acla, bringing various supplies, and the business of the enterprise was pressed with redoubled ardour, until, after a series of incredible toils and hardships, Vasco Nuñez had the satisfaction to behold two of his brigantines floating on the river Balsas.

As soon as they could be equipped for sea, he embarked in them with as many Spaniards as they could carry; and, issuing forth from the river, launched triumphantly on the great ocean he had discovered.

We can readily imagine the exultation of this intrepid adventurer, and how amply he was repaid for all his sufferings, when he first spread a sail upon that untraversed ocean, and felt that the range of an unknown world was open to him.

There are points in the history of these Spanish discoveries of the western hemisphere, that make us pause with wonder and admiration at the daring spirit of the men who conducted them, and the appalling difficulties surmounted by their courage and perseverance. We know few instances, however, more striking than this piece-meal transportation, across the mountains of Darien, of the first European ships that ploughed the waves of the Pacific; and we can readily excuse the boast of the old Castilian writers, when they exclaim, "that none but Spaniards could ever have conceived or persisted in such an undertaking; and no commander in the new world but Vasco Nuñez could have conducted it to a successful issue."*

Chapter XXV

Cruise of Vasco Nuñez in the Southern Sea—Rumours from Acla

The first cruise of Vasco Nuñez was to the groupe of Pearl Islands, on the principal one of which he disembarked the greater part of his crews, and despatched the brigantines to the main land to bring off the remainder. It was his intention to construct the other two vessels of his proposed squadron at this island. During the absence of the brigantines he ranged the island with his men, to collect provisions, and to establish a complete sway over the natives. On the return of his vessels, and while preparations were making for the building of the others, he embarked with a hundred men, and departed on a reconnoitering cruise to the eastward, towards the region pointed out by the Indians as abounding in riches.

Having passed about twenty leagues beyond the Gulf of San Miguel, the mariners were alarmed at beholding a great number of whales,

* Herrera, decad. 2. lib. ii. cap. 11.

which resembled a reef of rocks stretching far into the sea, and lashed by breakers. In an unknown ocean like this every unusual object is apt to inspire alarm. The seamen feared to approach these fancied dangers in the dark; Vasco Nuñez anchored, therefore, for the night under a point of land, intending to continue in the same direction on the following day. When the morning dawned, however, the wind had changed, and was contrary; whereupon he altered his course, and thus abandoned a cruise, which, if persevered in, might have terminated in the discovery of Peru! Steering for the main land, he anchored on that part of the coast governed by the cacique Chuchama, who had massacred Bernardo Morales and his companions, when reposing in his village. Here landing with his men, Vasco Nuñez came suddenly upon the dwelling of the cacique. The Indians sallied forth to defend their homes, but were routed with great loss; and ample vengeance was taken upon them for their outrage upon the laws of hospitality. Having thus avenged the death of his countrymen, Vasco Nuñez re-embarked and returned to Isla Rica.

He now applied himself diligently to complete the building of his brigantines, despatching men to Acla to bring the necessary stores and rigging across the mountains. While thus occupied, a rumour reached him that a new governor named Lope de Sosa was coming out from Spain to supersede Pedrarias. Vasco Nuñez was troubled at these tidings. A new governor would be likely to adopt new measures, or to have new favourites. He feared, therefore, that some order might come to suspend or embarrass his expedition; or that the command of it might be given to another. In his perplexity he held a consultation with several of his confidential officers.

After some debate, it was agreed among them that a trusty and intelligent person should be sent as a scout to Acla, under the pretence of procuring munitions for the ships. Should he find Pedrarias in quiet possession of the government, he was to account to him for the delay of the expedition; to request that the time allotted to it might be extended, and to request reinforcements and supplies. Should he find, however, that a new governor was actually arrived, he was to return immediately with the tidings. In such case it was resolved to put to sea before any contrary orders could arrive, trusting eventually to excuse themselves on the plea of zeal and good intentions.

Chapter XXVI

Reconnoitering expedition of Garabito—Stratagem of Pedrarias to entrap Vasco Nuñez

The person entrusted with the reconnoitering expedition to Acla was Andres Garabito, in whose fidelity and discretion Vasco Nuñez had implicit confidence. His confidence was destined to be fatally deceived. According to the assertions of contemporaries, this Garabito cherished a secret and vindictive enmity against his commander, arising from a simple but a natural cause. Vasco Nuñez had continued to have a fondness for the Indian damsel, daughter of the cacique Careta, whom he had received from her father as a pledge of amity. Some dispute arose concerning her on one occasion between him and Garabito, in the course of which he expressed himself in severe and galling language. Garabito was deeply mortified at some of his expressions, and, being of a malignant spirit, determined on a dastardly revenge. He wrote privately to Pedrarias, assuring him that Vasco Nuñez had no intention of solemnizing his marriage with his daughter, being completely under the influence of an Indian paramour; that he made use of the friendship of Pedrarias merely to further his own selfish views, intending, as soon as his ships were ready, to throw off an allegiance, and put to sea as an independent commander.

This mischievous letter Garabito had written immediately after the last departure of Vasco Nuñez from Acla. Its effects upon the proud and jealous spirit of the governor may easily be conceived. All his former suspicions were immediately revived. They acquired strength during a long interval that elapsed without tidings being received from the expedition. There were designing and prejudiced persons at hand, who perceived and quickened these jealous feelings of the governor. Among these was the Bachelor Corral, who cherished a deep grudge against Vasco Nuñez for having once thrown him into prison for his factious conduct; and Alonza de la Puente, the royal treasurer, whom Vasco Nuñez had affronted by demanding the repayment of a loan. Such was the tempest that was gradually gathering in the factious little colony of Darien.

The subsequent conduct of Garabito gives much confirmation to the charge of perfidy advanced against him. When he arrived at Acla he found that Pedrarias remained in possession of the government; for his intended successor had died in the very harbour. The conduct and conversation of Garabito was such as to arouse suspicions; he was arrested, and his papers and letters were sent to Pedrarias. When examined, he readily suffered himself to be wrought upon by threats of punishment and promises of pardon, and revealed all that he knew, and declared still more that he suspected and surmised, of the plans and intentions of Vasco Nuñez.

The arrest of Garabito, and the seizure of his letters, produced a great agitation at Darien. It was considered a revival of the ancient animosity between the governor and Vasco Nuñez, and the friends of the latter trembled for his safety.

Hernando de Arguello, especially, was in great alarm. He had embarked the most of his fortune in the expedition, and the failure of it would be ruinous to him. He wrote to Vasco Nuñez informing him of the critical posture of affairs, and urging him to put to sea without delay. He would be protected at all events, he said, by the Jeronimite Fathers at San Domingo, who were at that time all-powerful in the new world, and who regarded his expedition as calculated to promote the glory of God as well as the dominion of the king.* This letter fell into the hands of Pedrarias, and convinced him of the existence of a dangerous plot against his authority. He immediately ordered Arguello to be arrested; and now devised means to get Vasco Nuñez within his power. While the latter remained on the shores of the South Sea with his brigantines and his band of hearty and devoted followers, Pedrarias knew that it would be vain to attempt to take him by force. Dissembling his suspicions and intentions, therefore, he wrote to him in the most amicable terms, requesting him to repair immediately to Acla, as he wished to confer with him about the impending expedition. Fearing, however, that Vasco Nuñez might suspect his motives and refuse to comply, he at the same time ordered Francisco Pizarro to muster all the armed force he could collect, and to seek and arrest his late patron and commander wherever he might be found.

So great was the terror inspired by the arrest of Arguello, and by the general violence of Pedrarias, that, though Vasco Nuñez was a favourite with the great mass of the people, no one ventured to warn him of the danger that attended his return to Acla.

---

* In consequence of the eloquent representations made to the Spanish government by the venerable Las Casas, of the cruel wrongs and oppressions practised upon the Indians in the colonies, the Cardinal Ximenes, in 1516, sent out three Jeronimite Friars, chosen for their zeal and abilities, clothed with full powers to inquire into and remedy all abuses, and to take all proper measures for the good government, religious instruction, and effectual protection of the natives. The exercise of their powers at San Domingo made a great sensation in the new world, and, for a time, had a beneficial effect in checking the oppressive and licentious conduct of the colonists.

Chapter XXVII

Vasco Nuñez and the astrologer—His return to Acla

The old Spanish writers who have treated of the fortunes of Vasco Nuñez, record an anecdote which is worthy of being cited, as characteristic of the people and the age. Among the motley crowd of adventurers lured across the ocean by the reputed wealth and wonders of the New World, was an Italian astrologer, a native of Venice, named Micer Codro. At the time that Vasco Nuñez held supreme sway at Darien, this reader of the stars had cast his horoscope, and pretended to foretell his destiny. Pointing one night to a certain star, he assured him that in the year in which he should behold that star in a part of the heavens which he designated, his life would be in imminent jeopardy; but should he survive this year of peril, he would become the richest and most renowned captain throughout the Indies.

Several years, it is added, had elapsed since this prediction was made; yet, that it still dwelt in the mind of Vasco Nuñez, was evident from the following circumstance. While waiting the return of his messenger, Garabito, he was on the shore of Isla Rica one serene evening, in company with some of his officers, when, regarding the heavens, he beheld the fated star exactly in that part of the firmament which had been pointed out by the Italian astrologer. Turning to his companions, with a smile, "Behold," said he, "the wisdom of those who believe in soothsayers, and, above all, in such an astrologer as Micer Codro! According to his prophecy, I should now be in imminent peril of my life; yet, here I am, within reach of all my wishes; sound in health, with four brigantines and three hundred men at my command, and on the point of exploring this great Southern Ocean."

At this fated juncture, say the chroniclers, arrived the hypocritical letter from Pedrarias, inviting him to an interview at Acla! The discreet reader will decide for himself what credit to give to this anecdote, or rather, what allowance to make for the little traits of coincidence gratuitously added to the original fact by writers who delight in the marvellous. The tenor of this letter awakened no suspicion in the breast of Vasco Nuñez, who reposed entire confidence in the amity of the governor as his intended father-in-law, and appears to have been unconscious of any thing in his own conduct that could warrant hostility. Leaving his ships in command of Francisco Compañon, he departed immediately to meet the governor at Acla, unattended by any armed force.

The messengers who had brought the letter maintained at first a cautious silence as to the events which had transpired at Darien. They were gradually won, however, by the frank and genial manners of Vasco Nuñez, and grieved to see so gallant a soldier hurrying into the snare. Having crossed the mountains, and drawn near to Acla, their kind feelings got the better of their caution, and they revealed the true nature of their errand, and the hostile intentions of Pedrarias. Vasco Nuñez was struck with astonishment at the recital; but, being unconscious, it is said, of any evil intention, he could scarcely credit this sudden hostility in a man who had but recently promised him his daughter in marriage. He imagined the whole to be some groundless jealousy which his own appearance would dispel, and accordingly continued on his journey. He had not proceeded far, however, when he was met by a band of armed men, led by Francisco Pizarro. The latter stepped forward to arrest his ancient commander. Vasco Nuñez paused for a moment, and regarded him with a look of reproachful astonishment. "How is this, Francisco?" exclaimed he. "Is this the way you have been accustomed to receive me?" Offering no further remonstrance, he suffered himself quietly to be taken prisoner by his former adherent, and conducted in chains to Acla. Here he was thrown into prison, and Bartolome Hurtado, once his favourite officer, was sent to take command of his squadron.

Chapter XXVIII

Trial of Vasco Nuñez

Don Pedrarias concealed his exultation at the success of the stratagem by which he had ensnared his generous and confiding rival. He even visited him in prison, and pretended deep concern at being obliged to treat him with this temporary rigour, attributing it entirely to certain accusations lodged against him by the Treasurer Alonzo de la Puente, which his official situation compelled him to notice and investigate.

"Be not afflicted, however, my son!" said the hypocrite, "an investigation will, doubtless, not merely establish your innocence, but serve to render your zeal and loyalty towards your sovereign still more conspicuous."

While Pedrarias assumed this soothing tone towards his prisoner, he urged the Alcalde Mayor Espinosa to proceed against him with the utmost rigour of the law.

The charge brought against him of a treasonable conspiracy to cast off all allegiance to the crown, and to assume an independent sway on the borders of the Southern Sea, was principally supported by the confessions of Andres Garabito. The evidence is also cited of a soldier, who stood sentinel one night near the quarters of Vasco Nuñez on Isla Rica, and who, being driven to take shelter from the rain under the eaves of his house, overheard a conversation between that commander and certain of his officers, wherein they agreed to put to sea with the squadron on their own account, and to set the governor at defiance. This testimony, according to Las Casas, arose from a misconstruction on the part of the sentinel, who only heard a portion of their conversation, relating to their intention of sailing without waiting for orders, in case a new governor should arrive to supersede Pedrarias.

The governor in the meantime informed himself from day to day and hour to hour, of the progress of the trial, and, considering the evidence sufficiently strong to warrant his personal hostility, he now paid another visit to his prisoner, and, throwing off all affectation of kindness, upbraided him in the most passionate manner.

"Hitherto," said he, "I have treated you as a son, because I thought you loyal to your king, and to me as his representative, but as I find you have mediated rebellion against the crown of Castile, I cast you off from my affection, and shall henceforth treat you as an enemy."

Vasco Nuñez indignantly repelled the charge, and appealed to the confiding frankness of his conduct as a proof of his innocence. "Had I been conscious of my guilt," said he, "what could have induced me to come here and put myself into your hands? Had I meditated rebellion, what prevented me from carrying it into effect? I had four ships ready to weigh anchor, three hundred brave men at my command, and an open sea before me. What had I to do but to spread sail and press forward? There was no doubt of finding a land, whether rich or poor, sufficient for me and mine, far beyond the reach of your controul. In the innocence of my heart, however, I came here promptly, at your mere request, and my reward is slander, indignity and chains!"

The noble and ingenuous appeal of Vasco Nuñez had no effect on the prejudiced feelings of the governor: on the contrary, he was but the more exasperated against his prisoner, and ordered that his irons should be doubled.

The trial was now urged by him with increased eagerness. Lest the present accusation should not be sufficient to effect the ruin of his victim, the old inquest into his conduct as governor, which had remained suspended for many years, was revived, and he was charged anew with the wrongs inflicted on the Bachelor Enciso, and with the death of the unfortunate Nicuesa.

Notwithstanding all these charges the trial went on slowly, with frequent delays, for the Alcalde Mayor, Gaspar de Espinosa, seems to have had but little relish for the task assigned him, and to have needed frequent spurring from the eager and passionate governor. He probably considered the accused as technically guilty, though innocent of all intentional rebellion, but was ordered to decide according to the strict letter of the law. He therefore, at length, gave a reluctant verdict against Vasco Nuñez, but recommended him to mercy, on account of his great services, or entreated that, at least he might be permitted to appeal. "No!" said the unrelenting Pedrarias, "If he has merited death, let him suffer death!" He accordingly condemned him to be beheaded. The same sentence was passed upon several of his officers, who were implicated in his alleged conspiracy; among these was Hernando de Arguello, who had written the letter to Vasco Nuñez, informing him of the arrest of his messenger, and advising him to put to sea, without heeding the hostility of Pedrarias. As to the perfidious informer Garabito, he was pardoned and set at liberty.

In considering this case as far as we are enabled, from the imperfect testimony on record, we are inclined to think it one where passion and self-interest interfered with the pure administration of justice. Pedrarias had always considered Vasco Nuñez as a dangerous rival, and though his jealousy had been for some time lulled by looking on him as an intended son-in-law, it was revived by the suggestion that he intended to evade his alliance, and dispute his authority. His exasperated feelings hurried him too far to retreat, and, having loaded his prisoner with chains and indignities, his death became indispensable to his own security.

For our own part, we have little doubt, that it was the fixed intention of Vasco Nuñez, after he had only succeeded in the arduous undertaking of transporting his ships across the mountains, to suffer no capricious order from Pedrarias, or any other governor, to defeat the enterprise which he had so long meditated and for which he had so laboriously prepared. It is probable he may have expressed such general determination in the hearing of Garabito and of others of his companions. We can find ample excuse for such a resolution in his consciousness of his own deserts; his experience of past hindrances to his expedition, arising from the jealousy of others; his feeling of some degree of authority, from his office of Adelantado; and his knowledge of the favourable disposition and kind intentions of his sovereign towards him. We acquit him entirely of the senseless idea of rebelling against the crown; and suggest these considerations in palliation of any meditated disobedience of Pedrarias, should such a charge be supposed to have been substantiated.

Chapter XXIX

Execution of Vasco Nuñez (1517)

It was a day of gloom and horror at Acla, when Vasco Nuñez and his companions were led forth to execution. The populace were moved to tears at the unhappy fate of a man, whose gallant deeds had excited their admiration, and whose generous qualities had won their hearts. Most of them regarded him as the victim of a jealous tyrant; and even those who thought him guilty saw something brave and brilliant in the very crime imputed to him. Such, however, was the general dread inspired by the severe measures of Pedrarias, that no one dared lift up his voice, either in murmur or remonstrance.

The public crier walked before Vasco Nuñez, proclaiming, "This is the punishment inflicted by command of the king and his lieutenant, Don Pedrarias Davila, on this man, as a traitor and an usurper of the territories of the crown."

When Vasco Nuñez heard these words, he exclaimed, indignantly, "It is false! never did such a crime enter my mind. I have ever served my king with truth and loyalty, and sought to augment his dominions."

These words were of no avail in his extremity, but they were fully believed by the populace.

The execution took place in the public square of Acla; and we are assured by the historian, Oviedo, who was in the colony at the time, that the cruel Pedrarias was a secret witness of the bloody spectacle; which he contemplated from between the reeds of the wall of a house, about twelve paces from the scaffold!*

Vasco Nuñez was the first to suffer death. Having confessed himself and partaken of the sacrament, he ascended the scaffold with a firm step and a calm and manly demeanour; and, laying his head upon the block, it was severed in an instant from his body. Three of his officers,

---

* Oviedo, Hist. Ind. p. 2. cap. 9. MS.

Valderrabano, Botello, and Hernan Muños, were in like manner brought one by one to the block, and the day had nearly expired before the last of them was executed.

One victim still remained. It was Hernando de Arguello, who had been condemned as an accomplice, for having written the intercepted letter.

The populace could no longer restrain their feelings. They had not dared to intercede for Vasco Nuñez, knowing the implacable enmity of Pedrarias; but they now sought the governor, and, throwing themselves at his feet, entreated that this man might be spared, as he had taken no active part in the alleged treason. The day light, they said, was at an end, and it seemed as if God had hastened the night, to prevent the execution.

The stern heart of Pedrarias was not to be touched. "No," said he, "I would sooner die myself than spare one of them." The unfortunate Arguello was led to the block. The brief tropical twilight was past, and in the gathering gloom of the night the operations on the scaffold could not be distinguished. The multitude stood listening in breathless silence, until the stroke of the executioner told that all was accomplished. They then dispersed to their homes with hearts filled with grief and bitterness, and a night of lamentation succeeded to this day of horrors.

The vengeance of Pedrarias was not satisfied with the death of his victim; he confiscated his property and dishonoured his remains, causing his head to be placed upon a pole and exposed for several days in the public square.*

Thus perished, in his forty-second year, in the prime and vigour of his days and the full career of his glory, one of the most illustrious and deserving of the Spanish discoverers; a victim to the basest and most perfidious envy.

How vain are our most confident hopes, our brightest triumphs! When Vasco Nuñez from the mountains of Darien beheld the Southern Ocean revealed to his gaze, he considered its unknown realms at his disposal. When he had launched his ships upon its waters, and his sails were in a manner flapping in the wind, to bear him in quest of the wealthy empire of Peru, he scoffed at the prediction of the astrologer, and defied the influence of the stars. Behold him interrupted at the very moment of his departure, betrayed into the hands of his most invidious foe, the very enterprise that was to have crowned him with glory wrested into a crime, and himself hurried to a bloody and ignominious grave at the

* Oviedo, ubi sup.

foot, as it were, of the mountain from whence he had made his discovery! His fate, like that of his renowned predecessor, Columbus, proves that it is sometimes dangerous even to deserve too greatly.

THE FORTUNES
of
VALDIVIA AND HIS COMPANIONS

It was in the year 1512 that Valdivia, the Regidor of Darien, was sent to Hispaniola by Vasco Nuñez de Balboa for reinforcements and supplies for the colony. He set sail in a caravel, and pursued his voyage prosperously until he arrived in sight of the island of Jamaica. Here he was encountered by one of the violent hurricanes which sweep those latitudes, and driven on the shoals and sunken rocks called the Vipers, since infamous for many a shipwreck. His vessel soon went to pieces, and Valdivia and his crew, consisting of twenty men, escaped with difficulty in the boat, without having time to secure a supply either of water or provisions. Having no sails, and their oars being scarcely fit for use, they were driven about for thirteen days, at the mercy of the currents of those unknown seas. During this time their sufferings from hunger and thirst were indescribable. Seven of their number perished, and the rest were nearly famished when they were stranded on the eastern coast of Yucatan, in a province called Maya. Here they were set upon by the natives, who broke their boat in pieces, and carried them off captive to the cacique of the province, by whose orders they were mewed up in a kind of pen.

At first their situation appeared tolerable enough, considering the horrors from which they had escaped. They were closely confined, it is true, but they had plenty to eat and drink, and soon began to recover flesh and vigour. In a little while, however, their enjoyment of this good cheer met with a sudden check, for the unfortunate Valdivia, and four of his companions, were singled out by the cacique, on account of their improved condition, to be offered up to his idols. The natives of this coast in fact were cannibals, devouring the flesh of their enemies and of such strangers as fell into their hands. The wretched Valdivia and his fellow victims, therefore, were sacrificed in the bloody temple of the idol, and their limbs were afterwards served up at a grand feast held by the cacique and his subjects.

The horror of the survivors may be more readily imagined than described. Their hearts died within them when they heard the yells and howlings of the savages over their victims, and the still more horrible revelry of their cannibal orgies. They turned with loathing from the food set so abundantly before them, at the idea that it was but intended to fatten them for a future banquet.

Recovering from the first stupor of alarm, their despair lent them additional force. They succeeded in breaking in the night from the kind of cage in which they were confined, and fled to the depths of the forest. Here they wandered about forlorn, exposed to all the dangers and miseries of the wilderness; famishing with hunger, yet dreading to approach the haunts of men. At length their sufferings drove them forth from the woods into another part of the country, where they were again taken captive. The cacique of this province, however, was an enemy to the one from whom they had escaped, and of less cruel propensities. He spared their lives and contented himself with making them slaves, exacting from them the severest labour. They had to cut and draw wood, to procure water from a distance, and to carry enormous burthens. The cacique died soon after their capture, and was succeeded by another called Taxmar. He was a chief of some talent and sagacity, but he continued the same rigorous treatment of the captives. By degrees they sank beneath the hardships of their lot, until only two were left; one of them a sturdy sailor named Gonzalo Guerrero, the other a kind of clerical adventurer named Jeronimo de Aguilar. The sailor had the good luck to be transferred to the service of the cacique of the neighbouring province of Chatemal, by whom he was treated with kindness. Being a thorough son of the ocean, seasoned to all weathers, and ready for any chance or change, he soon accommodated himself to his new situation, followed the cacique to the wars, rose by his hardihood and prowess to be a distinguished warrior, and succeeded in gaining the heart and hand of an Indian princess.

The other survivor, Jeronimo de Aguilar, was of a different complexion. He was a native of Ecija, in Andalusia, and had been brought up to the church, and regularly ordained, and shortly afterwards had sailed in one of the expeditions to San Domingo, from whence he had passed to Darien.

He proceeded in a different mode from that adopted by his comrade, the sailor, in his dealings with the Indians, and in one more suited to his opposite calling. Instead of playing the hero among the men, and the gallant among the women, he recollected his priestly obligations to humility and chastity. Accordingly, he made himself a model of meekness and obedience to the cacique and his warriors, while he closed his eyes to the charms of the infidel women. Nay, in the latter respect, he reinforced his clerical vows by a solemn promise to God to resist all temptations of the flesh, so he might be delivered out of the hands of these Gentiles.

Such were the opposite measures of the sailor and the saint, and they appear to have been equally successful. Aguilar, by his meek obedience to every order, however arbitrary and capricious, gradually won the good will of the cacique and his family. Taxmar, however, subjected him to many trials before he admitted him to his entire confidence. One day when the Indians, painted and decorated in warlike style, were shooting at a mark, a warrior, who had for some time fixed his eyes on Aguilar, approached suddenly and seized him by the arm. "Thou seest," said he, "the certainty of these archers; if they aim at the eye, they hit the eye, if at the mouth, they hit the mouth—what wouldst thou think, if thou wert to be placed instead of the mark, and they were to shoot at and miss thee?"

Aguilar secretly trembled lest he should be the victim of some cruel caprice of the kind. Dissembling his fears, however, he replied with great submission, "I am your slave, and you may do with me as you please; but you are too wise to destroy a slave who is so useful and obedient." His answer pleased the cacique, who had secretly sent this warrior to try his humility.

Another trial of the worthy Jeronimo was less stern and fearful indeed, but equally perplexing. The cacique had remarked his unexampled discretion with respect to the sex, but doubted his sincerity. After laying many petty temptations in his way, which Jeronimo resisted with the self-denial of a saint, he at length determined to subject him to a fiery ordeal. He accordingly sent him on a fishing expedition accompanied by a buxom damsel of fourteen years of age: they were to pass the night by the sea-side, so as to be ready to fish at the first dawn of day, and were allowed but one hammock to sleep in. It was an embarrassing predicament—not apparently to the Indian beauty, but certainly to the scrupulous Jeronimo. He remembered, however, his double vow, and, suspending his hammock to two trees, resigned it to his companion, while, lighting a fire on the sea shore, he stretched himself before it on the sand. It was, as he acknowledged, a night of fearful trial, for his sandy couch was cold and cheerless, the hammock warm and tempting; and the infidel damsel had been instructed to assail him with all manner of blandishments and reproaches. His resolution, however, though often shaken, was never overcome; and the morning dawned upon him still faithful to his vow.

The fishing over, he returned to the residence of the cacique, where his companion, being closely questioned, made known the triumph of his self-denial before all the people. From that time forward he was held in great respect; the cacique especially treated him with unlimited confidence, entrusting to him the care, not merely of his house, but of his wives, during his occasional absence.

Aguilar now felt ambitious of rising to greater consequence among the savages, but this he knew was only to be done by deeds of arms. He had the example of the sturdy seaman, Gonzalo Guerrero, before his eyes, who had become a great captain in the province in which he resided. He entreated Taxmar therefore to entrust him with bow and arrows, buckler and war club, and to enroll him among his warriors. The cacique complied. Aguilar soon made himself expert at his new weapons, signalized himself repeatedly in battle, and, from his superior knowledge of the arts of war, rendered Taxmar such essential service, as to excite the jealousy of some of the neighbouring caciques. One of them remonstrated with Taxmar for employing a warrior who was of a different religion, and insisted that Aguilar should be sacrificed to their gods. "No," replied Taxmar, "I will not make so base a return for such signal services: surely the gods of Aguilar must be good, since they aid him so effectually in maintaining a just cause."

The cacique was so incensed at this reply that he assembled his warriors and marched to make war upon Taxmar. Many of the counsellors of the latter urged him to give up the stranger who was the cause of this hostility. Taxmar, however, rejected their council with disdain and prepared for battle. Aguilar assured him that his faith in the Christians' God would be rewarded with victory; he, in fact, concerted a plan of battle, which was adopted. Concealing himself, with a chosen band of warriors, among thickets and herbage, he suffered the enemy to pass by in making their attack. Taxmar and his host pretended to give way at the first onset. The foe rushed heedlessly in pursuit; whereupon Aguilar and his ambuscade assaulted them in the rear. Taxmar turned upon them in front; they were thrown in confusion, routed with great slaughter and many of their chiefs taken prisoners. This victory gave Taxmar the sway over the land, and strengthened Aguilar more than ever in his good graces.

Several years had elapsed in this manner, when intelligence was brought to the province of the arrival on the neighbouring coast of great vessels of wonderful construction, filled with white and bearded men, who fought with thunder and lightning. It was, in fact, the squadron of Francisco Hernandez de Cordova, then on a voyage of discovery. The tidings of this strange invasion spread consternation through the country, heightened, if we may credit the old Spanish writers, by a prophecy current among the savages of these parts, and uttered in former times by a priest named Chilam Cambal, who foretold that a white and bearded people would come from the region of the rising sun, who would overturn their idols and subjugate the land.

The heart of Jeronimo de Aguilar beat quick with hope when he heard of European ships at hand; he was distant from the coast, however, and perceived that he was too closely watched by the Indians to have any chance of escape. Dissembling his feelings, therefore, he affected to hear of the ships with perfect indifference, and to have no desire to join the strangers. The ships disappeared from the coast, and he remained disconsolate at heart, but was regarded with increased confidence by the natives.

His hopes were again revived in the course of a year or two by the arrival on the coast of other ships, which were those commanded by Juan de Grijalva, who coasted Yucatan in 1518; Aguilar, however, was again prevented by the jealous watchfulness of the Indians from attempting his escape, and when this squadron left the coast he considered all chance of deliverance at an end.

Seven years had gone by since his capture, and he had given up all hopes of being restored to his country and friends, when, in 1519, there arrived one day at the village three Indians, natives of the small island of Cozumel, which lies a few leagues in the sea, opposite the eastern coast of Yucatan. They brought tidings of another visit of white and bearded men to their shores, and one of them delivered a letter to Aguilar, which, being entirely naked, he had concealed in the long tresses of his hair which were bound round his head.

Aguilar received the letter with wonder and delight, and read it in presence of the cacique and his warriors. It proved to be from Hernando Cortez, who was at that time on his great expedition, which ended in the conquest of Mexico. He had been obliged by stress of weather to anchor at the island of Cozumel, where he learned from the natives that several white men were detained in captivity among the Indians on the neighbouring coast of Yucatan. Finding it impossible to approach the main land with his ships, he prevailed upon three of the islanders, by means of gifts and promises, to venture upon an embassy among their cannibal neighbours, and to convey a letter to the captive white men. Two of the smallest caravels of the squadron were sent under the command of Diego de Ordas, who was ordered to land the three messengers at the point of Cotoche, and to wait there eight days for their return.

The letter brought by these envoys informed the Christian captives of the force and destination of the squadron of Cortez, and of his having sent the caravels to wait for them at the point of Cotoche, with a ransom for their deliverance, inviting them to hasten and join him at Cozumel.

The transport of Aguilar on first reading the letter, was moderated when he reflected on the obstacles that might prevent him from profiting by this chance of deliverance. He had made himself too useful to the cacique to hope that he would readily give him his liberty, and he knew the jealous and irritable nature of the savages too well not to fear that even an application for leave to depart might draw upon him the severest treatment. He endeavoured, therefore, to operate upon the cacique through his apprehensions. To this end he informed him that the piece of paper which he held in his hand brought him a full account of the mighty armament that had arrived on the coast. He described the number of the ships and various particulars concerning the squadron, all which were amply corroborated by the testimony of the messengers. The cacique and his warriors were astonished at this strange mode of conveying intelligence from a distance, and regarded the letter as something mysterious and supernatural. Aguilar went on to relate the tremendous and superhuman powers of the people in these ships, who, armed with thunder and lightning, wreaked destruction on all who displeased them, while they dispensed inestimable gifts and benefits on such as proved themselves their friends. He, at the same time, spread before the cacique various presents brought by the messengers, as specimens of the blessings to be expected from the friendship of the strangers. The intimation was effectual. The cacique was filled with awe at the recital of the terrific powers of the white men, and his eyes were dazzled by the glittering trinkets displayed before him. He entreated Aguilar, therefore, to act as his ambassador and mediator, and to secure him the amity of the strangers.

Aguilar saw with transport the prospect of a speedy deliverance. In this moment of exultation, he bethought himself of the only surviving comrade of his past fortunes, Gonzalo Guerrero, and, sending the letter of Cortez to him, invited him to accompany him in his escape. The sturdy seaman was at this time a great chieftain in his province, and his Indian bride had borne him a numerous progeny. His heart, however, yearned after his native country, and he might have been tempted to leave his honours and dignities, his infidel wife and half savage offspring behind him, but an insuperable, though somewhat ludicrous, obstacle presented itself to his wishes. Having long since given over all expectation of a return to civilized life, he had conformed to the customs of the country, and had adopted the external signs and decorations that marked him as a warrior and a man of rank. His face and hands were indelibly painted or tattooed; his ears and lips were slit to admit huge Indian ornaments, and his nose was drawn down almost to his mouth by a massy ring of gold, and a dangling jewel.

Thus curiously garbled and disfigured, the honest seaman felt, that, however he might be admired in Yucatan, he should be apt to have a hooting rabble at his heels in Spain. He made up his mind, therefore, to remain a great man among the savages, rather than run the risk of being shown as a man monster at home.

Finding that he declined accompanying him, Jeronimo de Aguilar set off for the point of Cotoche, escorted by three Indians. The time he had lost in waiting for Guerrero had nearly proved fatal to his hopes, for when he arrived at the point, the caravels sent by Cortez had departed, though several crosses of reeds set up in different places gave tokens of the recent presence of Christians.

The only hope that remained was, that the squadron of Cortez might yet linger at the opposite island of Cozumel; but how was he to get there? While wandering disconsolately along the shore, he found a canoe, half buried in sand and water, and with one side in a state of decay; with the assistance of the Indians he cleaned it, and set it afloat, and on looking further he found the stave of a hogshead which might serve for a paddle. It was a frail embarkation in which to cross an arm of the sea, several leagues wide, but there was no alternative. Prevailing on the Indians to accompany him, he launched forth in the canoe and coasted the main land until he came to the narrowest part of the strait, where it was but four leagues across; here he stood directly for Cozumel, contending, as well as he was able, with a strong current, and at length succeeded in reaching the island.

He had scarce landed when a party of Spaniards, who had been lying in wait, rushed forth from their concealment, sword in hand. The three Indians would have fled, but Aguilar reassured them, and, calling out to the Spaniards in their own language, assured them that he was a Christian. Then, throwing himself on his knees, and raising his eyes streaming with tears to heaven, he gave thanks to God for having restored him to his countrymen.

The Spaniards gazed at him with astonishment: from his language he was evidently a Castilian, but to all appearance he was an Indian. He was perfectly naked; wore his hair braided round his head in the manner of the country, and his complexion was burnt by the sun to a tawny colour. He had a bow in his hand, a quiver at his shoulder, and a net-work pouch at his side in which he carried his provisions.

The Spaniards proved to be a reconnoitering party, sent out by Cortez to watch the approach of the canoe, which had been descried coming from Yucatan. Cortez had given up all hopes of being joined by the captives, the caravel having waited the allotted time at Cotoche, and returned without news of them. He had in fact made sail to prosecute his voyage, but fortunately one of his ships sprung a leak, which had obliged him to return to the island.

When Jeronimo de Aguilar and his companions arrived in presence of Cortez, who was surrounded by his officers, they made a profound reverence, squatted on the ground, laid their bows and arrows beside them, and touching their right hands, wet with spittle on the ground, rubbed them about the region of the heart, such being their sign of the most devoted submission.

Cortez greeted Aguilar with a hearty welcome, and raising him from the earth, took from his own person a large yellow mantle lined with crimson, and threw it over his shoulders. The latter, however, had for so long a time gone entirely naked, that even this scanty covering was at first almost insupportable, and he had become so accustomed to the diet of the natives, that he found it difficult to reconcile his stomach to the meat and drink set before him.

When he had sufficiently recovered from the agitation of his arrival among Christians, Cortez drew from him the particulars of his story, and found that he was related to one of his own friends, the licentiate Marcos de Aguilar. He treated him, therefore, with additional kindness and respect, and retained him about his person to aid him as an interpreter in his great Mexican expedition.

The happiness of Jeronimo de Aguilar at once more being restored to his countrymen, was doomed to suffer some alloy from the disasters that had happened in his family. Peter Martyr records a touching anecdote of the effect produced upon his mother by the tidings of his misfortune. A vague report reached her in Spain, that her son had fallen into the hands of cannibals. All the horrible tales concerning the treatment of these savages to their prisoners rushed to her imagination, and she went distracted. Whenever she beheld roasted meat, or flesh upon the spit, she would fill the house with her outcries. "Oh, wretched mother! oh, most miserable of women!" would she exclaim; "behold the limbs of my murdered son!"*

It is to be hoped that the tidings of his deliverance had a favourable effect upon her intellects, and that she lived to rejoice at his after fortunes. He served Hernando Cortez with great courage and ability

---

* P. Martyr, decad. iv. cap. 6.

throughout his Mexican conquests, acting sometimes as a soldier, sometimes as interpreter and ambassador to the Indians, and in reward of
his fidelity, and services, was appointed regidor, or civil governor of
the city of Mexico.

MICER CODRO, THE ASTROLOGER

The fate of the Italian astrologer, Micer Codro, who predicted the end of Vasco Nuñez, is related by the historian Oviedo, with some particulars that border upon the marvellous. It appears that, after the death of his patron, he continued for several years rambling about the New World, in the train of the Spanish discoverers; but intent upon studying the secrets of its natural history, rather than searching after its treasures.

In the course of his wanderings he was once coasting the shores of the Southern Ocean, in a ship commanded by one Geronimo de Valenzuela, from whom he received such cruel treatment as to cause his death, though, what the nature of the treatment was, we are not precisely informed.

Finding his end approaching, the unfortunate astrologer addressed Valenzuela in the most solemn manner: "Captain," said he, "you have caused my death by your cruelty; I now summon you to appear with me, within a year, before the Judgment Seat of God!"

The captain made a light and scoffing answer, and treated his summons with contempt.

They were then off the coast of Veragua, near the verdant islands of Zebaco, which lie at the entrance of the Gulf of Parita or Paria. The poor astrologer gazed wistfully with his dying eyes upon the green and shady groves, and entreated the pilot or mate of the caravel to land him on one of the islands, that he might die in peace. "Micer Codro," replied the pilot, "those are not islands, but points of land: there are no islands hereabout."

"There are, indeed," replied the astrologer, "two good and pleasant islands, well watered, and near to the coast, and within them is a great bay with a harbour. Land me, I pray you, upon one of these islands, that I may have comfort in my dying hour."

The pilot, whose rough nature had been touched with pity for the condition of the unfortunate astrologer, listened to his prayer, and conveyed him to the shore, where he found the opinion he had given of the character of the coast to be correct. He laid him on the herbage in the shade, where the poor wanderer soon expired. The pilot then dug a grave at the foot of a tree, where he buried him with all possible decency, and carved a cross on the bark to mark the grave.

Some time afterwards, Oviedo, the historian, was on the island with this very pilot, who showed him the cross on the tree, and gave his honest testimony to the good character and worthy conduct of Micer Codro. Oviedo, as he regarded the nameless grave, passed the eulogium of a scholar upon the poor astrologer: "He died," says he, "like Pliny, in the discharge of his duties, travelling about the world to explore the secrets of nature." According to his account, the prediction of Micer Codro held good with respect to Valenzuela, as it had in the case of Vasco Nuñez.—The captain died within the term in which he had summoned him to appear before the tribunal of God!*

* Vide Oviedo, Hist. Gen. lib. xxxix. cap. 2.

JUAN PONCE DE LEON,
Conqueror of Porto Rico, and
Discoverer of Florida

Chapter I

Reconnoitering expedition of Juan Ponce de Leon to the island of Boriquen (1508)

Many years had elapsed since the discovery and colonization of Hayti, yet its neighbouring island of Boriquen, or as the Spaniards called it, St. Juan (since named Porto Rico), remained unexplored. It was beautiful to the eye as beheld from the sea, having lofty mountains clothed with forest trees of prodigious size and magnificent foliage. There were broad fertile valleys also, always fresh and green; for the frequent showers and abundant streams in these latitudes, and the absence of all wintry frosts, produce a perpetual verdure. Various ships had occasionally touched at the island, but their crews had never penetrated into the interior. It was evident, however, from the number of hamlets and scattered houses, and the smoke rising in all directions from among the trees, that it was well peopled. The inhabitants still continued to enjoy their life of indolence and freedom, unmolested by the ills that overwhelmed the neighbouring island of Hayti. The time had arrived, however, when they were to share the common lot of their fellow savages, and to sink beneath the yoke of the white man.

At the time when Nicholas de Ovando, Governor of Hispaniola, undertook to lay waste the great province of Higuey, which lay at the eastern end of Hayti, he sent as commander of part of the troops a veteran soldier, named Juan Ponce de Leon. He was a native of Leon in Spain, and in his boyhood had been page to Pedro Nuñez de Guzman, Señor of Toral.* From an early age he had been schooled to war, and had served in the various campaigns against the Moors of Granada. He accompanied Columbus in his second voyage in 1493, and was afterwards, it is said, one of the partizans of Francisco Roldan, in his rebellion against the admiral. Having distinguished himself in various battles with the Indians, and acquired a name for sagacity as well as valour,

---

* Incas, Garcilaso de la Vega, Hist. Florida, tom. iv. cap. 37.

he received a command subordinate to Juan de Esquibel in the campaign against Higuey, and seconded his chief so valiantly in that sanguinary expedition, that, after the subjugation of the province, he was appointed to the command of it, as lieutenant of the Governor of Hispaniola.

Juan Ponce de Leon had all the impatience of quiet life and the passion for exploit of a veteran campaigner. He had not been long in the tranquil command of his province of Higuey, before he began to cast a wistful eye towards the green mountains of Boriquen. They were directly opposite, and but twelve or fourteen leagues distant, so as to be distinctly seen in the transparent atmosphere of the tropics. The Indians of the two islands frequently visited each other, and in this way Juan Ponce received the usual intelligence, that the mountains he had eyed so wistfully abounded with gold. He readily obtained permission from Governor Ovando to make an expedition to this island, and embarked in the year 1508 in a caravel with a few Spaniards and several Indian interpreters and guides.

After an easy voyage, he landed on the woody shores of the island, near to the residence of the principal cacique, Agueybanà. He found the chieftain seated in patriarchal style, under the shade of his native groves, and surrounded by his family, consisting of his mother, stepfather, brother and sister, who vied with each other in paying homage to the strangers. Juan Ponce, in fact, was received into the bosom of the family, and the cacique exchanged names with him, which is the Indian pledge of perpetual amity. Juan Ponce also gave Christian names to the mother and step-father of the cacique, and would fain have baptized them, but they declined the ceremony, though they always took a pride in the names thus given them.

In his zeal to gratify his guests, the cacique took them to various parts of the island. They found the interior to correspond with the external appearance. It was wild and mountainous, but magnificently wooded, with deep rich valleys fertilized by limpid streams. Juan Ponce requested the cacique to reveal to him the riches of the island. The simple Indian showed him his most productive fields of Yuca, groves laden with delicious fruit, the sweetest and purest fountains, and the coolest runs of water.

Ponce de Leon heeded but little these real blessings, and demanded whether the island produced no gold. Upon this the cacique conducted him to two rivers, the Manatuabon and the Zebuco, where the very pebbles seemed richly veined with gold, and large grains shone among the sand through the limpid water. Some of the largest of these were gathered by the Indians and given to the Spaniards. The quantity thus procured confirmed the hopes of Juan Ponce; and leaving several of his companions in the house of the hospitable cacique, he returned to Hayti to report the success of his expedition. He presented the specimens of gold to the Governor Ovando, who assayed them in a crucible. The ore was not so fine as that of Hispaniola, but, as it was supposed to exist in greater quantities, the governor determined on the subjugation of the island, and confided the enterprize to Juan Ponce de Leon.

Chapter II

Juan Ponce aspires to the government of Porto Rico (1509)

The natives of Boriquen were more warlike than those of Hispaniola; being accustomed to the use of arms from the necessity of repelling the frequent invasions of the Caribs. It was supposed, therefore, that the conquest of their island would be attended with some difficulty, and Juan Ponce de Leon made another, and as it were, a preparatory visit, to make himself acquainted with the country, and with the nature and resources of the inhabitants. He found the companions whom he had left there on his former visit, in good health and spirits, and full of gratitude towards the cacique Agueybanà, who had treated them with undiminished hospitality. There appeared to be no need of violence to win the island from such simple-hearted and confiding people. Juan Ponce flattered himself with the hopes of being appointed to its government by Ovando, and of bringing it peaceably into subjection. After remaining some time on the island, he returned to San Domingo to seek the desired appointment, but to his surprise, found the whole face of affairs had changed during his absence.

His patron, the governor Ovando, had been recalled to Spain, and Don Diego Columbus, son of the renowned discoverer, appointed in his place to the command at San Domingo. To add to the perplexities of Juan Ponce, a cavalier had already arrived from Spain, empowered by the king to form a settlement and build a fortress on the island of Porto Rico. His name was Christoval de Sotomayor; he was brother to the Count of Camina, and had been secretary to Philip I, surnamed the Handsome, king of Castile and father of Charles V.

Don Diego Columbus was highly displeased with the act of the king in granting these powers to Sotomayor, as it had been done without his knowledge and consent, and of course in disregard of his prerogative, as viceroy, to be consulted as to all appointments made within his jurisdiction. He refused, therefore, to put Sotomayor in possession of the island. He paid as little respect to the claims of Juan Ponce de Leon, whom he regarded with an ungracious eye as a favourite of his predecessor Ovando. To settle the matter effectually, he exerted what he considered his official and hereditary privilege, and chose officers to suit himself, appointing one Juan Ceron to the government of Porto Rico, and Miguel Diaz to serve as his lieutenant.*

Juan Ponce de Leon and his rival candidate, Christoval de Sotomayor, bore their disappointment with a good grace. Though the command was denied them, they still hoped to improve their fortunes in the island, and accordingly joined the crowd of adventurers that accompanied the newly appointed governor.

New changes soon took place in consequence of the jealousies and misunderstandings between King Ferdinand and the admiral as to points of privilege. The former still seemed disposed to maintain the right of making appointments without consulting Don Diego, and exerted it in the present instance; for, when Ovando, on his return to Spain, made favourable representation of the merits of Juan Ponce de Leon, and set forth his services in exploring Porto Rico, the king appointed him governor of that island, and signified specifically that Don Diego Columbus should not presume to displace him.

Chapter III

Juan Ponce rules with a strong hand—Exasperation of the Indians— Their experiment to prove whether the Spaniards were mortal

Juan Ponce de Leon assumed the command of the island of Boriquen in the year 1509. Being a fiery high-handed old soldier, his first step was to quarrel with Juan Ceron and Miguel Diaz, the ex-governor and his lieutenant, and to send them prisoners to Spain.†

* If the reader has perused the history of Columbus, he may remember the romantic adventure of this Miguel Diaz with a female cacique, which led to the discovery of the gold mines of Hayna, and the founding of the city of San Domingo.

† Herrera, decad. 1. lib. vii. cap. 13.

He was far more favourable to his late competitor, Christoval de Sotomayor. Finding him to be a cavalier of noble blood and high connexions, yet void of pretension, and of most accommodating temper, he offered to make him his lieutenant, and to give him the post of alcalde mayor, an offer which was very thankfully accepted.

The pride of rank, however, which follows a man even into the wilderness, soon interfered with the quiet of Sotomayor; he was ridiculed for descending so much below his birth and dignity, as to accept a subaltern situation to a simple gentleman in the island which he had originally aspired to govern. He could not withstand these sneers, but resigned his appointment, and remained in the island as a private individual; establishing himself in a village where he had a large repartimiento or allotment of Indians assigned to him by a grant from the king.

Juan Ponce fixed his seat of government in a town called Caparra, which he founded on the northern side of the island, about a league from the sea, in a neighbourhood supposed to abound in gold. It was in front of the port called Rico, which subsequently gave its name to the island. The road to the town was up a mountain, through a dense forest, and so rugged and miry that it was the bane of man and beast. It cost more to convey provisions and merchandize up this league of mountain, than it did to bring them from Spain.

Juan Ponce, being firmly seated in his government, began to carve and portion out the island, to found towns, and distribute the natives into repartimientos, for the purpose of exacting their labour.

The poor Indians soon found the difference between the Spaniards as guests, and the Spaniards as masters. They were driven to despair by the heavy tasks imposed upon them; for to their free spirits and indolent habits, restraint and labour were worse than death. Many of the most hardy and daring proposed a general insurrection, and a massacre of their oppressors; the great mass, however, were deterred by the belief that the Spaniards were supernatural beings and could not be killed.

A shrewd and sceptical cacique, named Brayoan, determined to put their immortality to the test. Hearing that a young Spaniard named Salzedo, was passing through his lands, he sent a party of his subjects to escort him, giving them secret instructions how they were to act. On coming to a river they took Salzedo on their shoulders to carry him across, but, when in the midst of the stream, they let him fall, and, throwing themselves upon him, pressed him under water until he was drowned. Then dragging his body to the shore, and still doubting his being dead, they wept and howled over him, making a thousand apologies for having fallen upon him, and kept him so long beneath the surface.

The cacique Brayoan came to examine the body and pronounced it lifeless; but the Indians, still fearing it might possess lurking immortality and ultimately revive, kept watch over it for three days, until it showed incontestable signs of putrefaction.

Being now convinced that the strangers were mortal men like themselves, they readily entered into a general conspiracy to destroy them.*

Chapter IV

Conspiracy of the caciques—Fate of Sotomayor

The prime mover of the conspiracy among the natives was Agueybanà, brother and successor to the hospitable cacique of the same name, who had first welcomed the Spaniards to the island, and who had fortunately closed his eyes in peace, before his native groves were made the scenes of violence and oppression. The present cacique had fallen within the repartimiento of Don Christoval de Sotomayor, and, though treated by that cavalier with kindness, could never reconcile his proud spirit to the yoke of vassalage.

Agueybanà held secret councils with his confederate caciques, in which they concerted a plan of operations. As the Spaniards were scattered about in different places, it was agreed that, at a certain time, each cacique should despatch those within his province. In arranging the massacre of those within his own domains, Agueybanà assigned to one of his inferior caciques the task of surprising the village of Sotomayor, giving him 3000 warriors for the purpose. He was to assail the village in the dead of the night, to set fire to the houses, and to slaughter all the inhabitants. He proudly, however, reserved to himself the honour of killing Don Christoval with his own hand.

Don Christoval had an unsuspected friend in the very midst of his enemies. Being a cavalier of gallant appearance and amiable and courteous manners, he had won the affections of an Indian princess, the sister of the cacique Agueybanà. She had overheard enough of the war council of her brother and his warriors to learn that Sotomayor was in

* Herrera, decad. 1. lib. viii. cap. 13.

danger. The life of her lover was more precious in her eyes than the safety of her brother and her tribe; hastening, therefore, to him, she told him all that she knew or feared, and warned him to be upon his guard. Sotomayor appears to have been of the most easy and incautious nature, void of all evil and deceit himself, and slow to suspect any thing of the kind in others. He considered the apprehension of the princess, as dictated by her fond anxiety, and neglected to profit by her warning.

He received, however, about the same time, information from a different quarter, tending to the same point. A Spaniard, versed in the language and customs of the natives, had observed a number gathering together one evening, painted and decorated, as if for battle. Suspecting some lurking mischief, he stripped and painted himself in their manner, and, favoured by the obscurity of the night, succeeded in mingling among them undiscovered. They were assembled round a fire performing one of their mystic war dances, to the chaunt of an areyto or legendary ballad. The strophes and responses treated of revenge and slaughter, and repeatedly mentioned the death of Sotomayor.

The Spaniard withdrew unperceived, and hastened to apprize Don Christoval of his danger. The latter still made light of these repeated warnings; revolving them, however, in his mind in the stillness of the night, he began to feel some uneasiness, and determined to repair in the morning to Juan Ponce de Leon, in his strong hold at Caparra. With his fated heedlessness, or temerity, however, he applied to Agueybanà for Indians to carry his baggage, and departed slightly armed, and accompanied by but three Spaniards, although he had to pass through close and lonely forests, where he would be at the mercy of any treacherous or lurking foe.

The cacique watched the departure of his intended victim, and set out shortly afterwards, dogging his steps at a distance through the forest, accompanied by a few chosen warriors. Agueybanà and his party had not proceeded far when they met a Spaniard named Juan Gonzalez, who spoke the Indian language. They immediately assailed him and wounded him in several places. He threw himself at the feet of the cacique, imploring his life in the most abject terms. The chief spared him for the moment, being eager to make sure of Don Christoval. He overtook that incautious cavalier in the very heart of the woodland, and stealing silently upon him burst forth suddenly with his warriors from the covert of the thickets, giving the fatal war whoop. Before Sotomayor could put himself upon his guard a blow from the war club of the cacique felled him to the earth, when he was quickly despatched by repeated blows. The four Spaniards who accompanied him shared his fate, being assailed, not merely by the warriors who had come in pursuit of them, but by their own Indian guides.

When Agueybanà had glutted his vengeance on this unfortunate cavalier, he returned in quest of Juan Gonzalez. The latter, however, had recovered sufficiently from his wounds to leave the place where he had been assailed, and dreading the return of the savages, had climbed into a tree and concealed himself among the branches. From thence, with trembling anxiety, he watched his pursuers as they searched all the surrounding forest for him. Fortunately they did not think of looking up into the trees, but, after beating the bushes for some time, gave up the search. Though he saw them depart, yet he did not venture from his concealment until the night had closed; he then descended from the tree, and made the best of his way to the residence of certain Spaniards, where his wounds were dressed. When this was done, he waited not to take repose, but repaired by a circuitous route to Caparra, and informed Juan Ponce de Leon of the danger he supposed to be still impending over Sotomayor, for he knew not that the enemy had accomplished his death. Juan Ponce immediately sent out forty men to his relief. They came to the scene of massacre, where they found the body of the unfortunate cavalier, partly buried, but with the feet out of the earth.

In the meantime the savages had accomplished the destruction of the village of Sotomayor. They approached it unperceived, through the surrounding forest, and entering it in the dead of the night, set fire to the straw-thatched houses, and attacked the Spaniards as they endeavoured to escape from the flames.

Several were slain at the onset, but a brave Spaniard, named Diego de Salazar, rallied his countrymen, inspirited them to beat off the enemy, and succeeded in conducting the greater part of them, though sorely mangled and harassed, to the strong hold of the Governor at Caparra. Scarcely had these fugitives gained the fortress, when others came hurrying in from all quarters, bringing similar tales of conflagration and massacre. For once a general insurrection, so often planned in savage life, against the domination of the white men, was crowned with success. All the villages founded by the Spaniards had been surprised, about a hundred of their inhabitants destroyed, and the survivors driven to take refuge in a beleaguered fortress.

Chapter V

War of Juan Ponce with the cacique Agueybanà

Juan Ponce de Leon might now almost be considered a governor without territories and a general without soldiers. His villages were smoking ruins, and his whole force did not amount to a hundred men, several of whom were disabled by their wounds. He had an able and implacable foe in Agueybanà, who took the lead of all the other caciques, and even sent envoys to the Caribs of the neighbouring islands, entreating them to forget all ancient animosities and to make common cause against these strangers—the deadly enemies of the whole Indian race. In the meantime the whole of this wild island was in rebellion, and the forests around the fortress of Caparra rang with the whoops and yells of the savages, the blasts of their war conchs, and the stormy roaring of their drums.

Juan Ponce was a staunch and wary old soldier, and not easily daunted. He remained grimly ensconced within his fortress, from whence he despatched messengers in all haste to Hispaniola, imploring immediate assistance. In the meantime, he tasked his wits to divert the enemy and keep them at bay. He divided his little force into three bodies of about thirty men each, under the command of Diego Salazar, Miguel de Toro, and Luis de Anasco, and sent them out alternately to make sudden surprises and assaults, to form ambuscades, and to practise the other stratagems of partizan warfare, which he had learnt in early life, in his campaigns against the Moors of Granada.

One of his most efficient warriors was a dog named Berezillo, renowned for courage, strength and sagacity. It is said that he could distinguish those of the Indians who were allies, from those who were enemies of the Spaniards. To the former he was docile and friendly, to the latter fierce and implacable. He was the terror of the natives, who were unaccustomed to powerful and ferocious animals, and did more service in this wild warfare, than could have been rendered by several soldiers. His prowess was so highly appreciated that his master received for him the pay, allowance and share of booty, assigned to a cross-bow man, which was the highest stipend given.*

---

* This famous dog was killed some years afterwards by a poisoned arrow, as he was swimming in the sea in pursuit of a Carib Indian. He left, however, a numerous progeny and a great name behind him; and his merits and exploits were long a favourite theme among the Spanish colonists. He was father to the renowned Leoncico, the faithful dog of Vasco Nuñez, which resembled him in looks and equalled him in prowess.

At length the stout old cavalier Juan Ponce was reinforced in his strong hold, by troops from Hispaniola, whereupon he sallied forth boldly to take revenge upon those who had thus held him in a kind of durance. His foe Agueybanà was at that time encamped in his own territories with more than five thousand warriors, but in a negligent unwatchful state, for he knew nothing of the reinforcements of the Spaniards, and supposed Juan Ponce shut up with his handful of men in Caparra. The old soldier, therefore, took him completely by surprise, and routed him with great slaughter. Indeed it is said the Indians were struck with a kind of panic when they saw the Spaniards as numerous as ever, notwithstanding the number they had massacred. Their belief in their immortality revived, they fancied that those whom they had slain had returned to life, and they despaired of victory over beings who could thus arise with renovated vigour from the grave.

Various petty actions and skirmishes afterwards took place, in which the Indians were defeated. Agueybanà, however, disdained this petty warfare, and stirred up his countrymen to assemble their forces, and by one grand assault to decide the fate of themselves and their island. Juan Ponce received secret tidings of their intent, and of the place where they were assembling. He had at that time barely eighty men at his disposal, but then they were cased in steel and proof against the weapons of the savages. Without stopping to reflect, the high mettled old cavalier put himself at their head, and led them through the forest in quest of the foe.

It was nearly sunset when he came in sight of the Indian camp, and the multitude of warriors assembled there made him pause, and almost repent of his temerity. He was as shrewd, however, as he was hardy and resolute. Ordering some of his men in the advance to skirmish with the enemy, he hastily threw up a slight fortification with the assistance of the rest. When it was finished he withdrew his forces into it, and ordered them to keep merely on the defensive. The Indians made repeated attacks but were as often repulsed with loss. Some of the Spaniards, impatient of this covert warfare, would sally forth in open field with pike and cross bow, but were called back within the fortification by their wary commander.

The cacique Agueybanà was enraged at finding his host of warriors thus baffled and kept at bay by a mere handful of Spaniards. He beheld the night closing in, and feared that in the darkness the enemy would escape. Summoning his choicest warriors round him, therefore, he led the way in a general assault, when, as he approached the fortress, he received a mortal wound from an arquebus, and fell dead upon the spot.

The Spaniards were not aware at first of the importance of the chief whom they had slain. They soon surmised it, however, from the confusion that ensued among the enemy, who bore off the body with great lamentations, and made no further attack.

The wary Juan Ponce took advantage of the evident distress of the foe, to draw off his small forces in the night, happy to get out of the terrible jeopardy into which a rash confidence had betrayed him. Some of his fiery spirited officers would have kept the field in spite of the overwhelming force of the enemy. "No, no," said the shrewd veteran; "it is better to protract the war than to risk all upon a single battle."

While Juan Ponce de Leon was fighting hard to maintain his sway over the island, his transient dignity was overturned by another power, against which the prowess of the old soldier was of no avail. King Ferdinand had repented of the step he had ill advisedly taken, in superseding the governor and lieutenant governor appointed by Don Diego Columbus. He became convinced, though rather tardily, that it was an infringement of the rights of the admiral, and that policy, as well as justice, required him to retract it. When Juan Ceron and Miguel Diaz, therefore, came prisoners to Spain, he received them graciously, conferred many favours on them to atone for their rough ejectment from office, and finally, after some time, sent them back, empowered to resume the command of the island. They were ordered, however, on no account to manifest rancour or ill will against Juan Ponce de Leon, or to interfere with any property he might hold, either in houses, lands, or Indians; but on the contrary, to cultivate the most friendly understanding with him. The king also wrote to the hardy veteran explaining to him, that this restitution of Ceron and Diaz had been determined upon in council, as a mere act of justice due to them, but was not intended as a censure upon his conduct, and that means should be sought to indemnify him for the loss of his command.

By the time the governor and his lieutenant reached the island, Juan Ponce had completed its subjugation. The death of the island champion, the brave Agueybanà, had in fact been a death-blow to the natives, and shows how much, in savage warfare, depends upon a single chieftain. They never made head of war afterwards; but, dispersing among their forests and mountains, fell gradually under the power of the Spaniards. Their subsequent fate was like that of their neighbours of Hayti. They were employed in the labour of the mines, and in other rude toils so repugnant to their nature that they sank beneath them, and, in a little while, almost all the aboriginals disappeared from the island.

Chapter VI

Juan Ponce de Leon hears of a wonderful country and miraculous fountain

Juan Ponce de Leon resigned the command of Porto Rico with tolerable grace. The loss of one wild island and wild government was of little moment, when there was a new world to be shared out, where a bold soldier like himself, with sword and buckler, might readily carve out new fortunes for himself. Besides, he had now amassed wealth to assist him in his plans, and, like many of the early discoverers, his brain was teeming with the most romantic enterprises. He had conceived the idea that there was yet a third world to be discovered, and he hoped to be the first to reach its shores, and thus secure a renown equal to that of Columbus.

While cogitating these things, and considering which way he should strike forth in the unexplored regions around him, he met with some old Indians, who gave him tidings of a country which promised, not merely to satisfy the cravings of his ambition, but to realize the fondest dreams of the poets. They assured him that, far to the north, there existed a land abounding in gold and in all manner of delights; but, above all, possessing a river of such wonderful virtue, that whoever bathed in it would be restored to youth! They added, that in times past, before the arrival of the Spaniards, a large party of the natives of Cuba had departed northward in search of this happy land and this river of life, and, having never returned, it was concluded that they were flourishing in renovated youth, detained by the pleasures of that enchanting country.

Here was the dream of the alchymist realised! one had but to find this gifted land and revel in the enjoyment of boundless riches and perennial youth! nay, some of the ancient Indians declared that it was not necessary to go so far in quest of these rejuvenating waters, for that, in a certain island of the Bahama groupe, called Bimini, which lay far out in the ocean, there was a fountain possessing the same marvellous and inestimable qualities.

Juan Ponce de Leon listened to these tales with fond credulity. He was advancing in life, and the ordinary term of existence seemed insufficient for his mighty plans. Could he but plunge into this marvellous fountain or gifted river, and come out with his battered war-worn body restored to the strength and freshness and suppleness of youth, and his head still retaining the wisdom and knowledge of age, what enterprises might be not accomplish in the additional course of vigorous years insured to him!

It may seem incredible, at the present day, that a man of years and experience could yield any faith to a story which resembles the wild fiction of an Arabian tale; but the wonders and novelties breaking upon the world in that age of discovery almost realised the illusions of fable, and the imaginations of the Spanish voyagers had become so heated, that they were capable of any stretch of credulity.

So fully persuaded was the worthy old cavalier of the existence of the region described to him, that he fitted out three ships at his own expense to prosecute the discovery, nor had he any difficulty in finding adventurers in abundance ready to cruise with him in quest of this fairy-land.*

Chapter VII

Cruise of Juan Ponce de Leon in search of the Fountain of Youth (1512)

It was on the 3rd of March, 1512, that Juan Ponce sailed with his three ships from the port of St. Germain in the island of Porto Rico. He kept for some distance along the coast of Hispaniola, and then, stretching away to the northward, made for the Bahama islands, and soon fell

---

* It was not the credulous minds of voyagers and adventurers alone that were heated by these Indian traditions and romantic fables. Men of learning and eminence were likewise beguiled by them: witness the following extract from the second decad of Peter Martyr, addressed to Leo X., then Bishop of Rome:—

"Among the islands on the north side of Hispaniola there is one about 325 leagues distant, as they say which have searched the same, in the which is a continual spring of running water, of such marvellous virtue that the water thereof being drunk, perhaps with some diet, maketh olde men young again. And here I must make protestation to your holiness not to think this to be said lightly or rashly, for they have so spread this rumour for a truth throughout all the court, that not only all the people, but also many of them whom wisdom or fortune hath divided from the common sort, think it to be true; but, if you will ask my opinion herein, I will answer, that I will not attribute so great power to nature, but that God hath no lesse reserved this prerogative to himself than to search the hearts of men," &c.—P. Martyr, decad. 2. cap. x. Lok's translation.

in with the first of the groupe. He was favoured with propitious weather and tranquil seas, and glided smoothly with wind and current along that verdant archipelago, visiting one island after another, until, on the fourteenth of the month, he arrived at Guanahani, or St. Salvador, where Christopher Columbus had first put his foot on the shores of the New World. His inquiries for the island of Bimini were all in vain, and as to the fountain of youth, he may have drank of every fountain, and river, and lake, in the archipelago, even to the salt pools of Turk's Island, without being a whit the younger.

Still he was not discouraged; but, having repaired his ships, he again put to sea and shaped his course to the north-west. On Sunday, the 27'th of March, he came in sight of what he supposed to be an island, but was prevented from landing by adverse weather. He continued hovering about it for several days, buffeted by the elements, until, in the night of the second of April, he succeeded in coming to anchor under the land, in thirty degrees eight minutes of latitude. The whole country was in the fresh bloom of spring; the trees were gay with blossoms, and the fields covered with flowers; from which circumstance, as well as from having discovered it on Palm Sunday, (Pascua Florida,) he gave it the name of Florida, which it retains to the present day. The Indian name of the country was Cautio.*

Juan Ponce landed, and took possession of the country in the name of the Castilian Sovereigns. He afterwards continued for several weeks ranging the coasts of this flowery land, and struggling against the gulf-stream and the various currents which sweep it. He doubled Cape Cañaveral, and reconnoitered the southern and eastern shores without suspecting that this was a part of Terra Firma. In all his attempts to explore the country, he met with resolute and implacable hosility on the part of the natives, who appeared to be a fierce and warlike race. He was disappointed also in his hopes of finding gold, nor did any of the rivers or fountains, which he examined, possess the rejuvenating virtue. Convinced, therefore, that this was not the promised land of Indian tradition, he turned his prow homeward on the fourteenth of June, with the intention, in the way, of making one more attempt to find the island of Bimini.

In the outset of his return he discovered a groupe of islets abounding with sea-fowl and marine animals. On one of them, his sailors, in the course of a single night, caught one hundred and seventy turtles, and might have taken many more, had they been so inclined. They likewise took fourteen sea wolves, and killed a vast quantity of pelicans

---

* Herrera, Hist. Ind., decad. 1. lib. ix. cap. 10.

and other birds. To this groupe Juan Ponce gave the name of the Tortugas, or Turtles, which they still retain.

Proceeding in his cruise, he touched at another groupe of islets near
the Lucayos, to which he gave the name of La Vieja, or the Old
Woman groupe, because he found no inhabitant there but one old
Indian woman.* This ancient sybil he took on board his ship to give
him information about the labyrinth of islands into which he was entering, and perhaps he could not have had a more suitable guide in the
eccentric quest he was making. Notwithstanding her pilotage, however,
he was exceedingly baffled and perplexed in his return voyage among
the Bahama islands, for he was forcing his way as it were against the
course of nature, and encountering the currents which sweep westward
along these islands, and the trade-wind which accompanies them. For
a long time he struggled with all kinds of difficulties and dangers; and
was obliged to remain upwards of a month in one of the islands,
to repair the damages which his ship had suffered in a storm.

Disheartened at length by the perils and trials with which nature
seemed to have beset the approach to Bimini, as to some fairy island
in romance, he gave up the quest in person, and sent in his place a
trusty captain, Juan Perez de Ortubia, who departed in one of the
other ships, guided by the experienced old woman of the isles, and by
another Indian. As to Juan Ponce, he made the best of his way back
to Porto Rico, where he arrived infinitely poorer in purse and wrinkled
in brow, by this cruise after inexhaustible riches and perpetual youth.

He had not been long in port when his trusty envoy, Juan Perez,
likewise arrived. Guided by the sage old woman, he had succeeded in
finding the long-sought-for Bimini. He described it as being large, verdant, and covered with beautiful groves. There were crystal springs and
limpid streams in abundance, which kept the island in perpetual verdure, but none that could restore to an old man the vernal greenness
of his youth.

Thus ended the romantic expedition of Juan Ponce de Leon. Like
many other pursuits of a chimera, it terminated in the acquisition of a
substantial good. Though he had failed in finding the fairy fountain of
youth, he had discovered in place of it the important country of
Florida.†

* Herrera, decad. 1. lib. ix.

† The belief of the existence, in Florida, of a river like that sought by Juan Ponce,
was long prevalent among the Indians of Cuba, and the caciques were anxious to
discover it. That a party of the natives of Cuba once went in search of it, and
remained there, appears to be a fact, as their descendants were afterwards to be
traced among the people of Florida. Las Casas says, that, even in his days, many

Chapter VIII

Expedition of Juan Ponce against the Caribs—His death (1514)

Juan Ponce de Leon now repaired to Spain, to make a report of his voyage to King Ferdinand. The hardy old cavalier experienced much raillery from the witlings of the court, on account of his visionary voyage, though many wise men had been as credulous as himself at the outset. The king, however, received him with great favour, and conferred on him the title of Adelantado of Bimini and Florida, which last was as yet considered an island. Permission was also granted him to recruit men either in Spain or in the colonies for a settlement in Florida; but he deferred entering on his command for the present, being probably discouraged and impoverished by the losses in his last expedition, or finding a difficulty in enlisting adventurers. At length another enterprise presented itself. The Caribs had by this time become a terror to the Spanish inhabitants of many of the islands, making descents upon the coasts and carrying off captives, who it was supposed were doomed to be devoured by these cannibals. So frequent were their invasions of the island of Porto Rico, that it was feared they would ultimately oblige the Spaniards to abandon it.

King Ferdinand, therefore, in 1514, ordered that three ships, well armed and manned, should be fitted out in Seville, destined to scour the islands of the Caribs, and to free the seas from those cannibal marauders. The command of the Armada was given to Juan Ponce de Leon, from his knowledge in Indian warfare, and his varied and rough experience which had mingled in him the soldier with the sailor. He was instructed in the first place to assail the Caribs of those islands most contiguous and dangerous to Porto Rico, and then to make war on those of the coast of Terra Firma, in the neighbourhood of Carthagena. He was afterwards to take the captaincy of Porto Rico, and to attend to the repartimientos or distributions of the Indians in conjunction with a person to be appointed by Diego Columbus.

The enterprise suited the soldier-like spirit of Juan Ponce de Leon, and the gallant old cavalier set sail full of confidence in January, 1515, and steered direct for the Caribbees, with a determination to give a wholesome castigation to the whole savage archipelago. Arriving at the

---

persisted in seeking this mystery, and some thought that the river was no other than that called the Jordan, at the point of St. Helena; without considering that the name was given to it by the Spaniards in the year 1520, when they discovered the land of Chicora.

island of Guadaloupe, he cast anchor, and sent men on shore for wood and water, and women to wash the clothing of the crews, with a party of soldiers to mount guard.

Juan Ponce had not been as wary as usual, or he had to deal with savages unusually adroit in warfare. While the people were scattered carelessly on shore, the Caribs rushed forth from an ambuscade, killed the greater part of the men, and carried off the women to the mountains.

This blow at the very outset of his vaunted expedition sank deep into the heart of Juan Ponce, and put an end to all his military excitement. Humbled and mortified, he set sail for the island of Porto Rico, where he relinquished all further prosecution of the enterprise, under pretext of ill health, and gave the command of the squadron to a captain named Zuñiga; but it is surmised that his malady was not so much of the flesh as of the spirit. He remained in Porto Rico as governor; but, having grown testy and irritable through vexations and disappointments, he gave great offence, and caused much contention on the island by positive and strong-handed measures, in respect to the distribution of the Indians.

He continued for several years in that island, in a state of growling repose, until the brilliant exploits of Hernando Cortez, which threatened to eclipse the achievements of all the veteran discoverers, roused his dormant spirit.

Jealous of being cast in the shade in his old days, he determined to sally forth on one more expedition. He had heard that Florida, which he had discovered, and which he had hitherto considered a mere island, was part of Terra Firma, possessing vast and unknown regions in its bosom. If so, a grand field of enterprise lay before him, wherein he might make discoveries and conquests to rival, if not surpass, the far-famed conquest of Mexico.

Accordingly in the year 1521, he fitted out two ships at the island of Porto Rico, and embarked almost the whole of his property in the undertaking. His voyage was toilsome and tempestuous, but at length he arrived at the wished-for land. He made a descent upon the coast with a great part of his men, but the Indians sallied forth with unusual valour to defend their shores. A bloody battle ensued, several of the Spaniards were slain, and Juan Ponce was wounded by an arrow, in the thigh. He was borne on board his ship, and, finding himself disabled for further action, set sail for Cuba, where he arrived ill in body and dejected in heart.

He was of an age where there is no longer prompt and healthful reaction either mental or corporeal. The irritations of humiliated pride and disappointed hope, exasperated the fever of his wound, and he died soon after his arrival at the island. "Thus fate," says one of the quaint old Spanish writers, "delights to reverse the schemes of man. The discovery that Juan Ponce flattered himself was to lead to a means of perpetuating his life, had the ultimate effect of hastening his death."

It may be said, however, that he has at least attained the shadow of his desire, since, though disappointed in extending the natural term of his existence, his discovery has ensured a lasting duration to his name.

The following epitaph was inscribed upon his tomb, which does justice to the warrior qualities of the stout old cavalier.

> Mole sub hac fortis requiescunt ossa Leonis,
> Qui vicit factis nomina magna suis.

It has thus been paraphrased in Spanish by the Licentiate Juan de Castellanos.

> Aqueste lugar estrecho
> Es sepulchro del varon,
> Que en el nombre fue Leon,
> Y mucho mas en el hecho.

"In this sepulchre rest the bones of a man, who was a lion by name, and still more by nature."

APPENDIX

CONTAINING

ILLUSTRATIONS AND DOCUMENTS

APPENDIX

No. I

Transportation of the remains of Columbus from St. Domingo to the Havana

At the termination of a war between France and Spain in 1795, all the Spanish possessions in the island of Hispaniola were ceded to France by the ninth article of the treaty of peace. To assist in the accomplishment of this cession a Spanish squadron was dispatched to the island at the appointed time, commanded by Don Gabriel de Aristizabal, lieutenant general of the royal armada. On the 11th December 1795 that commander wrote to the field marshal and governor, Don Joaquin Garcia, resident at St. Domingo, that being informed that the remains of the celebrated admiral Don Christopher Columbus lay in the Cathedral of that city, he felt it incumbent on him, as a Spaniard, and as commander in chief of his majesty's squadron of operations, to solicit the translation of the ashes of that hero to the Island of Cuba, which had likewise been discovered by him, and where he had first planted the standard of the cross. He expressed a desire that this should be done officially and with great care and formality, that it might not remain in the power of any one, by a careless transportation of these honoured remains, to lose a relique connected with an event which formed the most glorious epoch of Spanish history; and that it might be manifested to all nations that Spaniards, notwithstanding the lapse of ages, never ceased to pay all honours to the remains of that "worthy and adventurous General of the seas;" nor abandoned them, when the various public bodies representing the Spanish dominion emigrated from the Island. As he had not time without great inconvenience to consult the sovereign on this subject, he had recourse to the Governor, as royal vice patron of the Island, hoping that his solicitation might be granted and the remains of the admiral exhumed and conveyed to the island of Cuba, in the ship San Lorenzo.

The generous wishes of this high minded Spaniard met with warm concurrence on the part of the governor. He informed him in reply that the Duke of Veraguas, lineal successor of Columbus, had manifested the same solicitude, and had sent directions that the necessary measures should be taken at his expense; and had, at the same time, expressed a wish that the bones of the Adelantado, Don Bartholomew Columbus, should likewise be exhumed, transmitting inscriptions to be put upon the sepulchres of both. He added that although the King had given no orders on the subject, yet the proposition being so accordant with the grateful feelings of the Spanish nation, and meeting with the concurrence of all the authorities of the island, he was ready on his part to carry it into execution.

The commandant general Aristizabal then made a similar communication to the archbishop of Cuba, Don Fernando Portillo y Torres, whose metropolis was then the city of St. Domingo, hoping to receive his countenance and aid in this pious undertaking.

The reply of the archbishop was couched in terms of high courtesy towards the gallant commander and deep reverence for the memory of Columbus, and expressed a zeal in rendering this tribute of gratitude and respect to the remains of one, who had done so much for the glory of the nation.

The persons empowered to act for the Duke of Veraguas, the venerable dean and chapter of the Cathedral, and all the other persons and authorities to whom Don Gabriel de Aristizabal made similar communications, manifested the same eagerness to assist in the performance of this solemn and affecting rite.

The worthy commander Aristizabal, having taken all these preparatory steps with great form and punctilio, so as that the ceremony should be performed in a public and striking manner, suitable to the fame of Columbus, the whole was carried into effect with becoming pomp and solemnity.

On the 20th of December 1795 the most distinguished persons of the place, the dignitaries of the church, and civil and military officers, assembled in the metropolitan Cathedral. In the presence of this august assemblage a small vault was opened above the chancel, in the principal wall on the right side of the high altar. Within were found the fragments of a leaden coffin, a number of bones and a quantity of mould, evidently the remains of a human body. These were carefully collected and put into a case of gilded lead, about half an ell in length and breadth and a third in height, secured by an iron lock, the key of which was delivered to the archbishop. The case was enclosed in a coffin covered with black velvet, and ornamented with lace and fringe of gold. The whole was then placed in a temporary tomb or mausoleum.

On the following day there was another grand convocation at the Cathedral, when the vigils and masses for the dead were solemnly chaunted by the archbishop, accompanied by the commandant general of the armada, the Dominican and Franciscan friars and the friars of the Order of Mercy, together with the rest of the distinguished assemblage. After this a funeral sermon was preached by the archbishop.

On the same day at four o'clock in the afternoon, the coffin was transported to the ship with the utmost state and ceremony, with a civil, religious and military procession, banners wrapped in mourning, chaunts and responses and discharges of artillery. The most distinguished persons of the several orders took turn to support the coffin. The key was taken with great formality, from the hands of the archbishop by the Governor, and given into the hands of the commander of the armada, to be delivered by him to the Governor of the Havana, to be held in deposit until the pleasure of the king should be known. The coffin was received on board of a brigantine called the Discoverer, which, with all the other shipping, displayed mourning signals, and saluted the remains with the honours paid to an admiral.

From the port of St. Domingo the coffin was conveyed to the Bay of Ocoa, and there transferred to the ship San Lorenzo. It was accompanied by a portrait of Columbus, sent from Spain by the Duke of Veraguas, to be suspended close by the place where the remains of his illustrious ancestor should be deposited.

The ship immediately made sail and arrived at Havana in Cuba on the 15th of January 1796. Here the same deep feeling of reverence to the memory of the discoverer was evinced. The principal authorities repaired on board of the ship, accompanied by the superior naval and military officers. Every thing was conducted with the same circumstantial and solemn ceremonial. The remains were removed with great reverence, and placed in a felucca, in which they were conveyed to land in the midst of a procession of three columns of feluccas and boats in the royal service, all properly decorated, containing distinguished military and ministerial officers. Two feluccas followed, in one of which was a marine guard of honour, with mourning banners and muffled drums; and in the other were the commandant general, the principal minister of marine and the military staff. In passing the vessels of war in the harbour, they all paid the honours due to an admiral and captain general of the navy. On arriving at the mole, the remains were met by the Governor of the Island, accompanied by the Generals and the military staff. The coffin was then conveyed between files of soldiery which lined the streets to the obelisk in the place of arms, where it was received in a hearse prepared for the purpose. Here the remains were formally delivered to the Governor and captain general of the Island, the key given up to him, the coffin opened and examined, and the safe transportation of its contents authenticated. This ceremony being concluded it was conveyed in grand procession and with the utmost pomp to the Cathedral. Masses and the solemn ceremonies of the dead were performed by the Bishop, and the mortal remains of Columbus deposited with great reverence in the wall, on the right side of the grand altar. "All these honours and ceremonies," says the document from whence this notice is digested,* "were attended by the Ecclesiastical and secular dignitaries, the public bodies and all the nobility and gentry of Havana, in proof of the high estimation and respectful remembrance in which they held the hero who had discovered the New World, and had been the first to plant the standard of the cross on that island."

This is the last occasion that the Spanish nation has had to testify its feelings towards the memory of Columbus, and it is with deep satisfaction that the author of this work has been able to cite at large a ceremonial so solemn, affecting and noble in its details, and so honourable to the national character.

When we read of the remains of Columbus, thus conveyed from the port of St. Domingo, after an interval of nearly three hundred years, as sacred national reliques, with civic and military pomp and high religious ceremonial; the most dignified and illustrious men striving who most should pay them reverence we can not but reflect that it was from this very port he was carried off loaded with ignominious chains, blasted apparently in fame and fortune, and followed by the revilings of the rabble. Such honours, it is true, are nothing to the dead, nor can they atone to the heart, now dust and ashes, for all the wrongs and sorrows it may have suffered; but they speak volumes of comfort to the illustrious yet slandered and persecuted living, encouraging them bravely to bear with present injuries, by showing them how true merit outlives all calumny, and receives its glorious reward in the admiration of after ages.

* Navarrete Colec. tom. 2. p. 365.

No. II

Notice of the descendants of Columbus

On the death of Columbus his son Diego succeeded to his rights, as Viceroy and governor of the New World, according to the express capitulations between the sovereigns and his father. He appears, by the general consent of historians, to have been a man of great integrity, of respectable talents, and of a frank and generous nature. Herrera speaks repeatedly of the gentleness and urbanity of his manners, and pronounces him of a noble disposition and without deceit. This absence of all guile frequently laid him open to the stratagems of crafty men, grown old in deception, who rendered his life a continued series of embarrassments; but the probity of his character, with the irresistible power of truth, bore him through difficulties in which more politic and subtle men would have been entangled and completely lost.

Immediately after the death of the admiral, Don Diego came forward as lineal successor, and urged the restitution of the family offices and privileges, which had been suspended during the latter years of his father's life. If the cold and wary Ferdinand, however, could forget his obligations of gratitude and justice to Columbus, he had less difficulty in turning a deaf ear to the solicitations of his son. For two years Don Diego pressed his suit with fruitless diligence. He felt the apparent distrust of the monarch the more sensibly, from having been brought up under his eye, as a page in the royal household, where his character ought to be well known and appreciated. At length on the return of Ferdinand from Naples in 1508, he put him a direct question, with the frankness attributed to his character. He demanded "why his majesty would not grant to him as a favour, that which was his right, and why he hesitated to confide in the fidelity of one who had been reared in his house." Ferdinand replied that he could fully confide in him, but could not repose so great a trust, at a venture, in his children and successors. To this Diego rejoined, that it was contrary to all justice and reason to make him suffer for the sins of his children who never might be born.*

Still, though he had reason and justice on his side, the young admiral found it impossible to bring the wary monarch to a compliance. Finding all appeal to his ideas of equity or sentiments of generosity in vain, he solicited permission to pursue his claim in the ordinary course of law.

---

* Herrera, His. Ind. Decad. II. lib. 7. cap. 4.

The King could not refuse so reasonable a request and Don Diego commenced a process against King Ferdinand before the council of the Indies, founded on the repeated capitulations between the crown and his father, and embracing all the dignities and immunities ceded by them.

One ground of opposition to these claims was, that if the capitulation made by the Sovereigns, in 1492, had granted a perpetual viceroyalty to the admiral and his heirs, such grant could not stand; being contrary to the interest of the state, and to an express law, promulgated in Toledo in 1480, wherein it was ordained that no office, involving the administration of justice, should be given in perpetuity; that therefore the viceroyalty granted to the admiral could only have been for his life; and that even during that term, it had justly been taken from him for his misconduct. That such concessions were contrary to the inherent prerogatives of the crown, of which the government could not divest itself. To this Don Diego replied, that as to the validity of the capitulation, it was a binding contract, and none of its privileges ought to be restricted. That as by royal schedules, dated in Villa Franca, June 2nd, 1506, and Almazan, Aug. 28th 1507, it had been ordered that he (Don Diego) should receive the tenths, so equally ought the other privileges to be accorded to him. As to the allegation that his father had been deprived of his viceroyalty for his demerits, it was contrary to all truth. It had been audacity on the part of Bobadilla to send him a prisoner to Spain in 1500, and contrary to the will and command of the sovereigns, as was proved by their letter dated from Valencia de la Torre in 1502; in which they expressed grief at his arrest, and assured him that it should be redressed, and his privileges guarded entire to himself and his children.*

This memorable suit was commenced in 1508, and continued for several years. In the course of it the claims of Don Diego were disputed, likewise, on the plea that his father was not the original discoverer of Terra Firma, but only subsequently, of certain portions of it. This however was completely controverted by overwhelming testimony. The claims of Don Diego were minutely discussed and rigidly examined, and the unanimous decision of the council of the Indies in his favour, while it reflected honour on the justice and independence of that body, silenced many petty cavilers at the fair fame of Columbus.† Notwithstanding this decision, the wily monarch wanted neither means nor pretexts to delay the ceding of such vast powers, so repugnant to his

---

* Extracts from the Minutes of the Process, taken by the historian Muñoz, MS.

† Further mention will be found of this law suit in the article relative to Amerigo Vespucci.

cautious policy. The young admiral was finally indebted for his success in this suit to previous success attained in a suit of a different nature. He had become enamoured of Doña Maria de Toledo, daughter of Fernando de Toledo, grand commander of Leon, and niece to Don Fadrique de Toledo, the celebrated Duke of Alva, chief favourite of the king. This was aspiring to a high connexion. The father and uncle of the lady were the most powerful grandees of the proud Kingdom of Spain, and cousins german to Ferdinand. The glory, however, which Columbus had left behind, rested upon his children, and the claims of Don Diego, recently confirmed by the council, involved dignities and wealth sufficient to raise him to a level with the loftiest alliance. He found no difficulty in obtaining the hand of the lady, and thus was the foreign family of Columbus engrafted on one of the proudest races of Spain. The natural consequences followed. Diego had secured that magical power called "connexions" and the favour of Ferdinand, which had been so long withheld from him as the son of Columbus, shone upon him, though coldly, as the nephew of the duke of Alva. The father and uncle of his bride succeeded, though with great difficulty, in conquering the repugnance of the monarch, and after all, he but granted in part the justice they required. He ceded to Don Diego merely the dignities and powers enjoyed by Nicholas de Ovando, who was recalled, and he cautiously withheld the title of vice roy.

The recall of Ovando was not merely a measure to make room for Don Diego, it was the tardy performance of a promise made to Isabella on her death bed. The expiring queen had demanded it as a punishment for the massacre of her poor Indian subjects at Xaragua, and the cruel and ignominious execution of the female cacique Anacaona. Thus retribution was continually going its rounds in the checkered destinies of this island, which has ever presented a little epitome of human history; its errors, and crimes, and consequent disasters.

In complying with the request of the Queen, however, Ferdinand was favourable towards Ovando. He did not feel the same generous sympathies with his late consort, and, however Ovando had sinned against humanity in his treatment of the Indians, he had been a vigilant officer, and his very oppressions had in general proved profitable to the crown. Ferdinand directed that the fleet which took out the new governor, should return under the command of Ovando, and that he should retain undisturbed enjoyment of any property, or Indian slaves that might be found in his possession. Some have represented Ovando as a man far from mercenary. That the wealth wrung from the miseries of the natives, was for his sovereign, not himself; and it is intimated that one secret cause of his disgrace, was his having made an enemy of the all powerful and unforgiving Fonseca.*

The new admiral embarked at St. Lucar, June 9, 1509, with his wife, his brother Don Fernando, who was now grown to man's estate, and had been well educated, and his two uncles Don Bartholomew and Don Diego. They were accompanied by a numerous retinue of Cavaliers, with their wives, and of young ladies of rank and family, more distinguished, it is hinted, for high blood than large fortune, and who were sent out to find wealthy husbands in the New World.†

Though the king had not granted Don Diego the dignity of Viceroy, the title was generally given to him by courtesy, and his wife was universally addressed by that of Vice Queen.

Don Diego commenced his rule with a degree of splendour hitherto unknown in the colony. The Vice Queen, who was a lady of great desert, surrounded by the noble cavaliers, and the young ladies of family who had come in her retinue, established a sort of court which threw a degree of lustre over the half savage island. The young ladies were soon married to the wealthiest colonists and contributed greatly to soften those rude manners which had grown up in a state of society, hitherto destitute of the salutary restraint and pleasing decorum produced by female influence.

Don Diego had considered his appointment in the light of a Viceroyalty, but the King soon took measures which showed that he admitted of no such pretension. Without any reference to Don Diego, he divided the coast of Darien into two great provinces, separated by an imaginary line running through the Gulph of Uraba; appointing Alonzo de Ojeda governor of the eastern province, which he called New Andalusia; and Diego de Nicuesa, governor of the western province, which included the rich coast of Veragua, and which he called Castilla del Oro, or Golden Castile. Had the monarch been swayed by principles of justice and gratitude, the settlement of this coast would have been given to the Adelantado Don Bartholomew Columbus, who had assisted in the discovery of the country, and, together with his brother the admiral, had suffered so greatly in the enterprise. Even his superior abilities for the task should have pointed him out to the policy of the monarch; but the cautious and calculating Ferdinand knew the lofty spirit of the Adelantado, and that he would be disposed to demand high and dignified terms. He passed him by, therefore, and preferred more eager and accommodating adventurers.

* Charlevoix, ut supra, c. v. i. p. 272, id. 274.

† Las Casas, lib. ii. cap. 49. MS.

Don Diego was greatly aggrieved at this measure thus adopted without his participation or knowledge. He justly considered it an infringement of the capitulations granted and repeatedly confirmed to his father and his heirs. He had further vexations and difficulties with respect to the government of the island of St. Juan or Porto Rico, which was conquered and settled about this time; but after a variety of cross purposes the officers whom he appointed were ultimately recognised by the crown.

Like his father he had to contend with malignant factions in his government; for the enemies of the father transferred their enmity to the son. There was one Miguel Pasamonte, the king's treasurer, who became his avowed enemy, under the support and chiefly at the instigation of the bishop Fonseca, who continued to the son the implacable hostility which he had manifested to the father. A variety of trivial circumstances contributed to embroil him with some of the petty officers of the colony, and there was a remnant of the followers of Roldan who arrayed themselves against him.*

Two factions soon arose in the island, one of the admiral, the other of the treasurer Pasamonte. The latter affected to call themselves the party of the king. They gave all possible molestation to Don Diego, and sent home the most virulent and absurd misrepresentations of his conduct. Among others, they represented a large house with many windows, which he was building, as intended for a fortress, and asserted that he had a design to make himself sovereign of the island. King Ferdinand, who was now advancing in years, had devolved the affairs of the Indies in a great measure on Fonseca,† who had superintended them from the first, and he was greatly guided by the advice of that prelate, which was not likely to be favorable to the descendants of Columbus. The complaints from the colonies were so artfully enforced, therefore, that he established in 1510 a sovereign court at St. Domingo, called the royal audience, to which an appeal might be made from all sentences of the admiral, even in cases reserved hitherto exclusively for the crown. Don Diego considered this a suspicious and injurious measure intended to demolish his authority.

Frank, open, and unsuspicious, the young admiral was not formed for a contest with the crafty politicians arrayed against him; who were ready and adroit in seizing upon his slightest errors and magnifying them into crimes. Difficulties were multiplied in his path which it was out of his power to overcome. He had entered upon office full of

* Herrera, Decad. I. lib. vii. c. 12.
† Herrera, Decad. I. lib. vii. c. 12.

magnanimous intentions; determined to put an end to oppression and correct all abuses; all good men therefore had rejoiced at his appointment; but he soon found that he had overrated his strength and undervalued the difficulties awaiting him. He calculated from his own good heart, but he had no idea of the wicked hearts of others. He was opposed to the repartimientos of Indians, that source of all kinds of inhumanity, but he found all the men of wealth in the colony, and most of the important persons of the court, interested in maintaining them. He perceived that the attempt to abolish them would be dangerous and the result questionable: at the same time this abuse was a source of immense profit to himself. Self interest, therefore, combined with other considerations, and what at first appeared difficult, seemed presently impracticable. The repartimientos continued in the state in which he found them, excepting that he removed such of the superintendents as had been cruel and oppressive, and substituted men of his own appointment, who probably proved equally worthless. His friends were disappointed, his enemies encouraged; a hue and cry was raised against him, by the friends of those he had displaced, and it was even said that if Ovando had not died about this time, he would have been sent out to supplant Don Diego.

The subjugation and settlement of the island of Cuba in 1510, was a fortunate event in the administration of the present admiral. He congratulated King Ferdinand on having acquired the largest and most beautiful island in the world, without losing a single man. The intelligence was highly acceptable to the King, but it was accompanied by a great number of complaints against the admiral. Little affection as Ferdinand felt for Don Diego, he was still aware that most of these representations were false, and had their origin in the jealousy and envy of his enemies. He judged it expedient, however, in 1512 to send out Don Bartholomew Columbus with minute instructions to his nephew the admiral.

Don Bartholomew still retained the office of Adelantado of the Indies, although Ferdinand, through selfish motives, detained him in Spain, while he employed inferior men in voyages of discovery. He now added to his appointments the property and government of the little island of Mona during life, and assigned him a repartimiento of two hundred Indians, with the superintendence of the mines which might be discovered in Cuba, an office which proved very lucrative.*

Among the instructions given by the king to Don Diego, he directed that in consequence of the representations of the Dominican friars, the

* Charlevoix, Hist. St. Domingo, p. 321.

labour of the natives should be reduced to one third; that negro slaves should be procured from Guinea as a relief to the Indians;* and that Carib slaves should be branded on the leg to prevent other Indians from being confounded with them, and subjected to harsh treatment.†

The two governors Ojeda and Nicuesa, whom the king had appointed to colonize and command at the Isthmus of Darien in Terra Firma, having failed in their undertaking, the sovereign in 1514, wrote to Hispaniola, permitting the Adelantado Don Bartholomew, if so inclined, to take charge of settling the coast of Veragua and to govern that country under the admiral Don Diego, comformably to his privileges. Had the king consulted his own interest and the deference due to the talents and services of the Adelantado, this measure would have been taken at an earlier date. It was now too late. Illness prevented Don Bartholomew from executing the enterprise; and his active and toilsome life was drawing to a close.

Many calumnies having been sent home to Spain by Pasamonte and other enemies of Don Diego; and various measures, being taken by government which he conceived derogatory to his dignity and injurious to his privileges, he requested and obtained permission to repair to court that he might explain and vindicate his conduct. He departed accordingly on April 9th, 1515, leaving the Adelantado with the Vice Queen Doña Maria. He was received with great honour by the king, and he merited such a reception. He had succeeded in every enterprize he had undertaken or directed. The pearl fishery had been successfully established on the coast of Cubagua. The islands of Cuba and Jamaica had been subjected and brought under cultivation, without bloodshed. His conduct as governor had been upright; and he had only excited the representations made against him by endeavouring to lessen the oppression of the natives. The king ordered that all processes against him in the court of appeal and elsewhere, for damages done to individuals, in regulating the repartimientos, should be discontinued, and the cases sent to himself for consideration. But with all these favours, as the admiral claimed a share of the profits of the provinces of Castilla del Oro, saying that it was discovered by his father, as the names of its places such as Nombre de Dios, Porto Bello and El Retrete, plainly proved, the king ordered that interrogatories should be made among the mariners who had sailed with Christopher Columbus, in the hope of proving that he had not discovered the coast of Darien, or the Gulph of Uraba. "Thus," adds Herrera, "Don Diego was always involved in

* Herrera, Hist. Ind. Decad. I. lib. ix. cap. 5.
† Herrera, Hist. Ind. Decad. I. lib. ix. cap. 5.

litigations with the Fiscal, so that he might truly say he was heir to the troubles of his father."*

Not long after the departure of Don Diego from San Domingo, his uncle Don Bartholomew ended his active and laborious life. No particulars are given of his death, nor is there mention made of his age, which must have been advanced. King Ferdinand is said to have expressed great concern at the event, for he had a high opinion of the character and talents of the Adelantado: "a man," says Herrera, "of not less worth than his brother the admiral, and who, if he had been employed, would have given great proofs of it, for he was an excellent seaman, valiant and of a great heart."† Charlevoix attributes the inaction in which Don Bartholomew had been suffered to remain for several years, to the jealousy and parsimony of the king. He found the house already too powerful; and the Adelantado, had he discovered Mexico, was a man to make as good conditions as had been made by the admiral his brother.‡ It was said, observed Herrera, that the king rather preferred to employ him in his European affairs, though it could only have been to divert him from other objects. On his death the king resumed to himself the island of Mona, which he had given to him for life, and transferred his repartimiento of two hundred Indians to the Vice Queen, Doña Maria.

While the admiral, Don Diego, was pressing for an audience in his vindication at court, king Ferdinand died on the 23d of January 1516. His grandson and successor, prince Charles, afterwards the emperor Charles V., was in Flanders. The government rested for a time with cardinal Ximenes, who would not undertake to decide on the representations and claims of the admiral. It was not until 1520 that he obtained from the Emperor, Charles V., a recognition of his innocence of all the charges against him. The Emperor, finding that what Pasamonte and his party had written were notorious calumnies, ordered Don Diego to resume his charge, although the process with the Fiscal was still pending, and that Pasamonte should be written to, requesting him to forget all past passions and differences, and to enter into amicable relations with Don Diego. Among other acts of indemnification, he acknowledged his rights to exercise the office of Vice roy and governor in the island of Hispaniola, and in all parts discovered by his father.** His authority was, however, much diminished by new regulations and a

---

* Herrera, Decad. II. lib. i. cap. 7.

† Herrera, Decad. I. lib. x. cap. 16.

‡ Charlevoix, Hist. St. Domingo, lib. v.

** Herrera, Decad. II. lib. ix. cap. 7.

supervisor appointed over him, with the right to give information to the council against him, but with no other powers. Don Diego sailed in the beginning of September 1520 and on his arrival in St. Domingo, finding that several of the governors, presuming on his long absence, had arrogated to themselves independence, and had abused their powers, he immediately sent persons to supersede them, and demanded an account of their administration. This made him a host of active and powerful enemies, both in the colonies and in Spain.

Considerable changes had taken place in the island of Hispaniola during the absence of the admiral. The mines had fallen into neglect; the cultivation of the sugar cane having been found a more certain source of wealth. It became a by-word in Spain that the magnificent palaces, erected by Charles V at Madrid and Toledo, were built of the sugar of Hispaniola. Slaves had been imported in great numbers from Africa, being found more serviceable in the culture of the cane than the feeble Indians. The treatment of the poor Negroes was cruel in the extreme, and they seem to have had no advocates even among the humane. The slavery of the Indians had been founded on the right of the strong; but it was thought that the Negroes, from their colour, were born to slavery; and that from being bought and sold in their own country, it was their natural condition. Though a patient and enduring race, the barbarities inflicted on them at length roused them to revenge; and on the 27th of December 1522 there was the first African revolt in Hispaniola. It began in a sugar plantation of the admiral Don Diego, where about twenty slaves joined by an equal number from a neighboring plantation, got possession of arms, rose on their superintendants, massacred them and sallied forth upon the country. It was their intention to pillage certain plantations, to kill the whites, reinforce themselves by freeing their countrymen, and either to possess themselves of the town of Agua, or to escape to the mountains.

Don Diego set out from St. Domingo in search of the rebels, followed by several of the principal inhabitants. On the second day, he stopped on the banks of the river Nizao, to rest his party and to suffer reinforcements to overtake him. Here one Melchor de Castro, who accompanied the admiral, learnt that the negroes had ravaged his plantation, sacked his house, killed one of his men and carried off his Indian slaves. Without asking leave of the admiral, he departed in the night with two companions, visited his plantations, found all in confusion, and pursuing the Negroes, sent to the admiral for aid. Eight horsemen were hastily despatched to his assistance, armed with bucklers and lances, and having six of the infantry mounted behind them. De Castro had three horsemen beside this reinforcement, and at the head of this little band overtook the Negroes at break of day. The insurgents put themselves in battle array, armed with stones and Indian spears and uttering loud shouts and outcries. The Spanish horsemen braced their bucklers, couched their lances and charged them at full speed. The negroes were soon routed, and fled to the rocks, leaving six dead and several wounded. De Castro also was wounded in the arm. The admiral coming up assisted him in the pursuit of the fugitives. As fast as they were taken, they were hanged on the nearest trees, and remained suspended, as spectacles of terror to their countrymen. This prompt severity checked all further attempt at revolt among the African slaves. *

In the mean time the various enemies whom Don Diego had created, both in the colonies and in Spain, were actively and successfully employed. His old antagonist the treasurer Pasamonte had charged him with usurping almost all the powers of the royal audience, and with having given to the royal declaration, reestablishing him in his office of Vice roy, an extent never intended by the sovereign. These representations had weight at court, and in 1523 Don Diego received a most severe letter from the council of the Indies, charging him with the various abuses and excesses alleged against him, and commanding him, on pain of forfeiting all his privileges and titles, to revoke the innovations he had made, and restore things to their former state. To prevent any plea of ignorance of this mandate, the royal audience was enjoined to promulgate it, and to call upon all persons to conform to it, and to see that it was properly obeyed. The admiral received also a letter from the council informing him that his presence was necessary in Spain to give information as to the foregoing matters and advice relative to the reformation of various abuses and to the treatment and preservation of the Indians; he was requested, therefore, to repair to court without waiting for further orders.†

Don Diego understood this to be a peremptory recall and obeyed accordingly. On his arrival in Spain he immediately presented himself before the court at Victoria, with the frank and fearless spirit of an upright man, and pleaded his cause so well, that the sovereign and council acknowledged his innocence on all the points of accusation. He convinced them, moreover, of the exactitude with which he had discharged his duties; of his zeal for the public good and the glory of the crown, and that all the representations against him rose from the

---

* Herrera, Hist. Ind. Decad. III. lib. iv. cap. 9.

† Herrera, Hist. Ind. Decad. I. lib. v. cap. 4.

jealousy and enmity of Pasamonte and other royal officers in the colonies, who were impatient of any superior authority in the island to restrain them.

Having completely established his innocence and exposed the calumnies of his enemies, Don Diego trusted that he would soon obtain justice as to all his claims. As these, however, involved a participation in the profits of vast and richly productive provinces, he experienced the delays and difficulties usual with such demands; for it is only when justice costs nothing that it is readily rendered. His earnest solicitations at length obtained an order from the Emperor, that a commission should be formed, composed of the grand chancellor, the friar Loyasa, confessor to the Emperor and president of the royal council of the Indies, and a number of other distinguished personages. They were to inquire into the various points in dispute between the admiral and the Fiscal, and into the proceedings which had taken place in the council of the Indies, with the power of determining what justice required in the case.

The affair, however, was protracted to such a length, and accompanied by so many toils, vexations and disappointments, that the unfortunate Diego, like his father, died in the pursuit. For two years he had followed the court from city to city, during its migrations; from Victoria to Burgos, Valladolid, Madrid and Toledo. In the Winter of 1525, the Emperor set out from Toledo for Seville. The admiral undertook to follow him, though his constitution was broken by fatigue and vexation, and he was wasting under the attack of a slow fever. Oviedo the historian saw him at Toledo two days before his departure, and joined with his friends in endeavouring to dissuade him from a journey in such a state of health, and at such a season. Their persuasions were in vain. Don Diego was not aware of the extent of his malady: he told them that he should repair to Seville by the church of Our Lady of Guadaloupe, to offer up his devotions at that shrine, and he trusted through the intercession of the mother of God, soon to be restored to health.* He accordingly left Toledo in a litter on the 21st of February 1526, having previously confessed and taken the communion; and arrived the same day at Montalvan, distant about six leagues. There his illness increased to such a degree that he saw his end approaching. He employed the following day in arranging the affairs of his conscience and expired on February 23, being little more than fifty years of age: his premature death having been hastened by the griefs and troubles he had experienced. "He was worn out," says Herrera, "by following up his claims, and defending himself from the

---

* Charlevoix, Hist. St. Domingo, lib. 6.

calumnies of his competitors, who with many stratagems and devices sought to obscure the glory of the father and the virtue of the son."*

We have seen how the discovery of the New World rendered the residue of the life of Columbus a tissue of wrongs, hardships and afflictions; and how the jealousy and enmity he had awakened were inherited by his son. It remains to show briefly in what degree the anticipations of perpetuity, wealth and honour to his family were fulfilled.

When Don Diego Columbus died, his wife and family were at St. Domingo; he left two sons, Luis and Christopher, and three daughters, Maria, who afterwards married Don Sancho de Cardono; Juana, who married Don Luis de Cueva; and Isabella, who married Don George of Portugal, Count of Gelves. He had also a natural son named Christopher.†

After the death of Don Diego, his noble-spirited Vice Queen, left with a number of young children, endeavoured to assert and maintain the rights of the family. Understanding that, according to the privileges accorded to Christopher Columbus, they had a just claim to the vice royalty of the province of Veragua, as having been discovered by him, she demanded a licence from the royal audience of Hispaniola, to recruit men and fit out an armada to colonize that country. This the audience refused, and sent information of the demand to the Emperor. He replied that the Vice Queen should be kept in suspense, until the justice of her claim could be ascertained; as, although he had at various times given commissions to different persons to examine the doubts and objections which had been opposed by the Fiscal, no decision had ever been made.‡ The enterprize thus contemplated by the Vice Queen was never carried into effect.

Shortly afterwards she sailed for Spain to protect the claim of her eldest son Don Luis, then six years of age. Charles V. was absent, but she was most graciously received by the Empress. The title of admiral of the Indies was immediately conferred upon her son Don Luis, and the Emperor augmented his revenues and conferred other favours on the family. Charles V., however, could never be prevailed upon to give

---

* Herrera, Decad. III. lib. viii. cap. 15.

† Memorial ajustado sobre el estado de Vcragua. Charlevoix mentions another son called Diego, and calls one of the daughters Phillipine. Spotorno says that the daughter Maria took the veil, confounding her with a niece. These are trivial errors, merely noticed to avoid the imputation of inaccuracy. The account of the descendants of Columbus here given, accords with a genealogical tree of the family, produced before the council of the Indies in a great lawsuit for the estates.

‡ Herrera, Decad. IV. lib. ii. cap. 6.

Don Luis the title of Vice Roy, although that dignity had been decreed to his father, a few years previous to his death, as an hereditary right.*

In 1538 the young admiral Don Luis, then about eighteen years of age, was at court, having instituted proceedings before the proper tribunals for the recovery of the viceroyalty: two years afterwards, the suit was settled by arbitration, his uncle Don Fernando and Cardinal Loyasa, president of the council of the Indies, being umpires. By a compromise, Don Luis was declared captain general of Hispaniola, but with such limitations that it was little more than a bare title. Don Luis sailed for Hispaniola, but did not remain there long. He found his dignities and privileges mere sources of vexation, and finally entered into a compromise, which relieved himself and gratified the Emperor. He gave up all pretensions to the Vice Royalty of the New World, receiving in its stead, the titles of Duke of Veragua and Marquis of Jamaica.† He commuted also the claim to a tenth of the produce of the Indies for a pension of one thousand doubloons of gold.‡

Don Luis did not long enjoy the substitution of a certain, though moderate, revenue, for a magnificent but unproductive claim. He died shortly afterwards, leaving no other male issue than an illegitimate son named Christopher. He left two daughters by his wife Doña Maria de Mosquera, one named Phillippa and the other Maria, which last became a nun in the convent of St. Quirce at Valladolid.

Don Luis having no legitimate son was succeeded by his nephew Diego, son to his brother Christopher. A litigation took place between this young heir and his cousin Phillippa, daughter of the late Don Luis. The convent of St. Quirce also put in a claim on behalf of its inmate Doña Maria, who had taken the veil. Christopher, natural son to Don Luis, likewise became a prosecutor in the suit, but was set aside on account of his illegitimacy. Don Diego and his cousin Phillippa soon thought it better to join claims and persons in wedlock, than to pursue a tedious contest. They were married and their union was happy though not fruitful. Diego died without issue in 1578 and with him the legitimate male line of Columbus became extinct.

One of the most important lawsuits that the world has ever witnessed now arose for the estates and dignities descended from the great discoverer. Don Diego had two sisters, Francisca and Maria, the former of whom, and the children of the latter, advanced their several claims. To these parties was added Bernard Colombo of Cogoleto, who claimed

---

* Charlevoix, Hist. St. Domingo, lib. vi. p. 443.

† Charlevoix, Hist. St. Domingo, tom. i. lib. vi, p. 446.

‡ Spotorno, Hist. Colomb. p. 123.

as lineal descendant from Bartholomew Columbus the Adelantado, brother to the discoverer. He was, however, pronounced ineligible, as the Adelantado had no acknowledged, and certainly no legitimate offspring.

Baldassar or Balthazar Colombo of the house of Cuccaro and Conzano, in the Dukedom of Montferrat in Piedmont was an active and persevering claimant. He came from Italy into Spain, where he devoted himself for many years to the prosecution of this suit. He produced a genealogical tree of his family, in which was contained one Domenico Colombo, lord of Cuccaro, whom he maintained to be the identical father of Christopher Columbus the admiral. He proved that this Domenico was living at the requisite era, and produced many witnesses, who had heard that the navigator was born in the castle of Cuccaro; from whence, it was added, he and his two brothers had eloped at an early age, and had never returned.* A monk is also mentioned among the witnesses, who made oath that Christopher and his brothers were born in that castle of Cuccaro. This testimony was afterwards withdrawn by the prosecutor, as it was found that the monk's recollection must have extended back considerably upward of a century.† The claim of Balthazar was negatived. His proofs, that Christopher Columbus was a native of Cuccaro were rejected, as only hearsay or traditionary evidence. His ancestor Domenico, it appeared from his own showing, died in 1456; whereas it was established that Domenico, the father of the admiral, was living upwards of thirty years after that date.

The cause was finally decided by the council of the Indies on the 2d of December 1608. The male line was declared to be extinct. Don Nuño or Nugno Gelves de Portugallo was put in possession, and became Duke of Veragua. He was grandson to Isabella, third daughter of Don Diego (son of the discoverer) by his Vice Queen Doña Maria de Toledo. The descendants of the two elder sisters of Isabella had a prior claim, but their lines became extinct previous to this decision of the suit. The Isabella just named had married Don George of Portugal, count of Gelves. "Thus," says Charlevoix, "the dignities and wealth of Columbus passed into a branch of the Portuguese house of Braganza established in Spain, of which the heirs are entitled "*De Portugallo, Colon, duke de Veragua, marques de la Jamaica, y almirante de las Indias.*"‡

The suit of Balthazar Colombo of Cuccaro was rejected, under three different forms, by the council of the Indies; and his application for an allowance of support under the legacy of Columbus, in favour of poor

---

* Bossi, Hist. Colomb. Dissertations, p. 67.

† Bossi, Dissertation on the Country of Columbus, p. 63.

‡ Charlevoix, Hist. St. Domingo, tom. 1. lib. 6. p. 477.

relations, was also refused, although the other parties had assented to the demand.* He died in Spain, where he had resided many years in prosecution of this suit. His son returned to Italy, persisting in the validity of his claim; he said that it was in vain to seek justice in Spain; they were too much interested to keep those dignities and estates among themselves. But he gave out that he had received twelve thousand doubloons of gold in compromise from the other parties. Spotorno, under sanction of Ignazio de Giovanni, a learned canon, treats this assertion as a bravado to cover his defeat, being contradicted by his evident poverty.† The family of Cuccaro, however, still maintain their right, and express great veneration for the memory of their illustrious ancestor the admiral; and travellers occasionally visit their old castle in Piedmont with great reverence, as the birthplace of the discoverer of the New World.

No. III

Fernando Columbus

Fernando Columbus (or Colon, as he is called in Spain), the natural son and historian of the admiral, was born in Cordova. There is an uncertainty about the exact time of his birth. According to his epitaph, it must have been on the 28th September 1488, but according to his original papers, preserved in the library of the cathedral of Seville, and which were examined by Don Diego Ortiz de Zuñiga, historian of that city, it would appear to have been on the 29th of August 1487. His mother, Doña Beatrix Enriquez, was of a respectable family, but was never married to the admiral, as has been stated by some of his biographers.

Early in 1494 Fernando was carried to court, together with his elder brother Diego, by his uncle Don Bartholomew, to enter the royal household in quality of page to the prince Don Juan, son and heir to Ferdinand and Isabella. He and his brother remained in this situation until the death of the prince; when they were taken by queen Isabella as pages

* Bossi, Dissertation on the Country of Columbus.
† Spotorno, p. cxxvii.

into her own service. Their education of course was well attended to, and Fernando in after life give proofs of being a learned man.

In the year 1502, at the tender age of thirteen or fourteen years, Fernando accompanied his father in his fourth voyage of discovery and encountered all its singular and varied hardships with a fortitude that is mentioned with praise and admiration by the Admiral.

After the death of his father, it would appear that Fernando made two voyages to the New World; he accompanied the Emperor Charles V. also to Italy, Flanders and Germany; and, according to Zuñiga (Anales de Sevilla de 1539, No. 3.), travelled over all Europe and a part of Africa and Asia. Possessing talents, judgement and industry, these opportunities were not lost upon him, and he acquired much information in geography, navigation and natural history. Being of a studious habit and fond of books, he formed a select yet copious library of more than twenty thousand volumes, in print and in manuscript. With the sanction of the Emperor Charles V, he undertook to establish an academy and college of mathematics at Seville; and for this purpose commenced the construction of a sumptuous edifice without the walls of the city facing the Guadalquiver, in the place where the monastery of San Laureano is now situated. His constitution, however, had been broken by the sufferings he had experienced in his travels and voyages, and a premature death prevented the completion of his plan of the academy, and broke off other labours. He died at Seville on the 12th of July 1539, at the age, according to his epitaph, of fifty years, nine months, and fourteen days. He left no issue and was never married. His body was interred according to his request, in the cathedral of Seville. He bequeathed his valuable library to the same establishment.

Don Fernando devoted himself much to letters. According to the inscription on his tomb, he composed a work in four books or volumes, the title of which is defaced on the monument, and the work itself is lost. This is much to be regretted as according to Zuñiga, the fragments of the inscription specify it to have contained, among a variety of matter, historical, moral and geographical, notices of the countries he had visited, but especially of the New World, and of the voyages and discoveries of his father.

His most important and permanent work, however, was a history of the Admiral, composed in Spanish. It was translated into Italian by Alonzo de Ulloa, and from this Italian translation have proceeded the editions which have since appeared in various languages. It is singular that the work only exists in Spanish in the form of a retranslation from that of Ulloa, and full of errors in the orthography of proper names, and in dates and distances.

Don Fernando was an eye witness of some of the facts which he relates, particularly of the fourth voyage wherein he accompanied his father. He had also the papers and charts of his father, and recent documents of all kinds to extract from, as well as familiar acquaintance with the principal personages who were concerned in the events which he records. He was a man of probity and discernment, and writes more dispassionately than could be expected when treating of matters which affected the honour, the interests and happiness of his father. It is to be regretted, however, that he should have suffered the whole of his father's life previous to his discoveries, a period of about fifty six years, to remain in obscurity. He appears to have wished to cast a cloud over it, and only to have presented his father to the reader after he had rendered himself illustrious by his actions, and his history had become in a manner identified with the history of the world. His work, however, is an invaluable document, entitled to great faith, and is the corner stone of the history of the American continent.

No. IV

Age of Columbus

As the date I have assigned for the birth of Columbus, makes him about ten years older than he is generally represented, at the time of his discoveries, it is proper to state precisely my authority. In the valuable manuscript chronicle of the reign of the Catholic sovereigns, written by Andres Bernaldes, the curate of Los Palacios, there is a long tract on the subject of the discoveries of Columbus: it concludes with these words: *Murió en Valladolid, el año de 1506, en el mes de Mayo, in senectute bona, de edad 70 años, poco mas ó menos.* (He died in Valladolid in the year 1506, in the month of May, in a good old age, being seventy years old, a little more or less.) The curate of Los Palacios was a contemporary, and an intimate friend of Columbus, who was occasionally a guest in his house; no one was more competent, therefore, to form a correct idea of his age. It is singular, that, while the biographers of Columbus have been seeking to establish the epoch of his birth by various calculations and conjectures, this direct testimony of honest Andres Bernaldes has entirely escaped their notice, though some of them had his manuscript in their hands. It was first observed by my accurate friend Don Antonio Uguina in the course of his exact investigations, and has been pointed out and ably supported by Don Martin Fernandez de Navarrete, in the introduction to his valuable collection of voyages.

Various circumstances in the life of Columbus will be found to corroborate the statement of the curate; such, for example, as the increasing infirmities with which he struggled during his voyages, and which at last rendered him a cripple and confined him to his bed. The allusion to his advanced age in one of his letters to the sovereigns, wherein he relates the consolation he had received from a secret voice in the night season: *Tu vejez no impedira a toda cosa grande. Abrahan pasaba cien años cuando engendro a Isaac, &c.* (Thy old age shall be no impediment to any great undertaking. Abraham was above a hundred years old, when he begat Isaac, &c.) The permission granted him by the king the year previous to his death to travel on a mule, instead of a horse, on account of his *age* and infirmities; and the assertion of Oviedo, that at the time of his death he was quite old. (*era ya viejo.*)

This fact of the advanced age of Columbus throws quite a new coloring over his character and history. How much more extraordinary is the ardent enthusiasm which sustained him through his long career of solicitation, and the noble pride with which he refused to descend from his dignified demands, and to bargain about his proposition, though life was rapidly wasting in delays. How much more extraordinary is the hardihood with which he undertook repeated voyages into unknown seas, amidst all kinds of perils and hardships; the fortitude with which he bore up against an accumulation of mental and bodily afflictions, enough to have disheartened and destroyed the most youthful and robust, and the irresistible buoyancy of spirit with which to the last he still rose from under the ruined concerns and disappointed hopes and blasted projects of one enterprise, to launch into another, still more difficult and perilous.

We have been accustomed to admire all these things in Columbus when we considered him in the full vigor of his life; how much more are they entitled to our wonder as the achievements of a man, whom the weight of years and infirmities was pressing into the grave.

No. V

Lineage of Columbus

The ancestry of Christopher Columbus has formed a point of zealous controversy, which is not yet satisfactorily settled. Several honourable families, possessing domains in Placentia, Montferrat, and the different parts of the Genoese territories, claim him as belonging to their houses; and to these has recently been added the noble family of Colombo in Modena.* The natural desire to prove consanguinity with a man of distinguished renown, has excited this rivalry; but it has been heightened in particular instances, by the hope of succeeding to titles and situations of wealth and honour, when his male line of descendants became extinct. The investigation is involved in particular obscurity, as even his immediate relatives appear to have been in ignorance on the subject.

Fernando Columbus in his biography of the admiral, after a pompous prelude, in which he attempts to throw a vague and cloudy magnificence about the origin of his father, notices slightly the attempts of some to obscure his fame, by making him a native of various small and insignificant villages; and dwells with more complacency upon others, who make him a native of places in which there were persons of much honor of the name, and many sepulchral monuments with arms and epitaphs of the Colombos. He relates his having gone to the castle of Cucureo, to visit two brothers of the family of Colombo, who were rich and noble, the youngest of whom was above one hundred years of age, and who he had heard were relatives of his father; but they could give him no information upon the subject; whereupon he breaks forth into his professed contempt for these adventitious claims, declaring, that he thinks it better to content himself with dating from the glory of the admiral, than to go about inquiring whether his father "were a merchant or one who kept his hawks;"† since, adds he, of persons of similar pursuits, there are thousands who die every day, whose memory even among their own neighbours and relatives perishes immediately, without its being possible afterwards to ascertain even whether they existed.

After this and a few more expressions of similar disdain for these empty distinctions, he indulges in vehement abuse of Agostino Giustiniani, whom he calls a false historian, an inconsiderate, partial or malig-

---

* Spotorno, Hist. Mem. p. 5.

† Literally in the original *Cazador de Volateria*, a falconer. Hawking was in those days an amusement of the highest classes, and to keep hawks was almost a sign of nobility.

nant compatriot, for having in his Psalter traduced his father by saying that in his youth he had been employed in mechanical occupations.

As, after all this discussion, Fernando leaves the question of his father's parentage in all its original obscurity, yet appears irritably sensitive to any derogatory suggestions of others, his whole evidence tends to the conviction that he really knew nothing to boast of in his ancestry.

Of the nobility and antiquity of the Colombo family, of which the admiral probably was a remote descendant, we have some account in Herrera. "We learn," he says, "that the Emperor Otto the Second, in 940, confirmed to the counts Pietro, Giovanni and Alexandro Colombo, brothers, the feudatory possessions which they held within the jurisdiction of the cities of Ayqui, Savona, Aste, Montferrato, Turin, Viceli, Parma, Cremona and Bergamo, and all others which they held in Italy. It appears that the Colombos of Cuccaro, Cucureo, and Placentia were the same, and that the Emperor in the same year, 940, made donation to the said three brothers of the castles of Cuccaro, Conzano, Rosignano and others, and of the fourth part of Bistanio, which appertained to the Empire."[*]

One of the boldest attempts of those biographers bent on ennobling Columbus, has been to make him son of the lord of Cuccaro, a burgh of Montferrat in Piedmont, and to prove that he was born in his father's castle at that place; from whence he and his brothers eloped at an early age and never returned. This was asserted in the course of a process brought by a certain Baldasser, or Balthazar Colombo, resident in Genoa but originally of Cuccaro, claiming the title and estates, on the death of Diego Colon, Duke of Veragua, in 1578, the great grandson and last legitimate male descendant of the admiral. The council of the Indies decided against this claim to relationship. Some account of the law suit will be found in another part of this work.

This romantic story, like all others of the nobility of his parentage, is at utter variance with the subsequent events of his life, his long struggles with indigence and obscurity, and the difficulties he endured from the want of family connexions. How can it be believed, says Bossi, that this same man, who, in his most cruel adversities, was incessantly taunted by his enemies with the obscurity of his birth, should not reply to this reproach by declaring his origin, if he were really descended from the lords of Cuccaro, Conzano, and Rosignano? a circumstance which would have obtained him the highest credit with the Spanish nobility.[†]

The different families of Colombo which lay claim to the great

[*] Herrera, Decad. I. lib. I. cap. vii.
[†] Dissertation, &c.

navigator, seem to be various branches of one tree and there is little doubt of his appertaining remotely to the same respectable stock.

It appears evident, however, that Columbus sprang immediately from a line of humble but industrious citizens which had existed in Genoa, even from the time of Giacomo Colombo, the wool carder in 1311, mentioned by Spotorno, nor is this in any wise incompatible with the intimation of Fernando Columbus, that the family had been reduced from high estate to great poverty, by the wars of Lombardy. The feuds of Italy, in those ages, had broken down and scattered many of the noblest families, and while some branches remained in the lordly heritage of castles and domains, others were confounded with the humblest population of the cities.

No. VI

Birthplace of Columbus

There has been much controversy about the birthplace of Columbus. The greatness of his renown has induced various places to lay claim to him as a native, and from motives of laudable pride, for nothing reflects greater lustre upon a city than to have given birth to distinguished men. The original and long established opinion was in favour of Genoa; but such strenuous claims were asserted by the states of Placentia, and in particular of Piedmont, that the Academy of Sciences and Letters of Genoa was induced, in 1812, to nominate three of its members, Signors Serra, Carrega and Piaggio, commissioners, to examine into these pretensions.

The claims of Placentia had been first advanced in 1662, by Pietro Maria Campi, in the Ecclesiastical history of that place, who maintained that Columbus was a native of the village of Pradello in that vicinity. It appeared probable, on investigation, that Bertolino Colombo, great grandfather to the admiral, had owned a small property in Pradello, the rent of which had been received by Domenico Colombo of Genoa, and after his death by his sons Christopher and Bartholomew. Admitting this assertion to be correct, there was no proof that either the admiral, his father, or grand father had ever resided on that estate. The very circumstances of the case indicated, on the contrary, that their home was in Genoa.

The claim of Piedmont was maintained with more plausibility. It was shown that a Domenico Colombo was Lord of the castle of Cuccaro in Montferrat, at the time of the birth of Christopher Columbus, who, it was asserted, was his son, and born in his castle. Balthazar Colombo, a descendant of this person, instituted a law suit before the council of the Indies for the inheritance of the admiral when his male line became extinct. The council of the Indies decided against him, as is shown in an account of that process given among the illustrations of this history. It was proved that Domenico Colombo, father of the admiral, was resident in Genoa both before, and many years after, the death of this Lord of Cuccaro, who bore the same name.

The three commissioners appointed by the Academy of Science and Letters of Genoa to examine into these pretensions, after a long and diligent investigation, gave a voluminous and circumstantial report in favour of Genoa. An ample digest of their inquest may be found in the History of Columbus by Signor Bossi, who, in an able dissertation on the question, confirms their opinion. It may be added, in further corroboration, that Peter Martyr and Bartholomew Las Casas, who were contemporaries and acquaintances of Columbus, and Juan de Barros, the Portuguese historian, all make Columbus a native of the Genoese territories.

There has been a question fruitful of discussion among the Genoese themselves, whether Columbus was born in the city of Genoa, or in some other part of the territory. Finale and Oneglia, and Savona, towns on the Ligurian coast to the west, Boggiasco, Cogoleto, and several other towns and villages claim him as their own. His family possessed a small property at a village or hamlet called Terra Rossa; in Latin, Terra Rubra; which has induced some writers to assign his birth to one of those places. Bossi says that there is still a tower between Quinto and Nervi, which bears the title of Torre dei Colombi.* Bartholomew Columbus, brother to the admiral, styled himself of Terra Rubra in a Latin inscription on a map which he presented to Henry VII of England, and Fernando Columbus states, in his history of the admiral, that he was accustomed to subscribe himself in the same manner, before he attained to his dignities.

Cogoleto at one time bore away the palm. The families there claim the discoverer, and preserve a portrait of him. One or both of the two admirals named Colombo, with whom he sailed, are stated to have come from that place, and to have been confounded with him so as to have given support to this idea.†

---

* Bossi, French translation. Paris, 1824, p. 69.

† Idem.

Savona, a city in the Genoese territories, has claimed the same honour, and this claim has recently been very strongly brought forward. Signor Giovanni Battista Belloro, an advocate of Savona, has strenuously maintained his claim in an ingenious disputation, dated May 12th, 1826, in form of a letter to the Baron du Zach, editor of a valuable astronomical and geographical journal, published monthly at Genoa.*

Signor Belloro claims it as an admitted fact, that Domenico Colombo was for many years a resident and citizen of Savona, in which place one Christopher Columbus is shown to have signed a document in 1472.

He states that a public square in that city bore the name of Platea Columbi, toward the end of the fourteenth century; that the Ligurian government gave the name of "Jurisdizione di Columbi" to that district of the republic, under the persuasion that the great navigator was a native of Savona, and that Columbus gave the name of Savona to a little island adjacent to Hispaniola, among his earliest discoveries.

He quotes many Savonese writers, principally poets, and various historians and poets of other countries; and thus established the point that Columbus was held to be a native of Savona by persons of respectable authority. He lays particular stress on the testimony of the Magnifico Francisco Spinola, as related by the learned prelate Felippo Alberto Pollero, stating that he had seen the sepulchre of Christopher Columbus in the cathedral at Seville, and that the epitaph states him expressly to be a native of Savona. "Hic jacet Christophorus Columbus Savonensis."†

The proofs advanced by Signor Belloro show his zeal for the honour of his native city, but do not authenticate the fact he undertakes to establish. He shows clearly that many respectable writers believed Columbus to be a native of Savona; but a far greater number can be adduced, and many of them contemporary with the admiral, some of them his intimate friends, others his fellow citizens, who state him to have been born in the city of Genoa. Among the Savonese writers, Giulio Salinorio, who investigated the subject, comes expressly to the same conclusion. "Genova città nobilissima, era la patria de Colombo."

Signor Belloro appears to be correct in stating that Domenico, the father of the admiral, was several years resident in Savona. But it appears from his own dissertation, that the Christopher who witnessed the testament in 1472 styled himself of Genoa—"Christophorus Columbus Lane-

* Correspondence Astronom. Geograph. &c. de Baron du Zach, vol. 14. Cahier 6. Lettera 29. 1826.

† Felippo Alberto Pollero, Epicherema, cioé breve discorso per difesa di sua persona e carrattere, Torino, per Gio. Battista Zappata. MCDXCVI. (read 1696) in 4to. p. 47.

rius de Janua." This incident is stated by other writers, who presume this Christopher to have been the navigator on a visit to his father, in the interval of his early voyages. In as far as the circumstance bears on the point, it supports the idea that he was born at Genoa.

The epitaph on which Signor Belloro places his principal reliance entirely fails. Christopher Columbus was not interred in the Cathedral of Seville, nor was any monument erected to him in that edifice. The tomb to which the learned prelate Felippo Alberto Pollero alludes, may have been that of Fernando Columbus, son to the admiral, who, as has been already observed, was buried in the cathedral of Seville, to which he bequeathed his noble library. The place of his sepulture is designated by a broad slab of white marble, inserted in the pavement, with an inscription, partly in Spanish, partly in Latin, recording the merits of Fernando, and the achievements of his father. On either side of the epitaph is engraved an ancient Spanish Galley. The inscription quoted by Signor Belloro may have been erroneously written from memory by the magnifico Francisco Spinola, under the mistaken idea that he had beheld the sepulchre of the great discoverer. As Fernando was born at Cordova, the term Savonensis must have been another error of memory in the magnifico; no such word is to be found in the inscription.

This question of birthplace has also been investigated with considerable minuteness, and a decision given in favour of Genoa, by D. Gio. Battista Spotorno, of the royal university in that city, in his historical memoir of Columbus. He shews that the family of the Colombos had long been resident in Genoa. By an extract from the notarial register, it appeared that one Giacomo Colombo, a wool carder, resided without the gate of St. Andria in the year 1311. An agreement also, published by the academy of Genoa, proved that in 1489 Domenico Colombo possessed a house and shop, and a garden with a well, in the street of St. Andrew's gate, anciently without the walls, presumed to have been the same residence with that of Giacomo Colombo. He rented also another house from the monks of St. Stephen in the Via Mulcento, leading from the street of St. Andrew to the Strada Giulia.*

Signor Bossi states that documents lately found in the archives of the monastery of St. Stephen present the name of Domenico Colombo several times, from 1456 to 1459, and designate him as son of Giovanni Colombo, husband of Susanna Fontanarossa and father of Christopher, Bartholomew and Giacomo† (or Diego). He states also that the receipts of the canons show that the last payment of rent was made by Domenico

---

* Spotorno, Eng. transl. p. xi. xii.

† Bossi, French transl. p. 76.

Colombo for his dwelling in 1489. He surmises that the admiral was born in the before-mentioned house belonging to those monks, in Via Mulcento, and that he was baptized in the church of St. Stephen. He adds that an ancient manuscript was submitted to the commissioners of the Genoese academy, in the margin of which the notary had stated that the name of Christopher was on the register of the parish as having been baptized in that church.[*]

Andres Bernaldes, the curate of Los Palacios, who was an intimate friend of Columbus, says that he was of Genoa.[†] Agostino Giustiniani, a contemporary of Columbus, likewise asserts it in his Polyglot Psalter, published in Genoa in 1516. Antonio de Herrera, an author of great accuracy, who though not a contemporary, had access to the best documents, asserts decidedly that he was born in the city of Genoa.

To these names may be added that of Alexander Geraldini, brother to the nuncio, and instructor to the children of Ferdinand and Isabella, a most intimate friend of Columbus;[‡] also Antonio Gallo,[§] Bartolomeo Senarega[||] and Uberto Foglieta,[**] all contemporaries with the admiral, and natives of Genoa, together with an anonymous writer who published an account of his voyage of discovery at Venice in 1509.[¶] It is unnecessary to mention historians of later date agreeing in the same fact, as they must have derived their information from some of these authorities.

The question in regard to the birthplace of Columbus has been treated thus minutely, because it has been, and still continues to be, a point of warm controversy. It may be considered, however, as conclusively decided by the highest authority, the evidence of Columbus himself. In a testament executed in 1498, which has been admitted in evidence before the Spanish tribunals in certain law suits among his descendants, he twice declares that he was a native of the city of Genoa: "*Siendo yo nacido in Genova*," "I being born in Genoa;" and again he repeats the assertion, as a reason for enjoining certain conditions on his heirs, which manifest the interest he takes in his native place. "I command the said Don Diego, my son, or the person who inherits the said Mayorazgo (or entailed estate) that he maintain always in the city of Genoa a person of our lineage who shall have a house and a wife there, and to furnish him with an income on which he can live decently, as a person connected

---

*Ibid. p. 88.
† Cura de Los Palacios. MS. c. 118.
‡ Alex. Geraldini, Itin. ad Reg. sub Æquinoc.
§ Antonio Gallo, Annals of Genoa. Muratori, t. 23.
|| Senarega. Muratori, t. 24.
**Foglieta, Elog. Clar. Ligur.
¶ Grinæus, Nov. Orb.

with our family, and hold footing and root in that city as a native of it, so that he may have aid and favor in that city in case of need, *for from thence I came and there was born."* *

In another part of his testament he expresses himself with a filial fondness in respect to Genoa. "I command the said Don Diego, or whoever shall possess the said Mayorazgo, that he labour and strive always for the honour, and welfare and increase of the city of Genoa, and employ all his abilities and means in defending and augmenting the welfare and honour of her republic, in all matters which are not contrary to the service of the church of God, and the state of the King and Queen our sovereigns, and their successors."

An informal codicil executed by Columbus at Valladolid, May 4th, 1506, sixteen days before his death, was discovered about 1785, in the Corsini library at Rome. It is termed a military codicil from being made in the manner which the civil law allows to the soldier who executes such an instrument on the eve of battle, or in expectation of death. It was written on the blank page of a little breviary presented to Columbus by Pope Alexander VII. Columbus leaves the book "to his beloved country, the republic of Genoa."

He directs the erection of a hospital in that city for the poor, with provision for its support, and he declares that republic his successor in the admiralty of the Indies, in the event of his male line becoming extinct.

The authenticity of this paper has been questioned. It has been said that there was no probability of Columbus having resort to a usage with which he was most likely unacquainted. The objections are not cogent. Columbus was accustomed to the peculiarities of a military life, and he repeatedly wrote letters, in critical moments, as a precaution against some fatal occurrence that seemed to impend. The present codicil from its date, must have been written a few days previous to his death, perhaps at a moment when he imagined himself at extremity. This may account for any difference in the hand writing, especially as he was at times so affected by the gout in his hands as not to be able to write except at night. Particular stress has been laid on the signature, but it does not appear that he was uniform in regard to that, and it is a point to which any one who attempted a forgery would be attentive.

---

* "Item. Mando el dicho Don Diego mi hijo, o á la persona qui heredare el dicha mayorazgo, que tenga y sostenga siempre en la ciudad de Genova una persona de nuestro linage que tenga alli casa é muger, é le ordene renta con que pueda vivir honestamente, como persona tan llegada á nuestro linage, y haga pie y raiz en la dicha ciudad como natural della, porque podrá haber de la dicha ciudad ayuda e favor en las cosas del menester suyo, *pues que della salí y en ella nací.*"

It does not appear likewise that any advantage could have been obtained by forging the paper, or that any such was attempted.

In 1502, when Columbus was about to depart on his fourth and last voyage, he wrote to his friend doctor Nicolo Oderigo, formerly ambassador from Genoa to Spain, and forwarded to him copies of all his grants and commissions from the Spanish sovereigns, authenticated before the alcaldes of Seville. He at the same time, wrote to the bank of San Giorgio at Genoa, assigning a tenth of his revenues to be paid to that city in diminution of the duties on corn, wine, and other provisions.

Why should Columbus feel this strong interest in Genoa had he been born in any of the other Italian states which have laid claim to him? He was under no obligation to Genoa. He had resided there but a brief portion of his early life, and his proposition for discovery, according to some writers, had been scornfully rejected by that republic. There is nothing to warrant so strong an interest in Genoa, but the filial tie which links the heart of a man to his native place, however he may be separated from it by time or distance, and however little he may be indebted to it for favours.

Again: had Columbus been born in any of the towns and villages of the Genoese coast, which have claimed him for a native, why should he have made these bequests in favour of the *city* of Genoa, and not of his native town or village?

These bequests were evidently dictated by a mingled sentiment of pride and affection, which would be without all object if not directed to his native place. He was at this time elevated above all petty pride on the subject. His renown was so brilliant that it would have shed a lustre on any hamlet, however obscure; and the strong love of country here manifested would never have felt satisfied, until it had singled out the spot, and nestled down in the very cradle of his infancy. These appear to be powerful reasons, drawn from natural feeling, for deciding in favour of Genoa.

No. VII

The Colombos

During the early part of the life of Columbus, there were two other navigators, bearing the same name, of some rank and celebrity, with whom he occasionally sailed; their names occurring vaguely from time to time, during the obscure part of his career, have caused much perplexity to some of his biographers, who have supposed that they designated the discoverer. Fernando Columbus affirms them to have been family connexions,* and his father says, in one of his letters, "I am not the first admiral of our family."

These two were uncle and nephew: the latter being termed by historians Colombo the younger, (by the Spanish historians Colombo el mozo). They were in the Genoese service, but are mentioned, occasionally, in old chronicles as French commanders, because Genoa, during a great part of their time, was under the protection, or rather the sovereignty of France, and her ships and captains, being engaged in the expeditions of that power, were identified with the French marine.

Mention is made of the elder Colombo in Zurita's Annals of Arragon, (l. xix. p. 261.) in the war between Spain and Portugal, on the subject of the claim of the Princess Juana to the crown of Castile. In 1476 the King of Portugal determined to go to the Mediterranean coast of France, to incite his ally Louis XI to prosecute the war in the province of Guipuzcoa.

The King left Toro, says Zurita, on the 13th June, and went by the river to the city of Porto in order to await the armada of the King of France, the captain of which was Colon (Colombo), who was to navigate by the straits of Gibraltar to pass to Marseilles.

After some delays Colombo arrived, at the latter part of July, with the French armada, at Bermeo on the coast of Biscay, where he encountered a violent storm, lost his principal ship and ran to the coast of Galicia with an intention of attacking Ribaldo and lost a great many of his men. From thence he went to Lisbon to receive the King of Portugal, who embarked in the fleet in August with a number of his noblemen and took two thousand two hundred foot soldiers and four hundred and seventy horse to strengthen the Portuguese garrisons along the Barbary coast. There were in the squadron twelve ships and five caravels. After touching at Ceuta the fleet proceeded to Colibre, where the King dis-

---

* Hist. del Almirante, cap. 1.

embarked in the middle of September, the weather not permitting them to proceed to Marseilles (Zurita, l. xix. c. 51).

This Colombo is evidently the naval commander of whom the following mention is made by Jacques George Chaufepie in his supplement to Bayle (vol. ii. p. 126 of letter C.)

"I do not know what dependence," says Chaufepie, "is to be placed on a fact reported in the *Ducatiana* (part i. p. 143.) that Columbus was in 1474 captain of several ships for Louis XI and that, as the Spaniards had made at that time an irruption into Rousillon, he thought that for reprisal, and without contravening the peace between the two crowns, he could run down Spanish vessels. He attacked, therefore, and took two galleys of that nation, freighted on the account of various individuals. On complaints of this action being made to King Ferdinand, he wrote on the subject to Louis XI.: his letter is dated the 9 December, 1474. Ferdinand terms Christopher Columbus a subject of Louis; it was because, as is known, Columbus was a Genoese, and Louis was sovereign of Genoa, although that city and Savona were held of him in fief by the Duke of Milan."

It is highly probable that it was the squadron of this same Colombo of whom the circumstance is related by Bossi, and after him by Spotorno on the authority of a letter found in the archives of Milan, and written in 1476 by two illustrious Milanese gentlemen, on their return from Jerusalem. The letter states that in the previous year 1475, as the Venetian fleet was stationed off Cyprus to guard the island, a Genoese squadron, commanded by one Colombo, sailed by them with an air of defiance, shouting "Viva San Giorgia!" As the republics were then at peace they were permitted to pass unmolested.

Bossi supposes that the Colombo here mentioned was Christopher Columbus the discoverer; but it appears rather to have been the old Genoese admiral of that name, who according to Zurita was about that time cruising in the Mediterranean; and who, in all probability, was the hero of both the preceding occurrences.

The nephew of this Colombo, called by the Spaniards Colombo el mozo, commanded a few years afterwards a squadron in the French service, as will appear in a subsequent illustration, and Columbus may at various times have held an inferior command under both uncle and nephew, and been present on the above cited occasions.

No. VIII

Expedition of John of Anjou

About the time that Columbus had attained his twenty fourth year, his native city was in a state of great alarm and peril from the threatened invasion of Alphonso V of Arragon, King of Naples. Finding itself too weak to contend singly with such a foe, and having in vain looked for assistance from Italy, it placed itself under the protection of Charles VII of France. That monarch sent to its assistance John of Anjou, son of René or Renato, King of Naples, who had been dispossessed of his crown by Alphonso. John of Anjou, otherwise called the Duke of Calabria,* immediately took upon himself the command of the place, repaired its fortifications and defended the entrance of the harbour with strong chains. In the meantime Alphonso had prepared a large land force, and assembled an armament of twenty ships and ten galleys at Ancona on the frontiers of Genoa. The situation of the latter was considered eminently perilous, when Alphonso suddenly fell ill of a calenture and died; leaving the Kingdoms of Anjou and Sicily to his brother John and the kingdom of Naples to his son Ferdinand.

The death of Alphonso, and the subsequent division of his dominions, while they relieved the fears of the Genoese, gave rise to new hopes on the part of the house of Anjou; and the Duke John, encouraged by emissaries from various powerful partizans among the Neapolitan nobility, determined to make a bold attempt upon Naples for the recovery of the crown. The Genoese entered into his cause with spirit, furnishing him with ships, galleys, and money. His father René or Renato fitted out twelve galleys for the expedition in the harbour of Marseilles, and sent him assurance of an abundant supply of money and of the assistance of the king of France. The brilliant nature of the enterprize attracted the attention of the daring and restless spirits of the times. The chivalrous nobleman, the soldier of fortune, the hardy corsair, the bold adventurer, or the military partisan, enlisted under the banners of the Duke of Calabria. It is stated by historians that Columbus served in the armament from Genoa in a squadron commanded by one of the Colombos, his relations.

The expedition sailed in October 1459 and arrived at Sessa between the mouths of the Garigliano and the Volturno. The news of its arrival was the signal of universal revolt; the factious Barons and their vassals

---

* Duke of Calabria was the title of the son and heir apparent to the crown of Naples.

hastened to join the standard of Anjou, and the duke soon saw the finest provinces of the Neapolitan dominions at his command, and with his army and squadron menaced the city of Naples itself.

In the history of this expedition we meet with one hazardous action of the fleet in which Columbus had embarked.

The army of John of Anjou being closely invested by a superior force, was in a perilous predicament at the mouth of the Sarno. In this conjuncture, the captain of the armada landed with his men and scoured the neighborhood; hoping to awaken in the populace their former enthusiasm for the banner of Anjou, and perhaps to take Naples by surprize. A chosen company of Neapolitan infantry was sent against them. The troops from the fleet having little of the discipline of regular soldiery and much of the freebooting disposition of maritime rovers, had scattered themselves about the country, intent chiefly upon spoil. They were attacked by the infantry and put to the route, with the loss of many killed and wounded. Endeavouring to make their way back to the ships, they found the passes seized and blocked up by the people of Sorento, who assailed them with dreadful havoc. Their flight now became desperate and headlong; many threw themselves from rocks and precipices into the sea, and but a small portion regained the ships.

The contest of John of Anjou for the crown of Naples lasted four years. For a time fortune favoured him and the prize seemed almost within his grasp: but reverses succeeded; he was defeated at various points; the factious nobles, one by one, deserted him, and returned to their allegiance to Alphonso, and the Duke was finally compelled to retire to the Island of Ischia. Here he remained for some time guarded by eight galleys, which likewise harassed the bay of Naples.* In this squadron, which loyally adhered to him until he ultimately abandoned this unfortunate enterprize, Columbus is stated to have served.

No. IX

Capture of the Venetian galleys by Colombo the Younger

As the account of the sea fight, by which Fernando Columbus asserts that his father was first thrown upon the shores of Portugal, has been

* Colenuccio, Hist. Nap., lib. vii. cap. 17.

adopted by various respectable historians, it is proper to give particular reasons for discrediting it.

Fernando expressly says that it was in an action mentioned by Marco Antonio Sabelico in the eighth book of his tenth Decade. That the squadron in which Columbus served was commanded by a famous corsair called Columbus the younger (Colombo el Mozo) and that an embassy was sent from Venice to thank the King of Portugal for the succour he afforded to the Venetian captains and crews. All this is certainly recorded in Sabellicus, but the battle took place in 1485, after Columbus had *left* Portugal. Zurita in his annals of Arragon under the date of 1485, mentions this same action. He says "at this time four Venetian galleys sailed from the island of Cadiz, and took the route for Flanders; they were laden with merchandize from the Levant, especially from the island of Sicily, and, passing by Cape St. Vincent, they were attacked by a French corsair, son of Captain Colon (Colombo) who had seven vessels in his armada; and the galleys were captured the twenty first of August."*

A much fuller account is given in the life of King John II of Portugal by Garcia de Resende, who likewise records it as happening in 1485. He says the Venetian galleys were taken and robbed by the French and the captains and crews, wounded, plundered, and maltreated, were turned on shore at Cascoes. Here they were succoured by Doña Maria de Meneses, countess of Monsanto. When King John II heard of the circumstance, being much grieved that such an event should have happened on his coast; and being disposed to show his friendship for the republic of Venice, he ordered that the Venetian captains should be furnished with rich raiment of silk and costly cloths, and provided with horses and mules, that they might make their appearance before him in a style befitting themselves and their country. He received them with great kindness and distinction, expressing himself with princely courtesy, both as to themselves and the republic of Venice, and having heard their account of the battle, and of their destitute situation, he assisted them with a large sum of money to ransom their galleys from the French cruisers. The latter took all the merchandize on board of their ships, but King John prohibited any of the spoil from being purchased within his dominions. Having thus generously relieved and assisted the captains, and administered to the necessities of their crews, he enabled them all to return in their own galleys to Venice.

The dignitaries of the republic were so highly sensible of this munificence on the part of King John that they sent a stately embassy to that

---

* Zurita, Anales de Aragon, lib. xx. cap. 64.

monarch with rich presents and warm expressions of gratitude. Geronimo Donate was charged with this mission, a man eminent for learning and eloquence. He was honourably received and entertained by King John, and dismissed with royal presents, among which were genets and mules, with sumptuous trappings and caparisons, and many negro slaves richly clad.*

The following is the account of this action as given by Sabellicus in his History of Venice:†

"Erano andate quattro Galee delle quai Bartolommeo Minio era capitano. Queste navigando per l'Iberico mare, Colombo il più giovane, nipote de quel Colombo famoso corsale, fecesi incontro a' Veniziani di notte appresso il Sacro Promontorio, che chiamasi ora Capo di San Vincenzo, con sette navi guernite da combattere. Egli quantunque nel primo incontro avesse seco disposto d'opprimere le navi Veniziane, si ritenne però dal combattere sin al giorno, tuttavia per esser alla bataglia più acconcio così le seguia, che le prode del corsale toccavano le poppe de Veniziani. Venuto il giorno incontanente i Barbari diedero l'assalto. Sostennero i Veniziani allora l'empito del nemico, per numero di navi e di combattenti superiore, e durò il conflitto atroce per molte ore. Rare fiate fu combattuto contro simili nemici con tanta uccisione, perchè a pena si costuma d'attaccarsi contro di loro se non per occasione. Affermano alcuni, che vi furono presenti, esser morte delle ciurme Veniziane da trecento uomini. Altri dicono che fu meno. Morì in quella zuffa Lorenzo Michele capitano d'una galera, e Giovanni Delfino d'altro capitano fratello. Era durata la zuffa dal fare del giorno fin' ad ore venti, e erano le genti Veniziane mal trattate. Era gia la nave Delfina in potere de' nemici quando le altre ad una si renderono. Narrano alcuni, che furono di quel aspro conflitto partecipi, aver numerato nelle loro navi da prode a poppe ottanta valorosi uomini estinti, i quali dal nemico veduti, lo mossero a gemere e dire con sdegno, che così avevano voluto Veniziani. I corpi morti furono gettati nel mare, e i feriti posti nel lido. Quei che remasero vivi, seguirono con le nave il Capitano vittorioso sin' a Lisbona e ivi furono tutti licenziati. * * * * Quivi furono i Veniziani benignamente recevuti dal Re, gli infermi furono medicati, gli altri ebbero abiti

---

* Obras de Garcia de Resende, cap. 58. Avora, 1554.

† Marco Antonio Coccio, better known under the name of Sabellicus, a cognomen which he adopted on being crowned poet in the pedantic academy of Pomponius Lætus. He was a contemporary of Columbus, and makes brief mention of his discoveries in the eighth book of the tenth Ennead of his Universal History. By some writers he is called the Livy of his time; others accuse him of being full of misrepresentations in favour of Venice. The elder Scaliger charges him with venality, and with being swayed by Venetian gold.

e denari secondo la loro condizione. * * * * Oltre ciò vietò in tutto il Regno, che alcuno non comprasse della preda Veniziana, portata dai corsali. La nuova dell' avuta rovina non poco afflisse la città, erano perduti in quella mercatanzia da ducento mila ducati; ma il danno particolare degli uomini uccisi diede maggior afflizione."

Marc. Ant. Sabelico, Hist. Venet. Decad. IV. lib. 3.

No. X

Amerigo Vespucci

Among the earliest and most intelligent of the voyagers who followed the track of Columbus, was Amerigo Vespucci. He has been considered by many as the first discoverer of the southern continent, and by a singular caprice of fortune, his name has been given to the whole of the New World. It has been strenuously insisted, however, that he had no claim to the title of a discoverer, that he merely sailed in a subordinate capacity, in a squadron commanded by others, that the account of his first voyage is a fabrication, and that he did not visit the main land until after it had been discovered and coasted by Columbus. As this question has been made a matter of warm and voluminous controversy, it is proper to take a summary view of it in the present work.

Amerigo Vespucci was born in Florence, March 9th, 1451, of a noble, but not at that time a wealthy family: his father's name was Anastatio, his mother's was Elizabetta Mini. He was the third of their sons, and received an excellent education under his uncle, Georgio Antonio Vespucci, a learned friar, of the fraternity of San Marco, who was instructor to several illustrious personages of that period.

Amerigo Vespucci visited Spain and took up his residence in Seville, to attend to some commercial transactions on account of the family of the Medici of Florence; and to repair by his ingenuity the losses and misfortunes of an unskilful brother.*

The date of his arrival in Spain is uncertain but from comparing dates and circumstances mentioned in his letters, he must have been at Seville when Columbus returned from his first voyage.

Padre Stanislaus Canovai, professor of mathematics at Florence, who

---

* Bandini Vita d'Amerigo Vespucci.

has published the life and voyages of Amerigo Vespucci, says that he was commissioned by king Ferdinand and sent with Columbus in his second voyage in 1493. He states this on the authority of a passage in the Cosmography of Sebastian Munster, published at Basle in 1550;* but Munster mentions Vespucci as having accompanied Columbus in his first voyage; the reference of Canovai is therefore incorrect; and the suggestion of Munster is disproved by the letters of Vespucci, in which he states his having been stimulated by the accounts brought of the newly discovered regions. He never mentions such a voyage in any of his letters; which he most probably would have done, or rather would have made it the subject of a copious letter, had he actually performed it.

The first notice of a positive form which we have of Vespucci as resident in Spain is early in 1496. He appears, from documents in the royal archives at Seville, to have acted as agent or factor for the house of Juanoto Berardi, a rich Florentine merchant resident in Seville; who had contracted to furnish the Spanish sovereigns with three several armaments, of four vessels each, for the service of the newly discovered countries. He may have been one of the principals in this affair, which was transacted in the name of this established house. Berardi died in December 1495, and in the following January, we find Amerigo Vespucci attending to the concerns of the expedition, and settling with the masters of the ships for their pay and maintenance, according to the agreements made between them and the late Juanoto Berardi. On the 12th of January 1496, he received on this account, 10,000 maravedies from Bernardo Pinelo, the royal treasurer. He went on preparing all things for the dispatch of four caravels to sail under the same contract between the sovereigns and the house of Berardi, and sent them to sea on the 3d of February 1496; but on the 18th they met with a storm and were wrecked; the crews were saved with the loss of only three men.† While thus employed Amerigo Vespucci of course had occasional opportunity of conversing with Columbus, with whom, according to the expression of the admiral himself, in one of his letters to his son Diego, he appears to have been always on friendly terms. From these conversations, and from his agency in these expeditions, he soon became excited to visit the newly discovered countries, and to participate in enterprizes which were the theme of every tongue. Having made himself well acquainted with geographical and nautical science, he prepared to launch into the

* Cosm. Munst. p. 1108.

† These particulars are from manuscript memoranda, extracted from the royal archives, by the late accurate historian Muñoz.

career of discovery. It was not very long before he carried this design into execution.

In 1498 Columbus, in his third voyage, discovered the coast of Paria, on Terra Firma; which he at that time imagined to be a great island, but that a vast continent lay immediately adjacent. He sent to Spain specimens of pearls found on this coast, and gave the most sanguine accounts of the supposed riches of the country.

In 1499 an expedition of four vessels, under command of Alonzo de Ojeda, was fitted out from Spain, and sailed for Paria, guided by charts and letters sent to the government by Columbus. These were communicated to Ojeda by his patron, the bishop Fonseca, who had the superintendence of India affairs, and who furnished him also with a warrant to undertake the voyage.

It is presumed that Vespucci aided in fitting out the armament, and sailed in a vessel belonging to the house of Berardi, and in this way was enabled to take a share in the gains and losses of the expedition; for Isabella, as queen of Castile, had rigorously forbidden all strangers to trade with her transatlantic possessions, not even excepting the natives of the Kingdom of Arragon.

This squadron visited Paria and several hundred miles of the coast, which they ascertained to be Terra Firma. They returned in June 1500 and on the 18th of July in that year, Amerigo Vespucci wrote an account of his voyage to Lorenzo de Pier Francisco de Medici of Florence, which remained concealed in manuscript, until brought to light and published by Bandini in 1745.

In his account of this voyage, and in every other narrative of his different expeditions, Vespucci never mentions any other person concerned in the enterprize. He gives the time of his sailing, and states that he went with two caravels, which were probably his share of the expedition, or rather vessels sent by the house of Berardi. He gives an interesting narrative of the voyage and of the various transactions with the natives, which corresponds in many substantial points with the accounts furnished by Ojeda and his mariners of their voyage, in a law suit hereafter mentioned.

In May 1501, Vespucci, having suddenly left Spain, sailed in the service of Emanuel, King of Portugal; in the course of which expedition he visited the coast of Brazil. He gives an account of this voyage in a second letter to Lorenzo de Pier Francisco de Medici, which also remained in manuscript until published by Bartolozzi in 1789.*

No record or notice of any such voyage, undertaken by Amerigo

---

* Bartolozzi Recherche Historico. Firenze, 1789.

Vespucci, at the command of Emanuel, is to be found in the archives of the Torre do Tombo, the general archives of Portugal, which have been repeatedly and diligently searched for the purpose. It is singular also that his name is not to be found in any of the Portuguese historians, who in general were very particular in naming all navigators who held any important station among them or rendered any distinguished services. That Vespucci did sail along the coasts, however, is not questioned. His nephew after his death, in the course of evidence on some point in dispute, gave the correct latitude of Cape St. Augustine, which he said he had extracted from his uncle's journal.

In 1504, Vespucci wrote a third letter to the same Lorenzo de Medici containing a more extended account of the voyage just alluded to, in the service of Portugal. This was the first of his narratives that appeared in print. It appears to have been published in Latin in Strasburgh as early as 1505 under the title "Americus Vesputius, de Orbe Antarctica per Regem Portugalliæ pridem inventa."*

An edition of this letter was printed in Vicenza in 1507, in an anonymous collection of voyages edited by Francanzio di Monte Alboddo, an inhabitant of Vicenza. It was reprinted in Italian in 1508, at Milan, and also in Latin in a book entitled Itinerarium Portugalensium. In making the present illustration the Milan edition in Italian† has been consulted, and also a Latin translation of it, by Simon Grinæus, in his Novus Orbis, published at Basle in 1532. It relates entirely to the first voyage of Vespucci from Lisbon to the Brazils in 1501.

It is from this voyage to the Brazils that Amerigo Vespucci was first considered the discoverer of Terra Firma; and his name was at first applied to these southern regions, though afterwards extended to the whole continent. The merits of his voyage were, however, greatly exag-

---

* Panzer, tom. vi. p. 33. apud Esame critico, p. 88. Anotazione 1.

† This rare book in the possession of O. Rich, Esq. is believed to be the oldest printed collection of voyages extant. It has not the pages numbered, the sheets are merely marked with a letter of the alphabet at the foot of each eighth page. It contains the earliest account of the voyages of Columbus, from his first departure until his arrival at Cadiz in chains. The letter of Vespucci to Lorenzo de Medici occupies the fifth book of this little volume. It is stated to have been originally written in Spanish, and translated into Italian by a person of the name of Jocondo. An earlier edition is stated to have been printed in Venice by Alberto Vercellese in 1504. The author is said to have been Angelo Trivigiani, secretary to the Venetian ambassador in Spain. This Trivigiani appears to have collected many of the particulars of the voyages of Columbus from the manuscript Decades of Peter Martyr, who erroneously lays the charge of the plagiarism to Aloysius Cadamosto, whose voyages are inserted in the same collection. The book was entitled "Libretto di tutta la Navigazione del Re de Espagna, delle Isole, e Terreni nuovamente trovati."

gerated. The Brazils had been previously discovered, and formally taken possession of for Spain, in 1500, by Vicente Yañez Pinzon; and also in the same year, by Pedro Alvarez Cabral, on the part of Portugal; circumstances unknown, however, to Vespucci and his associates. The country remained in possession of Portugal, in conformity to the line of demarcation agreed on between the two nations.

Vespucci made a second voyage in the service of Portugal. He says that he commanded a caravel in a squadron of six vessels destined for the discovery of Malacca; which they had heard to be the great depôt and magazine of all the trade between the Ganges and the Indian sea. Such an expedition did sail about this time, under the command of Gonzalo Coelho. The squadron sailed according to Vespucci on the 10th of May 1503. It stopped at the Cape de Verde islands for refreshments, and afterwards sailed by the coast of Sierra Leone; but was prevented from landing by contrary winds and a turbulent sea. Standing to the southwest, they ran three hundred leagues, until they were three degrees to the southward of the Equinoctial line, where they discovered an uninhabited island, about two leagues in length and one in breadth. Here, on the 10th of August, by mismanagement, the commander of the squadron ran his vessel on a rock and lost her. While the other vessels were assisting to save the crew and property from the wreck, Amerigo Vespucci was despatched in his caravel to search for a safe harbour in the island. He departed in his vessel without his long-boat, and with less than half of his crew, the rest having gone in the boat to the assistance of the wreck. Vespucci found a harbour, but waited in vain for several days for the arrival of the ships. Standing out to sea, he met with a solitary vessel, and learnt that the ship of the commander had sunk, and the rest had proceeded onwards. In company with this vessel, he stood for the Brazils, according to a command of the King, in case that any vessel should be parted from the fleet. Arriving on the coast he discovered the famous bay of All Saints, where he remained upwards of two months, in hopes of being joined by the rest of the fleet. He at length ran 260 leagues farther south, where he remained five months building a fort and taking in a cargo of Brazil wood. Then leaving in the fortress a garrison of twenty four men with arms and ammunition, he set sail for Lisbon, where he arrived in June 1504.* The commander of the squadron, and the other four ships were never heard of afterwards.

Vespucci does not appear to have received the reward from the King of Portugal that his services merited, for we find him at Seville early in

---

* Letter of Vespucci to Soderini or Renato. Edit. of Canovai.

1505, on his way to the Spanish court, in quest of employment; and he was bearer of a letter from Columbus to his son Diego, dated February 5, which, while it speaks warmly of him as a friend, intimates his having been unfortunate. The following is the letter.

"My Dear Son,

"Diego Mendez departed from hence on Monday the third of this month. After his departure I conversed with Amerigo Vespucci, the bearer of this, who goes there (to court) summoned on affairs of navigation. Fortune has been adverse to him as to many others. His labours have not profited him so much as they reasonably should have done. He goes on my account, and with much desire to do something that may result to my advantage if within his power. I cannot ascertain here in what I can employ him, that will be serviceable to me, for I do not know what may be there required. He goes with the determination to do all that is possible for me. See in what he may be of advantage, and co-operate with him; that he may say and do every thing and put his plans in operation; and let all be done secretly that he may not be suspected. I have said every thing to him that I can say touching the business, and have informed him of the pay I have received, and what is due, &c."*

About this time Amerigo Vespucci received letters of naturalisation from King Ferdinand, and shortly afterwards he and Vicente Yañez Pinzon were named captains of an armada about to be sent out in the spice trade and to make discoveries. There is a royal order dated Toro, 11th April, 1507, for 12,000 maravedies, for an outfit for "Americo de Vespuche, resident of Seville." Preparations were made for this voyage and vessels procured and fitted out, but it was eventually abandoned. There are memoranda existing concerning it, dated in 1506, 1507, and 1508, from which it appears that Amerigo Vespucci remained at Seville, attending to the fluctuating concerns of this squadron, until the destination of the vessels was changed, their equipments were sold, and the accounts settled. During this time he had a salary of 30,000 maravedies. On the 22d of March 1508 he received the appointment of principal pilot, with a salary of 70,000 maravedies. His chief duties were to prepare charts, examine pilots, superintend the fitting out of expeditions, and prescribe the route that vessels were to pursue in their voyages to the New World. He appears to have remained at Seville and to have retained this office until his death on the 22d of February, 1512. His widow, Maria Corezo, enjoyed a pension of 10,000 maravedies. After

* Navarrete Colec. Viag. tom. i. p. 351.

his death, his nephew, Juan Vespucci, was nominated pilot with a salary of 20,000 maravedies commencing on the 22d of May 1512. Peter Martyr speaks with high commendation of this young man. "Young Vesputius is one to whom Americus Vesputius, his uncle, left the exact knowledge of the mariner's faculties, as it were by inheritance, after his death, for he was a very expert master in the knowledge of his carde, his compasse and the elevation of the pole starre by the quadrant. * * * * Vesputius is my very familiar friend and a wittie young man, in whose company I take great pleasure and therefore use him oftentymes for my guest. He hath also made many voyages into these coasts and diligently noted such things as he hath seen."*

Vespucci the nephew continued in this situation during the lifetime of Fonseca, who had been the patron of his uncle and his family. He was divested of his pay and his employ by a letter of the council dated the 18th of March 1525, shortly after the death of the Bishop. No further notice of Vespucci, is to be found in the archives of the Indies.

Such is a brief view of the career of Amerigo Vespucci; it remains to notice the points in controversy. Shortly after his return from his last expedition to the Brazils, he wrote a letter dated Lisbon, 4th of September 1504, containing a summary account of all his voyages. This letter is of special importance to the matters under investigation, as it is the only one known that relates to the disputed voyage, which would establish him as the discoverer of Terra Firma. It is presumed to have been written in Latin, and was addressed to René, duke of Lorraine, who assumed the title of king of Sicily and Jerusalem.

The earliest known edition of this letter was published in Latin in 1507, at St. Diez, in Lorraine. A copy of it has been found in the library of the Vatican (No. 9688) by the Abbé Cancellicri. In preparing the present illustration a reprint of this letter in Latin has been consulted, inserted in the Novus Orbis of Grinæus, published at Basle in 1532. The letter contains a spirited narrative of four voyages, which he asserts to have made to the New World. In the prologue he excuses the liberty of addressing king René, by calling to his recollection the ancient intimacy of their youth, when studying the rudiments of science together, under the paternal uncle of the voyager; and adds that if the present narrative should not altogether please his majesty, he must plead to him as Pliny said to Mecænas, "that he used formerly to be amused with his triflings."

In the prologue to this letter he informs René that affairs of commerce had brought him to Spain, where he had experienced the various changes

---

* Peter Martyr, Decad. III. lib. 5.—Eden's English Trans.

of fortune attendant on such transactions, and was induced to abandon that pursuit, and direct his labours to objects of a more elevated and stable nature. He therefore purposed to contemplate various parts of the world, and to behold the marvels which it contains. To this object both time and place were favourable, for King Ferdinand was then preparing four vessels for the discovery of new lands in the west, and appointed him among the number of those who went in the expedition. "We departed," he adds, "from the port of Cadiz, May 20, 1497, taking our course on the great gulph of ocean, in which voyage we employed eighteen months, discovering many lands and innumerable islands, chiefly inhabited, of which our ancestors make no mention."

A duplicate of this letter appears to have been sent at the same time (written, it is said, in Italian) to Piere Soderini, afterwards gonfalonier of Florence, which was some years subsequently published in Italy, not earlier than 1510, and entitled "Lettera de Amerigo Vespucci delle Isole nuovamente trovate in quatro suoi viaggi." We have consulted the edition of this letter in Italian inserted in the publication of Padre Stanislaus Canovai already referred to.

It has been suggested by an Italian writer that this letter was written by Vespucci to Soderini only, and the address altered to King René, through the flattery or mistake of the Lorraine editor; without perceiving how unsuitable the reference to former intimacy intended for Soderini was, when applied to a sovereign. The person making this remark can hardly have read the prologue to the Latin edition, in which the title of "your majesty" is frequently repeated, and the term "illustrious King" employed. It was first published also in Lorraine, the domains of René, and the publisher would not probably have presumed to take such a liberty with his sovereign's name. It becomes a question whether Vespucci addressed the same letter to king René and to Piere Soderini, both of them having been educated with him, or whether he sent a copy of this letter to Soderini, which subsequently found its way into print. The address to Soderini may have been substituted through mistake by the Italian publisher. Neither of the publications could have been made under the supervision of Vespucci.

The voyage specified in this letter as having taken place in 1497 is the great point in controversy. It is strenuously asserted that no such voyage took place, and that the first expedition of Vespucci to the coast of Paria was in the enterprise commanded by Ojeda in 1499. The books of the armadas existing in the archives of the Indies at Seville, have been diligently examined, but no record of such voyage has been found, nor any official documents relating to it. Those most experienced in Spanish colonial regulations insist that no command like that pretended by Vespucci could have been given to a stranger, till he had first received letters of naturalization from the sovereigns, for the Kingdom of Castile; and he did not obtain such until 1505, when they were granted to him as preparatory to giving him the command in conjunction with Pinzon.

His account of a voyage made by him in 1497, therefore, is alleged to be a fabrication for the purpose of claiming the discovery of Paria. Or rather it is affirmed that he has divided the voyage which he actually made with Ojeda in 1499 into two; taking a number of incidents from his real voyage, altering them a little, and enlarging them with descriptions of the countries and people, so as to make a plausible narrative, which he gives as a distinct voyage; and antedating his departure to 1497, so as to make himself appear the first discoverer of Paria.

In support of this charge various coincidences have been pointed out between his voyage, said to have taken place in 1497, and that described in his first letter to Lorenzo de Medici in 1499. These coincidences are with respect to places visited, transactions and battles with the natives, and the number of Indians carried to Spain and sold as slaves.

But the credibility of this voyage has been put to a stronger test. About 1508 a suit was instituted against the crown of Spain by Don Diego, son and heir of Columbus, for the government of certain parts of Terra Firma, and for a share in the revenue rising from them, conformably to the capitulations made between the sovereigns and his father. It was the object of the crown to disprove the discovery of the coast of Paria and the Pearl Islands by Columbus, as it was maintained that unless he had discovered them, the claim of his heir with respect to them would be of no validity.

In the course of this suit a particular examination of witnesses took place in 1512–13 in the Fiscal court. Alonzo de Ojeda and nearly a hundred other persons were interrogated on oath; that voyager having been the first to visit the coast of Paria after Columbus had left it, and that within a very few months. The interrogatories of these witnesses and their replies are still extant in the archives of the Indies at Seville, in a packet of papers entitled "Papers belonging to the admiral Don Luis Colon, about the conservation of his privileges from ann. 1515 to 1564." The author of the present work has two several copies of these interrogatories lying before him. One made by the late historian Muñoz, and the other made in 1826, and signed by Don Jose de la Higuera y Lara, keeper of the general archives of the Indies in Seville. In the course of this testimony the fact that Amerigo Vespucci accompanied Ojeda in this voyage of 1499 appears manifest, first from the deposition of Ojeda himself. The following are the words of the record: "In this voyage, which this said witness made, he took with him Juan de la Cosa and Morego Vespuche (Amerigo Vespucci) and other pilots."* Secondly, from the coincidence of many parts of the narrative of Vespucci with events in this voyage of Ojeda; among these coincidences, one is particularly striking. Vespucci in his letter to Lorenzo de Medici, and also in that to René or Soderini says that his ships, after leaving the coast of Terra Firma, stopped at Hispaniola, where they remained about two months and a half procuring provisions, during which time, he adds, we had many perils and troubles with the very Christians who were in that island with Columbus (and I believe through envy.)†

Now it is well known that Ojeda passed some time on the western end of the island, victualling his ships; and that serious dissensions took place between him and the Spaniards in those parts, and the party sent by Columbus under the command of Roldan to keep a watch upon his movements. If then Vespucci, as is stated upon oath, really accompanied Ojeda in this voyage, the inference appears almost irresistible, that he had not made the previous voyage in 1497. For the fact would have been well known to Ojeda; he would have considered Vespucci as the original discoverer, and would have had no motive for depriving him of the merit of it, to give it to Columbus, with whom Ojeda was not upon friendly terms.

Ojeda, however, expressly declares that the coast had been discovered by Columbus. On being asked how he knew the fact, he replied, because he saw the chart of the country discovered, which Columbus sent at the time to the king and queen, and that he came off immediately on a voyage of discovery and found what was therein set down as discovered by the admiral was correct.‡

Another witness, Bernaldo de Haro, states that he had been with the admiral, and had written (or rather copied) a letter for the admiral, to the King and Queen, designating, in an accompanying sea chart, the courses and steerings and winds by which he had arrived at Paria; and

---

* En este Viage que este dicho testigo hizo trujo consigo a Juan de la Cosa piloto e Morego Vespuche e otros pilotos.

† Per la necessitá del mantenimento fummo all' Isola d'Antiglia (Hispaniola) che é questa che discoperse Cristoval Columbo piú anni fá, dove facemmo molto mantenimento e stemmo due mesi e 17 giorni, dove passammo molti pericoli e travagli con li medesimi christiani que in questa isola stavanno col Colombo (credo per invidia). Letter of Vespucci. Edit. of Canovai.

‡ Preguntado como lo sabe, dijo, que lo sabe porque vió este testigo la figura que el dicho Almirante al dicho tiempo embió á Castilla al Rey e Reina nuestros Señores de lo que habia descubierto, y porque este testigo luego vino á descubrir y halló que era verdad lo que dicho tiene que el dicho Almirante descubrió. MS. Process of D. Diego Colon. pregunta 2.

that this witness had heard that from this chart others had been made, and that Pedro Alonzo, Niño, and Ojeda, and others who had since visited these countries, had been guided by the same.*

Francisco de Morales, one of the best and most credible of all pilots, testified that he saw a sea chart which Columbus had made of the coast of Paria, *and he believed that all governed themselves by it.*

Numerous witnesses in this process testify to the fact that Paria was first discovered by Columbus. Las Casas, who has been at the pains of counting them, says that the fact was established by twenty five eye-witnesses and sixty ear-witnesses. Many of them testify also, that the coast south of Paria, and that extending west of the island of Margarita away to Venezuela, which Vespucci states to have been discovered by himself in 1497, was now first discovered by Ojeda, and had never before been visited either by the admiral, "or any other Christian whatever."

Alonzo Sanchez de Carvajal says, that all the voyages of discovery which were made to the Terra Firma were made by persons who had sailed with the admiral, or been benefited by his instruction and directions, following the course he had laid down;† and the same is testified by many other pilots and mariners of reputation and experience.

It would be a singular circumstance if none of these witnesses, many of whom must have sailed in the same squadron with Vespucci along this coast in 1499, should have known that he had discovered and explored it two years previously. If that had really been the case, what motive could he have for concealing the fact? and why, if they knew it, should they not proclaim it? Vespucci states his voyage in 1497 to have been made with four caravels; that they returned in October 1498, and that he sailed again with two caravels in May 1499 (the date of Ojeda's departure). Many of the mariners would therefore have been present in both voyages. Why too should Ojeda and the other pilots, guide themselves by the charts of Columbus, when they had a man on

---

* Este testigo escrivió úna carta que el Almirante escriviera a el Rey e Reyna N.N.S.S. haciendo les saber las perlas e cosas que habia hallado, y le embió señalado con la dicha carta, in una carta de marear, los rumbos y vientos por donde habia llegado á la Paria, e que este testigo oyó decir como pr. aquella carta se habian hecho otras e por ellas habian venido Pedro Alonzo Merino (*Niño*) e Ojeda, e otros que despues han ido á aquellas partes. MS. Process of D. Diego Colon. pregunta 9.

† Que en todos los viages que algunos hicieron descubriendo en la dicha tierra ivan personas que ovieron navegado con el dicho Almirante y a ellos mostró muchas cosas de marear, y ellos por imitacion é industria del dicho Almirante las aprendian y aprendieron e seguendo ag°. que el dicho Almirante les habia mostrado, hicieron los viages que descubrieron en la Tierra Firma. Process, Pregunta 10.

board so learned in nautical science, and who from his own recent observations was practically acquainted with the coast? Not a word, however, is mentioned of the voyage and discovery of Vespucci by any of the pilots, though every other navigator and discoverer is cited; nor does there even a seaman appear who has accompanied him in his asserted voyage.

Another strong circumstance against the reality of this voyage is that it was not brought forward in this trial to defeat the claims of the heirs of Columbus. Vespucci states the voyage to have been undertaken with the knowledge and countenance of King Ferdinand; it must therefore have been avowed and notorious. Vespucci was living at Seville in 1508 at the time of the commencement of this suit, and for four years afterward, a salaried servant of the crown. Many of the pilots and mariners must have been at hand who sailed with him in his pretended enterprize. If this voyage had once been proved, it would completely have settled the question, as far as concerned the coast of Paria, in favour of the crown. Yet no testimony appears ever to have been taken from Vespucci while living; and when the interrogatories were made in the Fiscal court in 1512-13, not one of his seaman is brought up to give evidence. A voyage so important in its nature and so essential to the question in dispute is not even alluded to; while useless pains are taken to wrest evidence from the voyage of Ojeda, undertaken at a subsequent period.

It is a circumstance worthy of notice that Vespucci commences his first letter to Lorenzo de Medici in 1500, within a month after his return from the voyage he had actually made to Paria, and apologizes for his long silence, by saying that nothing had occurred worthy of mention ("e gran tempo che non ho scritto á vostra magnifizenza, e non lo ha causato altra cosa ne nessuna, salvo non mi essere occorso cosa degna di memoria") and proceeds eagerly to tell him the wonders he had witnessed in the expedition from which he had but just returned. It would be a singular forgetfulness to say that nothing had occurred of importance, if he had made a previous voyage of eighteen months in 1497-8 to this newly discovered world; and it would be almost equally strange, that he should not make the slightest allusion to it in this letter.

It has been the endeavour of the author to examine this question dispassionately; and after considering the statements and arguments advanced on either side he cannot resist a conviction that the voyage stated to have been made in 1497 did not take place, and that Vespucci has no title to the first discovery of the coast of Paria.

The question is extremely perplexing from the difficulty of assigning

sufficient motives for so gross a deception. When Vespucci wrote his
letters there was no doubt entertained but that Columbus had discovered
the main land in his first voyage, Cuba being always considered the
extremity of Asia, until circumnavigated in 1508. Vespucci may have
supposed Brazil, Paria and the rest of that coast part of a distinct continent, and have been anxious to arrogate to himself the fame of its
discovery. It has been asserted that on his return from his voyage to
the Brazils, he prepared a maritime chart, in which he gave his name to
that part of the main land; but this assertion does not appear to be well
substantiated. It would rather seem that his name was given to that
part of the continent by others, as a tribute paid to his supposed merit,
in consequence of having read his own account of his voyages.*

It is singular that Fernando, the son of Columbus, in his biography of
his father, should bring no charge against Vespucci of endeavouring to
supplant the admiral in this discovery. Herrera has been cited as the
first to bring the accusation, in his History of the Indies, first published
in 1601, and has been much criticised in consequence by the advocates
of Vespucci, as making the charge on his mere assertion. But in fact
Herrera did but copy what he found written by Las Casas, who had
the proceedings of the Fiscal court lying before him, and was moved
to indignation against Vespucci, by what he considered proofs of great
imposture.

It has been suggested that Vespucci was instigated to this deception,
at the time when he was seeking employment in the colonial service of
Spain; and that he did it to conciliate the Bishop Fonseca, who was

* The first suggestion of the name appears to have been in the Latin work already
cited, published in St. Diez in Lorraine in 1507, in which was inserted the letter of
Vespucci to king René. The author, after speaking of the other three parts of the
world, Asia, Africa, and Europe, recommends that the fourth shall be called
Amerige or America after Vespucci, whom he imagined its discoverer.

Note to the Revised Edition, 1848.—Humboldt, in his EXAMEN CRITIQUE,
published in Paris, in 1837, says: "I have been so happy as to discover, very
recently, the name and the literary relations of the mysterious personage who
(in 1507) was the first to propose the name of America to designate the new
continent, and who concealed himself under the Grecianized name of Hylacomylas."
He then, by a long and ingenious investigation, shows that the real name of this
personage was Martin Waldseemüller, of Fribourg, an eminent cosmographer,
patronized by René, duke of Lorraine; who no doubt put in his hands the letter
received by him from Amerigo Vespucci. The geographical works of Waldseemüller,
under the assumed name of Hylacomylas, had a wide circulation, went through
repeated editions, and propagated the use of the name America throughout the
world. There is no reason to suppose that this application of the name was in any
wise suggested by Amerigo Vespucci. It appears to have been entirely gratuitous
on the part of Waldseemüller.

desirous of any thing that might injure the interests of Columbus. In corroboration of this opinion, the patronage is cited which was ever shewn by Fonseca to Vespucci and his family. This is not, however, a satisfactory reason, since it does not appear that the Bishop ever made any use of the fabrication. Perhaps some other means might be found of accounting for this spurious narration, without implicating the veracity of Vespucci. It may have been the blunder of some editor, or the interpolation of some book maker, eager, as in the case of Trivigiani, with the manuscripts of Peter Martyr, to gather together disjointed materials and fabricate a work to gratify the prevalent passion of the day.

In the various editions of the letters of Vespucci the grossest variations and inconsistencies in dates will be found, evidently the errors of hasty and careless publishers. Several of these have been corrected by the modern authors who have inserted these letters in their works.* The same disregard to exactness which led to these blunders may have produced the interpolation of this voyage, garbled out of the letters of Vespucci and the accounts of other voyagers. This is merely suggested as a possible mode of accounting for what appears so decidedly to be a fabrication, yet which we are loth to attribute to a man of the good sense, the character and the reputed merit of Vespucci.

After all, this is a question more of curiosity than of real moment, although it is one of those perplexing points about which grave men will continue to write weary volumes until the subject acquires a fictitious importance from the mountain of controversy heaped upon it. It has become a question of local pride with the literati of Florence; and they emulate each other with patriotic zeal to vindicate the fame of their distinguished countryman. This zeal is laudable, when kept within proper limits; but it is to be regretted that some of them have so far been heated by controversy as to become irascible against the very memory of Columbus, and to seek to disparage his general fame, as if the ruin of it would add any thing to the reputation of Vespucci. This

---

* An instance of these errors may be cited in the edition of the letter of Amerigo Vespucci to King René, inserted by Grinæus in his Novus Orbis in 1532. In this Vespucci is made to state that he sailed from Cadiz, May 20, MCCCXCVII (1497), that he was eighteen months absent, and returned to Cadiz, October 15, MCCCCXCIX (1499), which would constitute an absence of twenty nine months. He states his departure from Cadiz on his second voyage, Sunday, May 11, MCCCCLXXXIX (1489), which would have made his second voyage precede his first by eight years. If we substitute 1499 for 1489, the departure on his second voyage would still precede his return from his first by five months. Canovai in his edition has altered the date of the first return to 1498, to limit the voyage to eighteen months.

is discreditable to their discernment and their liberality; it injures their cause and shocks the feelings of mankind, who will not willingly see a name, like that of Columbus, lightly or petulantly assailed in the course of these literary contests. It is a name consecrated in history, and is no longer the property of a city, or a state, or a nation, but of the whole world.

Neither should those who have a proper sense of the merit of Columbus put any part of his great renown at issue upon this minor dispute. Whether or not he was the first discoverer of Paria was a question of interest to his heirs, as a share in the government and revenues of that country depended upon it; but it is of no importance to his fame. In fact, the European who first reached the main land of the New World was most probably Sebastian Cabot, a native of Venice, sailing in the employ of England. In 1497 he coasted its shores from Labrador to Florida; yet the English have never set up any pretensions on his account.

The glory of Columbus does not depend upon the parts of the country he visited or the extent of coast along which he sailed, it embraces the discovery of the whole western world. With respect to him, Vespucci is as Yañez Pinzon, Bastides, Ojeda, Cabot, and the crowd of secondary discoverers, who followed in his track, and explored the realms to which he had led the way. When Columbus first touched a shore of the New World, even though a frontier island, he had achieved his enterprises; he had accomplished all that was necessary to his fame: the great problem of the ocean was solved; the world which lay beyond its western waters was discovered.

No. XI

Martin Alonzo Pinzon

In the course of the trial in the fiscal court, between Don Diego and the crown, an attempt was made to depreciate the merit of Columbus, and to ascribe the success of the great enterprise of discovery to the intelligence and spirit of Martin Alonzo Pinzon. It was the interest of the crown to do so, to justify itself in withholding from the heirs of Columbus the extent of his stipulated reward. The examinations of witnesses in this trial were made at various times and places, and upon a set of interrogatories formally drawn up by order of the fiscal. They took place upwards of twenty years after the first voyage of Columbus, and the witnesses testified from recollection.

In reply to one of the interrogatories, Arias Perez Pinzon, son of Martin Alonzo, declared, that, being once in Rome with his father on commercial affairs, before the time of the discovery, they had frequent conversations with a person learned in cosmography who was in the service of Pope Innocent VIII, and that being in the library of the pope, this person showed them many manuscripts, from one of which his father gathered intimation of these new lands; for there was a passage by an historian as old as the time of Solomon, which said, "Navigate the Mediterranean Sea to the end of Spain and thence towards the setting sun, in a direction between north and south, until ninety-five degrees of longitude, and you will find the land of Cipango, fertile and abundant, and equal in greatness to Africa and Europe." A copy of this writing, he added, his father brought from Rome with an intention of going in search of that land, and frequently expressed such determination; and that, when Columbus came to Palos with his project of discovery, Martin Alonzo Pinzon showed him the manuscript, and ultimately gave it to him just before he sailed.

It is extremely probable that this manuscript, of which Arias Perez gives so vague an account from recollection, but which he appears to think the main thing that prompted Columbus to his undertaking, was no other than the work of Marco Polo, which, at that time, existed in manuscript in most of the Italian libraries. Martin Alonzo was evidently acquainted with the work of the Venetian, and it would appear, from various circumstances, that Columbus had a copy of it with him in his voyages, which may have been the manuscript mentioned. Columbus had long before, however, had a knowledge of the work, if not by actual inspection, at least through his correspondence with Toscanelli in 1474, and had derived from it all the light it was capable of furnishing, before he ever came to Palos. It is questionable, also, whether the visit of Martin Alonzo to Rome, was not after his mind had been heated by conversations with Columbus in the convent of La Rabida. The testimony of Arias Perez is so worded as to leave it in doubt whether the visit was not in the very year prior to the discovery: "fue el dicho su padre á Roma aquel dicho año antes que fuese a descubrir." Arias Perez always mentions the manuscript as having been imparted to Columbus, after he had come to Palos with an intention of proceeding on the discovery.

Certain witnesses who were examined on behalf of the crown, and to whom specific interrogatories were put, asserted, as has already been mentioned in a note to this work, that had it not been for Martin Alonzo Pinzon and his brothers, Columbus would have turned back for Spain, after having run seven or eight hundred leagues; being disheartened at not finding land, and dismayed by the mutiny and menaces of his crew. This is stated by two or three as from personal knowledge, and by others from hearsay. It is said especially to have occurred on the 6th of October. On this day, according to the journal of Columbus, he had some conversation with Martin Alonzo, who was anxious that they should stand more to the southwest. The admiral refused to do so, and it is very probable that some angry words may have passed between them. Various disputes appear to have taken place between Columbus and his colleagues respecting their route, previous to the discovery of land; in one or two instances he acceded to their wishes, and altered his course, but in general he was inflexible in standing to the west. The Pinzons also, in all probability, exerted their influence in quelling the murmurs of their townsmen and encouraging them to proceed, when ready to rebel against Columbus. These circumstances may have become mixed up in the vague recollections of the seamen who gave the foregoing extravagant testimony, and who were evidently disposed to exalt the merits of the Pinzons at the expense of Columbus. They were in some measure prompted also in their replies by the written interrogatories put by order of the fiscal, which specified the conversations said to have passed between Columbus and the Pinzons, and notwithstanding these guides they differed widely in their statements, and ran into many absurdities. In a manuscript record in possession of the Pinzon family, I have even read the assertion of an old seaman, that Columbus, in his eagerness to compel the Pinzons to turn back to Spain, *fired upon their ships*, but, they continuing on, he was obliged to follow, and within two days afterwards discovered the island of Hispaniola.

It is evident the old sailor, if he really spoke conscientiously, mingled in his cloudy remembrance the disputes in the early part of the voyage, about altering their course to the southwest, and the desertion of Martin Alonzo, subsequent to the discovery of the Lucayos and Cuba, when, after parting company with the admiral, he made the island of Hispaniola.

The witness most to be depended upon as to these points of inquiry, is the physician of Palos, Garcia Fernandez, a man of education, who sailed with Martin Alonzo Pinzon as steward of his ship, and of course was present at all the conversations which passed between the commanders. He testifies that Martin Alonzo urged Columbus to stand more to the southwest, and that the admiral at length complied, but, finding no land in that direction, they turned again to the west; a statement which completely coincides with the journal of Columbus. He adds that the admiral continually comforted and animated Martin Alonzo, and all others in his company. (Siempre los consolaba el dicho Almirante esforzandolos al dicho Martin Alonzo e á todos los que en su compania iban.) When the physician was specifically questioned as to the conversations pretended to have passed between the commanders, in which Columbus expressed a desire to turn back to Spain, he referred to the preceding statement, as the only answer he had to make to these interrogatories.

The extravagant testimony before mentioned appears never to have had any weight with the fiscal; and the accurate historian Muñoz, who extracted all these points of evidence from the papers of the lawsuit, has not deemed them worthy of mention in his work. As these matters, however, remain on record in the archives of the Indies, and in the archives of the Pinzon family, in both of which I have had a full opportunity of inspecting them, I have thought it advisable to make these few observations on the subject; lest, in the rage for research, they might hereafter be drawn forth as a new discovery, on the strength of which to impugn the merits of Columbus.

No. XII

Rumour of the pilot said to have died in the house of Columbus

Among the various attempts to injure Columbus by those who were envious of his fame, was one intended to destroy all his merit as an original discoverer. It was said that he had received information of the existence of land in the western parts of the ocean, from a tempest tost pilot, who had been driven there by violent easterly winds, and who on his return to Europe had died in the house of Columbus, leaving in his possession the chart and journal of his voyage, by which he was guided to his discovery.

This story was first noticed by Oviedo, a contemporary of Columbus, in his History of the Indies published in 1535. He mentions it as a rumour circulating among the vulgar without foundation in truth.

Fernando Lopez de Gomara first brought it forward against Columbus, in his History of the Indies published in 1552. He repeats the rumour in the vaguest terms, manifestly from Oviedo, but without the contradiction given to it by that author. He says that the name and country of the pilot were unknown, some terming him an Andalusian, sailing between the Canaries and Madeira, others a Biscayan trading to England and France; and others a Portuguese voyaging between Lisbon and Mina on the coast of Guinea. He expresses equal uncertainty whether the pilot brought the caravel to Portugal, to Madeira, or to one of the Azores. The only point on which the circulators of the rumour agreed, was that he died in the house of Columbus. Gomara adds that by this event Columbus was led to undertake his voyage to the new countries.*

The other early historians who mention Columbus and his voyages, and were his contemporaries, viz. Sabellicus, Peter Martyr, Giustiniani, Bernaldes, commonly called the curate of Los Palacios, Las Casas, Fernando the son of the admiral, and the anonymous author of a voyage of Columbus, translated from the Italian into Latin by Madrignano,† are all silent in regard to this report.

Benzoni, whose History of the New World was published 1565, repeats the story from Gomara, with whom he was contemporary, but decidedly expresses his opinion, that Gomara had mingled up much falsehood, with some truth, for the purpose of detracting from the fame of Columbus, through jealousy that any one but a Spaniard should enjoy the honour of the discovery.‡

Acosta notices the circumstance slightly in his Natural and Moral History of the Indies, published in 1591 and takes it evidently from Gomara.§

Mariana in his History of Spain, published in 1592 also mentions it, but expresses a doubt of its truth and derives his information manifestly from Gomara.||

Herrera, who published his History of the Indies in 1601, takes no notice of the story. In not noticing it he may be considered as rejecting it; for he is distinguished for his minuteness; and was well acquainted with Gomara's history, which he expressly contradicts on a point of considerable interest.**

Garcilaso de la Vega, a native of Cusco in Peru, revived the tale with very minute particulars, in his Commentaries of the Incas, published in 1609. He tells it smoothly and circumstantially; fixes the date of the

---

*Gomara, Hist. Ind. cap. 14.

† Navigatio Christophori Columbi, Madrignano Interprete. It is contained in a collection of voyages, called Novus Orbis Regionum, edition of 1555, but was originally published in Italian, as written by Montalbodo Francanzano (or Francapano de Montaldo) in a collection of voyages entitled Nuovo Mondo, in Vicenza, 1507.

‡ Girolamo Benzoni, Hist. del Nuovo Mondo, lib. i. fo. 12. in Venetia, 1572.

§ Padre Joseph de Acosta, Hist. Ind. lib. i. cap. 19.

|| Juan de Mariana, Hist. España, lib. 26. cap. 3.

** Herrera, Hist. Ind. decad. II. lib. 3. cap. 1.

occurrence, 1484, "one year more or less;" states the name of the unfortunate pilot, Alonzo Sanchez de Huelva; the destination of his vessel, from the Canaries to Madeira; and the unknown land to which they were driven, the island of Hispaniola. The pilot, he says, landed, took an altitude, and wrote an account of all he saw, and all that had occurred in the voyage. He then took in wood and water, and set out to seek his way home. He succeeded in returning, but the voyage was long and tempestuous, and twelve died of hunger and fatigue, out of seventeen, the original number of the crew. The five survivors arrived at Tercera, where they were hospitably entertained by Columbus, but all died in his house, in consequence of the hardships they had sustained; the pilot was the last that died, leaving his host heir to his papers. Columbus kept them profoundly secret, and, by pursuing the route therein prescribed, obtained the credit of discovering the New World.[*]

Such are the material points of the circumstantial relation furnished by Garcilaso de la Vega, 120 years after the event. In regard to authority, he recollects to have heard the story when he was a child, as a subject of conversation between his father and the neighbours, and he refers to the histories of the Indies by Acosta and Gomara for confirmation. As the conversations to which he listened must have taken place sixty or seventy years after the date of the report, there had been sufficient time for the vague rumours to become arranged into a regular narrative, and thus we have not only the name, country, and destination of the pilot, but also the name of the unknown land to which his vessel was driven.

This account given by Garcilaso de la Vega has been adopted by many old historians, who have felt a confidence in the peremptory manner in which he relates it, and in the authorities to whom he refers.[†] These have been echoed by others of more recent date, and thus a weighty charge of fraud and imposture has been accumulated against Columbus,

[*] Commentarios de los Incas, lib. 1. cap. 3.

[†] Names of historians who have either adopted this story in detail, or the charge against Columbus, drawn from it.

Bernardo Aldrete, Antiguedad de España, lib. 4. cap. 17. p. 567.

Roderigo Caro, Antiguedad, lib. 3. cap. 76.

Juan de Solorzano, Ind. Jure, tom. i. lib. 1. cap. 5.

Fernando Pizarro, Varones Illust. del Nuevo Mundo, cap. 2.

Agostino Torniel, Annal. Sacr. tom. i. Ann. Mund. 1931, No. 48.

Pet. Damarez or De Mariz, Dial. 4. de Var. Hist. cap. 4.

Gregorio García, Orig. de los Indios, lib. i. cap. 4. § 1.

Juan de Torquemada, Monarch. Ind. lib. 18. cap. 1.

John Baptiste Riccioli, Geograf. Reform. lib. 3.

To this list of old authors may be added many others of more recent date.

apparently supported by a crowd of respectable accusers. The whole charge is to be traced to Gomara, who loosely repeated a vague rumour, without noticing the pointed contradiction given to it seventeen years before, by Oviedo, an ear-witness, from whose book he appears to have actually gathered the report.

It is to be remarked that Gomara bears the character among historians, of inaccuracy and of great credulity in adopting unfounded stories. *

It is unnecessary to give further refutation to this charge, especially as it is clear that Columbus communicated his idea of discovery to Paulo Toscanelli of Florence in 1474, ten years previous to the date assigned by Garcilaso de la Vega for this occurrence.

No. XIII

Martin Behem

This able geographer was born in Nuremberg in Germany about the commencement of the year 1430. His ancestors were from the circle of Pilsner in Bohemia; hence he is called by some writers, Martin of Bohemia; and the resemblance of his own name to that of the country of his ancestors frequently occasions a confusion in the appellation.

It has been said by some that he studied under Philip Bervalde the elder, and by others under John Muller, otherwise called Regiomontanus; though De Murr, who has made diligent inquiry into his history, discredits both assertions. According to a correspondence between Behem and his uncle, discovered of late years by De Murr, it appears that the

---

* Francisco Lopez de Gomara, Presbitero, Sevillano, escribio con elegante estilo acerca de las cosas de las Indies, pero dexandose llevar de falsas narraciones." Hijos de Sevilla, Numero ii, p. 42, Let. F. The same is stated in Bibliotheca Hispaña Nova, lib. i. p. 437.

"El Francisco Lopez de Gomara escrivio tantos borrones é cosas que no son verdaderas, de que ha hecho mucho daño a muchos escritores e coronistas, que despues del Gomara han escrito en las cosas de la Nueva España * * * es porque les ha hecho errar el Gomara." Bernal Diaz del Castillo, Hist. de la Conquest de la Nueva España, Fin de cap. 18.

"Tenia Gomara doctrina y estilo * * * pero empleose en ordinar sin discernimiento lo que halló escrito por sus antecesores, y dió credito á petrañas no solo falsas sino inverisimiles." Juan Bautista Muñoz, Hist. N. Mundo, Prologo, p. 18.

early part of his life was devoted to commerce; some have given him the credit of discovering the island of Fayal, but this is an error, arising probably from the circumstance that Job de Huertar, father in law of Behem, colonized that island in 1466.

He is supposed to have arrived at Portugal in 1481, while Alphonso V was still on the throne: it is certain that shortly afterwards he was in high repute for his science in the court of Lisbon, in so much that he was one of the council appointed by king John II to improve the art of navigation, and by some he has received the whole credit of the memorable service rendered to commerce by that council, in the introduction of the astrolabe into nautical use.

In 1484 King John sent an expedition under Diego Cam, as Barros calls him, Cano according to others, to prosecute discoveries along the coast of Africa. In this expedition Behem sailed as cosmographer. They crossed the equinoctial line, discovered the coast of Congo, advanced to twenty two degrees forty five minutes of south latitude,* and erected two columns on which were engraved the arms of Portugal, in the mouth of the river Zagra in Africa, which thence, for some time took the name of the River of Columns.†

For the services rendered on this and on previous occasions, it is said that Behem was knighted by King John in 1485 though no mention is made of such a circumstance in any of the contemporary historians. The principal proof of his having received this mark of distinction, is his having given himself the title on his own globe of *Eques Lusitanus.*

In 1486 he married at Fayal the daughter of Job de Huertar and is supposed to have remained there for some few years; where he had a son named Martin, born in 1489. During his residence at Lisbon and Fayal, it is probable the acquaintance took place between him and Columbus, to which Herrera and others allude; and the admiral may have heard from him some of the rumours circulating in the islands, of indications of western lands floating to their shores.

In 1491 he returned to Nuremberg to see his family, and while there, in 1492 he finished a terrestrial globe, considered a master piece in those days, which he had undertaken at the request of the principal magistrates of his native city.

In 1493 he returned to Portugal and from thence proceeded to Fayal.

In 1494 King John II, who had a high opinion of him, sent him to Flanders to his natural son Prince George, the intended heir of his crown. In the course of his voyage, Behem was captured and carried to

* Vasconcelos. lib. 4.

† Murr, Notice sur M. Behaim.

England, where he remained for three months detained by illness. Having recovered, he again put to sea, but was captured by a corsair and carried to France. Having ransomed himself, he proceeded to Antwerp and Bruges, but returned almost immediately to Portugal. Nothing more is known of him for several years, during which time it is supposed he remained with his family in Fayal, too old to make further voyages. In 1506 he went from Fayal to Lisbon, where he died.

The assertion that Behem had discovered the Western World previous to Columbus in the course of the voyage with Cam, was founded on the misinterpretation of a passage, interpolated in the chronicle of Hartmann Schedel, a contemporary writer. This passage mentions that when the voyagers were in the Southern Ocean, not far from the coast, and had passed the line, they came into another hemisphere, where, when they looked towards the east, their shadows fell towards the south, on their right hand; that here they discovered a new world unknown until then, and which for many years had never been sought, except by the Genoese and by them unsuccessfully.

"Hii duo, bono deorum auspicio, mare meridionale sulcantes, a littore non longe evagantes, superato circulo equinoctiali, in alterum orbem excepti sunt. Ubi ipsis stantibus orientem versus, umbra ad meridiem et dextram projiciebatur. Aperuêre igitur suâ industriâ alium orbem hactenus nobis incognitum et multis annis, a nullis quam Januensibus, licet frustra temptatum."

These lines are part of a passage which it is said is interpolated by a different hand in the original manuscript of the chronicle of Schedel. De Murr assures us they are not to be found in the German translation of the book by George Alt, which was finished the 5th of October 1493: but even if they were, they relate merely to the discovery which Diego Cam made of the southern hemisphere, previously unknown, and of the coast of Africa beyond the equator, all which appeared like a new world and as such was talked of at the time. The Genoese alluded to, who had made an unsuccessful attempt, were Antonio de Nolle, with Bartholomeo his brother, and Raphael de Nolle his nephew. Antonio was of a noble family, and, for some disgust, left his country and went to Lisbon with his before-mentioned relatives, in two caravels; sailing from whence in the employ of Portugal, they discovered the island of St. Jago, &c.*

This interpolated passage of Schedel was likewise inserted in the work De Europâ sub Frederico III of Æneas Silvius, afterwards pope Pius II, who died in 1464, long before the voyage in question. The misinterpretation of this passage first gave rise to the incorrect assertion, that Behem

---

* Barros, Decad. I. lib. ii. cap. 1. Lisbon, 1552.

had discovered the New World prior to Columbus; as if it were possible that such a circumstance could have happened without Behem's laying claim to the glory of the discovery, and without the world immediately resounding with so important an event. This error had been adopted by various authors without due examination; some of whom had likewise taken from Magellan the credit of having discovered the strait which goes by his name, and had given it to Behem. The error was too palpable to be generally prevalent, but it was suddenly revived in the year 1786 by a French gentleman of highly respectable character of the name of Otto, then resident of New York; who addressed a letter to Dr. Franklin, to be submitted to the Philosophical Society of Philadelphia, in which he undertook to establish the title of Behem to the discovery of the New World. His memoir was published in the Transactions of the American Philosophical Society, vol. 2, for 1786, article No. 35, and has been copied into the journals of most of the nations of Europe.

The authorities cited by M. Otto in support of his assertion are generally fallacious, and for the most part given without particular specification. His assertion has been diligently and satisfactorily refuted by Don Christoval Cladera.*

The grand proof of M. Otto is a globe which Behem made during his residence in Nuremberg in 1492, the very year that Columbus set out on his first voyage of discovery. This globe, according to M. Otto, is still preserved in the library of Nuremberg, and on it are painted all the discoveries of Behem, which are so situated that they can be no other than the coast of Brazil and the Straits of Magellan. This authority staggered many, and, if supported, would demolish the claims of Columbus.

Unluckily for M. Otto, in his description of the globe, he depended on the inspection of a correspondent. The globe in the library of Nuremberg was made in 1520 by John Schoener, professor of mathematics,† long after the discoveries and death of Columbus and Behem. The real globe of Behem made in 1492 does not contain any of the islands or shores of the New World, and thus proves that he was totally unacquainted with them. A copy or planisphere of Behem's globe is given by Cladera in his Investigations.

* Investigaciones Historicas, Madrid, 1794.
† Cladera, Investig. Hist. p. 115.

No. XIV

Voyages of the Scandinavians

Many elaborate dissertations have been written to prove that discoveries were made by the Scandinavians on the northern coast of America, long before the era of Columbus; but the subject appears still to be wrapped in much doubt and obscurity.

It has been asserted that the Norwegians as early as the ninth century discovered a great tract of land to the west of Iceland, which they called Grand Iceland, but this has been pronounced a fabulous tradition. The most plausible account is one given by Snorro Sturleson in his Saga or Chronicle of King Olaus. According to this writer, one Biorn of Iceland, sailing to Greenland in search of his father, from whom he had been separated by a storm, was driven by tempestuous weather far to the southwest, until he came in sight of a low country, covered with wood, with an island in its vicinity. The weather becoming favorable, he turned to the north east without landing, and arrived safe at Greenland. His account of the country he had beheld, it is said, excited the enterprize of Leif, son of Eric Rauda (or Redhead) the first settler of Greenland. A vessel was fitted out and Leif and Biorn departed alone in quest of this unknown land. They found a rocky and sterile island, to which they gave the name of Helleland, also a low sandy country covered with wood, to which they gave the name of Markland; and two days afterwards, they observed a continuance of the coast, with an island to the north of it. This last they described as fertile, well wooded, producing agreeable fruits, and particularly grapes, a fruit with which they were unacquainted. On being informed by one of their companions, a German, of its qualities and name, they called the country, from it, Vinland. They ascended a river well stored with fish, particularly salmon, and came to a lake from which the river took its origin, where they passed the winter. The climate appeared to them mild and pleasant; being accustomed to the rigorous climates of the north. On the shortest day, the sun was eight hours above the horizon; hence it has been concluded that the country was about the 49th degree of north latitude, and was either Newfoundland, or some part of the coast of North America, about the Gulph of St. Lawrence.[*] It is added that the relatives of Leif made several voyages to Vinland; that they traded with the natives for furs; and that in 1121 a Bishop named Eric went from Greenland to Vinland to convert the inhabitants to

[*] Forster's Northern Voyages, book ii. chap. 2.

256

Christianity. From this time, says Forster, we know nothing of Vinland, and there is every appearance that the tribe which still exists in the interior of Newfoundland, and which is so different from the other savages of North America, both in their appearance and mode of living, and always in a state of warfare with the Esquimaux of the northern coast, are descendants of the ancient Normans.

The author of the present work has not had the means of tracing this story to its original sources. He gives it on the authority of M. Malte-Brun, and Mr. Forster. The latter extracts it from the Saga or Chronicle of Snorro, who was born in 1179 and wrote in 1215; so that his account was formed long after the event is said to have taken place. Forster says, "the facts which we report have been collected from a great number of Icelandic manuscripts, and transmitted to us by Torfæus in his two works entitled Veteris Grœnlandiæ Descriptio, Hafnia, 1706, and Historia Winlandiæ Antiquæ, Hafnia, 1705." Forster appears to have no doubt of the authenticity of the facts. As far as the author of the present work has had experience in tracing these stories of early discoveries of portions of the New World, he has generally found them very confident deductions, drawn from very vague and questionable facts. Learned men are too prone to give substance to mere shadows, when they assist some preconceived theory. Most of these accounts, when divested of the erudite comments of their editors, have proved little better than the traditionary fables, noticed in another part of this work, respecting the imaginary islands of St. Borondon and of the Seven Cities.

There is no great improbability, however, that such enterprizing and roving voyagers as the Scandinavians, may have wandered to the northern shores of America, about the coast of Labrador, or the shores of Newfoundland; and if the Icelandic manuscripts said to be of the thirteenth century, can be relied upon as genuine, free from modern interpolation, and correctly quoted, they would appear to prove the fact. But granting the truth of the alleged discoveries, they led to no more result than would the interchange of communication between the natives of Greenland and the Esquimaux. The knowledge of them appears not to have extended beyond their own nation, and to have been soon neglected and forgotten by themselves.

Another pretension to an early discovery of the American continent has been set up, founded on an alleged map and narrative of two brothers of the name of Zeno of Venice; but it seems more invalid than those just mentioned. The following is the substance of this claim.

Nicolo Zeno, a noble Venetian, is said to have made a voyage to the north in 1380, in a vessel fitted out at his own cost, intending to visit

England and Flanders; but meeting with a terrible tempest, was driven for many days he knew not whither, until he was cast away upon Friseland, an island much in dispute among geographers, but supposed to be the Archipelago of the Ferroe islands. The shipwrecked voyagers were assailed by the natives, but rescued by Zichmni, a prince of the islands lying on the south side of Friseland, and duke of another district lying over against Scotland. Zeno entered into the service of this prince, and aided him in conquering Friseland and other northern islands. He was soon joined by his brother Antonio Zeno, who remained fourteen years in those countries.

During his residence in Friseland Antonio Zeno wrote to his brother Carlo in Venice giving an account of a report brought by a certain fisherman, about a land to the westward. According to the tale of this mariner, he had been one of a party who sailed from Friseland about twenty six years before, in four fishing boats. Being overtaken by a mighty tempest, they were driven about the sea for many days until the boat containing himself and six companions was cast upon an island called Estotiland, about one thousand miles from Friseland. They were taken by the inhabitants, and carried to a fair and populous city, where the King sent for many interpreters to converse with them, but none that they could understand, until a man was found who had likewise been cast away upon the coast, and who spoke Latin. They remained several days upon the island, which was rich and fruitful, abounding with all kinds of metals and especially gold.[*] There was a high mountain in the centre from which flowed four rivers, which watered the whole country. The inhabitants were intelligent and acquainted with the mechanical arts of Europe. They cultivated grain, made beer and lived in houses built of stone. There were Latin books in the King's library, though the inhabitants had no knowledge of that language. They had many cities and castles and carried on a trade with Greenland for pitch, sulphur and peltry. Though much given to navigation, they were ignorant of the use of the compass, and finding the Friselanders acquainted with it, held them in great esteem; and the king sent them with twelve barks to visit a country to the south called Drogeo. They had nearly perished in a storm, but were cast away upon the coast of Drogeo. They found the people to be cannibals and were on the point of being killed and devoured, but were spared on account of their great skill in fishing.

---

[*] This account is taken from Hackluyt, vol. iii. p. 123. The passage about gold and other metals is not to be found in the original Italian of Ramusio (tom. ii. p. 23), and is probably an interpolation.

The fisherman described this Drogeo as being a country of vast extent, or rather a new world; that the inhabitants were naked and barbarous, but that far to the south west there was a more civilized region and temperate climate, where the inhabitants had a knowledge of gold and silver, lived in cities, erected splendid temples to idols and sacrificed human victims to them, which they afterwards devoured.

After the fisherman had resided many years on this continent, during which time he had passed from the service of one chieftain to another, and traversed various parts of it, certain boats of Estotiland arrived on the coasts of Drogeo. The fisherman went on board of them, acted as interpreter, and followed the trade between the main land and Estotiland for some time, until he became very rich; then he fitted out a bark of his own and with the assistance of some of the people of the island, made his way back across the thousand intervening miles of ocean, and arrived safe at Friseland. The account he gave of these countries determined Zichmni, the prince of Friseland, to send an expedition thither, and Antonio Zeno was to command it. Just before sailing the fisherman who was to have acted as guide, died; but certain mariners who had accompanied him from Estotiland were taken in his place. The expedition sailed under the command of Zichmni; the Venetian Zeno merely accompanied it. It was unsuccessful. After having discovered an island called Icaria, where they met with a rough reception from the inhabitants, and were obliged to withdraw, the ships were driven by a storm to Greenland. No record remains of any further prosecution of the enterprize.

The countries mentioned in the account of Zeno were laid down on a map originally engraved on wood. The island of Estotiland has been supposed by M. Malte-Brun to be Newfoundland; its partially civilized inhabitants the descendants of the Scandinavian colonists of Vinland; and the Latin books in the king's library to be the remains of the library of the Greenland Bishop who emigrated thither in 1121. Drogeo, according to the same conjecture, was Nova Scotia and New England. The civilized people to the south west, who sacrificed human victims in rich temples, he surmises to have been the Mexicans or some ancient nation of Florida or Louisiana.

The premises do not appear to warrant this deduction. The whole story abounds with improbabilities; not the least of which is the civilization prevalent among the inhabitants; their houses of stone, their European arts, the library of their king, no traces of which were to be found on this subsequent discovery. Not to mention the information about Mexico, penetrating through the numerous savage tribes of a vast continent. It is proper to observe that this account was not published until 1558, long after the discovery of Mexico. It was given to the world by Francisco Marcolini, a descendant of the Zeni, from the fragments of letters said to have been written by Antonio Zeno to Carlo his brother. "It grieves me," says the editor, "that the book and divers other writings concerning these matters are miserably lost, for being but a child when they came to my hands, and not knowing what they were, I tore them and rent them in pieces, which now I cannot call to remembrance but to my exceeding great grief."[*]

This garbled statement by Marcolini, derived considerable authority by being introduced by Abraham Ortelius, an able geographer, in his Theatrum Orbis; but the whole story has been condemned by able commentators as a gross fabrication. Mr. Forster resents this as an instance of obstinate incredulity, saying that it is impossible to doubt the existence of the country of which Carlo, Nicolo and Antonio Zeno talk; as original acts in the archives of Venice prove that the chevalier undertook a voyage to the north; that his brother Antonio followed him; that Antonio traced a map which he brought back and hung up in his house, where it remained subject to public examination until the time of Marcolini, as an incontestable proof of the truth of what he advanced. Granting all this, it merely proves that Antonio and his brother were at Friseland and Greenland. Their letters never assert that Zeno made the voyage to Estotiland. The fleet was carried by a tempest to Greenland, after which we hear no more of him, and his account of Estotiland and Drogeo rests simply on the tale of the fisherman, after whose descriptions his map must have been conjecturally projected. The whole story resembles much the fables circulated shortly after the discovery of Columbus, to arrogate to other nations and individuals the credit of the achievement.

M. Malte-Brun intimates that the alleged discovery of Vinland may have been known to Columbus when he made a voyage in the North Sea in 1477,[†] and that the map of Zeno, being in the national library at London, in a Danish work, at the time when Bartholomew Columbus was in that city employed in making maps, he may have known something of it and have communicated it to his brother.[‡] Had M. Malte-Brun examined the history of Columbus with his usual accuracy, he would have perceived that in his correspondence with Paulo Toscanelli in 1474, he had expressed his intention of seeking India by a route directly to the west; his voyage to the north did not take place until

[*] Hackluyt, Collect. vol. iii. p. 127.

[†] Malte-Brun, Hist. de Géog. tom. i. lib. 17.

[‡] Ib. Géog. Universelle, tom. xiv. note sur la découverte de l'Amérique.

three years afterwards. As to the residence of Bartholomew in London, it was not until after Columbus had made his propositions of discovery to Portugal, if not to the courts of other powers. Granting therefore that he had subsequently heard the dubious stories of Vinland and of the fisherman's adventures, as related by Zeno, or at least by Marcolini, they evidently could not have influenced him in his great enterprize. His route had no reference to them, but was a direct western course, not toward Vinland and Estotiland and Drogeo, but in search of Cipango, and Cathay and the other countries described by Marco Polo as lying at the extremity of India.

No. XV

Circumnavigation of Africa by the ancients

The knowledge of the ancients with respect to the Atlantic coast of Africa is considered by modern investigators much less extensive than had been imagined, and it is doubted whether they had any practical authority for the belief that Africa was circumnavigable. The alleged voyage of Eudoxus of Cyzicus, from the Red Sea to Gibraltar, though recorded by Pliny, Pomponius Mela and others, is given entirely on the assertion of Cornelius Nepos, who does not tell from whence he derived his information. Posidonius (cited by Strabo) gives an entirely different account of this voyage and rejects it with contempt.*

The famous voyage of Hanno the Carthaginian is supposed to have taken place about a thousand years before the Christian era. The Periplus Hannonis remains, a brief and obscure record of this expedition, and a subject of great comment and controversy. By some it has been pronounced a fictitious work fabricated among the Greeks, but its authenticity has been ably vindicated. It appears to be satisfactorily proved, however, that the voyage of this navigator has been greatly exaggerated, and that he never circumnavigated the extreme end of Africa. Mons. de Bougainville† traces his route to a promontory which he named the West Horn, supposed to be Cape Palmas, about five or six degrees north of the Equinoctial line, from whence he proceeded to an-

---

* Gosselin, Recherches sur la Geographie des Anciens, tom. i, p. 162, &c.
† Memoirs de l'Acad. des Inscript. tom. xxvi.

other promontory, under the same parallel, which he called the South Horn, supposed to be Cape de Tres Puntas. Mons. Gosselin, however, in his Researches into the Geography of the Ancients (Tome i. p. 162 &c.), after a rigid examination of the Periplus of Hanno, determines that he had not sailed farther south than Cape Non. Pliny, who makes Hanno range the whole coast of Africa, from the Straits to the confines of Arabia, had never seen his Periplus, but took his idea from the works of Xenophon of Lampsaco. The Greeks surcharged the narration of the voyager with all kinds of fables, and on their unfaithful copies Strabo founded many of his assertions. According to M. Gosselin, the itineraries of Hanno, of Scylax, Polybius, Statius, Sebosus and Juba; the recitals of Plato, of Aristotle, of Pliny, of Plutarch, and the tables of Ptolemy all bring us to the same results, and, notwithstanding their apparent contradictions, fix the limit of southern navigation about the neighbourhood of Cape Non, or Cape Bojador.

The opinion that Africa was a peninsula, which existed among the Persians, the Egyptians, and perhaps the Greeks, several centuries prior to the Christian era, was not, in his opinion, founded upon any known facts; but merely on conjecture, from considering the immensity and unity of the ocean; or perhaps on mere ancient traditions; or on ideas produced by the Carthaginian discoveries beyond the Straits of Gibraltar, and those of the Egyptians beyond the Gulph of Arabia. He thinks that there was a very remote period, when geography was much more perfect than in the time of the Phœnicians and the Greeks, whose knowledge was but confused traces of what had previously been better known.

The opinion that the Indian Sea joined the ocean was admitted among the Greeks, and in the school of Alexandria, until the time of Hipparchus. It seemed authorized by the direction which the coast of Africa took after Cape Aromata, always tending westward, as far as it had been explored by navigators. It was supposed that the western coast of Africa rounded off to meet the eastern, and that the whole was bounded by the ocean much to the northward of the Equator. Such was the opinion of Crates, who lived in the time of Alexander, of Aratus, of Cleanthes, of Cleomedes, of Strabo, of Pomponius Mela, of Macrobius, and many others.

Hipparchus proposed a different system, and led the world into an error, which for a long time retarded the maritime communication of Europe and India. He supposed that the seas were separated into distinct basins, and that the eastern shores of Africa made a circuit round the Indian sea, so as to join those of Asia beyond the mouth of the Ganges. Subsequent discoveries, instead of refuting this error, only placed the junction of the continents at a greater distance. Marinus of Tyre and Ptolemy adopted this opinion in their works, and illustrated it in their maps, which for centuries controuled the general belief of mankind, and perpetuated the idea that Africa extended onward to the south pole, and that it was impossible to arrive by sea at the coasts of India. Still there were geographers who leaned to the more ancient idea of a communication between the Indian sea and the Atlantic Ocean. It had its advocates in Spain, and was maintained by Pomponius Mela and by Isidore of Seville. It was believed also by some of the learned in Italy in the thirteenth, fourteenth and fifteenth centuries, and thus was kept alive until it was acted upon so vigorously by Prince Henry of Portugal, and at length triumphantly demonstrated by Vasco de Gama, in his circumnavigation of the Cape of Good Hope.

No. XVI

Of the ships of Columbus

In remarking on the smallness of the vessels with which Columbus made his first voyage Dr. Robertson observes, that "in the fifteenth century the bulk and construction of vessels were accommodated to the short and easy voyages along the coast, which they were accustomed to perform." We have many proofs, however, that even anterior to the fifteenth century, there were large ships employed by the Spaniards, as well as by other nations. In an edict published in Barcelona in 1354 by Pedro IV, enforcing various regulations for the security of commerce, mention is made of Catalonian merchant ships of two and three decks and from 8,000 to 12,000 quintals burthen.

In 1419 Alonzo of Arragon hired several merchant ships to transport artillery, horses, &c. from Barcelona to Italy, among which were two, each carrying one hundred and twenty horses, which it is computed would require a vessel of at least 600 tons.

In 1463 mention is made of Venetian ship of 700 tons which arrived at Barcelona from England laden with wheat.

In 1497 a Castilian vessel arrived there being of 12,000 quintals burthen. These arrivals, incidentally mentioned among others of similar size, as happening at one port, shew that large ships were in use in those days*. Indeed, at the time of fitting out the second expedition of Columbus, there were prepared in the port of Bermeo a caracca of 1250 tons and four ships of from 150 to 450 tons burthen. Their destination, however, was altered, and they were sent to convoy Muley Boabdil, the last Moorish King of Granada, from the coast of his conquered territory to Africa.†

It was not for want of large vessels in the Spanish ports, therefore, that those of Columbus were of so small a size. He considered them best adapted to voyages of discovery, as they required but little depth of water, and therefore could more easily and safely coast unknown shores, and explore bays and rivers. He had some purposely constructed of a very small size for this service; such was the caravel which in his third voyage he dispatched to look out for an opening to the sea, at the upper part of the Gulph of Paria, when the water grew too shallow for his vessel of one hundred tons burthen.

The most singular circumstance with respect to the ships of Columbus, is that they should be open vessels; for it seems difficult to believe that a voyage of such extent and peril should be attempted in barks of so frail a construction. This, however, is expressly mentioned by Peter Martyr in his Decades, written at the time, and mention is made occasionally in the memoirs relative to the voyages, written by Columbus and his son, of certain of his vessels being without decks. He sometimes speaks of the same vessel as a ship and a caravel. There has been some discussion of late as to the precise meaning of the term caravel. The Chevalier Bossi, in his Dissertations on Columbus, observes that in the Mediterranean, caravel designates the largest class of ships of war among the Mussulmans, and that in Portugal it means a small vessel of from 120 to 140 tons burthen; but Columbus sometimes applies it to a vessel of forty tons.

Du Cange, in his Glossary, considers it a word of Italian origin. Bossi thinks it either Turkish or Arabic, and probably introduced into the European languages by the Moors. Mr. Edward Everett in a note to his Plymouth Oration considers that the true origin of the word is given in Ferrarii Origines Linguæ Italicæ: "Caravela, navigii minoris genus. Lat. Carabus; Græcè Κάραβος."

That the word caravel was intended to signify a vessel of a small size is evident from a naval classification made by king Alonzo in the middle of the thirteenth century. In the first class he enumerates Naos or large ships, which go only with sails; some of which have two masts and

---

* Capmany, Questiones Criticas, Quest. 6.
† Archives de Ind. en Sevilla.

others but one. In the second class smaller vesels, as Caraccas, Fustas, Ballenares, Pinezas, *Carabelas*, &c. In the third class vessels with sails and oars; as Galleys, Galeots, Tardantes and Saetias.*

Bossi gives a copy of a letter written by Columbus to Don Raphael Xansis, treasurer of the king of Spain; an edition of which exists in the public library at Milan. With this letter he gives several wood cuts of sketches made with a pen, which accompanied this letter, and which he supposes to have been from the hand of Columbus. In these are represented vessels which are probably caravels. They have high bows and sterns, with castles on the latter. They have short masts with large square sails. One of them, beside sails, has benches of oars, and is probably intended to represent a galley. They are all evidently vessels of small size and light construction.

In a work called "Recherches sur le Commerce" published in Amsterdam, 1779, is a plate representing a vessel of the latter part of the 15th century. It is taken from a picture in the church of S. Giovanni e Paolo in Venice. The vessel bears much resemblance to those said to have been sketched by Columbus: It has two masts, one of which is extremely small, with a latine sail. The main mast has a large square sail. The vessel has a high poop and prow, is decked at each end, and is open in the centre.

It appears to be the fact, therefore, that most of the vessels with which Columbus undertook his long and perilous voyages were of this light and frail construction; and little superior to the small craft which ply on rivers and along coasts in modern days.

No. XVII

Route of Columbus in his first voyage†

It has hitherto been supposed that one of the Bahama Islands at present bearing the name of San Salvador and which is also known as Cat Island, was the first point where Columbus came in contact with the

* Capmany, Quest. Crit.

† The author of this work is indebted for this able examination of the route of Columbus to an officer of the navy of the United States, whose name he regrets the not being at liberty to mention. He has been greatly benefited in various parts of this history, by nautical information from the same intelligent source.

New World. Navarrete, however, in his introduction to the "Collection of Spanish Voyages and Discoveries" recently published at Madrid, has endeavored to shew that it must have been Turk's Island, one of the same group, situated about 100 leagues (of 20 to the degree) S. E. of San Salvador. Great care has been taken to examine candidly the opinion of Navarrete, comparing it with the journal of Columbus, as published in the above mentioned work, and with the personal observations of the writer of this article, who has been much among these islands.

Columbus describes Guanahani, on which he landed and to which he gave the name of San Salvador, as being a beautiful island, and very large, as being level and covered with forests, many of the trees of which bore fruit; as having abundance of fresh water and a large lake in the centre; that it was inhabited by a numerous population; that he proceeded for a considerable distance in his boats along the shore, which tended to the N.N.E., and as he passed was visited by the inhabitants of several villages. Turk's Island does not answer to this description.

Turk's Island is a low key composed of sand and rocks, and lying north and south less than two leagues in extent. It is utterly destitute of wood and has not a single tree of native growth. It has no fresh water, the inhabitants depending entirely on cisterns and casks in which they preserve the rain; neither has it any lake, but several salt ponds which furnish the sole production of the island. Turk's Island cannot be approached on the east or north-east side in consequence of the reef that surrounds it. It has no harbor but has an open road on the west side, which vessels at anchor there have to leave and put to sea whenever the wind comes from any other quarter than that of the usual trade breeze of N.E. which blows over the island; for the shore is so bold that there is no anchorage except close to it and when the wind ceases to blow from the land, vessels remaining at their anchors would be swung against the rocks or forced high upon the shore by the terrible surf that then prevails. The unfrequented road of the Hawk's Nest at the south end of the island is even more dangerous. This island, which is not susceptible of the slightest cultivation, furnishes a scanty subsistence to a few sheep and horses. The inhabitants draw all their consumption from abroad with the exception of fish and turtle, which are taken in abundance, and supply the principal food of the slaves employed in the salt works. The whole wealth of the island consists in the produce of the salt ponds, and in the salvage and plunder of the many wrecks which take place in the neighborhood. Turk's Island, therefore, would never be inhabited in a savage state of society, where commerce does not exist, and where men are obliged to draw their subsistence from the spot which they people.

Again: when about to leave Guanahani, Columbus was at a loss to choose which to visit of a great number of islands in sight. Now there is no land visible from Turk's Island, excepting the two salt keys which lie south of it, and with it form the group known as Turk's Islands. The journal of Columbus does not tell us what course he steered in going from Guanahani to Concepcion but he states that it was five leagues distant from the former, and that the current was against him in sailing to it; whereas the distance from Turk's Island to the Gran Caico, supposed by Navarrete to be the Concepcion of Columbus, is nearly double, and the current sets constantly to the W.N.W. among these islands, which would be favourable in going from Turk's Island to the Caicos.

From Concepcion Columbus went next to an island, which he saw nine leagues off in a westerly direction, to which he gave the name of Fernandina. This Navarrete takes to be Little Inagua, distant no less than twenty two leagues from Gran Caico. Besides, in going to Little Inagua it would be necessary to pass quite close to three islands, each larger than Turk's Island, none of which are mentioned in the journal. Columbus describes Fernandina as stretching twenty eight leagues S.E. and N.W.: whereas Little Inagua has its greatest length of four leagues in a S.W. direction. In a word, the description of Fernandina has nothing in common with Little Inagua. From Fernandina Columbus sailed S.E. to Isabella, which Navarrete takes to be Great Inagua; whereas this latter bears S.W. from Little Inagua, a course differing 90° from the one followed by Columbus. Again: Columbus on the 20th of November takes occasion to say that Guanahani was distant eight leagues from Isabella: whereas Turk's Island is thirty five leagues from Great Inagua.

Leaving Isabella, Columbus stood W.S.W. for the island of Cuba and fell in with the Islas Arenas; this course drawn from Great Inagua, would meet the coast of Cuba about Port Nipe; whereas Navarrete supposes that Columbus next fell in with the keys south of the Jumentos, and which bear W.N.W. from Inagua, a course differing 45° from the one steered by the ships. After sailing for some time in the neighbourhood of Cuba, Columbus finds himself on the 14th of November in the sea of Nuestra Señora surrounded by so many islands that it was impossible to count them; whereas on the same day Navarrete places him off Cape Moa, where there is but one small island and more than fifty leagues distant from any group that can possibly answer the description.

Columbus informs us that San Salvador was distant from Port Principe forty five leagues, whereas Turk's Island is distant from the point, supposed by Navarrete to be the same, eighty leagues.

On taking leave of Cuba, Columbus remarks that he had followed its coast for an extent of 120 leagues; deducting twenty leagues for his having followed its windings there still remain 100. Now, Navarrete only supposes him to have coasted this island an extent of seventy leagues.

Such are the most important difficulties which the theory of Navarrete offers, and which appear insurmountable. Let us now take up the route of Columbus as recorded in his journal and with the best charts before us, examine how it agrees with the popular and traditional opinion that he first landed on the island of San Salvador.

We learn from the journal of Columbus that on the 11th of October 1492, he continued steering W.S.W. until sunset, when he returned to his old course of west, the vessels running at the rate of three leagues an hour. At ten o'clock he and several of his crew saw a light, which seemed like a torch carried about on land. He continued running on four hours longer and had made a distance of twelve leagues farther west when at two in the morning land was discovered ahead, distant two leagues. The twelve leagues which they ran since ten o'clock, with the two leagues distance from the land, form a total corresponding essentially with the distance and situation of Watling's Island from San Salvador; and it is thence presumed that the light seen at that hour was on Watling's Island, which they were then passing. Had the light been seen on land ahead and they had kept running on four hours at the rate of three leagues an hour, they must have run high and dry on shore. As the admiral himself received the royal reward for having seen this light, as the first discovery of land, Watling's Island is believed to be the point for which this premium was granted.

On making land the vessels were hove to until daylight of the same 12th of October; they then anchored off an island of great beauty, covered with forests and extremely populous.

It was called Guanahani by the natives but Columbus gave it the name of San Salvador. Exploring its coast where it ran to the N.N.E. he found a harbor capable of sheltering any number of ships. This description corresponds minutely with the S.E. part of the island known as San Salvador or Cat Island, which lies east and west, bending at its eastern extremity to the N.N.E. and has the same verdant and fertile appearance. The vessels had probably drifted into this bay at the S.E. side of San Salvador, on the morning of the 12th, while lying to for daylight; nor did Columbus while remaining at the island, or when sailing from it open the land so as to discover that what he had taken for its whole length, was but a bend at one end of it and that the main body of the island lay behind, stretching far to the N.W. From Guanahani, Columbus saw so many other islands that he was at a loss which next to visit. The Indians signified that they were innumerable and mentioned the names of above a hundred. He determined to go to the largest in sight, which appeared to be about five leagues distant; some of the others were nearer, and some further off. The island thus selected, it is presumed, was the present island of Concepcion; and that the others were that singular belt of small islands known as La Cadena (or the chain) stretching past the island of San Salvador in a S.E. and N.W. direction: the nearest of the groupe being nearer than Concepcion, while the rest are more distant.

Leaving San Salvador in the afternoon of the 14th for the island thus selected, the ships lay by during the night, and did not reach it until late in the following day; being retarded by adverse currents. Columbus gave this island the name of Santa Maria de la Concepcion: he does not mention either its bearings from San Salvador, or the course which he steered in going to it. We know that in all this neighborhood the current sets strongly and constantly to the W.N.W., and since Columbus had the current against him, he must have been sailing in an opposite direction or to the E.S.E. Besides, when near Concepcion, Columbus sees another island to the westward, the largest he had yet seen; but he tells us that he anchored off Concepcion and did not stand for this larger island because he could not have sailed to the west. Hence it is rendered certain that Columbus did not sail westward in going from San Salvador to Concepcion; for from the opposition of the wind, as there could be no other cause, he could not sail towards that quarter. Now, on reference to the chart we find the island, at present known as Concepcion, situated E.S.E. from San Salvador and at a corresponding distance of five leagues.

Leaving Concepcion on the 16th October, Columbus steered for a very large island seen to the westward nine leagues off, and which extended itself twenty eight leagues in a S.E. and N.W. direction. He was becalmed the whole day and did not reach the island until the following morning, 17th October. He named it Fernandina. At noon he made sail again with a view to run round it and reach another island called Samoet, but the wind being at S.E. by S., the course he wished to steer, the natives signified that it would be easier to sail round this island by running to the N.W. with a fair wind. He therefore bore up to the N.W. and having run two leagues found a marvellous port with a narrow entrance or rather with two entrances, for there was an island which shut it in completely, forming a noble basin within. Sailing out

of this harbor by the opposite entrance at the N.W. he discovered that
part of the island which runs east and west. The natives signified to him
that this island was smaller than Samoet and that it would be better
to return towards the latter. It had now become calm, but shortly after
there sprung up a breeze from W.N.W. which was ahead for the course
they had been steering; so they bore up and stood to the E.S.E. in order
to get an offing; for the weather threatened a storm, which however
dissipated itself in rain. The next day being the 18th October, they
anchored opposite the extremity of Fernandina.

The whole of this description answers most accurately the island of
Exuma, which lies south from San Salvador and S.W. by S. from Concepcion. The only inconsistency is that Columbus states that Fernandina bore nearly west from Concepcion and was twenty eight leagues
in extent. This mistake must have proceeded from his having taken the
long chain of keys called La Cadena for part of the same Exuma; which
continuous appearance they naturally assume when seen from Concepcion for they run in the same S.E. and N.W. direction. Their bearings
when seen from the same point, are likewise westerly as well as south-
westerly. As a proof that such was the case it may be observed that
after having approached these islands, instead of the extent of Fernandina being increased to his eye, he now remarks that it was twenty
leagues long, whereas before it was estimated by him at twenty eight;
he now discovers that instead of one island there were many and alters
his course southerly to reach the one that was most conspicuous.

The identity of the island here described with Exuma is irresistibly
forced upon the mind. The distance from Concepcion, the remarkable
port with an island in front of it, and farther on its coast turning off to
the westward are all so accurately delineated, that it would seem as
though the chart had been drawn from the description of Columbus.

On the 19th October the ships left Fernandina steering S.E. with
the wind at north. Sailing three hours on this course they discovered
Samoet to the east and steered for it, arriving at its north point before
noon. Here they found a little island surrounded by rocks with another
reef of rocks lying between it and Samoet. To Samoet Columbus gave
the name of Isabella, and to the point of it opposite the little island,
that of Cabo del Isleo; the cape at the S.W. point of Samoet Columbus
called Cabo de Laguna, and off this last his ships were brought to
anchor. The little island lay in the direction from Fernandina to Isabella, east and west. The coast from the small island lay westerly twelve
leagues to a cape which Columbus called Fermosa from its beauty;
this he believed to be an island apart from Samoet or Isabella with another one between them. Leaving Cabo Laguna, where he remained

until the 20th October, Columbus steered to the N.E. towards Cabo del Isleo but meeting with shoals inside the small island he did not come to anchor until the day following. Near this extremity of Isabella they found a lake from which the ships were supplied with water.

This island of Isabella or Samoet agrees so accurately in its description with Isla Larga, which lies east of Exuma, that it is only necessary to read it with the chart unfolded to become convinced of the identity.

Having resolved to visit the island which the natives called Cuba and described as bearing W.S.W. from Isabella, Columbus left Cabo del Isleo at midnight, the commencement of the 24th October and shaped his course accordingly to the W.S.W. The wind continued light, with rain, until noon, when it freshened up, and in the evening Cape Verde, the S.W. point of Fernandina, bore N.W. distant seven leagues. As the night became tempestuous he lay to until morning, drifting according to the reckoning two leagues.

On the morning of the 25th he made sail again to W.S.W., until nine o'clock, when he had run five leagues; he then steered west until three, when he had run eleven leagues, at which hour land was discovered, consisting of seven or eight keys lying north and south, and distant five leagues from the ships. Here he anchored the next day, south of these islands, which he called Islas de Arena; they were low, and five or six leagues in extent.

The distances run by Columbus, added to the departure taken from Fernandina and the distance from these islands of Arena at the time of discovering, give a sum of thirty leagues. This sum of thirty leagues is about three less than the distance from the S.W. point of Fernandina or Exuma, whence Columbus took his departure, to the group of Mucaras, which lie east of Cayo Lobo on the grand bank of Bahama, and which correspond to the description of Columbus. If it were necessary to account for the difference of three leagues in a reckoning, where so much is given on conjecture, it would readily occur to a seaman that an allowance of two leagues for drift, during a long night of blowy weather, is but a small one. The course from Exuma to the Mucaras is about S.W. by W. The course followed by Columbus differs a little from this, but as it was his intention on setting sail from Isabella to steer W.S.W. and since he afterwards altered it to west, we may conclude that he did so in consequence of having been run out of his course to the southward while lying to the night previous.

Oct. 27—At sunrise Columbus set sail from the isles Arenas or Mucaras for an island called Cuba, steering S.S.W. At dark, having made seventeen leagues on that course, he saw the land, and hove his ships to until morning. On the 28th he made sail again at S.S.W., and entered a beautiful river with a fine harbour, which he named San Salvador. The journal in this part does not describe the localities with the minuteness with which every thing has hitherto been noted; the text also is in several places obscure.

This port of San Salvador we take to be the one now known as Caravelas Grandes, situated eight leagues west of Nuevitas del Principe. Its bearings and distance from the Mucaras coincide exactly with those run by Columbus, and its description agrees, as far as can be ascertained by charts, with the port which he visited.

Oct. 29.—Leaving this port Columbus stood to the west and having sailed six leagues he came to a point of the island running N.W., which we take to be the Punta Gorda; and ten leagues farther another stretching easterly, which will be Punta Curiana. One league farther he discovered a small river and beyond this another very large one, to which he gave the name of Rio de Mares. This river emptied into a fine basin resembling a lake, and having a bold entrance; it had for landmarks two round mountains at the S.W. and to the W.N.W. a bold promontory, suitable for a fortification, which projected far into the sea. This we take to be the fine harbor and river situated west of Point Curiana; its distance corresponds with that run by Columbus from Caravelas Grandes, which we have supposed identical with Port San Salvador. Leaving Rio de Mares the 30th of October, Columbus stood to the N.W. for fifteen leagues when he saw a cape, to which he gave the name of Cabo de Palmas. This, we believe, is the one which forms the eastern entrance to Laguna de Moron. Beyond this cape was a river, distant, according to the natives, four days' journey from the town of Cuba; Columbus determined therefore to make for it.

Having lain to all night he reached the river on the 31st of October but found that it was too shallow to admit his ships. This is supposed to be what is now known as Laguna de Moron. Beyond this was a cape surrounded by shoals, and another projected still farther out. Between these two capes was a bay capable of receiving small vessels. The identity here of the description with the coast near Laguna de Moron seems very clear. The cape east of Laguna de Moron coincides with Cape Palmas, the Laguna de Moron with the shoal river described by Columbus; and in the western point of entrance with the island of Cabrion opposite it we recognise the two projecting capes he speaks of, with what appeared to be a bay between them. This all is a remarkable combination, difficult to be found any where but in the same spot which Columbus visited and described. Further, the coast from the port of San Salvador had run west to Rio de Mares, a distance of seventeen leagues, and from Rio de Mares it had extended N.W. fifteen leagues to

Cabo de Palmas; all of which agrees fully with what has been here supposed. The wind having shifted to north, which was contrary to the course they had been steering, the vessels bore up and returned to Rio de Mares.

On the 12th of November the ships sailed out of Rio de Mares to go in quest of Babeque, an island believed to abound in gold and to lie E. by S. from that port. Having sailed eight leagues with a fair wind they came to a river, in which may be recognised the one which lies just west of Punta Gorda. Four leagues farther they saw another, which they called Rio del Sol. It appeared very large but they did not stop to examine it as the wind was fair to advance. This we take to be the river now known as Sabana. Columbus was now retracing his steps and had made twelve leagues from Rio de Mares; but in going west from Port San Salvador to Rio de Mares he had run seventeen leagues. San Salvador therefore remains five leagues east of Rio del Sol, and accordingly on reference to the chart we find Caravelas Grandes situated a corresponding distance from Sabana.

Having run six leagues from Rio del Sol, which makes in all eighteen leagues from Rio de Mares, Columbus came to a cape which he called Cabo de Cuba, probably from supposing it to be the extremity of that island. This corresponds precisely in distance from Punta Curiana with the lesser island of Guajava, situated near Cuba, and between which and the greater Guajava Columbus must have passed in running in for Port San Salvador. Either he did not notice it from his attention being engrossed by the magnificent island before him, or as is also possible his vessels may have been drifted through the passage, which is two leagues wide, while lying to the night previous to their arrival at Port San Salvador.

On the 13th of November, having hove to all night, in the morning the ships passed a point two leagues in extent and then entered into a gulf that made into the S.S.W. and which Columbus thought separated Cuba from Bohio. At the bottom of the gulf was a large basin between two mountains. He could not determine whether or not this was an arm of the sea, for not finding shelter from the north wind, he put to sea again. Hence it would appear that Columbus must have partly sailed round the smaller Guajava, which he took to be the extremity of Cuba, without being aware that a few hours' sail would have taken him by this channel to Port San Salvador, his first discovery in Cuba, and so back to the same Rio del Sol which he had passed the day previous. Of the two mountains seen on both sides of this entrance the principal one corresponds with the peak called Alto de Juan Daune, which lies seven leagues west of Punta de Maternillos. The wind continuing north, he stood east fourteen leagues from Cape Cuba, which we have supposed the lesser island of Guajava. It is here rendered sure that the point of Little Guajava was believed by him to be the extremity of Cuba; for he speaks of the land mentioned as lying to leeward of the above mentioned gulf as being the island of Bohio, and says that he discovered twenty leagues of it running E.S.E. and W.N.W.

On the 14th November, having lain to all night with a N.E. wind, he determined to seek a port and if he found none to return to those which he had left in the island of Cuba; for it will be remembered that all east of Little Guajava he supposed to be Bohio. He steered E. by S. therefore six leagues and then stood in for the land. Here he saw many ports and islands, but as it blew fresh with a heavy sea he dared not enter but ran the coast down N.W. by W. for a distance of eighteen leagues, where he saw a clear entrance and a port, into which he stood S.S.W. and afterwards S.E., the navigation being all clear and open. Here Columbus beheld so many islands that it was impossible to count them. They were very lofty and covered with trees. Columbus called the neighboring sea Mar de Nuestra Señora, and to the harbor near the entrance to these islands he gave the name of Puerto del Principe. This harbor he says he did not enter until the Sunday following, which was four days after. This part of the text of Columbus's journal is confused, and there are also anticipations, as if it had been written subsequently or mixed together in copying; it appears evident that while lying to the night previous with the wind at N.E., the ships had drifted to the N.W. and been carried by the powerful current of the Bahama channel far in the same direction. When they bore up, therefore, to return to the ports which they had left in the island of Cuba, they fell in to leeward of them, and now first discovered the numerous group of islands of which Cayo Romano is the principal. The current of this channel is of itself sufficient to have carried the vessels to the westward a distance of 20 leagues, which is what they had run easterly since leaving Cape Cuba or Guajava, for it had acted upon them during a period of thirty hours. There can be no doubt as to the identity of these keys with those about Cayo Romano, for they are the only ones in the neighborhood of Cuba that are not of a low and swampy nature, but large and lofty. They enclose a free, open navigation and abundance of fine harbors, in late years the resort of pirates who found security and concealment for themselves and their prizes in the recesses of these lofty keys. From the description of Columbus the vessels must have entered between the islands of Baril and Pacedon, and sailing along Cayo Romano on a S.E. course, have reached in another day their old cruising ground in the neighborhood of lesser Guajava. Not only Columbus does not tell us here of his having changed his anchorage amongst these keys, but his journal does not even mention his having anchored at all until the return from the ineffectual search after Babeque. It is clear from what has been said, that it was not in Port Principe that the vessels anchored on this occasion, but it could not have been very distant, since Columbus went from the ships in his boats on the 18th November to place a cross at its entrance. He had probably seen the entrance from without when sailing east from Guajava on the 13th of November. The identity of this port with the one now known as Neuvitas el Principe seems certain from the description of its entrance. Columbus, it appears, did not visit its interior.

On the 19th November the ships sailed again in quest of Babeque. At sunset Port Principe bore S.S.W. distant seven leagues, and having sailed all night at N.E. by N. and until ten o'clock of the next day (20th November) they had run a distance of fifteen leagues on that course. The wind blowing from E.S.E., which was the direction in which Babeque was supposed to lie, and the weather being foul, Columbus determined to return to Port Principe, which was then distant twenty five leagues. He did not wish to go to Isabella, distant only twelve leagues, lest the Indians whom he had brought from San Salvador, which lay eight leagues from Isabella, should make their escape. Thus in sailing N.E. by N. from near Port Principe Columbus had approached within a short distance of Isabella. That island was then according to his calculations thirty seven leagues from Port Principe; and San Salvador was forty five leagues from the same point. The first differs but eight leagues from the truth, the latter nine; or from the actual distance of Neuvitas el Principe from Isla Larga and San Salvador. Again, let us now call to mind the course made by Columbus in going from Isabella to Cuba; it was first W.S.W., then west, and afterwards S.S.W. Having consideration for the different distances run on each, these yield a medium course not materially differing from S.W. Sailing then S.W. from Isabella, Columbus had reached Port San Salvador on the coast of Cuba. Making afterwards a course of N.E. by N. from off Port Principe he was going in the direction of Isabella. Hence we deduce that Port San Salvador on the coast of Cuba lay west of Port Principe, and the whole combination is thus bound together and established. The two islands seen by Columbus at ten o'clock of the same 20th November must have been some of the keys which lie west of the Jumentos. Running back towards Port Principe, Columbus made it at dark, but found that he had been carried to the westward by the currents. This furnishes a sufficient proof of the strength of the current in the Bahama channel, for it will be remembered that he ran over to

Cuba with a fair wind. After contending for four days, until the 24th November, with light winds against the force of these currents, he arrived at length opposite the level island whence he had set out the week before when going to Babeque.

We are thus accidentally informed that the point from whence Columbus started in search of Babeque was the same island of Guajava the lesser, which lies west of Neuvitas el Principe. Further—at first he dared not enter into the opening between the two mountains, for it seemed as though the sea broke upon them; but having sent the boat ahead the vessels followed in at S.W. and then W. into a fine harbor. The level island lay north of it and with another island formed a secure basin capable of sheltering all the navy of Spain. This level island resolves itself then into our late Cape Cuba, which we have supposed to be Little Guajava, and the entrance east of it becomes identical with the gulf above mentioned which lay between two mountains, one of which we have supposed the Alto de Juan Daune, and which gulf appeared to divide Cuba from Bohio. Our course now becomes a plain one. On the 26th of November Columbus sailed from Santa Catalina (the name given by him to the port last described) at sunrise and stood for the cape at the S.E. which he called Cabo de Pico. In this it is easy to recognise the high peak already spoken of as the Alto de Juan Daune. Arrived off this he saw another cape distant fifteen leagues, and still farther another five leagues beyond it, which he called Cabo de Campana. The first must be that now known as Point Padre, the second Point Mulas; their distances from Alto de Juan Daune are underrated; but it requires no little experience to estimate correctly the distances of the bold headlands of Cuba as seen through the pure atmosphere that surrounds the island.

Having passed Point Mulas in the night, on the 27th, Columbus looked into the deep bay that lies S.E. of it and seeing the bold projecting headland that makes out between Port Nipe and Port Banes, with those deep bays on each side of it, he supposed it to be an arm of the sea dividing one land from another with an island between them.

Having landed at Taco for a short time, Columbus arrived in the evening of the 27th at Baracoa, to which he gave the name of Puerto Santo. From Cabo del Pico to Puerto Santo, a distance of sixty leagues, he had passed no fewer than nine good ports and five rivers to Cape Campana; and thence to Puerto Santo eight more rivers each with a good port; all of which may be found on the chart between Alto de Juan Daune and Baracoa. By keeping near the coast he had been assisted to the S. E. by the eddy current of the Bahama channel. Sailing from Puerto Santo or Baracoa on the 4th of December, he reached the extremity of Cuba the following day and striking off upon a wind to the S.E. in search of Babeque, which lay to the N.E., he came in sight of Bohio, to which he gave the name of Hispaniola.

On taking leave of Cuba Columbus tells us that he had coasted it a distance of 120 leagues. Allowing twenty leagues of this distance for his having followed the undulations of the coast, the remaining 100 measured from Point Maysi fall exactly upon Cabrion Key, which we have supposed the western boundary of his discoveries.

The astronomical observations of Columbus form no objection to what has been here advanced, for he tells us that the instrument which he made use of to measure the meridian altitudes of the heavenly bodies was out of order and not to be depended upon. He places his first discovery, Guanahani, in the latitude of Ferro, which is about 27° 30' north. San Salvador we find in 24° 30', and Turk's Island in 21° 30'; both are very wide of the truth but it is certainly easier to conceive an error of three than one of six degrees.

Laying aside geographical demonstration, let us now examine how historical records agree with the opinion, here supported, that the island of San Salvador was the first point where Columbus came in contact with the New World. Herrera, who is considered the most faithful and authentic of Spanish historians, wrote his History of the Indies towards the year 1600. In describing the voyage of Juan Ponce de Leon made to Florida in 1512 he makes the following remarks:* "Leaving Aguada in Porto Rico, they steered to the N.W. by N. and in five days arrived at an island called El Viejo in latitude 22° 30' north. The next day they arrived at a small island of the Lucayos, called Caycos. On the eighth day they anchored at another island called Yaguna in 24°, on the eighth day out from Porto Rico. Thence they passed to the island of Manuega in 24° 30', and on the eleventh day they reached Guanahani, which is in 25° 40' north. This island of Guanahani was the first discovered by Columbus on his first voyage and which he called San Salvador." This is the substance of the remarks of Herrera and is entirely conclusive as to the location of San Salvador. The latitudes, it is true, are all placed higher than we now know them to be, that of San Salvador being such as to correspond with no other land than that now known as the Berry Islands, which are seventy leagues distant from the nearest coast of Cuba, whereas Columbus tells us that San Salvador was only forty five leagues from Port Principe. But in those infant days of navigation the instruments for measuring the altitudes of the heavenly bodies and the tables of de-

* Herrera, Hist. Ind. Decad. i. lib. 9. cap. 10.

clinations for deducing the latitude must have been so imperfect as to place the most scientific navigator of the time below the most mechanical one of the present.

The second island arrived at by Ponce de Leon in his north-western course was one of the Caycos; the first one, then, called El Viejo, must have been Turk's Island, which lies S.E. of the Caycos. The third island they came to was probably Mariguana; the fourth Crooked Island, and the fifth Isla Larga. Lastly they came to Guanahani, the San Salvador of Columbus. If this be supposed identical with Turk's Island, where do we find the succession of islands touched at by Ponce de Leon on his way from Porto Rico to San Salvador?* No stress has been laid in these remarks on the identity of name which has been preserved to San Salvador, Concepcion and Port Principe with those given by Columbus, though traditional usage is of vast weight in such matters. Geographical proof of a conclusive kind, it is thought, has been advanced to enable the world to remain in its old hereditary belief that the present island of San Salvador is the spot where Columbus first set foot upon the New World. Established opinions of the kind should not be lightly molested; it is a good old rule that ought to be kept in mind in curious research as well as territorial dealings, "Do not disturb the ancient landmarks."

* In the first chapter of Herrera's description of the Indies, appended to his history, is another scale of the Bahama islands, which corroborates the above. It begins at the opposite end, at the N.W., and runs down to the S.E. It is thought unnecessary to cite it particularly.

Note to the Revised Edition of 1848.—The Baron de Humboldt, in his Examen critique de l'histoire de la geographie du nouveau continent," published in 1837, speaks repeatedly in high terms of the ability displayed in the above examination of the route of Columbus, and argues at great length and quite conclusively in support of the oninion contained in it. Above all, he produces a document hitherto unknown, and the great importance of which had been discovered by M. Valeknaer and himself in 1832. This is a map made in 1500 by that able mariner Juan de la Cosa, who accompanied Columbus in his second voyage and sailed with other of the discoverers. In this map, of which the Baron de Humboldt gives an engraving, the islands as laid down agree completely with the bearings and distances given in the journal of Columbus, and establishes the identity of San Salvador, or Cat Island, and Guanahani.

"I feel happy," says M. de Humboldt, "to be enabled to destroy the incertitudes (which rested on this subject) by a document as ancient as it is unknown; a document which confirms irrevocably the arguments which Mr. Washington Irving has given in his work against the hypotheses of the Turk's Island."

In the present revised edition the author feels at liberty to give the merit of the very masterly paper on the route of Columbus, where it is justly due. It was furnished him at Madrid by the late commander Alexander Slidell Mackenzie, of the

No. XVIII

Principles upon which the sums mentioned in this work have been reduced into modern currency

In the reign of Ferdinand and Isabella the mark of silver, which was equal to eight ounces or to fifty castellanos, was divided into sixty five reals, and each real into thirty four maravedies; so that there were 2,210 maravedies in the mark of silver. Among other silver coins there was the real of eight, which, consisting of eight reals, was within a small fraction the eighth part of a mark of silver, or one ounce. Of the gold coins then in circulation, the castellano or *dobla de la Vanda* was worth 490 maravedies and the ducado 383 maravedies.

If the value of the maravedi had remained unchanged in Spain down to the present day, it would be easy to reduce a sum of the time of Ferdinand and Isabella, into a correspondent sum of current money; but by the successive depreciations of the coin of Vellon, or mixed metals, issued since that period, the *real* and maravedi of Vellon, which had replaced the ancient currency, were reduced towards the year 1700 to about a third of the value of the old *real* and maravedi, now known as the *real* and maravedi of silver. As however the ancient piece of eight reals was equal approximately to the ounce of silver, and the duro or dollar of the present day, is likewise equal to an ounce, they may be considered identical. Indeed, in Spanish America, the dollar, instead of being divided into twenty reals as in Spain, is divided into only eight parts, called reals, which evidently represent the real of the time of Ferdinand and Isabella, as the dollar does the real of eight. But the ounce of silver was anciently worth 276¼ maravedies; the dollar, therefore, is likewise equal to 276¼ maravedies. By converting then the sums mentioned in this work into maravedies, they have been afterwards reduced into dollars by dividing by 276¼.

There is still, however, another calculation to be made, before we can arrive at the actual value of any sum of gold and silver mentioned in former times. It is necessary to notice the variation which has taken place in the value of the metals themselves. In Europe, previous to the discovery of the New World, an ounce of gold commanded an amount of food or labour which would cost three ounces at the present day; hence an ounce of gold was then estimated at three times its present

---

United States navy, whose modesty shrunk from affixing his name to an article so calculated to do him credit, and which has since challenged the high eulogiums of men of nautical science.

value. At the same time an ounce of silver commanded an amount which at present costs four ounces of silver. It appears from this, that the value of gold and silver varied with respect to each other, as well as with respect to all other commodities. This is owing to there having been much more silver brought from the New World, with respect to the quantity previously in circulation, than there has been of gold. In the fifteenth century one ounce of gold was equal to about twelve of silver and now, in the year 1827 it is exchanged against sixteen.

Hence in giving an idea of the relative value of the sums mentioned in this work, it has been found necessary to multiply them by 3 when in gold and by 4 when expressed in silver.*

It is expedient to add that the dollar is reckoned in this work at 100 cents of the United States of North America, and four shillings and sixpence of England.

No. XIX

Prester John

Said to be derived from the Persian *Prestegani* or *Perestigani*, which signifies apostolique; or *Preschtak-Geham*, angel of the world. It is the name of a potent Christian monarch of shadowy renown, whose dominions were placed by writers of the middle ages sometimes in the remote parts of Asia and sometimes in Africa, and of whom such contradictory accounts were given by the travelers of those days that the very existence either of him or his kingdom came to be considered doubtful. It now appears to be admitted, that there really was such a potentate in a remote part of Asia. He was of the Nestorian Christians, a sect spread throughout Asia, and taking its name and origin from Nestorius, a Christian patriarch of Constantinople.

The first vague reports of a Christian potentate in the interior of Asia, or as it was then called India, were brought to Europe by the Crusaders, who it is supposed gathered them from the Syrian merchants who traded to the very confines of China.

In subsequent ages, when the Portuguese in their travels and voyages discovered a Christian king among the Abyssinians, called Baleel-

---

* See Caballero, Pesos y Medidas. J. B. Say, Economic Politique.

Gian, they confounded him with the potentate already spoken of. Nor was the blunder extraordinary, since the original Prester John was said to reign over a remote part of India; and the ancients included in that name Ethiopia and all the regions of Africa and Asia bordering on the Red Sea and on the commercial route from Egypt to India.

Of the Prester John of India we have reports furnished by William Ruysbrook, commonly called Rubruquis, a Franciscan friar sent by Louis IX, about the middle of the thirteenth century to convert the Grand Khan. According to him, Prester John was originally a Nestorian priest, who on the death of the sovereign made himself king of the Naymans, all Nestorian Christians. Carpini, a Franciscan friar, sent by pope Innocent in 1245 to convert the Mongols of Perisa, says, that Ocoday, one of the sons of Ghengis Khan of Tartary, marched with an army against the Christians of Grand India. The king of that country, who was called Prester John, came to their succor. Having had figures of men made of bronze, he had them fastened on the saddles of horses, and put fire within, with a man behind with a bellows. When they came to battle these horses were put in the advance, and the men who were seated behind the figures, threw something into the fire, and blowing with their bellows, made such a smoke that the Tartars were quite covered with it. They then fell on them, dispatched many with their arrows, and put the rest to flight.

Marco Polo (1271) places Prester John near the great wall of China, to the north of Chan-si, in Teudich, a populous region full of cities and castles.

Mandeville (1332) makes Prester sovereign of Upper India (Asia), with four thousand islands tributary to him.

When John II, of Portugal, was pushing his discoveries along the African coast, he was informed that 350 leagues to the east of the kingdom of Benin in the profound depths of Africa, there was a puissant monarch, called Ogave, who had spiritual and temporal jurisdiction over all the surrounding kings.

An African prince assured him, also, that to the east of Timbuctoo there was a sovereign who professed a religion similar to that of the Christians, and was king of a Mosaic people.

King John now supposed he had found traces of the real Prester John, with whom he was eager to form an alliance religious as well as commercial. In 1487 he sent envoys by land in quest of him. One was a gentleman of his household, Pedro de Covilham; the other, Alphonso de Paiva. They went by Naples to Rhodes, thence to Cairo, thence to Aden on the Arabian Gulf above the mouth of the Red Sea.

Here they separated with an agreement to rendezvous at Cairo. Alphonso de Paiva sailed direct for Ethiopia; Pedro de Covilham for the Indies. The latter passed to Calicut and Goa, where he embarked for Sofala on the eastern coast of Africa, thence returned to Aden, and made his way back to Cairo. Here he learned that his coadjutor, Alphonso de Paiva, had died in that city. He found two Portuguese Jews waiting for him with fresh orders from king John not to give up his researches after Prester John until he found him. One of the Jews he sent back with a journal and verbal accounts of his travels. With the other he set off again for Aden; then to Ormuz, at the entrance of the Gulf of Persia, where all the rich merchandise of the East was brought to be transported thence by Syria and Egypt into Europe.

Having taken note of every thing here, he embarked on the Red Sea, and arrived at the court of an Abyssinian prince named Escander, (the Arabic version of Alexander,) whom he considered the real Prester John. The prince received him graciously, and manifested a disposition to favor the object of his embassy, but died suddenly, and his successor Naut refused to let Covilham depart, but kept him for many years about his person, as his prime councilor, lavishing on him wealth and honors. After all, this was not the real Prester John; who, as has been observed, was an Asiatic potentate.

No. XX

Marco Polo*

The travels of Marco Polo or Paolo furnish a key to many parts of the voyages and speculations of Columbus, which without it would hardly be comprehensible.

Marco Polo was a native of Venice who in the thirteenth century, made a journey into the remote, and at that time unknown regions of the East and filled all Christendom with curiosity by his account of the

---

* In preparing the first edition of this work for the press the author had not the benefit of the English translation of Marco Polo, published a few years since, with admirable commentaries, by William Marsden, F.R.S. He availed himself, principally, of an Italian version in the Venetian edition of Ramusio (1606), the French translation by Bergeron, and an old and very incorrect Spanish translation. Having since procured the work of Mr. Marsden he has made considerable alterations in these notices of Marco Polo.

countries he had visited. He was preceded in his travels by his father Nicholas and his uncle Maffeo Polo. These two brothers were of an illustrious family in Venice and embarked about the year 1255, on a commercial voyage to the East. Having traversed the Mediterranean and through the Bosphorus, they stopped for a short time at Constantinople, which city had recently been wrested from the Greeks by the joint arms of France and Venice. Here they disposed of their Italian merchandise, and, having purchased a stock of jewelry, departed on an adventurous expedition to trade with the western Tartars, who, having overrun many parts of Asia and Europe, were settling and forming cities in the vicinity of the Wolga. After traversing the Euxine to Soldaia, (at present Sudak,) a port in the Crimea, they continued on, by land and water, until they reached the military court, or rather camp of a Tartar prince, named Barkah, a descendant of Ghengis Khan, into whose hands they confided all their merchandise. The barbaric chieftain, while he was dazzled by their precious commodities, was flattered by the entire confidence in his justice manifested by these strangers. He repaid them with princely munificence, and loaded them with favors during a year that they remained at his court. A war breaking out between their patron and his cousin Hulagu, chief of the eastern Tartars, and Barkah being defeated, the Polos were embarrassed how to extricate themselves from the country and return home in safety. The road to Constantinople being cut off by the enemy, they took a circuitous route, round the head of the Caspian Sea, and through the deserts of Transoxiana, until they arrived in the city of Bokhara, where they resided for three years.

While here there arrived a Tartar nobleman who was on an embassy from the victorious Hulagu to his brother the Grand Khan. The ambassador became acquainted with the Venetians, and finding them to be versed in the Tartar tongue and possessed of curious and valuable knowledge, he prevailed upon them to accompany him to the court of the emperor, situated as they supposed, at the very extremity of the East. After a march of several months, being delayed by snow-storms and inundations, they arrived at the court of Cublai, otherwise called the Great Khan, which signifies King of Kings; being the sovereign potentate of the Tartars. This magnificent prince received them with great distinction; he made enquiries about the countries and princes of the West, their civil and military government, and the manners and customs of the Latin nations. Above all he was curious on the subject of the Christian religion. He was so much struck by their replies that, after holding a council with the chief persons of his kingdom, he entreated the two brothers to go on his part as ambassadors to the Pope, to entreat him to send a hundred learned men well instructed in the Christian faith, to impart a knowledge of it to the sages of his empire. He also entreated them to bring him a little oil from the lamp of our Saviour in Jerusalem, which he concluded must have marvellous virtues. It has been supposed, and with great reason, that under this covert of religion, the shrewd Tartar sovereign veiled motives of a political nature. The influence of the pope in promoting the crusades had caused his power to be known and respected throughout the East; it was of some moment, therefore, to conciliate his good will. Cublai Khan had no bigotry nor devotion to any particular faith, and probably hoped, by adopting Christianity to make it a common cause between himself and the warlike princes of Christendom, against his and their inveterate enemies, the soldan of Egypt and the Saracens.

Having written letters to the pope, in the Tartar language, he delivered them to the Polos, and appointed one of the principal noblemen of his court to accompany them in their mission. On their taking leave he furnished them with a tablet of gold on which was engraved the royal arms; this was to serve as a passport, at sight of which the governors of the various provinces were to entertain them, to furnish them with escorts through dangerous places, and render them all other necessary services at the expense of the Great Khan.

They had scarce proceeded twenty miles, when the nobleman who accompanied them fell ill, and they were obliged to leave him and continue on their route. Their golden passport procured them every attention and facility, throughout the dominions of the Great Khan. They arrived safely at Acre in April 1269. Here they received news of the recent death of pope Clement IV, at which they were much grieved, fearing it would cause delay in their mission. There was at that time in Acre a legate of the holy chair, Tebaldo de Vesconti of Placentia, to whom they gave an account of their embassy. He heard them with great attention and interest, and advised them to await the election of a new Pope, which must soon take place, before they proceeded to Rome on their mission. They determined in the interim to make a visit to their families, and accordingly departed for Negropont and from thence to Venice, where great changes had taken place in their domestic concerns during their long absence. The wife of Nicholas, whom he had left pregnant, had died in giving birth to a son, who had been named Marco.

As the contested election for the new pontiff remained pending for two years, they were uneasy, lest the Emperor of Tartary should grow impatient at so long a postponement of the conversion of himself and his people; they determined, therefore, not to wait the election of a

Pope, but to proceed to Acre, and get such dispatches and such ghostly ministry for the Grand Khan as the legate could furnish. On this second journey, Nicholas Polo took with him his son Marco, who afterwards wrote an account of these travels.

They were again received with great favour by the legate Tebaldo, who, anxious for the success of their mission, furnished them with letters to the Grand Khan, in which the doctrines of the Christian faith were fully expounded. With these, and with a supply of the holy oil from the sepulchre, they once more set out in September 1271, for the remote parts of Tartary. They had not long departed, however, when missives arrived from Rome informing the legate of his own election to the holy chair. He took the name of Gregory X and decreed that in future on the death of a Pope, the cardinals should be shut up in conclave until they elected a successor; a wise regulation, which has since continued, enforcing a prompt decision and preventing intrigue.

Immediately on receiving intelligence of his election he despatched a courier to the king of Armenia requesting that the two Venetians might be sent back to him if they had not departed. They joyfully returned and were furnished with new letters to the Khan. Two eloquent friars also, Nicholas Vincenti and Gilbert de Tripoli, were sent with them, with powers to ordain priests and Bishops and to grant absolution. They had presents of crystal vases and other costly articles, to deliver to the Grand Khan, and thus well provided, they once more set forth on their journey.*

Arriving in Armenia, they ran great risks of their lives from the war which was raging, the soldan of Babylon having invaded the country. They took refuge for some time with the superior of a monastery. Here the two reverend fathers, losing all courage to prosecute so perilous an enterprize, determined to remain, and the Venetians continued their journey. They were a long time on the way, and exposed to great hardships and sufferings from floods and snow storms, it being the winter season. At length they reached a town in the dominions of the Khan. That Potentate sent officers to meet them at forty days' distance from the court and to provide quarters for them during their journey.† He received them with great kindness, was highly gratified with the result of their mission, and with the letters of the Pope, and having received

---

* Ramusio, tom. iii.

† Bergeron, by a blunder in his translation from the original Latin, has stated that the Khan sent 40,000 men to escort them. This has drawn the ire of the critics upon Marco Polo, who have cited it as one of his monstrous exaggerations.

from them some oil from the lamp of the holy sepulchre, he had it locked up and guarded as a precious treasure.

The three Venetians, father, brother and son, were treated with such distinction by the Khan, that the courtiers were filled with jealousy. Marco soon, however, made himself popular and was particularly esteemed by the emperor. He acquired the four principal languages of the country, and was of such remarkable capacity, that, notwithstanding his youth, the Khan employed him in missions and services of importance, in various parts of his dominions, some to the distance of even six months' journey. On these expeditions he was industrious in gathering all kinds of information respecting that vast empire; and from notes and minutes made for the satisfaction of the Grand Khan, he afterwards composed the history of his travels.

After about seventeen years' residence in the Tartar court the Venetians felt a longing to return to their native country. Their patron was advanced in age and could not survive much longer, and after his death, their return might be difficult if not impossible. They applied to the Grand Khan for permission to depart, but for a time met with a refusal, accompanied by friendly upbraidings. At length a singular train of events operated in their favor; an embassy arrived from a Mogul Tartar prince, who ruled in Persia, and who was grand nephew to the emperor. The object was to entreat, as a spouse, a princess of the imperial lineage. A granddaughter of Cublai Khan, seventeen years of age, and of great beauty and accomplishments, was granted to the prayer of the prince, and departed for Persia with the ambassadors, and with a splendid retinue, but after traveling for some months, was obliged to return on account of the distracted state of the country.

The ambassadors despaired of conveying the beautiful bride to the arms of her expecting bridegroom, when Marco Polo returned from a voyage to certain of the Indian islands. His representations of the safety of a voyage in those seas, and his private instigations, induced the ambassadors to urge the Grand Khan for permission to convey the princess by sea to the gulf of Persia, and that the Christians might accompany them, as being best experienced in maritime affairs. Cublai Khan consented with great reluctance, and a splendid fleet was fitted out and victualed for two years, consisting of fourteen ships of four masts, some of which had crews of two hundred and fifty men.

On parting with the Venetians the munificent Khan gave them rich presents of jewels, and made them promise to return to him after they had visited their families. He authorized them to act as his ambassadors to the principal courts of Europe, and, as on a former occa-

sion, furnished them with tablets of gold, to serve, not merely as passports, but as orders upon all commanders in his territories for accommodations and supplies.

They set sail therefore in the fleet with the oriental princess and her
attendants and the Persian ambassadors. The ships swept along the
coast of Cochin China, stopped for three months at a port of the island
of Sumatra near the western entrance of the straits of Malacca, waiting
for the change of the monsoon to pass the bay of Bengal. Traversing
this vast expanse they touched at the island of Ceylon and then crossed
the strait to the southern part of the great peninsula of India. Thence
sailing up the Pirate coast, as it is called, the fleet entered the Persian
gulf and arrived at the famous port of Olmuz, where it is presumed
the voyage terminated, after eighteen months spent in traversing the
Indian seas.

Unfortunately for the royal bride who was the object of the splendid
naval expedition, her bridegroom, the Mogul king, had died some time
before her arrival, leaving a son named Ghazan, during whose minority
the government was administered by his uncle Kai-Khatu. According to
the directions of the regent, the princess was delivered to the youthful
prince, son of her intended spouse. He was at that time at the head of
an army on the borders of Persia. He was of a diminutive stature but
of a great soul, and, on afterwards ascending the throne, acquired renown for his talents and virtues. What became of the Eastern bride,
who had traveled so far in quest of a husband, is not known; but every
thing favorable is to be inferred from the character of Ghazan.

The Polos remained some time in the court of the regent, and then
departed, with fresh tablets of gold given by that prince, to carry them
in safety and honor through his dominions. As they had to traverse
many countries where the traveler is exposed to extreme peril, they appeared on their journeys as Tartars of low condition, having converted
all their wealth into precious stones and sewn them up in the folds
and linings of their coarse garments. They had a long, difficult and
perilous journey to Trebizond, whence they proceeded to Constantinople, thence to Negropont, and, finally, to Venice, where they arrived
in 1295, in good health, and literally laden with riches. Having heard
during their journey of the death of their old benefactor Cublai Khan,
they considered their diplomatic functions at an end, and also that they
were absolved from their promise to return to his dominions.

Ramusio, in his preface to the narrative of Marco Polo, gives a
variety of particulars concerning their arrival, which he compares to
that of Ulysses. When they arrived at Venice, they were known by no-

body. So many years had elapsed since their departure without any
tidings of them, that they were either forgotten or considered dead.
Besides, their foreign garb, the influence of southern suns, and the
similitude which men acquire to those among whom they reside for
any length of time, had given them the look of Tartars rather than
Italians.

They repaired to their own house, which was a noble palace, situated in the street of St. Giovanne Chrisostomo, and was afterwards
known by the name of La Corte de la Milione. They found several of
their relatives still inhabiting it, but they were slow in recollecting the
travellers, not knowing of their wealth and probably considering them,
from their coarse and foreign attire, poor adventurers returned to be a
charge upon their families. The Polos, however, took an effectual mode
of quickening the memories of their friends, and ensuring themselves
a loving reception. They invited them all to a grand banquet. When
their guests arrived, they received them richly dressed in garments of
crimson satin of oriental fashion. When water had been served for the
washing of hands, and the company were summoned to table, the
travellers who had retired appeared again in still richer robes of crimson damask. The first dresses were cut up and distributed among the
servants, being of such length that they swept the ground; "which,"
says Ramusio, "was the mode in those days with dresses worn within
doors." After the first course they again retired, and came in dressed
in crimson velvet; the damask dresses being likewise given to the domestics; and the same was done at the end of the feast with their
velvet robes; when they appeared in the Venetian dress of the day.
The guests were lost in astonishment and could not comprehend the
meaning of this masquerade; when, having dismissed all the attendants,
Marco Polo brought forth the coarse Tartar dresses in which they had
arrived: slashing them in several places with a knife and ripping open
the seams and lining, there tumbled forth rubies, sapphires, emeralds,
and diamonds, and other precious stones, until the whole table glittered with inestimable wealth acquired from the munificence of the
Grand Khan, and conveyed in this portable form through the perils of
their long journey.

"The company," observes Ramusio, "were out of their wits with
amazement, and now clearly perceived what they had at first doubted,
that these in very truth were those honoured and valiant gentlemen the
Polos, and accordingly paid them great respect and reverence."

The account of this curious feast is given by Ramusio on traditional
authority; having heard it many times related by the illustrious Gasparo

Malipiero, a very ancient gentleman, and a senator, of unquestionable veracity, who had it from his father, who had it from his grandfather, and so on up to the fountain head.

When the fame of this banquet and of the wealth of the travellers came to be divulged throughout Venice, all the city, noble and simple, crowded to do honor to the extraordinary merit of the Polos. Maffeo, who was the eldest, was admitted to the dignity of the magistracy. The youth of the city came every day to visit and converse with Marco Polo, who was extremely amiable and communicative. They were insatiable in their inquiries about Cathay and the Grand Khan, which he answered with great courtesy, giving them details with which they were vastly delighted; and as he always spoke of the wealth of the Grand Khan in round numbers, they gave him the name of Messer Marco Milioni.

Some months after their return, Lampa Doria, commander of the Genoese navy, appeared in the vicinity of the island of Curzola with seventy galleys. Andrea Dandolo, the Venetian admiral, was sent against him. Marco Polo commanded a galley of the fleet. His usual good fortune deserted him. Advancing the first in the line with his galley and not being properly seconded, he was taken prisoner, thrown in irons and carried to Genoa. Here he was detained for a long time in prison and all offers of ransom rejected. His imprisonment gave great uneasiness to his father and uncle, fearing that he might never return. Seeing themselves in this unhappy state with so much treasure and no heirs, they consulted together. They were both very old men, but Nicolo, observes Ramusio, was of a galliard complexion; it was determined he should take a wife. He did so, and to the wonder of his friends, in four years had three children.

In the mean while the fame of Marco Polo's travels had circulated in Genoa. His prison was daily crowded with nobility and he was supplied with every thing that could cheer him in his confinement. A Genoese gentleman who visited him every day at length prevailed upon him to write an account of what he had seen. He had his papers and journals sent to him from Venice, and with the assistance of his friend or, as some will have it, his fellow-prisoner, produced the work which afterwards made such a noise throughout the world.

The merit of Marco Polo at length procured him his liberty. He returned to Venice, where he found his father with a house full of children. He took it in good part, followed the old man's example, married, and had two daughters, Moretta and Fantina. The date of the death of Marco Polo is unknown; he is supposed to have been, at the time, about seventy years of age. On his death-bed he is said to have been exhorted by his friends to retract what he had published, or at least, to disavow those parts commonly regarded as fictions. He replied indignantly that so far from having exaggerated, he had not told one half of the extraordinary things of which he had been an eye-witness.

Marco Polo died without male issue. Of the three sons of his father by the second marriage, one only had children, viz. five sons and one daughter. The sons died without leaving issue; the daughter inherited all her father's wealth and married into the noble and distinguished house of Trevesino. Thus the male line of the Polos ceased in 1417, and the family name was extinguished.

Such are the principal particulars known of Marco Polo, a man whose travels for a long time made a great noise in Europe and will be found to have had a great effect on modern discovery. His splendid account of the extent, wealth, and population of the Tartar territories filled every one with admiration. The possibility of bringing all those regions under the dominion of the church and rendering the Grand Khan an obedient vassal to the holy chair, was for a long time a favorite topic among the enthusiastic missionaries of Christendom, and there were many saints-errant who undertook to effect the conversion of this magnificent infidel.

Even at the distance of two centuries, when the enterprizes for the discovery of a new route to India, had set all the warm heads of Europe madding about those remote regions of the East, the conversion of the Grand Khan became again a popular theme; and it was too speculative and romantic an enterprize not to catch the vivid imagination of Columbus. In all his voyages he will be found continually to be seeking after the territories of the Grand Khan, and even after his last expedition, when nearly worn out by age, hardships and infirmities, he offered, in a letter to the Spanish monarchs, written from a bed of sickness, to conduct any missionary to the territories of the Tartar Emperor who would undertake his conversion.

No. XXI

The work of Marco Polo

The work of Marco Polo is stated by some to have been originally written in Latin,* though the most probable opinion is that it was written in the Venetian dialect of the Italian. Copies of it in manuscript were multiplied and rapidly circulated; translations were made into various languages; until the invention of printing enabled it to be widely diffused throughout Europe. In the course of these translations and successive editions the original text, according to Purchas, has been much vitiated, and it is probable many extravagancies in numbers and measurements with which Marco Polo is charged, may be the errors of translators and printers.

When the work first appeared it was considered by some as made up of fictions and extravagancies; and Vossius assures us that even after the death of Marco Polo he continued to be a subject of ridicule among the light and unthinking, insomuch that he was frequently personated at masquerades by some wit or droll, who, in his feigned character related all kinds of extravagant fables and adventures. His work, however, excited great attention among thinking men, containing evidently a fund of information concerning vast and splendid countries, before unknown to the European world. Vossius assures us that it was at one time highly esteemed among the learned. Francis Pepin, author of the Brandenburgh version, styles Polo a man commendable for his piety, prudence and fidelity. Athanasius Kircher, in his account of China, says, that none of the ancients have described the kingdoms of the remote East with more exactness. Various other learned men of past times have borne testimony to his character, and most of the substantial points of his work have been authenticated by subsequent travellers. The most able and ample vindication of Marco Polo, however, is to be found in the English translation of his work, with copious notes and commentaries, by William Marsden, F.R.S. He has diligently discriminated between what Marco Polo relates from his own observation, and what he relates as gathered from others; he points out the errors that have arisen from misinterpretations, omissions or interpretations of translators, and he claims all proper allowance for the superstitious coloring of parts of the narrative from the belief, prevalent among the most wise and learned of his day, in miracles and magic. After perusing

---

* Prevost, Hist. des Voyages, tom. xxvii. lib. 4. cap. 3. Paris, 1549.

the work of Mr. Marsden, the character of Marco Polo rises in the esti-mation of the reader. It is evident that his narration, as far as related from his own observations, is correct, and that he had really traversed a great part of Tartary and China, and navigated in the Indian seas. Some of the countries and many of the islands, however, are evidently described from accounts given by others, and in these accounts are generally found the fables which have excited incredulity and ridicule. As he composed his work after his return home, partly from memory and partly from memorandums, he was liable to confuse what he had heard with what he had seen, and thus to give undue weight to many fables and exaggerations which he had received from others.

Much has been said of a map brought from Cathay by Marco Polo, which was conserved in the convent of St. Michale de Murano in the vicinity of Venice, and in which the Cape of Good Hope and the island of Madagascar were indicated; countries which the Portuguese claim the merit of having discovered two centuries afterwards. It has been suggested also that Columbus had visited the convent and examined this map, from whence he derived some of his ideas concerning the coast of India. According to Ramusio, however, who had been at the convent and was well acquainted with the Prior, the map preserved there was one copied by a Friar from the original one of Marco Polo, and many alterations and additions had since been made by others' hands, so that for a long time it lost all credit with judicious people, until on compar-ing it with the work of Marco Polo, it was found in the main to agree with his descriptions.* The Cape of Good Hope was doubtless among the additions made subsequent to the discoveries of the Portuguese.†
Columbus makes no mention of this map, which he most probably would have done had he seen it. He seems to have been entirely guided by the one furnished by Paulo Toscanelli, and which was apparently pro-jected after the original map, or after the descriptions of Marco Polo, and the maps of Ptolemy.

When the attention of the world was turned towards the remote parts of Asia in the fifteenth century and the Portuguese were making their attempts to circumnavigate Africa, the narration of Marco Polo again rose to notice. This, with the travels of Nicolo le Comte, the Venetian,

*Ramusio, vol. ii. p. 17.
† Mr. Marsden, who has inspected a splendid fac simile of this map preserved in the British Museum, objects even to the fundamental part of it: "where," he observes, "situations are given to places that seem quite inconsistent with the descriptions in the travels and cannot be attributed to their author, although inserted on the supposed authority of his writings." Marsden's M. Polo. Introd. p. xlii.

and of Hieronimo da San Stefano, a Genoese, are said to have been the principal lights by which the Portuguese guided themselves in their voyages.*

Above all, the influence which the work of Marco Polo had over the mind of Columbus gives it particular interest and importance. It was evidently an oracular work with him. He frequently quotes it, and on his voyages, supposing himself to be on the Asiatic coast, he is continually endeavouring to discover the islands and main lands described in it, and to find the famous Cipango.

It is proper therefore to specify some of those places and the manner in which they are described by the Venetian traveller, that the reader may more fully understand the anticipations which were haunting the mind of Columbus in his voyages among the West Indian islands, and along the coast of Terra Firma.

The winter residence of the Great Khan, according to Marco Polo, was in the city of Cambalu, or Kanbalu, (since ascertained to be Pekin), in the province of Cathay. This city, he says, was twenty four miles square, and admirably built. It was impossible, according to Marco Polo, to describe the vast amount and variety of merchandize and manufactures brought there; it would seem as if there were enough to furnish the universe.

"Here are to be seen in wonderful abundance the precious stones, the pearls, the silks, and the diverse perfumes of the East; scarce a day passes that there does not arrive nearly a thousand cars laden with silk, of which they make admirable stuffs in this city."

The palace of the Great Khan is magnificently built and four miles in circuit. It is rather a groupe of palaces. In the interior it is resplendent with gold and silver; and in it are guarded the precious vases and jewels of the sovereign. All the appointments of the Khan for war, for the chace, for various festivities are described in gorgeous terms.

But though Marco Polo is magnificent in his description of the Province of Cathay and its imperial city of Cambalu, he outdoes himself when he comes to describe the province of Mangi. This province is supposed to be the southern part of China. It contained, he says, twelve hundred cities. The capital, Quinsai, supposed to be the city of Hangcheu, was twenty five miles from the sea, but communicated, by a river, with a port situated on the sea coast, and had great trade with India.

The name Quinsai, according to Marco Polo, signifies the city of

* Hist. des Voyages, tom. xl. lib. 11. ch. 4.

heaven; he says he has been in it, and examined it diligently, and affirms it to be the largest in the world; and so it undoubtedly is, if the measurement of the traveller is to be taken literally, for he declares that it is one hundred miles in circuit. This seeming exaggeration has been explained by supposing him to mean Chinese miles or *li*, which are to the Italian miles in proportion of three to eight; and Mr. Marsden observes that the walls even of the modern city, the limits of which have been considerably contracted, are estimated by travelers at sixty *li*. The ancient city has evidently been of immense extent, and as Marco Polo could not be supposed to have measured the walls himself, he has probably taken the loose and incorrect estimates of the inhabitants. He describes it also as built upon little islands like Venice, and has twelve thousand stone bridges,* the arches of which are so high that the largest vessels can pass under them without lowering their masts. It has, he affirms, three thousand baths, and six hundred thousand families, including domestics. It abounds with magnificent houses, and has a lake thirty miles in circuit within its walls, on the banks of which are superb palaces of people of rank.† The inhabitants of Quinsai are very voluptuous and indulge in all kinds of luxuries and delights, particularly the women, who are extremely beautiful. There are many merchants and artisans, but the masters do not work, they employ servants to do all their labour. The province of Mangi was conquered by the Great Khan, who divided it into nine kingdoms, appointing to each a tributary king. He drew from it an immense revenue, for the country abounded in gold, silver, silks, sugars, spices and perfumes.

Zipangu, Zipangri, or Cipango

Fifteen hundred miles from the shores of Mangi, according to Marco Polo, lay the great island of Zipangu, by some written Zipangri, and by

---

* Another blunder in translation has drawn upon Marco Polo the indignation of George Hornius, who, in his Origin of America, iv. 3, exclaims, "Who can believe all that he says of the city of Quinsay? As for example, that it has stone bridges twelve thousand miles high!" &c. It is probable that many of the exaggerations in the accounts of Marco Polo are in fact the errors of his translators. Mandeville, speaking of this same city, which he calls Cansai, says it is built on the sea like Venice and has 1200 bridges.

† Sir George Staunton mentions this lake as being a beautiful sheet of water, about three or four miles in diameter; its margin ornamented with houses and gardens of Mandarines, together with temples, monasteries for the priests of Fo, and an imperial palace.

Columbus Cipango.* Marco Polo describes it as abounding in gold, which however, the king seldom permits to be transported out of the island. The king has a magnificent palace covered with plates of gold as in other countries the palaces are covered with sheets of lead or copper. The halls and chambers are likewise covered with gold; the windows adorned with it; the very floors paved with it, sometimes in plates of thickness of two fingers. The island also produces vast quantities of the largest and finest pearls, together with a variety of precious stones, so that in fact it abounds in riches. The Great Khan made several attempts to conquer this island but in vain, which is not to be wondered at if it be true what Marco Polo relates, that the inhabitants had certain stones of a charmed virtue inserted between the skin and the flesh of their right arms, which, through the power of diabolical enchantments rendered them invulnerable. The island was an object of diligent search to Columbus.

About the island of Zipangu or Cipango, and between it and the coast of Mangi, the sea, according to Marco Polo, is studded with small islands to the number of seven thousand four hundred and forty, of which the greater part are inhabited. There is not one which does not produce odoriferous trees, and perfumes in abundance. Columbus thought himself at one time in the midst of these islands.

These are the principal places described by Marco Polo, which occur in the letters and journals of Columbus. The island of Cipango was the first land he expected to make and he intended to visit afterwards the province of Mangi; and to seek the Great Khan in his city of Cambalu in the province of Cathay.

Unless the reader can bear in mind these sumptuous descriptions of Marco Polo, of countries teeming with wealth and cities whose very domes and palaces flamed with gold, he will have but a faint idea of the splendid anticipations which filled the imagination of Columbus, when he discovered, as he supposed, the extremity of Asia.

It was this confident expectation of soon arriving at these countries, and realizing the accounts of the Venetian, that induced him to hold

---

* Supposed to be those islands collectively called Japan. They are named by the Chinese Ge-pen, the terminating syllable *gu* added by Marco Polo, is supposed to be the Chinese word *kue*, signifying kingdom, which is commonly annexed to the names of foreign countries. As the distance of the nearest part of the southern island from the coast of China near Ning-po, is not more than five hundred Italian miles, Mr. Marsden supposes Marco Polo in stating it to be 1500 miles, means Chinese miles or li, which are in the proportion of somewhat more than one-third of the former.

forth those promises of immediate wealth to the sovereigns, which caused so much disappointment, and brought upon him the frequent reproach of exciting false hopes and indulging in wilful exaggeration.

No. XXII

Sir John Mandeville

Next to Marco Polo, the travels of Sir John Mandeville, and his account of the territories of the Great Khan, along the coast of Asia, seem to have been treasured up in the mind of Columbus.

Mandeville was born in the city of St. Albans. He was devoted to study from his earliest childhood and after finishing his general education, applied himself to medicine. Having a great desire to see the remotest parts of the earth, then known, that is to say, Asia and Africa, and above all to visit the Holy Land, he left England in 1332 and passing through France, embarked at Marseilles. According to his own account he visited Turkey, Armenia, Egypt, Upper and Lower Libya, Syria, Persia, Chaldea, Ethiopia, Tartary, Amazonia, and the Indies, residing in their principal cities. But most, he says, he delighted in the Holy Land, where he remained for a long time, examining it with the greatest minuteness, and endeavouring to follow all the traces of our Saviour. After an absence of thirty four years he returned to England, but found himself forgotten and unknown by the greater part of his countrymen and a stranger in his native place. He wrote a history of his travels in three languages, English, French and Latin, for he was master of many tongues. He addressed his work to Edward III. His wanderings do not seem to have made him either pleased with the world at large or contented with his home. He railed at the age, saying that there was no more virtue extant; that the church was ruined, error prevalent among the clergy, simony upon the throne, and in a word that the devil reigned triumphant. He soon returned to the continent and died at Liege in 1372. He was buried in the abbey of the Gulielmites in the suburbs of that city, where Ortelius in his Itinerarium Belgiæ says that he saw his monument, on which was the effigy, in stone, of a man with a forked beard and his hands raised towards his head (probably folded as in prayer, according to the manner of old tombs) and a lion at his feet. There was an inscription stating his name, quality and calling, viz. professor of medicine, that he was very pious, very learned, and very charitable to the poor, and that after having travelled over the whole world, he had died at Liege. The people of the convent shewed also his spurs and the housings of the horses which he had ridden in his travels.

The descriptions given by Mandeville of the Grand Khan, of the province of Cathay and the city of Cambalu, are no less splendid than those of Marco Polo. The royal palace was more than two leagues in circumference. The grand hall had twenty four columns of copper and gold. There were more than three hundred thousand men occupied and living in and about the palace, of which more than one hundred thousand were employed in taking care of ten thousand elephants and of a vast variety of other animals, birds of prey, falcons, parrots and paroquets. On days of festival there were even twice the number of men employed. The title of this potentate in his letters was, "Khan, the son of God, exalted possessor of all the earth, master of those who are masters of others." On his seal was engraved "God reigns in heaven, Khan upon earth."

Mandeville has become proverbial for indulging in a traveller's exaggerations, yet his accounts of the countries which he visited have been found far more veracious than had been imagined. His descriptions of Cathay, and the wealthy province of Mangi, agreeing with those of Marco Polo, had great authority with Columbus.

No. XXIII

The Zones

The zones were imaginary bands or circles in the heavens producing an effect of climate on corresponding belts on the globe of the earth. The polar circles and the tropics mark these divisions.

The central region, lying beneath the track of the sun, was termed the torrid zone; the two regions between the tropics and the polar circles were termed the temperate zones, and the remaining parts between the polar circles and the poles, the frigid zones.

The frozen regions near the poles were considered uninhabitable and unnavigable on account of the extreme cold. The burning zone, or rather the central part of it, immediately about the equator, was considered uninhabitable, unproductive and impassable, in consequence of the excessive heat. The temperate zones lying between them, were supposed to be fertile and salubrious, and suited to the purposes of life.

The globe was divided into two Hemispheres by the equator, an imaginary line encircling it at equal distance from the poles. The whole of the world known to the ancients was contained in the temperate zone of the northern Hemisphere.

It was imagined that if there should be inhabitants in the temperate zone of the southern Hemisphere, there could still be no communication with them on account of the burning zone which intervened.

Parmenides, according to Strabo, was the inventor of this theory of the five zones, but he made the torrid zone extend on each side of the equator beyond the tropics. Aristotle supported this doctrine of the zones. In his time nothing was known of the extreme northern parts of Europe and Asia, nor of interior Ethiopia, and the southern part of Africa, extending beyond the tropic of Capricorn to the Cape of Good Hope. Aristotle believed that there was habitable earth in the southern Hemisphere, but that it was for ever divided from the part of the world already known, by the impassable zone of scorching heat at the equator.*

Pliny supported the opinion of Aristotle concerning the burning zones. "The temperature of the central region of the earth," he observes, "where the sun runs his course is burnt up as with fire. The temperate zones which lie on either side can have no communication with each other in consequence of the fervent heat of this region."†

Strabo (lib. xi.), in mentioning this theory gives it likewise his support, and others of the ancient philosophers as well as the poets might be cited, to shew the general prevalence of the belief.

It must be observed that, at the time when Columbus defended his proposition before the learned at Salamanca, the ancient theory of the burning zone had not yet been totally disproved by modern discovery. The Portuguese, it is true, had penetrated within the tropics, but though the whole of the space between the tropic of Cancer and that of Capricorn, in common parlance was termed the torrid zone, the uninhabitable and impassable part, strictly speaking, according to the doctrine of the ancients, only extended a limited number of degrees on each side of the Equator; forming about a third, or at most the half of the zone. The proofs which Columbus endeavoured to draw therefore from the

* Aristotle, Met. ii. cap. 5.
† Pliny, lib. i. cap. 61.

voyages made to St. George la Mina were not conclusive with those who were bigoted to the ancient theory, and who placed this scorching region still farther southward and immediately about the Equator.

No. XXIV

Of the Atalantis of Plato

The island Atalantis is mentioned by Plato in his dialogue of Timæus. Solon, the Athenian lawgiver, is supposed to have travelled into Egypt. He is in an ancient city on the Delta, the fertile island formed by the Nile, and is holding converse with certain learned priests on the antiquities of remote ages, when one of them gives him a description of the island of Atalantis and of its destruction, which he describes as having taken place before the conflagration of the world by Phaeton.

This island, he was told, had been situated in the Western Ocean, opposite to the Straits of Gibraltar. There was an easy passage from it to other islands, which lay adjacent to a large continent exceeding in size all Europe and Asia. Neptune settled in this island, from whose son Atlas its name was derived, and he divided it among his ten sons. His descendants reigned here in regular succession for many ages. They made irruptions into Europe and Africa, subduing all Libya as far as Egypt and all Europe to Asia Minor.

They were resisted, however, by the Athenians, and driven back to their Atlantic territories. Shortly after this there was a tremendous earthquake and an overflowing of the sea, which continued for a day and a night. In the course of this the vast island of Atalantis and all its splendid cities and warlike nations were swallowed up and sunk to the bottom of the sea, which spreading its waters over the chasm formed the Atlantic Ocean. For a long time, however, the sea was not navigable on account of rocks and shelves, of mud and slime, and of the ruins of that drowned country.

Many, in modern times, have considered this a mere fable; others suppose that Plato, while in Egypt, had received some vague accounts of the Canary Islands, and on his return to Greece, finding those islands so entirely unknown to his countrymen, had made them the seat of his political and moral speculations. Some, however, have been disposed to give greater weight to this story of Plato. They imagine that such an island may really have existed, filling up a great part of the Atlantic, and that the continent beyond it was America, which in such case was not unknown to the ancients. Kircher supposes it to have been an island extending from the Canaries to the Azores; that it was really engulphed in one of the convulsions of the globe, and that those small islands are mere shattered fragments of it.

As a further proof that the New World was not unknown to the ancients many have cited the singular passage in the Medea of Seneca, which is wonderfully apposite, and shews at least how nearly the warm imagination of a poet may approach to prophecy. The predictions of the ancient oracles were rarely so unequivocal.

> Venient annis
> Sæcula seris, quibus Oceanus
> Vincula rerum laxet, et ingens
> Pateat tellus, Typhisque novos
> Detegat orbes, nec sit terris
> Ultima Thule.

Gosselin in his able research into the voyages of the ancients, supposes the Atalantis of Plato to have been nothing more nor less than one of the nearest of the Canaries, viz. Fortaventura or Lancerote.

No. XXV

The Imaginary Island of St. Brandan

One of the most singular geographical illusions on record is that which for a long while haunted the imaginations of the inhabitants of the Canaries. They fancied they beheld a mountainous island, of about ninety leagues in length, lying far to the westward. It was only seen at intervals, but in perfectly clear and serene weather. To some it seemed one hundred leagues distant, to others forty, to others only fifteen or eighteen.*

On attempting to reach it, however, it somehow or other eluded the search and was nowhere to be found. Still there were so many eye-witnesses of credibility who concurred in testifying to their having seen it,

* Feyjoo, Theatro Critico, tom. iv. d. 10. sect. 29.

and the testimony of the inhabitants of different islands agreed so well as to its form and position, that its existence was generally believed; and geographers inserted it in their maps. It is laid down on the globe of Martin Behem, projected in 1492, as delineated by M. De Murr, and it will be found in most of the maps of the time of Columbus, placed commonly about 200 leagues west of the Canaries. During the time that Columbus was making his proposition to the court of Portugal, an inhabitant of the Canaries applied to King John II for a vessel to go in search of this island. In the archives of the Torre do Tombo,* also, there is a record of a contract made by the crown of Portugal with Fernando de Ulmo, cavalier of the royal household, and captain of the island of Tercera, wherein he undertakes to go at his own expense, in quest of an island, or islands, or Terra Firma, supposed to be the Island of the Seven Cities; on condition of having jurisdiction over the same, for himself and his heirs, allowing one tenth of the revenues to the King. This Ulmo, finding the expedition above his capacity, associated one Juan Alphonso del Estreito in the enterprize. They were bound to be ready to sail with two caravels in the month of March 1487.† The fate of their enterprize is unknown.

The name of St. Brandan, or Borondon, given to this imaginary island from time immemorial, is said to be derived from a Scotch abbot who flourished in the sixth century, and who is called sometimes by the foregoing appellations, sometimes San Blandano or St. Blandanus. In the martyrology of the order of St. Augustine, he is said to have been the patriarch of 3,000 monks. About the middle of the sixth century, he accompanied his disciple, St. Maclovio or St. Malo in search of certain islands possessing the delights of Paradise, which they were told existed in the midst of the ocean and were inhabited by infidels. These most adventurous saints-errant had wandered for a long time upon the ocean, and at length landed upon an island called Ima. Here St. Malo found the body of a giant lying in a sepulchre. He resuscitated him and had much interesting conversation with him, the giant inform- ing him that the inhabitants of that island had some notions of the Trinity, and moreover giving him a gratifying account of the torments which Jews and pagans suffered in the infernal regions. Finding the giant so docile and reasonable, St. Malo expounded to him the doctrines of the Christian religion, converted him and baptized him by the name of Mildum. The giant, however, either through weariness of life, or

* Lib. iv. de la Chancelaria del Rey Don Juan II. fol. 101.
† Torre do Tombo, Lib. das Ylhas, f. 119.

eagerness to enjoy the benefits of his conversion, begged permission, at the end of fifteen days, to die again, which was granted him.

According to another account, the giant told them, he knew of an island in the ocean defended by walls of burnished gold, so resplendent that they shone like crystal, but to which there was no entrance. At their request, he undertook to guide them to it, and taking the cable of their ship, threw himself into the sea. He had not proceeded far, however, when a tempest rose and obliged them all to return, and shortly after the giant died.* A third legend makes the saint pray to heaven on Easter day, that they may be permitted to find land where they may celebrate the offices of religion with becoming state; an island immediately appears, on which they land, perform a solemn mass and the sacrament of the Eucharist; after which reimbarking and making sail, they behold to their astonishment the supposed island suddenly plunge to the bottom of the sea, being nothing else than a monstrous whale.†

When the rumour circulated of an island seen from the Canaries, which always eluded the search, the legends of St. Brandan were revived and applied to this unapproachable land. We are told also that there was an ancient Latin manuscript in the archives of the Cathedral church of the Grand Canary, in which the adventures of these saints were recorded. Through carelessness, however, this manuscript has disappeared.‡ Some have maintained that this island was known to the ancients and was the same mentioned by Ptolemy among the Fortunate or Canary Islands, by the names of Aprositus,** or the Inaccessible; and which according to friar Diego Philipo, in his book on the Incarnation of Christ, shews that it possessed the same quality in ancient times of deluding the eye and being unattainable to the feet of mortals.|| But whatever belief the ancients may have had on the subject, it is certain that it took a strong hold on the faith of the moderns during the prevalent rage for discovery; nor did it lack abundant testimonials. Don Joseph de Viera y Clavijo says there never was a more difficult paradox nor problem in the science of geography; since to affirm the existence of this island is to trample upon sound criticism, judgement, and reason; and to deny it, one must abandon tradition and experience,

---

* Fr. Gregorio Garcia, Origen de los Indios, lib. i. cap. 9.

† Sigeberto. Epist. ad Tietmar. Abbat.

‡ Nuñez de la Pena, Conquist de la Gran Canaria.

** Ptolemy, lib. iv. tom. iv.

|| Fr. D. Philipo, lib. viii. fol. 25.

and suppose that many persons of credit had not the proper use of their senses.*

The belief in this island has continued long since the time of Columbus. It was repeatedly seen and by various persons at a time, always in the same place and of the same form. In 1526 an expedition set off for the Canaries in quest of it, commanded by Fernando de Troya and Fernando Alvarez. The cruized in the wonted direction, but in vain, and their failure ought to have undeceived the public. "The phantasm of the island, however," says Viera, "had such a secret enchantment for all who beheld it, that the public preferred doubting the good conduct of the explorers, than their own senses." In 1570 the appearances were so repeated and clear that there was a universal fever of curiosity awakened among the people of the Canaries and it was determined to send forth another expedition. That they might not appear to act upon light grounds, an exact investigation was previously made of all the persons of talent and credibility who had seen these apparitions of land; or who had other proofs of its existence.

Alonzo de Espinosa, governor of the island of Ferro, accordingly made a report in which more than one hundred witnesses, several of them persons of the highest respectability, deposed that they had beheld the unknown island about forty leagues to the north west of Ferro; that they had contemplated it with calmness and certainty, and had seen the sun set behind one of its points.

Testimonials of still greater force came from the islands of Palma and Teneriffe. There were certain Portuguese who affirmed that, being driven about by a tempest, they had come upon the island of St. Borondon. Pedro Vello, who was the pilot of the vessel, asserted that having anchored in a bay, he landed with several of the crew. They drank fresh water in a brook, and beheld in the sand the print of footsteps, double the size of those of an ordinary man, and the distance between them was in proportion. They found a cross nailed to a neighboring tree, near to which were three stones placed in form of a triangle, with signs of fire having been made among them, probably to cook shellfish. Having seen much cattle and sheep grazing in the neighborhood, two of their party, armed with lances, went into the woods in pursuit of them. The night was approaching, the heavens began to lower, and a harsh wind arose. The people on board the ship cried out that she was dragging her anchor, whereupon Vello entered the boat, and hurried on board. In an instant they lost sight of land, being, as it were, swept away in the hurricane. When the storm had passed away and sea and

* Hist. Isl. Can. lib. i. cap. xxviii.

sky were again serene, they searched in vain for the island; not a trace of it was to be seen, and they had to pursue their voyage, lamenting the loss of their two companions who had been abandoned in the wood.*

A learned licentiate, Pedro Ortiz de Funez, inquisitor of the Grand Canary, while on a visit at Teneriffe, summoned several persons before him, who testified having seen the island. Among them was one Marcos Verde, a man well known in those parts. He stated that in returning from Barbary, and arriving in the neighborhood of the Canaries, he beheld land which, according to his maps and calculations could not be any of the known islands. He concluded it to be the far famed St. Borondon. Overjoyed at having discovered this land of mystery, he coasted along its spellbound shores, until he anchored in a beautiful harbor, formed by the mouth of a mountain ravine. Here he landed with several of his crew. It was now, he said, the hour of the Ave Maria, or of vespers. The sun being set, the shadows began to spread over the land. The voyagers having separated, wandered about in different directions, until out of hearing of each other's shouts. Those on board, seeing the night approaching, made signal to summon back the wanderers to the ship. They reembarked, intending to resume their investigations on the following day. Scarcely were they on board, however, when a whirlwind came rushing down the ravine, with such violence as to drag the vessel from her anchor, and hurry her out to sea; and they never saw any thing more of this hidden and inhospitable island.

Another testimony remains on record in a manuscript of one Abreu Galindo; but whether taken at this time does not appear. It was that of a French adventurer, who, many years before, making a voyage among the Canaries was overtaken by a violent storm which carried away his masts. At length the furious winds drove him to the shores of an unknown island covered with stately trees. Here he landed with part of his crew, and choosing a tree proper for a mast, cut it down and began to shape it for his purpose. The guardian power of the island, however, resented as usual this invasion of his forbidden shores. The heavens assumed a dark and threatening aspect, the night was approaching and the mariners fearing some impending evil abandoned their labour, and returned on board. They were borne away as usual from the coast and the next day arrived at the island of Palma.†

The mass of testimony collected by official authority in 1570 seemed

---

* Nuñez de la Pena, lib. i. cap. l. Viera. Hist. Isl. Can. tom. i. cap. xxviii.

† Nuñez, Conquista de la Gran Canaria. Viera. Hist. &c.

so satisfactory, that another expedition was fitted out in the same year in the island of Palma; it was commanded by Fernando de Villalobos, regidor of the island; but was equally fruitless with the preceding. St. Borondon seemed disposed only to tantalize the world with distant and serene glimpses of his ideal paradise; or to reveal it amidst storms to tempest tost mariners, but to hide it completely from the view of all who diligently sought it. Still the people of Palma adhered to their favorite chimera. Thirty four years afterwards, in 1605, they sent another ship on the quest, commanded by Gaspar Perez de Acosta, an accomplished pilot accompanied by the Padre Lorenzo Pinedo, a holy Franciscan friar, skilled in natural science. St. Borondon, however, refused to reveal his island to either monk or mariner. After cruizing about in every direction, sounding, observing the skies, the clouds, the winds, every thing that could furnish indications, they returned without having seen any thing to authorize a hope.

Upwards of a century now elapsed without any new attempt to seek this fairy island. Every now and then, it is true, the public mind was agitated by fresh reports of its having been seen. Lemons and other fruits, and the green branches of trees, which floated to the shores of Gomera and Ferro, were pronounced to be from the enchanted groves of St. Borondon. At length in 1721 the public infatuation again rose to such a height that a fourth expedition was sent, commanded by Don Gaspar Dominguez, a man of probity and talent. As this was an expedition of solemn and mysterious import, he had two holy Friars as apostolical chaplains. They made sail from the island of Teneriffe towards the end of October, leaving the populace in an indescribable state of anxious curiosity. The ship, however, returned from its cruize as unsuccessful as all its predecessors.

We have no account of any expedition being since undertaken, though the island still continued to be a subject of speculation, and occasionally to reveal its shadowy mountains to the eyes of favoured individuals. In a letter written from the island of Gomera, 1759, by a Franciscan monk to one of his friends, he relates having seen it from the village of Alaxero at six in the morning of the third of May. It appeared to consist of two lofty mountains with a deep valley between; and on contemplating it with a telescope, the valley or ravine appeared to be filled with trees. He summoned the curate, Antonio Joseph Manrique, and upwards of forty other persons, all of whom beheld it plainly.*

Nor is this island delineated merely in ancient maps of the time of

---

* Viera, Hist. Isl. Can. tom. i. cap. xxviii.

Columbus. It is laid down as one of the Canary Islands in a French map published in 1704, and Mons. Gautier in a geographical chart annexed to his Observations on Natural History, published in 1755, places it five degrees to the west of the island of Ferro, in the 29th degree of N. latitude.*

Such are the principal facts existing relative to the island of St. Brandan. Its reality was for a long time a matter of firm belief. It was in vain that repeated voyages and investigations proved its non-existence: the public, after trying all kinds of sophistry, took refuge in the supernatural, to defend their favourite chimera. They maintained that it was rendered inaccessible to mortals by divine providence, or by diabolical magic. Most inclined to the former. All kinds of extravagant fancies were indulged concerning it:† some confounded it with the fabled island of the Seven Cities, situated somewhere in the bosom of the ocean, where, in old times, seven bishops and their followers had taken refuge from the Moors. Some of the Portuguese imagined it to be the abode of their lost king Sebastian. The Spaniards pretended that Roderick, the last of their Gothic kings, had fled thither from the Moors, after the disastrous battle of the Guadalete. Others suggested that it might be the seat of the terrestrial paradise; the place where Enoch and Elijah remained in a state of blessedness until the final day; and that it was made at times apparent to the eyes, but invisible to the search of mortals. Poetry, it is said, has owed to this popular belief one of its beautiful fictions; and the garden of Armida, where Rinaldo was detained enchanted, and which Tasso places in one of the Canary Islands, has been identified with the imaginary St. Borondon.‡

The learned father Feyjoo** has given a philosophical solution to this geographical problem. He attributes all these appearances, which have been so numerous and so well authenticated as not to admit of doubt, to certain atmospherical deceptions, like that of the Fata Morgana, seen at times in the straits of Messina, where the city of Reggio and its surrounding country is reflected in the air above the neighbouring sea; a phenomenon which has likewise been witnessed in front of the city of Marseilles. As to the tales of the mariners who had landed on these forbidden shores and been hurried from thence in whirlwinds and tempests, he considers them as mere fabrications.

As the populace, however, reluctantly give up any thing that partakes

* Viera, Hist. Isl. Can. tom. i. cap. 28.

† Viera, ubi sup.

‡ Viera, Hist. Isl. Can.

** Theatro Critico, tom. iv. d. 10.

of the marvellous and mysterious, and as the same atmospherical phenomena which first gave birth to the illusion may still continue, it is not improbable that a belief in the island of St. Brandan may still exist among the ignorant and credulous of the Canaries and that they at times behold its fairy mountains rising above the distant horizon of the Atlantic.

No. XXVI

The Island of the Seven Cities

One of the popular traditions concerning the ocean which were current during the time of Columbus, was that of the Island of the Seven Cities. It was recorded in an ancient legend that at the time of the conquest of Spain and Portugal by the Moors, when the inhabitants fled in every direction to escape from slavery, seven Bishops, followed by a great number of their people, took shipping and abandoned themselves to their fate, on the high seas. After tossing about for some time, they landed upon an unknown island in the midst of the ocean. Here the Bishops burnt the ships, to prevent the desertion of their followers, and founded seven cities. Various pilots of Portugal, it was said, had reached that island at different times, but had never returned to give any information concerning it, having been detained, according to subsequent accounts, by the successors of the bishops, to prevent pursuit. At length, according to common report, at the time that prince Henry of Portugal was prosecuting his discoveries, several seafaring men presented themselves one day before him, and stated that they had just returned from a voyage, in the course of which they had landed upon the island. The inhabitants, they said, spoke their language, and carried them immediately to church, to ascertain whether they were Catholics, and were rejoiced at finding them of the true faith. They then made earnest inquiries to know whether the Moors still retained possession of Spain and Portugal. While part of the crew were at church, the rest gathered sand on the shore for the use of the kitchen, and found, to their surprise, that one-third of it was gold. The islanders were anxious that the crew should remain with them a few days, until the return of their governor, who was absent; but the mariners, afraid of being detained, embarked and made sail. Such was the story they told prince Henry, hoping to receive reward for their intelligence. The prince expressed displeasure at their hasty departure from the island, and ordered them to return and procure further information; but the men, apprehensive no doubt of having the falsehood of their tale discovered, made their escape, and nothing more was heard of them.*

This story had much currency. The Island of the Seven Cities was identified with the island mentioned by Aristotle as having been discovered by the Carthaginians; and was put down in the early maps about the time of Columbus under the name of Antilla.

At the time of the discovery of New Spain, reports were brought to Hispaniola of the civilization of the country; that the people wore clothing; that their houses and temples were solid, spacious, and often magnificent; and that crosses were occasionally found among them. Juan de Grivalja being despatched to explore the coast of Yucatan, reported that in sailing along it, he beheld with great wonder stately and beautiful edifices of lime and stone, and many high towers that shone at a distance.† For a time the old tradition of the seven cities was revived, and many thought that they were to be found in the same part of New Spain.

No. XXVII

Discovery of the Island of Madeira

The discovery of Madeira by Macham rests principally upon the authority of Francisco Alcaforado, an esquire of prince Henry of Portugal, who composed an account of it for that prince. It does not appear to have obtained much faith among Portuguese historians. No mention is made of it in Barros; he attributes the first discovery of the island to Juan Gonzalez and Tristram Vaz, who he said descried it from Porto Santo, resembling a cloud on the horizon.‡

The abbé Prevost, however, in his General History of Voyages, vol. 6, seems inclined to give credit to the account of Alcaforado. "It was

* Hist. del Almirante, cap. 10.

† Torquemada, Monarquia Indiana, lib. iv. cap. 4. Origen de los Indios, por Fr. Gregorio Garcia, lib. iv. cap. 20.

‡ Barros, Asia, Decad. I. lib. i. cap. 3.

composed," he observes, "at a time when the attention of the public would have exposed the least falsities, and no one was more capable than Alcaforado of giving an exact detail of this event, since he was of the number of those who participated in the second discovery." The narrative, as originally written, was overcharged with ornaments and digressions. It was translated into French and published in Paris in 1671. The French translator had retrenched the ornaments but scrupulously retained the facts. The story, however, is cherished in the island of Madeira, where a painting in illustration of it is still to be seen. The following is the purport of the French translation; I have not been able to procure the original of Alcaforado.

During the reign of Edward III of England, a young man of great courage and talent named Robert Macham fell in love with a young lady of rare beauty of the name of Anne Dorset. She was his superior in birth, and of a proud and aristocratic family; but the merit of Macham gained him the preference over all his rivals. The family of the young lady, to prevent her making an inferior alliance, obtained an order from the king to have Macham arrested and confined, until by arbitrary means they married his mistress to a man of quality. As soon as the nuptials were celebrated, the nobleman conducted his beautiful and afflicted bride to his seat near Bristol. Macham was now restored to liberty. Indignant at the wrongs he had suffered, and certain of the affections of his mistress, he prevailed upon several friends to assist him in a project for the gratification of his love and his revenge. They followed hard on the traces of the new married couple to Bristol. One of the friends obtained an introduction into the family of the nobleman in quality of a groom. He found the young bride full of tender recollections of her lover and of dislike to the husband thus forced upon her. Through the means of this friend, Macham had several communications with her, and concerted means for their escape to France, where they might enjoy their mutual love unmolested.

When all things were prepared, the young lady rode out one day accompanied only by the fictitious groom, under pretence of taking the air. No sooner were they out of sight of the house than they galloped to an appointed place on the shore of the channel, where a boat awaited them. They were conveyed on board a vessel which lay with anchor a-trip and sails unfurled, ready to put to sea. Here the lovers were once more united. Fearful of pursuit the ship immediately weighed anchor; they made their way rapidly along the coast of Cornwall, and Macham anticipated the triumph of soon landing with his beautiful prize on the shores of gay and gallant France. Unfortunately an adverse and stormy wind arose in the night; at day break they found themselves out of sight of land; the mariners were ignorant and inexperienced; they knew nothing of the compass, and it was a time when men were unaccustomed to traverse the high seas. For thirteen days the lovers were driven about on a tempestuous ocean, at the mercy of wind and wave. The fugitive bride was filled with terror and remorse, and looked upon this uproar of the elements as the anger of heaven directed against her. All the efforts of her lover could not remove from her mind a dismal presage of some approaching catastrophe.

At length the tempest subsided. On the fourteenth day at dawn the mariners perceived what appeared to be a tuft of wood rising out of the sea. They joyfully steered for it, supposing it to be an island. They were not mistaken. As they drew near the rising sun shone upon noble forests, the trees of which were of a kind unknown to them. Flights of birds also came hovering about the ship, and perched upon the yards and rigging without any signs of fear.

The boat was sent on shore to reconnoitre and soon returned with such accounts of the beauty of the country, that Macham determined to take his drooping companion to the land, in hopes her health and spirits might be restored by refreshment and repose. They were accompanied on shore by the faithful friends who had assisted in their flight. The mariners remained on board to guard the ship.

The country was indeed delightful. The forests were stately and magnificent; there were trees laden with excellent fruits, others with aromatic flowers; the waters were cool and limpid; the sky serene, and there was a balmy sweetness in the air. The animals that they met with shewed no signs of alarm or ferocity, from which they concluded that the island was uninhabited. On penetrating a little distance they found a sheltered meadow, the green bosom of which was bordered by laurels and refreshed by a mountain brook which ran sparkling over pebbles. In the centre was a majestic tree, the wide branches of which afforded shade from the rays of the sun. Here Macham had bowers constructed and determined to pass a few days; hoping that the sweetness of the country, and the serene tranquillity of this delightful solitude would recruit the drooping health and spirits of his companion.

Three days, however, had scarcely passed, when a violent storm arose from the north east and raged all night over the island. On the succeeding morning Macham repaired to the sea side, but nothing of his ship was to be seen and he concluded that it had foundered in the tempest.

Consternation fell upon the little band, thus left in an uninhabited island in the midst of the ocean. The blow fell most severely on the timid and repentant bride. She had reproached herself with being the cause of all their misfortunes, and from the first had been haunted by dismal forebodings. She now considered them about to be accomplished, and her horror was so great as to deprive her of speech: she expired in three days without uttering a word.

Macham was struck with despair at beholding the tragical end of this tender and beautiful being. He upbraided himself, in the transports of his grief, with tearing her from her home, her country and her friends, to perish upon a savage coast. All the efforts of his companions to console him were in vain; he died within five days, broken-hearted, begging as a last request that his body might be interred beside that of his mistress, at the foot of a rustic altar which they had erected under the great tree. They set up a large wooden cross on the spot, on which was placed an inscription written by Macham himself, relating in a few words his piteous adventure, and praying any Christians who might arrive there to build a chapel in the place dedicated to Jesus the Saviour.

After the death of their commander, his followers consulted about the means to escape from the island. The ship's boat remained on the shore. They repaired it and put it in a state to bear a voyage, and then made sail, intending to return to England. Ignorant of their situation, and carried about by the winds, they were cast upon the coast of Morocco, where, their boat being shattered upon the rocks, they were captured by the Moors and thrown into prison. Here they understood that their ship had shared the same fate, having been driven from her anchorage in the tempest and carried to the same inhospitable coast, where all her crew were made prisoners.

The prisons of Morocco were in those days filled with captives of all nations, taken by their cruisers. Here the English prisoners met with an experienced pilot, a Spaniard of Seville, named Juan de Morales. He listened to their story with great interest, inquired into the situation and description of the island they had discovered; and subsequently, on his redemption from prison, communicated the circumstances, it is said, to prince Henry of Portugal.

There is a difficulty in the above narrative of Alcaforado in reconciling dates. The voyage is said to have taken place during the reign of Edward III, which commenced in 1327, and ended in 1378. Morales, to whom the English communicated their voyage, is said to have been in the service of the Portuguese in the second discovery of Madeira in 1418 and 1420. Even if the voyage and imprisonment had taken place in the last year of king Edward's reign this leaves a space of forty years.

Hakluyt gives an account of the same voyage, taken from Antonio

Galvano. He varies in certain particulars. It happened, he says, in the year 1344 in the time of Peter IV of Arragon. Macham cast anchor in a bay since called after him Machio. The lady being ill, he took her on shore, accompanied by some of his friends, and the ship sailed without them. After the death of the lady, Macham made a canoe out of a tree and ventured to sea in it with his companions. They were cast upon the coast of Africa, where the Moors, considering it as a kind of miracle, carried them to the king of their country, who sent him to the king of Castile. In consequence of the traditional accounts remaining of this voyage, Henry II of Castile sent people in 1395 to rediscover the island.

No. XXVIII

Las Casas

Bartholomew Las Casas, bishop of Chiapa, so often cited in all histories of the New World, was born at Seville in 1474, and was of French extraction. The family name was Casaus. The first of the name who appeared in Spain, served under the standard of Ferdinand III surnamed the Saint, in his wars with the Moors of Andalusia. He was at the taking of Seville from the Moors, when he was rewarded by the King, and received permission to establish himself there. His descendants enjoyed the prerogatives of nobility, and suppressed the letter *u* in their name, to accommodate it to the Spanish tongue.

Antonio, the father of Bartholomew, went to Hispaniola with Columbus in 1493 and returned rich to Seville in 1498.* It has been stated by one of the biographers of Bartholomew Las Casas, that he accompanied Columbus in his third voyage in 1498, and returned with him in 1500.† This, however, is incorrect. He was during that time, completing his education at Salamanca, where he was instructed in Latin, dialectics, logic, metaphysics, ethics and physics, after the supposed method and system of Aristotle. While at the university, he had as a servant an Indian slave given him by his father, who had received him from Columbus. When Isabella, in her transport of virtuous indignation, ordered the Indian slaves to be sent back to their country, this one was

* Navarrete, Colec. Viag. tom. i. Introd. p. lxx.
† T. A. Llorente, Œuvres de Las Casas, p. 11. Paris, 1822.

taken from Las Casas. The young man was aroused by the circumstance, and on considering the nature of the case, became inflamed with a zeal in favour of the unhappy Indians, which never cooled throughout a long and active life. It was excited to tenfold fervour, when at about the age of twenty eight years, he accompanied the commander Ovando to Hispaniola in 1502 and was an eye witness to many of the cruel scenes which took place under his administration. The whole of his future life, a space exceeding sixty years, was devoted to vindicating the cause and endeavouring to meliorate the sufferings of the natives. As a missionary he traversed the wilderness of the New World in various directions, seeking to convert and civilize them; as a protector and champion, he made several voyages to Spain, vindicated their wrongs before courts and monarchs, wrote volumes in their behalf, and exhibited a zeal, and constancy, and intrepidity worthy of an apostle. He died at the advanced age of ninety two years and was buried at Madrid at the church of the Dominican convent of Atocha, of which fraternity he was a member.

Attempts have been made to decry the consistency and question the real philanthropy of Las Casas, in consequence of one of the expedients to which he resorted to relieve the Indians from the cruel bondage imposed upon them. This occurred in 1517, when he arrived in Spain on one of his missions to obtain measures in their favour from government. On his arrival in Spain he found Cardinal Ximenes, who had been left regent on the death of king Ferdinand, too ill to attend to his affairs. He repaired therefore to Valladolid, where he awaited the coming of the new monarch Charles, archduke of Austria, afterwards the Emperor Charles V. He had strong opponents to encounter in various persons high in authority, who holding estates and repartimientos in the colonies were interested in the slavery of the Indians; among those and not the least animated, was the Bishop Fonseca, president of the council of the Indies.

At length the youthful sovereign arrived, accompanied by various Flemings of his court, particularly his grand chancellor, Doctor Juan de Selvagio, a learned and upright man, whom he consulted on all affairs of administration and justice. Las Casas soon became intimate with the chancellor, and stood high in his esteem, but so much opposition arose on every side, that he found his various propositions for the relief of the natives but little attended to. In his doubt and anxiety he had now recourse to an expedient which he considered as justified by the circumstances of the case.* The chancellor Selvagio and the other

---

* Herrera clearly states this as an expedient adopted when others failed. "Bar-

Flemings who had accompanied the youthful sovereign, had obtained from him, before quitting Flanders licences to import slaves from Africa to the colonies; a measure which had recently in 1516 been prohibited by a decree of Cardinal Ximenes, while acting as regent. The chancellor, who was a humane man, reconciled it to his conscience by a popular opinion that one negro could perform, without detriment to his health, the labour of several Indians, and that, therefore, it was a great saving of human suffering. So easy it is for interest to wrap itself up in plausible argument. He might, moreover, have thought the welfare of the Africans but little affected by the change. They were accustomed to slavery in their own country, and they were said to thrive in the New World. "The Africans," observes Herrera, "prospered so much in the island of Hispaniola, that it was the opinion unless a negro should happen to be hanged, he would never die; for as yet none had been known to perish from infirmity. Like oranges, they found their proper soil in Hispaniola, and it seemed even more natural to them than their own native Guinea."[*]

Las Casas finding all other means ineffectual, endeavoured to turn these interested views of the grand chancellor to the benefit of the Indians. He proposed that the Spaniards, resident in the colonies might be permitted to procure negroes for the labour of the farms and the mines, and other severe toils, which were above the strength, and destructive of the lives of the natives.[†] He evidently considered the poor Africans as little better than mere animals; and he acted like others, on an arithmetical calculation of diminishing human misery, by substituting one strong man for three or four of feebler nature. He moreover esteemed the Indians as a nobler and more intellectual race of beings and their preservation and welfare of higher importance to the general interests of humanity.

It is this expedient of Las Casas, which has drawn down severe censure upon his memory. He has been charged with gross inconsistency, and even with having originated "this inhuman traffic in the New World." This last is a grievous charge; but historical facts and dates remove the original sin from his door, and prove that the practice existed in the colonies and was authorized by royal decree long before he took a part in the question.

---

tholomé de Las Casas viendo que sus conceptos hallaban in todas partes dificultad, i que las opiniones que tenia, por mucha familiaridad que havia seguido, i gran credito can al grand Canciller, no podian haber efecto, *se volvio a otros expedientes,"* &c.—Decad. II. lib. ii. cap. xx.

[*] Herrera, Hist. Ind. D. II. lib. iii. cap. iv.

[†] Idem, D. II. lib. ii. cap. xx.

Las Casas did not go to the New World until 1502. By a royal ordinance passed in 1501, negro slaves were permitted to be taken there, provided they had been born among Christians.* By a letter written by Ovando dated 1503, it appears there were numbers in the island of Hispaniola at that time, and he entreats that none more might be permitted to be brought. In 1506, the Spanish government forbade the introduction of Negro slaves from the Levant, or those brought up with the Moors, and stipulated that none should be taken to the colonies but those from Seville, who had been instructed in the Christian faith, that they might contribute to the conversion of the Indians.† In 1510, king Ferdinand being informed of the physical weakness of the Indians ordered fifty Africans to be sent from Seville to labour in the mines.‡ In 1511 he ordered that a great number should be procured from Guinea, and transported to Hispaniola, understanding that one negro could perform the work of four Indians.** In 1512 and 1513, he signed further orders relative to the same subject. In 1516 Charles V granted licences to the Flemings to import negroes to the colonies. It was not until the year 1517, that Las Casas gave his sanction to the traffic. It already existed, and he countenanced it solely with the view to having the hardy Africans substituted for the feeble Indians. It was advocated at the same time, and for the same reasons by the Jeronimite Friars, who were missionaries in the colonies. The motives of Las Casas were purely benevolent, though founded on erroneous notions of justice. He thought to permit evil, that good might spring out of it; to choose between two existing abuses, and to eradicate the greater by resorting to the lesser. His reasoning, however fallacious it may be, was considered satisfactory and humane by some of the most learned and benevolent men of the age, among whom was the cardinal Adrian, afterwards elevated to the papal chair, and characterized by gentleness and humanity. The traffic was permitted; enquiries were made as to the number of slaves required, which was limited to four thousand; and the Flemings obtained a monopoly of the trade which they afterwards farmed out to the Genoese.

Dr. Robertson in noticing this affair, draws a contrast between the conduct of the cardinal Ximenes, and that of Las Casas, strongly to the disadvantage of the latter. "The cardinal," he observes, "when solicited to encourage this commerce, peremptorily rejected the proposition, be-

* Herrera, Hist. Ind. D. II, lib. ii. cap. viii.
† Herrera, D. I. lib. vi. cap. 20.
‡ Idem, Hist. Ind. D. I. lib. viii. cap. ix.
** Idem, D. I. lib. ix. cap. v.

cause he perceived the iniquity of reducing one race of men to slavery, when he was consulting about the means of restoring liberty to another; but Las Casas from the inconsistency natural to men who hurry with headlong impetuosity towards a favourite point, was incapable of making this distinction. In the warmth of his zeal to save the Americans from the yoke, he pronounced it to be lawful and expedient to impose one still heavier upon the Africans."*

This distribution of praise and censure is not perfectly correct. Las Casas had no idea that he was imposing a heavier, nor so heavy, a yoke upon the Africans. The latter were considered more capable of labour, and less impatient of slavery. While the Indians sunk under their tasks, and perished by thousands in Hispaniola, the negroes, on the contrary, throve there. Herrera, to whom Dr. Robertson refers as his authority, assigns a different motive, and one of mere finance, for the measure of cardinal Ximenes. He says, that he ordered that no one should take negroes to the Indies, because, as the natives were decreasing, and it was known that one negro did more work than four of them, there would probably be a great demand for African slaves, and a tribute might be imposed upon the trade, from which would result profit to the royal treasury.† This measure was presently after carried into effect, though subsequent to the death of the cardinal, and licences were granted by the sovereign for pecuniary considerations. Flechier, in his life of Ximenes, assigns another, but a mere political motive for this prohibition. The cardinal, he says, objected to the importation of negroes into the colonies, as he feared they would corrupt the natives, and, by confederacies with them, render them formidable to government. De Marsolier, another biographer of Ximenes, gives equally politic reasons for this prohibition. He cites a letter written by the cardinal on the subject, in which he observed that he knew the nature of the negroes: they were a people capable, it was true, of great fatigue, but extremely prolific and enterprising; and that, if they had time to multiply in America, they would infallibly revolt, and impose on the Spaniards the same chains which they had compelled them to wear.‡ These facts, while they take from the measure of the cardinal that credit for exclusive philanthropy which has been bestowed upon it, manifest the clear foresight of that able politician, whose predictions with respect

* Robertson, Hist. America, p. 3.

† "Porque como iban faltando los Indios, i se conocia, que un Negro trabajaba mas que quatro, por lo qual habia, gran demanda de ellos, parecia que se podia poner algun tributo en la saca, de que resultaria provecho á la real hacienda." Herrera, Decad. II. lib. ii. cap. 8.

‡ De Marsolier, Hist. du Ministère du Cardinal Ximenes, lib. vi. Toulouse, 1694.

to negro revolt have been so strikingly fulfilled in the island of Hispaniola.

Cardinal Ximenes, in fact, though a wise and upright statesman, was
not troubled with scruples of conscience on these questions of natural
right; nor did he possess more toleration than his contemporaries, towards savage and infidel nations. He was grand inquisitor of Spain and
was very efficient during the latter years of Ferdinand in making slaves
of the refractory Moors of Granada. He authorized, by express instructions, expeditions to seize and enslave the Indians of the Caribbee
Islands, whom he termed only suited to labour, enemies of the Christians, and cannibals. Nor will it be considered a proof of a gentle and
tolerant policy, that he introduced the tribunal of the Inquisition into
the New World. These circumstances are not cited to cast reproach
upon the character of cardinal Ximenes, but to show how incorrectly
he has been extolled at the expense of Las Casas. Both of them must
be judged in connexion with the customs and opinions of the age in
which they lived.

Las Casas was the author of many works, but few of which have
been printed. The most important is a General History of the Indies,
from the discovery to the year 1520, in three volumes. It exists only in
manuscript, but is the fountain from which Herrera and most of the
other historians of the New World have drawn large supplies. The work,
though prolix, is valuable, as the author was an eye witness of many
of the facts, had others from persons who were concerned in the transactions recorded, and possessed copious documents. It displays great
erudition, though somewhat crudely and diffusely introduced. His history was commenced in 1527 at fifty three years of age and was finished
in 1559, when eighty five. As many things are set down from memory
there is occasional inaccuracy, but the whole bears the stamp of sincerity and truth. The author of the present work, having had access to
this valuable manuscript, has made great use of it, drawing forth many
curious facts hitherto neglected; but he has endeavoured to consult it
with caution and discrimination, collating it with other authorities, and
omitting whatever appeared to be dictated by prejudice or over heated
zeal.

Las Casas has been accused of high colouring and extravagant dec-
lamation, in those passages which relate to the barbarities practised on
the natives; nor is the charge entirely without foundation. The same
zeal in the cause of the Indians is expressed in his writings that shone
forth in his actions; always pure, often vehement; and occasionally un-
seasonable; still, however, when he errs it is on a generous and right-
eous side. If one tenth part of what he says he "witnessed with his

own eyes" be true, and his veracity is above all doubt, he would have been wanting in the natural feelings of humanity, had he not expressed himself in terms of indignation and abhorrence.

In the course of his work, when Las Casas mentions the original papers lying before him from which he drew many of his facts, it makes one lament that they should be lost to the world. Beside the journals and letters of Columbus, he says he had numbers of the letters of the Adelantado, Don Bartholomew, who wrote better than his brother and whose writings must have been full of energy. Above all he had the map, formed from study and conjecture, by which Columbus sailed on his first voyage. What a precious document would this be for the world! These writings may still exist neglected and forgotten among the rubbish of some convent in Spain. Little hope can be entertained of discovering them in the present stage of degeneracy of the cloister. The monks of Atocha, in a recent conversation with one of the royal princes, betrayed an ignorance that this illustrious man was buried in their convent, nor can any of the fraternity point out his place of sepulture to the stranger.*

The publication of this work of Las Casas has not been permitted in Spain, where every book must have the sanction of a censor before it is committed to the press. The horrible pictures it exhibits of the cruelties inflicted on the Indians, would it was imagined excite an odium against their conquerors. Las Casas himself seems to have doubted the expediency of publishing it, for in 1560, he made a note with his own hand, which is preserved in the two first volumes of the original, mentioning that he left them in confidence to the college of the order of the Predicadores of St. Gregorio, in Valladolid, begging of its prelates, that no secular person, nor even the collegians, should be permitted to read his history for the space of forty years; and that after that term it might be printed, if consistent with the good of the Indies and of Spain.†

For the foregoing reason the work has been cautiously used by Spanish historians, passing over in silence, or with brief notice, many passages of disgraceful import. This feeling is natural, if not commendable; for the world is not prompt to discriminate between individuals and the nation of whom they are but a part. The laws and regulations for

---

* In this notice the author has occasionally availed himself of the interesting memoir of Mons. T. A. Llorente, prefixed to his collection of the works of Las Casas; collating it with the History of Herrera, from which its facts are principally derived.

† Navarrete, Colec. Viag. tom. i. Introd. p. lxxv.

the government of the newly discovered countries, and the decisions of the council of the Indies on all contested points, though tinctured in some degree with the bigotry of the age, were distinguished for wisdom, justice, and humanity, and do honour to the Spanish nation. It was only in the abuse of them by individuals, to whom the execution of the laws was entrusted, that these atrocities were committed. It should be remembered also that the same nation which gave birth to the sanguinary and rapacious adventurers who perpetrated these cruelties, gave birth likewise to the early missionaries like Las Casas, who followed the sanguinary course of discovery, binding up the wounds inflicted by their countrymen: men who in a truly evangelical spirit braved all kinds of perils and hardships and even death itself, not through a prospect of temporal gain or glory but through a desire to meliorate the condition and save the souls of barbarous and suffering nations. The dauntless enterprizes and fearful peregrinations of many of these virtuous men, if properly appreciated, would be found to vie in romantic daring with the heroic achievements of chivalry, with motives of a purer and far more exalted nature.

No. XXIX

Peter Martyr

Peter Martir, or Martyr, of whose writings much use has been made in this history, was born at Anghierra in the territory of Milan, in Italy, on the second of Febuary 1455. He is commonly termed Peter Martyr of *Angleria,* from the Latin name of his native place. He is one of the earliest historians that treat of Columbus, and was his contemporary and intimate acquaintance. Being at Rome in 1487, and having acquired a distinguished reputation for learning, he was invited by the Spanish ambassador, the Count de Tendilla, to accompany him to Spain. He willingly accepted the invitation and was presented to the sovereigns at Saragossa. Isabella amidst the cares of the war with Granada, was anxious for the intellectual advancement of her kingdom, and wished to employ Martyr to instruct the young nobility of the royal household. With her peculiar delicacy, however, she first made her confessor, Hernando de Talavera, enquire of Martyr in what capacity he desired to serve her. Contrary to her expectation Martyr replied, "in the profession of arms." The Queen complied, and he followed her in her campaigns, as one of her household and military suite, but without distinguishing himself, and perhaps without having any particular employ in a capacity so foreign to his talents. After the surrender of Granada, when the war was ended, the Queen, through the medium of the Grand Cardinal of Spain, prevailed upon him to undertake the instruction of the young nobles of her court.

Martyr was acquainted with Columbus while making his application to the Sovereigns, and was present at his triumphant reception by Ferdinand and Isabella in Barcelona, on his return from his first voyage. He was continually in the royal camp, during the war with the Moors, of which his letters contain many interesting particulars. He was sent ambassador extraordinary by Ferdinand and Isabella in 1501 to Venice and thence to the grand Soldan of Egypt. The Soldan in 1490 or 1491 had sent an embassy to the Spanish Sovereigns, threatening that, unless they desisted from the war against Granada, he would put all the Christians in Egypt and Syria to death, overturn all their temples, and destroy the holy sepulchre at Jerusalem. Ferdinand and Isabella pressed the war with tenfold energy, and brought it to a triumphant conclusion in the next campaign, while the Soldan was still carrying on a similar negotiation with the Pope. They afterwards sent Peter Martyr ambassador to the Soldan to explain and justify their measure. Martyr discharged the duties of his embassy with great ability; obtained permission from the Soldan to repair the holy places at Jerusalem; and an abolition of various extortions to which Christian pilgrims had been subjected. While on this embassy he wrote his work De Legatione Babylonica, which includes a history of Egypt in those times.

On his return to Spain, he was rewarded with places and pensions, and in 1524 was appointed a minister of the council of the Indies. His principal work is an account of the discoveries of the New World in eight Decades, each containing ten chapters. They are styled Decades of the New World or Decades of the Ocean, and, like all his other works, were originally written in Latin, though since translated into various languages. He had familiar access to letters, papers, journals and narratives of the early discoverers, and was personally acquainted with many of them, gathering particulars from their conversation. In writing his Decades, he took great pains to obtain information from Columbus himself, and from others, his companions.

In one of his epistles (No. 153, January 1494, to Pomponius Lætus) he mentions having just received a letter from Columbus, by which it appears he was in correspondence with him. Las Casas says that great credit is to be given to him in regard to those voyages of Columbus, although his Decades contain some inaccuracies relative to subsequent events in the Indies. Muñoz allows him great credit as an author contemporary with his subject, grave, well cultivated, instructed in the facts of which he treats, and of entire probity. He observes, however, that his writings, being composed on the spur or excitement of the moment, often related circumstances which subsequently proved to be erroneous; that they were written without method or care, often confusing dates and events, so that they must be read with some caution.

Martyr was in the daily habit of writing letters to distinguished persons, relating the passing occurrences of the busy court and age in which he lived. In several of these Columbus is mentioned, and also some of the chief events of his voyages, as promulgated at the very moment of his return. These letters not being generally known or circulated, or frequently cited, it may be satisfactory to the reader to have a few of the main passages which relate to Columbus. They have a striking effect in carrying us back to the very time of the discoveries.

In one of his epistles, dated Barcelona May 1st, 1493, and addressed to C. Borromeo, he says, "Within these few days a certain Christopher Columbus has arrived from the western antipodes; a man of Liguria, whom my sovereigns reluctantly entrusted with three ships, to seek that region, for they thought that what he said was fabulous. He has returned and brought specimens of many precious things, but particularly gold, which those countries naturally produce."*

In another letter, dated likewise from Barcelona in September following, he gives a more particular account. It is addressed to count Tendilla, governor of Granada, and also to Hernando Talavera, archbishop of that diocess and the same to whom the propositions of Columbus had been referred by the Spanish sovereigns.

"Arouse your attention, ancient sages," says Peter Martyr in his epistle; "listen to a new discovery. You remember Columbus the Ligurian, appointed in the camp by our sovereigns to search for a new hemisphere of land at the western antipodes. You ought to recollect, for you had some agency in the transaction; nor would the enterprize, as I think, have been undertaken without your counsel. He has returned in safety, and relates the wonders he has discovered. He exhibits gold as proof of the mines in those regions; gosampine cotton also, and aromatics, and pepper more pungent than that from Caucasus. All these things, together with scarlet dye wood, the earth produces spontaneously. Pursuing the western sun from Gades five thousand miles, of each a thousand paces, as he relates, he fell in with sundry

---

* Opus Epist. P. Martyris Anglerii. Epist. 131.

islands and took possession of one of them, of greater circuit, he asserts, than the whole of Spain. Here he found a race of men living
contented in a state of nature, subsisting on fruits and vegetables, and
bread formed from roots. * * * * These people have kings, some greater
than others, and they war occasionally among themselves, with bows
and arrows, or lances sharpened and hardened in the fire. The desire of
command prevails among them, though they are naked. They have wives
also. What they worship, except the divinity of heaven, is not ascertained," &c.*

In another letter, dated likewise in September 1493 and addressed to
the cardinal and vice-chancellor Ascanius Sforza, he says:

"So great is my desire to give you satisfaction, illustrious prince, that
I consider it a gratifying occurrence in the great fluctuations of events,
when any thing takes place among us in which you may take an interest. The wonders of this terrestrial globe, round which the sun makes
a circuit in the space of four and twenty hours, have, until our time,
as you are well aware, been known only in regard to one hemisphere,
merely from the Golden Chersonesus to our Spanish Gades. The rest
has been given up as unknown by cosmographers; and if any mention
of it has been made, it has been slight and dubious. But now, O blessed
enterprize! under the auspices of our sovereigns, what has hitherto lain
hidden since the first origin of things, has at length begun to be developed. The thing has thus occurred. Attend, illustrious prince! A certain Christopher Columbus, a Ligurian, despatched to those regions
with three vessels by my sovereigns, pursuing the western sun above
five thousand miles from Gades, achieved his way to the antipodes.
Three and thirty successive days they navigated, with nought but sky
and water. At length from the masthead of the largest vessel in which
Columbus himself sailed, those on the look out proclaimed the sight of
land. He coasted along six islands, one of them, as all his followers
declare, beguiled perchance by the novelty of the scene, is larger than
Spain." Martyr proceeds to give the usual account of the productions of
the islands, and the manners and customs of the natives, particularly
the wars which occurred among them; "as if *meum* and *tuum* had been
introduced among them as among us, and expensive luxuries, and the
desire of accumulating wealth; for what, you will think, can be the
wants of naked men? What further may succeed," he adds, "I will hereafter signify. Farewell."†

In another letter dated Valladolid, February 1st, 1494, to Hernando

* Idem, Epist. 134.
† Idem, Epist. 135.

de Talavera, archbishop of Granada, he observes, "The King and Queen, on the return of Columbus to Barcelona, from his honourable enterprize, appointed him admiral of the ocean sea, and caused him, on account of his illustrious deeds, to be seated in their presence; an honour and a favour, as you know, the highest with our sovereigns. They have despatched him again to those regions, furnished with a fleet of eighteen ships. There is prospect of great discoveries at the western antarctic antipodes."*

In a subsequent letter to Pomponius Lætus dated from Alcala de Henares, December 9th, 1494, he gives the first news of the success of this expedition.

"Spain," says he, "is spreading her wings, augmenting her empire and extending her name and glory to the antipodes. * * * * Of eighteen vessels despatched by my sovereigns with the admiral Columbus, in his second voyage to the western hemisphere, twelve have returned, and have brought gosampine cotton, huge trees of dye wood, and many other articles held with us as precious, the natural productions of that hitherto hidden world: and beside all other things, no small quantity of gold. O wonderful Pomponius! Upon the surface of that earth are found rude masses of native gold, of a weight that one is afraid to mention. Some weigh 250 ounces, and they hope to discover others of a much larger size, from what the naked natives intimate, when they extol their gold to our people. Nor are the Lestrigonians or Polyphemi, who feed on human flesh, any longer doubtful. Attend—but beware! lest they rise in horror before thee! When he proceeded from the Fortunate Islands, now termed the Canaries, to Hispaniola, the island on which he first set foot, turning his prow a little toward the south, he arrived at innumerable islands of savage men, whom they call cannibals or Caribbees; and these, though naked, are courageous warriors. They fight skilfully with bows and clubs, and have boats hollowed from a single tree, yet very capacious, in which they make fierce descents on neighbouring islands, inhabited by milder people. They attack their villages, from which they carry off the men and devour them."†

Another letter to Pomponius Lætus on the same subject, has been cited at large in the body of this work. It is true these extracts give nothing that has not been stated more at large in the Decades of the same author; but they are curious as the very first announcements of the discoveries of Columbus, and as showing the first stamp of these

* Idem, Epist. 141.
† Idem, Epist. 147.

extraordinary events upon the mind of one of the most learned and liberal men of the age.

A collection of the letters of Peter Martyr was published in 1530, under the title of Opus Epistolarum Petri Martyris Anglerii; it is divided into thirty eight books, each containing the letters of one year. The same objections have been made to his letters as to his Decades, but they bear the same stamp of candour, probity and great information. They possess peculiar value from being written at the moment, before the facts they record were distorted or discoloured by prejudice or misrepresentation. His works abound in interesting particulars not to be found in any contemporary historian. They are rich in thought, but still richer in fact, and are full of urbanity, and of the liberal feeling of a scholar, who has mingled with the world. He is a fountain from which others draw and from which, with a little precaution, they may draw securely. He died in Valladolid in 1526.

No. XXX

Oviedo

Gonzalo Fernandez de Oviedo y Valdes, commonly known as Oviedo, was born in Madrid, 1478, and died in Valladolid in 1557 aged seventy nine years. He was of a noble Asturian family, and in his boyhood (in 1490) was appointed one of the pages to Prince Juan, heir apparent of Spain, the only son of Ferdinand and Isabella. He was in this situation at the time of the siege and surrender of Granada, was consequently at court at the time that Columbus made his agreement with the Catholic sovereigns, and was in the same capacity at Barcelona, and witnessed the triumphant entrance of the discoverer attended by a number of the natives of the newly found countries.

In 1513 he was sent out to the New World by Ferdinand to superintend the gold foundries. For many years he served there in various offices of trust and dignity, both under Ferdinand and his grandson and successor Charles V. In 1535 he was made alcayde of the fortress of St. Domingo in Hispaniola, and afterwards was appointed historiographer of the Indies. At the time of his death he had served the crown upwards of forty years, thirty four of which were passed in the colonies, and he had crossed the ocean eight times, as he mentions in various parts of his writings. He wrote several works: the most important is a Chronicle of the Indies in fifty books, divided into three parts. The first part, containing nineteen books, was printed at Seville in 1535, and reprinted in 1547 at Salamanca, augmented by a twentieth book containing shipwrecks. The remainder of the work exists in manuscript. The printing of it was commenced at Valladolid in 1557, but was discontinued in consequence of his death. It is one of the unpublished treasures of Spanish colonial history.

He was an indefatigable writer, laborious in collecting and recording facts, and composed a multitude of volumes, which are scattered through the Spanish libraries. His writings are full of events which happened under his own eye, or were communicated to him by eye witnesses; but he was deficient in judgement and discrimination. He took his facts without caution, and often from sources unworthy of credit. In his account of the first voyage of Columbus, he falls into several egregious errors, in consequence of taking the verbal information of a pilot named Hernan Perez Matteo, who was in the interest of the Pinzons and adverse to the admiral. His work is not much to be depended upon in matters relative to Columbus. When he treats of a more advanced period of the New World, from his own actual observation, he is much more satisfactory, though he is accused of listening too readily to popular fables and misrepresentations. His account of the natural productions of the New World and of the customs of its inhabitants is full of curious particulars; and the best narratives of some of the minor voyages which succeeded those of Columbus, are to be found in the unpublished part of his work.

No. XXXI

Cura de Los Palacios

Andres Bernaldes, or Bernal, generally known by the title of the Curate of *Los Palacios*, from having been Curate of the town of Los Palacios from about 1488 to 1513, was born in the town of Fuentes, and was for some time chaplain to Diego Deza, archbishop of Seville, one of the greatest friends to the application of Columbus. Bernaldes was well acquainted with the admiral, who was occasionally his guest, and in 1496 left many of his manuscripts and journals with him, which the

Curate made use of in a history of the reign of Ferdinand and Isabella, in which he introduced an account of the voyages of Columbus. In his narrative of the Admiral's coasting along the southern side of Cuba, the Curate is more minute and accurate than any other historian. His work exists only in manuscript, but is well known to historians, who have made frequent use of it. Nothing can be more simple and artless than the account which the honest curate gives of his being first moved to undertake his chronicle. "I who wrote these chapters of memoirs," he says, "being for twelve years in the habit of reading a register of my deceased grandfather, who was notary public of the town of Fuentes, where I was born, I found therein several chapters recording certain events and achievements which had taken place in his time; and my grandmother his widow, who was very old, hearing me read them said to me, 'And thou, my son, since thou art not slothful in writing, why dost thou not write, in this manner, the good things which are happening at present in thy own day, that those who come hereafter may know them, and marveling at what they read may render thanks to God.'

"From that time," continues he, "I proposed to do so, and as I considered the matter, I said often to myself, 'if God gives me life and health I will continue to write until I behold the kingdom of Granada gained by the Christians;' and I always entertained a hope of seeing it, and did see it: great thanks and praises be given to our Saviour Jesus Christ! And because it was impossible to write a complete and connected account of all things that happened in Spain, during the matrimonial union of the king Don Ferdinand, and the queen Doña Isabella, I wrote only about certain of the most striking and remarkable events, of which I had correct information, and of those which I saw or which were public and notorious to all men."*

The work of the worthy curate, as may be inferred from the foregoing statement, is deficient in regularity of plan; the style is artless and often inelegant, but it abounds in facts not to be met with elsewhere, often given in a very graphical manner, and strongly characteristic of the times. As he was contemporary with the events and familiar with many of the persons of his history, and as he was a man of probity and void of all pretension, his manuscript is a document of high authenticity. He was much respected in the limited sphere in which he moved, "yet," says one of his admirers, who wrote a short preface to this chronicle, "he had no other reward than that of the curacy of Los Palacios, and the place of chaplain to the archbishop Don Diego Deza."

In the possession of O. Rich, esq. of Madrid, is a very curious manu-

* Cura de los Palacios, cap. 7.

script chronicle of the reign of Ferdinand and Isabella already quoted in this work, made up from this history of the Curate of Los Palacios and from various other historians of the times, by some contemporary writer. In his account of the voyage of Columbus, he differs in some trivial particulars from the regular copy of the manuscript of the Curate. These variations have been carefully examined by the author of this work, and wherever they appear to be for the better, have been adopted.

No. XXXII

*"Navigatione del re de Castiglia delle Isole e
Paese Nuovamente Ritrovate"*

"Navigatio Christophori Colombi"

The above are the titles in Italian and in Latin of the earliest narrative of the first and second voyages of Columbus that appeared in print. It was anonymous and there are some curious particulars in regard to it. It was originally written in Italian by Montalbodo Fracanzo, or Fracanzano, or by Francapano de Montabaldo, for writers differ in regard to the name, and was published in Vicenza in 1507, in a collection of voyages entitled Mondo Novo, e Paese Nuovamente Ritrovate.

The collection was republished at Milan in 1508, both in Italian and in a Latin translation made by Archangelo Madrignano, under the title of Itinerarium Portugallensium; this title being given, because the work related chiefly to the voyages of Luigi Cadamosto, a Venetian in the service of Portugal.

The collection was afterwards augmented by Simon Grinæus with other travels, and printed in Latin at Basle in 1533,* by Hervagio, entitled, Novus Orbis Regionum, &c. The edition of Basle, 1555, and the Italian edition of Milan in 1508, have been consulted in the course of this work.

Peter Martyr (Decad. II. cap. 7.) alludes to this publication under the first Latin title of the book, Itinerarium Portugallensium, and accuses the author, whom by mistake he terms Cadamosto, of having stolen the materials of his book from the three first chapters of his first Decade

* Bibliotheca Pinello.

of the Ocean, of which he says, he granted copies in manuscript to several persons, and in particular to certain Venetian ambassadors. Martyr's Decades were not published until 1516, excepting the first three, which were published in 1511, at Seville.

This narrative of the voyages of Columbus is referred to by Gio. Batista Spotorno, in his Historical Memoir of Columbus, as having been written by a companion of Columbus.

It is manifest from a perusal of the narrative, that though the author may have helped himself freely from the manuscript of Martyr, he must have had other sources of information. His description of the person of Columbus, as a man tall of stature and large of frame, of a ruddy complexion and oblong visage is not copied from Martyr nor from any other writer. No historian had indeed preceded him except Sabellicus, in 1504, and the portrait agrees with that subsequently given of Columbus in the biography written by his son.

It is probable that this narrative, which appeared only a year after the death of Columbus, was a piece of literary job work, written for the collection of voyages published at Vicenza; and that the materials were taken from oral communication, from the account given by Sabellicus, and particularly from the manuscript copy of Martyr's first Decade.

No. XXXIII

Antonio de Herrera

Antonio Herrera de Tordesillas, one of the authors most frequently cited in this work, was born in 1565 of Roderick Tordesillas and Agnes de Herrera, his wife. He received an excellent education and entered into the employ of Vespasian Gonzago, brother to the Duke of Mantua, who was viceroy of Naples for Philip the Second of Spain. He was for some time secretary to this statesman, and entrusted with all his secrets. He was afterwards grand historiographer of the Indies to Philip II, who added to that title a large pension. He wrote various books, but the most celebrated is a General History of the Indies or American Colonies in four volumes, containing eight decades. When he undertook this work, all the public archives were thrown open to him, and he had access to documents of all kinds. He has been charged with great precipitation in the production of his two first volumes, and with negligence in not making sufficient use of the indisputable sources of information thus placed within his reach. The fact was that he met with historical tracts lying in manuscript, which embraced a great part of the first discoveries, and he contented himself with stating events as he found them therein recorded. It is certain that a great part of his work is little more than a transcript of the manuscript history of the Indies by Las Casas, sometimes reducing and improving the language when tumid, omitting the impassioned sallies of the zealous father, when the wrongs of the Indians were in question, and suppressing various circumstances degrading to the character of the Spanish discoverers. The author of the present work has therefore frequently put aside the history of Herrera, and consulted the source of his information, the manuscript history of Las Casas.

Muñoz observes "that in general Herrera did little more than join together morsels and extracts, taken from various parts, in the way that a writer arranges chronologically the materials from which he intends to compose a history." He adds, "that had not Herrera been a learned and judicious man, the precipitation with which he put together these materials, would have led to innumerable errors." The remark is just, yet it is to be considered that to select and arrange such materials judiciously, and treat them learnedly, was no trifling merit in the historian.

Herrera has been accused also of flattering his nation, exalting the deeds of his countrymen and softening and concealing their excesses. There is nothing very serious in this accusation. To illustrate the glory of his nation is one of the noblest offices of the historian, and it is difficult to speak too highly of the extraordinary enterprizes and splendid actions of the Spaniards in those days. In softening their excesses, he fell into an amiable and pardonable error, if it were indeed an error, for a Spanish writer to endeavour to sink them in oblivion.

Vossius passes a high eulogium on Herrera. "No one," he says, "has described with greater industry and fidelity the magnitude and boundaries of provinces, the tracts of sea, positions of capes and islands, of ports and harbours, the windings of rivers and dimensions of lakes, the situation and peculiarities of regions, with the appearance of the heavens, and the designation of places suitable for the establishment of cities." He has been called among the Spaniards, the prince of the historians of America, and it is added that none have risen since his time capable of disputing with him that title. Much of this praise will appear exaggerated by such as examine the manuscript histories, from which he transferred chapters and entire books, with very little alteration, to his volumes; and a great part of the eulogiums passed on him for his work on the Indies will be found really due to Las Casas, who has too long been eclipsed by his copyist. Still, Herrera has left voluminous proofs of industrious research, extensive information and great literary talent. His works bear the mark of candour, integrity and a sincere desire to record the truth.

He died in 1625, at sixty years of age, after having obtained from Philip IV the promise of the first charge of secretary of state that should become vacant.

No. XXXIV

Bishop Fonseca

The singular malevolence displayed by Bishop Juan Rodriguez de Fonseca toward Columbus and his family, and which was one of the secret and principal causes of their misfortunes, has been frequently noticed in the course of this work. It originated, as has been shewn, in some dispute between the admiral and Fonseca at Seville, in 1493, on account of the delay in fitting out the armament for the second voyage, and in regard to the number of domestics to form the household of the admiral. Fonseca received a letter from the sovereigns tacitly reproving him, and ordering him to shew all possible attention to the wishes of Columbus, and to see that he was treated with honour and deference. Fonseca never forgot this affront, and, what with him was the same thing, never forgave it. His spirit appears to have been of that unhealthy kind which has none of the balm of forgiveness; and in which a wound once made forever rankles. The hostility thus produced continued with increasing virulence throughout the life of Columbus and at his death was transferred to his son and successor. This persevering animosity has been illustrated in the course of this work by facts and observations cited from authors, some of them contemporary with Fonseca, but who were apparently restrained, by motives of prudence, from giving full vent to the indignation which they evidently felt. Even at the present day a Spanish historian would be cautious of expressing his feelings freely on the subject, lest they should prejudice his work in the eyes of the ecclesiastical censors of the press. In this way bishop Fonseca has in a great measure escaped the general odium his conduct merited.

This prelate had the chief superintendence of Spanish colonial affairs, both under Ferdinand and Isabella and the Emperor Charles V. He was an active, and intrepid, but selfish, overbearing and perfidious man. His administration bears no marks of enlarged and liberal policy; but is full of traits of arrogance and meanness. He opposed the benevolent attempts of Las Casas to ameliorate the condition of the Indians, and to obtain the abolition of repartimientos; treating him with personal haughtiness and asperity.* The reason assigned is that Fonseca was enriching himself by those very abuses, retaining large numbers of the miserable Indians in slavery to work in his possessions in the colonies.

To shew that his character has not been judged with undue severity, it is expedient to point out his invidious and persecuting conduct towards Hernando Cortez. The Bishop, while ready to foster rambling adventurers who came forward under his patronage, had never the head or the heart to appreciate the merits of illustrious commanders like Columbus and Cortez.

At a time when disputes arose between Cortez and Diego Velazquez, governor of Cuba, and the latter sought to arrest the conqueror of Mexico in the midst of his brilliant career, Fonseca, with entire disregard of the merits of the case, took a decided part in favour of Velazquez. Personal interest was at the bottom of this favour; for a marriage was negotiated between Velazquez and a sister of the Bishop.† Complaints and misrepresentations had been sent to Spain by Velazquez of the conduct of Cortez, who was represented as a lawless and unprincipled adventurer, attempting to usurp absolute authority in New Spain. The true services of Cortez had already excited admiration at court, but such was the influence of Fonseca, that, as in the case of Columbus, he succeeded in prejudicing the mind of the sovereign against one of the most meritorious of his subjects. One Christoval de Tapia, a man destitute of talent or character, but whose great recommendation was his having been in the employ of the Bishop,‡ was invested with powers similar to those once given to Bobadilla, to the prejudice of Columbus. He was to enquire into the conduct of Cortez, and in case he thought fit, to seize him, sequestrate his property and supersede him in command. Not content with the regular official letters furnished to Tapia,

* Herrera, D. II. lib. ii. cap. 3.
† Herrera, D. III. lib. iv. cap. 9.
‡ Idem, D. III. lib. i. cap. 15.

the Bishop, shortly after his departure, sent out Juan Bono de Quexo with blank letters signed by his own hand, and with others directed to various persons, charging them to admit Tapia for governor and assuring them that the king considered the conduct of Cortez as disloyal. Nothing but the sagacity and firmness of Cortez prevented this measure from completely interrupting if not defeating his enterprises; and he afterwards declared, that he had experienced more trouble and difficulty from the menaces and affronts of the ministers of the king than it cost him to conquer Mexico.*

When the dispute between Cortez and Velazquez came to be decided upon in Spain, in 1522, the father of Cortez, and those who had come from New Spain as his procurators, obtained permission from cardinal Adrian, at that time governor of the realm, to prosecute a public accusation of the bishop. A regular investigation took place before the council of the Indies of their allegations against its president. They charged him with having publicly declared Cortez a traitor and a rebel: with having intercepted and suppressed his letters addressed to the king, keeping his majesty in ignorance of their contents and of the important services he had performed, while he diligently forwarded all letters calculated to promote the interest of Velazquez: with having prevented the representations of Cortez from being heard in the council of the Indies, declaring that they should never be heard there while he lived: with having interdicted the forwarding of arms, merchandise and reinforcements to New Spain: and with having issued orders to the office of the India House at Seville to arrest the procurators of Cortez and all persons arriving from him, and to seize and detain all gold that they should bring. These and various other charges of similar nature were dispassionately investigated. Enough were substantiated to convict Fonseca of the most partial, oppressive and perfidious conduct, and the cardinal consequently forbade him to interfere in the cause between Cortez and Velazquez, and revoked all the orders which the bishop had issued, in the matter, to the India House of Seville. Indeed Salazar, a Spanish historian, says that Fonseca was totally divested of his authority as president of the council, and of all control of the affairs of New Spain, and adds that he was so mortified at the blow, that it brought on a fit of illness, which well nigh cost him his life.†

The suit between Cortez and Velazquez was referred to a special tribunal, composed of the grand chancellor and other persons of note, and was decided in 1522. The influence and intrigues of Fonseca being

---

* Herrera, Hist. Ind., decad. iii. lib. iv. cap. 3.
† Salazar, Conq. de Mexico, lib. i. cap. 2.

no longer of avail, a triumphant verdict was given in favor of Cortez, which was afterwards confirmed by the emperor Charles V, and additional honors awarded him. This was another blow to the malignant Fonseca, who retained his enmity against Cortez until his last moment, rendered still more rancorous by mortification and disappointment.

A charge against Fonseca, of a still darker nature than any of the preceding, may be found lurking in the pages of Herrera, though so obscure as to have escaped the notice of succeeding historians. He points to the bishop as the instigator of a desperate and perfidious man, who conspired against the life of Hernando Cortez. This was one Antonio de Villafaña, who fomented a conspiracy to assassinate Cortez, and elect Francisco Verdujo, brother-in-law of Velazquez, in his place. While the conspirators were waiting for an opportunity to poniard Cortez, one of them, relenting, apprized him of his danger. Villafaña was arrested. He attempted to swallow a paper containing a list of the conspirators, but being seized by the throat, a part of it was forced from his mouth containing fourteen names of persons of importance. Villafaña confessed his guilt, but tortures could not make him inculpate the persons whose names were on the list, who he declared were ignorant of the plot. He was hanged by order of Cortez.* In the investigation of the disputes between Cortez and Velazquez this execution of Villafaña was magnified into a cruel and wanton act of power; and in their eagerness to criminate Cortez, the witnesses on the part of Velazquez declared that Villafaña had been instigated to what he had done by letters from bishop Fonseca! (Que se movió a lo que hizo con cartas del Obispo de Burgos.)† It is not probable that Fonseca had recommended assassination, but it shews the character of his agents and what must have been the malignant nature of his instructions, when these men thought that such an act would accomplish his wishes.

Fonseca died at Burgos on the 4th of November 1524 and was interred at Coca.

* Herrera, Hist. Ind. D. III. lib. i. cap. 1.
† Idem, D. III. lib. iv. cap. 3.

No. XXXV

On the situation of the terrestrial paradise

The speculations of Columbus on the situation of the terrestrial paradise, extravagant as they may appear, were such as have occupied many grave and learned men. A slight notice of their opinions on this curious subject may be acceptable to the general reader and may take from the apparent wildness of the ideas expressed by Columbus.

The abode of our first parents was anciently the subject of anxious inquiry; and, indeed, mankind have always been prone to picture some place of perfect felicity, where the imagination, disappointed in the coarse realities of life, might revel in an elysium of its own creation. It is an idea not confined to our religion, but is found in the rude creed of the most savage nations, and it prevailed generally among the ancients. The speculations concerning the situation of the garden of Eden resemble those of the Greeks concerning the garden of the Hesperides; that region of delight, which they forever placed on the most remote verge of the known world, which their poets embellished with all the charms of fiction, after which they were continually longing and which they could never find. At one time it was in the Grand Oasis of Arabia. The exhausted travellers, after traversing the parched and sultry desert, hailed this verdant spot with rapture; they refreshed themselves under its shady bowers, and beside its cooling streams, as the crew of a tempest tost vessel repose on the shores of some green island in the deep; and from its being thus isolated amidst an ocean of sand, they gave it the name of the Island of the Blessed. As geographical knowledge increased, the situation of the Hesperian gardens was continually removed to a greater distance. It was transferred to the borders of the great Syrtis in the neighborhood of Mount Atlas. Here, after traversing the frightful deserts of Barca, the traveller found himself in a fair and fertile country watered by rivulets and gushing fountains. The oranges and citrons transported hence to Greece, where they were as yet unknown, delighted the Athenians by their golden beauty and delicious flavour, and they thought none but the garden of the Hesperides could produce such glorious fruit. In this way the happy region of the ancients was transported from place to place, still in the remote and obscure extremity of the world, until it was fabled to exist in the Canaries, thence called the Fortunate or the Hesperian Islands. Here it remained, because discovery advanced no further, and because these islands were so distant and so little known, as to allow full latitude to the fictions of the poet.*

In like manner the situation of the terrestrial Paradise, or Garden of Eden was long a subject of earnest inquiry and curious disputation, and occupied the laborious attention of the most learned theologians. Some placed it in Palestine or the Holy Land; others in Mesopotamia, in that rich and beautiful tract of country embraced by the wanderings of the Tigris and the Euphrates; others in Armenia, in a valley surrounded by precipitous and inaccessible mountains, and imagined that Enoch and Elijah were transported thither, out of the sight of mortals, to live in a state of terrestrial bliss, until the second coming of our Saviour. There were others who gave it situations widely remote, such as in the Trapoban of the ancients, at present known as the island of Ceylon; or in the island of Sumatra; or in the Fortunate or Canary Islands; or in one of the islands of Sunda; or in some favoured spot under the equinoctial line.

Great difficulty was encountered by these speculators to reconcile the allotted place with the description given in Genesis of the Garden of Eden; particularly of the great fountain which watered it and which afterwards divided itself four rivers, the Pison or Phison, the Gihon, the Euphrates and the Hiddekel. Those who were in favor of the Holy Land supposed that the Jordan was the great river which afterwards divided itself into the Phison, Gihon, Tigris and Euphrates, but that the sands have choked up the ancient beds by which those streams were supplied; that originally the Phison traversed Arabia Deserta and Arabia Felix, from whence it pursued its course to the Gulph of Persia; that the Gihon bathed northern or Stony Arabia and fell into the Arabian Gulph or the Red Sea; that the Euphrates and the Tigris passed by Eden to Assyria and Chaldea, from whence they discharged themselves into the Persian Gulph.

By most of the early commentators the river Gihon is supposed to be the Nile. The source of this river was unknown, but was evidently far distant from the spots whence the Tigris and the Euphrates arose. This difficulty, however, was ingeniously overcome, by giving it a subterranean course of some hundreds of leagues from the common fountain, until it issued forth to day light in Abyssinia.† In like manner subterranean courses were given to the Tigris and Euphrates, passing under the Red Sea, until they sprang forth in Armenia as if just issuing from one common source. So also those who placed the terrestrial Paradise

* Gosselin, Recherches sur la Géog. des Anciens, t. i.
† Feyjoo, Theatro Critico, lib. vii. § 2.

in islands, supposed that the rivers which issued from it, and formed those heretofore named, either traversed the surface of the sea, as fresh water by its greater lightness may float above the salt; or that they flowed through deep veins and channels of the earth, as the fountain of Arethusa was said to sink into the ground in Greece and rise in the island of Sicily, while the river Alpheus, pursuing it, but with less perseverance, rose somewhat short of it in the sea.

Some contended that the deluge had destroyed the Garden of Eden, and altered the whole face of the earth, so that the rivers had changed their beds and had taken different directions from those mentioned in Genesis; others, however, among whom was St. Augustine, in his commentary upon the Book of Genesis, maintained that the terrestrial Paradise still existed, with its original beauty and delights, but that it was inaccessible to mortals, being on the summit of a mountain of stupendous height, reaching into the third region of the air and approaching the moon, being thus protected by its elevation from the ravages of the deluge.

By some this mountain was placed under the equinoctial line, or under that band of the heavens metaphorically called by the ancients "the table of the sun,"* comprising the space between the tropics of Cancer and Capricorn, beyond which the sun never passed in his annual course. Here would reign a uniformity of nights and days and seasons, and the elevation of the mountain would raise it above the heats and storms of the lower regions. Others transported the Garden beyond the equinoctial line, and placed it in the southern hemisphere; supposing that the Torrid zone might be the flaming sword appointed to defend its entrance against mortals. They had a fanciful train of argument to support their theory. They observed that the terrestrial Paradise must be in the noblest and happiest part of the globe; that part must be under the noblest part of the heavens; as the merits of a place do not so much depend upon the virtues of the earth as upon the happy influences of the stars and the favorable and benign aspect of the heavens. Now, according to philosophers, the world was divided into two hemispheres. The southern they considered the head, and the northern the feet or under part. The right hand the east, from whence commenced the movement of the primum mobile, and the left the west, towards which it moved. This supposed, they observed that it was manifest that as the head of all things natural and artificial, is always the best and noblest part, governing the other parts of the body, so the south, being the head of the earth, ought to be superior and nobler than either east, or west,

---

* Herodot. lib. iii.   Virgil, Georg. i.   Pomp. Mela, lib. iii. cap. x.

or north; and in accordance with this they cited the opinion of various philosophers, among the ancients, and more especially that of Ptolemy, that the stars of the southern hemisphere were larger, more resplendent, more perfect and of course of greater virtue and efficacy than those of the northern; an error universally prevalent, until disproved by modern discovery. Hence they concluded that in this southern hemisphere, in this head of the earth, under this purer and brighter sky, and these more potent and benignant stars, was placed the terrestrial Paradise.

Various ideas were entertained as to the magnitude of this blissful region. As Adam and all his progeny were to have lived there, had he not sinned, and as there would have been no such thing as death to thin the number of mankind, it was inferred that the terrestrial Paradise must be of great extent to contain them. Some gave it a size equal to Europe or Africa, others gave it the whole southern hemisphere. St. Augustine supposed that as mankind multiplied, numbers would be translated, without death, to heaven; the parents, perhaps, when their children had arrived at mature age; or portions of the human race at the end of certain periods, and when the population of the terrestrial paradise had attained a certain amount.* Others supposed that mankind, remaining in a state of primitive innocence, would not have required so much space as at present. Having no need of rearing animals for subsistence, no land would have been required for pasturage; and the earth not being cursed with sterility, there would have been no need of extensive tracts of country to permit of fallow land and the alternation of crops required in husbandry. The spontaneous and never failing fruits of the Garden would have been abundant for the simple wants of man. Still, that the human race might not be crowded, but might have ample space for recreation and enjoyment, and the charms of variety and change, some allowed at least a hundred leagues of circumference to the Garden.

St. Basilius† in his eloquent discourse on Paradise, expatiates with rapture on the joys of this sacred abode, elevated to the third region of the air and under the happiest skies. There a pure and never failing pleasure is furnished to every sense. The eye delights in the admirable clearness of the atmosphere, in the verdure and beauty of the trees, and the never withering bloom of the flowers. The ear is regaled with

---

* St. August. lib. ix. cap. 6. Sup. Genesis.

† St. Basilius was called the Great. His works were read and admired by all the world, even by Pagans. They are written in an elevated and majestic style with great splendour of idea and vast erudition.

the singing of the birds, the smell with the aromatic odours of the land. In like manner the other senses have each their peculiar enjoyments. There the vicissitudes of the seasons are unknown, and the climate unites the fruitfulness of summer, the joyful abundance of autumn, and the sweet freshness and quietude of spring. There the earth is always green, the flowers are ever blooming, the waters limpid and delicate; not rushing in rude and turbid torrents, but welling up in crystal fountains and winding in peaceful and silver streams. There no harsh and boisterous winds are permitted to shake and disturb the air and ravage the beauty of the groves; there prevails no melancholy nor darksome weather, no drowning rain nor pelting hail, no forked lightning nor rending and resounding thunder; no wintry pinching cold nor withering and panting summer heat, nor any thing else that can give pain or sorrow or annoyance; but all is bland, and gentle and serene; a perpetual youth and joy reigns throughout all nature and nothing decays and dies.

The same idea is given by St. Ambrosius in his book on paradise,[*] an author likewise consulted and cited by Columbus. He wrote in the fourth century and his touching eloquence, and graceful yet vigorous style ensured great popularity to his writings. Many of these opinions are cited by Glanville, usually called Bartholomeus Anglicus, in his work De Proprietatibus Rerum, a work with which Columbus was evidently acquainted. It was a species of encyclopedia of the general knowledge current at the time, and likely to recommend itself to a curious and enquiring voyager. This author cites an assertion as made by St. Basilius and St. Ambrosius, that the water of the fountain which proceeds from the garden of Eden falls into a great lake, with such a tremendous noise that the inhabitants of the neighborhood are born deaf: and that from this lake proceed the four chief rivers mentioned in Genesis.[†]

This passage, however, is not to be found in the Hexameron of either Basilius or Ambrosius, from which it is quoted; neither is it in the Oration on Paradise by the former, nor in the letter on the same subject written by Ambrosius to Ambrosius Sabinus. It must be a misquotation by Glanville. Columbus, however, appears to have been struck with it,

[*] St. Ambros. Opera. Edit. Coignard. Parisiis, MDCXC.

[†] "Paradisus autem in Oriente, in altissimo monte, de cujus cacumine cadentes aquæ, maximum faciunt lacum, que in suo casu tantum faciunt strepitum et fragorem, quod omnes incolæ, juxta prædictum lacum, nascuntur surdi, ex immoderato sonitu seu fragore sensum auditus in parvulis corrumpente. *Ut dicit Basilius in Hexameron, similiter et Ambros.* Ex illo lacu, velut ex uno fonte, procedunt illa flumina quatuor, Phison qui et Ganges, Gyon qui et Nilus dicitur, et Tigris ac Euphrates." Bart. Angl. de Proprietatibus Rerum, lib. xv. cap. cxii. Francofurti, 1540.

and Las Casas is of opinion that he derived thence his idea that the vast body of fresh water which filled the Gulph of La Ballena, or Paria, flowed from the fountain of Paradise, though from a remote distance; and that in this gulph, which he supposed in the extreme part of Asia, originated the Nile, the Tigris, the Euphrates and the Ganges, which might be conducted under the land and sea by subterraneous channels, to the places where they spring forth on the earth and assume their proper names.

I forebear to enter into various other of the voluminous speculations which have been formed relative to the terrestrial paradise; and, perhaps, it may be thought that I have already said too much on so fanciful a subject; but to illustrate clearly the character of Columbus, it is necessary to elucidate those veins of thought passing through his mind while considering the singular phenomena of the unknown regions he was exploring, and which are often but slightly and vaguely developed in his journals and letters. These speculations, likewise, like those concerning fancied islands in the ocean, carry us back to the time and make us feel the mystery and conjectural charm that reigned over the greatest part of the world, and which have since been completely disspelled by modern discovery. Enough has been cited to shew that in his observations concerning the terrestrial Paradise, Columbus was not indulging in any fanciful and presumptuous chimeras, the offspring of a heated and disordered brain. However visionary his conjectures may seem, they were all grounded on written opinions held little less than oracular in his day; and they will be found on examination to be far exceeded by the speculations and theories of sages held illustrious for their wisdom and erudition in the school and the cloister.

No. XXXVI

Will of Columbus

In the name of the most holy Trinity, who inspired me with the idea, and afterwards made it perfectly clear to me, that I could navigate and go to the Indies from Spain, by traversing the ocean westwardly; which I communicated to the King Don Ferdinand and to the Queen Doña Isabella, our sovereigns; and they were pleased to furnish me the necessary equipment of men and ships, and to make me their admiral over the said ocean, in all parts lying to the west of an imaginary line drawn from pole to pole, a hundred leagues west of the Cape de Verde and Azore Islands; also appointing me their Viceroy and governor over all continents and islands that I might discover beyond the same line westwardly; with the right of being succeeded in the said offices by my eldest son and his heirs for ever; and a grant of the tenth part of all things found in the said jurisdiction; and of all rents and revenues arising from it; and the eighth of all the lands and every thing else, together with the salary corresponding to my rank of admiral, Viceroy, and governor, and all other emoluments accruing thereto, as is more fully expressed in the title and agreement sanctioned by their Highnesses.

And it pleased the Lord Almighty that in the year one thousand four hundred and ninety two I should discover the continent of the Indies and many islands, among them Hispaniola, which the Indians call Ayte, and the Monicongos, Cipango. I then returned to Castile to their Highnesses, who approved of my undertaking a second enterprize for further discoveries and settlements; and the Lord gave me victory over the Island of Hispaniola, which extends six hundred leagues, and I conquered it and made it tributary; and I discovered many islands inhabited by cannibals, and seven hundred to the west of Hispaniola, among which is Jamaica, which we call Santiago; and three hundred and thirty three leagues of continent from south to west, besides a hundred and seven to the north, which I discovered in my first voyage; together with many islands as may more clearly be seen by my letters, memorials and maritime charts. And as we hope in God that before long a good and great revenue will be derived from the above islands and continent, of which, for the reasons aforesaid, belong to me the tenth and the eighth, with the salaries and emoluments specified above; and considering that we are mortal, and that it is proper for every one to settle his affairs and to leave declared to his heirs and successors the property he possesses or may have a right to: Wherefore I have concluded to make an entailed estate (mayorazgo) out of the said eighth of the lands, places, and revenues, in the manner which I now proceed to state.

In the first place, I am to be succeeded by Don Diego, my son, who in case of death without children is to be succeeded by my other son Ferdinand; and should God dispose of him also without leaving children, and without my having any other son, then my brother Don Bartholomew, is to succeed; and after him his eldest son; and if God should dispose of him without heirs he shall be succeeded by his sons from one to another for ever, or in the failure of a son to be succeeded

by Don Ferdinand, after the same manner, from son to son successively; or, in their place by my brothers Bartholomew and Diego. And
should it please the Lord that the estate, after having continued some
time in the line of any of the above successors, should stand in need of
an immediate and lawful male heir, the succession shall then devolve
to the nearest relation, being a man of legitimate birth, and bearing
the name of Columbus, derived from his father and his ancestors. This
entailed estate shall in no wise be inherited by a woman, except in
case that no male is to be found either in this or any other quarter of
the world of my real lineage, whose name as well as that of his ancestors
shall have always been Columbus. In such an event (which may God
forefend) then the female of legitimate birth most nearly related to the
preceding possessor of the estate, shall succeed to it; and this is to be
under the conditions herein stipulated at foot, which must be understood to extend as well to Don Diego my son, as to the aforesaid and
their heirs, every one of them, to be fulfilled by them; and failing to do
so, they are to be deprived of the succession, for not having complied
with what shall herein be expressed and the estate to pass to the person most nearly related to the one who held the right; and the person
thus succeeding shall in like manner forfeit the estate, should he also
fail to comply with the said conditions; and another person, the nearest of my lineage, shall succeed, provided he abide by them, so that
they may be observed for ever in the form prescribed. This forfeiture
is not to be incurred for trifling matters, originating in lawsuits, but
in important cases when the glory of God or my own, or that of my
family may be concerned, which supposes a perfect fulfilment of all the
things hereby ordained, all which I recommend to the courts of justice.
And I supplicate his holiness who now is, and those that may succeed
in the holy church, that if it should happen that this my will and testament has need of his holy order and command for its fulfilment, that
such order be issued in virtue of obedience and under penalty of ex-
communication, and that it shall not be in any wise disfigured. And
I also pray the King and Queen, our sovereigns, and their eldest born,
Prince Don Juan, our lord, and their successors, for the sake of the
services I have done them, and because it is just, that it may please
them not to permit this my will and constitution of my entailed estate
to be in any way altered, but to leave it in the form and manner which
I have ordained, for ever; for the greater glory of the Almighty, and
that it may be the root and basis of my lineage and a memento of the
services I have rendered their Highnesses; that being born in Genoa
I came over to serve them in Castile and discovered to the west of
Terra Firma, the Indies and islands before mentioned. I accordingly

pray their Highnesses to order that this my privilege and testament be held valid, and be executed summarily and without any opposition or demur, according to the letter. I also pray the grandees of the realm and the lords of the council, and all others having administration of justice, to be pleased not to suffer this my will and testament to be of no avail, but to cause it to be fulfilled as by me ordained; it being just that a noble, who has served the King and Queen and the Kingdom, should be respected in the disposition of his estate by will, testament, institution of entail or inheritance, and that the same be not infringed either in whole or in part.

In the first place, my son Don Diego and all my successors and descendants, as well as my brothers Bartholomew and Diego, shall bear my arms, such as I shall leave them after my days, without inserting any thing else in them; and they shall be their seal to seal withal. Don Diego my son, or any other who may inherit his estate, on coming into possession of the inheritance, shall sign with the signature which I now make use of, which is an X. with an S. over it, and an M. with a Roman A. over it, and over that an S., and then a Greek Y. with an S. over it, with its lines and points, as is my custom, as may be seen by my signatures, of which there are many, and it will be seen by the present one.

He shall only write "the Admiral," whatever other titles the King may have conferred on him; this is to be understood as respects his signature, but not the enumeration of his titles, which he can make at full length if agreeable; only the signature is to be "the Admiral."

The said Don Diego or any other inheritor of this estate, shall possess my offices of Admiral of the Ocean, which is to the west of an imaginary line, which his highness ordered to be drawn, running from pole to pole a hundred leagues beyond the Azores and as many more beyond the Cape de Verde Islands, over all which I was made, by their order, the Admiral of the Sea, with all the preeminences held by Don Henrique in the Admiralty of Castile, and they made me their governor and Viceroy perpetually, and for ever, over all the islands and main land discovered or to be discovered, for myself and heirs, as is more fully shewn by my treaty and privilege as above mentioned.

Item: The said Don Diego, or any other inheritor of this estate, shall distribute the revenue which it may please our Lord to grant him in the following manner under the above penalty.

First, of the whole income of this estate, now and at all times, and of whatever may be had or collected from it, he shall give the fourth part annually to my brother Don Bartholomew Columbus, Adelantado of the Indies; and this is to continue till he shall have acquired an income of a million of maravedies, for his support and for the services he has rendered and will continue to render to this entailed estate; which million he is to receive, as stated, every year, if the said fourth amount to so much and that he have nothing else; but if he possess a part or the whole of that amount in rents, that henceforth he shall not enjoy the said million nor any part of it, except that he shall have in the said fourth part unto the said quantity of a million, if it should amount to so much; and as much as he shall have of revenue beside the fourth part, whatever sum of maravedies of known rent from property or perpetual offices, the said quantity of rent or revenue from property or offices shall be discounted, and from the said million shall be reserved whatever marriage portion he may receive with any female he may espouse, so that whatever he may receive in marriage with his wife, no deduction shall be made on that account from the said million, but only for whatever he may acquire, or may have over and above his wife's dowry: and when it shall please God that he or his heirs and descendants shall derive from their property and offices a revenue of a million arising from rents, neither he nor his heirs shall enjoy any longer any thing from the said fourth part of the entailed estate, which shall remain with Don Diego or whoever may inherit it.

Item,—From the revenues of the said estate or from any other fourth part of it (should its amount be adequate to it) shall be paid every year to my son Ferdinand two millions, till such time as his revenue shall amount to two millions, in the same form and manner as in the case of Bartholomew, who as well as his heirs are to have the million or the part that may be wanting.

Item,—The said Don Diego or Don Bartholomew shall make, out of the said estate for my brother Diego, such provision as may enable him to live decently, as he is my brother, to whom I assign no particular sum, as he has attached himself to the church, and that will be given him which is right and this to be given him in a mass, and before any thing shall have been received by Ferdinand my son or Bartholomew my brother or their heirs, and also according to the amount of the income of the estate. And in case of discord, the case is to be referred to two of our relations, or other men of honour, and should they disagree among themselves, they will choose a third person as arbitrator, being virtuous and not distrusted by either party.

Item,—All this revenue which I bequeath to Bartholomew, to Ferdinand, and to Diego, shall be delivered to, and received by them as prescribed under the obligation of being faithful and loyal to Diego my son or his heirs, they as well as their children: and should it appear that they or any of them had proceeded against him in any thing touching his honour, or the prosperity of the family or of the estate, either in word or deed, whereby might come a scandal and debasement to my family, and a detriment to my estate; in that case nothing farther shall be given to them or him from that time forward, in as much as they are always to be faithful to Diego and to his successors.

Item,—As it was my intention when I first instituted this entailed estate to dispose, or that my son Diego should dispose for me, of the tenth part of the income in favour of necessitous persons, as a tithe and in commemoration of the Almighty and Eternal God, and persisting still in this opinion, and hoping that his high Majesty will assist me and those who may inherit it in this or the New World, I have resolved that the said tithe shall be paid in the manner following:

First,—It is to be understood that the fourth part of the revenue of the estate which I have ordained and directed to be given to Don Bartholomew, till he have an income of one million, includes the tenth of the whole revenue of the estate; and that in proportion as the income of my brother Don Bartholomew shall increase, as it has to be discounted from the revenue of the fourth part of the entailed estate, that the said revenue shall be calculated, to know how much the tenth part amount to, and the part which exceeds what is necessary to make up the million for Don Bartholomew, shall be received by such of my family as may most stand in need of it, discounting it from the said tenth, if their income do not amount to fifty thousand maravedies; and should any of these come to have an income to this amount, such a part shall be awarded them as two persons chosen for the purpose, may determine along with Don Diego or his heirs. Thus it is to be understood that the million which I leave to Don Bartholomew comprehends the tenth of the whole revenue of the estate, which revenue is to be distributed among my nearest and most needy relations in the manner I have directed; and when Don Bartholomew have an income of one million and that nothing more shall be due to him on account of said fourth part, then Don Diego my son, or the person who may be in possession of the estate, along with two other persons which I shall herein point out, shall inspect the accounts, and so direct that the tenth of the revenue shall still continue to be paid to the most necessitous members of my family that may be found in this or any other quarter of the world, who shall diligently be sought out; and they are to be paid out of the fourth part from which Don Bartholomew is to derive his million, which sums are to be taken into account and deducted from the said tenth, which should it amount to more, the overplus, as it arises from the fourth part, shall be given to the most necessitous persons, as aforesaid, and should it not be sufficient, that Don Bartholomew shall have it until his own estate goes on increasing, leaving the said million in part or in the whole.

Item,—The said Don Diego my son, or whoever may be the inheritor, shall appoint two persons of conscience and authority and most nearly related to the family, who are to examine the revenue and its amount carefully, and to cause the said tenth to be paid out of the fourth from which Don Bartholomew is to receive his million, to the most necessitous members of my family that may be found here or elsewhere, whom they shall look for diligently upon their consciences, and as it might happen that the said Don Diego, or others after him, for reasons which may concern their own welfare, or the credit and support of the estate, may be unwilling to make known the full amount of the income; nevertheless, I charge him on his conscience to pay the sum aforesaid, and I charge them on their souls and consciences not to denounce or make it known except with the consent of Don Diego or the person that may succeed him; but let the above tithe be paid in the manner I have directed.

Item,—In order to avoid all disputes in the choice of the two nearest relations who are to act with Don Diego or his heirs, I hereby elect Don Bartholomew my brother for one, and Don Fernando my son for the other; and when these two shall enter upon the business, they shall choose two other persons among the most trusty and most nearly related, and these again shall elect two others when it shall be question of commencing the examination. And thus it shall be managed with diligence from one to the other, as well in this as in the other of government, for the service and glory of God and the benefit of the said entailed estate.

Item,—I also enjoin Diego or any one that may inherit the estate to have and maintain in the city of Genoa one person of our lineage to reside there with his wife and appoint him a sufficient revenue to enable him to live decently as a person closely connected with the family, of which he is to be the root and basis in that city, from which great good may accrue to him, in as much as I was born there and came from thence.

Item,—The said Don Diego, or whoever shall inherit the estate, must remit in bills, or in any other way, all such sums as he may be able to save out of the revenue of the estate, and direct purchases to be made in his name, or that of his heirs, in a stock in the Bank of St. George, which gives an interest of six per cent. and is secure money, and this shall be devoted to the purposes I am about to explain.

Item,—As it becomes every man of rank and property to serve God either personally or by means of his wealth, and as all monies deposited with St. George are quite safe and Genoa is a noble city and powerful by sea, and as at the time that I undertook to set out upon the discovery of the Indies it was with the intention of supplicating the King and Queen, our Lords, that whatever moneys should be derived from the said Indies should be invested in the conquest of Jerusalem, and as I did so supplicate them; if they do this, it will be well: if not, at all events the said Diego or such person as may succeed him in this trust, to collect together all the money he can and accompany the King our Lord should he go to the conquest of Jerusalem, or else go there himself with all the force he can command; and in pursuing this intention it will please the Lord to assist towards the accomplishment of the plan, and should he not be able to effect the conquest of the whole, no doubt he will achieve it in part. Let him therefore collect and make a fund of all his wealth in St. George of Genoa, and let it multiply there till such time as it may appear to him that something of consequence may be effected as respects the project on Jerusalem; for I believe that when their Highnesses shall see that this is contemplated they will wish to realize it themselves, or will afford him, as their servant and vassal, the means of doing it for them.

Item,—I charge my son Diego and my descendants, especially whoever may inherit this estate, which consists as aforesaid, of the tenth of whatsoever may be had or found in the Indies and the eighth part of the lands and rents, all which together with my rights and emoluments as Admiral, Viceroy and governor, amount to more than twenty-five per cent.,—I say, that I require of him to employ all this revenue, as well as his person and all the means in his power, in well and faithfully serving and supporting their Highnesses or their successors, even to the loss of life and property; since it was their Highnesses, next to God, who first gave me the means of getting and achieving this property, although it is true I came over to these realms to invite them to the enterprize, and that a long time elapsed before any provision was made for carrying it into execution; which, however, is not surprising, as this was an undertaking of which all the world was ignorant, and no one had any faith in it, wherefore I am by so much the more indebted to them, as well as because they have since also much favoured and promoted me.

Item,—I also require of Diego or whosoever may be in possession of the estate, that in the case of any schism taking place in the church of God, or that any person of whatever class or condition should attempt to despoil it of its property and honours, they hasten to offer at the feet of his Holiness, that is, if they are not heretics (which God forbid!), their persons, power and wealth for the purpose of suppressing such schism and preventing any spoliation of the honour and property of the church.

Item,—I command the said Diego, or whosoever may possess the said estate, to labour and strive for the honour, welfare and aggrandizement of the city of Genoa, and to make use of all his power and means in defending and enhancing the good and credit of that republic, in all things not contrary to the service of the church of God, or the high dignity of the King and Queen our Lords, and their successors.

Item,—The said Diego or whoever may possess or succeed to the estate, out of the fourth part of the whole revenue, from which as aforesaid is to be taken the tenth, when Don Bartholomew or his heirs shall have saved the two millions or part of them, and when the time shall come of making a distribution among our relations, shall apply and invest the said tenth in providing marriages for such daughters of our lineage as may require it, and in doing all the good in their power.

Item,—When a suitable time shall arrive, he shall order a church to be built in the Island of Hispaniola, and in the most convenient spot, to be called Santa Maria de la Concepcion, to which is to be annexed an hospital upon the best possible plan, like those of Italy and Castile, and a chapel is to be erected to say mass in for the good of my soul and those of my ancestors and successors, with great devotion, since no doubt it will please the Lord to give us a sufficient revenue for this and the aforementioned purposes.

Item,—I also order Diego my son, or whosoever may inherit after him, to spare no pains in having and maintaining in the Island of Hispaniola four good professors of theology to the end and aim of their studying and labouring to convert to our holy faith the inhabitants of the Indies; and in proportion as by God's will the revenue of the estate shall increase in the same degree shall the number of teachers and devout persons increase, who are to strive to make Christians of the natives, in attaining which no expense should be thought too great: and in commemoration of all that I hereby ordain, and of the foregoing, a monument of marble shall be erected in the said church of La Concepcion, in the most conspicuous place, to serve as a record of what I here enjoin on the said Diego, as well as to other persons who may look upon it, which marble shall contain an inscription to the same effect.

Item,—I also require of Diego my son and whosoever may succeed him in the estate, that every time and as often as he confess, he first shew this obligation or a copy of it to the confessor, praying him to read it through, that he may be enabled to inquire respecting its ful-filment, from which will redound great good and happiness to his soul.

S.

S. A. S.

X. M. Y.

EL ALMIRANTE

No. XXXVII

Signature of Columbus

As every thing respecting Columbus is full of interest, his signature has been a matter of some discussion. It partook of the pedantic and bigoted character of the age, and perhap of the peculiar character of the man, who, considering himself mysteriously elected and set apart from among men for certain great purposes, adopted a correspondent formality and solemnity in all his concerns. His signature was as follows.

S.

S.   A.   S.

X.   M.   Y.

XPO   FERENS.

The first half of the signature, XPO (for CHRISTO), is in Greek letters; the second, FERENS, is in Latin. Such was the usage of those days, and even at present both Greek and Roman letters are used in signatures and inscriptions in Spain.

The cyphers or initials above the signature are supposed to repre-sent a pious ejaculation. To read them one must begin with the lower letters and connect them with those above. Signor Gio. Batista Spotorno conjectures them to mean either Xristus (Christus), Sancta Maria, Yo-sephus, or Salva me, Xristus, Maria, Yosephus. The North-American Review for April 1827, suggests the substitution of Jesus for Josephus, but the suggestion of Spotorno is most probably correct, as a common Spanish ejaculation is "Jesus Maria y José."

It was an ancient usage in Spain, and it has not entirely gone by, to accompany the signature with some words of religious purport. One object of this practice was to shew the writer to be a Christian. This was of some importance in a country in which Jews and Mahometans were proscribed and persecuted.

Don Fernando, son to Columbus, says that his father, when he took his pen in hand, usually commenced by writing "Jesus cum Maria sit nobis in via," and the book which the admiral prepared and sent to the sovereigns, containing the prophecies which he considered as referring to his discoveries and to the rescue of the holy sepulchre, begins with the same words. This practice is akin to that of placing the initials of pious words above the signature, and gives great probability to the mode in which they have been decyphered.

No. XXXVIII

A visit to Palos

[The following narrative was actually commenced, by the author of this work, as a letter to a friend, but unexpectedly swelled to its present size. He has been induced to insert it here from the idea that many will feel the same curiosity to know something of the present state of Palos and its inhabitants that led him to make the journey.]

Seville. 1828.

Since I last wrote to you I have made, what I may term, an American Pilgrimage, to visit the little port of Palos in Andalusia, where Columbus fitted out his ships, and whence he sailed for the discovery of the New World. Need I tell you how deeply interesting and gratifying it has been to me? I had long meditated this excursion, as a kind of pious, and, if I may so say, filial duty of an American, and my intention was quickened when I learnt that many of the edifices, mentioned in the History of Columbus, still remained in nearly the same state in which they existed at the time of his sojourn at Palos, and that the descendants of the intrepid Pinzons, who aided him with ships and money, and sailed with him in the great voyage of discovery, still flourished in the neighbourhood.

The very evening before my departure from Seville on the excursion, I heard that there was a young gentleman of the Pinzon family studying law in the city. I got introduced to him, and found him of most prepossessing appearance and manners. He gave me a letter of introduction to his father, Don Juan Fernandez Pinzon, resident of Moguer, and the present head of the family.

As it was in the middle of August, and the weather intensely hot, I hired a calesa for the journey. This is a two-wheeled carriage, resembling a cabriolet, but of the most primitive and rude construction; the harness is profusely ornamented with brass, and the horse's head decorated with tufts and tassels and dangling bobs of scarlet and yellow worsted. I had, for calesero, a tall, long-legged Andalusian, in short jacket, little round-crowned hat, breeches decorated with buttons from the hip to the knees, and a pair of russet leather bottinas or spatter-dashes. He was an active fellow, though uncommonly taciturn for an Andalusian, and strode along beside his horse, rousing him occasionally to greater speed by a loud malediction or a hearty thwack of his cudgel.

In this style, I set off late in the day to avoid the noontide heat, and after ascending the lofty range of hills that borders the great valley of the Guadalquiver, and having a rough ride among their heights, I descended about twilight into one of those vast, silent, melancholy plains, frequent in Spain, where I beheld no other signs of life than a roaming flock of bustards, and a distant herd of cattle, guarded by a solitary herdsman, who, with a long pike planted in the earth, stood motionless in the midst of the dreary landscape, resembling an Arab of the desert. The night had somewhat advanced when we stopped to repose for a few hours at a solitary venta or inn, if it might so be called, being nothing more than a vast low-roofed stable, divided into several compartments for the reception of the troops of mules and arrieros (or carriers) who carry on the internal trade of Spain. Accommodation for the traveller there was none—not even for a traveller so easily accommodated as myself. The landlord had no food to give me, and as to a bed, he had none but a horse cloth, on which his only child, a boy of eight years old, lay naked on the earthen floor. Indeed the heat of the weather and the fumes from the stables made the interior of the hovel insupportable, so I was fain to bivouac on my cloak on the pavement at the door of the venta, where, on waking after two or three hours of sound sleep, I found a contrabandista (or smuggler) snoring beside me, with his blunderbuss on his arm.

I resumed my journey before break of day, and had made several leagues by ten o'clock, when we stopped to breakfast, and to pass the sultry hours of midday in a large village, from whence we departed about four o'clock, and, after passing through the same kind of solitary country, arrived just after sunset at Moguer. This little city (for at present it is a city) is situated about a league from Palos, of which place it has gradually absorbed all the respectable inhabitants, and, among the number, the whole family of the Pinzons.

So remote is this little place from the stir and bustle of travel, and so destitute of the show and vainglory of this world, that my calesa, as it rattled and jingled along the narrow and ill-paved streets, caused a great sensation; the children shouted and scampered along by its side, admiring its splendid trappings of brass and worsted, and gazing with reverence at the important stranger who came in so gorgeous an equipage.

I drove up to the principal posada, the landlord of which was at the door. He was one of the very civilest men in the world, and disposed to do every thing in his power to make me comfortable; there was only one difficulty, he had neither bed nor bed-room in his house. In fact it was a mere venta for muleteers, who are accustomed to sleep on the ground with their mule cloths for beds and pack-saddles for pillows. It was a hard case, but there was no better posada in the place. Few people travel for pleasure or curiosity in these out-of-the-way parts of Spain, and those of any note are generally received into private houses. I had travelled sufficiently in Spain to find out that a bed, after all, is not an article of indispensable necessity, and was about to bespeak some quiet corner where I might spread my cloak, when fortunately the landlord's wife came forth. She could not have a more obliging disposition than her husband, but then—God bless the women!—they always know how to carry their good wishes into effect. In a little while a small room, about ten feet square, that had formed a thoroughfare between the stables and a kind of shop or bar room, was cleared of a variety of lumber, and I was assured that a bed should be put up there for me. From the consultations I saw my hostess holding with some of her neighbour gossips, I fancied the bed was to be a kind of piece-meal contribution among them for the credit of the house.

As soon as I could change my dress, I commenced the historical researches which were the object of my journey, and inquired for the abode of Don Juan Fernandez Pinzon. My obliging landlord himself volunteered to conduct me thither, and I set off full of animation at the thoughts of meeting with the lineal representative of one of the co-adjutors of Columbus.

A short walk brought us to the house, which was most respectable in its appearance, indicating easy, if not affluent, circumstances. The door, as is customary in Spanish villages, during summer, stood wide open. We entered with the usual salutation or rather summons, "Ave Maria!" A trim Andalusian handmaid answered to the call, and, on our inquiring for the master of the house, led the way across a little

patio or court, in the center of the edifice, cooled by a fountain surrounded by shrubs and flowers, to a back court or terrace, likewise set
out with flowers, where Don Juan Fernandez was seated with his family, enjoying the serene evening in the open air.

I was much pleased with his appearance. He was a venerable old
gentleman, tall, and somewhat thin, with fair complexion and grey
hair. He received me with great urbanity, and on reading the letter
from his son, appeared struck with surprise to find I had come quite to
Moguer, merely to visit the scene of the embarkation of Columbus; and
still more so on my telling him, that one of my leading objects of
curiosity was his own family connection; for it would seem that the
worthy cavalier had troubled his head but little about the enterprises
of his ancestors.

I now took my seat in the domestic circle, and soon felt myself quite
at home, for there is generally a frankness in the hospitality of Spaniards, that soon puts a stranger at his ease beneath their roof. The wife
of Don Juan Fernandez was extremely amiable and affable, possessing
much of that natural aptness for which the Spanish women are remarkable. In the course of conversation with them I learnt, that Don Juan
Fernandez, who is seventy-two years of age, is the eldest of five
brothers, all of whom are married, have numerous offspring, and live
in Moguer and its vicinity, in nearly the same condition and rank of
life as at the time of the discovery. This agreed with what I had previously heard, respecting the families of the discoverers. Of Columbus
no lineal and direct descendant exists; his was an exotic stock that
never took deep and lasting root in the country; but the race of the
Pinzons continues to thrive and multiply in its native soil.

While I was yet conversing, a gentleman entered, who was introduced to me as Don Luis Fernandez Pinzon, the youngest of the
brothers. He appeared between fifty and sixty years of age, somewhat
robust, with fair complexion and grey hair, and a frank and manly de-
portment. He is the only one of the present generation that has followed the ancient profession of the family; having served with great
applause as an officer of the royal navy, from which he retired, on his
marriage, about twenty-two years since. He is the one, also, who takes
the greatest interest and pride in the historical honours of his house,
carefully preserving all the legends and documents of the achievements
and distinctions of his family, a manuscript volume of which he lent to
me for my inspection.

Don Juan now expressed a wish that, during my residence in Moguer,
I would make his house my home. I endeavoured to excuse myself, alleg-
ing, that the good people at the posada had been at such extraordinary

trouble in preparing quarters for me, that I did not like to disappoint them. The worthy old gentleman undertook to arrange all this, and, while supper was preparing, we walked together to the posada. I found that my obliging host and hostess had indeed exerted themselves to an uncommon degree. An old ricketty table had been spread out in a corner of the little room as a bedstead, on top of which was propped up a grand *cama de luxo*, or state bed, which appeared to be the admiration of the house. I could not, for the soul of me, appear to undervalue what the poor people had prepared with such hearty good will, and considered such a triumph of art and luxury; so I again entreated Don Juan to dispense with my sleeping at his house, promising most faithfully to make my meals there whilst I should stay at Moguer, and as the old gentleman understood my motives for declining his invitation, and felt a good-humoured sympathy in them, we readily arranged the matter. I returned therefore with Don Juan to his house and supped with his family. During the repast a plan was agreed upon for my visit to Palos, and to the convent La Rabida, in which Don Juan volunteered to accompany me and be my guide, and the following day was allotted to the expedition. We were to breakfast at a hacienda, or country seat, which he possessed in the vicinity of Palos, in the midst of his vineyards, and were to dine there on our return from the convent. These arangements being made, we parted for the night; I returned to the posada highly gratified with my visit, and slept soundly in the extraordinary bed which, I may almost say, had been invented for my accommodation.

On the following morning, bright and early, Don Juan Fernandez and myself set off in the calesa for Palos. I felt apprehensive at first, that the kind-hearted old gentleman, in his anxiety to oblige, had left his bed at too early an hour, and was exposing himself to fatigues unsuited to his age. He laughed at the idea, and assured me that he was an early riser, and accustomed to all kinds of exercise on horse and foot, being a keen sportsman, and frequently passing days together among the mountains on shooting expeditions, taking with him servants, horses, and provisions, and living in a tent. He appeared, in fact, to be of an active habit, and to possess a youthful vivacity of spirit. His cheerful disposition rendered our morning drive extremely agreeable; his urbanity was shown to every one whom we met on the road; even the common peasant was saluted by him with the appellation of *caballero*, a mark of respect ever gratifying to the poor but proud Spaniard when yielded by a superior.

As the tide was out we drove along the flat grounds bordering the Tinto. The river was on our right, while on our left was a range of hills, jutting out into promontories, one beyond the other, and covered with vineyards and fig-trees. The weather was serene, the air soft and balmy, and the landscape of that gentle kind calculated to put one in a quiet and happy humour. We passed close by the skirts of Palos, and drove to the hacienda, which is situated at some little distance from the village, between it and the river. The house is a low stone building, well whitewashed, and of great length; one end being fitted up as a summer residence, with saloons, bed-rooms, and a domestic chapel; and the other as a bodega or magazine for the reception of the wine produced on the estate.

The house stands on a hill, amidst vineyards, which are supposed to cover a part of the site of the ancient town of Palos, now shrunk to a miserable village. Beyond these vineyards, on the crest of a distant hill, are seen the white walls of the convent of La Rabida rising above a dark wood of pine trees.

Below the hacienda flows the river Tinto, on which Columbus embarked. It is divided by a low tongue of land, or rather the sand bar of Saltes, from the river Odiel, with which it soon mingles its waters, and flows on to the ocean. Beside this sand bar, where the channel of the river runs deep, the squadron of Columbus was anchored, and from thence he made sail on the morning of his departure.

The soft breeze that was blowing scarcely ruffled the surface of this beautiful river; two or three picturesque barks, called mysticks, with long latine sails, were gliding down it. A little aid of the imagination might suffice to picture them as the light caravels of Columbus, sallying forth on their eventful expedition, while the distant bells of the town of Huelva, which were ringing melodiously, might be supposed as cheering the voyagers with a farewell peal.

I cannot express to you what were my feelings on treading the shore which had once been animated with the bustle of departure, and whose sands had been printed by the last footstep of Columbus. The solemn and sublime nature of the event that had followed, together with the fate and fortunes of those concerned in it, filled the mind with vague yet melancholy ideas. It was like viewing the silent and empty stage of some great drama when all the actors had departed. The very aspect of the landscape, so tranquilly beautiful, had an effect upon me; and as I paced the deserted shores by the side of a descendant of one of the discoverers, I felt my heart swelling with emotions and my eyes filling with tears.

What surprised me was, to find no semblance of a sea-port; there was neither wharf nor landing-place—nothing but a naked river bank, with the hulk of a ferry-boat, which I was told carried passengers to

Huelva, lying high and dry on the sands, deserted by the tide. Palos, though it has doubtless dwindled away from its former size, can never have been important as to extent and population. If it possessed warehouses on the beach, they have disappeared. It is at present a mere village of the poorest kind, and lies nearly a quarter of a mile from the river, in a hollow among hills. It contains a few hundred inhabitants, who subsist principally by labouring in the fields and vineyards. Its race of merchants and mariners is extinct. There are no vessels belonging to the place, nor any show of traffic, excepting at the season of fruit and wine, when a few mysticks and other light barks anchor in the river to collect the produce of the neighbourhood. The people are totally ignorant, and it is probable that the greater part of them scarce know even the name of America. Such is the place from whence sallied forth the enterprise for the discovery of the western world!

We were now summoned to breakfast in a little saloon of the hacienda. The table was covered with natural luxuries produced upon the spot—fine purple and muscatel grapes from the adjacent vineyard, delicious melons from the garden, and generous wines made on the estate. The repast was heightened by the genial manners of my hospitable host, who appeared to possess the most enviable cheerfulness of spirit and simplicity of heart.

After breakfast we set off in the calesa to visit the Convent of La Rabida, about half a league distant. The road, for a part of the way, lay through the vineyards, and was deep and sandy. The calesero had been at his wits end to conceive what motive a stranger like myself, apparently travelling for mere amusement, could have in coming so far to see so miserable a place as Palos, which he set down as one of the very poorest places in the whole world; but this additional toil and struggle through deep sand to visit the old Convent of La Rabida, completed his confusion—"Hombre!" exclaimed he, "es una ruina! no hay mas que dos frailes!"—"Zounds! why it's a ruin! there are only two friars there!" Don Juan laughed, and told him that I had come all the way from Seville precisely to see that old ruin and those two friars. The calesero made the Spaniard's last reply when he is perplexed—he shrugged his shoulders and crossed himself.

After ascending a hill and passing through the skirts of a straggling pine wood, we arrived in front of the convent. It stands in a bleak and solitary situation, on the brow of a rocky height or promontory, overlooking to the west a wide range of sea and land, bounded by the frontier mountains of Portugal, about eight leagues distant. The convent is shut out from a view of the vineyard of Palos by the gloomy forest of pines already mentioned, which cover the promontory to the east, and darken the whole landscape in that direction.

There is nothing remarkable in the architecture of the convent; part of it is Gothic, but the edifice, having been frequently repaired, and being whitewashed, according to a universal custom in Andalusia, inherited from the Moors, has not that venerable aspect which might be expected from its antiquity.

We alighted at the gate where Columbus, when a poor pedestrian, a stranger in the land, asked bread and water for his child! As long as the convent stands, this must be a spot calculated to awaken the most thrilling interest. The gate remains apparently in nearly the same state as at the time of his visit, but there is no longer a porter at hand to administer to the wants of the wayfarer. The door stood wide open, and admitted us into a small court yard. From thence we passed through a Gothic portal into the chapel, without seeing a human being. We then traversed two interior cloisters, equally vacant and silent, and bearing a look of neglect and dilapidation. From an open window we had a peep at what had once been a garden, but that had also gone to ruin; the walls were broken and thrown down; a few shrubs, and a scattered fig-tree or two were all the traces of cultivation that remained. We passed through the long dormitories, but the cells were shut up and abandoned; we saw no living thing except a solitary cat stealing across a distant corridor, which fled in a panic at the unusual sight of strangers. At length, after patrolling nearly the whole of the empty building to the echo of our own footsteps, we came to where the door of a cell, being partly open, gave us the sight of a monk within, seated at a table writing. He rose, and received us with much civility, and conducted us to the superior, who was reading in an adjacent cell. They were both rather young men, and, together with a noviciate and a lay-brother, who officiated as cook, formed the whole community of the convent.

Don Juan Fernandez communicated to them the object of my visit, and my desire also to inspect the archives of the convent, to find if there was any record of the sojourn of Columbus. They informed us that the archives had been entirely destroyed by the French. The younger monk, however, who had perused them, had a vague recollection of various particulars concerning the transactions of Columbus at Palos, his visit to the convent, and the sailing of his expedition. From all that he cited, however, it appeared to me that all the information on the subject contained in the archives, had been extracted from Herrera and other well known authors. The monk was talkative and eloquent, and soon diverged from the subject of Columbus, to one which he considered of infinitely greater importance—the miraculous image of the Virgin possessed by their convent, and known by the name of "Our Lady of La Rabida." He gave us a history of the wonderful way in which the image had been found buried in the earth, where it had lain hidden for ages, since the time of the conquest of Spain by the Moors; the disputes between the convent and different places in the neighbourhood for the possession of it; the marvellous protection it extended to the adjacent country, especially in preventing all madness, either in man or dog, for this malady was anciently so prevalent in this place as to gain it the appellation of La Rabia, by which it was originally called; a name which, thanks to the beneficent influence of the Virgin, it no longer merited or retained. Such are the legends and reliques with which every convent in Spain is enriched, which are zealously cried up by the monks, and devoutly credited by the populace.

Twice a year on the festival of our Lady of La Rabida, and on that of the patron saint of the order, the solitude and silence of the convent are interrupted by the intrusion of a swarming multitude, composed of the inhabitants of Moguer, of Huelva, and the neighbouring plains and mountains. The open esplanade in front of the edifice resembles a fair, the adjacent forest teems with the motley throng, and the image of our Lady of La Rabida is borne forth in triumphant procession.

While the friar was thus dilating upon the merits and renown of the image, I amused myself with those day dreams, or conjurings of the imagination, to which I am a little given. As the internal arrangements of convents are apt to be the same from age to age, I pictured to myself this chamber as the same inhabited by the guardian, Juan Perez de Marchena, at the time of the visit of Columbus. Why might not the old and ponderous table before me be the very one on which he displayed his conjectural maps, and expounded his theory of a western route to India? It required but another stretch of the imagination to assemble the little conclave around the table; Juan Perez the friar, Garci Fernandez the physician, and Martin Alonzo Pinzon the bold navigator, all listening with rapt attention to Columbus, or to the tale of some old seaman of Palos, about islands seen in the western parts of the ocean.

The friars, as far as their poor means and scanty knowledge extended, were disposed to do every thing to promote the object of my visit. They showed us all parts of the convent, which however, has little to boast of, excepting the historical associations connected with it. The library was reduced to a few volumes, chiefly on ecclesiastical subjects, piled promiscuously in the corner of a vaulted chamber, and covered with dust. The chamber itself was curious, being the most ancient part of the edifice, and supposed to have formed part of a temple in the time of the Romans.

We ascended to the roof of the convent to enjoy the extensive prospect it commands. Immediately below the promontory on which it is situated, runs a narrow but tolerably deep river, called the Domingo Rubio, which empties itself into the Tinto. It is the opinion of Don Luis Fernandez Pinzon, that the ships of Columbus were careened and fitted out in this river, as it affords better shelter than the Tinto, and its shores are not so shallow. A lonely bark of a fisherman was lying in this stream, and not far off, on a sandy point, were the ruins of an ancient watch tower. From the roof of the convent, all the windings of the Odiel and the Tinto were to be seen, and their junction into the main stream, by which Columbus sallied forth to sea. In fact the convent serves as a landmark, being, from its lofty and solitary situation, visible for a considerable distance to vessels coming on the coast. On the opposite side I looked down upon the lonely road, through the wood of pine trees, by which the zealous guardian of the convent, Fray Juan Perez, departed at midnight on his mule, when he sought the camp of Ferdinand and Isabella in the Vega of Granada, to plead the project of Columbus before the queen.

Having finished our inspection of the convent, we prepared to depart, and were accompanied to the outward portal by the two friars. Our calesero brought his rattling and ricketty vehicle for us to mount; at sight of which one of the monks exclaimed, with a smile, "Santa Maria! only to think! A calesa before the gate of the convent of La Rabida!" And, indeed, so solitary and remote is this ancient edifice, and so simple is the mode of living of the people in this bye-corner of Spain, that the appearance of even a sorry calesa might well cause astonishment. It is only singular that in such a bye-corner the scheme of Columbus should have found intelligent listeners and coadjutors, after it had been discarded, almost with scoffing and contempt, from learned universities and splendid courts.

On our way back to the hacienda, we met Don Rafael, a younger son of Don Juan Fernandez, a fine young man, about twenty-one years of age, and who, his father informed me, was at present studying French and mathematics. He was well mounted on a spirited grey horse, and dressed in the Andalusian style, with the little round hat and jacket. He sat his horse gracefully, and managed him well. I was pleased with the frank and easy terms on which Don Juan appeared to live with

his children. This I was inclined to think his favourite son, as I understood he was the only one that partook of the old gentleman's fondness
for the chase, and that accompanied him in his hunting excursions.

A dinner had been prepared for us at the hacienda, by the wife of
the capitaz, or overseer, who, with her husband, seemed to be well
pleased with this visit from Don Juan, and to be confident of receiving
a pleasant answer from the good-humoured old gentleman whenever
they addressed him. The dinner was served up about two o'clock, and
was a most agreeable meal. The fruits and wines were from the estate,
and were excellent; the rest of the provisions were from Moguer, for
the adjacent village of Palos is too poor to furnish any thing. A gentle
breeze from the sea played through the hall, and tempered the summer
heat. Indeed I do not know when I have seen a more enviable spot
than this country retreat of the Pinzons. Its situation on a breezy hill,
at no great distance from the sea, and in a southern climate, produces
a happy temperature, neither hot in summer nor cold in winter. It
commands a beautiful prospect, and is surrounded by natural luxuries.
The country abounds with game, the adjacent river affords abundant
sport in fishing, both by day and night, and delightful excursions for
those fond of sailing. During the busy seasons of rural life, and especially at the joyous period of vintage, the family pass some time
here, accompanied by numerous guests, at which times, Don Juan assured me, there was no lack of amusements, both by land and water.

When we had dined, and taken the siesta, or afternoon nap, according to the Spanish custom in summer time, we set out on our return
to Moguer, visiting the village of Palos in the way. Don Rafael had
been sent in advance in procure the keys of the village church, and to
apprise the curate of our wish to inspect the archives. The village consists principally of two streets of low whitewashed houses. Many of the
inhabitants have very dark complexions, betraying a mixture of African
blood.

On entering the village, we repaired to the lowly mansion of the
curate. I had hoped to find him some such personage as the curate in
Don Quixote, possessed of shrewdness and information in his limited
sphere, and that I might gain some anecdotes from him concerning his
parish, its worthies, its antiquities, and its historical events. Perhaps I
might have done so at any other time, but, unfortunately, the curate
was something of a sportsman, and had heard of some game among the
neighbouring hills. We met him just sallying forth from his house, and,
I must confess, his appearance was picturesque. He was a short, broad,
sturdy, little man, and had doffed his cassock and broad clerical beaver,

for a short jacket and a little round Andalusian hat; he had his gun in hand, and was on the point of mounting a donkey which had been led forth by an ancient withered handmaid. Fearful of being detained from his foray, he accosted my companion the moment he came in sight. "God preserve you, Señor Don Juan! I have received your message, and have but one answer to make. The archives have all been destroyed. We have no trace of any thing you seek for—nothing—nothing. Don Rafael has the keys of the church. You can examine it at your leisure—Adios, caballero!" With these words the galliard little curate mounted his donkey, thumped his ribs with the butt end of his gun, and trotted off to the hills.

In our way to the church we passed by the ruins of what had once been a fair and spacious dwelling, greatly superior to the other houses of the village. This, Don Juan informed me, was an old family possession, but since they had removed from Palos it had fallen to decay for want of a tenant. It was probably the family residence of Martin Alonzo or Vicente Yañez Pinzon, in the time of Columbus.

We now arrived at the Church of St. George, in the porch of which Columbus first proclaimed to the inhabitants of Palos the order of the sovereigns, that they should furnish him with ships for his great voyage of discovery. This edifice has lately been thoroughly repaired, and, being of solid mason work, promises to stand for ages, a monument of the discoverers. It stands outside of the village, on the brow of a hill, looking along a little valley toward the river. The remains of a Moorish arch prove it to have been a mosque in former times; just above it, on the crest of the hill, is the ruin of a Moorish castle.

I paused in the porch, and endeavoured to recall the interesting scene that had taken place there, when Columbus, accompanied by the zealous friar Juan Perez, caused the public notary to read the royal order in presence of the astonished alcaldes, regidors, and alguazils; but it is difficult to conceive the consternation that must have been struck into so remote a little community, by this sudden apparition of an entire stranger among them, bearing a command that they should put their persons and ships at his disposal, and sail with him away into the unknown wilderness of the ocean.

The interior of the church has nothing remarkable, excepting a wooden image of St. George vanquishing the Dragon, which is erected over the high altar, and is the admiration of the good people of Palos, who bear it about the streets in grand procession on the anniversary of the saint. This groupe existed in the time of Columbus, and now flourishes in renovated youth and splendour, having been newly painted and gilded, and the countenance of the saint rendered peculiarly blooming and lustrous.

Having finished the examination of the church, we resumed our seats in the calesa and returned to Moguer. One thing only remained to fulfill the object of my pilgrimage. This was to visit the chapel of the Convent of Santa Clara. When Columbus was in danger of being lost in a tempest on his way home from his great voyage of discovery, he made a vow, that, should he be spared, he would watch and pray one whole night in this chapel; a vow which he doubtless fulfilled immediately after his arrival.

My kind and attentive friend, Don Juan, conducted me to the convent. It is the wealthiest in Moguer, and belongs to a sisterhood of Franciscan nuns. The chapel is large, and ornamented with some degree of richness, particularly the part about the high altar, which is embellished by magnificent monuments of the brave family of the Puerto Carreros, the ancient lords of Moguer, and renowned in Moorish warfare. The alabaster effigies of distinguished warriors of that house, and of their wives and sisters, lie side by side, with folded hands, on tombs immediately before the altar, while others recline in deep niches on either side. The night had closed in by the time I entered the church, which made the scene more impressive. A few votive lamps shed a dim light about the interior; their beams were feebly reflected by the gilded work of the high altar, and the frames of the surrounding paintings, and rested upon the marble figures of the warriors and dames lying in the monumental repose of ages. The solemn pile must have presented much the same appearance when the pious discoverer performed his vigil, kneeling before this very altar, and praying and watching throughout the night, and pouring forth heartfelt praises for having been spared to accomplish his sublime discovery.

I had now completed the main purpose of my journey, having visited the various places connected with the story of Columbus. It was highly gratifying to find some of them so little changed though so great a space of time had intervened; but in this quiet nook of Spain, so far removed from the main thoroughfares, the lapse of time produces but few violent revolutions. Nothing, however, had surprised and gratified me more than the continued stability of the Pinzon family. On the morning after my excursion to Palos, chance gave me an opportunity of seeing something of the interior of most of their households. Having a curiosity to visit the remains of a Moorish castle, once the citadel of Moguer, Don Fernandez undertook to show me a tower which served as a magazine of wine to one of the Pinzon family. In seeking for the key we were sent from house to house of nearly the whole connexion. All appeared to be living in that golden mean equally removed from the wants and superfluities of life, and all to be happily interwoven by kind and cordial habits of intimacy. We found the females of the family generally seated in the patios, or central courts of their dwellings, beneath the shade of awnings and among shrubs and flowers. Here the Andalusian ladies are accustomed to pass their mornings at work, surrounded by their handmaids, in the primitive, or rather, oriental style. In the porches of some of the houses I observed the coat of arms granted to the family by Charles V, hung up like a picture in a frame. Over the door of Don Luis, the naval officer, it was carved on an escutcheon of stone, and coloured. I had gathered many particulars of the family also from conversation with Don Juan, and from the family legend lent me by Don Luis. From all that I could learn, it would appear that the lapse of nearly three centuries and a half has made but little change in the condition of the Pinzons. From generation to generation they have retained the same fair standing and reputable name throughout the neighbourhood, filling offices of public trust and dignity, and possessing great influence over their fellow citizens by their good sense and good conduct. How rare is it to see such an instance of stability of fortune in this fluctuating world, and how truly honourable is this hereditary respectability, which has been secured by no titles or entails, but perpetuated merely by the innate worth of the race! I declare to you that the most illustrious descents of mere titled rank could never command the sincere respect and cordial regard with which I contemplated this staunch and enduring family, which for three centuries and a half has stood merely upon its virtues.

As I was to set off on my return to Seville before two o'clock, I partook of a farewell repast at the house of Don Juan, between twelve and one, and then took leave of his household with sincere regret. The good old gentleman, with the courtesy, or rather the cordiality of a true Spaniard, accompanied me to the posada, to see me off. I had dispensed but little money in the posada—thanks to the hospitality of the Pinzons—yet the Spanish pride of my host and hostess seemed pleased that I had preferred their humble chamber, and the scanty bed they had provided me, to the spacious mansion of Don Juan; and when I expressed my thanks for their kindness and attention, and regaled mine host with a few choice cigars, the heart of the poor man was overcome. He seized me by both hands and gave me a parting benediction, and then ran after the calesero, to enjoin him to take particular care of me during my journey.

Taking a hearty leave of my excellent friend Don Juan, who had been unremitting in his attentions to me to that last moment, I now set off on my wayfaring, gratified to the utmost with my visit, and full of kind and grateful feelings toward Moguer and its hospitable inhabitants.

No. XXXIX

Manifesto of Alonzo de Ojeda

The following curious formula, composed by learned divines in Spain, was first read aloud by the friars in the train of Alonzo de Ojeda, as a prelude to his attack on the savages of Carthagena, and was subsequently adopted by the Spanish discoverers in general, in their invasions of Indian countries.

"I, Alonzo de Ojeda, servant of the high and mighty kings of Castile and Leon, civilizers of barbarous nations, their messenger and captain, notify and make known to you, in the best way I can, that God our Lord, one and eternal, created the heavens and earth, and one man and one woman, from whom you, and we, and all the people of the earth, were and are descendants, procreated, and all those who shall come after us; but the vast number of generations which have proceeded from them in the course of more than five thousand years that have elapsed since the creation of the world, made it necessary that some of the human race should disperse in one direction, and some in another, and that they should divide themselves into many kingdoms and provinces, as they could not sustain and preserve themselves in one alone. All these people were given in charge, by God our Lord, to one person, named Saint Peter, who was thus made lord and superior of all the people of the earth, and head of the whole human lineage; whom all should obey, wherever they might live, and whatever might be their law, sect, or belief: he gave him also the whole world for his service and jurisdiction; and though he desired that he should establish his chair in Rome, as a place most convenient for governing the world, yet he permitted that he might establish his chair in any other part of the world, and judge and govern all the nations, Christians, Moors, Jews, Gentiles, and whatever other sect or belief might be. This person was denominated Pope, that is to say, Admirable, Supreme,

Father and Guardian, because he is father and governor of all mankind. This holy father was obeyed and honoured as lord, king, and superior of the universe, by those who lived in his time, and, in like manner, have been obeyed and honoured all those who have been elected to the pontificate; and thus it has continued unto the present day, and will continue until the end of the world.

"One of these pontiffs, of whom I have spoken, as lord of the world, made a donation of these islands and continents of the ocean sea, and all that they contain, to the Catholic kings of Castile, who, at that time, were Ferdinand and Isabella, of glorious memory, and to their successors, our sovereigns, according to the tenor of certain papers, drawn up for the purpose (which you may see, if you desire). Thus His Majesty is king and sovereign of these islands and continents by virtue of the said donation, and, as king and sovereign, certain islands, and almost all, to whom this has been notified, have received His Majesty, and have obeyed and served, and do actually serve him. And, moreover, like good subjects, and with good will, and without any resistance or delay, the moment they were informed of the foregoing, they obeyed all the religious men sent among them to preach and teach our holy faith; and these of their free and cheerful will, without any condition or reward, became Christians, and continue so to be. And His Majesty received them kindly and benignantly, and ordered that they should be treated like his other subjects and vassals. You also are required and obliged to do the same. Therefore, in the best manner I can, I pray and entreat you, that you consider well what I have said, and that you take whatever time is reasonable to understand and deliberate upon it, and that you recognise the Church for sovereign and superior of the universal world, and the supreme pontiff, called Pope, in her name, and His Majesty, in his place, as superior and sovereign king of the islands and Terra Firma by virtue of said donation; and that you consent that these religious fathers declare and preach to you the foregoing; and if you shall so do, you will do well, and will do that to which you are bounden and obliged; and His Majesty, and I, in his name, will receive you with all due love and charity, and will leave you your wives and children free from servitude, that you may freely do with them and with yourselves whatever you please and think proper, as have done the inhabitants of the other islands. And, beside this, His Majesty will give you many privileges and exemptions, and grant you many favours. If you do not do this, or wickedly and intentionally delay to do so, I certify to you that, by the aid of God, I will forcibly invade and make war upon you in all parts and modes that I can, and will subdue you to the yoke and obedience of the Church and of His

Majesty; and I will take your wives and children, and make slaves of them, and sell them as such, and dispose of them as His Majesty may command; and I will take your effects, and will do you all the harm and injury in my power, as vassals who will not obey or receive their sovereign, and who resist and oppose him. And I protest that the deaths and disasters, which may in this manner be occasioned, will be the fault of yourselves, and not of His Majesty, nor of me, nor of these cavaliers who accompany me. And of what I here tell you, and require of you, I call upon the notary here present to give me his signed testimonial."

THE END.

EDITORIAL APPENDIX

Textual Commentary,
Discussions, and Lists by
James W. Tuttleton

LIST OF ABBREVIATIONS

The following symbols have been used in the editorial apparatus to designate the manuscripts and previously published texts of *Companions of Columbus* and *The Life and Voyages of Christopher Columbus* (indicated by the suffix C).

MS	Manuscript of *Companions of Columbus* (Irving holograph)
1E	First English edition (London: John Murray, 1831)
1A	First American edition (Philadelphia: Carey & Lea, 1831)
1F	First French edition (Paris: Galignani, 1831)
ARE	Author's Revised Edition, vol. 5 (New York: G. P. Putnam, 1848)
MS1aC	Fragments, in Irving's hand, of printer's copy for first American edition of *The Life and Voyages of Christopher Columbus*
MS1eC	Printer's copy, largely in the hand of five Spanish scribes, for first English edition
MS2eC	Irving's corrections in a copy of first English edition
MS3aC	Printer's copy for third American edition
ur-MS3aC	The first stage of correction of the copy of 2EC that became MS2aC, as indicated by scribal transcriptions of MS2eC. This is a hypothetical document which is not extant.
1EC	First English edition (London: John Murray, 1828)
1AC	First American edition (New York: G. & C. Carvill, 1828)
2EC	Second English edition (London: John Murray, [1828?])
2AC	Second American edition (New York: G. & C. Carvill, 1831)
2AsuC	Fragmentary manuscript revisions of *Columbus* at Sunnyside
3AC	Third American edition (New York: Putnam, 1848–1849); ARE
T	Twayne edition

EXPLANATORY NOTES

The following notes, keyed to page and line numbers in the text, are intended to provide historical, biographical, cultural, and bibliographical information of a variety of kinds.

3.3   History of Columbus] Washington Irving's *A History of the Life and Voyages of Christopher Columbus* was first published in London in four volumes by John Murray in 1828. The first American edition, in three volumes, was published in February of the same year by G. & C. Carvill in New York. Two four-volume editions, based on the first English edition, were also published in Paris, by A. Galignani and Baudry.

3.9   Paria] Paria, a peninsula on the Cumana, or "Pearl Coast" of Venezuela, was famous among the explorers for its pearl fishery.

3.9   Cubaga] Cubaga (Pearl Island) is a small island northwest of the Golfo de las Perlas. Settled about 1512, Cubaga was a major source of pearls. See Charles Alexander, *Geography of Margarita and Adjacent Islands* (Berkeley: University of California Publications in Geography, 1958).

3.10   Veragua] Veragua, the "gold coast" of the Isthmus of Panama, was discovered by Columbus in 1502. The region was possibly named for the *quebi*, or chief, of the region.

3.10   Aurea Chersonesus] Greek: "golden peninsula." The Golden Chersonese (the peninsula of Malaya) was believed by the Jewish historian Josephus to be the site of King Solomon's mines, the source of fabulous treasures of gold. Since, to the medieval mind, gold was believed to be engendered by heat (silver by cold), and since Columbus had found a considerable amount of gold in torrid Central America, he believed the Isthmus of Panama to lie somewhere near Ophir, the peninsula of Malaya, and King Solomon's mines. In a letter to King Ferdinand from Jamaica in July, 1503, Columbus argued that the mines of the Aurea were one and the same with those of Veragua, and lay only twenty days' journey to the west. See Martín Fernandez de Navarrete, *Colección de los viajes y descubrimientos que hicieron por mar los Españoles* (Madrid, 1825–29), I, 457; Flavius Josephus, *Jewish Antiquities* (Cambridge, Mass., 1934), V, 660–61.

3.13   Terra Firma]   Because Columbus thought he had discovered
India, the Spanish New World discoveries were officially designated
the "Islas y Tierra Firme" of the Indies of the Ocean Sea. The islands
are the Antilles or the West Indies. The Tierra Firme, or mainland,
designated that part of the South American continent on the southern
coast of the Caribbean Sea between the peninsula of Paria on the east
to Central America on the west. As the explorers extended their knowledge of the continental coastline, the denotation of Tierra Firme
changed accordingly.

3.16–17   Caribbean sea]   So named after the Caribs, a race of warlike
natives of the Lesser Antilles who practiced cannibalism and scarifica-
tion. The original name, "Calinago" or "Calino," was corrupted by
Columbus to "Caribales," from which the English word "cannibal" is
derived. Such word corruptions, particularly in place names, were
predictably common, so that Thomas Jefferys, royal geographer in
the mid-eighteenth century, complained: "what strangled jargon and
changes have been caused by a bad pronunciation of foreign names,
when used by persons utterly strangers to the language" (*The West-
India Atlas or A Compendius Description of the West-Indies by the
late Thomas Jefferys, Geographer to the King* [London, 1799], p. ii).
Juan Lopez de Velasco, in his *Geografía descripcion universal de las
Indias, recopilada...desde el ano de 1571 al de 1574*, called the
Caribbean the "Gulf of Cannibals," as most Spaniards informally
termed it. But Jefferys observed that "It has been sometimes called
the *Caribbean-Sea*, which name it would be better to adopt, than to
leave this space quite anonymous" (p. 6).

3.17   His last and most disastrous voyage]   Columbus voyaged to the
New World four times. On the famous first voyage he sailed from
Palos, Spain, with three small ships, the *Santa Maria*, commanded by
Columbus; the *Pinta*, commanded by Martín Pinzón; and the *Nina*,
commanded by Vicente Yáñez Pinzón. On October 12, 1492, he
sighted San Salvador and, coasting the islands, Cuba and Hispaniola.
On the second voyage, which got under way in October 1493, he
discovered the Lesser Antilles, Puerto Rico, and the Virgin Islands.
In 1498, on his third voyage, Columbus sighted Trinidad, to the south
of the Caribbean islands, and the continental coastline of Venezuela.
Sent back to Spain in chains for his wretched mismanagement of the
colony at Hispaniola, Columbus regained his freedom and tried to
repair his fortunes and reputation by a fourth voyage in 1502. A principal object of all of the Spanish mariners was to explore the Tierra
Firme to discover whether there were a passage through or around
it to the Spice Lands of the Far East. On his fourth and last voyage,

Columbus discovered the coast of Honduras in Central America and enlarged Spanish knowledge of the mainland but found no strait to India. He returned to Spain and suffered eventual eclipse. As a result of the junta at Burgos in 1508, King Ferdinand therefore commissioned Yáñez Pinzón and Diaz de Solís to "follow the navigation for the discovery of that canal or open sea which you are sent to discover and which I wish to be sought." See *Colección de documentos inéditos relativos al descubrimiento, conquista, y organización de las antiguas posesiones españolas de America y Oceania* (Madrid, 1874), XXII, 8–9. Needless to say, Pinzón and Diaz de Solís also failed to find the strait. Irving's claim that Columbus's fourth voyage was undertaken with the "express purpose" of discovering the strait is the traditional view, supported, for example, by Samuel Eliot Morison's *Admiral of the Ocean* (Boston, 1942): "But the Admiral of the Ocean Sea must seek the strait. That's what he came for" (II, 338). This claim has been challenged by historian Carl O. Sauer, however, who describes the royal instructions to Columbus of March 14, 1502, as merely "a commission to discover and trade without indicating direction or destination." Sauer argues that "it was not to the end of discovering the strait that the voyage was undertaken nor did the proof of his error [in mistaking Panama for Malaya] enter the mind of Columbus. He returned in the belief that he had found the Golden Chersonese. As it had been from the first landing on the Bahamas, gold was what he wanted, the gold that admitted souls to Paradise" (*The Early Spanish Main* [Berkeley, 1966], pp. 121–43).

3.18 imaginary strait] The "imaginary geography" of the medieval mariners is discussed in L. Sprague de Camp and Willy Ley's *De la Atlántida a El Dorado* (Barcelona, 1960).

3.19 Southern Ocean] Prior to Nuñez de Balboa's discovery of the Pacific (1513), the Spanish believed the sea to be one, the Ocean Sea. In a north-to-south expedition across the province of Darien in the Isthmus of Panama, Balboa discovered "the other sea," which he called Mar del Sur, or Southern Ocean (the Pacific). As a consequence, "Mar del Norte" was adopted to designate the Atlantic and the as yet unnamed Caribbean Sea.

3.22 Darien] Generally, the eastern region of Panama. Specifically that part of the Isthmus of Panama between the Gulf of Darien on the east and the Gulf of San Miguel on the west.

4.7 cavalgada] Spanish: *cabalgada*; from Latin: *caballus*, "horse." This obsolete term denotes a ride, march, or raid on horseback.

4.10–11 Castilian cavalier] Castile, a former kingdom in central and northern Spain, so named for the many castles built there by Christian nobles who recaptured it in the eighth and ninth centuries from the Moors. Originally a province of the kingdom of Leon, the capital of which was Burgos, Castile gained its autonomy by the tenth century. By the end of the fifteenth century, the Castilian cavaliers (literally, horsemen) had completely expelled the Moors from Spain, after the conquest of Granada, unified the nation under the joint rule of Ferdinand and Isabella, and made Madrid the capital and Castilian the literary language of modern Spain.

4.21 treaty with the sovereigns]   The commission (the *Título* or title of April 30, 1492) confirmed the titles and offices conferred on Columbus by the crown, namely, that he should be the royal "Almirante de las dichas Islas, ó Tierra-firme" as well as their "Visorey" and "Gobernador." (Cf. Navarrete's *Colección de los viajes y descubrimientos que hicieron por mar los Españoles* [Madrid, 1825], I, 14. Morison translates the title thus: "Whereas you, *Cristóbal Colón*, are setting forth by our command . . . to discover and acquire certain islands and mainland in the ocean sea . . . it is just and reasonable that, since you are exposing yourself to this danger in our service, you be rewarded therefor, . . . it is our will and pleasure that you the said *Cristóbal Colón* after you have discovered and acquired the said islands and mainland . . . or any of them, shall be our Admiral of the said islands and mainland which you may thus discover and acquire, and shall be our Admiral and Viceroy and Governor therein, and shall be empowered henceforward to call and entitle yourself *Don Cristóbal Colón*, and his heirs and successors forever may be so entitled, and enjoy the offices of Admiral of the Ocean Sea, Viceroy and Governor of the said islands and mainland" (*Admiral of the Ocean Sea*, I, 139). For a discussion of the hereditary titles of Columbus as viceroy, governor, captain general, and admiral, see Mario Góngora's *El estado en el derecho indiano, época de fundación, 1492–1570* (Santiago de Chile, 1951).

4.32 the banner of Ferdinand and Isabella]   The marriage in 1469 of Ferdinand V of Aragon (1452–1516) and Isabella I of Castile (1451–1504) unified all of the kingdoms of Spain except Navarre and Moorish Granada. Determined to Christianize all of Andalusia, a region of southern Spain, the Catholic monarchs defeated Granada in 1492 and established the Spanish Inquisition which expelled or executed Spanish Jews and Moslems who would not become Christians. Under the joint rule of *los Reyes Católicos*, as they are called, Spain became a colonial empire and a maritime power rivaling France and England. See W. H. Prescott's *History of the Reign of Ferdinand and Isabella, the Catholic* (1838) and Irving's *A Chronicle of the Con-*

quest of Granada (1829). For a contemporary history of that period, used in manuscript by Irving, the interested reader should consult Andres Bernaldes, *Memorias del reinado de los reyes catolicos*, ed. Manuel Gomez-Moreno and Juan de M. Carriazo (Madrid, 1962). For a more recent study of these monarchs, see Jean Hippolyte Mariéjol's *The Spain of Ferdinand and Isabella*, trans. and ed. Benjamin Keen (New Brunswick, N.J., 1961) and J. H. Elliott, *Imperial Spain, 1469–1716* (London, 1963).

4.39   caravel] From the Spanish "carabela," the term generally designates a Spanish or Portuguese sailing vessel of medium tonnage particularly used in trading. Columbus's *Nina, Pinta,* and *Santa Maria,* for example, were lateen-rigged caravels built for Flemish and Mediterranean trade. See E. Keble Chatterton's "Caracks and Caravels," in *The Ship Under Sail: The Splendour of the Sailing Ship Through the Ages* (Philadelphia: n.d.), p. 65. See appendix No. 16, "Of the Ships of Columbus."

5.24–25 Navarrete] *Colección de los viages y descubrimientos, que hicieron por mar los españoles desde fines de siglo XV, con varios documentos inéditos concernientes a la historia de la marina castellana y de los establecimientos españoles en indias,* ed. Martin Fernandez de Navarrete, 3 vols. (Madrid, 1825–1829).

5.27   Oviedo's General History, which only exists in manuscript] It has since been published, for example, in the Biblioteca de Autores Españoles series. See Gonzalo Fernandez de Oviedo, *Historia general y natural de las indias,* ed. Juan Perez de Tudela Bueso, 5 vols. (Madrid, 1959).

5.30–31 law case between Don Diego Columbus and the crown] In 1508 Don Diego, the son of Columbus, instituted a suit to recover the titles conferred by the crown on his father and his heirs. Irving summarizes the suit in appendix no. 2, "Notice of the Descendants of Columbus."

5.32   Archives of the Indias] The Archivo General de Indias at Seville. Readers interested in the Spanish materials from which Irving composed his *Companions of Columbus* should consult William R. Shepherd's *Guide to Materials for the History of the United States in Spanish Archives* (Washington, D.C., 1907), James Alexander Robertson's *List of Documents in Spanish Archives Relating to the History of the United States* (Washington, D.C., 1910), the sources Irving acknowledges here in the introduction, and the collections of books and manuscripts in the Archivo General de Indias at Seville; and the Archivo Historico Nacional, Biblioteca de Departamento de Fomento, Biblioteca-Museo de Ultramar, Biblioteca Nacional, Biblioteca Real

(Biblioteca de Palacio), Depósito Hidrográfico, and the Real Academia de la Historia, all in Madrid.

5.35 Herrera] Antonio de Herrera y Tordesillas, *Historia General de los Hechos de los Castellanos, en las Islas, y Tierra-Firme de el Mar Oceano*, 10 vols. (Asuncion de Paraguay, n.d.).

5.35 Las Casas] Fray Bartolomé de las Casas, *Historia de las Indias*, ed. Agustin Millares Carlo, 3 vols. (Mexico-Buenos Aires, 1951).

5.35 Gomara] Francisco Lopez de Gomara, *La historia general de las Indias*, 2 vols. (Anvers, 1554).

5.36 Peter Martyr] Pedro Mártir de Anglería, *Décadas del Nuevo Mundo* (Buenos Aires, 1944). *De orbe Novo Petri Martyris* was first published in Latin; Irving used the Lok translation. Joseph H. Sinclair's bibliography of published editions of *De Orbe Novo* lists English translations by Lok as appearing in 1597, 1620, 1626, and 1812. The library of Obadiah Rich, however, contained none of these translations. "Manuscripts and Printed Books in the Possession of Obadiah Rich, Esq.," published by the House of Representatives (document 37, dated December 27, 1827, p. 10) does list, however, this entry: "Martyr, Decades of the New World, translated by Eden and Lok, London, 1555." This is doubtless the edition Irving used. Its full entry should read: Mártir de Anglería (Pedro), *The Decades of the New World or West India, conteyning the nauigations and conquests of the Spanyards, with the particular description of the questions of the spanyards, with the particular description of the most ryche and large landes and islands lately found in the West Ocean perteyning to the inheritance of the Kings of Spayne. In the which the diligent reader may not only consyder what commodities may hereby chaunce to the hole Christian world in tyme to come, but also learn many secreates touchynge the lande, the sea, and the starres, very necessarie to knowe to all such as shal attempt any nauigations, or otherwise have delite to behold the strange and wonderffull woorkes of God and Nature. Written in the latine tounge by Peter Martyr of Angleria, and translated into Englysche by Richarde Eden, Londini in aedibus Guilhelmi Powell anno 1555.* See Sinclair's "Bibliografía de Pedro Martir" in the *Boletin de la Academia Nacional de Historia, Sociedad Ecuatoriana de Estudios Americanos* 10, nos. 27–29 (1930).

5.41 Don Manuel Josef Quintana] Spanish diplomat and man of letters, Quintana was born in Madrid on April 11, 1772, and died there on March 11, 1857. His *Vidas de españoles célebres* was a three-volume study of the biographies of famous Spaniards. The first volume, which appeared in 1807, contained the lives of El Cid, Guzmán el Bueno, Roger de Lauria, El príncipe de Viana, and of Gonzalve de Cordoue.

Volume 2, which appeared in 1830, contained the lives of Vasco Nuñez de Balboa and Francisco Pizarro. The third volume of lives, published in 1833, recounted the lives of Fray Bartolomé de las Casas and Don Alvaro de Luna. Quintana's sources were generally those which Irving used: Martyr, Navarrete, Gomara, Herrera, Las Casas, and Oviedo. Quintana does cite some sources Irving appears not to have used: Juan Cristobal Calvet de Stella's *De rebus indicis*, Fray Pedro Simon's *Noticias historiales de las conquistas de Tierra-Firme*, and various other unpublished relations of Pedrarias and the death of Vasco Nuñez. A translation of the second volume of the *Vidas*, by Margaret Hodson, appeared in Edinburgh and London in 1832 under the title *Lives of Vasco Nuñez de Balboa, and Francisco Pizarro*. For an account of Quintana's contribution to Spanish letters, see E. M. Piñyro's *M. J. Quintana, ensayo critico y biográfico* (Paris-Madrid, 1892) and *Obras inéditas de Quintana, precedidas de una biografía por su subrino M. J. Quintana y de un juicio critico por don Manuel Cañete* (Madrid, 1872).

7.9 character and exploits of Alonzo de Ojeda] Ojeda is discussed in Irving's life of Columbus: book 6, chapters 2, 7, 12; book 8, chapters 3–4, 6–7; and book 12, chapters 5–6.

7.13 Cuenca in New Castile] A province of central Spain occupying the eastern part of the ancient kingdom of New Castile.

7.21 School of Arms] For a discussion of the military training and weaponry of the period of the Spanish conquests, see Albert María Salas, *Las armas de la conquista* (Buenos Aires, 1950).

8.16 cousin german] A first cousin.

8.17–18 first inquisitors of Spain] A royal Spanish Inquisition was created in 1480 by Ferdinand and Isabella. Organized of local tribunals with a supreme council at Madrid (the *Suprema*), the Spanish Holy Office offered Mohammedans and Jews in Spain the choice of conversion or exile. Under the Grand Inquisitor General Jiminez de Cisneros, even the descendants of the *conversos* were persecuted, not to speak of mystics, Albigensians, Illuminati, and infidels. See H. C. Lea, *History of the Inquisition of Spain*, 5 vols. (London, 1905–1908), Luis Fernández de Retana's *Cisneros y su siglo*, 2 vols. (Madrid, 1929–1930), Zacarios García Villada's *Cisneros, según sus íntimos* (Madrid, 1920), and José Barcía Mercadel's *Cisneros (1436–1517)* (Madrid, 1941).

8.20 Fonseca] For an account of his life, see Irving's appendix no. 34 and Mariano Alcocer y Martínez's *Juan Rodríguez de Fonseca* (Valladolid, 1926).

8.26 small Flemish painting]   See book 8, chapter 3 of Irving's life of Columbus.

8.39 terrestrial paradise]   The Garden of Eden, for which the Spanish mariners were on the lookout. For a discussion of the opinions of the learned theorists, see "On the situation of the terrestrial paradise," appendix no. 35, of Irving's life of Columbus.

9.14 territories appertaining to Portugal]   Portugal dominated maritime explorations in the early fifteenth century. Under the leadership of Prince Henry, Portuguese explorers coasted the Atlantic shore of Africa in search of India, gold, ivory, and spices. With the death of Henry, however, Spain became the Iberian maritime leader. See C. Raymond Beazley's "Prince Henry of Portugal and His Political, Commercial, and Colonizing Work," *American Historical Review* 17 (1911–1912), 252–67, and Edgar Presage's *The Portuguese Pioneers* (London, 1933).

9.26 the stipulated privileges of the admiral.]   Columbus's treaty with the crown is conveniently summarized in Mario Góngora's *El estado en el derecho indiano, época de fundácion (1492–1570)* (Santiago de Chile, 1951), pp. 43–44.

10.8 Juan de la Cosa]   For further information on the life of this able seaman, see Segundo de Ispizúa's "Juan de la Cosa," *Cultura hispanoamérica* 8, no. 62 (1918), Enrique de Leguina y Vidal's *Hijos ilustres de Santander: Juan de la Cosa* (Madrid, 1877), and Antonio Ballesteros y Beretta's *La Marina Cantabra y Juan de la Cosa* (Santander, 1954).

10.9 Biscayan]   A native of Biscay, a Basque maritime province of northern Spain.

10.17–18 Amerigo Vespucci]   Vespucci (1451–1512), a free-lance Spanish merchant and adventurer, allegedly undertook an expedition to the New World in May, 1497, after the king had withdrawn the exclusive rights of Columbus to New World exploration. On this voyage he was claimed to have discovered the New World, eight days before John Cabot reached the mainland of America; for this achievement the country was named after him. Vespucci's voyage with Ojeda began on May 16, 1499; they returned to Spain on September 8, 1500. After service under the crown in Portugal, Vespucci was appointed *piloto mayor* of Spain in 1508, an office he held until his death. See appendix no. 10, "Amerigo Vespucci."

10.21 His importance]   The attitude of most historians is that Vespucci's claim to have discovered America is invalid. Clements Markham, who edited Vespucci's letters, observes: "The evidence against Vespucci is cumulative and quite conclusive. His first voyage is a fabrication. He cannot be acquitted of the intention of appropriating for himself the glory of having first discovered the mainland. The impartial and upright Las Casas, after carefully weighing the evidence, found him guilty. This verdict has been, and will continue to be, confirmed by posterity." See *The Letters of Amerigo Vespucci and Other Documents Illustrative of His Career*, trans. and ed. Clements R. Markham (London, 1894), p. xxxix; Roberto Levillier's *América la bien llamada*, 2 vols. (Buenos Aires, 1948); and Germán Arciniegas's *Amerigo and the New World: The Life and Times of Amerigo Vespucci*, trans. Harriet de Onís (New York, 1955).

10.29 the Canaries] The Canary Islands, a Spanish archipelago in the Atlantic, sixty miles west of Africa, purchased by Ferdinand and Isabella in 1476, formed the staging area for Spanish vessels bound on New World voyages. Gomara is one of the seven major islands which make up the Canaries.

11.3 Surinam] A country east of Venezuela, formerly Dutch Guiana.

11.6 Oronoko] A river in northern South America, approximately 1,500 miles long, which empties into the Gulf of Paria; so called from the Spanish misrendering of the Carib name for the river—Ibirinoco. Columbus, who discovered the river, told Queen Isabella that the mouth of the river was the gateway to the terrestrial paradise, and for many years thereafter it drew Spanish explorers like Diego de Ordaz in search of the valley of El Dorado.

11.9 Trinidad] One of the largest of the British West Indian islands (discovered by Columbus in 1496), Trinidad is six miles off the coast of Venezuela, in the Gulf of Paria. See F. Eversley, *The Trinidad Reviewer* (London, 1900).

12.19 Boca del Drago] Translated Dragon's Mouth, this is the strait between the isthmus of Paria and Trinidad.

12.22 Curiana] A shoreline province on the Gulf of Pearls lying between the isthmus of Paria on the east and Cabo Codera on the west.

12.23 Margarita] An island in the Caribbean Sea twelve miles north of the peninsula of Araya, Margarita (Spanish for "pearl") was discovered by Columbus in 1498 and named for the royal princess.

12.26 Maracapana] A province due east of Cumana, near modern Barcelona, Venezuela.

12.31 cassava bread] Derived from bitter and sweet yucca (manioc); the roots were grated or boiled and baked into flat cakes. Since cassava bread kept from spoilage almost indefinitely, it was highly valued by the mariners and even became an item of tribute from the natives in lieu of gold.

13.2   cannibals]   The "Indians" whom Columbus and his fellow mariners first encountered were a homogeneous culture of natives occupying the Greater Antilles (Cuba, Haiti, Puerto Rico, and Jamaica) and the Bahama Islands. Anthropologically, they were northern Arawaks, separated from the Arawaks of South America by the Caribs of the Lesser Antilles, who followed them northward probably only a few generations before the Spanish discoveries. The Panamanian natives were of the Chibchan race and culture. A major distinction between these groups was their political organization (the Arawaks and Chibchans had a class-structured society based on heredity), but the Spaniards called all hostile natives Caribs, especially if they practiced cannibalism and used poisoned arrows.

14.11   Curazao]   Curaçao, an island in the Dutch West Indies, forty miles from the northern coast of Venezuela, discovered and occupied by Ojeda in 1499 and abandoned by the Spanish in 1527. The history of this island is discussed in DeVeer's *La Colonie de Curaçao* (Le Pays Bas, 1898).

14.13   Penthesilea]   In classical mythology, a celebrated queen of the Amazons, daughter of Ares. She came to the aid of Priam in the last year of the Trojan War and was slain by Achilles after she had displayed great acts of valor.

14.13   Antæus]   In classical mythology, a giant, the son of Poseidon and Ge. He was invincible as long as he remained in contact with his mother, Earth (Ge). But Hercules discovered the source of his strength, lifted him from the earth, and crushed him in the air.

15.39–40   Maracaibo]   A seaport on the Gulf of Venezuela.

17.5   Cape Maracaibo]   The modern Peninsula de la Guajira.

17.7   Cape de la Vela]   A cape on the northernmost peninsula of modern Colombia, east of the Bahia de Portete.

17.8   the state of his vessels]   One of the formidable problems of the Spanish mariners was the shipworm, a boring bivalve mollusk of the family *Teredidae*, which attached itself to the hulls of ships in New World waters and literally chewed them to pieces. See Paul Bartsch's *A Monograph of the American Shipworms* (Washington, 1922), pp. 1–51.

17.11   Hispaniola]   Española ("the Spanish Island"), also called St. Domingo, is the largest of the Antilles or Caribbean islands, now composed of the Dominican Republic and Haiti. The earliest Spanish settlement in the New World, Hispaniola was quickly depleted of its gold and native population and was abandoned except as the base of operations for West Indian and South American voyages of exploration.

17.17   dye wood]   Brazilwood. Another item of tribute exacted from the natives in lieu of gold, brazilwood was shipped to Spain as a source of colonial revenue.

17.19   Yaquimo]   A port in Southern Hispaniola in the old province of Bainoa, near modern Jacmel.

17.22   the quondam rebel]   See Irving's life of Columbus, book 11, chapter 4.

17.32   John Cabot]   A Venetian sailor (1450–1498), but born in Genoa as Giovanni Caboto, Cabot set sail from Bristol on May 2, 1497, aboard the *Mathew* with eighteen men. After fifty-two days at sea, Cabot discovered North America on June 24, along the coast of Cape Breton Island. Cabot made a second voyage under the authority of Henry VII in May, 1498, in search of Cipangu (Japan) and the spice lands of Asia but discovered, instead, the coasts of Nova Scotia and New England. He died shortly after his return to England.

19.1   Niño]   For a sketch of the life of Pedro Alonzo Niño, see the entry in *Diccionario de Historia España* (Madrid, 1952), II, 649.

19.7   Palos]   The base of New World explorations was principally four Spanish ports on the Atlantic coast in Andalusia: Port St. Mary (Puerto de Santa María), on the Bay of Cadiz; Sanlúcar de Barrameda, on the mouth of the Guadalquivir; the convergence of the Tinto and Odiel rivers at the towns of Palos, Moguer, and Huelva; and the harbor of Lepe.

21.13   Cauchieto]   Caquetío, a province of aboriginal Venezuela to the east of Lago de Maracaibo and south of the Peninsula de Paraguana.

21.14   guanin]   *Guañín,* an alloy of gold and copper much prized by the Arawaks, according to Las Casas, for its odor. See his *Historia de las Indias,* vol. 1, chap. 67.

21.28   injured in boring]   King Ferdinand complains in the letter of May 3, 1509, to Nicolas de Ovando, governor of Hispaniola, that the shipment of pearls is damaged from clumsy boring. See *Colección de documentos inéditos* (Madrid, 1874), XXXI, 428.

21.31   Bayonne in Gallicia]   A small Atlantic seaport town in the province of Coruna in Galicia just north of the Portuguese border at approximately 42° of latitude and 11° of longitude.

22.18   his family]   For a discussion of the remarkable Pinzon family, see appendix no. 11, José Maria Aensio's *Martín Alonso Pinzón, estudio historica* (Madrid, 1892), and Cesáro Fernández Duro's *Pinzón en el descubrimiento de las Indias* (Madrid, 1892).

23.15   Cape de Verde Islands]   A crescent-shaped archipelago belonging to Portugal, situated off the West African coast some 280 miles west by southwest from Senegal.

23.33–34 Cape St. Augustine] Formerly known as Santa Maria de la Consolacion, this cape stands on the remote eastern tip of Brazil, near the mouth of the Pernambuco.

25.18 Amazon] The greatest of the river systems of South America, the Amazon was discovered in 1500 by Vicente Yañez Pinzon. Known among the Spanish as Rio Santa Maria de la Mar Dulce, Rio Grande, and El Ryo Marañon, the Amazon was first navigated from the Andes to the sea in 1541 by Francisco Orellana (ca. 1490–1546). Orellana named it Amazonas after a savage battle with the Tapuyans, a tribe famous among the Indians for its women warriors. See "The Voyage of Francisco de Orellana down the River of the Amazons," translated by C. R. Markham from Antonio de Herrera's *Historia general de las Indias occidentales*, Hakluyt Society Publications, vol. 24 (1899).

25.32 the Bahamas] A British crown colony in the West Indies, the Bahamas were discovered by Columbus on October 12, 1492 (O. S.) when he landed at Guanahani, which he renamed San Salvador (Watling Island). See J. M. Wright, *History of the Bahama Islands*, ed. G. B. Shattuck (New York, 1905), and A. Dean Peggs, *A Short History of the Bahamas* (Nassau, 1952).

27.13 Juan Diaz de Solis] For a sketch of the life of this mariner, (?–1516), see José Toribio Medina, *Juan Díaz de Solís* (Santiago de Chile, 1897).

27.14 Lebrija] A town in southern Spain in the province of Sevilla to the west of the Sierra de Gibalbín.

27.26–27 A Castile...Pinzon] Translation: "To Castile and Leon, Pinzon gave the New World."

28.18 notary] The *escribano* was authorized to take depositions, as a sworn official of the crown, and to authenticate the claims made therein. Many of the witnesses, for example, Francisco Pizarro, could neither read nor write; it was therefore in the crown's interest, in protecting its legal claims, to require the presence of a notary to record and authenticate the discoveries.

28.18 Triana] A suburb to the southwest of Seville, across the Guadalquiver River.

29.19 Francisco de Bobadilla] A protégé of the king, Bobadilla (?–1502) was designated examiner and governor of the Indies in 1499, replacing Columbus.

30.2 Alguazil Mayor] The chief constable or peace officer in the settlement.

31.24 maravedies] Former gold coins issued by the Moors in Spain.

32.24 Valfermoso] An obsolete Spanish compound of *valle* ("valley") and *hermoso* ("beautiful"): beautiful valley.

33.14   Bahio Honda]   A bay on the northernmost tip of Colombia on the Peninsula de la Guajira, to the east of the Cape de la Vela.

33.29   cacique]   The Arawak and Chibchan peoples were organized by hereditary classes under a ruler called a *cacique*.

33.32   lombards]   From the obsolete Spanish *lombarda*, the term signifies a military engine used against the natives.

36.17–18   Aurea Chersonesus]   See above, note for 3.10.

36.30   the Adelantado]   El Adelantado ("the leader") was the name generally identifying Bartholomew Columbus, from the office conferred on him by his brother Columbus and confirmed by Ferdinand and Isabella.

37.11   Nestor]   A wise counsellor; from Greek legend, the wisest and oldest of the Greeks in Homer's Trojan War.

38.7   Moresco]   Moorish.

38.17   Governor Ovando]   Nicolas de Ovando (1460?–1518), of noble lineage, friend and protégé of the king, was appointed governor of the Indies in 1501 and relieved by Don Diego Columbus in 1509. For a full account of his life see Ursula Lamb's *Frey Nicolas de Ovando, gobernador de las Indias, 1501–1509* (Madrid, 1956).

38.25   New Andalusia]   The name given to the region of modern Colombia extending from the middle of the Gulf of Urabá eastward to the Cape de la Vela.

39.28   Bachelor]   Martin Fernandez de Enciso, entitled to be called El Bachiller by reason of his university studies, was author of *Suma de Geographia* (1519), a navigating manual and summary of contemporary knowledge of geography.

39.29   castellanos]   The castellano, an ancient Spanish coin, was worth the fiftieth part of a gold mark.

40.5   Alcalde Mayor]   From the Arabic *al-quadi*: *Cadi*, "judge," this Spanish title signified the mayor or chief justice of the peace of a town or settlement.

40.28   arbitrament]   Arbitration.

40.33   pistole]   A former gold coin of Spain equal to two escudos.

41.18   Juan de Esquibel]   Accompanying Columbus on his second voyage, Esquibel settled in Hispaniola and distinguished himself as a conquistador of Hispaniola in the time of Ovando and of Jamaica under Don Diego Columbus.

41.19   Higuey]   Aboriginal Hispaniola was divided into five provinces. Higuey was one of the ten subdivisions of Caizcimu, the southeastern province.

43.7   Francisco Pizarro]   Pizarro (ca. 1471–1541) sailed with Ojeda from Hispaniola to Urabá, journeyed to the Pacific with Balboa's party, discovered Peru, and explored the kingdoms of the sun. He was assassinated by Spanish rivals in Lima in 1541.

43.8   Cortez]   Hernán (Hernando) Cortés (1485–1547), was born in Medellín in Extramadura, sailed to Hispaniola in 1504, explored Cuba with Velasquez in 1511, landed in Yucatan in 1519, and defeated Montezuma and the Aztecs in 1521. See F. A. MacNutt's *Hernando Cortés and the Conquest of Mexico, 1485–1547* (London, 1909).

43.12   Carthagena]   The seaport capital of Bolivar, Colombia, in South America.

43.27   Gulf of Uraba]   The Gulf of Darien on the northwestern Atlantic coast of Colombia, where the Rio Atrato enters the Bahia Colombia.

43.29   Estremadura]   A region composed of central and western Portugal and of western Spain. From *extrema ora*, or Land's End, this region designated the far western lands bordering on the Atlantic.

44.9   a certain formula]   For a discussion of the papal bulls authorizing the Christianization of the New World, see Luis Weckmann's *Las bulas alejandrinas de 1493 y la teoría política del papado medieval: Estudio sobre la supremacía papal sobre islas, 1091–1493* (Mexico City, 1949) and F. Mateos, "Bulas portugesas y españolas sobre descubrimientos geográficas," *Missionalia hispánica* 19 (1962), 5–35, 129–168. For a discussion of the techniques by which the missionaries implemented the papal bulls, see Johann Specker's *Die Missionsmethode in Spanisch-Amerika im 16. Jahrhundert, mit besonderer Berücksichtigung der Konzilien und Synoden* (Schöneck, 1953). For a discussion of what one historian has called "the mystical, crusading, apocalyptical, and messianic mentality" of early Spanish explorations, see John L. Phelan's *The Millennial Kingdom of the Franciscans in the New World* (Berkeley, 1956).

45.16   "Santiago!"]   As a war cry, "Santiago!" was an invocation to the patron saint of the Spanish, St. James, who was believed to have Christianized Spain in New Testament times.

48.8   one so small of frame]   The figure of Napoleon doubtless accounts for the admiration of many nineteenth-century writers for the exploits of short men like Nicuesa and Ojeda. Emily Foster described Irving in her journal as "neither tall nor slight"; he was, in fact, five feet seven inches tall.

50.2   San Sebastian]   This village was located on the eastern coast of the Gulf of Urabá, near Nicocli, on the Punta Urabá.

51.9   poisoned weapons]   One of the distinguishing features of the Carib Indians was their use of poisoned arrows. The poison was extracted from the sap of the manchineel tree; the points were made of fishbone, tortoise shell, or fire-hardened wood. See *Handbook of South*

American Indians, ed. Julian H. Steward (Washington, 1948), IV, 559.

53.36 Cape Tiburon] An island cape at the western extremity of Hispaniola at the entrance of the Canal of Gonave, near the island and bay of Caimitos in the Republic of Haiti.

54.5 Charlevoix] Pierre François Xavier de Charlevoix (1682–1761), a French Jesuit, is the author of a history of San Domingo.

56.10 trover and conversion] Trover is an action for the recovery of the value of personal property wrongly converted by another to his own use; conversion is the unauthorized assumption and exercise of rights over personal property which belongs to another.

57.22 Hayti] Haiti, a Caribbean republic occupying the western third of the island of Hispaniola, the other territory being occupied by the Dominican Republic. Haiti was so called from the Arawak name Quizquella (Quisqueya), "a thing than which there is nothing greater" or "mainland," a reference to the size of the island.

60.8 areytos] Popular songs of the ancient Indians of the Caribbean, often accompanied by dancing.

63.3 Coanabo] One of the principal caciques, or chiefs, of Hispaniola. His character and conduct, and particularly his massacre of Spaniards and his capture by Ojeda, are recounted in Irving's life of Columbus.

64.25 coup-de-main] Literally, in French, a blow from the hand; any sudden attack.

66.9 Francisco Roldan] For a discussion of the conspiracy and rebellion of Roldan, see Irving's life of Columbus, book 11, chapters 4–6; book 12, chapters 1–6.

69.23 Chagres] The Rio Chagres flows into the Atlantic in the area of the Canal Zone.

72.19 Puerto Bello] A port on the Caribbean coast of Panama just to the east of Nombre de Dios.

74.18–19 Vasco Nuñez de Balboa] For a discussion of the life of Balboa, see Angel de Altolaguirre y Duvale's *Vasco Nuñez de Balboa* (Madrid, 1914); Octavio Mendez Pereira's *Balboa*, ed. Everett W. Hesse (New York, 1944); and Kathleen Romoli's *Balboa of Darien: Discoverer of the Pacific* (New York, 1953).

74.29–30 Salvatierra] One of the fifteen towns of ancient Hispaniola, Salvatierra de la Sabana was situated in the native province of Guacayarima, in the present Département du Sud of Haiti.

76.11 maize] For a discussion of maize, which became the staple food for the Spaniards after this episode, see Oviedo's *Sumario*, chapter 4, and Carl O. Sauer's *The Early Spanish Main*, pp. 241, 244. A white and a red wine were made on the South American continent from maize grain, yucca, palm fruit, pineapples, and other fruits. But such alco-

holic drinks were not known on many of the Caribbean islands to the
north.

77.2   locum tenens]   A temporary substitute.

77.3   letter patent]   In law, a written or printed document issued by a
sovereign power, conferring upon a patentee some right, such as the
right of command over a district.

78.14   taking gold in nets]   For the report of this unusual method of
recovering gold, see Angel de Altolaguirre's *Vasco Nuñez de Balboa*
(Madrid, 1914), pp. 64–66, documents 30–31. The Bachelor Enciso's
account, in the Barlow translation of ca. 1541, illuminates Irving's
sources: "In cenw thei make moche salt. The people be strong and
warly, and use bowes and arowes w^t poison, and go all nakyd bothe
men and women, and when eny of their principalles die, wch be called
casyques, thei open his bodye and take out his bowelles and wasshe
him with certeine things and oynt him, and upon that thei put cotton
dyed of divers colours wch clyngeth to his bodie, and so covered thei
put him in a hamaca wch is ther bedde, and that thei hange w^{t}in the
house wher thei make their fyre and so the dead doeie drieth. In this
lond on cenw is moche gold among the indies, and thei saie it is
fett from a certein mountayne from whens the river of cenw cometh
from certein places that thei call murri-cubra and cuda, and when
it rayne thei traverse the river w^t nettes, and when the water encreseth
it bryngeth downe the golde from the mountaynes in graynes some as
bigge as an egge and some more and some lesse, and from thens thei
bryng it to cenw and then thei work it" (Martin Fernandez de Enciso,
El Bachiller, *Suma de Geographia* [1519], translated by Roger Barlow
as *A Brief Summe of Geographie*, ed. E. G. R. Taylor [London, 1932],
p. 174.

79.35–41   Respondieron . . . ostros]   The passage may be translated as:
"He replied to me: In what I said that there was only one God, that
he governed heaven and earth, and that he was Lord of all, it appeared
well to them and that it ought to be so; but as to my statement that
the Pope was lord of all the universe in lieu of God, and that he had
conferred that land upon the King of Castile, they said that the Pope
must have been drunk when he did so, for he gave what was not his
own, and that the king who asked for and accepted such a gift must
be some idiot, since he asked for the property of others and came there
to take it" (Martin Fernandez de Enciso, *Suma de Geographia* [Seville,
1519]. The full title is *Suma de geographia que trata de todas las parti-
das & trata largamé del arte del marear: juntaméte con la espera en
romáce: con el regimiéto del sol & del norte: nueuamente hecha* (Seville: Jacobo Cróberger, 1519).

81.37–38   Santa Maria de la Antigua del Darien]   Located inland from the Gulf of Uraba just north of the Atrato River, Santa Maria de la Antigua del Darien was a staging area for Spanish explorations on the Tierra Firme to the south and west.

83.8   Valdivia]   Pedro de Valdivia was born in Villanueva de la Serena (Extramadura) in 1497, and died in Tucapel (Chile) in 1554.

83.8   regidor]   In Spain, a magistrate, alderman, director, prefect, or governor.

85.24   the stork]   In the classical bestiaries storks were notorious for their rapacity. Chaucer follows Bartholomaeus's *De Proprietatibus Rerum* (xii, 8) and Aelian's *De Natura Animalium* (viii, 20) in regarding the stork as "the wrekere of avouterye" (*The Parlement of Foulys*, l. 361).

87.30   Zamudio]   When the Spaniards found themselves without a commander, they formed, as the law required, a council to elect alcaldes, regidors, and other officials. In the colony at La Antigua, Vasco Nuñez de Balboa and Martín Zamudio were elected alcaldes, Juan de Valdivia was elected regidor, and Bartolomé Hurtado was made alguazil mayor.

87.37   taled out]   counted out.

91.28   Valdivia]   For the life of Pedro de Valdivia, son of Pedro Oncas de Melo and Doña Isabel Gutíerrez de Valdivia, see *Proceso de Valdivia*, published for Barros Arana (Santiago de Chile, 1874), and Rosa Arciniega, *Don Pedro de Valdivia* (Santiago, 1943).

92.10   Coyba]   While Coiba would appear to have been a province in central Panama, due south of Veragua, Charles L. G. Anderson has argued that there was no such district: "When the Old Admiral [Columbus, in November, 1502] arrived at Puerto Bello and Nombre de Dios, he inquired of the natives whence came their gold, and they replied *coiba*, meaning far land, or far road. Columbus believed the word was the name of a district, which came to be called 'Coyba la Rica'–'the Rich Coiba'" (*Life and Letters of Vasco Nuñez de Balboa* [New York, 1941], p. 312). Careta was both the name of the region and the name of its cacique. The region lay some eighty to a hundred miles west of the Gulf of Uraba, just to the west of Darien.

93.16   Ponca]   For the character of Ponca, see Anderson's *Life and Letters of Vasco Nuñez de Balboa* (New York, 1941), pp. 159–60.

95.2   Comagre]   The province of the cacique Comagre lay to the north of Careta at approximately 78° of longitude by 9° of latitude. Martyr, following the account of Colmenares, is the source of the report of the plain of twelve leagues. Sauer observes that "The province of Comagre was mainly in the upper part of the Bayano drainage, but also extended north across the low coastal range to the Caribbean . . ." (*The Early Spanish Main* [Berkeley, 1966], p. 221).

95.23–24 the bodies of his ancestors and relatives] Oviedo is the most trustworthy source of these data on the burial customs of the Panamanian Indians. Archaeologist Samuel K. Lothrop has pointed out that "burial was a rite reserved for the nobility as well as for such wives, retainers, and captives as were selected to accompany their lords to another world. The living destined for the grave either took poison voluntarily, were buried alive while stupefied by intoxication, or were killed in some unspecified manner. Bodies of the common people were abandoned to the beasts and birds." Lothrop also observes that among some ruling families it was the custom to dessicate and preserve the bodies of the chiefs, usually by surrounding them with fires until the bodies dried out. The dessicated bodies were either seated in order around the walls of a special room or house or were placed in hammocks. See Lothrop's "The Archaeology of Panama," in *Handbook of South American Indians*, ed. Julian H. Steward (Washington, D.C., 1948), IV, 145–46.

96.24 Tubanamà] The province of Tubanamà lay further to the west of Comagre, between Pocorosa to the east and the Gulf of San Blas on the west.

98.2 Dobayba] The search for the fabulous gold of the cacique Dabeiba caused Balboa to turn back from the isthmus of Panama to the South American continent. Dabeiba lay some seventy miles south of the Gulf of Uraba on the Rio Sucio, which emptied into the Atrato.

99.8–9 Rio Grande de San Juan] So named because it was discovered by Balboa on St. John's Day, June 24, 1512, this river system—the Rio Atrato in modern geography—had no less than six or seven, perhaps as many as ten, mouths emptying into the Gulf of Uraba.

100.10 Rio Negro] One of the tributaries of the Rio Atrato, seventy miles south of the Gulf of Uraba, at the Isla de Canela.

100.14 Abibeyba] The province of Abibeiba was some sixty miles from the Rio Negro and the Isla de Canela, south of the Gulf of Uraba. For a discussion of the barbacoas or tree houses which sometimes accommodated more than 200 persons, see Gregorio Hernandez de Alba's "The Cultures of Northwest South America: Sub-Andean Tribes of the Cauca Valley," in *Handbook of South American Indians*, ed. Steward, IV, 315.

101.13 Bartolome Hurtado] Alguazil mayor of Antigua under Balboa.

102.15 Fulvia] For the story of this Indian beauty, see Charles L. G.

Anderson's *Life and Letters of Vasco Nuñez de Balboa* (New York, 1941), pp. 94–95.

104.30 Alonzo Perez de la Rua] For an account of the Hurtado–Perez de la Rua affair, see Antonio de Herrera's *Historia General*, vol. 2, bk. 9, chap. 13.

107.17 arquebusses] An early type of portable gun, of varying sizes, fielded on a tripod, carriage, trestle, or forked rest; so named from the German "hook-gun," from the hook, cast along with it, by which it was sometimes attached to the carriage.

108.4 pirogues] A pirogue or piragua (Carib for "dug-out") is a long narrow canoe hollowed out from the trunk of a single tree, occasionally rigged with sails.

108.38 pechry] A fishing ground or sea (French: pêcherie, from *pêcher*, "to fish")

110.3 the first negroes ever found in the new world] It was Martyr's assumption that these strange Negroes to the south were African slaves who had been shipwrecked in the islands. Sauer, however, argues that they might have come across the Pacific: "The report by the officials of the Santa Maria noted black men of large stature, long beards, and frizzy hair, who fought with clubs and were cannibals, all of which are Melanesian traits. This is the earliest intimation that there may have been landings in the New World from distant parts of the South Seas by men who were accustomed to venture into the open ocean" (*The Early Spanish Main* [Berkeley, 1966], p. 269).

111.32–33 *Te Deum laudamus*] The opening words ("Thee, God, we praise") of an ancient Latin hymn of praise in the form of a psalm, sung as a thanksgiving on special occasions, as after a victory or a deliverance, as well as at Matins and Morning Prayer.

112.29–30 the 26th of September, 1513] The date is in error; Oviedo apparently erred in transcribing Balboa's journal. Modern historians have revised it to September 27. Cf. Sauer, *The Early Spanish Main*, p. 232.

114.37 Saint Michael] Bahia San Miguel is located near La Palma, Panama, on the Pacific.

116.14 the stormy season] The season of hurricanes (from the Arawak word *huracan*) in the West Indies lasts from June to October; the number varies between two and twenty-one in an apparently cyclical pattern.

117.21 the rapid rising of the water] The scientific study of tides, unknown in the sixteenth century, was initiated in 1687 when Newton's *Principia* applied the general theory of gravitation to ocean movements.

Spanish mariners of the sixteenth century were able to deduce, however, from the height of the inrolling tides that the Southern Sea was indeed a major ocean and not a lake or minor sea. On the eastern coast of the Isthmus of Panama the force of the Atlantic tides was broken by the island system of the Caribbean. On the western coast, however, the high inrolling Pacific tides implied an open sea matching the Atlantic in size.

119.6 marks of gold] A former money of account in Europe, equal to eight ounces.

120.26 Isla Rica] An island in the Archipelago de las Perlas, south of the Canal Zone in the Pacific.

122.3 Crœsus] King of Lydia in the sixth century B.C.; proverbial for his fabulous wealth.

127.2 Pedrarias Davila] For the career of this governor, see Pablo Alvarez Rubiano's *Pedrarias Dávila* (Madrid, 1944).

129.2 Castilla del Oro] The province of Darien in Panama.

129.20 argonauts] the legendary heroes of Greece who sailed with Jason in the *Argo* in quest of the Golden Fleece; hence, any nautical explorer, particularly in search of gold.

130.1 Licentiate] One authorized, through a license formally attesting his professional competence, to perform some function, in this case to perform judicial duties.

130.5 the late Queen Isabella] The queen had died in 1504.

130.37 Æsopus] A myth developed in the lifetime of Æsopus representing him as an ugly hunchback and buffoon. In the Middle Ages the legends of Æsopus were woven by Maximus Planudes into a kind of romance representing Æsopus as a monster of greed and physical deformity.

134.28 university of Salamanca] The University of Salamanca grew up around the estate of the monastic order attached to the cathedral in the fifteenth century. Many important documents relative to New World voyages are preserved there, for example, a contemporary map of the region by Juan de la Cosa (a photographic copy of it may be seen in Charles Gibson's *Spain in America* [New York, 1966], p. 80ff.). An interesting sidelight on the university appears in James Boswell's *Life of Samuel Johnson*: "He this evening again recommended to me to perambulate Spain. I said it would amuse him to get a letter from me dated at Salamancha. JOHNSON: 'I love the University of Salamancha; for when the Spaniards were in doubt as to the lawfulness of their conquering America, the University of Salamancha gave it as their opinion that it was not lawful.' He spoke this with great emotion, and with that generous warmth which dictated the lines in his *London*, against Spanish encroachment." For an early history of the University, see Pedro Chacon's *Breve Relaccion*.

136.21   Corobari]   A river along the delta between Darien and Abraime, near the Gulf of Uraba.

137.21   Diego Velasquez]   Born at Cuellar in Segovia, Velasquez (1465–1524) sailed with Columbus in 1493, became Governor Ovando's lieutenant in Hispaniola, established a base at Cuba in 1511, and assumed the rank of Lieutenant Governor of Cuba. He died there in 1524. See I. A. Wright's *The Early History of Cuba, 1492–1586* (New York, 1916) and Carlos M. Trelles, *El adelantade Diego Velásquez* (Havana, 1934).

140.3   the ancient harpies]   In classical mythology, ravenous, filthy creatures having the head of a woman and the body of a bird; by extension, any grasping, rapacious person, especially a scolding, bad-tempered woman.

146.31   Peru]   The name ("Piru" in some early Spanish manuscripts) given to that South American country in the sixteenth century. Of uncertain origin, it is said to have been derived by a misrendering of the Indian word "Pelu' 'or "Biru" (river).

149.14   Zenu]   The province of Sinu lay to the west of the Gulf of Uraba on the Rio Sunu.

149.37   the smelting-house]   For a discussion of the native smelting and metalwork, see Paul B. Bergsøe's *The Gilding Process and the Metallurgy of Copper and Lead among the Pre-Columbian Indians*, trans. F. C. Reynolds (Copenhagen, 1938) and *The Metallurgy and Technology of Gold and Platinum among the Pre-Columbian Indians*, trans. F. C. Reynolds (Copenhagen, 1937).

152.2   Balsas]   The native name was Chucunaque.

156.13–14   the Jeronimite Fathers]   A missionary order founded by St. Jerome (Eusebius Hieronymus, ca. 340–420 A.D.).

164.18   Maya]   The province of Maya is on the northern coast of modern Honduras, due south of Isla Guanaja.

165.24   Chatemal]   A province probably in the region of the Bahia Chetumal, separating Mexico from Honduras.

165.31   Ecija in Andalusia]   A city on the Rio Genil famed for its church architecture and scenic environs. See Andres Hovindo's *Historia de Ecija y sus santos* and M. Serrano's *Monumentos de los pueblos de la provincia Sevilla* (Seville, 1911).

166.29   but one hammock to sleep in]   Aside from its tempting uses, the hanging bed of the West Indies was the subject of a great deal of native superstition. The aborigines would not eat figs on a hammock

for fear that it would rot, nor would they eat any fish with teeth, for
fear that the hammock would soon wear through. See "Hammock or
Hamac," in Chambers's *Cyclopedia: Or an Universal Dictionary of
Arts and Sciences* (London, 1728), I, 204–5.

167.38   Francisco Hernandez de Cordova]   Born in 1475, Cordova accompanied Pedrarias to Castillo de Oro in 1514, took an expedition
into Nicaragua in 1524, and died there in 1526.

168.20   Cozumel]   An island off the eastern coast of Mexico just south
of the Yucatan channel.

168.26–27   Hernando Cortez]   The conqueror of Mexico, Cortez was
born in Estremadura in 1485, studied law at the University of Salamanca, undertook an expedition to Mexico, and defeated the forces
of the Aztec empire in 1521. See Salvador de Madariaga's *Hernán
Cortés: Conqueror of Mexico*, 2d ed. (Buenos Aires, 1955) and M.
Collis's *Cortés and Montezuma* (London, 1954).

173.20   Zebaco]   Isla Cebaco is due west of the Peninsula de Azuero off
the Pacific shore of Panama.

175.6   Boriquen]   San Juan (Bautista) de Puerto Rico was called Boriquen by the natives.

177.32   Philip I]   Philip (1478–1506) was king of Spain by marriage in
1496 to Joanna, the daughter of King Ferdinand and Isabella.

177.33   Charles V]   Charles V (1500–1558), the son of Philip I and
Joanna, acceded to joint rule with Joanna in 1518. He formally abdi-
cated his Spanish kingdoms in 1556 and retired to private life. See
W. Robertson's *History of the Emperor Charles V* (New York, 1829).

178.28   old soldier]   In 1509 Ponce de Leon was about forty-nine.

179.12–13   repartimiento]   By application to the corregidor, alcalde
mayor, or other political authority, a Spanish rancher could receive
an assignment of Indian laborers to work his *encomienda* for a designated period. The institution for the distribution or assignment of
these Indian workers was called the *repartimiento*. See F. A. Kirkpat-
rick's "Repartimiento-Encomienda," *Hispanic American Historical Review* 19 (1939), 372–79 and Silvio Zavala's *La encomienda indiana*
(Madrid, 1935) and *De encomiendas y propiedad territorial en algunas regiones de la América española* (Mexico, 1940). On the problem
of slavery see Jose Antonio Saco's *Historia de la esclavitud de la raza
africana en el nuevo mundo y en especial en los países Américo-
hispanos*, 2 vols. (Barcelona, 1879–1883).

186.20   a river of such wonderful virtue]   For a discussion of Ponce
de Leon's search, see Leonardo Olschki's "Ponce de Leon's Fountain
of Youth: History of a Geographic Myth," *Hispanic American Historical Review* 21 (1941), 361–85.

186.31 Bahama groupe] A chain of islands north of Cuba and Hispaniola. Bimini is due east of Miami Beach, Florida.

187.18 St. Germain] A port in the Mayaguez district of southwestern
Puerto Rico.

188.4 Guanahani, or St. Salvador] Sometimes called Watling's Island,
in the Bahamas chain.

188.8–9 Turk's Island] One of a number of small islands at the southeastern line of the Bahamas, due north of Hispaniola.

188.19 Palm Sunday] Ponce de Leon discovered Florida on March 27,
1513. Ferdinand V appointed him governor of "the Island of Florida"
in 1514. See F. A. Ober's *Juan Ponce de Leon* (New York, 1908).

189.1–2 Tortugas] Off the north coast of Haiti, Tortugas was inhabited by large tortoises (Spanish *tortugas*).

189.4 Lucayos] The Islas Lucayas are the Bahamas.

190.28–29 Carthagena] Cartagena, Colombia.

191.1 Guadaloupe] One of the southernmost leeward islands southwest of Puerto Rico and north of eastern Venezuela.

348.33 the Pinzon family] This illustrious family, which has continued
into the twentieth century at Huelva and Moguer, is distinguished by
such modern sons as Admiral Luis Hernández Pinzón and Captain
José Luis H. Pinzón. The latter called a conference in March, 1918, to
vindicate Martín Alonzo Pinzón's reputation from an unflattering
role in which he was represented in a film about Christopher Columbus. See José Luis Pinzón, *Conferencia ... sobre el tema "Martín
Alonzo Pinzón y su participación en el descubrimiento de América*
(Madrid, 1918).

349.9 calesero] The Spanish term for a driver of a calash, or light
two-horse carriage having four low wheels and an enclosed cab for
passengers.

349.11 bottinas] Bottines, leggings, buskins, or large boots partly
covering the leg; spatterdashes are long gaiters or chaps, which protect the trousers from mud while riding.

352.7 *cama de luxo*] The choicest bed or couch.

352.17 the convent La Rabida] For the story of this celebrated Fran-
ciscan convent, in relation to Columbus, see Evaristo de la Paliza y
José Pérez's *La Rábida y Cristóbal Colón* (Huelva, 1855), and P. José
Coll's *Colón y la Rábida*, 2d ed. (Madrid, 1892).

353.23 mysticks] Misticos, coasting vessels of the Mediterranean, having two sails.

356.29–30 Juan Perez de Marchena] For his role in the story, see
"La Rabida," in *Enciclopedia Universal Ilustrada*, vol. 49 (Barcelona,
1923), pp. 57–61.

359.9 galliard] Archaic, meaning lively or gay, from the spirited sixteenth-century dance for two, to a triple rhythm.

363.7 One of these pontiffs] Alexander VI acceded to the papal chair in 1492 and ruled until 1503. He was succeeded by Pius III (1503), Julius II (1503–1513), and Leo X (1513–1522).

TEXTUAL COMMENTARY

In establishing a text of *Companions of Columbus* and of the appendixes to *Columbus* which most reflects Irving's final intention, the editor has adopted W. W. Greg's theory of copy-text as the basis on which to formulate his rationale for editorial decisions affecting both accidentals and substantives. That theory is set forth in "The Rationale of Copy-Text," *Studies in Bibliography* 3 (1950–1951), 19–36, and is applied to the editions of nineteenth-century American authors by the *Statement of Editorial Principles and Procedures* prepared by the Center for Editions of American Authors, Modern Language Association of America (revised edition, 1972). The terminology used is Fredson Bowers's as set forth in his *Principles of Bibliographical Description* (Princeton, 1949). "Accidentals" is intended to mean those textual variants affecting form (e.g., spelling, punctuation, capitalization, hyphenization, etc.); "substantives" refers to those variants affecting meaning (e.g., word changes).

THE MANUSCRIPT

The manuscript of *Companions of Columbus* is contained in two bound volumes housed in the Clifton Waller Barrett collection of the University of Virginia Library. The manuscript numbers 498 leaves, divided by book and chapters, but lacking a title page and a table of contents (although "Irving's Companions of Columbus 2 vols" and "Companions of Columbus" are lightly penciled in, apparently in Irving's hand, on the first leaf of both volumes). (The second volume commences with the story of Vasco Nuñez de Balboa.)

The manuscript, written in Irving's hand, is incomplete, lacking title page, introduction, table of contents, a few sections (e.g., chapter 2 of Ojeda's third voyage), stray leaves, and breaking off in the midst of chapter 24 of Balboa's story, at 151.38. The final twelve chapters are missing. It is written in pen and pencil, in a variety of blue and black inks, some now faded to brown, with extensive corrections, insertions, deletions, and tracings over of words and phrases, indicating that the manuscript was composed over a long period of time in various physical circumstances. The manuscript leaves are written on one side only, as intended fair copy, but there are many canceled sentences and trial phrases on the versos. These, together with the frequent marginal corrections and interlineations, cut-and-paste additions, and repaginations, suggest the long process of Irving's revision and the roughness of the copy finally given to Murray's printer, C. Roworth, of Bell Yard, Temple Bar.

The manuscript paper, which varies in size from 7⅝₁₆ x 4½ inches to 7¹¹⁄₁₆ x 4¹¹⁄₁₆ inches, is of various shades of white and off-white fading into bluish tints, and of various grades, wove and laid, with and without chain and watermarks. From a variety of watermarks, the dating of the composition of the manuscript can be partly confirmed. These watermarks include the following: "1829," "–29," "G. WILMOT 1830," "M P," "RTA 18–," "–FELL," a crowned oval encircling a lion, erect, with a staff, "SMITH & WALLNUTT," "J W II" and "–TMAN" (the last two apparently referring to J. Whatman, London papermaker). The Smith and Wallnutt paper bears the imprint of the London stationer Dobbs. Additional confirmation of the date of the composition, between 1829 and 1831, is afforded by the edging of the paper: most of it is plain, some is gold-edged, but a number of leaves bear a black border. This paper was the official mourning paper for embassy correspondence during July and August of 1830, after the death of King George IV.

The manuscript of *Companions of Columbus* was clearly printer's copy for the first English edition, for it bears all the usual printshop evidences of direct use: the pages are frequently folded, inkstained, and marked with notes to the printer, printer's brackets, and the names and initials of three compositors in the printshop of Roworth–Brown, McCulloch, and one J. E. None of the corrected proofsheets of this first English edition survives. Consequently, the precise character of Irving's proof alterations, as opposed to unauthorized printer's alterations, cannot be determined. Nor are there copies of any of Irving's handwritten instructions to the printer—such as those he supplied in the case of *Mahomet*—to guide the modern editor. Consequently, in establishing a "definitive" text of *Companions* and the appendixes to *Columbus* for the Twayne edition, the editor relies on what can be inferred from the data developed from multiple collations of the manuscripts and the significant printed editions of the works published during Irving's lifetime.

These data, fully tabulated below, suggest that the appropriate copy-text for *Companions* is the manuscript discussed above—at least for that part of the text for which the manuscript is extant. For those portions of the text where the manuscript is missing, the first English edition, set from the manuscript and published in London in 1831 by John Murray, has been chosen as copy-text. The rationale for choosing the manuscript, rather than one of the printed forms of the text (except where the manuscript is missing), is set forth in the following paragraphs.

Since the manuscript is reasonably fair copy—certainly it was printer's copy—it most closely reflects Irving's intention in composing the text. The manuscript is that version of the text most free of corruptions invariably introduced by copyeditors, house stylists, and printers in the printing process. Bowers and others have shown that the history of printed texts generally reveals—from impression to impression and edition to edition—the gradual deterioration of those forms in the manuscript which most reflect the author's characteristic style. The rationale of the CEAA copy-text theory obliges an editor to recover the author's manuscript practice and to present it in a corrected form. Wherever later printed texts give irrefutable evidence of the author's revision, such changes—whether they be in accidentals or substantives—are accepted as reflecting the author's later, or even final, intention.

In the Twayne edition, therefore, the manuscript will serve as the copy-text for accidentals (which are most easily corrupted in the styling and printing process) and for substantive forms, appropriately emended according to Irving's revisions in later printed texts. The first American edition (published in Philadelphia in 1831 by Carey and Lea) was set from proofslips of the first English edition and, in addition to containing a number of nonauthorial substantive variants, was extensively styled by the printer. Since Irving had no opportunity to correct the proof of the first American edition, it has no textual authority. Similarly, the Author's Revised Edition, published in New York in 1849 by Putnam, extensively modernized and Americanized its accidentals. Set from pages of the first English edition (determined by collations), it is even further removed from manuscript forms and is without authority in accidentals, except in cases where manuscript is lacking (see 151.38–192.19, 348.12–364.10).

The manuscripts and all authorized printed editions of *Companions* and of the appendixes to *Columbus* published during Irving's lifetime have been collated according to the following pattern: (1) sight collation of Irving's holograph MS (University of Virginia Library) with a photocopy of it; (2) four sight collations of the photocopy of the MS with 1E (New York Public Library, Lenox Library, "Checked May 1913") and 1E (University of Wisconsin Library, Rare Book Room); (3) three machine collations of 1E (TxU Irv8, copy 1) with 1E (TxU Irv8, copies 2–4), University of Texas Library; (4) sight collation of 1E (NYPL, Lenox Library "Checked May 1913") with 1E (Fales Collection, New York University); (5) sight collation of 1A (Tuttleton, inscribed "John S. Tenney, 1831" with the bookplate of Hobart Van Zandt Bosworth with 1E (NYPL, Lenox Library "Checked May 1913"); (6) sight collation of 1F (NYPL, Astor Library, KBS) with 1E (NYPL, Lenox Library "Checked May 1913"); (7) two sight collations of 1E (NYPL, Lenox Library "Checked May 1913") with 1849 ARE (Tuttleton, inscribed "Edward Barstow Sargent"); (8) two machine collations of 1F (New York Public Library, Astor Library, KBS, and University of Wisconsin Library E123.1721); (9) two machine collations of 1A with 1835 Carey, Lea and Blanchard reprint of 1A (University of Wisconsin Rare Books CA 2799 and Wisconsin Historical Society F813.I72; and NYPL, Lenox Library, Duyckinck Collection, American History Division, and NYPL 197843B, American History Division, inscribed "Donated by R. Matlack"); (10) four machine collations of 1A (University of Wisconsin Rare Books CA 2799 and NYU Library, inscribed "John L. Tumey"; University of Wisconsin Rare Books CA 2799 and Tuttleton, bookplate Hobart Van Zandt Bosworth; University of Wisconsin Rare Books 2799 and NYU Library E123.I72; University of Texas Library Rare Book Room and Tuttleton, bookplate of Hobart Van Zandt Bosworth); (11) two sight collations of MS1eC (Carl and Lily Pforzheimer Library, NYC) with a photocopy of 1EC (University of Virginia Library); (12) machine collation of 1EC (Fales Collection, NYU, and University of Virginia Library); (13) sight collation of 1EC (Fales Collection, NYU, photocopy) with 1EC (Berg Collection, NYPL, no. 10272); (14) sight collation of 1EC (Fales Collection, NYU, photocopy) with 1EC (NYPL, American History Division, no. 55503); (15) sight collation of 1EC (University of Virginia, photocopy) with 1AC (NYPL, AHD, inscribed "Gordon Lester Ford," no. 174572); (16) machine collation of 1EC (Berg Collection, NYPL no. 10272) with 2EC (Fales Collection, NYU); (17) sight collation of a photocopy of MS2eC (University of Virginia Library) with 1EC (Fales Collection, NYU); (18) sight collation of 1EC (University of Virginia Library, photocopy) with 1837A (McElroy, inscribed "Is. S. Geger, July 17, 1837"); (19) sight collation of 1EC (University of Virginia Library, photocopy) with 1AC (NYPL, American History Division); (20) sight collation of 1AC (NYPL, American History Division) with 2AC (NYPL, American History Division); (21) sight collation of 1AC (NYPL, American History Division) with 1837A ("McElroy, inscribed "Is. S. Geger, July 17, 1837"); (22) sight collation of 1AC (NYPL, AHD, inscribed "Gordon Lester Ford") with MS2eC (University of Virginia Library); (23) sight collation of 1EC (Fales Collection, NYU) with 1EC (NYPL, Berg Collection); (24) sight collation of MS3aC (McElroy microfilm) with 3AC (Tuttleton, inscribed "Edward Barstow Sargent"); (25) sight collation of MS2eC (University of Virginia Library) with MS3aC (McElroy microfilm); (26) sight collation of MS3aC (McElroy) with 1851 3AC ("Author's Revised Version," inscribed "John McElroy"); (27) sight collation of 1EC (Fales Collection, NYU) with 2EC (NYPL, American History Division); (28) sight collation of 1EC (Fales Collection, NYU with 1849 ARE (Tuttleton, inscribed "Edward Barstow Sargent"); (29) sight collation of 1EC (Fales Collection, NYU) with 1851 ARE (inscribed "John McElroy"); (30) sight collation of 1837A (McElroy, inscribed "Is. S. Geger, July 17, 1837") with 1849 ARE (Tuttleton, inscribed "Edward Barstow Sargent"); (31) machine collation of 1849 ARE (Tuttleton, inscribed "Edward Barstow Sargent") with 1850 ARE (inscribed "Ralph Aderman"); (32) machine collation of 1850 ARE (inscribed "Ralph Aderman") with 1851 ARE (inscribed "John McElroy").

TREATMENT OF SUBSTANTIVES

Irving's preparation of the first English edition of *Companions* reflects his habit of making extensive alterations in the proofsheets of the text. The more than three hundred substantive differences between 1E and MS, which served as printer's copy, take the form of additions, substitutions, and deletions, affecting fact, diction, syntax, and paragraph structure. Moreover, these substantive variations comprise a rich fund of primary data upon which the establishment of his text and an assessment of Irving's art, in the process of revision, can be made. A full tabulation of these substantive variations between MS and 1E may be found below in the List of Emendations and the List of Rejected Substantives.

For the present, however, some idea of Irving's method of revising 1E proofsheets may be inferred from the following discussion of his substitutions. Nearly sixty changes involve extensive rewriting of substantial phrases, of whole sentences, and even complete paragraphs. Almost always these changes result in clear improvements of style, marked by greater clarity, directness, and force. An instance of such improvement may be found at the opening of chapter 7 of Ojeda's third voyage, where Irving's manuscript reading—"Though Alonzo de Ojeda was pronounced out of danger, yet he still lay disabled by his wound"—is changed in proofs to "Alonzo de Ojeda, though pronounced out of danger, was still disabled by his wound" (53.3–4). Here awkward rhythm and the unhappy sequence of liquids and assonantal vowels is satisfactorily revised. Again, Irving first wrote that Ojeda's neurotic fear that he would starve to death induced him "to take precautions against his own anticipated fate"; in proofs, Irving revised the sentence to read that his fear induced Ojeda "to set by an extra portion for himself, as a precaution against his anticipated fate" (54.24–25). In discussing Lope de Olano's fear of Nicuesa's anger, Irving wrote that Olano hoped to avoid punishment "by making interest with his fellow officers to induce them to intercede in his behalf"—a syntactically awkward and verbose phrase, which was changed in proofs to read "by persuading his fellow officers to intercede in his behalf" (70.23–24).

Even more impressive instances of his substantive revisions in the syntax of individual MS sentences and of paragraph and chapter contraction—most of them too long to quote and compare here—may be found in the List of Rejected Substantives. Of especial interest is Irving's long tribute to the faithful Juan de la Cosa, appended to the account of his death (compare the List of Rejected Substantives with 62.9–63.21); and the account of the famine at Carthagena, expanded from a score of lines to a powerful and affecting narrative of very nearly five pages (compare the List of Rejected Substantives with 75.9–77.20).

In addition to these sentence and paragraph revisions in the proofs of 1E, collations of the MS and 1E reveal more than 115 occasions when Irving revised in the effort to gain greater clarity and precision in diction. Some suggestion of the effect of these words or phrase substitutions may be gathered from a study of the contexts in which "politic" is substituted for "worthy" (150.11), "Dismayed" for "Discouraged" (147.1), "multitude" for "rabble" (87.15), "senses" for "ears" (42.26), "disposed" for "determined" (33.20), and so on. The MS reading—"Such is the cupidity of human nature"—compared with the revision of the proofs—"Such was the cupidity of the colonists" (148.29)—suggests Irving's conscious unwillingness to let too broad a generalization stand in the final text. His alteration of the specific "Twelve" to the general "Numbers" (109.5), on the other hand, indicates Irving's consciousness that too precise a specification of the number of men who fell ill in Darien would diminish the impact of that heroic expedition. Some of these substitutions, it is worth noting, involve corrections of fact—for example, "Maracaibo" for "Coquibacoa" (14.9), "1497" for "1797" (17.32), and "Hernando" for "Fernando" (151.19).

Such substitutions of single words, phrases, and sentences—often involving some expansion of the text—account for most of Irving's revisions in the proofs of 1E. There are more than fifty instances, however, where the simple addition of one or more words occurs. At 26.7 "they made" is expanded to "they again made"; "of paper" is expanded to "of documents and writing" (26.37); "he" to "the latter" (34.19); "his surviving" to "his only surviving" (46.16); "were as" to "were said to be as" (78.12); "further" to "still more" (78.15); "emptied" to "emptied itself"

(100.9); "them by" to "them, with great agility, by" (100.20–21); and so on. Almost all of these additions, like the previously discussed substitutions, constitute distinct improvements lending greater accuracy, precision, and rhythmical fluency to the style of the work.

In about forty cases, Irving's revisions may be categorized as deletions of one or more words. It is not surprising that, statistically, deletions are less significant than substitutions or additions, since Irving often treated his proofsheets as a rough draft to be expanded and polished. For example, "the songs and shouts of the delighted natives" is condensed to "their songs and shouts" (16.21); "As the natives appeared to be gentle and pacific Ojeda determined" to "Ojeda determined" (33.19); "remittances of revenue" to "remittances" (92.6); "sacraficed at the shrine of the divinity" to "sacrificed at its shrine" (98.24); "had hitherto been accustomed to absolute command" to "had always absolute command" (141.11); and "fire which was kept up" is compressed to "fire kept up" (146.42). Inevitably, Irving's deletions make for greater compactness in the sentences where such excisions occur, although the overall effect of his revisions of the 1E proofs, as I have indicated, is in the direction of expansion.

Of the more than three hundred substantive variations between MS and 1E, the editor has accepted some 280 1E readings on the ground that they overwhelmingly reflect Irving's apparent revisions in proof, and are not unauthorized compositorial changes or changes introduced by Murray copyeditors. Since no proofsheets survive, absolute certainty in every case is impossible. Nevertheless, some 1E readings are clearly unwarranted. They are usually instances of the printer's failure correctly to read the manuscript before him. A full list of them is recorded in the List of Rejected Substantives. For the present, however, it may be noted that 1E gives "Nations," while MS gives "Natives" (10.27); Irving himself caught this 1E compositor's misreading of the MS and changed it to "Natives" when he prepared the revision for ARE. (In all T chapter rubrics common nouns are lowercased.) At 15.29 the MS "prisoner" is changed in 1E to "prisoners"—an unapproved instance, the editor judges, of Murray house styling. At 64.15 the MS reading "entreated that" is unaccountably shortened to "entreated." Since the conjunction is appropriately grammatical, it is restored on the ground that its deletion is an unwarranted compositor's omission. Similarly, the MS plural "cargoes" at 69.24 is unaccountably shortened to "cargo," though the context clearly suggests the preferability of the plural. At 70.15–16 Irving deliberately crossed out the definite article in the phrase "the supply." It is possible that Irving might have changed his mind again, in reading the proofs, and restored the definite article. But there is no evidence to support this conjecture; instead, the editor judges that the compositor did not follow Irving's MS instruction and printed a canceled reading. At 73.24, the editor restores "in every defile," which has greater idiomatic authority than the unaccountable change to "at every defile." At 119.22 MS gives "Further" in the chapter title; it is unaccountably changed to "Farther" in 1E. Since 1E gives "Further" in the chapter title in the table of contents, it is restored at 119.22. At 139.20 the compositor misread MS "huge" for "large"; at 140.26 he misread "previous" for "perilous"; and at 146.29 he misread "retired" for "returned." In all of these cases, the clear textual and contextual evidence warrants preserving MS substantives altered in the printing process.

Machine collations of 1E reveal no variation in the substantives of that text. Apparently Irving's revision of the proofsheets was completed before the text passed from proof into final print. To anticipate the later discussion of accidentals, it should be noted here that machine collations of 1E reveal only one variation in the accidentals of the text of 1E: one collated text of 1E (TxU Irv8, copy 4) lacks a tilde in "Niño" at 19.14, owing, the editor judges, to a loosened piece of type. Collation of TxU Irv8, copy 4, and "NYPL Lenox Library (Checked May 1913)" reveal a number of discrepancies of a single kind: the tilde in "Nuñez" in the running head is missing in thirteen cases. These variations suggest two possibilities: that the former is a lightly corrected text, or that at different times during the printing process a number of tilde type fonts dropped out of the frame. In either case, these insignificant variations affect only the appurtenances of the text, not the text itself. The editor judges that the latter explanation—lost type fonts—is the correct one and that there is no necessity to infer two states of the text. He therefore reasons that while *Companions* exists in slightly variant states, there appears to be only a single impression of the text in the first English edition.

While no proofsheets survive to document the process of Irving's revisions in preparing 1E, the state of those proofsheets may be partially reconstructed from the evidence supplied by collations of MS, 1E, and 1A. This evidence suggests that Irving revised duplicate sets of 1E proofs: from one set, 1E was printed in London; from the other, 1A was later set into print for the Philadelphia firm of Carey & Lea. The text of the duplicate set kept in England was published some two months earlier than 1A, to establish Irving's English copyright. The text set from proofsheets sent to Philadelphia, however, does not correspond in every substantive particular to 1E. In fact, in twenty-two cases, 1A substantives correspond exactly to MS substantives—though it is clear that 1A was not set from MS. These substantive correspondences between MS and 1A may be accounted for in two ways. First, Irving may have failed to record on the duplicate proofsheets sent to America these twenty-two changes, possibly through oversight. Or, second, he may have made additional revisions on his original proofsheets *after* the duplicates had been sent to Philadelphia, thereby creating these crucial differences. In view of the large number of changes he made in revising 1E proofs, the editor judges that his failure to record these twenty-two changes in the proof sent to America was probably an authorial oversight.

A study of these instances in which the MS and 1A readings deviate from 1E confirms the tact and critical intelligence evident in those substitutions, additions, and deletions which have been discussed above. Examples of those revisions which did not find their way into the printed form of 1A are more than a dozen substitutions: "outcast" for "traytor" (93.16); "likewise" for "also" (97.25); "put into" for "thrown into" (105.42); "danger" for "peril" (107.18); "rest" for "people" (111.33); "issued" for "given" (122.26). Though MS is missing for the introduction and the final twelve chapters, there are a number of differences between 1A and 1E that imply original MS readings which Irving revised when working on the proofsheets of 1E. In all probability, the MS read "the discoverers" at 4.29–30, for that reading appears in 1A, but in 1E is revised to "the heroes of these remoter adventures." Similarly, MS must have read "tale" at 5.16, for this substantive appears in 1A; it was revised to "romance" in 1E. At 363.40, the 1A reading "powerfully" almost certainly represents the MS reading, for which Irving substituted "forcibly" in the 1E proofs.

A half dozen of these readings in which MS and 1A correspond, but differ from 1E, represent additions of one or more words: "elapsed" in MS and 1A is revised to "had elapsed" (104.16); parentheses are added at 106.8–9; and 1A's "the rabble" is almost surely identical with the MS reading (now missing), expanded in 1E to "a hooting rabble" (170.5–6). Eight of the correspondences between MS and 1A represent readings from which deletions were made in the final stages of 1E: "Coyba, the dominions of Careta" is condensed to "Coyba" (93.10); "pray to him that he will guide" to "pray to him to guide" (111.21); and "too much" to "visibly" (122.29). These evidences of the incompletely revised proofsheets of 1E, from which 1A was set, throw additional clear, if indirect, light on Irving's method while revising.

In judging the substantive variants revealed in collations of the MS, 1E, and 1A, the editor has inferred from the evidence that most variations between the MS copy-text and 1E or 1A reflect Irving's final revision of proofsheets, in 1831, when *Companions of Columbus* came out of the Roworth printshop.

The editor has been similarly rigorous in selecting among the substantive variations between MS, 1E, and ARE. Nevertheless, a comparison of MS, 1E, and ARE reveals nearly two hundred instances where Irving's ARE revisions require emendations of the copy-text. As one might well imagine, Irving, working at a rapid pace to prepare a revised, multivolume edition of his works for Putnam, made few substantive additions to *Companions of Columbus*. The editor counts less than half a dozen instances in which the text is expanded by one or more words. Most of these are of minor significance. At 86.29 Irving expands by altering the mood of the verb from "thought" to "should think"; the phrase "of innocence" is expanded to "of his innocence" (159.24); and the 1E error "if desire" is corrected, by expansion, to "if you desire" (363.12).

More extensive and rhetorically significant, however, are Irving's substitutions. In preparing the "Author's Revised Edition" for Putnam, Irving made nearly sixty brief substitutions, usually a word or two, lending greater precision, vigor, or force. For example, he changed "agreed" to "arranged" (40.8); "discoveries" to "discoverers" (46.35); "headlong" to "headstrong" (46.40); "furious" to "heedless" (52.10).

By far the most statistically and stylistically significant revisions which distinguish ARE from MS and 1E are deletions of one or more words. In this respect, the revisions of 1E and ARE represent an extraordinary contrast, since the overwhelming majority of revisions of 1E proofs represent additions. Indeed, the more than 130 deletions clearly indicate that ARE is a more compressed and compact narrative, comparatively free of some of the expansive stylistic features of the first English edition. All of these excisions cannot be listed here. They may be inspected in the List of Emendations. But some idea of these deletions is suggested by Irving's shortening of "noted of the early commanders" to "noted commanders" (4.30); of "spirit and a daring eye" to "spirit" (8.3); of "several who had just" to "several just" (10.5). In addition, "some of which were peopled" is shortened to "some peopled" (13.9); "savage warriors" to "savages" (13.11); "vengeance that had been wreaked" to "vengeance wreaked" (14.4); "he immediately charged" to "he charged" (15.25); "all others that they" to "all they" (16.8); and "difficulty from this perilous situation" to "difficulty" (25.23). "From hence," "from whence," and "from thence" are regularly shortened to "hence," "whence," and "thence" (e.g., at 11.4, 17.28, 38.29). These phrases are so consistently abbreviated, in fact, that the editor judges them instances of Putnam house styling. They are therefore rejected in favor of the MS readings.

To summarize this discussion of substantives: the editor has presented MS as the appropriate copy-text for the establishment of the text of this Twayne edition. With substantive variants, copy-text readings are retained when MS evidence suggests that the 1E compositor misread his printer's copy. Copy-text readings are emended (1) when variants suggest Irving's revisions in the 1E proofsheets; (2) when ARE variants indicate Irving's revisions of 1E for the Putnam edition; and (3) when there are clear, egregious errors which Irving would have corrected had he noticed them in the process of either revision or proofreading (e.g., the error of "Gabriel" for "Rafael" at 358.26). Every substantive emendation is noted in the List of Emendations, and the rationale for kinds of emendation is explained in the Discussions of Adopted Readings. *No silent emendations have been knowingly made. Every alteration is listed in the notes.*

TREATMENT OF ACCIDENTALS

In the treatment of accidentals, the editor has observed the same conservative principles that govern his treatment of the substantives of the copy-text. Just as MS forms the basis of substantive readings, emended to incorporate substantives from the 1E and ARE, so MS forms the basis for the accidentals of the Twayne edition. In determining the accidentals of the Twayne edition, the editor has compared MS with the postcopy-text accidentals in 1E, 1A, and ARE. The accidentals of MS cannot be wholly accepted for the Twayne edition. Examination of the MS reveals that Irving wrote rapidly and carelessly, often omitting punctuation, hyphens, and capitals and was often wildly erratic in his spelling. Since he trusted the proofreaders or printer to provide the appropriate forms, and since he revised his proofsheets in order to polish the punctuation, as well as improve the phrasing, there are literally thousands of discrepancies between the slipshod accidentals of MS and the published accidentals of 1E. But since no proofsheets of 1E survive, the editor cannot determine whether 1E accidentals represent Murray house styling or Irving's revision of accidentals in the proof stage. We may assume as a principle of style that Irving's final intention was to produce a work both accurate and consistent in its accidentals. The editor has been tempted, therefore, to impose consistent and accurate readings. This temptation has been resisted, since many of the MS inconsistencies, as an examination of the internal evidence reveals, are characteristic of Irving's holograph practice. Moreover, many of his inconsistencies are actually testaments to the richness, diversity, and variety of his style. The editor judges that the appearance of variant spellings may be intentional. English/American variants in spelling enrich the text and should not, because they cannot, be reconciled. In addition, since one cannot tell whether Irving's irregularities in the MS accidentals are intentional, or whether they are imperfectly realized efforts on his part to anticipate Murray's house style, the editor is faithful to the copy-text. (No extant information about either Murray's printer, the shop of C. Roworth, or about Roworth's compositors [aside from their names or initials], is available to assist the editor in his determination of the accidentals.)

Comparisons of 1E and 1A, and 1E and ARE, which Irving prepared for Putnam in 1849, reveal, like the collation of MS and 1E, variations in accidentals numbering in the thousands. Most of these variations are instances of Carey and Lea's and Putnam's house styling, which radically altered the punctuation of MS and 1E and Americanized or modernized Irving's rather British and sometimes oldstyle spelling. For example, ARE changes "chequered" to "checkered," "valour" to "valor," "colour" to "color," "enterprize" to "enterprise," "labour" to "labor," "honour" to "honor," "harbour" to "harbor," "swoln'" to "swollen," "stoccade" to "stockade." "Vigour," "succour," "clamour," "relique," and "despatch" are similarly modernized or Americanized in spelling.

The ARE alterations of the accidentals of 1E, from which ARE was set, are judged to be examples of Putnam's house style, and cannot thus be accepted as reflecting Irving's authorial practice, although he may have acquiesced in them, if indeed he saw them at all in the ARE proofsheets. (Neither the printer's copy nor the proofsheets of ARE are extant.)

However, not every spelling irregularity of the copy-text is sanctioned simply because it appears in MS or 1E. Some of Irving's inconsistencies in spelling may be emended with confidence, especially those involving proper names—even though no list survives of proper names separately handed to the printer. In several cases the Spanish forms of proper names which Irving found in his historical sources survive in the MS and 1E. On most occasions, however, these names are emended in the Twayne text. The editor judges that Irving intended accuracy and anglicized regularly in the spelling of these names, and he therefore emends "Jozef" to "Josef" (5.34), "Encisco" to "Enciso" (xii.25, xii.29, xii.33), "Darian" to "Darien" xiii.9), "Nuñes" to "Nuñez" (xiii.26), "Vegara" to "Vergara" (33.1), "Roderigo" to "Rodrigo" (84.3), "Espanoles" to "Españoles" (113.32), "Nunez" to "Nuñez" (151.14), "Chuchamà" to "Chuchama" (154.10), "Cortes" to "Cortez" (168.20), "Aguaybanà" to "Agueybanà" (183.2).

Several kinds of evidence have been considered in determining Irving's intended spelling. In an overwhelming number of instances the copy-text is inconsistent and requires emendation. For example, at 151.14 and at scores of other places, MS omits the tilde in "Nuñez"; since

Irving sometimes spells it with the tilde, the copy-text is emended to supply it. Since the copy-text overwhelmingly prefers "Vergara," "Vegara" at 33.1 is emended. For most of these spelling irregularities, there is sufficient internal evidence in the copy-text to support judicious emendation. Where irregularities are such that no statistical probability of the correct spelling, based on the number of observed instances, can be inferred, the editor has appealed to the accidentals forms of ARE. Ordinarily, between the internal evidence of MS and the spelling accidentals Irving presumably sanctioned in the revisions for ARE, the editor can find a sure guide in determining the spelling accidentals for proper names. For example, at 84.3, MS, 1E, and 1A give "Roderigo." (At 83.22, the 1E spelling is "Rodrigo.") ARE is the only printed text to give "Rodrigo" at 84.3, an indication to the editor that Irving himself caught and corrected the 1E error in preparing ARE printer's copy. This correction supplements other internal evidence, therefore warranting emendation of the copy-text at 84.3. Wherever irregularities in MS find their way into 1E and ARE, the problem is more complicated, since Irving, the Murray copyreaders, and the ARE Putnam copyreaders were insufficiently attentive to catch the inconsistency. In such cases, the editor has sought to establish the correct spelling by examination of Irving's sources.

Turning from the spelling of proper names to Irving's spelling in general, we are on more uncertain ground. As Henry Pochmann has shown in the Textual Commentary of the Twayne edition of *Mahomet*, considerable uncertainty exists as to the dictionary, if any, Irving relied upon in the years immediately preceding the publication of *Voyages and Discoveries of the Companions of Columbus*. One fact is clear, however, from the accidentals of MS. Irving's MS spellings reveal a pronounced tendency toward the anglicization of a number of words which are preserved intact in 1E. This is not surprising, since Irving had been abroad for a number of years and because he was doubtless trying to accommodate his spelling to the house style of his British publisher, John Murray.

With respect to "-our" versus "-or" spellings, Irving tends to prefer the British form—presenting "ardour," "armour," "clamour," "colour," "discolour," "endeavour," "favour," "harbour," "labour," "rumour," "succour," "valour," and 'vigour." For a number of words, however, Irving's spelling in inconsistent, and the MS features both forms of "favor," "favorite," "honor," and "splendor." Yet the "-or" form is invariably given for "neighbor," "neighborhood," "favorable," and "demeanor." As Irving's MS practice generally corresponds with Murray's house style, there is a marked consistency between MS and 1E in the spelling of all of these terms; emendation of "valour" (175.33) is required only once,

an alteration which harmonizes the copy-text here with the eight observed instances of "valour" listed in the notes.

With respect to "-ise" versus "-ize" forms, Irving's MS spellings are
extraordinarily consistent. Thus the copy-text gives, for example, "com-
prize," "recognize," "apprize," "authorize," "colonize," and "realize." The
copy-text also gives "baptize," "signalize," "stigmatize," "fertilize," "idol-
ize," "civilize," "patronize," and "solemnize."

Irving's practice with *z* spellings merits a further note. MS offers a
number of interesting old-style spellings: "bruize," "cruize," "pauze,"
"surprize," and "enterprize." In 1E, an effort was made by Murray copyreaders to transpose these into *s* spellings. For example, 1E gives "bruised"
(92.19), "cruise" (187.12), "paused" (15.8), "surprised" (24.34), and
"enterprise" (69.40). In a number of cases, however, 1E failed to anglicize these *z* spellings. For example, "cruizings" survives in 1E at 19.9,
forms of "enterprize" at 8.10, 19.28, and 22.29; and "surprized" at 15.23.
The editor takes the position that these older "-ize" spellings are permissible variants recognized in the literature and lexicographies of the early
nineteenth century, and do not require emendation of the copy-text.

With respect to "-se" and "-ce" spellings, the copy-text is consistent,
offering "pretence," "defence," and "offence," "dispence," and "suspence."
All of these copy-text forms stand without emendation, as does the
noun "licence."

Other instances of copy-text forms, some of them irregular, are these:
MS prefers "entrusted" 137.30 and "entreated" (48.28); "lustre" (144.31),
"supervisor" (33.36) but "superseder" (29.19); and "connection" (351.11)
but "connexions" (37.28–29). These stand without emendation.

A few additional examples will serve to characterize Irving's sometimes British, sometimes oldstyle, and frequently irregular spelling in
the copy-text. MS offers "chaunting" (16.4), "controul" (107.4), "relique" (59.29), "ascendancy" (19.17), "transcendant" (131.13), "alchymist" (186.27), "chequered" (5.11), "cigars" (361.38)—ARE gives the
Americanized "segars." "Waylayed" (80.23), "hamac" (16.14), "centinel"
(51.22), "shew" (81.27), and "traytor" (93.22) also characterize the
MS spelling.

The editor is similarly conservative in establishing the appropriate
hyphenations for the Twayne edition. Irregularities in hyphenation, like
irregularities in spelling, generally stand without emendation—unless
it is clear from substantial internal evidence that Irving clearly preferred
one form over another. In a few cases, apparently single words are
improperly broken into two words. The editor judges these, on the
basis of additional internal evidence, to be instances of Irving's hasty
composition, and the forms are appropriately emended and noted. Two

other categories of hyphenation remain to be discussed. A number of possible single-word compounds in MS and 1E are apparently broken by line-end word division. The Discussions of Adopted Readings supplies the evidence on which emendations in such cases, are made. The second category is two-word forms without hyphenation. MS, for example, gives "peace offerings" (15.12) and "unlooked for" (86.25–26). Such items are not emended to hyphenate; no editor should impose his own system of punctuation on an author. To do so is to tamper with and corrupt the text as compositors often do.

Alterations in the copy-text punctuation are made with comparable caution. As with other forms of the accidentals, MS is the basis for the accidentals of the Twayne edition, but the copy-text has required emendation from time to time when Irving, writing rapidly and carelessly, supplied what, in then contemporary usage, could be called erroneous punctuation, and when Irving failed to provide necessary punctuation. Here and there, as noted in the List of Emendations, the copy-text has been emended to supply a comma after nonrestrictive adjective clauses and phrases; to supply a necessary comma concluding parenthetical matter; to supply a necessary comma after long introductory adverbial clauses; to supply a semicolon to correct a comma splice; to provide needed concluding quotation marks; to raise or lower the case; to spell out ampersands; to join compounds wrongly separated; to provide needed hyphens in compounds, particularly for compound adjectives modifying a noun; to provide necessary tildes in Spanish terms; to provide omitted apostrophes; to provide needed periods after abbreviations; to anglicize names inadvertently spelled in the Spanish way; and to correct Irving's sometimes eccentric spelling. Of the approximately 1,200 emendations of the copy-text, nearly 1,000 constitute emendations of the accidentals of the MS. This high number of required emendations is in itself evidence that Irving worked hastily and in a slipshod fashion, intending the proofsheets to constitute an intermediate form of the text (a later version, as it were, of the MS), on which extensive corrections could be made. Most of the emendations I have noted were, in fact, made for 1E—probably by Irving, between September and December, 1830, when he worked over the proofs in London.

Yet many of the accidentals variations between MS and 1E cannot be accepted in T. For one thing, much of the 1E spelling constitutes an anglicization of Irving's spelling. It may be remarked that Irving tended to provide English spellings in any event and that he wished to appear in a form acceptable to his English public. But the aim of T has been to provide, insofar as possible, what Irving actually wrote, purged, of course, of gross errors. For another, Murray's house stylist clearly pointed the text—through commas and semicolons—much more heavily than was Irving's habit in MS. It might be remarked that Irving intended his copyeditor to point the text for him—and there is evidence in the letters, especially touching *Columbus*, indicating that he sought the assistance of others in readying the text of 1EC. But as the proof-sheets of 1E and 1EC do not survive, it is not possible to distinguish Irving's pointing in the proofs from his copyeditor's. T, therefore, starts, as it were, from scratch—and seeks to provide only necessary punctuation. It may be pointed out that the T editor has usually found 1E to be a sure guide in establishing contemporary practice, and many of the T emendations will be found to have an example in 1E or even ARE. But he has tended to resist the invitation to regularize Irving's punctuation on the ground that to emend more fully would be to tamper with the accidentals of the copy-text, and thereby to nullify the reason for choosing a copy-text in the first place.

Yet, despite the T editor's generally conservative treatment of accidentals, the copy-text requires extensive emendation. Irving, for example, regularly misspelled forms of "maritime" (9.3), "sacrifice" (11.18), "seize" (24.40), "disastrous" (26.9), "grievous" (26.11), "harass" (33.39), "receive" (45.21), "allege" (127.27), "deceive" (58.6), "Nicuesa" (66.41), "separate" (67.10), 'inveigled" (88.2), "Caribbean" (88.33), "weigh" (95.42), etc. Some of these misspellings even survive into 1E and ARE. They are here corrected in T.

Irving's capitals present hundreds of occasions where the necessity of emending must be determined. Fortunately, the editor is on somewhat surer ground here than in the case of other accidentals, since it may be more convincingly argued that Irving wanted consistency in the case forms of his text and since the element of "permissible variants" (e.g., in spelling) is not as great a factor in case usage. Therefore, statistical incidence can be invoked more confidently in determining the appropriate case form. Yet Irving was notoriously inconsistent in his handling of case forms, and frequently raised the case, or lowered it, on mere (apparent) whim. Moreover—especially in the case forms of *A, C, G, K, M, N, O, R, S, V,* and *W*—it is often well nigh impossible to distinguish his lower from his upper cases. The T editor has tended to rely on the conservative principle that doubtful cases should be referred to Irving's characteristic habits and to contemporary usage; thus terms like "Christian" are raised in case (4.14), and common nouns like "brigantine" (108.12–13), which appear in mid-sentence, are lowered.

The necessity of selecting a sloppily written manuscript as copy-text has therefore resulted in extensive emendations of the copy-text and an extensive apparatus for the List of Emendations. Nevertheless, it should be observed that the editor has worked very conservatively and emended far fewer times than Irving—or his copyeditors at Murray's and Putnam's—saw fit to do. Another modern editor might have emended far more (or less) often than I have. An emendation is an aesthetic as well as textual decision, and, about the aesthetic dimension of editing, *de gustibus non est disputandem*. In any event, every decision to emend has been listed in the List of Emendations, and the Discussions of Adopted Readings offers an explanation for many of the choices made.

One further problem in the accidentals and substantives of the Twayne edition of *Voyages and Discoveries of the Companions of Columbus* remains to be discussed. When Irving prepared *Columbus* and *Companions* for the Author's Revised Edition, he grouped the two works in a three-volume subset within that fifteen-volume series. In grouping these two works, he appended the thirty-five illustrations and documents pertaining to the *Columbus* volume to the end of the third of the three-volume set, that volume containing *Companions*. Inserted between the final chapter of *Companions* and its two appendixes ("A Visit to Palos" and "Manifesto of Ojeda") are these thirty-five appendixes touching the life and history of the great original discoverer. Although the editor of *Companions* has selected MS, emended from 1E and ARE, as the copy-text for the Twayne edition, he and John McElroy, who has edited *Columbus* for the Twayne edition, have collaborated in offering the two works together, in the form in which they finally appeared in the Author's Revised Edition. In deciding to follow Irving's procedure in preparing that edition, they have been guided by the Textual Editor, Edwin T. Bowden, and the editorial board of the Twayne Edition. Responsibility for establishing the text of *Columbus*, together with the apparatus, Introduction, and Textual Commentary, has been the province of John McElroy. Responsibility for establishing the text of the *appendixes* of *Columbus* rests with the editor of the present volume, James W. Tuttleton. What follows is a description of the principal manuscripts and printed texts of the appendixes of *Columbus*, together with a discussion of the rationale employed in establishing the text of the Twayne edition.

THE APPENDIXES OF COLUMBUS

The several manuscripts and printed texts of *The Life and Voyages of Christopher Columbus* have already been fully described by John Harmon McElroy in his edition of the text in this series (1981). But since the illustrations and documents concerning *Columbus* are appended to this Twayne edition of *Companions of Columbus* (as they were in the 1848 Putnam Author's Revised Edition three-volume subset), a brief description of the manuscript appendixes and a discussion of the copy-text is in order here. For a fuller discussion the reader is referred to McElroy's excellent account of the composition and transmission of the text.

The illustrations touching Columbus that constitute the primary basis for the copy-text here, except where otherwise indicated, are bound into the fifth (and final) volume of the complete manuscript of *Columbus* (MS1eC), now housed in the Carl and Lily Pforzheimer Library in New York City. These appendixes were numbered in manuscript and in some cases renumbered by Irving or his scribes to achieve the proper final sequence. It would appear that Irving prepared a duplicate manuscript simultaneously or perhaps even before MS1eC, to be used as printer's copy for the first American edition of the work (New York: G. & C. Carvill, 1828), but that duplicate mnauscript (MS1aC), entirely in Irving's hand, is extant only in fragments, none of the illustrations surviving. MS1eC is therefore of primary value in determining the copy-text, for it became the printer's copy of the first English edition (London: John Murray, 1828), designated here 1EC.

The manuscript of these appendixes is in six hands, one of them Irving's. The others, Spanish scribes in Madrid, have been identified by McElroy as Joachim de Mendizábal, Manuel Ruiz, Joseph Garcia Cavallero, Don Guillermo Ireland, and one other, unknown. A variety of blue and black inks, some faded now into a reddish-brown, are used on a variety of paper weights and grades, rag wove and unwove, with and without chain and water marks, including apparently expensive cream yellow foolscap, various hues of white and off-white, shading into bluish tints. The paper size is predominantly 8 by 11¾ inches, although "Route of Columbus" measures 5½ x 8¼ inches, and five sheets of "Peter Martyr" measure 7 x 9¾ inches. There are 282 leaves, written largely on one side only, at various times and places, including one unidentified leaf, touching various bequests of Columbus, which was inadvertently bound-in with the texts of these appendixes. The handwriting of the manuscript ranges from Irving's careless scrawl to the formal penmanship of the Spanish scribes whose calligraphy was an aid to legibility for the typesetters. Most of these leaves are fair copy intended for the printer. Some, however, are cut-and-paste indications of Irving's perpetual (and sometimes heavy) revisions as he proofread and corrected the work of his copyists, whose peculiar errors in the transcription of English indicate Spanish linguistic interference. None of the paper is dated, but the manuscript pages bear the following watermarks: Ysidro, Esteuan, Ynfantado, Manuel, YEB, Capellades, Angel, Polo, RRS & FRF, Mortorell, and Serra; and on some leaves there are four single initials within a

floral garland—J, B, E, and Y. These are all apparently papers of
Spanish manufacture, reflecting Irving's residence in Seville and Madrid
while he composed these appendixes and had them copied. No con-
clusions as to the dating of the composition of these illustrations can be
derived from the manuscript alone. Two sheets are of German origin
and bear the watermark of a profile head of the emperor within a circle,
with the legend around the medallion reading FRANZ DER II KAISER VON
OESTERREICH.

This manuscript of the appendixes was clearly that copy from which
1EC was set, inasmuch as it bears all the evidence of print-house handling: it is heavily folded, inkstained, and fingerprinted by the compositors,
with penciled brackets signifying different gatherings and compositorial
units. The first three volumes of 1EC, it is interesting to note, were
published by W. Clowes, a London printer for John Murray; and marginal notations in the manuscript of the text of *Columbus* identify at least
three of the compositors working for that house: Heming, King, and
Underwood. But the fourth volume of 1EC, which contains the appendixes, as well as sixty-four pages of the text proper (the conclusion),
was printed by Thomas Davison, whose compositors left no indication
of their identities on the manuscript.

The sequence and numbers of the appendixes in the bound Pforzheimer five-volume manuscript, and their manuscript length, are as
follows: "Route of Columbus in His First Voyage" (33 pages); "Transportation of the Remains of Columbus from St. Domingo to the Havanna"
(9 pages); "Notice of the Descendants of Columbus" (33 pages); "Fernando Columbus" (3 pages); "Lineage of Columbus" (6 pages); "Birthplace of Columbus" (14 pages); "The Colombos" (4 pages); "Expedition
of John of Anjou" (4 pages); "Capture of the Venetian Galleys" (5 pages);
"Amerigo Vespucci" (7 pages); "Rumour of the Pilot Said to Have Died
in the House of Columbus" (6 pages); "Martin Behem" (8 pages); "Voyages of the Scandinavians" (13 pages); "Circumnavigation of Africa by
the Ancients" (6 pages); "Principles Upon Which the Sums Mentioned
in This Work Have Been Reduced into Modern Currency" (3 pages);
"Marco Polo" (15 pages); "The Work of Marco Polo" (10 pages); "Sir
John Mandeville" (3 pages); "The Zones" (3 pages); "Of the Atalantis
of Plato" (3 pages); "The Imaginary Isle of St. Brandan" (14 pages);
"The Island of the Seven Cities" (3 pages); "Discovery of the Island of
Madeira" (10 pages); "Las Casas" (5 pages); "Ships of Columbus" (30
pages, page 7 missing); "Martin Alonzo Pinzon" (15 pages); "Peter
Martyr" (11 pages); "Cura de los Palacios" (1 page); "Oviedo" (3
pages); "'Navigatione del Re de Castiglia delle Isole e Paese Nuovamente Ritrovate,' 'Navigatio Christophori Colombi'" (3 pages); "Antonio

Herrera" (4 pages); "Bishop Fonseca" (7 pages); "Of the Situation of the Terrestrial Paradise" (14 pages); "Will of Columbus" (18 pages); and "Signature of Columbus" (2 pages).

A number of these illustrations or appendixes to *Columbus*, though properly numbered, were bound-in out of sequence in the Pforzheimer volume, specifically "Route of Columbus in His First Voyage," which precedes all others, doubtless because of its smaller paper size; "Martin Alonzo Pinzon" and "Ships of Columbus" were inadvertently bound-in after "Las Casas." "Oviedo" and "Cura de los Palacios" are also transposed in binding. In addition to dislocations of whole appendixes, in the binding process, groups of leaves also became misplaced in handling, possibly in the printshop, possibly in the bindery. In "Amerigo Vespucci," the manuscript breaks off at 233.34–35, at the end of the paragraph ending "hereafter mentioned" and the paragraph beginning "In May, 1501" and is bound in just after "Ships of Columbus." In "Circumnavigation of Africa by the Ancients," the manuscript is dislocated at 261.14 between "apparent" and "contradictions" and the rest of the appendix is misbound into "Las Casas." At the same time, "Las Casas" breaks off at 316.13 between "New World." and "These"—the conclusion wrongly bound-in as the conclusion to "Circumnavigation of Africa by the Ancients." Manuscript pages 13 and 14 of "Las Casas" are transposed in binding. On the verso of manuscript page 3 of "'Navigatione del Re de Castiglia'" incidentally, is a canceled phrase reading "magnificent houses and has a lake thirty miles in circuit. [Paragraph] Within its walls on the bank"—an indication of Irving's "trying out a phrase" to inspect its effectiveness, a technique much more common on the versos of the *Companions* manuscript than on that of *Columbus*, since the former was not copied by scribes.

PRINTED EDITIONS OF COLUMBUS

The first edition of *Columbus*, together with the appendixes which are included here, was published in London in four volumes by John Murray in 1828, while Irving was still resident in Spain. The negotiations and terms between author and publisher, together with the circumstances touching on the correction and revision of the proofsheets, have already been fully detailed by John Harmon McElroy in the Textual Commentary to the Twayne edition of *Columbus*. Here it is sufficient to note that the first English edition, which I shall designate as 1EC (so as to distinguish it in this text from 1E, the abbreviation for the first English edition of *Companions of Columbus*, with other forms of the *Columbus* likewise bearing the C suffix), was full of altered phrases and words as well as typographical and factual errors which caused Irving, in far-away Madrid, considerable irritation and embarrassment.

When Irving saw 1EC, he immediately undertook the task of restoring his phrasing where called for and of correcting and revising it for a second edition. This revision, on the pages of 1EC (together with some cut-and-paste holograph additions), produced a version of the text that I have designated MS2eC. The correspondence of John Murray with Irving just after the publication of 1EC did not reveal to Irving that Murray in fact produced a second English edition (2EC), an edition that went to press before Murray received Irving's corrections. MS2eC is thus a list of changes and revisions never used in correcting or preparing 2EC. It is apparent from collations of 1EC and 2EC that, for the appendixes alone, there are some forty-three variations: fifteen represent mere resettings; seven represent substantive variations; and twenty-one represent variations in the accidentals.

These variations in the texts of 1EC and 2EC (also dated 1828 and not indicated on the title page as a new or revised edition) suggest that someone at the printshop of Thomas Davison or in the House of Murray, or perhaps Irving's independent agent (but not Irving, since he was off in Spain)—someone, in any event, proofread and corrected both the manuscript (MS1eC) and 1EC and ordered changes and re-settings never seen or sanctioned by Irving for 2EC. A list of them may be discovered by consulting the List of Rejected Substantives, the List of Emendations, and the Discussions of Adopted Readings.

As remarked above, Irving prepared a duplicate of MS1eC, which I have designated MS1aC; it became printer's copy for 1AC, the first American edition. Only fragments of MS1aC, all in Irving's hand, survive. Here one may parenthetically remark that many of Irving's restorations of MS1eC readings in MS2eC are identical with readings in 1AC, suggesting that MS2eC was prepared with the original manuscript before him. Revisions and corrections of 1AC became the basis for 2AC, published by the Carvills in New York in 1831. It is not clear who supervised the printing of 1AC and 2AC, for which proofsheets do not survive. But it clearly was not Irving, for 1AC and 2AC show considerable styling of the accidentals of the text, if we may assume that the accidentals of MS1aC were identical with those of MS2eC. Thus, the early American printings of *Columbus* have slight textual authority: none in the case of accidentals, yet confirming evidence in the case of identical substantives present in MS2eC but different in 1EC and 2EC.

Toward the end of his career, Irving prepared a fully revised text of *Columbus* for the 1848 Author's Revised Edition published in New York by G. P. Putnam. Printer's copy for this edition, which I have designated 3AC, was a conflation of texts involving 2AC and a missing revision of MS2eC–2EC that McElroy designates ur-MS3a (here designated ur-MS3aC). This form of the text, no longer extant, can be inferred from MS3aC, which evolved from it and became 3AC printer's copy. In the preparation of his edition, McElroy has selected MS3aC–3AC as the copy-text for the Twayne edition. The soundness of his reasoning is fully evident in his Textual Commentary, to which the reader is referred for fuller information.

It is worth observing that the 1848 Author's Revised Edition was a uniform set of Irving's collected works in fifteen volumes that aimed for, among other things, uniformity of style in the accidentals of the text. Consequently, McElroy observes that, between the four fifths of the extant MS3aC and 3AC, there are some 2,787 differences in accidentals and that, in revising and proofing the text of 3AC, Irving passively acquiesced in substantives that apparently did not originate with his pen. That Putnam's house styled the accidentals of the text and that Irving may not have realized that some substantive readings were corruptions of his own manuscript prose is irresistibly suggested by the evidence of multiple collations. Consequently, establishing the author's final intention may be achieved by approaching the textual data from several theoretical angles, of which McElroy's approach represents a successful model for the resolution of the problems of the thousands of differentiae that are obliged to be considered in establishing the Twayne edition of *Columbus*.

THE COPY-TEXT OF THE APPENDIXES

Although the text of 1EC is marked by Murray house styling, printer's alterations, and unauthorized changes in the substantives, its status as the *first* printed edition based on a partly authorial holograph makes it natural to consider the manuscript-printer's copy (MS1eC) as providing a basis for the accidentals of the appendixes. For one thing, as a unitary text, having been composed by Irving at roughly a single time and place and partly copied under his supervision and corrected by him, MS1eC lacks the admixtures of accidentals with no authority evident in later composite revisions made onto the tear-pages of the various English and American editions. It is therefore possible, using MS1eC for the accidentals, to reconstruct Irving's own intentions, at the time of composition, without the corruptions of the Murray, Carvill, and Putnam house styles in punctuation, capitalization, etc. For that reason, MS1eC serves as copy-text for the appendixes.

Even so, MS1eC cannot simply be reproduced in its accidentals. The sections of the manuscript in Irving's own hand, and particularly his revisions of the scribal copy, are sometimes rushed, rough, and slipshod in the accidentals, reflecting his usual habit of leaving it to others to copyedit his texts or to make his own corrections on the proofsheets (which in this case he never saw). Moreover, there are many errors in names, dates, and other facts; and, it seems fair to conclude, his Spanish coypists frequently introduced errors into their copies that Irving did not notice when he went over their work. Consequently, while MS1eC is generally acceptable for accidentals, these accidentals are emended, where necessary, based upon collations with MS2eC (Irving's correction of 1EC), 1AC, and MS3aC-3AC. In particular, Irving's own revisions and changes, resulting in those alterations noted from MS2eC and 3AC, give a clear and subsequent indication of how he wanted the text to appear in its accidentals, wherever the accidentals are specifically submitted to revision.

The accidentals of MS1eC, it may be remarked here, give the work a decidedly British and sometimes old-style flavor, although—as might be expected of an American author who had lived long in England—there is considerable inconsistency in his choices among "our–or" and "ise –ize" spellings, and such alternates as "sepulchre–sepulture," "checkered–chequered," "chant–chaunt," and "relique–relic." Irving's capitalization, moreover, reflects the same inconsistencies noted in the discussion of the manuscript of *Companions of Columbus*. Sometimes he does, sometimes he does not, capitalize such titles as "Admiral," and sometimes it is impossible to tell whether or not the letter is a capital. On the whole, emendations of MS1eC are treated conservatively here, although there is a substantial number of cases where, from the evidence of Irving's revisions later, emendations must be made.

On the matter of substantives, MS1eC serves as copy-text, although here, for obvious reasons supported by McElroy's description of the evolution of MS3aC-3AC, MS1eC must be emended to incorporate substantive changes Irving made in producing MS2eC and MS3aC–3AC. In several cases noted below, it should be remarked, Irving's subsequent revision of the substantives in MS2eC and MS3aC–3AC involved a revision of the attendant accidentals as well; and where this has occurred, the accidentals of MS3aC–3AC take priority as copy-text readings.

The first important text to have an effect on the emendation of substantives is MS2eC, which is, as I have indicated, Irving's attempt to restore MS1eC readings on tear-sheets of 1EC, and to provide corrected, revised, and new material for an intended second English edition. Irving's revisions in MS2eC range from simple word substitution, deletion, and addition to the complete rewriting of whole appendixes and the addition of a wholly new appendix. In some cases Irving's changes represent the mere restoration of words or phrases found in MS1eC and changed without his authority in 1EC and 2EC. At 195.40 for example, "convocation" appears in MS1eC, is changed to "commemoration" in 1EC, and is restored in MS2eC. In such cases, the MS1eC readings are transmitted through MS2eC to 3AC. In other cases, the revisions in MS2eC are simple matters of slightly altered punctuation, in pencil or pen, changes in a word or phrase, corrections of spellings or dates, or substitutions of accurate footnotes, and a full list of these changes is given in the apparatus.

Other changes, however, are more thoroughgoing and deserve fuller discussion. On the basis of new information, or correct information, or for stylistic reasons, Irving often rewrote extensive passages, like the opening two paragraphs, in his own hand, of "The Colombos" (see the List of Emendations [225.11–18]). Apparently his revisions were sometimes preceded by intermediate drafts; for example, the revision at the end of "The Colombos" beginning "It is highly probable" (226.19) is in the hand of a scribe. The last paragraph of "Amerigo Vespucci" is also extensively rewritten in Irving's hand. (See the List of Emendations for 245.16–25). The very brief "Martin Alonzo Pinzon" in MS1eC is completely revised, expanded, and rewritten in MS2eC, doubtless owing to Irving's growing interest in the life of this companion of Columbus, whose story he was very probably researching and writing at the same time for *Companions of Columbus*. Irving prefixes an instruction to this appendix—"To be inserted in place of Illustration No X of the first edition"—which is clearly addressed to the printer of the new edition. As remarked, however, Murray proceeded to print 2EC before he received Irving's revisions.

A like instruction to the printer is prefixed to the MS2eC appendix of "Route of Columbus in His First Voyage," in which Irving instructs that the completely rewritten appendix be "inserted in place of the printed article Vol 4." This appendix is unusually interesting in that the whole essay as it appears in 1EC was apparently written by Alexander Slidell Mackenzie, a naval officer and friend of Irving, who was more capable than Irving of determining, from the islands and charts, what Columbus's exact route might have been. The appendix in MS1eC is, in the editor's judgment, a clumsily written piece of prose, full of stylistic solecisms and incongruities. In a footnote to the appendix, Irving observes that "The author of this work is indebted for this able examination of the route of Columbus to an officer of the navy in the United States, whose name he regrets the not being at liberty to mention. He has been greatly benefited, in various parts of this history, by nautical information from the same intelligent source" (264.32–35). The editor judges Mackenzie actually to have written the appendix, which Irving then copied out in his own hand. While both MS1eC and MS2eC are in Irving's hand, the latter is apparently Irving's attempt to polish up what I take to be Mackenzie's clumsy original, which Irving felt to reflect on him as a stylist.

Paradoxically, however, the MS2eC revision must be rejected by the editor as a source of emendation to the copy-text for this appendix. For the final printed text of this appendix, 3AC, is based on the text of MS1eC rather than that of MS2eC. Whether Irving forgot, in 1848, that he had completely rewritten this appendix and that it had been already printed in earlier American editions; or whether, as a tribute to Mackenzie, he deliberately retained the essay in its original MS1eC form, cannot be known. His appended "Note to the Revised Edition of 1848," however, suggests the latter. For Mackenzie is identified by name as the young American naval officer who had written a paper in Madrid two decades before on Columbus's route to the New World. In any event, the theory of copy-text requires that the editor present that text of this appendix most nearly reflecting the author's final intention. And since Irving prepared MS3aC for the printing of 3AC, and included the MS1eC version, the revision in MS2eC must be rejected. Since line collation is impracticable, however, the rejected version of this appendix is printed *in toto* in the List of Rejected Substantives.

The appendixes of "Marco Polo" and "The Work of Marco Polo" are also extremely revised in MS2eC, both in Irving's hand and in that of a scribe, in order to reflect new information about the medieval explorer unavailable to Irving when he first wrote those appendixes. Comparably long passages are also rewritten, in Irving's hand, in two final appendixes, the "Cura de los Palacios" and "Bishop Fonseca." Although the canceled passages in these four appendixes are rather lengthy, the editor presents them entire in the apparatus as indications of Irving's tireless efforts to improve the style and substance of this important work of his middle career.

One other important revision in the MS2eC remains to be noted. Inserted into MS2eC is the text of a completely new illustration, in Irving's hand, entitled "Age of Columbus." It is designated number 4, and has stood in that position in all printed forms of the text subsequent to 2EC. This version of the appendix becomes the copy-text, and substantive emendations from MS3aC–3AC are incorporated into it.

Although the Author's Revised Edition is a major revision of Irving's oeuvre, apparently Irving was largely satisfied with the revisions of the appendixes he had made in MS2eC, and in MS3aC offered comparatively few changes for the Putnam edition. Yet some idea of Irving's revisions for 3AC may be derived from the following discussion. As usual they include the expected substitutions, deletions, and additions of words and phrases. Instances of shortened phrases appear at 199.16 where "and that none" is shortened to "and none"; at 227.14 where "and had assembled" is condensed to "and assembled." At 228.19 the manuscript gives "many it is said, seized with a kind of fury, threw"; and 3AC gives "many threw." Occasionally phrases are expanded, as at 287.40, words are substituted, as at 287.36, or a spelling is corrected. At certain points all major texts differ, as at 225.31, where MS1eC gives "lost a large part," 1EC gives "lost many," 1AC gives "lost a many" and 3AC gives "lost a great many."

By far the most important substantive variations between 3AC and previous forms of the text are in its additions. One significant addition takes the form of a footnote to the conclusion of number 17, "Route of Columbus," which defends Irving's analysis of Columbus's route, on the basis of new authoritative information, and identifies Mackenzie as the naval officer, unnamed in MS1eC, who assisted Irving in the preparation of the original appendix. More significant, however, is the addition of a wholly new appendix, number 19, "Prester John," which appears for the first time in print in 3AC. For these additions MS3aC–3AC provides the copy-text.

To conclude, MS1eC is the copy-text for the Twayne edition of the appendixes, both for substantives and accidentals, which are nevertheless emended on the authority of later forms which inescapably reflect Irving's revisions of the text. The List of Emendations, the List of Rejected Substantives, and the Discussions of Adopted Readings offer a record of decisions to emend or not to emend. The aim in every case of substantive variation has been, on the copy-text rationale of Greg and Bowers, to present in the Twayne edition a text most nearly approximating Irving's final intention.

In preparing the Twayne text, proof was read five times in an effort to detect and eliminate errors in the setting copy or in the printing process. Modesty and experience remind me, however, of the old adage, which may be paraphrased: "No edition is complete until Error hath set upon it his Imprimatur."

Although Irving's text is faithfully and critically rendered, no effort is made to reproduce exactly the so-called appurtenances of the text— that is, such typographical details as the precise arrangement of the title and half-title pages and other preliminary matter, pagination and lineation, the footnote symbols as they occur in prior texts, the display capitals and the capitalized text letters following them, or the exact typography of the chapter titles, running heads, table of contents, synoptic chapter headings, and end-of-chapter notes or indexes. Except for these details, then, the Introduction, the Textual Commentary, and the accompanying Discussions of Adopted Readings, together with the Lists of Emendations, Rejected Substantives, and End-of-Line Hyphenation, are designed to provide the reader with all the data needed to reconstruct the copytext and to follow the steps by which the Twayne texts of *Companions of Columbus* and the appendixes to *Columbus* were established. Beyond this, the assembled evidence is designed not only to enable the reader so minded to examine and consider the bases on which all editorial decisions were made but to reconsider them, if he chooses, and in the process to see the relationships that exist among the several texts from the earliest draft of Irving's manuscripts to a reasonably close approximation of the printed texts the author intended them to be.

DISCUSSIONS OF ADOPTED READINGS

In these discussions of decisions to emend or not to emend, the symbols designating manuscripts and texts are those found in the List of Abbreviations, p. 367. The page and line figures are keyed in each case to a word or words in the text to which the discussion refers. A bracket separates the key word or words from the comment that follows.

xi.11   natives] ARE; Nations 1E, 1F. The copy-text is here emended on the authority of ARE, which corrects the 1E compositor's apparent misreading of lost printer's copy.

xii.18   shipwreck] ARE; Ship-wreck 1E, 1F. Since the copy-text hyphenation represents line-end word division (Ms preferring shipwreck at 66.32), the copy-text is here emended.

xii.25   Enciso] 1F, ARE; Encisco 1E. The copy-text misprint is corrected, here and at xii.29.

xii.33   downfall] ARE; downfal 1E, 1F. The copy-text misprint is here corrected.

xiii.9   Darien] 1F, ARE; Darian 1E. The copy-text misprint is here corrected.

xiii.16   the Pacific] 1E, 1F, ARE. It should be noted that the full chapter title (116.8) in 1E, 1F, and ARE reads "Adventures of Vasco Nunez on the borders of the Pacific Ocean."

xiii.17   Further] 1E, 1F, ARE. Note that the copy-text reads "Farther" in the chapter title at 119.22.

xiii.17   Nuñez.] 1E, 1F, ARE. Note that the copy-text chapter title at 119.22 is "Nunez on the borders of the Pacific Ocean.—(1513.)"

xiii.26   Nuñez] 1F, ARE; Nunes 1E. Since the Ms and 1E overwhelmingly prefer Nuñez, the copy-text is here emended.

xiii.29   Golden] ARE; Gold 1E, 1F. Since the copy-text prefers "Golden" at xiii.7, the term is here emended.

xiv.32   Notice] 3AC; Account MS1eC. The text is here emended. An additional authority is Irving's revision for the MS2eC.

xiv.34   Age of Columbus] 3AC; missing in MS1eC. The text is here emended on the authority of Irving's insertion of this illustration in MS2eC and subsequent editions.

xv.16   Prester John] 3AC; missing in MS1eC. The text is here emended on the authority of 3AC, for which this illustration was written.

2.4–9   Venient annis . . . Ultima Thule] This passage from Seneca's *Medea* appears on the title page of all four volumes of *Columbus* in both the first English edition (London: Murray, 1828) and the three-volume "Author's Revised Edition" (New York: George P. Putnam, 1849) of *The Life and Voyages of Christopher Columbus; To Which Are Added Those of His Companions*. Frank J. Miller translates the passage thus: "There will come an age in the far-off years when Ocean shall unloose the bonds of things, when the whole broad earth shall be revealed, when Tethys shall disclose new worlds and Thule not be the limit of the lands" (*Seneca's Tragedies* [London: William Heinemann, 1916], I, 261).

3.9   first fruits] 1A; first-fruits 1E, 1F, ARE. Since the hyphen never otherwise appears with this term (cf. 9.8, 39.30, and 130.29), the copy-text is here emended.

4.14   Christian] ARE; christian 1E, 1A, 1F. The copy-text is emended here to bring the case into conformity with usual contemporary 1E capitalization practice, e.g., at MS 115.16.

4.29   arsenal] ARE; arsenals 1E, 1A, 1F. The alteration of the word from plural to singular is presumed to have Irving's authority.

4.30   noted commanders] ARE; noted of the early commanders 1E, 1A, 1F. This verbal compression is typical of Irving's revision for ARE.

4.36   seaman] ARE; sea-man in 1E and 1F represents line-end word division. Irving's preference is seaman, as in 10.5, 19.7, and 26.18.

4.40   new world] 1E; New World ARE. The copy-text is not emended since MS, while inconsistent, rarely elevates the cases.

5.1   vain-glorious] 1E; vainglorious ARE. The copy-text here is not emended owing to Irving's irreconcilable inconsistency; vainglory appears at 63.13, and 350.4 and vain gloriously at 61.19.

5.32   Archives] ARE; archives 1E, 1A; achives 1F. The copy-text is here emended since the 1E preference is for uppercase, as in 5.34.

5.34   Josef] 1A; Jozef 1E, 1F, ARE. The copy-text is emended on the authority of the proper spelling at 113.32.

7.33–34   lib. i. cap.] ARE; l.i.c. 1E, 1A, 1F. Here and in subsequent footnotes to the text, the T edition will emend the copy-text to provide ARE's fuller and clearer abbreviations for volume, chapter, and tome.

8.3   spirit that] ARE; spirit and a daring eye that MS, 1E, 1A, 1F. The copy-text is here emended; ARE represents Irving's revision for greater compression.

8.10   enterprizing] MS, 1E; enterprising 1F, ARE. In all MS forms of this word Irving preferred the z spelling, where it occasionally survives Murray house styling (e.g., here, at 9.28, 19.16, 19.28, and 177.7).

8.15   connexions] MS; connections 1E. The copy-text invariably prefers the Anglicized spelling, e.g., at 37.28–29 and 179.2–3.

8.19   Bishop] MS; bishop 1E, 1A, 1F, ARE. The copy-text ordinarily capitalizes the term. Where it does not, the case is raised, as noted.

9.3   maritime] 1A, 1F, ARE; maratime MS, 1E. Irving's misspelling is here emended.

10.33   Colec.] ARE; Collec. MS, 1E, 1A, 1F. The spelling of the Spanish word, abbreviated, is proper in ARE; the copy-text is therefore emended.

11.4   From hence] MS; Hence ARE. Here—and at 12.22, 17.27, 25.32, 36.18, 38.29, 112.22, 122.14, 125.7, 138.14, 148.17, 151.11, 152.26, 163.1, 165.33, and 183.16–17—a Putnam house editor apparently deleted the "unnecessary" preposition. T preserves it.

11.26–27   residence, from the maladies engendered by the heat of the climate in their crowded habitations.] 1E, 1A, 1F, ARE; residence, as the living thus crowded for a length of time in that hot climate, was apt to engender maladies. MS. The variation of 1E from MS here suggests Irving's revision of the proofsheets.

12.14–15   a treatment, by which Amerigo Vespucci declares he
                saw many cured.] ARE; a treatment, adds Amerigo
                Vespucci, by which we saw many cured. MS, 1E, 1A,
                1F. The ARE reading is a clear improvement of the
                syntax; Irving's revision is the basis for this emenda-
                tion of the copy-text.

12.32   entirely] MS; certainly 1E. The compositor's misread-
                ing is here corrected.

12.33   superhuman] 1A, ARE; super-human 1E, 1F; super
                human MS. On the analogy of MS "supernatural"
                (52.4) the copy-text is emended.

13.9   some peopled] ARE; some of which were peopled MS,
                1E, 1A, 1F. The ARE reading, which is the basis for
                emendation of the copy-text here, reflects Irving's
                characteristic tightening and compression of his prose
                style for the ARE.

13.18   oarsmen] 1A, ARE; oars-men 1E, 1F; oars men MS.
                The hyphenation in 1E apparently represents line-
                end word division. Since other compounds with "man"
                or "men" usually appear as one word in MS (e.g., at
                19.7, 26.18, and 356.37), and since the two-word form
                may represent authorial carelessness, the copy-text is
                here emended

14.9   Maracaibo] 1E, 1A, 1F, ARE; Coquibacoa MS. This
                manuscript error Irving apparently caught and cor-
                rected in 1E proofs.

14.25   part,] ARE; part MS, 1E, 1A, 1F. The copy-text is
                here emended, on the example of ARE, to supply the
                necessary punctuation to set off the prepositional
                phrase.

15.8   Spaniards'] T; Spaniards MS, 1E, 1A, 1F, ARE. The
                copy-text is here emended to supply the necessary
                apostrophe for the genetive case.

15.12   peace offerings] The copy-text never hyphenates the
                term; cf. 33.25, 123.30, and 144.27.

15.29   prisoner] MS; prisoners 1E, 1A, 1F, ARE. Since the
                MS singular is appropriately idiomatic, 1E is presumed
                to be an instance of Murray house styling.

15.31   and the two girls] 1E, 1A, 1F, ARE; and two of the
                girls MS. The 1E reading is resumed to be evidence
                of Irving's revision of the 1E proofsheets.

15.31   dexterously] MS, 1E, 1A, 1F; dextrously ARE. The copy-text is inconsistent (preferring "dextrous" at 52.5). No principle of emendation is available.

16.8–11   beauty. Neither ... daughters.] 1E, 1A, 1F, ARE; beauty. The men, moreover, were singularly devoid of jealousy, offering their wives and daughters to the strangers in the most hospitable manner, and shewing signs of surprize and chagrin if their friendly offers were rejected. MS. The 1E variation from MS here suggests that Irving revised the passage in 1E proofs.

16.22   that] MS; which ARE. Here, and at other places noted in the List of Rejected Substantives, a Putnam copy-editor has needlessly altered Irving's characteristic conjunction.

16.40   Crown] 1E; The case is here raised to conform to usual MS practice with this word, e.g., at 24.1, 29.37, and 35.25.

17.36–37   This was the first discovery of the main land of America.] In a burst of national enthusiasm, someone associated with the first American edition (Philadelphia: Carey and Lea, 1831) caused this sentence to be set in italics. However tempted, the editor respects the authority of the copy-text, which is not italicized.

18.5–7   discoveries, . . . importance.] ARE; discoveries. MS. This ARE revision is typical of Irving's chapter-end expansion.

19.7   Moguer,] ARE; Moguer MS. The ARE comma appropriately sets off the prepositional phrase; the copy-text is therefore emended.

19.34   law suit] MS; the copy-text is inconsistent, preferring this form at 138.4, but lawsuit at 36.7.

21.15–16   at a number . . . fortress, the whole] ARE; at a place where there was a kind of fortress protecting a number of houses and gardens situated on a river, the whole MS, 1E, 1A, 1F. The ARE version here is accepted as an instance of Irving's revision for the Putnam edition.

21.28   East] 1A, 1E, ARE; east MS. Since the copy-text tends to capitalize the term as a synonym for the Orient (cf. at 8.38 and 112.1), the copy-text is therefore emended.

24.1–2   he observed on the beach the print of footsteps, of gigantic size] ARE; he observed on the beach the print of footsteps, which seemed of gigantic size MS, 1E, 1F; he observed the print of footsteps on the beach which seemed of gigantic size 1A. Here Irving's characteristic compression of style for the ARE is evident; the copy-text is therefore emended.

26.23 imposition practiced] ARE; imposition that had been practiced MS. Another instance of Irving's phrasal compression in ARE.

27.5 colonize] MS, 1E, 1A, 1F, ARE. While Irving prefers some "s" British spellings, he invariably prefers the *z* spelling for this word.

32.7 Coquibacoa,] ARE; Coquibacoa MS, 1E, 1A. The copy-text is here emended, on the example of ARE, to supply the necessary comma.

33.1 Vergara] 1A, 1F, ARE; Vegara MS, 1E. Irving's MS misspelling, which survives in 1E, is here corrected.

33.38 mean time] 1E; meantime MS. Except for this one instance, MS invariably prefers the two-word form; e.g., at 70.22, 97.26, 109.14, 114.6, 120.25, 133.31, 135.37, and 141.29. Hence, the copy-text is emended.

37.5–7 voyagers; . . . friend] ARE; voyagers, and he was known to possess a stanch friend at Court in the Bishop Fonseca MS; voyagers; and it was thought that an application on his part would be attended with success, for he was known to possess a staunch friend at court in the Bishop Fonseca 1E, 1A, 1F. The ARE reading is the basis for emendation here in every particular.

38.25 Vela,] 1F, ARE; Vela MS, 1E, 1A. The copy-text is here emended, on the example of ARE, to supply the necessary punctuation.

39.30 civilized] MS. In all forms of the word Irving preferred the *z* spelling, which sometimes survives Murray house styling (e.g., 57.10, 91.6, 112.6, 112.7, 169.39, and 362.14).

40.12 high mettled] T here follows the author's revision in 1E proofs, but rejects the 1E hyphenation, which probably represents Murray's house style.

40.16 Jamaica,] ARE; Jamaica MS, 1E, 1A. The copy-text is here emended, on the example of ARE, to supply the necessary comma.

40.22 court,] ARE; court MS, 1E, 1A. The copy-text is here

emended, on the example of ARE, to supply the necessary comma.

40.27   brave,]   ARE; brave MS, 1E, 1A. The copy-text is here
emended, on the example of ARE, to supply the necessary comma.

41.33   Veragua,]   ARE; Veragua MS, 1E, 1A. The copy-text is
here emended, on the example of ARE, to supply the
necessary comma.

43.39   or]   MS; nor ARE. Here and elsewhere, as noted in the
List of Rejected Substantives, correlative conjunctions
in ARE have been improperly negatived by a Putnam copyeditor.

45.36   was surrounded]   MS, 1E, 1A, 1F; were surrounded
ARE. The ARE reading is rejected as a Putnam alteration not reflecting Irving's intention.

46.35   discoverers]   ARE; discoveries 1E, 1A, 1F. The ARE
reading is here accepted on the ground that Irving
preferred "discoverers" as making clearer sense. (The
MS lacks this sentence.)

46.40   headstrong]   ARE; head-long 1E, 1F; headlong 1A.
"Headstrong" in ARE is accepted here as a more
appropriate synonym for "rash"; the copy-text is therefore emended. (The MS lacks this adjective.)

53.37   cassava]   T; casava MS. The MS elsewhere invariably
doubles the s; cf. 12.31, 58.12, 58.19 and 133.25.

57.28   villages]   MS; villagers 1E, 1A, ARE. One is inclined
to suspect that the 1E compositor misread MS. The
copy-text is therefore not emended.

59.25   Chapter XI]   1E; missing in MS.

62.18   Chapter XIII]   1E, 1A, 1F, ARE; Chap 12 MS. The
chapter numbers underwent reordering, probably in
Irving's revision of 1E proofslips, since he needed to
insert the matter of chapter 12, which is missing in
the manuscript.

63.26   waylaid]   ARE; way-laid 1E, 1A, 1F; way layed MS.
The MS was so extensively revised here that T accepts
the ARE reading, since MS sometimes prefers waylayed.

63.31   rout]   1F, ARE; route 1E, 1A. The 1E printer's error
is here corrected. Missing in MS.

63.36   hardships and]   ARE; hardships he had sustained, and
1E, 1A, 1F; missing in MS.

64.15 entreated that] MS; entreated 1E, 1A, 1F, ARE. The MS reading is here retained as appropriately grammatical.

64.17 *"that . . . grave."*] 1E. The editor here accepts the italics of 1E, not present in MS.

65.4 Chapter I] T; Chap 1 MS. The chapter number, omitted in all printed forms of the text, is here retained.

69.11 days'] 1F, ARE; days MS, 1E, 1A. Here the copy-text is emended to provide the necessary apostrophe.

69.24 cargoes] MS; cargo 1E, 1A, 1F, ARE. The plural designation was apparently dropped by the 1E compositor.

70.15–16 a supply] MS; the supply 1E, 1A, 1F, ARE. Irving's manuscript deliberately crosses out "the" and substitutes "a"; the MS reading is therefore restored as representing Irving's intended reading.

73.24 in every defile] MS; at every defile 1E, 1A, 1F, ARE. The 1E reading is here rejected in favor of the greater idiomatic character of the MS reading.

73.29 sallied] MS, 1E, 1A, 1F; sailed ARE. Though ARE beguiles here, the editor preserves the copy-text's "sallied." Like the sullied/solid flesh of Hamlet, the nearness of sallied/sailed suggests an ARE compositor's misreading of printer's copy. "Sallied" has, moreover, greater verbal vigor and connotative appropriateness to "armament" and "flushed with the consciousness of power."

74.38–73.5 surprize . . . encounter] 1E, 1A, 1F, ARE; surprize and indignation of the Bachelor, who threatened to put him on the first uninhabited island they should encounter.* MS. Irving apparently decided not to supply the footnote, implied by the asterisk, and revised the sentence in proofslips. MS preference for the *z* spelling is the rationale for the emendation.

75.9–77.20 harbour of Carthagena. . . . Valenzuela.] The manuscript here contains matter listed in List of Emendations. Irving apparently added that lengthy passage to indicate how pacific the Indians could be. But in doing so he made chapter 6 too long. He therefore broke chapter 6 at the end of the episode on the peaceful Indians and shifted the encounter of Pizarro

	and Ojeda's men to chapter 7, though the MS contains it in chapter 6.
78.25	compunction] MS, 1E, 1A, 1F; compunctions ARE. The ARE reading is rejected as not idiomatic, a probable compositor's error.
79.41	otros,"] 1A, 1F; otros, 1E, ARE. The copy-text (here 1E) is emended to supply the necessary end quotation marks.
80.35	previous] ARE; previously MS, 1E, 1A, 1F. The copy-text is here emended since Irving apparently intended, in the ARE revision, an adjective modifying ["to this"], rather than an adverb, to modify "sailed."
90.12–13	Nuñez, who . . . favorite] 1E; T follows the 1E revision here, except that MS "favorite" is retained.
90.30	skillfully] T here restores the 1E revision of the MS spelling.
92.12	cacique] ARE; Cacique MS, 1E, 1A, 1F. The copy-text is here emended to lower case since it ordinarily does not present a capital for this term. Cf. 194.8, 220.2, 324.10, 326.13.
93.10	Coyba. The cacique] 1E, 1F, ARE; Coyba, the dominions of Careta. The cacique MS, 1A. The identical reading of MS and 1A here suggests that 1A was set from proofsheets of 1E, which Irving revised after sending duplicate sheets to America.
93.16	outcast] 1E, 1F, ARE; traytor MS; traitor 1A. Again 1A appears to have been set from 1E proofslips which Irving later revised.
96.5	porch. "Why," said he, "should] ARE; porch. Before the strangers could recover from their astonishment at this sudden act, he thus addressed them, "Why should 1E, 1F; porch. Before the Spaniards . . . should MS, 1A. The appearance of "Spaniards" in 1A and MS again indicates that the proofslips of 1E were revised in London after duplicates had been sent to Carey & Lea in America.
96.11	South. "Beyond these] T here retains MS punctuation.
96.29–97.2	The youthful cacique . . . by the idea.] 1E, 1A, 1F, ARE. In MS these two paragraphs are reversed. A close study of the sequence of the narrative confirms

the rightness of Irving's reordering of the two paragraphs. The copy-text is therefore emended.

96.29   further] MS, 1E, 1A, 1F; farther ARE. There is no reason to emend the copy-text here since the ARE compositor, presumably, misread his printer's copy or followed Putnam house style.

97.25   likewise] 1E, 1F, ARE; also MS, 1A. The appearance of "also" in 1A again suggests that 1E was revised after a duplicate set of proofslips was sent to Carey & Lea in America.

100.11   Black River] ARE; black river MS, 1E, 1A, 1F. The terms are emended to uppercase on the authority of customary case usage, e.g., at 101.14 and 101.25.

100.24–29   These habitations . . . fishing] 1E, 1A, 1F, ARE; *missing in* MS.

101.13   Dobayba, . . . favorite] T here retains MS spelling of "favorite."

102.40–103.1   Foiled . . . and concerted] 1E, 1F, ARE; Foiled in this and other attempts of the kind, Zemaco resorted to the conspiracy with the neighboring caciques with which the settlement was menaced. (*New paragraph*) Five caciques had joined in the confederacy. They had prepared a hundred canoes; had amassed provisions for an army; and had concerted MS, 1A. The close correspondence between the MS and 1A here suggests that the duplicate proofslips of 1E, sent to Carey & Lea, were afterward corrected for the 1E edition. Still, the MS and 1A differ here somewhat: 1A begins a new paragraph with "Five" and provides the missing MS period after "confederacy," both changes thought by the editor to have no authority.

103.27   abandoned] 1E, 1F, ARE; might have abandoned MS, 1A. Again, 1E proofslips, from which 1A was set, were later revised in London.

104.16   had elapsed] 1E, 1F, ARE; elapsed MS, 1A. Here again the 1E proofs, from which 1A had been set, were later corrected for 1E.

104.30–31   honour, and peculiarly gifted with the] ARE; honour, who seems to have peculiarly possessed the MS, 1E, 1A, 1F. The ARE version is here accepted as Irving's revision, in every particular but one, the spelling "honor," which is rejected in favour of MS "honour."

105.42 ringleaders] 1A, 1F, ARE; ring leaders MS, 1E. The copy-text is here emended to conform with the contemporary compounding practice.

105.42 put into] 1E, 1F, ARE; thrown in MS, 1A. Again, 1A was set from incompletely corrected proofslips of 1E.

106.8–9 (to . . . gold)] 1E, 1F, ARE; to . . . gold MS, 1A. The absence of parentheses in 1A again suggests the incompletely corrected proofslips from which it was set.

106.27 Zamudio,] 1F, ARE; Zamudio MS, 1E, 1A. The copy-text is here emended to supply appropriate appositive punctuation.

107.16 resolute, vigorous, and devoted] 1E, 1F, ARE; resolute and vigorous, and those most devoted MS, 1A. Again, 1A suggests the incompletely corrected 1E proofslips from which 1A was set.

107.18 danger] 1E, 1F, ARE; peril MS, 1A. Again 1A was clearly set from 1E proofslips to which Irving later made revisions for 1E.

108.7 dominion] 1E, 1F, ARE; dominions MS, 1A. Additional evidence that 1A was set from 1E proofslips Irving corrected after sending duplicate proofs to Carey & Lea.

111.21 pray to him to guide] 1E; pray to him that he will guide MS, 1A. Again, 1A suggests the incompletely corrected 1E proofslips from which 1A was set.

111.22 and which] 1E; and in which MS, 1A. Again, 1A suggests the incompletely corrected 1E proofslips from which 1A was set.

111.33 rest] 1E, 1F, ARE; people MS, 1A. Again, 1A suggests the incompletely corrected proofslips from which 1A was set.

112.3–5 savage? . . . the Spaniards] 1E, 1F, ARE; Indian? The latter could hardly be the case, for the natives had told the Spaniards 1A; Indian? Yet the natives had talked MS. The appearance of "Indian" in MS and 1A again suggests the incompletely corrected 1E proofslips from which 1A was set.

112.30 spent] 1E, 1F, ARE; been MS, 1A. Again, the correspondence of MS and 1A suggests the incompletely corrected 1E proofslips from which 1A was set.

112.30 days in] 1E, 1F, ARE; days MS, 1A. The correspondence of MS and 1A suggests the incompletely corrected 1E proofslips from which 1A was set.

113.28   pounds'] ARE; pounds MS, 1E, 1A, 1F. The copy-text is here emended, on the example of ARE, to supply the necessary apostrophe.

114.8   Escaray] 1E, 1F, ARE; Esceray MS; Escary 1A. The copytext is emended to correct Irving's misspelling in the MS.

114.10   days'] 1F, ARE; days MS, 1A, 1E. The copy-text is here emended to provide the necessary apostrophe.

115.9   Doña] T here retains the MS spelling of Doña Juana.

115.22   Equinoctial] T; equinoctial MS, 1A, 1F, ARE; equinoxial 1E. The copy-text case is here emended to conform with usual MS practice, e.g., at 25.9 and 27.2.

115.32   they] ARE; they all MS, 1E, 1A, 1F. The copy-text is here emended on the authority of ARE.

116.10   quantity] MS; quantities ARE. The ARE reading probably represents Putnam house styling.

116.26   Finding] 1E, 1F, ARE; Seeing MS, 1A. The form "Seeing" in 1A suggests the incompletely corrected proofslips of the copy-text from which 1A was set.

117.7   sight, in] ARE; sight, as if swallowed in MS, 1E, 1A, 1F. The copy-text is here emended on the authority of ARE.

118.27   superhuman] 1A, ARE; super human MS; super-human 1E, 1F. The MS two-word form was probably a careless error; MS gives superhuman at 12.33.

119.14   burthens] MS, 1E, 1A, 1F; burdens ARE. Here, and at 119.17, 121.14, 123.21 and 165.17, ARE substitutes "burdens" and "burden." These are presumed to be instances of Putnam house styling; the copy-text is therefore not emended.

119.19   awakened] ARE; filled him with MS, 1E, 1A, 1F. The copy-text is here emended on the authority of ARE.

119.22   Further] MS, 1F; Farther 1E, 1A, ARE. The copy-text is not emended here. 1E is presumed to be a compositor's error since it diverges from the MS and since the 1E table of contents (xiii.17) gives "Further."

122.26   issued] 1E, 1F, ARE; given MS, 1A. The MS and 1A reading here suggests the incompletely corrected 1E proofslips from which 1A was set.

122.29   visibly] 1E, 1F, ARE; too much MS, 1A. Again, the

MS and 1A reading suggests the incompletely corrected 1E proofslips from which 1A was set.

122.29–30   remains accordingly a]   1E, 1F, ARE; remains a MS, 1A. Again, the identical readings in MS and 1A suggest the 1E proofs, incompletely corrected, from which 1A was set.

128.32   countermanded]   MS, 1A, ARE; counter-manded 1E, 1F. The hyphenation in 1E represents line-end word division; the copy-text is therefore not emended.

129.5   to Don Pedrarias.]   1E, 1A, 1F, ARE; *missing in* MS.

129.24   objects]   1F, ARE; object, 1E, 1A; *missing in* MS. The copy-text is here emended on the authority of ARE.

129.26   crossbows]   1E, 1A; cross-bows 1F, ARE; *missing in* MS. Though the MS gives "cross bows" at 107.17, usage is inconsistent and no principle of emendation can be inferred from the copy-text.

129.30   Islands]   1F; islands 1E, 1A, ARE; *missing in* MS. The copy-text is here emended to capitalize the term.

131.13   transcendant]   1E, 1F; transcendent 1A, ARE; *missing in* MS. The spelling "transcendant" in the copy-text (1E) is presumed not to be a compositor's error, since the copy-text is consistent in preferring "ascendant" or "ascendancy" throughout (e.g., 19.17, 40.37, 57.19); the copy-text is therefore not emended.

134.2   Don]   1E, 1A, 1F, ARE; *missing in* MS.

134.26   Alcalde Mayor]   1A, 1F; alcalde mayor MS, 1E, ARE. The copy-text is here emended on the authority of usual MS practice, e.g., at 127.29, 130.2 and 130.18.

139.20   huge]   MS; large 1E, 1A, 1F, ARE. 1E is presumed to be a compositor's misreading of the MS, which gives inescapably, if not clearly, "huge."

140.26   previous]   MS; perilous 1E, 1A, 1F, ARE. 1E is presumed to be the compositor's misreading of the MS, which unmistakably gives "previous."

145.16   pounds']   ARE; pounds MS, 1E, 1A, 1F. The copy-text is here emended, on the example of ARE, to supply the necessary apostrophe.

146.29   retired]   MS; returned 1E, 1A, 1F, ARE. The manuscript reading, misconstrued by the 1E compositor, is here restored.

148.33   passed]   T; past MS, 1E, 1A, 1F, ARE. The correct preterit form is here supplied by the T editor.

150.14   Nuñez] 1A, 1F, ARE; Nunez MS, 1E. The copy-text is
              here and passim emended to supply the necessary
              tilde.

153.21   Islands] 1F, ARE; islands 1E, 1A. The copy-text is
              here emended on the example of ARE. There is no
              MS for chapters 25 and after; hence 1E becomes
              copy-text.

154.10   Chuchama] 1A; Chuchamà 1E, 1F, ARE. The copy-
              text is here emended to delete the accent, since in no
              other instance in MS or 1E is the name accented;
              cf. 145.27–28, 145.31.

154.25   expedition;] 1A, 1F, ARE; expedition, 1E. The copy-
              text is here emended, since it appears to suffer broken
              type in all inspected copies, to restore the semicolon.

155.5   Andres] 1A, 1F, ARE; Francisco 1E. The copy-text is
              here emended on the example of ARE and the cor-
              rect form of the name in the copy-text at 142.37.

157.9   foretell] 1A, ARE; foretel 1E, 1F. The copy-text is
              here emended to correct the misprint.

157.27   Southern Ocean] T; southern ocean 1E, 1A, 1F, ARE.
              The copy-text is here emended to supply capitals,
              which normally appear with this term in MS and 1E,
              e.g., at 3.19, 27.15, 120.41, 138.14, 151.9, and 162.31.

159.4   Andres] 1A, 1F, ARE; Andrez 1E. The copy-text is
              here emended to correct the spelling of the name.

164.4   Regidor] T; regidor 1E, 1A, 1F, ARE. The copy-text
              is here emended to bring the case into conformity
              with usual capitalization of "Regidor" (e.g., at 91.28
              and 97.9.

166.28   sea-side] 1E, 1A, 1F, ARE. Though the form "sea
              side" appears in the MS at 48.6, the only other ob-
              served instance of the word, no principle of emenda-
              tion is possible.

166.38   overcome] 1A, ARE; over-come 1E, 1F. The hyphena-
              tion in 1E here apparently represents line-end word
              division.

167.34   when intelligence] 1E, 1F, ARE; when, in 1517, in-
              telligence 1A. This 1A reading is rejected on the
              grounds that it represents a reading in the 1E proof-
              slips, from which 1A was set, which Irving later
              deleted.

168.21   tidings] 1A, 1F, ARE; tiding 1E. The copy-text is emended on the greater frequency, in general usage, of the plural form. Cf. 1E "tidings" at 171.29.

168.23   concealed in] 1E, 1F, ARE; concealed it in 1A. The 1A reading is rejected as reflecting the incompletely corrected proofslips of 1E, from which it was set.

168.27   Cortez] 1F, ARE; Cortes 1E, 1A. In two instances (43.8 and 171.31) the Anglicized z spelling appears; in nine other cases (168.40, 169.32, 170.12, 170.15, 170.41–171.1, 171.2, 171.8, 171.13, and 171.21) the Spanish spelling survives Murray house styling. In the editor's judgment, the copy-text should be emended in these nine cases; ample warrant for this view inheres in the two 1E Anglicized forms and Irving's manifest preference for "Cortez" in ARE.

170.5–6   a hooting rabble] 1E, 1F, ARE; the rabble 1A. The 1A reading apparently represents the incompletely corrected proofslips from which 1A was set.

170.20   hogshead] 1A, ARE; hogs-head 1E, 1F. The intention of the copy-text cannot be determined here, since the hyphenation in 1E occurs at line end; nevertheless, the editor judges that Irving preferred the one-word form, since he passed it in revising ARE proofs. The copy-text is therefore emended.

171.36   son!"*] 1A, 1F, ARE; son!* 1E. The copy-text is here emended to supply the missing quotation marks.

173.20   Gulf of Parita or Paria] ARE; Gulf of Parita or Paris 1E, 1F; Gulf of Paria 1A. The copy-text is here emended to correct the 1E misspelling. The 1A omission of "Parita or" is presumed to have no authority.

173.25   hereabout] 1A; here-about 1E, 1F, ARE. The hyphenation in 1E and ARE occurs at line end and presumably represents simple word division; the copy-text is therefore emended.

175.14   frosts] ARE; frost 1E, 1A, 1F. The copy-text is here emended, on the authority of ARE, to substitute the plural form.

175.33   valour] 1A, 1F; valor 1E, ARE. This is the sole appearance of the American "-or" spelling in the copy-text. Since Irving overwhelmingly prefers "valour" (e.g., at 124.36, 126.18, 128.7), the 1E copy-text is therefore emended.

177.23   some time] 1A, ARE; sometime 1E, 1F. The copy-text is here emended to separate two words run together, presumably to justify the line.

177.32   I,] 1A, 1F, ARE; I. 1E. The copy-text is here emended on the authority of ARE, to delete the period and to substitute the comma necessary to set off the appositive. Cf. MS and 1E usage at 37.16.

178.16   King] T; king 1E, 1A, 1F, ARE. The copy-text is here emended to supply the capital, which usually appears with the proper name in MS and 1E (e.g., at 30.3, 36.15, 36.21, and 92.6).

180.6   incontestable] ARE; incontestible 1E, 1A, 1F. The copy-text is here emended, on the authority of ARE, to correct the spelling of the suffix.

181.16   areyto] ARE; Areyto 1E, 1A, 1F. The common noun is here lowercased on the example of ARE.

181.19   apprize] 1E. The copy-text is here not emended since the z spelling doubtless represents Irving's MS form.

183.2   Agueybanà] 1A, ARE; Aguaybana 1E, 1F. Here, and at 183.7, the copy-text is emended to correct the spelling, which is correctly given at 180.11, 180.19, 181.31 and 182.3.

183.12   Caparra] 1F, ARE; Caparra, 1E, 1A. The copy-text is here emended, on the authority of ARE, to delete the unnecessary comma.

184.14   grave.] Though ARE runs this and the following paragraph together, the revision is presumed to be without Irving's sanction since it creates an unusually long paragraph and lacks the unity of 1E; the copy-text is therefore not emended.

184.30   withdrew] 1A, 1F, ARE; with-drew 1E, 1F. The hyphenation of 1E is presumed to represent line-end word division; the copy-text is therefore not emended.

185.33   death-blow] 1E; death blow 1A; deathblow 1F, ARE. The 1E hyphenation, at line-end here, cannot be emended since there are no other instances of the form in the copy-text available for comparison.

186.17   realize] 1E. The copy-text is not emended although it otherwise supplies the British s spelling, e.g., at 186.27 and 187.6. The z form doubtless is a survival from the lost MS.

187.18   port] ARE; Port 1E, 1A, 1F. The copy-text is here

emended, to lowercase, on the authority of ARE and usual 1E practice, e.g., at 348.21.

187.20   northward] 1A, 1F, ARE; north-ward 1E. The hyphenation in the copy-text is judged by the editor to be line-end hyphenation dividing the word; cf. "westward" at 189.11, "eastward" at 69.5, and "northwestward" at 108.6.

187.35   men,"] 1A, 1F, ARE; men, 1E. The copy-text is here emended to supply the necessary quotation marks.

188.4   Salvador] ARE; Salvador's 1E, 1A, 1F. The copy-text is here emended on the authority of ARE.

188.7   have drank] 1E, 1A, ARE; have drunk 1F. Since the verb form in 1E was acceptable in 1831, the copy-text is not emended.

188.33   tradition,] 1A, 1F, ARE; tradition; 1E. The copy-text is here emended, on the authority of ARE, to supply the comma.

189.4   to which] 1E; to whom ARE. The copy-text is not emended since ARE appears to represent Putnam misreading of printer's copy.

189.6   sybil] 1E, 1A, 1F; sibyl ARE. Though the 1E spelling is less frequent than "sibyl," the copy-text is not emended.

190.35   archipelago] 1F; Achipelago 1E, 1A; Archipelago ARE. The copy-text is here emended to correct the obvious 1E misprint and to lowercase, in conformity with usual MS and 1E practice, e.g., at 188.3 and 188.8.

191.18   distribution] ARE; distributions 1E, 1A, 1F. The copy-text is here emended, on the authority of ARE, to provide the singular number.

191.32   undertaking] 1A, ARE; under-taking 1E, 1F. The hyphenation here in 1E presumably represents line-end word division.

191.33   wished-for] 1A, ARE; wished for 1E, 1F. The copy-text is here emended on the example of ARE and 1E hyphenation at 139.8.

192.1   fate,"] 1A, 1F, ARE; fate" 1E. The copy-text is here emended, on the authority of ARE, to supply the necessary comma.

192.10   requiescunt] 1E, 1F, ARE; requiescat 1A. Though "requiescat" is a grammatical form indicating the subjunctive mood of the verb, Irving's translation clearly indicates the indicative third-person plural; consequently, the copy-text is not emended.

APPENDIXES

194.6–7   to France] The text here gives the MS1eC reading, altered as indicated in 1EC and 2EC, and restored by Irving in MS2eC and 3AC.

194.16   translation of the ashes] The present reading reflects the MS1eC (and possibly MS1aC as well), which 1EC and 2EC unaccountably alter. Irving restores the MS1eC forms in MS2eC, which become the basis then for the 3AC reading.

196.17   San] The copy-text is here emended to provide the proper form, which is accurately given at 194.31.

197.6   notice is digested] This reading, which seems inferior to the 1EC "account is taken," was restored by Irving in MS2eC and became the basis for the 3AC reading.

198.29–30   in him, but could] This reading reflects one of Irving's few revisions for the text of 3AC, most substantive variations between MS1eC and 3AC being first recorded in MS2eC.

199.24   Valencia] This spelling, revised for 3AC, constitutes only one of hundreds of errors or alternative forms in the accidentals of MS1eC, particularly in Latin, Spanish, and Italian.

200.27–30   Anacaona . . . disasters.] This reading is typical of Irving's additions to the copy-text in preparing MS2eC.

201.28   Nicuesa] The text is emended, here and at 89.15, to correct a spelling error that survives in all texts prior to the Twayne edition.

208.21   1525] The reading of 1525 in 2EC and 1825 in 1EC testifies to the existence of two English editions.

208.29   Our Lady] The copy-text is here emended to capitalize fully a term erratically treated in each of the printed texts, but which Irving's ambiguous manuscript case forms suggest as possible capitals.

218.21   Academy . . . Letters] The case is here raised since Irving, in the haste of composition, did not always bother to capitalize proper names, expecting to do it on the proofsheets, if it had not already been done for him by the printer or copyeditor.

219.7–9 shown . . . proved.] The successive revisions of this passage, provided in the List of Emendations, indicate succinctly the evolution of this text.

222.8 Bernaldes] The text is here emended to correct the spelling, which is inaccurate at this point in all other printed forms of the text.

227.28–34 The brilliant . . . relations.] The MS2eC reading is rejected inasmuch as it does not find its way into 3AC. The editor assumes that, since Irving rejected the MS2eC substantive, the Twayne editor must follow suit.

229.9 1485] The date 1685 in 3AC is clearly an error and is here rejected.

236.21–22 Vicente Yañez Pinzon] The 3AC reading is here rejected. Pinzon's first name was misspelled in MS1eC, canceled in 1EC and 2EC, restored as the misspelling "Vincente" in MS2eC, and the error passed undetected into 3AC.

239.37 Jose] The form given here is based on MS1eC, as well as on the cognate form of the name in *Companions* (5.34). Compositorial misreading produced "Tote" in 1EC; but Irving's MS2eC correction "Josef" he himself rejected in 3AC.

245.26–248.18 No . . . Columbus] T here substitutes for MS1eC the extensively revised appendix in the form of the text found in MS2eC and 3AC. Irving's superscription in MS2eC reads "To be inserted in the place of Illustration No X of the first edition." The full text of the canceled MS1eC appendix is given in List of Emendations.

264.26 No. XVII] In the case of this appendix, the text is that of MS1eC, emended to incorporate or substitute substantives from 3AC. Readers should be aware, however, that a complete revision, in holograph, was completed by Irving for MS2eC. It is headed by this instruction to the printer: "to be inserted in place of the printed article vol. 4." Although this revision reflects a later state of the MS1eC text, Irving either forgot about his revision in preparing 3AC or else rejected it. For the text of 3AC is based on 1EC, slightly revised for minor stylistic improvement, rather than on MS2eC. Although the grounds for basing T on MS2eC are tempting, the editor judges 3AC to have a determinative authority over the substantives of this text. This judgment is supported by the editor's belief that the appendix of the "Route of Columbus in the First Voyage" in MS1eC is in fact the work of Alexander Slidell Mackenzie, as the *Note to the Revised Edition of 1848*" (277.26) suggests. If MS1eC represents Mackenzie's version of Columbus's route, a fact suggested by the stylistic infelicities and internal evidence like the phrasing "the writer of this article, who has been much among these islands" (265.8–9), MS2eC was Irving's effort to polish up Mackenzie's prose style. Why then did not Irving reproduce his MS2eC revision in 3AC? One can only surmise, on the basis of his "Note," that his retention of the MS1eC form of the appendix was Irving's tribute to and acknowledgment of his old friend. For the sake of comparison, the MS2eC revision is printed *in toto* in the List of Rejected Substantives.

277.26   *Note*]   Irving's revisions for the 3AC are, in the appendixes, relatively minor. Such notes account for much of the substance of the additions to the text.

281.29–35   "In preparing . . . Polo]   This MS2eC addition is in Irving's hand.

282.5–33   Constantinople . . . East.]   The MS2eC revision of 1EC, on the authority of which 3AC was based, and on which these emendations are given, is not principally in Irving's hand. Except for the headnote of instruction to the printer and the paragraph beginning "After a march" the holograph revision is in the flowing hand of an unknown professional scribe.

285.8–287.8 services . . . afterwards]   Here, as before, the handwriting of the MS2eC revision is that of Irving's scribe, except for a manuscript link, beginning "Ramusio, in his preface," and occasional corrections of the scribe's spelling or of Irving's own script.

285.14   years']   The copy-text is here emended to supply the necessary apostrophe.

288.40–289.10	Fantina . . . extinguished] The revision of the MS2eC passage is in the hand of Irving's scribe.
290.29–291.11	travellers . . . others] Except for occasional interlinear corrections and the appended note at 296.25, all extensive MS2eC revisions in this appendix are in the hand of Irving's scribe.
290.38	Prevost, Hist.] The editor judges that the 3AC deletion of "Prevost" to have been an oversight. The MS1eC name is therefore retained in T.
294.34–41	*Supposed . . . former] This MS2eC addition is in Irving's hand.
298.6	island Atalantis] The discrepancy here between the 1EC and 2EC readings offers additional evidence that Murray took *Columbus* into a second edition, without Irving's knowledge.
317.38	T. A.] The text is here emended to correct the initials, which Irving himself corrected at 311.34.
325.6–39	Nothing . . . Deza."] This extensive MS2eC addition is in Irving's hand.
330.25	sister] T follows the copy-text rather than the MS2eC, which emends the term to "niece," since Irving himself rejected "niece" in 3AC.
331.6–332.9	and he . . . perfidious] This extensive MS2eC revision is in Irving's hand.
332.23	Velasquez] The copy-text is here emended, on the authority of MS2eC. Irving's correction of "Alvarez" was apparently overlooked by the compositor of 3AC and by Irving himself when reading proof.
344.39	is secure] The 3AC reading of "in secure" is probably a compositor's error.
345.38	whosoever] Here, and at 432.12 and 435.8, the copy-text is emended to supply the correct nominative case for the pronoun, on the ground that Irving would doubtless have corrected the improper case had he noticed it.
346.26	calesero] The misspelling is corrected here, and at 354.24, 354.34, and 361.40. The copy-text gives the correct spelling at 457.15.
350.13	bed-room] 1E, 1A, 1F, ARE. Here and at 353.8 hyphenation occurs in 1E at line-end. Since there are no other observed forms of the word in the copy-text, it is impossible to determine Irving's intention. Conse-

quently, the editor takes the conservative position, warranted by ARE hyphenation in both cases, that Irving intended to hyphenate the term.

350.15   pack-saddles]   1E, 1A, 1F, ARE. The form here appears in 1E as line-end hyphenation. Since ARE preserves the hyphen in midline, the editor judges the hyphenated form to have Irving's sanction; the copy-text is therefore not emended.

350.17   out-of-the-way parts]   1E, 1A, 1F; out-of-the-way-parts ARE. In 1E the hyphen between "the" and "way" appears at the end of the line; the additional hyphen in ARE, between "way" and "parts" is believed to be the ARE compositor's error and is rejected.

350.20   indispensable]   1A, 1F, ARE; indispensible 1E. The copy-text misspelling is here corrected.

352.2   gentleman]   1A, 1F, ARE; gentlemen 1E. The misprint in the copy-text is here corrected.

353.7   whitewashed]   T; white-washed 1E, 1A, 1F, ARE. Though in all printed forms here the term is hyphenated, the copy-text is emended since 1E represents line-end word-division: at 355.5 and 358.29 the copy-text gives "whitewashed."

353.37   shores]   ARE; shore 1E, 1A, 1F. The copy-text is here emended, on the authority of ARE, to indicate the plural.

353.41   landing-place]   1E, 1A, 1F, ARE. Since 1E hyphenates the term at line-end, it is impossible to declare Irving's intention as other than the form given here; consequently the copy-text is not emended.

354.35   himself.]   This and the following paragraph are run together in ARE to the detriment of the unity and coherence of Irving's paragraph structures. The editor judges the joining of these paragraphs to be without authorial sanction; the copy-text is therefore not emended.

354.41   vineyard]   1A, ARE; vine-yard 1E, 1F. The hyphenation here represents line-end word division; since the copy-text otherwise prefers "vineyard" (e.g., 354.7, 354.17), the copy-text is emended.

355.1   pines already mentioned,]   ARE; pines which I have mentioned, 1E, 1A, 1F. The copy-text is here emended on the authority of ARE.

355.6   Moors, has not] ARE; Moors, it has not 1E, 1A, 1F.
           The copy-text is here emended on the authority of
           ARE.

355.20   fig-tree] 1A, 1F, ARE; fig tree 1E. The copy-text is here
           emended on the authority of 1E hyphenation of the
           term at 365.23 and Irving's approval of the hyphen
           in ARE.

356.35   physician] 1A, ARE; Physician 1E, 1F. The copy-text
           is here emended on the authority of ARE, to lower
           the unnecessary uppercase.

357.20   Perez,] 1F, ARE; Perez 1E, 1A. The copy-text is here
           emended, on the authority of ARE, to supply the
           appositive comma.

358.26   Don Rafael] Irving's error in the name is here cor-
           rected. He almost certainly means that Don Rafael of
           357.36 and 359.8. Irving's diary for August 13, 1828,
           mentions meeting "in route Don Rafael on horse-
           back, son of Don Juan, 21 years of age. Studying Fren
           & mathematics. Din with Don Juan & Rafael at the
           Hacienda" (Penny, p. 52). This diary entry, in the
           context of "A Visit to Palos," suggests additional evi-
           dence for emending "Gabriel" to "Rafael" here.

361.3   interwoven] The editor judges that 1E here repre-
           sents line-end word division; the copy-text is there-
           fore emended on the authority of ARE.

361.10   V,] The copy-text is emended here on the authority
           of ARE.

363.12   if you desire] The copy-text is emended to provide
           the pronoun which must have been inadvertently
           deleted in the 1E proofslips.

363.30   of said] The copy-text is here emended on the author-
           ity of ARE: an identical phrase, not emended in ARE,
           occurs at 363.14. But the editor takes the conservative
           position that Irving may not have intended emenda-
           tion at 363.14. The copy-text in that instance is there-
           fore not emended.

363.40   forcibly] The 1A reading of "powerfully," here re-
           jected, suggests the incompletely corrected 1E proof-
           slips from which 1A was set; consequently, the copy-
           text is not emended.

364.10   THE END.] 1E; the absence of "THE END." in ARE
           does not convince the editor that Irving intended its

deletion from the text. Since "A Visit to Palos" and "Manifesto of Alonzo de Ojeda" were separated from the text, in ARE, by the inclusion of thirty-seven intervening appendixes relative to *Columbus*, it is presumed that "THE END." was inadvertently dropped.

LIST OF EMENDATIONS

The numbers before each note indicate the page and line. Chapter numbers, chapter or section titles, epigraphs, author's chapter or section summaries, texts, quotations, and footnotes are included in the line count. Only running heads are omitted from the count.

The reading to the left of the bracket is the portion of the text under consideration or discussion and represents an accepted reading that differs from the copy-text. The source of the reading is identified by the symbol after the bracket.

The reading after the semicolon is the rejected reading of the copy-text and any other text in which that reading occurs; if other alternatives are also available, they are recorded following that reading.

The swung (wavy) dash ~ represents the same word, words, or characters that appear before the bracket, and is used in recording punctuation variants; the caret ∧ indicates that a mark of punctuation is omitted. T signifies that a decision to emend or not to emend has been made on the authority of the editor of the Twayne edition. Some of these editorial decisions are explained in the Discussions of Adopted Readings, which include decisions to emend as well as some decisions not to emend. Discussion is identified by an asterisk*. Brief notes in the List of Emendations itself are italicized.

*xi.10	natives]	ARE; Nations 1E, 1F
*xii.18	shipwreck]	ARE; Ship-wreck 1E
*xii.25	Enciso]	ARE; Encisco 1E
xii.29	Enciso]	ARE; Encisco 1E
xii.33	Enciso]	ARE; Encisco 1E
*xii.33	downfall]	ARE; downfal 1E
xiii.9	Darien]	ARE; Darian 1E
*xiii.17	Nuñez]	ARE; Nuñes 1E
*xiii.29	Golden]	ARE; Gold 1E
xiv.31	Havana]	ARE; Havanna MS
*xiv.32	Notice]	ARE; Account 1EC
*xiv.34	Age of Columbus]	ARE; Missing in 1EC
*xv.16	Prester John]	ARE; Missing in 1EC

*3.9   first fruits]   T; ~-~ 1E
*4.14   Christian]   ARE; christian 1E
*4.29   arsenal]   ARE; arsenals 1E
*4.30   noted commanders]   ARE; noted of the early com-
                  manders 1E
*4.36   seaman]   ARE; sea-man 1E
*5.32   Archives]   ARE; archives 1E; achives 1F
*5.34   Josef]   T; Jozef 1E
7.5   CHAPTER I.]   1E, ARE; Chap 1. MS
7.8   History]   1E, ARE; history MS
7.14   service]   1E, 1A, ARE; Service MS
7.19   Christian]   ARE; christian MS, 1E
7.20   and]   1E, 1A, ARE; & MS. *Emended also at* 7.30, 12.4,
                  13.6, 13.13, 14.31, 15.22, 17.15, 17.16, 19.15, 20.17,
                  20.24, 20.36, 20.38, 21.6, 21.33, 22.2, 22.21, 23.10,
                  25.1, 26.5, 26.10, 26.32, 29.10, 29.21, 29.38, 31.25,
                  31.30, 31.32, 31.32, 32.12, 32.21, 32.24, 32.26, 32.34,
                  32.39, 33.22, 34.2, 34.13, 34.23, 34.25, 34.33, 34.35,
                  35.6, 36.30, 37.5, 41.13, 45.4, 47.9, 49.1, 53.10, 53.16,
                  55.6, 61.37, 64.24, 66.26, 67.33, 74.12, 78.27, 80.33,
                  84.24, 85.2, 85.5, 88.21, 90.18, 90.18, 91.14, 91.17,
                  96.39, 97.11, 98.30, 99.22, 101.3, 102.36, 105.28, 105.32,
                  105.37, 106.21, 106.22, 107.37, 108.21, 108.25, 109.6,
                  109.8, 109.21, 109.35, 110.28, 112.20, 114.28, 115.33,
                  116.31, 117.26, 119.22, 121.6, 122.5, 122.34, 124.9,
                  125.24, 125.24, 126.32, 135.8, 135.15, 135.19, 135.33,
                  136.23, 138.27, 138.83, 140.9, 140.9, 140.14, 141.3,
                  141.4, 145.15, 145.38, 146.37, 147.24, 147.36, 147.38,
                  149.21 149.28, 212.30, 213.36, 213.42, 214.3, 214.8,
                  214.12, 229.20, 308.21, 310.40, 319.18, 324.34, 325.1,
                  325.4, 339.3, 341.1, and 344.23.
7.22   country]   1E, 1A, ARE; Country MS
7.24   Celi,]   1E, 1A, ARE; ~; MS
*7.33–34   lib. i. cap.]   ARE; l.i.c. MS, 1E
*8.3   spirit that]   ARE; spirit and a daring eye that MS,
                  1E, 1A
8.8   Celi, as page,]   1E, 1A, ARE; ~∧ ~∧ MS
8.14   separate]   1E, 1A, ARE; seperate MS
8.17   friar, one]   ARE; friar, who was one MS, 1E, 1A
8.25   History]   1E, ARE; history MS
8.33   court,]   1E, 1A, ARE; ~∧ MS
8.37   in drugs and]   ARE; with drugs & MS; ~ and 1E, 1A

8.37	in gold and] ARE; with gold & MS; ~ and 1E, 1A
8.38	in oriental] ARE; with oriental MS, 1E, 1A
*9.3	maritime] 1A, ARE; maratime MS, 1E
9.20–21	Sovereigns] 1E, 1A, ARE; Sovreigns MS. *Emended also at* 16.36, 26.20, 26.29, 28.19, 29.38–39, 31.21, 31.28, 44.11, 44.21, 44.23–24, 73.1, and 78.38.
9.40	tom.] ARE; t. MS, 1E, 1A. *Emended also at* 10.33, 11.39, 11.40, 16.34, 20.40, 22.34.
10.4	St.] 1E, 1A, ARE; ~ₐ MS. *Emended also at* 23.33, 27.6, 28.12, 44.18, and 146.22.
10.5	several just] ARE; several who had just MS, 1E, 1A
10.9	or, . . . termed,] 1E, 1A, ARE; ~ₐ . . . ~ₐ MS
10.15	if,] 1E, 1A, ARE; ~ₐ MS
10.21	sailed,] 1E, 1A, ARE; ~ₐ MS
10.27	Spain—] 1E, 1A; Spain. MS; SPAIN.— ARE
10.27	Paria—] 1E; Paria. MS; PARIA.— ARE
*10.33	Colec.] ARE; Collec. MS, 1E, 1A
11.3	Surinam.*] 1E, 1A, ARE; ~ₐ* MS
11.4	of the gulph] T; to the gulph MS; to the Gulf 1E, ARE
11.9	at Trinidad] ARE; at the Island of Trinidad MS, 1E, 1A
11.18	sacrifices] 1E, 1A, ARE; sacrafices MS
11.18	but, he adds,] 1E, 1A, ARE; ~ₐ ~ ~ₐ MS
11.21	and were proof] 1E, ARE; and proof MS
*11.26–27	residence, . . . habitations.] 1E, ARE; residence, as the living thus crowded for a length of time in that hot climate, was apt to engender maladies. MS
11.31	are noted] 1E, ARE; are so noted MS
12.3	coast, . . . end,] 1E, 1A, ARE; ~ₐ . . . ~ₐ MS
12.6	when,] 1E, 1A, ARE; ~ₐ MS
*12.14–15	a treatment, . . . many cured.] ARE; a treatment, adds Amerigo Vespucci, by which we saw many cured. MS, 1E, 1A.
12.18	parts] 1E, 1A, ARE; part MS
12.18	Trinidad and] 1E, 1A, ARE; Trinidad & MS
12.18	Gulph] T; gulph MS; Gulf 1E, 1A, ARE
12.19	Dragon's] 1E, 1A, ARE; Dragons MS
12.24	pearl] 1E, 1A, ARE; Pearl MS
12.26	Maracapana,] 1E, 1A, ARE; ~ₐ MS
12.29	natives] 1E, 1A, ARE; Natives MS
12.31	seamen] 1E, 1A, ARE; Seamen MS
12.33	Spaniards,] 1E, 1A, ARE; ~ₐ MS

*12.33   superhuman]   1A, ARE; Super-human 1E; Super human MS

12.34   favour,]   1E; favour MS; favor 1A, ARE

13.5   Ojeda]   ARE; Alonzo de Ojeda MS, 1E, 1A

13.7   vessels, as]   ARE; vessels, therefore, as MS, 1E, 1A

*13.9   some peopled]   ARE; some of which were peopled MS, 1E, 1A

13.9   uninhabited, supposed]   ARE; uninhabited, and which are supposed MS, 1E, 1A

13.11   savages]   ARE; savage warriors MS, 1E, 1A

13.16   The show]   ARE; This show MS, 1E, 1A

13.18   paterero]   1E, 1A, ARE; peterero MS

13.18   Besides]   ARE; Beside MS, 1E, 1A

*13.18   oarsmen,]   ARE; oars-men 1E; oars men MS

13.22   advance,]   1E, 1A, ARE; $\sim_\wedge$ MS

13.24   this,]   1E, 1A, ARE; $\sim_\wedge$ MS

13.24   up and]   ARE; up in the boats and MS, 1E, 1A

13.25   smoke the]   ARE; smoke of these unknown weapons the MS, 1E, 1A

13.27   with a]   ARE; with that MS, 1E, 1A

13.35   ordered]   ARE; ordered them MS, 1E, 1A

14.4   vengeance wreaked]   ARE; vengeance that had been wreaked MS, 1E, 1A

14.6   wounds.]   1E, 1A, ARE; $\sim_\wedge$ MS

*14.9   Maracaibo]   1E, 1A, ARE; Coquibacoa MS

14.10   recovered,]   1E, 1A, ARE; $\sim_\wedge$ MS

14.12   giants]   1E, 1A, ARE; Giants MS

14.13   Penthesilea]   1E, 1A, ARE; Pantasilia MS

14.13   Antæus]   1E, 1A, ARE; Antaus MS

14.15   East]   1E, 1A, ARE; east MS

14.21   coast,]   ARE; $\sim_\wedge$ MS, 1E, 1A

*14.25   part,]   ARE; $\sim_\wedge$ MS, 1E, 1A

14.29   discrepancy]   ARE; discrepance MS, 1E, 1A

14.31   law suit]   1E, 1A; Law suit MS; lawsuit ARE

15.25   he charged]   ARE; he immediately charged MS, 1E, 1A

15.30   ships,]   1E, 1A, ARE; $\sim_\wedge$ MS

15.30   them,]   1E, 1A, ARE; $\sim_\wedge$ MS

*15.31   and the two girls]   1E, 1A, ARE; and two of the girls MS

15.34   inhabitants,]   1E, 1A, ARE; $\sim_\wedge$ MS

15.37   gulf,]   1E, 1A, ARE; $\sim_\wedge$ MS

15.40   Here, in]   1E, ARE; Here Ojeda, in MS

15.40	he sent] 1E, ARE; sent MS
16.7	forms;] ARE; ~∧ MS, 1E, 1A
16.8	all they] ARE; all others that they MS, 1E, 1A
*16.8–11	beauty . . . daughters.] 1E, ARE; beauty. The men, moreover, were singularly devoid of jealousy, offering their wives and daughters to the strangers in the most hospitable manner, and shewing signs of surprize and chagrin if their friendly offers were rejected. MS
16.12–13	ship, . . . aroused,] 1E, 1A, ARE; ~∧ . . . ~∧ MS
16.21	their . . . shouts] 1E, ARE; the songs and shouts of the delighted natives. MS
16.26	them,] 1E, 1A, ARE; ~∧ MS
16.27	which,] 1E, 1A, ARE; ~∧ MS
16.27	the Indians "plunged] 1E, ARE; "they plunged MS
16.29	mirth,] 1E, 1A, ARE; ~∧ MS
*16.40	Crown] 1E, 1A, ARE; crown MS
17.5	Maracaibo,] 1E, 1A, ARE; ~∧ MS
17.5	pursued his] 1E, ARE; pursued his his MS
17.6	port, and] 1E, 1A, ARE; port & MS
17.7	de la] 1E, 1A, ARE; dela MS
17.8	There] 1E, ARE; Here MS
17.9	at not meeting] 1E, ARE; of meeting MS
17.11	course,] 1E, ARE; ~∧ MS
17.15	alleged] 1E, 1A, ARE; alledged MS
17.21	intrusion,] 1E, 1A, ARE; ~∧ MS
17.21	Francisco] ARE; Francesco MS, 1E, 1A
17.32	Cabot, a Venetian,] 1E, 1A, ARE; ~∧ ~∧ MS
17.31	1497] 1E, ARE; 1797 MS
18.1	ducats] 1E, 1A, ARE; Ducats MS
18.2	armament,] 1E, 1A, ARE; ~∧ MS
18.4–5	this latter] 1E, ARE; this MS
*18.5–7	discoveries, . . . importance.] ARE; discoveries. MS, 1E, 1A
*19.7	Moguer,] 1E, 1A, ARE; ~∧ MS
19.27	the cradle] ARE; the original cradle MS, 1E, 1A
20.2–3	afterwards] ARE; after MS, 1E, 1A
20.3	Drago,] 1E, 1A, ARE; ~∧ MS
20.17	and make] ARE; and to make MS, 1E, 1A
20.26	tearing] 1E, ARE; severing MS
20.26	body,] 1E, 1A, ARE; ~∧ MS
20.29	pearls] 1E, 1A, ARE; Pearls MS

20.40	cap.] ARE; c. MS, 1E, 1A. *Emended also at* 52.41, 136.33, 136.34, 140.41 and 142.38
21.4	which,] 1E, 1A, ARE; $\sim_\wedge$ MS
21.7	Firma] 1E, 1A, ARE; firma MS
21.10	pearls,] 1E, 1A, ARE; $\sim_\wedge$ MS
21.11	beauty,] 1E, 1A, ARE; $\sim_\wedge$ MS
21.13	trading,] 1E, 1A, ARE; $\sim_\wedge$ MS
*21.15–16	at a number . . . fortress, the whole] ARE; at a place where there was a kind of fortress protecting a number of houses and gardens situated on a river, the whole MS, 1E, 1A
*21.28	East] 1E, 1A, ARE; east MS
21.30	success,] 1E, 1A, ARE; $\sim_\wedge$ MS
22.8	maritime] 1E, 1A, ARE; maratime MS
22.14	History] 1E, ARE; history MS
22.18	cloud this may have thrown over his] ARE; cloud of disgrace may have overshadowed his MS, 1E, 1A
22.22	hostility,] 1E, 1A, ARE; $\sim_\wedge$ MS
22.27	recommendations to] ARE; recommendations they could have to MS, 1E, 1A
22.34	decad. i. lib. iv. cap. 5] ARE; d.i.l.iv.c.v. MS, 1E, 1A
23.5	Yañez] 1E, 1A, ARE; Yanez MS
23.6	squadron;] 1E, 1A, ARE; $\sim$, MS
23.15	Islands] 1E, 1A, ARE; islands MS
23.15	southwest] 1E, 1A, ARE; South-west MS
23.16	leagues,] 1E, 1A, ARE; $\sim_\wedge$ MS
23.22–23	to the south . . . star] 1E, ARE; for some polar star to the South MS
23.26	Cross] 1E, 1A, ARE; cross MS
23.31	the 28th] 1E, 1A, 1F, ARE; the 20 MS
23.37	landed,] 1E, 1A, ARE; $\sim_\wedge$ MS
*24.1–2	he observed . . . gigantic size] ARE; he observed on the beach the print of footsteps, which seemed of gigantic size MS, 1E; he observed the print of footsteps on the beach which seemed of gigantic size 1A
24.4	coast,] 1E, 1A, ARE; $\sim_\wedge$MS
24.13	contempt,] 1E, 1A, ARE; $\sim_\wedge$ MS
24.17	size,] 1E, 1A, ARE; $\sim_\wedge$ MS
24.20	coast,] 1E, 1A, ARE; $\sim_\wedge$ MS
24.21	northwest] 1E, 1A, ARE; north west MS
24.29	seize] 1E, 1A, ARE; sieze MS
24.31	handled] ARE; he handled MS, 1E, 1A

24.35	comrades] 1E, 1A, ARE; comerades MS
24.40	seizing] 1E, 1A, ARE; siezing MS
25.13	people,] 1E, 1A, ARE; ~∧ MS
25.18	Marañon,] ARE; river Marañon; MS, 1E; river Mara-non 1A
25.20	which,] 1E, 1A, ARE; ~∧ MS
25.22	noise,] 1E, 1A, ARE; ~∧ MS
25.23	difficulty] ARE; difficulty from this perilous situation MS, 1E, 1A
25.25	natives,] 1E, 1A, ARE; ~∧ MS
25.28	Polar] 1E, 1A, ARE; polar MS
25.29	coast,] 1E, 1A, ARE; ~∧ MS
25.30	Gulf] 1E, 1A, ARE; gulf MS
25.31	Drago,] 1E, 1A, ARE; ~∧ MS
25.31	23rd] 1E, 1A, ARE; 23 MS
25.31	island] 1E, 1A, ARE; Island MS
26.6	Hispaniola. Having] 1E, ARE; Hispaniola, where, having MS
26.7	gale,] 1E, 1A, ARE; ~∧ MS
26.7	they again made] 1E, ARE; they made MS
26.9	disastrous] 1E, 1A, ARE; desasterous MS
26.9–10	yet made] ARE; that had yet been made MS, 1E, 1A
26.11	grievous] 1E, 1A, ARE; grevious MS
26.14	the terrors] 1E, ARE; the original terrors MS
26.21	seized] 1E, 1A, ARE; siezed MS. *Emended also at* 26.26, 35.3, 50.18, 55.9, 70.26, 104.37, 105.8, 105.38, 105.42, 143.11, and 148.15.
*26.23	imposition practiced] ARE; imposition that had been practiced MS, 1E, 1A
26.25	sacrifice] 1E, 1A, ARE; sacrafice MS
26.25	at a public] 1E, 1A, ARE; at public MS
26.35	the expenses] 1E, 1A, ARE; the protection MS
26.36	bury] 1E, 1A, ARE; ~, MS
26.37	of documents and writings] 1E, 1A, ARE; of paper MS
27.13	Solis,] 1E, 1A, ARE; ~∧ MS
27.15	to lead . . . Ocean] 1E, 1A, ARE; to connect the Atlantic & Pacific Ocean MS
27.20	dignity of a] 1E, 1A, ARE; dignity of the MS
28.4	Notwithstanding] 1E, 1A; 1500 Notwithstanding MS
28.7–8	each in its turn represented] ARE; each of which, in its turn, was represented MS, 1E, 1A
28.9	townsman] 1E, 1A, ARE; towns man MS

28.13	southwest] 1E, 1A, ARE; Southwest MS
28.19	maritime] 1E, 1A, ARE; maratime MS
29.14	bands,] 1E, 1A, ARE; $\sim_\wedge$ MS
29.18	road.] 1E, 1A, ARE; $\sim_\wedge$ MS
29.19	superseder 1E, 1A, ARE; superceder MS
29.26	traffic] 1E, 1A, ARE; dealings MS
29.26–27	was for . . . procuring] 1E, 1A, ARE; was to procure MS
29.31	shipwreck] 1E, 1A, ARE; Shipwreck MS
30.6	Colec. tom.] ARE; Collec. t. 1E; Colle. T. MS
31.4	The] 1E, 1A, ARE; 1502 The MS
31.7	fire, . . . spirit] 1E, 1A, ARE; fire, and sanguine swelling spirit MS
31.12	southern] 1E, 1A, ARE; Southern MS
31.13	province] 1E, 1A, ARE; Island MS
31.14	ships,] 1E, 1A, ARE; $\sim_\wedge$ MS
31.18	trade] 1E, 1A, ARE; traffic MS
31.27	discovery] 1E, 1A, ARE; Discovery MS
31.34	tom. iii. Document x.] ARE; t. iii. document x. MS, 1E, 1A
32.2	territory] 1E, 1A, ARE; islands MS
32.4	Seville,] 1E, 1F, ARE; $\sim_\wedge$ MS
32.4	Campos,] 1E, 1A, ARE; $\sim_\wedge$ MS
*32.7	Coquibacoa,] 1E, 1A, ARE; $\sim_\wedge$ MS
32.9	1st,] 1E, 1A, ARE; 1st MS
32.10	Campo; 2d,] 1E, 1A, ARE; $\sim_\wedge$ $\sim_\wedge$ MS
32.11	Vergara; 3d, The] 1E, 1A, ARE; Vergara. 3d. the MS
32.11	caravel] 1E, 1A, ARE; Caravel MS
32.12	Ojeda,] 1E, 1A, ARE; $\sim_\wedge$ MS
32.12	4th, the caravel] 1E, 1A, ARE; 4th the Caravel MS
32.18	Gulf] 1E, 1A, ARE; gulf MS
32.19	Margarita,] 1E, 1A, ARE; $\sim_\wedge$ MS
32.19–20	Guevara, was separated] 1E, 1A, ARE; Guevara was seperated MS
32.25	supplies,] 1E, 1A, ARE; $\sim_\wedge$ MS
32.32	directions,] 1E, 1A, ARE; $\sim_\wedge$ MS
32.33	natives.] 1E, 1A, ARE; $\sim_\wedge$ MS
*33.1	Vergara] 1E, 1A, ARE; Vegara MS
33.9	supplies,] 1E, 1A, ARE; $\sim$; MS
33.19	Ojeda determined] 1E, 1A, ARE; As the natives appeared to be gentle and pacific Ojeda determined MS
33.20	disposed] 1E, 1A, ARE; determined MS

33.23	Indians] 1E, 1A, ARE; natives MS
33.26	associates,] 1E, 1A, ARE; ~∧ MS
33.34	barter,] 1E, 1A, ARE; ~∧ MS
33.35	ransom,] 1E, 1A, ARE; ~∧ MS
33.35	plunder,] 1E, 1A, ARE; ~∧ MS
*33.38	mean time] 1E; meantime MS
33.39	harass] 1E, 1A, ARE; harrass MS
34.1	settlement,] 1E, 1A, ARE; ~∧ MS
34.2	country,] 1E, 1A, ARE; ~∧ MS
34.5	parties about] 1E, 1A, ARE; parties, ranged about MS
34.9	box,] 1E, 1A, ARE; ~∧ MS
34.10	supervisor] 1E, 1A, ARE; Supervisor MS
34.17–18	box. Being . . . Vergara,] 1E, 1A, ARE; ~∧ ~ . . . ~∧ MS
34.19	the latter] 1E, 1A, ARE; he MS
34.23	sacrificed] 1E, 1A, ARE; sacraficed MS
34.27–28	him, therefore, . . . to convey him] ARE; him therefore of their intention to convey him 1E; him therefore that they should convey him MS
34.37	arrangement,] 1E, 1A, ARE; ~∧ MS
34.40	Crown] 1E, 1A, ARE; crown MS
34.40	would] 1E, 1A, ARE; should MS
34.42	plan] 1E, 1A, ARE; ~, MS
35.2	San] 1E, 1A, ARE; St. MS
35.8	stone's] 1E, 1A, ARE; stones MS
35.23	parties,] 1E, 1A, ARE; ~∧ MS
35.26	Sovereign] 1E, 1A, ARE; Sovreign MS. *Emended also at* 36.29, 37.27, 79.8, 79.17, and 103.3.
35.33	labyrinths] 1E, 1A, ARE; labarynths MS
36.17	Veragua] 1E, 1A, ARE; Veraguas MS
36.23	conceived] 1E, 1A, ARE; concieved MS
36.27	Veragua] 1E, 1A, ARE; Veraguas MS
37.1	adventurers,] 1E, 1A, ARE; ~∧ MS
37.2	individual ready] ARE; individual who might be ready MS, 1E, 1A
*37.5–7	voyagers; . . . friend] ARE; voyagers, and he was known to possess a stanch friend at court in the Bishop Fonseca MS; voyagers; and it was thought that an application on his part would be attended with success, for he was known to possess a staunch friend at court in the Bishop Fonseca 1E
37.10	pilot] 1E, 1A, ARE; Pilot MS

37.10   Cosa,] 1E, 1A, ARE; ~∧ MS
37.12   conceived] 1E, 1A, ARE; concieved MS
37.15   aid] 1E, 1A, ARE; back MS
37.21   who,] 1E, 1A, ARE; ~∧ MS
37.39   house ARE; houses 1E; *Missing in* MS
37.41   decad. ii. cap. 10] ARE; Decade ii. c. 10 1E
38.1   combined] ARE; seem to have combined MS, 1E, 1A
38.1   Nicuesa] 1E, 1A, ARE; Nicuessa MS. *Emended also*
             at 39.21, 40.14, 40.21, 40.27, 41.31, 41.36, 41.42,
             42.10, 42.20, 48.28, 48.31, 66.36, 66.41, 68.5, 68.15,
             69.16, 69.19, 69.25, 72.7, 72.15, 72.33, 72.40, 73.12,
             73.16, 83.22, 83.26, 84.27, 85.20, 85.23, 85.26, 85.30,
             85.39, 86.12, 86.25, 87.11, 87.33, 87.39, 87.40, 88.9,
             88.27, 88.36, 88.41, 89.3, 92.38, 106.34, 150.21.
38.1   a complete] ARE; as a complete MS, 1E, 1A
38.3   form and] 1E, 1A, ARE; form and for MS
38.3   for bodily] 1E, 1A, ARE; for his MS
38.5–8   exercises . . . fashion] ARE; ~ had inherited ~ 1E;
             exercises, common to the Spanish cavaliers of those
             days, the reliques of their warfare with the Moors.
             He was noted for his vigour and adroitness in the
             jousts or tilting matches after the Moresco fashion MS
38.10   viol; besides] ARE; viol; beside 1E; viol; add to MS
38.10   caracole] 1E, 1A, ARE; caricol MS
38.12   Such were] 1E, 1A, ARE; Such are MS
38.20   both] ARE; both of the candidates MS, 1E, 1A
*38.25   Vela,] ARE; ~∧ MS, 1E, 1A
38.26   west] 1E, 1A, ARE; West MS
38.27   Dios,] 1E, 1A, ARE; ~∧ MS
39.3   Veragua] 1E, 1A, ARE; Veraguas MS
39.11   Carribee] 1E, 1A, ARE; Carribbee MS
39.11   islands,] 1E, 1A, ARE; ~∧ MS
39.13   deemed] 1E, 1A, ARE; considered MS
39.15   mankind,] 1E, 1A, ARE; ~∧ MS
39.31   and flourished] 1E, 1A, ARE and that it flourished MS
40.5   chief] 1E, 1A, ARE; cheif MS
40.8   arranged] ARE; agreed MS
*40.11–12   supplies; . . . high mettled] 1E, 1A, ARE; supplies;
             these he was to put on board a ship purchased by
             himself, and then proceed to join his high mettled MS
*40.16   Jamaica,] ARE; ~∧ MS
*40.22   court,] ARE; ~∧ MS, 1E, 1A

°40.27	brave,] ARE; ∼∧ MS, 1E, 1A
40.30	fighting for] 1E, 1A, ARE; fighting about MS
41.20	island] 1E, 1A, ARE; Island MS
°41.33	Veragua,] 1E, 1A, ARE; ∼∧ MS
41.41	Columbus;] 1E, 1A, ARE; ∼∧ MS
42.1	was an] 1E, 1A, ARE; was MS
42.1	harassed] 1E, 1A, ARE; harrassed MS
42.9	atrip] ARE; a trip MS, 1E; a-trip 1A
42.10–11	perplexities artfully] ARE; perplexities which had been artfully MS, 1E, 1A
42.21–22	At this . . . quarter.] 1E, 1A, ARE; At this critical moment a thing almost miraculous operated to his relief. MS.
42.26	senses] 1E, 1A, ARE; ears MS
42.29–30	other . . . person] 1E, 1A, ARE; other familiar of the law should get upon his traces MS
43.7–8	Pizarro, afterwards] ARE; Pizarro, who was afterwards MS, 1E, 1A
43.10	by an] 1E, 1A, ARE; by MS
43.12	Carthagena] 1E, 1A, ARE; Carthagina MS
43.20–21	The warning was] 1E, 1A, ARE; The caution of Juan de la Cosa was MS (*New paragraph*)
43.27	where] 1E, 1A, ARE; were MS
43.30	infantry,] 1E, 1A, ARE; Infantry MS
43.37	and,] 1E, 1A, ARE; ∼∧ MS
43.40	Peru,] 1E, 1A, ARE; ∼∧ MS
44.9	formula recently] ARE; formula which had recently been MS 1E, 1A
44.10	I,] 1E, 1A, ARE; ∼∧ MS
44.25	Christian] 1E, 1A, ARE; christian MS
44.26	sovereignty] 1E, 1A, ARE; sovreignty MS
44.28	seizure] 1E, 1A, ARE; siezure MS
44.40	lib. ii. cap.] ARE; l. ii. c. MS, 1E, 1A
45.3	patroness,] 1E, 1A, ARE; ∼∧ MS
45.10	lieutenant,] 1E, 1A, ARE; ∼∧ MS
45.13–14	enemy, where] 1E, 1A, ARE; enemy, were MS
45.15	lances,] 1E, 1A, ARE; ∼∧ MS
45.21	received] 1E, 1A, ARE; recieved MS
45.32	other,] 1E, 1A, ARE; ∼∧ MS
45.34	yells,] 1E, 1A, ARE; ∼∧ MS
46.9	enemy,] 1E, 1A, ARE; ∼∧ MS
46.16	his only surviving] 1E, 1A, ARE; his surviving MS

46.16	"Brother,"] 1E, 1A, ARE; "~ˏ" MS
46.18	fate!"] 1E, 1A, ARE; ~." MS
46.19–40	Thus fell . . . inroad] 1E, 1A, ARE; (*No paragraph*) The soldier complied, and survived to tell the heroic end of this veteran navigator and most loyal and devoted friend. He was the only one that escaped of seventy Spaniards who had followed Ojeda in this inroad. MS
*46.35	discoverers] ARE; discoveries 1E, 1A
*46.40	headstrong] ARE; head-long 1E; headlong 1A; *missing in* MS
47.3	disastrous] 1E, 1A, ARE; desasterous MS
47.3	shore,] 1E, 1A, ARE; ~ˏ MS
47.5	wilderness;] 1E, 1A, ARE; ~ˏ MS
47.6	forest spread] 1E, 1A, ARE; forest seemed to spread MS
47.14	about . . . up] 1E, 1A, ARE; almost giving up MS
47.20	mangroves,] 1E, 1A, ARE; ~ˏ MS
47.33	"Llegaron] 1E, 1A, ARE; ˏ~ MS
47.36	espada] 1E, 1A, ARE; Espada MS
47.36	roḋela] 1E, 1A, ARE; Rodela MS
47.40	lib. ii. cap.] ARE; l. ii. c. MS, 1E, 1A
47.40	lib. vii. cap. 15] ARE; l. vii. cap. xv. MS, 1E, 1A
48.12	Virgin . . . had,] 1E, 1A, ARE; virgin . . . had MS
48.15	commander,] 1E, 1A, ARE; ~ˏ MS
48.19	enmity,] 1E, 1A, ARE; ~ˏ MS
48.34	brother."†] 1E, ARE; ~.*" MS
49.9	parrots] 1E, 1A, ARE; Parrots MS
49.17	ran] ARE; they ran MS, 1E, 1A
49.20	vengeance,] 1E, 1A, ARE; ~ˏ MS
49.21	employed,] 1E, 1A, ARE; ~ˏ MS
50.3–4	lieutenant] 1E, 1A, ARE; Lieutenant MS
50.5	disastrous] 1E, 1A, ARE; disasterous MS
50.16	and, . . . thought,] 1E, 1A, ARE; ~ˏ . . . ~ˏ MS
50.16	lions] 1E, 1A, ARE; Lions MS
50.17	venomous] 1E, 1A, ARE; venemous MS
50.18	river,] 1E, 1A, ARE; ~ˏ MS
50.19	alligator] 1E, 1A, ARE; alligater MS
50.25	savages] 1E, 1A, ARE; Savages MS
50.31	and urging] 1E, 1A, ARE; but urging MS
50.39	decad. l. lib. vii. cap] ARE; d. l. vii. c MS, 1E, 1A
51.11	gold,] 1E, 1A, ARE; ~ˏ MS

51.13	savages] 1E, 1A, ARE; Savages MS
51.15	San Sebastian] ARE; St. Sebastian MS, 1E, 1A
51.30	harass] 1E, 1A, ARE; harrassed MS
52.3	from fugitive] 1E, 1A, ARE; of fugitive MS
52.5	fact,] 1E, 1A, ARE; ~∧ MS
52.10	heedless] ARE; furious MS, 1E, 1A
52.13	savages] 1E, 1A, ARE; Savages MS
52.18	Holy Virgin] 1E, 1A, ARE; holy virgin MS
52.24	caused] 1E, 1A, ARE; had MS
52.28	vow] 1E, 1A, ARE; vow to God MS
52.32	that they] 1E, 1A, ARE; they MS
52.33	vinegar] 1E, 1A, ARE; Vinegar MS
53.3–4	Alonzo . . . wound, and] 1E, 1A, ARE; Though Alonzo de Ojeda was pronounced out of danger, yet he still lay disabled by his wound; and MS
53.8	sea] 1E, 1A, ARE; Sea MS
53.13	ship] 1E, 1A, ARE; Ship MS
53.14	commander's] 1E, 1A, ARE; commanders MS
53.24	harassed] 1E, 1A, ARE; harrassed MS
53.31	thus qualified,] 1E, 1A, ARE; thus fitted out MS
53.34	While casting] 1E, 1A, ARE; While they were casting MS
53.35	Sebastian,] 1E, 1A, ARE; ~∧ MS
*53.37	cassava bread] ARE; casava bread MS; Casava bread 1E; cassava-bread 1F
53.38	ship] 1E, 1A, ARE; Ship MS
53.40	seize] 1E, 1A, ARE; sieze MS
54.3	place,] 1E, 1A, ARE; ~∧ MS
54.3	weighed] 1E, 1A, ARE; wieghed MS
54.5	vessel;] 1E, 1A, ARE; ~, MS
54.24–25	to set . . . certain] 1E, 1A, ARE; to take precautions against his own anticipated fate; certain MS
54.32	lib. viii. cap.] ARE; l. viii. c. MS, 1E, 1A
55.26	energy, ability,] 1E, 1A, ARE; ~∧ ~∧ MS
55.33	Mayor,] 1E, 1A, ARE; ~∧ MS
55.34	made,] 1E, 1A, ARE; ~∧ MS
55.37	Sebastian] 1E, 1A, ARE; Sebastians MS
56.4	Disastrous] 1E, 1A, ARE; Disasterous MS
56.5–6	a quarrel] ARE; a fierce quarrel MS, 1E, 1A
56.11	downright] 1E, 1A, ARE; down right MS
56.28	as a soldier] ARE; as soldier MS, 1E, 1A
56.33	vessel . . . westward that all] ARE; vessel had been

	already swept so far to the westward that all 1E; vessel was already swept so far to westward all MS
56.35	Borne] 1E, 1A, ARE; Bore MS
57.2	ashore] ARE; on shore MS, 1E, 1A
57.3	southern] 1E, 1A, ARE; Southern MS
57.9	might] 1E, 1A, 1F, ARE; would MS
57.16	Ojeda,] 1E, 1A, ARE; ~∧ MS
57.23	taskmasters] 1E, 1A, ARE; task masters MS
57.28–29	strangers.] 1E, 1A, ARE; ~; MS
57.35	coast. The Savannahs] 1E, 1A, ARE; coast, the Savannahs MS
58.2	oozy] 1E, 1A, ARE; oosy MS
58.4–5	soil . . . themselves] 1E, 1A, ARE; soil, continually flattering themselves MS
58.6	deceived] 1E, 1A, ARE; decieved MS
58.12	cassava] 1E, 1A, ARE; Cassava MS
58.19	cassava] 1E, 1A, ARE; Cassava MS
58.24	Madonna] 1E, 1A, ARE; Madona MS
58.26	mangrove] 1E, 1A, ARE; Mangrove MS
58.27	and, kneeling,] 1E, 1A, ARE; ~∧ ~∧ MS
58.30	Nay,] 1E, 1A, ARE; ~∧ MS
58.41	lib. ii. cap.] ARE; l. ii. c. MS, 1E, 1A
59.3	men] 1E, 1A, ARE; ~, MS
59.6	mangrove trees,] 1E, ARE; Mangrove trees MS
59.10	and, . . . it,] 1E, ARE; ~∧ . . . ~∧ MS
59.24	worshipped] 1E, ARE; worshiped MS
60.34	cap. 61, . . . decad i. lib. ix. cap.] ARE; c. 61, . . . d.l.l.ix.c. MS, 1E, 1A
61.9	seems almost] ARE; seems to have been almost MS, 1E, 1A
61.15	Esquibel,] 1E, ARE; ~∧ MS
61.19	vaingloriously] ARE; vain gloriously MS; vain-gloriously 1E
61.29–30	buffeted] ARE; buffetted MS, 1E
61.34–35	and here . . . dealing] 1E, 1A, ARE; and here it is worthy of remark the singular difference we perceive in the character and conduct of these Spanish adventurers when dealing MS
61.37	sacrifices] 1E, 1A, ARE; sacrafices MS
62.2	vindictive,] 1E, ARE; ~∧ MS
62.2	Esquibel,] 1E, 1A, ARE; ~∧ MS
62.10–17	vessel . . . vengeance] 1E, 1A, ARE; vessel, and for their recent violence towards Ojeda. The latter, how-

ever, observes Las Casas, was not a man to make accusations. With all his faults, he did not harbour malice. He was quick and fiery; his sword leapt from its scabbard on the least provocation; but after the first flash all was over & if he cooled upon an injury, he never sought for vengeance.

The offences of Talavera and his gang, however, were not destined to escape unpunished. The Admiral Don Diego Columbus sent over a party of soldiers to Jamaica to arrest them; they were brought to San Domingo and tried for Piracy; and Talavera and several of his principal accomplices were hanged.*
(*Footnote*) *Las Casas. Hist Ind. L2. C. 61. MS

*62.18   CHAPTER XIII.]   1E, 1A, ARE;   Chap 12. MS

62.28–64.21   Anxious for. . . . His story]   1E, 1A, ARE;   He now endeavoured to fit out another armament but it was all vain. He was doomed to experience the fate that too often attends upon dashing projectors. The world is dazzled by them for a time; they are heroes while successful, but misfortune dissipates the charm and the hero sinks into the adventurer. So is fared with Ojeda. He had figured in San Domingo as the conqueror of Coanabo; the commander of a squadron; the governor of a province; His prowess & exploits were the theme of every tongue. He had set sail in vaunting style, threatening the life of Esquibel and setting the vice roy at defiance. Every one thought he was about to accomplish wonders. A few months had elapsed and behold him in the streets of San Domingo, a shipwrecked, disappointed man. The disasters of his colony were known, his situation was considered desperate. His former friends dreading some new demand upon their purses, looked coldly on him; and his schemes that were once thought full of genius and promise, were now pronounced wild ill-concerted and ruinous.

But though his friends were cool his enemies were active. Many of the crew of Talavera infested the city of San Domingo and harboured the most malignant enmity to Ojeda, whom they looked upon as the cause of the death of their leader. A number of these miscreants waylayed and attacked him one

night, as he was returning home at a late hour. Instead of flying Ojeda shewed his usual spirit. Drawing
his sword & setting his back against a wall he defended himself against the whole gang, and, not
content with beating them off, he pursued them
through the street sword in hand, and then returned
tranquilly and unharmed to his lodgings.

This is the last achievement that is recorded of him.
His embarrassments increased, his popularity was
at an end, and he sank into that obscurity that gathers round a ruined man. It is probable that ill health
contributed to quench that sanguine and fiery spirit,
that had hitherto been the secret of his fortunes, for
we are told he fell ill of a malady arising from the
various hardships he had endured, and from the
wound received at San Sebastians, which had been
imperfectly cured.

Gomara, in his history of the Indias, affirms that
Ojeda turned monk and died in the convent of San
Francisco; but Las Casas, who knew him, and was
at San Domingo at the time makes no mention of the
fact as he certainly would have done had it taken
place. He confirms, however, the story of the striking
reverse in his character and fortunes, for there is no
ruin so complete as that of a towering spirit humiliated and broken down. He died so poor, says Las
Casas, that there he did not leave money enough to
provide for his interment. His last request presents
a wholesome comment on his life. He entreated that
his body might be buried in the monastery of San
Francisco, just at the portal, in humble expiation of
his past pride, "that everyone who entered might
tread upon his grave."

Such was the fate of Alonzo de Ojeda, one of the
most extraordinary of the Spanish discoverers. With
all his faults, who does not forget them at the threshold of his humble and untimely grave! His story MS

*63.26   waylaid]   ARE; way layed MS; way-laid 1E
*63.31   rout]   ARE; route 1E
*63.36   hardships and]   ARE; hardships he had sustained, and
          1E
64.2   Indies]   1E, ARE; Indias MS
*64.17   *"that . . . grave."*]   1E, ARE; *no italics in MS*

64.22	lively] 1E, 1A, ARE; livly MS
64.23	chequered] 1E; checquered MS, 1A; checkered ARE
64.25	"was] 1E, 1A, ARE; $_\wedge\sim$ MS
64.25	coup-de-main] 1E, ARE; $\sim_\wedge\sim_\wedge\sim$ MS
64.27	or ambition] 1E, 1A; nor ambition ARE; an ambition MS
64.33	San Domingo] ARE; S. Doming. MS, 1E
*65.4	CHAPTER I.] ARE; Chap. 1. MS; missing in 1E
65.8	voyage,] 1E, ARE; $\sim_\wedge$ MS
65.12	stand] 1E, 1A, ARE; keep MS
65.12	squadron] 1E, 1A, ARE; Squadron MS
65.13	and,] 1E, 1A, ARE; $\sim_\wedge$ MS
65.16	brigantines] 1E, 1A, ARE; Brigantines MS
65.21	into which] 1E, 1A, ARE; in which MS
65.30	fate,] 1E, ARE; $\sim_\wedge$ MS
65.32	tree,] 1E, ARE; $\sim_\wedge$ MS
66.7	brigantines] 1E, 1A, ARE; Brigantines MS
66.9	and,] 1E, 1A, ARE; $\sim_\wedge$ MS
66.10	apprehensions] 1E, 1A, ARE; suspicions MS
66.11	brigantines] 1E, 1A, ARE; Brigantines MS
66.12–13	uneasiness, however,] 1E, 1A ,ARE; $\sim_\wedge$ $\sim_\wedge$ MS
66.14	Veragua,] 1E, 1A, ARE; $\sim_\wedge$ MS
66.15	intended] 1E, 1A, ARE; proposed MS
66.27	they would] 1E, 1A, ARE; they should MS
66.28	to apply . . . provisions] 1E, 1A, ARE; to ascort them in search of provisions MS
66.32	whether,] 1E, 1A, ARE; $\sim_\wedge$ MS
66.33	step would take] 1E, 1A, ARE; step took MS
67.3	page,] 1E, ARE; $\sim_\wedge$ MS
67.4	companions,] 1E, ARE; $\sim_\wedge$ MS
67.8	time,] 1E, ARE; $\sim_\wedge$ MS
67.9	march, they] 1E, 1A, ARE; march, however, they MS
67.10	separated] 1E, 1A, ARE; seperated MS
67.14	consternation,] 1E, 1A, ARE; $\sim_\wedge$ MS
67.24	They were on a] 1E, 1A, ARE; On a MS
67.24	swampy] 1E, 1A, ARE; savage MS
67.26	them,] 1E, 1A, ARE; $\sim_\wedge$ MS
68.13	island] 1E, 1A, ARE; Island MS
68.15	followers,] 1E, 1A, ARE; $\sim_\wedge$ MS
68.35	brigantines] 1E, 1A, ARE; Brigantines MS
69.6	and, . . . opinion,] 1E, 1A, ARE; $\sim_\wedge \ldots \sim_\wedge$ MS
69.9	night,] 1E, 1A, ARE; $\sim_\wedge$ MS

*69.11   days'] ARE; ∼∧ MS, 1E, 1A
69.22   brigantines] 1E, 1A, ARE; Brigantines MS
69.26   and, . . . lieutenant,] 1E, ARE; ∼∧ . . . ∼∧ MS
69.31   storm,] 1E, ARE; ∼∧ MS
69.38   ships,] 1E, 1A, ARE; ∼; MS
69.38   purpose, . . . said,] 1E, 1A, ARE; ∼∧ . . . ∼∧ MS
70.8   brigantine] 1E, 1A, ARE; Brigantine MS
70.17   revived,] 1E, ARE; ∼∧ MS
70.23–24   commander, . . . intercede] 1E, 1A, ARE; commander
      by making interest with his fellow officers to induce
      them to intercede MS
70.26   arrived,] 1E, ARE; ∼∧ MS
70.29   Olano . . . but] 1E, 1A, 1F; ∼ favor ∼ ARE; Olano
      interceded in his behalf, but MS
71.6   appeared,] 1E, ARE; ∼∧ MS
71.9   with them] ARE; with him MS, 1E, 1A
71.9   Domingo,] 1E, 1A, ARE; ∼∧ MS
71.27   laden,] 1E, 1A, ARE; ∼∧ MS
71.29   Harassed] 1E, 1A, ARE; Harrassed MS
71.29   fatigues,] 1E, 1A, ARE; ∼∧ MS
71.33   genial] 1E, 1A, ARE; generous MS
71.34   harassing] 1E, 1A, ARE; harrassing MS
72.2   indispensable to] 1E, 1A, ARE; indispensible for MS
72.4   Indian in] 1E, 1A, ARE; Indian already in MS
72.5   were] ARE; they were MS, 1A, 1E
72.14   Nuñez,] 1E, 1A, ARE; ∼∧ MS
72.16   sailor, who] 1E, 1A, ARE; sailor, on board, who MS
72.24   Porto Bello] ARE; Portobello 1E, 1A
72.31–35   Bastimientos (or . . .).] 1E, 1A, ARE; Bastimientos.
      (or . . .) MS
72.35–36   under which] 1E, 1A, ARE; with which MS
72.36   everything] ARE; every thing MS, 1E, 1A
72.40   and,] 1E, 1A, ARE; . . . ∼∧ MS
72.41   decad. i . . . cap.] ARE; D. i . . . c. MS, 1E, 1A
73.3   exigency,] 1E, 1A, ARE; ∼∧ MS
73.4   Spaniards,] 1E, 1A, ARE; ∼∧ MS
73.10–11   and they were] 1E, 1A, ARE; and were MS
73.13   for those] 1E, 1A, ARE; for the men MS
73.16   united,] 1E, 1A, ARE; ∼∧ MS
73.20   Badajos,] 1E, 1A, ARE; ∼∧ MS
73.23–24   villages and barren] 1E, 1A, ARE; villages; barren MS
74.4   the last] 1E, 1A, ARE; last MS

74.10	sailing,] 1E, 1A, ARE; ~_∧ MS
74.11	hangers-on] 1E, 1A, ARE; hangers on MS
74.11	debt,] 1E, 1A, ARE; ~_∧ MS
74.13	everyone] 1E, 1A, ARE; every one MS
74.23–26	Martyr, . . . a mere] 1E, 1A, ARE; Martyr speaks of him as a "master of fence" which may either be interpreted as a skillful swordsman, or a teacher of the Science of Arms. He calls him also a "rash royster" and intimates that he was a mere MS
74.35–36	vessel, . . . voyage. When] 1E, 1A, ARE; vessel, as provisions for the voyage, without the knowledge of the Bachelor Enciso. When MS
74.37	Nuñez] 1A, 1E, ARE; Nunez MS. *Emended also at* 75.6, 87.32, 90.18, 91.15, 92.2, 93.21, 94.1, 94.9, 94.27, 95.6, 95.34, 95.37, 96.18, 96.33, 98.2, 98.4, 100.14, 101.11, 102.30, 102.36, 106.25, 108.3, 109.4, 110.7, 111.16, 111.30, 113.4, 113.6, 113.11, 114.3, 114.36, 115.38, 116.9, 116.29, 117.42, 118.14, 118.23, 119.10, 119.30, 120.3, 120.18, 120.40, 121.17, 121.19, 122.11, 122.30, 122.36, 124.7, 124.12, 124.30, 124.37, 125.23, 125.34, 125.37, 126.15, 126.36, 127.5, 127.16, 128.15, 133.16, 133.28, 136.2, 137.31, 138.8, 138.16, 138.20, 138.30, 138.35, 140.39, 141.11, 141.27, 142.18, 142.30, 143.1, 143.5, 143.11, 143.18, 149.7, 150.28, 151.2, and 151.14.
*74.38–75.3	surprize . . . encounter.] 1E, 1A, 1F, ARE; surprize and indignation of the Bachelor, who threatened to put him on the first uninhabited island they should encounter.* MS
75.3	him.] 1E, 1A, ARE; ~_∧ MS
75.4	God,"] 1E, 1A, ARE; ~_∧" MS
75.5	things."] 1E, 1A, ARE; ~._∧ MS
*75.9–77.20	harbour of Carthagena . . . Valenzuela] 1E, 1A, ARE; harbour of Carthagena and had not been there long when a brigantine anchored in the port. On going on board Enciso was astonished to find that it was manned by the followers of Ojeda. He at first suspected that they had deserted; his indignation as a magistrate was immediately awakened, and he determined to sieze them and inflict on them the severity of the law. On conversing with their commander Francisco Pizarro, however, the latter shewed him his

letter patent, signed by Ojeda, related to him the disasterous catastrophe of the colony of San Sebastian. They had continued in the fortress the fifty days stipulated with Ojeda, but receiving no succour and hearing no tidings of him, determined to embark. They were seventy in number and the two brigantines which had been left with them were incapable of taking so many. They came to the forlorn agreement, therefore, to remain until famine, sickness and the poisoned arrows of the Indians should reduce their number to the capacity of the brigantines. A brief space of time was sufficient for the purpose. They then prepared for the voyage. Four mares which had been kept alive as terrors to the Indians were killed and salted for sea stores. Then taking whatever other articles of provision remained, they embarked and made sail. One Brigantine was commanded by Pizarro, the other one by Valenzuela. MS

77.21	when, . . . storm,] 1E, 1A, ARE; $\sim_\wedge$ . . . $\sim_\wedge$ MS
77.25	sailors,] 1E, 1A, ARE; Sailors MS
77.29	brigantine] 1E, 1A, ARE; Brigantine MS
77.31	disastrous] 1E, 1A, ARE; disasterous MS
77.35	decad. i. lib. vii. cap.] 1A; d.l.l.vii.c. MS, 1E, ARE
78.3–7	The Bachelor . . . worthy] 1E, 1A, ARE; While at anchor in the harbour of Carthagena the Bachelor Enciso was inspired with the passion for adventure, so prevalent among the Spanish discoverer, and undertook an enterprize that would have been worthy MS
78.10	by torrents] 1E, 1A, ARE; by the torrents MS
78.12	were . . . as] 1E, 1A, ARE; were as MS
78.15	still more] 1E, 1A, ARE; further MS
78.17	sepulture] 1E, 1A, ARE; Sepulture MS
78.17	country, whither] 1E, 1A, ARE; country. Hither MS
78.20–23	It appeared . . . determined] 1A, 1F, ARE; The Enterprizing Bachelor immediately determined MS
78.24	sepulchres! . . . did] 1E, 1A, 1F, ARE; sepulchres; where he expected to find immense spoil from the golden ornaments buried with the dead for many generations. Neither did MS
78.25	dead] 1E, 1A, 1F, ARE; grave MS

78.26–27	infidels . . . according] 1E, 1A, 1F, ARE; infidels, and buried according MS
78.29	Enciso] 1E, 1A, ARE; The Bachelor MS
78.31–35	The Bachelor . . . to be read] 1E, 1A, ARE; The Bachelor, who in a true spirit of his calling mingled the civilian with the soldier, proceeded according to the legal form recently enjoined by the crown. He caused to be read MS
79.1	that, as] 1E, 1A, ARE; $\sim_\wedge \sim$ MS
79.1–2	God the Sovereign] 1E, 1A, ARE; god the Sovreign MS
79.3–5	the doctrine . . . they observed] 1E, 1A, ARE; the doctrine of the pope being regent of the world in place of God, and as to his grant of their country to the King of these strangers, they observed MS
79.6–7	been . . . mad] 1E, 1A, ARE; been MS
79.9–15	if this . . . menaced] 1E, 1A, ARE; if this pope and King came there they would serve them as they had done others of their enemies, whose heads they pointed out to the bachelor, elevated on poles. (*New paragraph*) Enciso menaced MS
79.17–18	Bachelor, . . . law,] 1E, 1A, ARE; $\sim_\wedge \ldots \sim_\wedge$ MS
79.19	them,] 1E, 1A, ARE; $\sim_\wedge$ MS
79.22	sepulchres] 1E, 1A, ARE; Sepulchres MS
79.25	arrows,] 1E, 1A, ARE; $\sim_\wedge$ MS
79.28	disastrous] 1E, 1A, ARE; disasterous MS
79.29–30	and, . . . ships,] 1E, 1A, ARE; $\sim_\wedge \ldots \sim_\wedge$ MS
79.33	in 1519 . . . &c.] 1E, 1A, ARE; in 1519 MS
79.33	*de Geographia,*] 1E, 1A, ARE; *Geographica* MS
*79.41	otros,"] 1E, ARE; $\sim,_\wedge$ 1E
80.1	Chapter IX] 1E, 1A, ARE; Chap. 8. MS
80.12	Pizarro;] 1E, 1A, ARE; $\sim$, MS
80.12	flour, . . . biscuit,] 1E, 1A, ARE; $\sim_\wedge \ldots \sim_\wedge$ MS
80.18	vanishing . . . fortress] 1E, 1A, ARE; vanishing. On landing he found the fortress MS
80.21	swine,] 1E; $\sim_\wedge$ MS
80.22	failing,] 1E; $\sim_\wedge$ MS
80.33–35	Nuñez . . . informed] 1E, 1A, ARE; Nuñez stepped forward; the same absconding debtor who had been smuggled on board in the cask. He informed MS
80.38	side,] 1E; $\sim_\wedge$ MS

80.39	country] 1E, 1A, ARE; accountry MS
81.9	Zemaco. He sent] ARE; Zemaco. When he heard of the approach of the Spaniards, he sent MS, 1E, 1A
81.10	safety, . . . posting] 1E, 1A, ARE; safety and posted MS
81.11	height,] 1E, 1A, ARE; ~∧ MS
81.15	to . . . whose] 1E, 1A, ARE; to the holy Virgin, by the name of Our Lady of Antigua, whose MS
81.17–21	to offer . . . they] 1E, 1A, ARE; to offer jewels of gold and silver, the spoils of the heathen, at her shrine. Doubting also that his men MS
81.22	oath . . . turn] 1E, 1A, ARE; oath not to turn MS
81.27	resistance,] 1E, 1A, ARE; ~∧ MS
81.28	triumph,] 1E, 1A, ARE; triumph and MS
81.30–31	country; . . . food] 1E, 1A, ARE; country. He thus collected food MS
81.32–33	His heart . . . elated by] 1E, 1A, ARE; The Bachelor was elated by MS
81.33	booty;] 1E, 1A, ARE; ~. MS
81.34	disasters,] 1E, ARE; ~∧ MS
81.36	government] 1E, 1A, ARE; Government MS
81.36–37	village; . . . fulfillment] 1E, 1A, ARE; ~∧ . . . fulfilment MS
81.37	de la] 1E, 1A, ARE; el MS
82.1	CHAPTER X.] 1E, 1A, ARE; Chap. 9. MS
82.23	Nicuesa,] 1E, 1A, ARE; ~∧ MS
82.24	allotted] 1E, 1A, ARE; alotted MS
82.25	therefore,] 1E, 1A, ARE; ~∧ MS
82.26–27	usurpation.] 1E, 1A, ARE; ~.* MS
82.29	easily] 1E, 1A, ARE; readily MS
82.30–32	Bachelor . . . him] 1E, 1A, ARE; Bachelor found the chair of authority suddenly wrested from under him MS
83.1	CHAPTER XI.] 1E, 1A, ARE; Chap. 10. MS
83.14	life,] 1E, 1A, ARE; ~∧ MS
83.19	at signals] ARE; at these signals MS, 1E, ARE
83.19	shores,] 1E, 1A, ARE; ~∧ MS
83.20	manner, and in] 1E, 1A, ARE; manner. In MS
83.21–22	They . . . Rodrigo] 1E, 1A, ARE; They were commanded by one Rodrigo MS
83.23	disastrous] 1A, 1E, ARE; disasterous MS
83.26	Sebastian] 1E, 1A, ARE; Sebastians MS
83.36	law,] 1E, 1A, ARE; ~∧ MS

83.37	ambassadors,] 1E, 1A, ARE; $\sim_\wedge$ MS
84.1	CHAPTER XII.] 1E, 1A, ARE; Chap. 11. MS
84.3	Rodrigo] 1E, ARE; Roderigo MS, 1A
84.3–4	westward, . . . harbour,] 1E, 1A, ARE; $\sim_\wedge$ . . . $\sim_\wedge$ MS
84.5	discovered] 1E, 1A, ARE; descried MS
84.6	sea. It was] ARE; sea. On making up to it, he found that it was MS, 1E, 1A
84.8	Dios,] 1E, 1A, ARE; $\sim_\wedge$ MS
84.9	overshadowed] ARE; over shadowed MS; over- shadowed 1A
84.16	emaciated, and] 1E, 1A, ARE; emaciated & MS
84.29	the envoys] 1E, 1A, ARE; envoys MS
84.29	Darien,] 1E, 1A, ARE; $\sim_\wedge$ MS
84.40	decad. xi. lib. i.] ARE; d. ll. l. i. 1E, 1A
85.3	individuals,] 1E, 1A, ARE; $\sim_\wedge$ MS
85.5	monopolies] 1E, 1A, ARE; reservations MS
85.8	ambassadors] 1E, 1A, ARE; embassadors MS
85.10	conversation held] ARE; conversation which they held MS, 1E, 1A
85.17	for at . . . hands!"] 1E, 1A, ARE; for from . . . hands." MS
85.18	subtle] 1E, 1A, ARE; subtel MS
85.19	to depart] ARE; their departure MS, 1E, 1A
85.22	they,] 1E, 1A, ARE; $\sim_\wedge$ MS
85.26–27	instanced . . . disposition.] 1E, 1A, ARE; instanced his tyrannous and ungrateful disposition in the manner in which he had treated Olana. MS
85.27–28	disposition. (*Paragraph*) The] 1E, 1A, ARE; *No paragraph* MS
85.28	Bachelor] 1E, 1A, ARE; Bachellor MS
85.30	treasures . . . refunded] 1E, 1A, ARE; treasures to be refunded MS
85.35	forward] 1E, 1A, ARE; forward one MS
85.42	you,"] 1E, 1A, ARE; $\sim_\wedge$" MS
86.10–13	But . . . obviousness] 1E, 1A, ARE; But there is a relief and you hold it in your hands. If it was an error to invite Nicuessa to Darien, it is easily reme- died by not receiving him." The obviousness MS
86.15	CHAPTER XIII.] 1E, 1A, ARE; Chap. 12. MS
86.17	Darien,] 1E, 1A, ARE; $\sim_\wedge$ MS
86.20	Nuñez, waiting] 1E, 1A, ARE; Nuñez, and waiting MS
86.20	waiting, . . . supposed,] 1E, 1A, ARE; $\sim_\wedge$ . . . $\sim_\wedge$ MS

86.21	honour] 1E, 1A; honours MS; honor ARE
86.22	voice,] 1E, 1A, ARE; ~∧ MS
86.27	request;] 1E, 1A, ARE; ~∧ MS
86.29	should think] ARE; thought MS, 1E, 1A
86.29–30	entreaties only] ARE; entreaties were vain; they only MS, 1E, 1A
86.30–31	replies, . . . venture] 1E, 1A, ARE; replies, accompanied by threats should he venture MS
86.32	on, he] ARE; on, therefore, he MS, 1E, 1A
86.34	people] 1E, 1A, ARE; rabble MS
87.15	multitude] 1E, 1A, ARE; rabble MS
87.19	refused,] 1E, 1A, ARE; ~∧ MS
87.19	in one] 1E, 1A, ARE; in in one MS
87.23	Dios] 1E, 1A, ARE; dios MS
87.25	cavalier. His] 1E, 1A, ARE; cavalier, and that his own measure of exclusion might be abandoned. His MS
87.26	a noisy] 1E, 1A, ARE; one noisy MS
87.27	Benitez,] 1E, 1A, ARE; ~; MS
87.30–31	patronage . . . until] 1E, 1A, ARE; patronage felt himself emboldened to bluster. His voice rose with the general clamour, keeping above the voices of his companions, until MS
87.30	Zamudio] 1E, 1A, ARE; Zamudio also MS
87.32–33	merely . . ! we] 1E, 1A, ARE; more bawling—"No—no—no! we MS
87.37	lashes,] 1E, 1A, ARE; ~∧ MS
87.39	brigantine] 1E, 1A, ARE; brigantines MS
87.41	lib. ii. cap.] ARE; l. ii. c. MS, 1E, 1A
88.1	brigantines,] 1E, 1A, ARE; ~∧ MS
88.2	inveigled] 1E, ARE; inviegeled MS; enveigled 1A
88.3	to reinstate] 1E, 1A, ARE; to receive MS
88.5	Zamudio, who seized] 1E, 1A, ARE; ~; ~ MS
88.9	In vain that] ARE; It was in vain that MS, 1E, 1A
88.11	him; in vain that] ARE; him; it was in vain that MS, 1E, 1A
88.14	discarded] 1E, 1A, ARE; illstarred MS
88.21	Caribbean] 1E, 1A, ARE; Carribbean MS
88.24	brigantine] 1E, 1A, ARE; Brigantine MS
88.25–26	Spaniards, . . . shore of Cuba,] 1E, 1A, ARE; Spaniards . . . Shores of Cuba MS
88.26	tree:] ARE; ~∧ MS; ~;– 1E, 1A

88.29	however,] 1E, 1A, ARE; ~∧ MS
88.33	Caribbean] 1E, 1A, ARE; Carribbean MS
88.40	Casas,] 1E, 1A, ARE; ~∧ MS
89.1	which,] 1E, 1A, ARE; ~∧ MS
89.4–5	same . . . be] 1E, 1A, ARE; same, he concludes, might be MS
89.6	cap.] ARE; c. MS, 1E, 1A
90.2	DISCOVERER] 1E, 1A, ARE; The Discoverer MS
90.5	disastrous] 1E, 1A, ARE; disasterous MS
90.6–7	Balboa, . . . daring,] 1E, 1A, ARE; ~∧ . . . ~∧ MS
90.12	but met] ARE; but he met MS, 1E, 1A
*90.12–13	Nuñez, . . . favorite] 1E, 1A, ARE; Nunez. The latter was a great favorite MS
90.15–16	susceptible,] 1E, 1A, ARE; ~∧ MS
90.16	Spaniards,] 1E, 1A, ARE; ~∧ MS
90.17	are easily dazzled] 1E, 1A, ARE; were easily dazzled MS
90.23	might] 1E, 1A, ARE; may MS
90.27	law] 1E, 1A, ARE; Law MS
*90.30	skillfully; but . . . men] ARE; ~ skilfully ~ 1E, 1A; skillfully, but he had to deal with men MS
90.34	guilty, therefore, and] ARE; guilty therefore, and thrown 1E; guilty & thrown MS
91.15	permission . . . to] 1E, 1A, ARE; permission to MS
91.22	Nuñez,] 1E, 1A, ARE; Nunez MS
91.26	and, as] 1E, 1A, ARE; ~∧ MS
91.27–28	friend, . . . Valdivia] 1E, 1A, ARE; friend . . . Baldivia MS
91.30	Pasamonte,] 1E, 1A, ARE; ~∧ MS
92.6	remittances] 1E, 1A, 1F, ARE; remittances of revenue MS
*92.12	cacique] 1E, 1A, ARE; Cacique MS
92.12	who cherished] 1E, 1A, 1F, ARE; who still cherished MS
92.21	assault, made] ARE; assault, they made MS, 1E, 1A
92.31	brigantines] 1E, 1A, ARE; Brigantines MS
92.35	brigantines] 1E, 1A, ARE; Brigantines MS
*93.10	Coyba. . . . cacique] 1E, 1F, ARE; Coyba, the dominions of Careta. The cacique MS, 1A
93.14	colony,] 1E, 1A, ARE; ~∧ MS
*93.16	outcast] 1E, 1F, ARE; traytor MS; traitor 1A
93.25	and,] 1E, 1A, ARE; ~∧ MS

93.26   children,]   1E, 1A, ARE; ～∧ MS
93.32   said he to]   1E, 1A, 1F, ARE; said he reproachfully to
                  MS
93.32   Nuñez,]   1E, 1A, ARE; ～∧ MS
93.33–34   were not fed]   1E, 1A, ARE; have not been fed MS
93.37   free, therefore, with]   1E, 1A, ARE; free with MS
93.38   friends.]   1E, 1A, ARE; ～: MS
93.41   people!]   1E, 1A, ARE; ～∧ MS
94.2   a strong alliance]   1E, 1A, ARE; strong alliances MS
94.5   engaging, moreover,]   1E, 1A, ARE; ～∧ ～∧ MS
94.8   Darien,]   1E, 1A, ARE; ～∧ MS
94.21   was,]   1E, 1A, ARE; ～∧ MS
94.33   decad. 3. cap. vi]   ARE; D. 3. c. vi MS, 1E, 1A
95.3   name,]   1E, 1A, ARE; ～; MS
95.17   interwoven]   1E, 1A, ARE; inter woven MS
95.17–18   to cause surprize]   T; to cause surprise; ARE; to fill
                  the Spaniards with surprise 1A, 1E; to fill the Span-
                  iards with surprize MS
95.18–19   apartments]   1E, 1A, ARE; appartments MS
95.21   maize]   1E, 1A, ARE; Maize MS
95.24   ancestors]   1E, 1A, ARE; ～, MS
95.28–29   not with religious]   ARE; not a species of religious MS,
                  1E, 1A
95.30   The eldest son of the cacique was]   ARE; Among the
                  sons of the cacique, the eldest was   MS, 1E, 1A
95.36   slaves, captives taken]   ARE; slaves, being captives
                  that he had taken MS, 1E, 1A
95.36   in the]   1E, 1A, ARE; in MS
95.42   weighing]   1E, 1A, ARE; wieghing MS
96.3   beings whom]   1E, 1A, ARE; beings he MS
*96.5   porch. "Why," said he, "should]   ARE; Before the
                  strangers could recover from their astonishment at
                  this sudden act, he thus addressed them, Why should
                  1E; porch. Before the Spaniards should MS, 1A
96.8   perils,]   1E, 1A, ARE; ～∧ MS
96.10–11   he, . . . south.]   1E, 1A, ARE; he . . . South. MS
96.11   these]   1E, 1A, ARE; them MS
96.13   them,]   1E, 1A, ARE; ～∧ MS
96.14   southern]   1E, 1A, ARE; Southern MS
96.16   plentiful]   1E, 1A, ARE; plenty MS
96.17   south]   1E, 1A, ARE; South MS
96.17   iron]   1E, 1A, ARE; Iron MS

96.18	Vasco] ARE; Struck with this intelligence, Vasco MS, 1E, 1A
96.19–20	task," . . . prince,] 1E, 1A, ARE; ~$_\wedge$" . . . ~$_\wedge$ MS
96.25	days'] ARE; ~$_\wedge$ MS, 1E, 1A
*96.29–97.2	The youthful . . . the idea.] 1E, 1A, 1F, ARE; These two paragraphs are inverted in MS.
96.30	captives taken] ARE; captives whom he had taken MS, 1E, 1A
96.32	He moreover offered] ARE; The prince, moreover, offered MS, 1E, 1A
96.34	father's] 1E, 1A, ARE; fathers MS
96.38–39	which, if accomplished,] 1E, 1A, ARE; ~$_\wedge$ ~ ~$_\wedge$ MS
97.3–4	He hastened. . . . Before] 1E, 1A, ARE; Being bent upon this splendid enterprize, Vasco Nuñez hastened his return to Darien to make the necessary preparation. Before MS
97.10	arrived from] ARE; arrived there from MS, 1E, 1A
97.13	thunder, lightning,] 1E, 1A, ARE; ~$_\wedge$ ~$_\wedge$ MS
97.16	Valdivia] 1E, 1A, ARE; Valdibia MS
*97.25	likewise] 1E, 1F, ARE; also MS, 1A
98.4	Valdivia] 1E, 1A, ARE; Valdibia MS
98.5	prompted foraging] ARE; prompted him to undertake foraging MS, 1E, 1A
98.5	excursions] 1A, 1E, ARE; incursions MS
98.7–8	rumours . . . situated] 1E, 1A; rumours which beguiled the Spanish adventurers with the idea of golden realms in the interior of this unknown land, was one about a province called Dobayba situated MS; rumors ~ ARE
98.10	Gulf] 1E, 1A, ARE; gulf MS
98.16	possessions] 1E, 1A, ARE; lands MS
98.16	worshippers] 1E, 1A, ARE; worshipers MS
98.21	pilgrimage,] 1E, 1A, ARE; ~$_\wedge$ MS
98.24	sacrificed] 1E, 1A, ARE; sacraficed MS
98.24	at its shrine] 1E, 1A, ARE; at the shrine of the divinity MS
98.25	time,] 1E, 1A, ARE; ~$_\wedge$ MS
98.27	punishment,] 1E, 1A, ARE; ~$_\wedge$ MS
98.30	failing,] 1E, 1A, ARE; ~$_\wedge$ MS
98.32	sacrifices] 1E, 1A, ARE; sacrafices MS
98.35	walls . . . golden] 1E, 1A, ARE; walls being full of golden MS

98.38   cap . . . cap.]   ARE; c. vi. Idem. d. 7. c. x. MS, 1E, 1A
99.4   Golden Temple]   1E, 1A, ARE; Golden temple MS
99.7   and,]   1E, 1A, ARE; ~∧ MS
99.9   John, also]   1E, 1A, ARE; John, since MS
99.14   ascended,]   1E, 1A, ARE; ~∧ MS
99.20   Vasco]   1E, 1A, ARE; *No paragraph in MS*
99.30–100.1   and made . . . to the]   1E, 1A, ARE; and returned down
                  the river to the   MS
99.31–41   *In . . . companions]   1E, 1A, ARE; missing in MS
100.7   into what is termed the Grand River]   ARE; into what
                  was termed the Grand River 1E, 1A; into the Grand
                  River   MS

100.9   emptied itself]   1E, 1A, ARE; emptied MS
100.10   waters,]   1E, 1A, ARE; ~∧ MS
*100.11   Black River]   1A, ARE; black river MS, 1E
100.14   Abibeyba]   1E, 1A, ARE; Abibea MS
100.16–20   immense . . . wind.]   1E, 1A, ARE; immense trees.
                  They were constructed of wood and trees curiously
                  interlaced, and though sufficiently strong, were so
                  pliant as to yield uninjured, to the motion of the
                  branches when agitated by the wind. MS
100.20–21   them, . . . by]   1A, 1E, ARE; them by MS
100.22   man's]   1E, 1A, ARE; mans MS
100.30   the Indians]   1E, 1A, ARE; they MS
100.31   former]   1E, 1A, ARE; Spaniards MS
100.34   threatened, . . . down,] 1E, 1A, ARE; ~∧ . . . ~∧ MS
100.35   and]   1E, 1A, ARE; with MS
101.10   overrun]   1E, 1A, ARE; over run MS
101.14   Negro,]   1E, 1A, ARE; ~∧ MS
*101.16   Dobayba; . . . favorite]   1E, ARE; Dobayba, for some
                  time a favorite   MS
101.20   Hurtado,]   1E, 1A, ARE; ~∧ MS
101.28   River]   1E, 1A, ARE; river MS
101.28   freighted,]   1E, 1A, ARE; ~∧ MS
101.28   River]   1E, 1A, ARE; river MS
101.30   cacique]   1E, 1A, ARE; Cacique MS
101.32   Spaniards,]   1E, 1A, ARE; ~∧ MS
102.5   River and]   1E, 1A, ARE; river & MS
102.11   intelligence;]   1E, 1A, ARE; ~∧ MS
102.26   the Spaniard]   1E, 1A, ARE; Vasco Nuñez MS
102.26   on her]   ARE; upon her MS 1E, 1A
102.32   cacique]   1E, 1A, ARE; Cacique MS

102.34	settlement] 1E, 1A, ARE; Settlement MS
102.35	the Spaniard] 1E, 1A, ARE; Vasco Nuñez MS
102.38	And the Indians were] ARE; The Indians were therefore 1E, 1A; The Indians were, therefore, MS
*102.40–103.1	Foiled . . . concerted] 1E, 1F, ARE; Foiled . . . conspiracy with the neighboring caciques with which the settlement was menaced. (*New paragraph*)Five caciques had joined in the confederacy. They had prepared a hundred canoes; had amassed provisions for an army, and had concerted MS; *New paragraph* ~ Five ~ 1A
103.7	men,] 1E, 1A, ARE; ~ₐ MS
103.22	Valdivia] 1E, 1A, ARE; Valdibia MS
*103.27	abandoned] 1E, ARE; might have abandoned MS, 1A
103.27	fate.] 1E, 1A, ARE; ~* MS
103.28	harassed] 1E, 1A, ARE; harrassed MS
103.31	determined . . . all] 1E, 1A, ARE; determined to sail, himself, to communicate all MS
104.1	colony,] 1E, 1A, ARE; ~ₐ MS
104.6	containing extravagant] ARE; containing the most extravagant MS, 1E, 1A
*104.16	had elapsed] 1E, ARE; elapsed MS, 1A
104.18	adventurers] 1E, 1A, ARE; ~, MS
104.27	River] 1E, 1A, ARE; river MS
104.28–29	oppressive] 1E, 1A, ARE; oppression MS
*104.30–31	honour, and peculiarly gifted with the] T; honor, . . . the ARE; honour, who seems to have peculiarly possessed the MS, 1E, 1A
105.2	adversaries] 1E, 1A, ARE; ~, MS
105.6	debate,] 1E, 1A, ARE; ~ₐ MS
105.15	yet unshared] ARE; which yet remained unshared MS, 1E, 1A
105.24	ringleader] 1E, 1A, ARE; ring leader MS
105.26	seize] 1E, 1A, ARE; sieze MS
105.33	swore] 1E, 1A, ARE; ~, MS
105.36	"Vasco] 1E, 1A, ARE; ₐ~ MS
105.36	Nuñez,"] 1E, 1A, ARE; Nunez,ₐ MS
*105.42	ringleaders] 1E, 1A, ARE; ring leaders MS
*105.42	put into] 1E, 1F, ARE; thrown in MS, 1A
106.1	recalled] 1E, 1A, ARE; ~, MS
106.3	pseudo-commander] 1E, ARE; ~ₐ ~ MS, 1A
106.5	Hispaniola,] ARE; ~ₐ MS, 1E, 1A

*106.8–9   (to . . . gold)]   1E, ARE; ∧~ . . . ~∧ MS, 1A
 106.14   treasurer]   1E, 1A, ARE; Treasurer MS
 106.16   Sovereign]   1E, 1A, ARE; sovreign MS
 106.18   with]   1E, 1A, ARE; ~, MS
 106.21   ringleaders]   1E, 1A, ARE; ring leaders MS
 106.27   received]   1E, 1A, ARE; recieved MS
*106.27   colleague, the Alcalde Zamudio,]   ARE; ~∧ ~ alcalde
                ~∧ MS
 106.29   throne . . . succeeded]   1E, 1A, ARE; throne; had suc-
                ceeded MS
 107.11   Fame,]   1E, 1A, ARE; ~∧ MS
 107.13   enterprize.]   T; enterprize: MS; enterprise. 1E, 1A, ARE
*107.16   resolute, . . . devoted]   1E, 1F, ARE; resolute and
                vigorous, and those most devoted MS, 1A
*107.18   danger]   1E, 1F, ARE; peril MS, 1A
 107.35   a number]   1E, 1A, ARE; a considerable number MS
 107.40   Ocean.]   1E, 1A, ARE; ~∧ MS
 107.41   cap.]   ARE; c. MS, 1E, 1A
 108.4   brigantine]   1E, 1A, ARE; Brigantine MS
 108.4   pirogues]   1E, 1A, ARE; Pirogues MS
*108.7   dominion]   1E, ARE; dominions MS, 1A
 108.12–13   brigantine]   1E, 1A, ARE; Brigantine MS
 108.16   upon . . . and]   1E, 1A, ARE; upon the spirit of Vasco
                Nuñez, and MS
 108.21   toilsome.]   ARE; toilsome in the extreme. MS, 1E, 1A
 108.21   with]   1E, 1A, ARE; by MS
 108.21   Spaniards,]   1E, 1A, ARE; ~∧ MS
 108.22   weight]   1E, 1A, ARE; wieght MS
 108.27   village]   1E, 1A, ARE; Village MS
 108.38   pechry]   1E, 1A, ARE; Pechry MS
 108.38   sea]   1E, 1A, ARE; Sea MS
 109.2   ridge,]   1E, 1A, ARE; ~∧ MS
 109.5   Numbers]   1E, 1A, ARE; Twelve MS
 109.16   Quaraquà]   1E, ARE; Quaraqua MS, 1A
 109.17   were entering]   1E, 1A, ARE; entering MS
 109.30   Quaraquà]   1E, ARE; Quaraqua MS, 1A
 109.35   and,]   1E, 1A, ARE; ~∧ MS
 109.36–37   bloodhounds]   1A, ARE; blood hounds MS, 1E
 109.41   decad. . . lib. . . cap.]   ARE; d. . . l. . . c. MS, 1E, 1A
 110.2   "These,"]   1E, 1A, ARE; ∧~∧∧ MS
 110.4   discovered."†]   ARE; discovered.+ MS
 110.6   Quaraquà]   1E, ARE; Quaraqua MS, 1A

110.10	so disabled] 1E, 1A, ARE; disabled MS
110.10	wounds received] ARE; wounds they had received MS, 1E, 1A
110.14	long-sought] 1E, 1A, ARE; ~∧~ MS
110.23	The] 1E, 1A, ARE; 1513 The MS
110.24	village . . . . It was] 1E, 1A, ARE; village to scale the last mountain height that intervened between them and the sight of the Unknown Sea. It was MS
110.27	days'] 1E, 1A, ARE; ~∧ MS
110.27	Quaraquà] 1E, ARE; Quaraqua MS, 1A
110.30	shipwreck,] 1E, 1A, ARE; ~∧ MS
111.3	o'clock] 1E, 1A, ARE; oclock MS
111.3	they emerged] 1E, 1A, ARE; they came to the loftiest region of the mountain, and emerged MS
111.4–5	struggled . . . alone] 1E, 1A, ARE; struggled. The bald summit of the mountain alone MS
111.10–11	summit . . . prospect] 1E, 1A, ARE; summit, a boundless prospect MS
111.19	Behold, my friends,] 1E, 1A, ARE; ~∧ ~∧ MS
111.21	pray . . . guide] 1E, 1F, ARE; pray to him that he will guide MS, 1A
*111.22	and which] 1E, 1F, ARE; and in which MS, 1A
111.26	Indies] 1E, 1A, ARE; Indias MS
111.29	Catholic] 1E, 1A, ARE; catholic MS
111.31	to death] 1E, 1A, ARE; to the death MS
111.32–33	*Laudamus*–] T; ~∧ MS; ~, 1E, 1A, ARE
*111.33	rest] 1E, 1F, ARE; people MS, 1A
111.36	that mountain] ARE; that wild mountain MS, 1E, 1A
111.37–40	and must . . . studded] 1E, 1A, ARE; and opened a boundless field for conjecture. Was this the great Indian Ocean studded MS
112.1	gorgeous] 1E, 1A, ARE; splendid MS
112.3–5	savage? . . . Spaniards of] 1E, 1F, ARE; Indian? The latter could hardly be the case, for the natives had told the spaniards 1A; Indian? Yet the natives had talked of MS
112.7–9	who . . . this] 1E, 1A, ARE; having peculiar laws and customs and arts, and sciences; forming as it were a world within themselves, intercommuning by this MS
112.10–11	continents; . . . independence of] 1E, 1A, ARE; continents, and totally ignorant and independent of MS

112.13   Such . . . suggested]   1E, 1A, ARE; Such were the
                ideas naturally suggested MS
112.14–15   It was . . . that]   1E, 1A, ARE; The prevalent belief of
                the Spaniards, however, was that MS
112.15   Christians]   1E, 1A, ARE; christians MS
112.18   Sovereigns]   T; Sovreigns MS; sovereigns, 1E, 1A
112.24   Sovereigns]   T; sovreigns MS; sovereigns 1E, 1A
112.27   monuments,]   1E, 1A, ARE; ~∧ MS
*112.30   spent]   1E, 1F, ARE; been MS, 1A
*112.30   days in]   1E, 1F, ARE; days MS, 1A
112.32   present, . . . said,]   1E, 1A, ARE; ~∧ . . . ~∧ MS
112.33   days']   1E, ARE; ~∧ MS, 1A
112.38   obstacles,]   1E, 1A, ARE; ~∧ MS
113.1–2   could have subdued]   1E, 1A, ARE; could subdue MS
113.9   who,]   1E, 1A, ARE; ~∧ MS
113.14   flash]   1E, 1A, ARE; ~, MS
113.25   therefore,]   1E, 1A, ARE; ~∧ MS
*113.28   pounds']   ARE; ~∧ MS, 1E, 1A
113.32   Españoles]   ARE; Espanoles MS, 1A, 1E
113.32   Célebres,]   1E, 1A, ARE; Celebres MS
114.4   guides]   1E,1 A, ARE; Indian guides MS
114.5   Quaraquà]   1E, ARE; Quaraqua MS, 1A
*114.7–8   Pizarro, . . . Escaray,]   1E, 1A, ARE; ~∧ . . . Esceray∧
                MS; ~∧ . . . Escary 1A
*114.10   days']   ARE; ~∧ MS, 1E, 1A
114.11–12   water being in]   1E, 1A, ARE; water in MS
114.13–14   far . . . came]   1E, 1A, ARE; far on land, the tide,
                came MS
114.26   Quaraquà]   1E, ARE; Quaraqua ME, 1A
114.27   repose]   1E, 1A, ARE; ~, MS
114.31   forests,]   1E, 1A, ARE; ~∧ MS
114.37   saint's]   1E, 1A, ARE; Saints MS
114.40   decad. . . .lib. . . . cap.]   ARE; d . . . l . . . c. MS,
                1E, 1A
115.8   voice:]   1E, 1A, ARE; ~; MS
115.9   Ferdinand and Doña Juana]   1E, ARE; Fernando and
                Doña Juana MS; Ferdinand and Donna Juanna 1A
115.10   Arragon]   1E, 1A, ARE; Aragon MS
115.16   if other]   1E, 1A, ARE; if any other MS
115.16   prince or captain]   1E, 1A, ARE; Prince, or Captain
                MS
115.16   Christian] ARE; christian MS, 1E, 1A

115.19	Sovereigns] T; Sovreigns MS; sovereigns 1E, 1A, ARE
115.20	Indian islands, and Terra Firma] ARE; Indias, islands, and terra firma MS, 1E, 1A
115.21	northern and southern] ARE; Northern and Southern MS, 1E, 1A
115.21	seas] 1E, 1A, ARE; Seas MS
*115.22	Equinoctial] T; equinoctial MS, ARE; equinoxial 1E, 1A
115.23	Cancer and Capricorn] 1A, ARE; cancer and capricorn MS, 1E
115.31	Sovereigns] T; Sovreigns MS; sovereigns 1E, 1A, ARE
*115.32	they] ARE; they all MS, 1E, 1A
115.40	made] 1E, 1A, ARE; made made MS
115.40–41	Three Persons . . . Trinity] 1E, 1A, ARE; three persons . . . trinity MS
116.5	lands—a scene] 1E, 1A, ARE; ~. a Scene MS
116.14	sea] 1E, 1A, ARE; ~, MS
116.15	October, November, and December] 1E, ARE; Octobre, Novembre and Decembre MS
116.18	These] 1E, 1A, ARE; His MS
116.21	monarchs] 1E, 1A, ARE; Monarchs MS
*116.26	Finding] 1E, ARE; Seeing MS, 1A
116.32	on] 1E, 1A, ARE; into MS
116.33	Oviedo's] 1E, 1A, ARE; Oviedos MS
117.1	cacique's] 1E, 1A, ARE; caciques MS
*117.7	sight, in] ARE; sight, as if swallowed in MS, 1E, 1A
117.18	isthmus] 1E, 1A, ARE; Isthmus MS
117.24	Nothing, . . . said,] 1E, 1A, ARE; ~ ∧ . . . ~ ∧ MS
117.26	gulf] 1E, 1A, ARE; Gulf MS
117.32	sea,] 1E, 1A, ARE; ~ ∧ MS
117.33	became] ARE; was MS, 1E, 1A
117.34	the retiring waves] 1E, 1A, ARE; the waves beating MS
118.2	repair,] 1E, 1A, ARE; ~ ∧ MS
118.5	stalks] 1E, 1A, ARE; stalkes MS
118.8	leaks. When re-embarked] ARE; leaks that remained. When they re embarked MS; When they re-embarked 1E, 1A
118.9	water's] 1E, 1A, ARE; waters MS
118.11	from hunger] ARE; from the pangs of hunger MS, 1E, 1A
118.17	swords] 1E, 1A, ARE; sword MS

118.18	abundance,] 1E, 1A, ARE; ~∧ MS
118.25	Túmaco] 1E, 1A, ARE; Tumaco MS
118.25	savage,] 1E, 1A, ARE; ~∧ MS
*118.27	superhuman] 1A, ARE; super human MS; super-human 1E
118.38	pearls] 1E, 1A, ARE; pearl MS
119.2	eye-witnesses] 1E, 1A, ARE; eye witnesses MS
119.3	sea] 1E, 1A, ARE; Sea MS
119.12	south] 1E, 1A, ARE; South MS
119.16	tapir . . . lama] 1E, 1A, ARE; Tapir . . . Lama MS
119.18	great] 1E, 1A, ARE; Great MS
*119.19	awakened] ARE; filled him with MS, 1E, 1A
119.20	him.] 1E, 1A, ARE; ~∧ MS
119.24	Lest] 1E, 1A, ARE; 1513 Lest MS
119.26	Túmaco] 1E, 1A, ARE; Tumaco MS
119.28–29	the paddles] 1E, 1A, ARE; their paddles MS
119.31	might be] 1E, 1A, ARE; might MS
119.31	Sovereigns] T; Sovreigns MS; sovereigns 1E, 1A
119.33	Departing] 1E, ARE; *No paragraph in MS*
120.3	gulf,] 1E, 1A, ARE; ~∧ MS
120.5	hand,] 1E, 1A, ARE; ~∧ MS
120.6	it,] 1E, 1A, ARE; ~∧ MS
120.7	St. Michael's] 1E, 1A, ARE; St Michaels MS
120.10	one of] 1E, 1A, ARE; of MS
120.12	man's] 1E, 1A, ARE; mans MS
120.23	when, . . . allies,] 1E, 1A, ARE; ~∧ . . . ~∧ MS
120.27	Pearl] 1E, 1A, ARE; pearl MS
120.28	he] ARE; Vasco Nunez MS; Vasco Nuñez 1E, 1A
120.28	Túmaco] 1E, 1A, ARE; Tumaco MS
120.31	Túmaco] 1E, 1A, ARE; Tùmaco MS
120.36	river,] 1E, 1A, ARE; ~∧ MS
121.2	Túmaco] 1E, 1A, ARE; Tùmaco MS
121.13	be] 1E, ARE; lay MS, 1A
121.15–16	separate] 1E, 1A, ARE; seperate MS
121.25	heat,] 1E, 1A, ARE; ~∧ MS
121.31	while,] 1E, 1A, ARE; ~∧ MS
121.31	course,] 1E, 1A, ARE; ~∧ MS
121.32	glen,] 1E, 1A, ARE; ~∧ MS
122.3	Crœsus] 1E, 1A, ARE; Crosus MS
122.7	gold.] 1E, 1A, ARE; ~∧ MS
122.8	Poncra] 1E, 1A, ARE; Poncras MS
122.19	even, . . . said,] 1E, 1A, ARE; ~∧ . . . ~∧ MS

122.25   companions,]   1E, 1A, ARE; ~∧ MS
*122.26   issued]   1E, 1A, ARE; given MS, 1A
122.28   alleged]   1E, 1A, ARE; alledged MS
*122.29   visibly]   1E, 1F, ARE; too much MS, 1A
*122.29–30   remains accordingly a]   1E, 1F, ARE; remains a MS, 1A
122.31   staid]   1E, 1F, ARE; remained MS, 1A
122.37   "Behold,"]   1E, 1A, ARE; ∧~∧" MS
122.41   decad. . . cap.]   ARE; d. . . c. MS, 1E, 1A
123.1–2   worshipped]   1E, 1A, ARE; worshiped MS
123.9   forests;]   1E, 1A, ARE; ~, MS
123.9   it,]   1E, 1A, ARE; ~∧ MS
123.14–27   excessively . . . places, the]   1E, 1A, ARE; excessively
                from hunger. The villages on this elevated part of the
                mountains, were scattered and poor, poor and nearly
                destitute of provisions. They held no communication
                with each other, each contenting itself with the scanty
                produce of its own height and forests. Some were
                certainly deserted; at other places, the MS
123.16   country, and]   1E, 1A, ARE; country they were about
                to traverse, and MS
123.33   spirits . . . length]   1E, 1A, ARE; spirits. Indeed they
                were suffering the punishment of their avarice, for
                they had laden their Indians with gold instead of
                provisions, thinking the latter of far inferior value.
                As the Indians could carry but small burdens, and
                had to be fed from the common stock it had soon been
                exhausted. Their sufferings became so great that
                many of their Indian companions sank down and
                perished by the way. At length MS
124.4   the]   1E, 1A, ARE; these MS
124.5   of the]   1E, 1A, ARE; of these MS
124.10   of any]   ARE; that would attend any MS, 1E, 1A
124.14   weapons,]   1E, 1A, ARE; ~∧ MS
124.15   armies]   1A, 1E, ARE; warriors MS
124.16   upon]   ARE; to venture upon MS, 1E, 1A
124.20   departed secretly]   ARE; departed silently and secretly
                MS, 1E, 1A
124.21   through the forests and the]   ARE; through the laba-
                rynths the forests & the MS; through the labrinths of
                the forests and the 1E, 1A
124.23   Tubanamà]   1E, ARE; Tubanama MS, 1A
124.24   days']   1E, 1A, ARE; days MS

124.25–26   suddenly, and captured] ARE; suddenly, and with
              success, so as to surprize and capture MS; suddenly,
              and with success, so as to surprise and capture 1E, 1A
124.27   Tubanamà lost] ARE; When Tubanamà found him-
              self a prisoner in the hands of the Spaniards, he
              lost MS, 1E; When Tubanama found himself a pris-
              oner in the hands of the Spaniards, he lost 1A
124.27–28   allies beholding] ARE; allies of Vasco Nunez behold-
              ing MS; allies of Vasco Nuñez beholding 1E, 1A
124.28   captive, urged] ARE; captive, now urged MS, 1E, 1A
124.33   he, "to] 1E, 1A, ARE; he to MS
125.13   neighborhood] 1A, ARE; neighborhood for the pur-
              pose of collecting it and which might also facilitate
              communciation between the Seas. MS
125.23   men, Nuñez] 1E, 1A, ARE; ~∧ Nunez MS
125.28   toilfully,] 1E, 1A, ARE; ~∧ MS
125.29   Comagre.] 1E, 1A, ARE; ~∧ MS
125.30   had been] 1E, 1A, ARE; was MS
125.30   son,] 1E, 1A, ARE; ~∧ MS
125.31   who had] 1E, 1A, ARE; had MS
125.32   Christianity] 1E, 1A, ARE; christianity MS
125.33   hospitality,] 1E, 1A, ARE; ~∧ MS
125.34   soldier's] 1E, 1A, ARE; soldiers MS
125.41   cap.] ARE; c. MS, 1E, 1A
126.1   brigantine] 1E, 1A, ARE; Brigantine MS
126.2   Darien,] 1E, 1A, ARE; ~∧ MS
126.2   day.] 1A, 1E, ARE; ~, MS
126.4   Sea] 1E, 1A, ARE; sea MS
126.6   companions left] ARE; companions he had left MS,
              1E, 1A
126.21–24   followers . . . and] 1E, 1A, ARE; followers, watching,
              fighting, fasting, and labouring with them, treating
              them with frank affability, visiting and consoling such
              as were sick or infirm and MS
126.26   precaution;] 1E, 1A, ARE; ~, MS
126.36   "Behold,"] 1E, 1A, ARE; "Behold" MS
126.36   Martyr,] 1E, 1A, ARE; ~∧ MS
127.7   Sovereign] T; Sovreign MS; sovereign 1E, 1A, ARE
127.11   Sovereign] T; Sovreign MS; sovereign 1E, 1A, ARE
127.20   March, a] ARE; March. The MS; ~; ~ 1E 1A
127.27   alleged] 1E, 1A, ARE; alledged MS
127.34   Davila,] 1E, 1A, ARE; ~∧ MS

128.13	Comagre,] 1E, 1A, ARE; ~∧ MS
128.15	discovery] 1E, 1A, ARE; Discovery MS
128.32–34	expedition. . . . dreams] 1E, 1A, ARE; expedition. Nothing could equal the disappointment of the Spanish cavaliers at having their dreams MS
128.35	them,] 1E, 1A, ARE; ~∧ MS
129.3	cavaliers,] 1E, 1A, ARE; ~∧ MS
*129.24	objects] ARE; object MS, 1E, 1A
*129.30	Islands] T; islands MS, 1E, 1A, ARE
129.41	lib. . . . cap.] ARE; l . . . c. MS, 1E, 1A
130.11–12	she . . . daughters] ARE; she had a family of four sons and four daughters, whom she had left behind in Spain MS, 1E, 1A
132.18	Gulf] 1A, ARE; gulf 1E
133.12	Bishop] T; bishop 1E, 1A, ARE
133.17	Darien,] 1E, 1A, ARE; ~∧ MS
133.26	palace] 1E, 1A, ARE; Palace MS
133.27	cavaliers,] 1E, 1A, ARE; ~; MS
*134.2	Don Pedrarius] 1A, 1E, ARE; Pedrarius MS
134.5	as public] 1E, 1A, ARE; as the public MS
134.13	unexpected] 1E, 1A, ARE; unsexpected MS
134.14	his whole] 1E, 1A, ARE; whole MS
134.19	Islands] 1E, 1A, ARE; islands MS
134.23	purposes,] 1E, 1A, ARE; ~∧ MS
134.26	Espinosa,] 1E, 1A, ARE; ~∧ MS
*134.26	Alcalde] 1E, 1A, ARE; an Alcalde MS
134.30	Quevedo,] 1E, 1A, ARE; ~∧ MS
134.31	Now,] 1E, 1A, ARE; ~∧ MS
134.35	fact,] 1E, 1A, ARE; ~∧ MS
134.35	Under . . . prelate] 1E, 1A, ARE; Under his influence MS
135.1	conducted,] 1E, 1A, ARE; ~∧ MS
135.3	whom] 1E, 1A, ARE; ~, MS
135.8	the inquisition] ARE; this inquisition MS, 1E, 1A
135.32	Isabella] T; Isabel MS, 1E, ARE
135.39	severity,] 1E, 1A, ARE; ~∧ MS
135.42	Sea] 1E, 1A, ARE; sea MS
136.17	kind,] 1E, 1A, ARE; ~∧ MS
136.19	speedily;] 1E, 1A, ARE; ~, MS
136.27	calamities;] 1E, 1A, ARE; ~, MS
136.28	them;] 1E, 1A, ARE; ~∧ MS
137.11	brocade,] 1E, 1A, ARE; ~∧ MS

137.20	flee] 1E, 1A, ARE; fly MS
137.21	Velasquez,] 1E, 1A, ARE; ∼∧ MS
137.22	island; others] 1E, 1A, ARE; island, but MS
137.23	health,] 1E, 1A, ARE; ∼∧ MS
137.32	inquiry,] 1E, 1A, ARE; ∼∧ MS
138.5	man's] 1E, 1A, ARE; mans MS
138.7	check given] ARE; check which had been given MS, 1E, 1A
138.12	and make provisions] ARE; and to make the requisite provisions MS, 1E, 1A
138.12	isthmus] 1E, 1A, ARE; Isthmus MS
138.13	founding of a] T; founding a MS, 1E, 1A, 1F, ARE
138.19	Ayora,] 1E, 1A, ARE; ∼∧ MS
138.22–23	harassed and] 1E, 1A, ARE; harrassed & MS
138.26	seizing] 1E, 1A, ARE; siezing MS
138.31	Ayora] 1E, 1A, ARE; ∼, MS
138.32	resistance;] 1E, 1A, ARE; ∼, MS
138.32	caciques] 1E, 1A, ARE; the caciques MS
138.33	friends,] 1E, 1A, ARE; ∼∧ MS
138.35	disastrous] 1E, 1A, ARE; disasterous MS
138.39	likely] ARE; that would be likely MS, 1E, 1A
138.40	fitting] ARE; likely MS, 1E, 1A
138.41	lib. . . . cap.] ARE; l . . . c. MS, 1E, 1A
139.7	temple,] 1E, 1A, ARE; ∼∧ MS
139.8	continued a] ARE; continued to form a MS, 1E, 1A
139.11	temple] 1E, 1A, ARE; Temple MS
139.11	therefore,] 1E, 1A, ARE; ∼∧ MS
139.21–22	vampire; alligators] 1E, 1A, ARE; Vampire; Alligators MS
139.23	dragons!] 1E, 1A, ARE; Dragons! MS
139.29	Indians,] 1E, 1A, ARE; ∼∧ MS
139.31	houses,] 1E, 1A, ARE; houses and MS
139.32	roots,] 1E, 1A, ARE; ∼; MS
140.3	and one] 1E, 1A, ARE; one MS
140.8	mountains,] 1E, 1A, ARE; ∼∧ MS
140.11	and,] 1E, 1A, ARE; ∼∧ MS
140.13	tradition,] 1E, 1A, ARE; ∼∧ MS
140.17	them,] 1E, 1A, ARE; ∼∧ MS
140.19	Several of the] 1E, 1A, ARE; The MS
140.29	and,] 1E, 1A, ARE; ∼∧ MS
140.31	Temple] 1E, 1A, ARE; temple MS
140.33	a swarm] ARE; an immense swarm MS, 1E, 1A

140.35	Some,] 1E, 1A, ARE; ~∧ MS
141.2	night,] 1E, 1A, ARE; ~∧ MS
141.3	river,] 1E, 1A, ARE; ~∧ MS
141.6	the fearful] ARE; these fearful MS, 1E, 1A
141.11	Nuñez,"] 1E, 1A, ARE; ~∧∧ MS
141.11	had . . . command] 1E, 1A, ARE; had hitherto been accustomed to absolute command MS
141.14	different."] 1E, 1A, ARE; different. MS
141.20	colony] 1E, 1A, ARE; Colony MS
141.30	hands,] 1E, 1A, ARE; ~∧ MS
141.32	circumstance,] 1E, 1A, ARE; ~∧ MS
142.2	Sovereign.] T; Sovreign, MS; sovereign 1E, 1A
142.4	letter,] 1E, 1A, ARE; ~∧ MS
142.6	Mayor,] 1E, 1A, ARE; ~∧ MS
142.9	inquest still] ARE; inquest which was still MS, 1E, 1A
142.11	indignantly,] 1E, 1A, ARE; ~∧ MS
142.11	presumptuous] 1E, 1A, ARE; presumptious MS
142.15	Sovereign] T; Sovreign MS; sovereign 1E, 1A
142.26	Bishop] T; bishop MS, 1E, 1A, ARE
142.27	present,] 1E, 1A, ARE; ~∧ MS
142.37	juncture,] 1E, 1A, ARE; ~∧ MS
143.20	harassing] 1E, 1A, ARE; harrassing MS
143.20	Pedrarias.] 1E, 1A, ARE; ~∧ MS
143.23	disastrous] 1E, 1A, ARE; disasterous MS
143.26	to permit] ARE; to go still further, and to permit MS, 1E, 1A
143.29	expedition, and was] 1E, 1A, ARE; expedition. He was MS
143.30	Islands] 1E, 1A, ARE; islands MS
144.7	shores] 1E, 1A, ARE; Shores MS
144.12	Peñalosa;] 1E, 1A, ARE; ~, MS
144.16	island . . . archipelago] 1E, 1A, ARE; Island . . . Archipelago MS
144.16–17	which, . . . fishery,] 1E, 1A, ARE; ~∧ . . . ~∧ MS
144.24	unavailing,] 1E, 1A, ARE; ~∧ MS
144.30	weighing] 1E, 1A, ARE; wieghing MS
144.33	and,] 1E, 1A, ARE; ~∧ MS
144.37	Spaniards,] 1E, 1A, ARE; ~∧ MS
144.38	you," . . . he,] 1E, 1A, ARE; you, . . . he MS
145.3	main land,] 1E, 1A, ARE; ~∧ MS
145.6	direction, . . . said,] 1E, 1A, ARE; ~∧ . . . ~∧ MS
145.6	inexhaustible] 1E, 1A, ARE; inexhaustable MS

145.10	while] 1E, 1A, ARE; as MS
145.13	island,] 1E, 1A, ARE; ~ₐ MS
*145.16	pounds'] ARE; ~ₐ MS, 1E, 1A
145.20	Tutibrà] ARE, 1E; Tutibàr MS; Tutibar 1A
145.26	their] 1E, 1A, ARE; his MS
145.35	islands] 1E, 1A, ARE; Islands MS
145.37	suspicions;] 1E, 1A, ARE; ~, MS
145.41	decad. . . . lib. . . . cap. . . . Peter . . . decad. . . . cap.] ARE; c . . .l . . . c . . . P . . . d . . . c. MS, 1E, 1A
146.2	Chirucà] 1E, 1A, ARE; Chiruca MS
146.7	Tutibrà] 1E, ARE; Tutibar MS; Tutibra 1A
146.11	caciques,] 1E, 1A, ARE; ~ₐ MS
146.23	cruelty;] 1E, 1A, ARE; ~, MS
146.28	that,] 1E, 1A, ARE; the MS
146.29	night,] 1E, 1A, ARE; ~ₐ MS
146.32	discoverers;] 1E, 1A, ARE; ~, MS
146.41	harassed] 1E, 1A, ARE; harrassed MS
146.42	fire kept up] 1E, 1A, ARE; fire which was kept up MS
147.1	Dismayed] 1E, 1A, ARE; Discouraged MS
147.2	hastened] 1E, 1A, ARE; determined MS
147.5	harassing] 1E, 1A, ARE; harrassing MS
147.9	deceive] 1E, 1A, ARE; decieve MS
147.10	Velasquez,] 1E, 1A, ARE; ~ₐ MS
147.11	grievously] 1E, 1A, ARE; greviously MS
147.11	Unable,] 1E, 1A, ARE; ~ₐ MS
147.13	savages,] 1E, 1A, ARE; ~ₐ MS
147.22	goaded,] 1E, 1A, ARE; ~ₐ MS
147.31	until,] 1E, 1A, ARE; ~ₐ MS
147.33	squadrons.] 1E, 1A, ARE; ~ₐ MS
147.34	despaired] ARE; began to despair MS, 1E, 1A
147.42	these] 1E, 1A, ARE; those MS
148.2	fen] 1E, 1A, ARE; fens MS
148.16–17	and, . . . St. Michael,] 1E, 1A, ARE; ~ₐ . . . ~ₐ MS
148.18	time . . . mountains] 1E, 1A, ARE; time for home by a different route across the mountains. MS
148.21	in a battered] 1E, 1A, ARE; in battered MS
148.28	ducats.] 1E, 1A, ARE; ~ₐ MS
148.29	Such . . . colonists] 1E, 1A, ARE; Such is the cupidity of human nature MS
148.30	islands] 1E, 1A, ARE; Islands MS
148.32	of the] ARE; of all the MS, 1E, 1A

148.32	adventurers] 1E, 1A, ARE; ~, MS
148.33	passed] T; past MS, 1E, 1A, ARE
148.35	decad. . . . lib. . . . cap.] ARE; d . . . l . . . c. MS, 1E, 1A
149.14	Zenu,] 1E, 1A, ARE; ~∧ MS
149.23	Tubanamà,] 1E, ARE; Tubanama MS, 1A
149.26	losses,] 1E, 1A, ARE; ~∧ MS
149.27	harassed] 1E, 1A, ARE; harrassed MS
149.30	kept . . . mountains,] 1E, 1A, ARE; kept a look out upon the mountains MS
149.31–33	trees . . . Savannahs] 1E, 1A, ARE; trees, and the long waving grass of the Savannahs MS
149.34	sea,] 1E, 1A, ARE; ~∧ MS
149.38	This was] 1E, 1A, ARE; This MS
149.38	who] 1E, 1A, ARE; he MS
149.39	proclaimed,] 1E, 1A, ARE; ~∧ MS
150.1	harassed] 1E, 1A, ARE; harrassed MS
150.2	evils,] 1E, 1A, ARE; ~∧ MS
150.4–5	proofs . . . highly] 1E, 1A, ARE; proofs of his services being highly MS
150.7	colony . . . necessity] 1E, 1A, ARE; colony since he had come into power, and of the necessity MS
150.10	ruins.] 1E, 1A, ARE; ~∧ MS
150.11	politic] 1E, 1A, ARE; worthy MS
150.12	that] 1E, 1A, ARE; a MS
150.16	Sovereign. "But] T; Sovreign; But MS; sovereign. "But 1E, 1A, ARE
150.16	persist,] 1E, 1A, ARE; ~∧ MS
150.18	friend?] 1E, 1A, ARE; ~. MS
150.19	son-in-law] 1E, 1A, ARE; ~∧~∧~ MS
150.23	toils,] 1E, 1A, ARE; ~∧ MS
151.6	son-in-law] 1E, 1A, ARE; ~∧~∧~ MS
151.10	Careta,] 1E, 1A, ARE; ~∧ MS
*151.19	Hernando] 1E, 1A, ARE; Fernando MS
151.22	great] 1E, 1A, ARE; considerable MS
151.25	Acla,] 1E, 1A, ARE; ~∧ MS
151.27	seaboard] 1E, 1A, ARE; seabord MS
152.24	party did] ARE; party was absent and did 1E, 1A
152.27–28	with roots gathered in] ARE; with such roots as they could gather in 1E
152.40–41	until, after] ARE; until at length, after 1E, 1A

*153.21	Islands] ARE; islands 1E, 1A
153.33	were alarmed] ARE; were filled with apprehension 1E, 1A
153.34	decad. . . . lib. . . . cap.] ARE; d . . . l . . . c. 1E, 1A
*154.10	Chuchama] 1A; Chuchamà 1E, ARE
*154.25	expedition;] 1A, 1F, ARE; ~, MS
*155.5	Andres] 1A, 1F, ARE; Francisco 1E
155.20	and put] ARE; and to put 1E, 1A, 1F
155.35	perfidy advanced] ARE; perfidy that has been advanced 1E, 1A, 1F
156.22	be vain] ARE; be in vain 1E, 1A, 1F
156.25	to confer with] ARE; to hold a conference with 1E, 1A, 1F
*157.9	foretell] 1A, ARE; fortel 1E, 1F
*157.27	Southern Ocean] T; southern ocean 1E, 1A, 1F, ARE
*159.4	Andres] 1A, 1F, ARE; Andrez 1E
159.7	his house] ARE; the house 1E, 1A, 1F
159.24	of his innocence] ARE; of innocence 1E, 1A, 1F
160.4	Alcalde Mayor] 1A, 1F; Alcalde mayor 1E; alcalde mayor ARE
160.21	testimony on record] ARE; testimony that remains on record 1E, 1A, 1F
160.22	self-interest] 1F, ARE; ~∧~ 1E, 1A
160.26	and dispute] ARE; and to dispute 1E, 1A, 1F
161.13	dared lift] ARE; dared to lift 1E, 1A, 1F
161.33	cap.] ARE; c. 1E, 1A, 1F
*164.4	Regidor] T; regidor 1E, 1A, 1F, ARE
166.25	self-denial] 1F, ARE; ~∧~ 1E, 1A
166.33	sea shore] 1A; ~-~ 1E, 1F, ARE
*166.38	overcome] 1A, ARE; ~-~ 1E, 1F
167.39	tidings] 1A, 1F, ARE; tiding 1E
*168.27	Cortez] 1F, ARE; Cortes 1E, 1A
169.31	Gonzalo] ARE; Gonsalo 1E, 1A, 1F
*170.20	hogshead] 1A, ARE; hogs-head 1E, 1F
170.32	on] ARE; upon 1E, 1A, 1F
171.5	sprung] ARE; had sprung 1E, 1A, 1F
171.29	effect produced] ARE; effect that had been produced 1E, 1A, 1F
171.30	reached] ARE; had reached 1E, 1A, 1F
171.31	tales concerning] ARE; tales that circulated in Spain 1E, 1A, 1F
*171.36	son!"*] 1A, 1F, ARE; son!* 1E

171.40	cap.] ARE; c. 1E, 1A, 1F
173.9	Southern Ocean] 1F, ARE; Southern ocean 1E, 1A
*173.20	Gulf of Parita or Paria] ARE; Gulf of Parita or Paris 1E; Gulf of Paria 1A
*173.25	hereabout] 1A; here-about 1E, 1F, ARE
174.11	lib. . . . cap.] ARE; l . . . c. 1E, 1A, 1F
*175.14	frosts] ARE; frost 1E, 1A, 1F
*175.33	valour] 1A, 1F; valor 1E, ARE
175.34	tom. . . . cap.] ARE; t. . . . c. 1E, 1A, 1F
176.34–35	Yuca, . . . fruit] ARE; Yuca, the groves laden with the most delicious fruit 1E, 1A, 1F
*177.23	some time] 1A, ARE; sometime 1E, 1F
*177.32	I,] ARE; I. 1E, 1A, 1F
*178.16	King] T; king 1E, 1A, 1F, ARE
178.34	lib. . . . cap.] ARE; l . . . c. 1E, 1A, 1F
*180.6	incontestable] ARE; incontestible 1E, 1A, 1F
180.34	lib. . . . cap.] ARE; l . . . c. 1E, 1A, 1F
*181.16	areyto] ARE; Areyto 1E, 1A, 1F
*183.2	Agueybanà] 1A, ARE; Aguaybanà 1E, 1F
*183.12	Caparra] 1F, ARE; ~, 1E, 1A
183.19	and keep] ARE; and to keep 1E, 1A, 1F
*184.30	withdrew] 1A, 1F, ARE; with-drew 1E
186.8	Besides] ARE; Beside 1E, 1A, 1F
186.12	thus secure] ARE; thus to secure 1E, 1A, 1F
187.18	port] ARE; Port 1E, 1A, 1F
187.24	Bishop] 1A; bishop 1E, 1F, ARE
*187.35	men,"] 1A, 1F, ARE; ~,∧ 1E
187.35	decad. . . . cap.] ARE; d . . . c. 1E, 1A, 1F
*188.4	Salvador] ARE; Salvador's 1E, 1A, 1F
*188.33	tradition,] 1A, ARE; ~; 1E
188.41	decad. . . . lib. . . . cap.] ARE; d . . . l . . . c. 1E, 1A
189.36	decad. . . . lib.] ARE; d . . . l. 1E, 1A
190.20	King Ferdinand, therefore, in] ARE; At length King Ferdinand, in 1E, 1A
*190.35	archipelago] T; Achipelago 1E, 1A; Archipelago ARE
*191.18	distribution] ARE; distributions 1E, 1A
191.20	Cortez] ARE; Cortes 1E, 1A
*191.32	undertaking] 1A, ARE; under-taking 1E
*191.33	wished-for] 1A, ARE; ~∧~ 1E
191.40	where] ARE; when 1E, 1A
*192.1	fate,"] 1A, ARE; ~∧" 1E

APPENDIXES

194.1	APPENDIX] 3AC; *missing in MS1eC*; APPENDIX, CONTAINING *ILLUSTRATIONS AND DOCUMENTS* 1EC
194.4	Havana] 3AC; Havanna MS1eC, 1EC
194.6–7	to France] 3AC; to the French crown MS1eC
194.7	ninth] 3AC; 9th MS1eC
194.8	squadron] 3AC; Squadron MS1eC
194.10	general] 1EC; General MS1eC
194.15	majesty's squadron] 1EC; Majesties Squadron MS1eC
194.16	solicit] 1EC; Solicit MS1eC
194.22	history] 1EC, 2EC, 3AC; arms MS1eC
194.24	remains] 3AC; memory MS1eC
195.2	bones] 1EC, 2EC, MS2eC, MS3AC, 3AC; ashes MS1eC, 1AC
195.2	Adelantado] 3AC; adelantado MS1eC
195.3	exhumed, transmitting] MS3AC, 3AC, 1EC, 2EC; exhumed, and transported, sending MS1eC
195.9	general] 1EC; General MS1eC
195.10	Cuba,] 1EC; ∼∧ MS1eC
195.29	place, the] 1EC, 2EC, MS3AC, 3AC; place, both the MS1eC
195.32	high] 1EC, 2EC, MS2eC, 3AC; grand MS1eC
195.38	gold] 1EC; Gold MS1eC
195.42	general] 1EC; General MS1eC
196.1	friars] 1EC; Friars MS1eC
196.2	Order of Mercy] 1EC; order of mercy MS1eC
196.4	four o'clock] 1EC; 4 oclock MS1eC
196.5	civil,] 1EC; ∼∧ MS1eC
196.6	banners wrapped in mourning] 3AC; banners covered with crape MS1eC
196.13	brigantine] 1EC; Brigantine MS1eC
196.15	an admiral] 1EC, 3AC; an effective admiral MS1eC
196.17	San Lorenzo] MS2eC, 3AC; St. Lorenzo MS1eC
196.30	feluccas] 1EC; Feluccas MS1eC
196.30	in one of which] 1EC, 3AC; in which MS1eC
196.32	the other] 1EC, 3AC; another Felucca MS1eC
196.32	general] 1EC; General MS1eC
196.34	general] 1EC; General MS1eC
196.39	hearse] 3AC; herse 1EC; pantheon MS1eC
196.40	general] 1EC; General MS1eC

197.5	"All] 1EC; $_\wedge\sim$ MS1eC
197.5	ceremonies,"] 1EC; $\sim,_\wedge$ MS1eC
197.6	"were] 1EC; $_\wedge\sim$ MS1eC
197.8	Havana] 3AC; Havanna MS1eC, 1EC
197.9	New World] 1EC; new world MS1eC
197.10	on] 1EC, 2EC, 3AC; in MS1eC
197.16	When we] 3AC; *No paragraph in MS1eC*
197.18	civic] MS2eC, MS3AC, 3AC; civil MS1eC, 1EC, 2EC
197.23	honours, it is true,] 1EC; $\sim_\wedge$ $\sim_\wedge$ MS1eC
197.30	Colec. tom] 3AC; Collec. t. MS1eC
198.4	New World] 1EC; new world MS1eC
198.10	laid him open] 3AC; exposed him 1EC; lay him open MS1eC
198.10	grown old] 1EC, 2EC, MS2EC, MS3AC, 3AC; grey MS1eC
198.29	house."] 3AC; $\sim$?" MS1eC
198.29–30	in him, but could] 3AC; in himself, but that he could MS1eC
198.33	born.*] 3AC; born. MS1eC
198.37	course] 3AC; courts MS1eC
198.38	*Herrera . . . cap 4.] 3AC; *missing in MS1eC*
199.4	embracing] 3AC; comprehending MS1eC
199.8	interest of the state] 1EC; 3AC; common good MS1eC
199.10	justice] 1EC; Justice MS1eC
199.10	that therefore] 3AC; therefore that MS1eC
199.16	and none] 3AC; and that none MS1eC
199.17	dated in Villa] 3AC; dated Villa MS1eC
199.20	accorded] 3AC; granted MS1eC
199.24	Valencia] 3AC; Valentia MS1eC
199.26	guarded] 3AC; preserved MS1eC
199.27	suit] 1EC, 2EC, MS2eC, MS3AC, 3AC; process MS1eC
199.34	independence] 1EC; independance MS1eC
199.36	wily] 1EC, 2EC, 3AC; eviley MS1eC
199.38	Minutes] 1E; minutes MS1eC
199.38	Muñoz] 3AC; Muños MS1eC
199.39	relative to] 3AC; on MS1eC
200.3	Doña] 3AC; Donna MS1eC
200.4	Fernando] 3AC; Ferdinando MS1eC
200.9–10	and the . . . Diego,] 3AC; and his claims MS1eC; and the claims MS2eC
200.11	him] 3AC; Diego MS1eC
200.13	races] 1EC, 2EC, MS2eC, MS3AC, 3AC; stocks MS1eC

200.16	been so long] 3AC; so long been MS1eC
200.21	Nicholas] 3AC; Nicolas MS1eC
200.25	death] 1EC; Death MS1eC
200.27–30	Anancaona. Thus . . . disasters.] 3AC; Anacaona. MS1eC
200.31	request] 1EC, 2EC, 3AC; bequest MS1eC
200.31	Queen,] T; ~$_\wedge$ MS1eC; queen, 1EC
200.32	favourable towards] 1EC, 2EC, 3AC; considerate of MS1eC
201.3	St. Lucar] 3AC; San Lucar MS1eC
201.3	June 9,] 1EC; ~$_\wedge$ MS1eC
201.4	man's] 1EC; mans MS1eC
201.7	and of young] 3AC; and young MS1eC
201.9	New World] 1EC; new world MS1eC
201.11	given] 1EC, 3AC; accorded MS1eC
201.14	desert] 1EC; merit MS1eC
201.25	Darien] 1EC; Darian MS1eC
201.26	Gulph] T; gulph MS1eC; gulf 1EC; Gulf 3AC
201.27	New Andalusia] 1EC; new andalusia MS1eC
201.27–28	and Diego] MS3AC, 3AC; and a cavalier, named Diego 1EC; and a cavalier, by the name of Diego MS1eC
201.28	Nicuesa] T; Nicuessa MS1eC, 3AC
201.32	Adelantado] 3AC; adelantado MS1eC
201.37	Adelantado] 3AC; adelantado MS1eC
201.38	by,] 1EC; ~$_\wedge$ MS1eC
202.5	Rico] 1EC; rico MS1eC
202.7	officers . . . appointed] 1EC, 3AC; officers appointed by himself MS1eC
202.10–11	government . . . son] 1EC, 3AC; government; and indeed he inherited them from the admiral. MS1eC
202.11	Pasamonte] 3AC; Passamonte MS1eC
202.19	Pasamonte] 3AC; Passamonte MS1eC
202.25	advancing] 3AC; advanced MS1eC
202.29	enforced,] 3AC; ~$_\wedge$ MS1eC
202.37	seizing upon] 3AC; laying hold of MS1eC
202.38	path which] 1EC; ~, ~ MS1eC
202.41	lib.] 3AC; l. MS1eC
203.5	wicked hearts] 3AC; wickedness MS1eC; wicked MS2eC
203.5–6	He was opposed to the] 3AC; he opposed the MS1eC
203.10	abuse] 3AC; injustice MS1eC
203.32	Adelantado] 3AC; adelantado MS1eC

203.37	superintendence] 1EC; superintendance MS1eC
203.41	Charlevoix, . . . 321] 3AC; Charleroix, . . . 331. MS1eC
204.1	reduced to] ARE; reduced MS1eC, 1EC
204.4	them, and] 1EC, 2EC, 3AC; them and and MS1eC
204.5	Nicuesa] T; Nicuessa MS1eC, 3AC
204.8	Adelantado] 3AC; adeantado MS1eC
204.8	Bartholomew, if] 3AC; Bartholomew Columbus, if MS1eC
204.11	talents] 3AC; talent MS1eC
204.12	Adelantado] 3AC; adelantado MS1eC
204.16	Pasamonte] 3AC; Passamonte MS1eC
204.21	on April 9th, 1515] 1EC; in April 9th 1515 MS1eC
204.21	Adelantado] 3AC; adelantado MS1eC
204.22	Doña] 3AC; Dona MS1eC
204.26	bloodshed. His] T; bloodshed; his 1EC; blood shed. His MS1eC
204.36	Bello] T; ~, 1EC; bello MS1eC
204.36	El] 1EC; el MS1eC
204.39	Darien] 1EC; Darian MS1eC
204.39	Gulph] T; Gulf 3AC; gulf 1EC; gulph MS1eC
204.39	Herrera,] 1EC; ~ₐ MS1eC
204.41	Decad. I. lib. ix. cap. 5] T; D. I. l. ix. c.5 MS1eC
205.4	Don Bartholomew] 3AC; Bartholomew MS1eC
205.5	age,] 3AC; ~ₐ MS1eC
205.6	advanced,] 1AC, MS3AC, 3AC; much MS2eC; great 1EC, 2EC
205.8	Adelantado: "a man] 3AC; adelantado. He was a man MS1eC
205.11	valiant and] T; valient ~ MS1eC; ~, ~ 1EC
205.11	of great heart] 3AC; of noble mind MS1eC; of a noble mind 1EC
205.11	Charlevoix] 3AC; Charleroix MS1eC
205.13	house] 3AC; family MS1eC
205.14	Adelantado] 3AC; adelantado MS1eC
205.16	brother. It] 3AC; *New paragraph in MS1eC*
205.18–19	resumed to himself] 3A; resumed the government of MS1eC
205.19	for life] 3AC; for his life MS1eC
205.20	two hundred] 1EC; 200 MS1eC
205.21	Doña] 3AC; Dona MS1eC
205.22	an audience] 1EC, 2EC, MS2eC, 3AC; a hearing MS1eC

205.24	prince] 1EC, 2EC, 3AC; the prince MS1eC
205.25	V., was] 1EC; V, MS1eC
205.28	V.,] 1EC; V, MS1eC
205.29	Pasamonte] 3AC; Passamonte MS1eC
205.32	Pasamonte] 3AC; Passamonte MS1eC
205.33	passions] 3AC; vexations MS1eC
205.34	relations] 3AC; intercourse MS1eC
205.35	acknowledged] 1EC; ackowledged MS1eC
205.36	parts] 3AC; places MS1eC
205.38	Herrera,] 1EC; ~$_\wedge$ MS1eC
205.38	cap.] 3AC; c. MS1eC
205.39	Herrera,] 1EC; ~$_\wedge$ MS1eC
205.39	cap.] 3AC; c. MS1eC
205.40	Charlevoix, . . . lib.] 3AC; Charleroix . . . l. MS1eC
205.41	Herrera,] 1EC; ~$_\wedge$ MS1eC
205.41	lib. . . . cap.] 3AC; l. . . . c. MS1eC
206.5	themselves independence] 1EC, 3AC; themselves an independance MS1eC
206.22	them] 3AC; the negroes MS1eC
206.26	on their superintendants] 3AC; against their masters MS1eC
206.28	the whites] 3AC; the Spaniards MS1eC
206.30	to escape to] 1EC, 2EC, 3AC; to make for MS1eC
206.31	Don Diego . . . search] 3AC; When tidings were brought to Don Diego at St. Domingo of this revolt, he set out in search MS1eC
206.33	banks] 3AC; bank MS1eC
206.33	suffer] 3AC; to give time for MS1eC
206.34	Castro,] 3AC; ~$_\wedge$ MS1eC
206.35	plantation] 3AC; plantations MS1eC
206.35–36	his house] 1EC, 2EC, 3AC; the house MS1eC
206.37	in] 1EC; on MS1eC
206.38	confusion,] 1EC; ~$_\wedge$ MS1eC
206.38–39	pursuing the] 1EC, 2EC, 3AC; getting on the traces of MS1eC
206.41	six . . . infantry] 1EC, 2EC, 3AC; six infantry MS1eC
206.41	De Castro] 3AC; Decastro MS1eC
207.3	loud] 1EC, 2EC, 3AC; great MS1eC
207.5	charged them] 1EC, 2EC, 3AC; charged on them MS1eC
207.8	As . . . they] 1EC, 2EC, 3AC; As they MS1eC
207.9	suspended] 1EC, 2EC, MS2eC, 3AC; hanging MS1eC

207.11	African] 1EC; african MS1eC
207.12	whom] 1EC, 2EC, 3AC; who MS1eC
207.14	Pasamonte] 3AC; Passamonte MS1eC
207.18–19	a most . . . letter] 1EC, 2EC, 3AC; an overwhelming letter MS1eC
207.19	Indies] 1EC; Indias MS1eC
207.20	on pain] 3AC; under penalty MS1eC
207.22	and restore] 3AC; and to restore MS1eC
207.23	enjoined] 1EC; enjoyned MS1eC
207.27	as to the] 1EC, 2EC, 3AC; of the MS1eC
207.29	requested,] 1EC; ∼∧ MS1eC
207.34	upright] 1EC, 2EC, MS2eC, MS3AC, 3AC; honourable MS1eC
207.36	them,] 1EC; ∼∧ MS1eC
207.36	exactitude] 3AC; fidelity MS1eC
207.38	rose] 3AC; arose MS1eC
207.39	Herrera,] 1EC; ∼∧ MS1eC
207.40	Herrera,] 1EC; ∼∧ MS1eC
207.40	Hist. Ind., Decad I, lib. v. cap. 4.] 3AC; D. I. l. v. c. 4. MS1eC
208.1	Pasamonte] 3AC; Passamonte MS1eC
208.6	claims] 1EC, 2EC, MS2eC, 3AC; pretentions MS1eC
208.8	demands] 1EC, 2EC, 3AC; claims MS1eC
208.12	Indies] 1EC; Indias MS1eC
208.15	proceedings] 1EC, 2EC, 3AC; processes MS1eC
208.15	place in] 3AC; place before MS1eC
208.15	Indies] 1EC; Indias MS1eC
208.23–24	he . . . fever] 3AC; a fever was preying on his vitals MS1eC, 1AC; he was wasting away under the attack of a slow fever. 1EC, 2EC
208.24	historian] 1EC; Historian MS1eC
208.25–26	endeavouring] 3AC; endeavours MS1eC
208.28–29	Seville by] 3AC; Seville, passing by MS1eC
208.29	Our Lady] T; our Lady 3AC; our lady MS1eC
208.31	restored to] 1EC, 2EC, 3AC; reestablished in MS1eC, 1AC
208.32	21st of] 1EC, 2EC, 3AC; 21 MS1eC
208.32	confessed] 1EC, 2EC, 3AC; confessed himself MS1eC
208.33	Montalvan,] 1EC; ∼∧ MS1eC
208.36	23,] 1EC; ∼∧ MS1eC
208.38–41	"He . . . Herrera, "by] 1EC; He was exhausted, says Herrera, by MS1eC

208.40   Charlevoix, . . . lib.]   3AC; Charleroix . . . l. MS1eC
209.3   New World]   1EC; new world MS1eC
209.9   sons,]   1EC; ~∧ MS1eC
209.10   Cardono;]   3AC; Cordova 1EC; Cardona 1AC, MS2eC;
                Cardova MS1eC
209.11   Cueva;]   3AC; Cuera, MS1eC
209.11   George]   3AC; Giorge MS1eC
209.12   Portugal,]   1EC; ~∧ MS1eC
209.14   noble-spirited.]   1EC, 2EC, 3AC; spirited MS1eC
209.24   commissions]   ARE; commission MS1eC, 1EC
209.26   the enterprize]   T; the spirited enterprize MS1eC; the
                enterprise 1EC
209.29–30   her eldest]   3AC; the eldest MS1eC
209.31   Indies]   1EC; Indias MS1eC
209.33   family.]   1EC; ~∧ MS1eC
209.34   Herrera,]   3AC; ~∧ MS1eC
209.35   Charlevoix]   3AC; Charleroix MS1eC
209.36   called]   3AC; named MS1eC
209.36   Phillipine]   3AC; Philippine MS1eC
209.40   Indies]   1EC; Indias MS1eC
209.41   cap.]   3AC; c. MS1eC
209.41   Herrera,]1EC; ~∧ MS1eC
210.4   having . . . tribunals]   1EC, 2EC, 3AC; at court push-
                ing vigorously a process in the royal fiscal court, for
                the recovery of the Vice royalty. MS1eC
210.6   arbitration, his]   1EC; abritration. His MS1eC
210.6   Cardinal]   3AC; cardinal MS1eC
210.6   Loyasa,]   1EC; ~∧ MS1eC
210.7   Indies, being]   1EC; Indias being MS1eC
210.8   captain general]   T; Captain General MS1eC
210.8   of Hispaniola]   1EC, 2EC, 3AC; of the island of His-
                paniola MS1eC
210.14   Duke . . . Marquis]   3AC; duke . . . marquis MS1eC
210.15   Indies]   1EC; Indias MS1eC
210.17   the]   3AC; this MS1eC
210.21   Phillippa]   3AC; Philippa MS1eC
210.21   which last]   3AC; who MS1eC
210.25   Phillippa]   3AC; Philippa MS1eC
210.29   Phillippa]   3AC; Philippa MS1eC
210.30   join . . . persons]   3AC; join their claims and interests
                MS1eC

210.34–35	lawsuits . . . arose] 1EC, 3AC; lawsuits now arose that the world has ever witnessed MS1eC
210.39	Charlevoix . . . lib.] 3AC; Charleroix . . . l. MS1eC
210.40	Charlevoix, Hist. St. Doming., tom. l. lib. vi. p. 446] 3AC; Ib. c. i. lib. vi. pp. 446–7. MS1eC
210.41	Spotorno,] 1EC; ~∧ MS1eC
211.1	Adelantado] 1EC; adelantado MS1eC
211.3	Adelantado] 3AC; adelantado MS1eC
211.4	Baldassar] 3AC; Baldasser MS1eC
211.4	Balthazar] 3AC; Balthasar MS1eC
211.6	Spain,] 1EC; ~∧ MS1eC
211.7	for many] 3AC; during many MS1eC
211.8	Domenico] 3AC; Dominico MS1eC
211.9	Cuccaro,] 1EC; ~∧ MS1eC
211.10	Domenico] 3AC; Dominico MS1eC
211.17	monk's] 1EC; monks MS1eC
211.18	Balthazar] 3AC; Balthasar MS1eC
211.20	Domenico] 3AC; Dominico 1EC; Dominico, MS1eC
211.22	Domenico] 3AC; Dominico MS1eC
211.24	Indies] 1EC; Indias MS1eC
211.25	Nuño] 3AC; Nuno MS1eC
211.30	lines] 3AC; progeny MS1eC
211.30	suit] 1EC, 2EC, 3AC; process MS1eC
211.31	the Isabella just named] 3AC; The first named Isabella MS1eC
211.32	"Thus,"] 1EC; "Thus" MS1eC
211.32	Charlevoix] 3AC; Charleroix MS1eC
211.34	of which the heirs] 1EC, 2EC, 3AC; whose posterity MS1eC, 1AC
211.35	*marques*] 3AC; marquis MS1eC
211.35	*Indias.*"‡] T; Indias* MS1eC; Indias*. 1EC
211.36	Balthazar] 3AC; Balthasar MS1eC
211.37	Indies] 1EC; Indias MS1eC
211.39	Colomb] 3AC; Columb MS1eC
211.40	Bossi, . . . Columbus] 3AC; Bossi . . . Columb MS1eC
211.41	Charlevoix . . . tom. lib.] 3AC; Charleroix . . . t. . . . l. MS1eC
212.10	Cuccaro,] 1EC; ~∧ MS1eC
212.14	New World] 1EC; new world MS1eC
212.17	Spain), the] 1EC; Spain) the MS1eC
212.21	library of the cathedral of] 3AC; church at MS1eC

212.22	Zuñiga,] 1EC; ~ᴧ MS1eC
212.24	mother,] 1EC; ~ᴧ MS1eC
212.24	Enriquez,] 1EC; ~ᴧ MS1eC
212.29	and] 1EC; & MS1eC
212.32	Bossi,] 1EC; ~ᴧ MS1eC
212.33	Spotorno,] 1EC; ~ᴧ MS1eC
213.6	praise and] 1EC, 2EC, 3AC; pride & MS1eC
213.8	New World] 1EC; new world MS1eC
213.8–9	He accompanied . . . also to] 3AC; He also accompanied the emperor Charles V. to MS1eC
213.9	Anales] 1EC; anales MS1eC
213.10	1539] 3AC; 1593 MS1eC, 1EC
213.16	academy and] 1EC; Academy & MS1eC
213.19–20	the monastery . . . situated] 1EC; at present is situated the monastery of San Laureano. MS1eC
213.23	12th of] 3AC; 12th MS1eC, 1EC
213.24	fifty . . . nine . . . fourteen] 1EC, 3AC; 50 . . . 9 . . . 14 MS1eC
213.26	cathedral of] 3AC; cathedral church of MS1eC
213.27	establishment.] MS2eC, MS3AC, 3AC; establishment. "It was put," says Zuñiga, "in the Chapter-House of the church, a building which had formerly served for a royal chapel, and is adorned with book-cases of mahogany, beautifully carved, and the walls and vaults are painted in fresco; in which it remains, forgotten and neglected, yet withheld from the world*." 1EC, 2EC; establishment. "It was put," says Zuñiga, in the Chapter-House of the church, a building which had formerly served for a royal chapel, and is adorned with book-cases of mahogany, beautifully carved, and the walls and vaults are painted in fresco; in which it remains the sport of time, but forgotten and less frequented than its master desired; difficult to be enjoyed and easy to be consumed."* MS1eC, 1AC. *The source of this rejected passage is footnoted in 1EC as Zuñiga, Annales de Sevilla, l. xiv. p. 496."*
213.29	books] 1EC; Books MS1eC
213.33	moral and] T; moral & MS1eC; ~, ~ 1EC
213.34	New World] 1EC; new world MS1eC
213.37	admiral, composed] 3AC; admiral, which he composed MS1eC
213.38	translation have proceeded] 3AC; translation, or rather

	from the version of it again into Spanish, have proceeded MS1eC
213.40	the form] 3AC; form MS1eC, 1EC
213.41	and full] MS2eC, 3AC; and it is full MS1eC, 1EC, 1AC, 2EC
214.5	events] 3AC; event MS1eC
214.8	interests] 3AC; interest MS1eC
216.1	No. V] 3AC; No. IV. MS1eC
216.6	houses] 1EC, 2EC, MS2eC, 3AC; lines MS1eC
216.12	investigation] 1EC, 3AC; case MS1eC
216.20–21	and epitaphs] 1EC; & Epitaphs MS1eC
216.21	Colombos.] 1EC; Colombo's. MS1eC
216.22	Cucureo] 3AC; Cugureo MS1eC
216.28–29	"were . . . hawks;"†] 1EC; were . . . hawkes;* MS1eC
216.31	perishes] 1EC, 2EC, MS2eC, 3AC; perish MS1eC
216.35	Spotorno,] 1EC; ~∧ MS1eC
216.36	falconer.] 1EC; Falconer. MS1eC
217.3	father's] 1EC; fathers MS1eC
217.5–6	to the conviction that] 1EC, 2EC, 3AC; to convince one that MS1eC
217.9	says,] 1EC; ~∧ MS1eC
217.9	Second,] 1EC; ~∧ MS1eC
217.18	Empire."*] T; Empire.* MS1eC; empire*." 1EC
217.21	to prove] 3AC; to state MS1eC
217.21	and to . . . born] 1EC, 2EC, 3AC; and that he was born MS1eC
217.22	place; . . . he] 3AC; place. From hence it is said Columbus MS1eC
217.24	Baldasser, or Balthazar] 3AC; Baldassarre, or Balthasar MS1eC
217.31	his life] 3AC; the admiral's life MS1eC
217.34	who] 1EC, 2EC, MS3AC, 3AC; whom MS1eC
217.34–35	was . . . enemies] 1EC, 2EC, 3AC; they did not cease to reproach MS1eC
217.40	Herrera,] 1EC; ~. MS1eC
217.40	lib. . . . cap.] 3AC; l. . . . c. MS1eC
217.41	Dissertation,] 1EC; ~∧ MS1eC
218.3	evident] 3AC; probable MS1eC
218.5	Colombo . . . 1311] 1EC, 2EC, 3AC; Colombo, in 1311, the wool carder MS1eC
218.13	No. VI.] 3AC; No. V. MS1eC
218.14	Birthplace] 1EC; Birth place MS1eC

218.21   Academy . . . Sciences . . . Letters]   3AC; academy . . .
              sciences . . . letters MS1eC
218.23   Piaggio,]   1EC; ~∧ MS1eC
218.25   Pietro]   3AC; Petro MS1eC
218.30   Domenico]   3AC; Dominico MS1eC
219.2   Domenico]   3AC; Dominico MS1eC
219.4   born]   1EC; borne MS1eC
219.4   Balthazar]   3AC;   Baltazar   MS1eC;   Baltasar   1EC;
              Balthasar 2EC
219.4   Colombo,]   1EC; ~∧ MS1eC
219.6   Indies]   1EC; Indias MS1eC
219.7–9   shown . . . proved]   3AC; shown in the preceding ac-
              count of his claim. It was proved 1EC; shewn in
              the preceding account of that process given among
              the illustrations of this history. It was in proof MS1eC
219.10   after,]   1EC; ~∧ MS1eC
219.12–13   Academy . . . Science . . . Letters]   3AC; academy . . .
              science . . . letters MS1eC
219.16   History]   1EC; history MS1eC
219.27–29   hamlet . . . Nervi, which]   MS2eC; hamlet between
              Quinto and Nervi, which 1EC; hamlet between Quinto
              and Nervi, called Terra Rossa; in Latin, Terra Rubra;
              which 3AC
219.30   Colombi.* Bartholomew]   3AC; *New paragraph in*
              MS1eC
219.31   Latin]   1EC; latin MS1eC
220.4   12th,]   1EC; ~∧ MS1eC
220.5   editor]   1EC; Editor MS1eC
220.6   geographical]   1EC; Geographical MS1eC
220.6   journal . . . Genoa.*]   3AC; journal*. MS1eC
220.11   fourteenth]   1EC; 14th MS1eC
220.19   authority. He]   3AC; *New paragraph in MS1eC*
220.22   epitaph]   1EC; Epitaph MS1eC
220.32   città]   3AC; citta MS1eC
220.33   Belloro]   3AC; Bellero MS1eC; Ballero 1AC
220.33   Domenico]   3AC; Dominico MS1eC
220.36   styled]   1EC; stiled MS1eC
220.36   *Christophorus*]   3AC; Christopherus MS1eC
220.37   Geograph. &c. de]   3AC; Geograph du MS1eC
220.38   Lettera . . . 1826]   3AC; Lettera 29. Genes. 1826 MS1eC
220.40   carrattere]   3AC; carattere MS1eC
220.40   1696]   3AC; 1694 MS1eC

221.1	*Janua.*"] 1EC; ~._∧ MS1eC
221.2	navigator on] 3AC; navigator, when on MS1eC
221.4	at] 1EC, 2EC, 3AC; in MS1eC
221.5	Belloro] 3AC; Bellero MS1eC
221.9–10	who, as has been . . . was] 3AC; who was MS1eC
221.10	buried] 1EC; burried MS1eC
221.11–13	library. The . . . inscription] 3AC; library. A monument was erected to his memory in that church. The inscription MS1eC
221.16	Belloro] 3AC; Bellero MS1eC
221.16	written from] 3AC; written down from MS1eC
221.20	magnifico; . . . inscription] 3AC; magnifico. MS1eC
221.21	birthplace] 1EC; birth place MS1eC
221.22–23	Gio. Battista] MS2eC; Gio Battista 3AC; Giovan' Batista MS1eC
221.25	notarial] 3AC; notaries MS1eC; notariat 1EC; notary's 1AC
221.27	Andria] 3AC; Andrea MS1eC
221.29	Andrew's] 1EC; Andrews MS1eC
221.32	Via] 1EC, 2EC, 3AC; lane MS1eC
221.36	Colombo,] 1EC; ~_∧ MS1eC
221.40	Spotorno,] 3AC; ~_∧ MS1eEC
221.41	Bossi,] 1EC; ~_∧ MS1eC
222.2	born in the] 3AC; born in that MS1eC; born in a 1EC
222.2	those monks in Via] 3AC; the monks, in the lane MS1eC; the monks, situate in Via 1EC
222.6	parish] 1EC; Parish MS1eC
222.8	Andres] 3AC; Andreas 1EC; Andrez MS1eC, 1AC
222.8	Bernaldes] T; Bernaldez MS1eC, 1EC, 3AC
222.17	Foglieta] 3AC; Foglietto MS1eC
222.22	birthplace] 1EC; birth place MS1eC
222.32	Don Diego,] 1EC, 2EC, 3AC; Diego MS1eC
222.36	Ibid.] 1EC; Ib. MS1eC
222.37	de . . . cap.] 3AC; do . . . c. MS1eC
222.40	Senarega] 3AC; Senaraya MS1eC
222.41	Foglieta] 3AC; Foglietto MS1eC
222.42	Grinæus] MS2eC; Grineus MS1eC, 1EC, 3AC
223.2	*for*] 1EC; for MS1eC
223.2	in] 1EC, 2EC, 3AC; from MS1eC
223.8	abilities] 1EC, 2EC, 3AC; forces MS1eC
223.9	republic, . . . are not] 1EC, 2AC; republic, not being contrary to the service MS1eC

223.12   Valladolid,]   1EC; ~∧ MS1eC
223.14–16   made . . . on]   1EC, 3AC; made after the custom of
                officers who executed such testaments frequently
                MS1eC
223.19   country,]   1EC; ~∧ MS1eC
223.22   Indies]   1EC; Indias MS1eC
223.24   a usage]   1EC, 2EC, 3AC; a military usage MS1eC
223.33   night]   1EC, 3AC; nights MS1eC
223.35   point to]   1EC, 2EC, 3AC; point on MS1eC
223.36   á la]   3AC; a la MS1eC
223.38   é muger]   3AC; y muger MS1eC
223.38   pueda]   3AC; puede MS1eC
223.39   á nuestro]   3AC; a nuestro MS1eC
223.40   podrá]   3AC; podra MS1eC
223.40   dicha]   3AC; dicho MS1eC
224.2   any such was]   1EC, 3AC; any was MS1eC
224.29–30   singled . . . spot]   1EC, 2EC, 3AC; singled out MS1eC
224.30   down in]   1EC, 3AC; down, as it were, in MS1eC
225.1   No. VII]   3AC; No. VI MS1eC
225.2   Colombos]   1EC; Colombos's MS1eC
225.5–10   sailed; . . . family."]   3AC; sailed. According to Fernando
                Columbus (Hist. del Almirante, Ch. 1.) they were
                relatives of his father; and Columbus, in one of his
                letters, says, "I am not the first admiral of our family."
                MS1eC
225.11–18   These two . . . Colombo in]   3AC; These were uncle
                and nephew: the latter is termed by historians, Co-
                lombo the younger (by the Spanish historians, Colom-
                bo el Mozo). The elder of them was in the French
                service; probably he entered it at the time that Genoa
                was under the protection, or rather the domination,
                of France. It is said that he was engaged in the expe-
                ditions of John of Anjou against Naples, and that
                Columbus sailed with him.
                    Mention is made of the elder Colombo in MS1eC
225.18   Zurita's]   2EC, 3AC; Zuritas MS1eC; Zuriata's 1EC
225.19   Portugal,]   1EC; ~∧ MS1eC
225.20   Princess]   3AC; princiness MS1eC
225.21   Mediterranean]   1EC; mediterranean MS1eC
225.23   Guipuzcoa]   3AC; Guipuzcao MS1eC
225.24   Zurita, . . . June,]   1EC; Zurita on the 13 June MS1eC
225.26   France,]   1EC; ~∧ MS1eC

225.26	(Colombo),] 1EC; ~∧ MS1eC
225.28–29	July, . . . armada,] 1EC; ~∧ . . . ~∧ MS1eC
225.29	Bermeo] 3AC; Bormeo MS1eC
225.31	lost a great many] 3AC; lost a many MS2eC; lost a large part MS1eC; lost many 1EC
225.32	receive] 1EC, 2EC, 3AC; take MS1eC
225.34	thousand] 1EC; ~, MS1eC
225.36	caravels. After] 3AC; *New paragraph in MS1eC*
225.38	Hist . . . 1.] 3AC; *Missing in MS1eC*
226.2	Zurita,] 1EC; ~∧ MS1eC
226.4	Jacques George de Chaufepie] 3AC; Jacques George Chaufepies MS1eC; Jacques George Chaufpie MS2eC
226.6	Chaufepie, "is] 3AC; Chaufepies is MS1eC
226.7	(part i. p. 143.) that] 1EC; (part 1. p. 143 which cites annot: on the Hist Charles VI) that MS1eC
226.10	crowns,] 1EC; ~∧ MS1eC
226.11	attacked, therefore,] 1EC; ~∧ ~∧ MS1eC
226.12	galleys] 1EC; Galleys MS1eC
226.12	nation,] 1EC; ~∧ MS1eC
226.14	XI.:] 1E; XI, MS1eC
226.19–37	It is highly probable . . . occasions] 3AC; missing in 2EC; It is highly probable that the squadron of this same Colombo which appeared in the Levant in 1475 and 1476, and on one occasion attacked the Venetian squadron stationed to protect the island of Cyprus; mention of which was made in a letter of two Milanese gentlemen to the duke of Milan, dated 1476, cited by Bossi, and after him by Spotorno.
	The nephew of this Colombo, called by the Spaniards Colombo el Mozo, commanded, likewise, a few years afterwards, a squadron in the French service, and became formidable in the Mediterranean, as will appear in a subsequent illustration. The names of these two Colombos, uncle and nephew, appearing vaguely at intervals during the obscure period of the admiral's life, have been confounded with his name by historians. Fernando Columbus says that his father sailed for several years with Colombo the younger*. It is probable that he may, at various times, have had an inferior command in the squadron of both uncle and nephew, and that he may have been pres-

	ent on the above cited occasions. / *Hist. del Almir-
	ante, c. v. MS1eC, 1EC
226.25	Colombo] 3AC; Columbus MS2eC
227.8	VII] 1E; 7th MS1eC
227.13	meantime] 1EC; mean time MS1eC
227.14	galleys] 3AC; Galleys MS1eC
227.16	eminently] 3AC; imminently MS1eC
227.19	dominions] 1EC, 2EC, 3AC; power MS1eC
227.23	to make . . . Naples] 1EC, 2EC, 3AC; to dash boldly upon Naples MS1eC
227.24	entered . . . spirit] 1EC; 2EC, 3AC; entered spiritedly into his cause, MS1eC
227.25	galleys] 3AC; Galleys MS1eC
227.30	corsair,] 1EC, 2EC, 3AC; corsair, warriors MS1eC
227.30–31	the bold . . . partisan] 1EC, 2EC, 3AC; of every description, who either panted for honour or lived by the sword, MS1eC
227.33	Colombos,] 1EC, ~∧ MS1eC
227.35	expedition sailed] 3AC; expedition against Naples MS1eC
227.37	revolt] 1EC; ~, MS1eC
227.38–39	heir . . . Naples] 3AC; heir of the king of Naples, being similar to that of prince of Wales in England. MS1eC
228.8	scoured] 3AC; occupied MS1eC
228.11–12	A chosen . . . having] 3AC; The troops from the fleet were sent against them. Having MS1eC; A Chosen company of infantry were sent against them. The band . . . having 1AC
228.13–14	rovers, had] 3AC; they had MS1eC
228.15	They . . . infantry] 1EC, 2EC, 3AC; They were set upon by the foot soldiers MS1eC
228.19	many threw] 3AC; many, it is said, seized with the madness of despair, threw 1EC; many, it is said, seized with a kind of fury, threw MS1eC
228.20	regained] 1EC, 2EC, 3AC; were able to regain MS1eC
228.23	grasp:] 1EC; ~, MS1eC
228.23	succeeded;] 1EC; ~, MS1eC
228.24	points;] 1EC; ~, MS1eC
228.25–26	Alphonso, . . . island] 1EC, 2EC, 3AC; Alphonso, until the Duke had to retire to the Island MS1eC
228.27	galleys] 1EC; Galleys MS1eC

228.27	harassed] 1EC; harrassed MS1eC
228.29	Columbus . . . served] 3AC; it is supposed Columbus may have served MS1eC
228.34	Colenuccio, Hist. . . . 17.] 3AC; Colnucio, . . . 17. 1EC; Colnucio Hist . . . 17 MS1eC
229.6	Mozo) and] 1EC; mozo) & MS1eC
229.7	embassy] 1EC; ambassy MS1eC
229.8	Venetian] 1EC; Venitian MS1eC
229.9	Sabellicus] 3AC; Sabelicus MS1eC, 1EC
229.9	1485, after] 3AC; 1485, a year after MS1eC
229.11–13	"at . . . were] 1EC; "at this time there sailed four Venitian Galleys . . . Cadiz, which took the route for Flanders and were MS1eC
229.14	Cape] 1EC; cape MS1eC
229.16	galleys] 1EC; Galleys MS1eC
229.19	Resende] 3AC; Reesende MS1eC
229.20	Venetian galleys] 1EC; Venitian Galleys MS1eC
229.21	maltreated,] 1EC; ~∧ MS1eC
229.23	Meneses,] 1EC; ~∧ MS1eC
229.26	Venetian] 1EC; Venitian MS1eC
229.33	galleys] 1EC; Galleys MS1eC
229.38	galleys] 1EC; Galleys MS1eC
229.40	embassy] 1EC; ambassy MS1eC
229.41	Zurita, . . . 64] 3AC; Zurita, lib. ss. c. 64. MS1eC
229.41	Anales] 3AC; Annales MS1eC
230.2	Donate] 3AC; Donato MS1eC
230.4	genets] 1EC; Genets MS1eC
230.8	History] 1EC; history MS1eC
230.9	"Erano] 1EC; ∧~ MS1eC
230.9	andate] 3AC; andati MS1eC
230.9	quattro] 3AC; quatro MS1eC
230.9	Bartolommeo] 3AC; Bartolomeo MS1eC
230.10	navigando] 3AC; navicando MS1eC
230.10	più] 3AC; piu MS1eC
230.11	nipote di] 3AC; nepote di MS1eC
230.11	Veniziani] 3AC; Venetiani MS1eC
230.12	che chiamasi] 3AC; chiamasi MS1eC
230.12	ora] 3AC; hora MS1eC
230.13	Vincenzo] 3AC; Vicenzo MS1eC
230.14	avesse] 3AC; haber MS1eC
230.14	disposto] 3AC; disposti MS1eC
230.14	Veniziane] 3AC; Venetiane MS1eC

230.15	ritenne] 3AC; retenne MS1eC
230.15	dal] 3AC; da MS1eC
230.15	esser] 3AC; essa MS1eC
230.17	Veniziani] 3AC; Venitiani MS1eC
230.17	incontanente] 3AC; incontanenti MS1eC
230.17–18	l'assalto. Sostennero] 3AC; l'assalto, sostennero MS1eC
230.18	Veniziani] 3AC; Venetiani MS1eC
230.18	allora] 3AC; allhora MS1eC
230.18–19	di . . . di] 3AC; de' . . . de' MS1eC
230.19	ore] 3AC; hore MS1eC
230.19	Rare] 3AC; Rari MS1eC
230.20	fu] 3AC; fù MS1eC
230.20	tanta] 3AC; tanto MS1eC
230.20	perchè] 3AC; perche MS1eC
230.21	d'attaccarsi] 3AC; d'attacarsi MS1eC
230.21	se non] 3AC; si non MS1eC
230.21–22	occasione. Affermano] 3AC; occasione, affermano MS1eC; occasione. Affirmano 1EC
230.22	morte] 3AC; morti MS1eC
230.22	Veniziane] 3AC; Venitiane MS1eC
230.23	uomini. Altri] 3AC; huomini. (*New paragraph*) Altre MS1eC
230.23	che fu] 3AC; que fù MS1eC
230.24	d'altro] 3AC; de l'altro MS1eC
230.25	ore] 3AC; hore MS1eC
230.26	e] 3AC; et MS1eC
230.26	genti Veniziane] 3AC; gente Venetiane MS1eC
230.27	de'] 3AC; de MS1eC
230.27	ad una] 3AC; ad una ad una MS1eC
230.28	di] 3AC; de MS1eC
230.28	aspro] 3AC; aspero MS1eC
230.28	partecipi] 3AC; participi MS1eC
230.29	prode] 3AC; prodo MS1eC
230.29	uomini] 3AC; huomini MS1eC
230.29	quali] 3AC; quai MS1eC
230.30	e dire] 3AC; i dire MS1eC
230.30	così] 3AC; cosi MS1eC
230.30	avevano] 3AC; havevano MS1eC
230.30	Veniziani] 3AC; Venitiane MS1eC
230.31	mare, e i] 3AC; mare et i MS1eC
230.31	lido] 3AC; lito MS1eC
230.32	vivi,] 3AC; vivi MS1eC

230.33	e] 3AC; et MS1eC
230.33	licenziati] 3AC; licentiate MS1eC
230.33	Veniziani] 3AC; Venitiane MS1eC
230.34	dal] 3AC; del MS1eC
230.34	infermi] 3AC; infirme MS1eC
230.34	ebbero abiti] 3AC; hebbero habiti MS1eC
230.35	Resende, cap. 58. Avora] 3AC; Reesende, c. 58. Evora MS1eC
230.36	Coccio] 3AC; Cocceio MS1eC
230.39	Ennead] 3AC; Decade MS1eC; Enneada 1AC
230.40	Livy] 3AC; Titus Livy MS1eC
231.1	condizione] 3AC; conditione MS1eC
231.2	Veniziana] 3AC; Venitiana MS1eC
231.2	dai] 3AC; da i MS1eC
231.3	avuta] 3AC; havuta MS1eC
231.3	città 3AC; citta MS1eC
231.4	mercatanzia] 3AC; mercatantia MS2eC; mercutantia MS1eC
231.4	mila] 3AC; milo MS1eC
231.4	particolare] 3AC; particulare MS1eC
231.5	degli] 3AC; de gli MS1eC
231.5	uomini] 3AC; huomini MS1eC
231.5	afflizione] 3AC; afflitione MS1eC
231.6	lib] 3AC; l MS1eC
231.7	No. X.] 3AC; No. IX MS1eC
231.13	New World] 1EC; new world MS1eC
231.16	in a squadron] 3AC; in squadrons MS1eC
231.16	and that] 1EC, 2EC, 3AC; and that his first visit to the main land was after MS1eC
231.17	until] 1EC, 2EC, MS2eC, MS3AC, 3AC; was MS1eC
231.20	9th,] 1EC; 9th MS1eC
231.20	1451,] 1EC; ~∧ MS1eC
231.22	mother's] 1EC, 2EC, 3AC; mother MS1eC
231.22	Elizabetta] 3AC; Elisabetta MS1eC
231.34	d'Amerigo] 3AC; D'Amerigo MS1eC
232.4	Cosmography] 3AC; cosmography MS1eC
232.21	expedition] 3AC; expeditions MS1eC
232.23	12th of] 3AC; 12th MS1eC
232.24	maravedies] T; maravedis MS1eC
232.25	Pinelo,] 3AC; ~∧ MS1eC
232.27–28	3d of February] 3AC; 3ᵈ february MS1eC
232.30	opportunity] 3AC; opportunities MS1eC

233.9   guided by]   3AC; with the assistance of MS1eC
233.11–12   superintendence]   3AC; superintendance MS1eC
233.16–18   for . . . trade]   1EC, 3AC; as it was strictly prohibited
                 by Isabella as queen of Castile for any stranger from
                 trading MS1eC, 1AC
233.20   coast,]   3AC; ~∧ MS1eC
233.23   de]   3AC; di MS1eC
233.24   concealed]   1EC, 2EC, 3AC; buried MS1eC, 1AC
233.34   hereafter]   3AC; here in after MS1eC
233.36   Emanuel,]   3AC; ~∧ MS1eC
233.39   remained]   1EC, 2EC, 3AC; lay MS1eC
233.41   Firenze,]   3AC; ~∧ MS1eC
234.7   however,]   3AC; ~∧ MS1eC
234.7   sail]   1EC, 2EC, 3AC; voyage MS1eC
234.9   latitude]   3AC; altitude MS1eC
234.12–13   the voyage . . . Portugal]   1EC, 2EC, 3AC; the voyage
                 in the service of Portugal, just alluded to MS1eC
234.14   Latin]   3AC; latin, MS1eC
234.15   Vesputius,]   3AC; ~∧ MS1eC
234.16   Regem]   3AC; regem MS1eC
234.16   inventa]   3AC; invento MS1eC
234.17   edition]   1EC, 2EC, MS2eC, MS3AC, 3AC; addition
                 MS1eC
234.20   Latin]   3AC; latin MS1eC
234.20   Itinerarium]   3AC; Itinerarum MS1eC
234.22   Latin]   3AC; latin MS1eC
234.23   Orbis]   3AC; orbis MS1eC
234.29   Panzer,]   3AC; ~∧ MS1eC
234.29   critico,]   3AC; ~∧ MS1eC
234.43   *nuovamente*]   3AC; nuevamente MS1eC
235.9   depôt]   3AC; depot MS1eC
235.14   was]   1EC; were MS1eC
235.14–15   and . . . coast of]   1EC, 2EC, 3AC; and afterwards,
                 through the improvidence and obstinacy of the com-
                 mander Coelho, they went reconnoitering the coast of
                 Sierra Leone, but were MS1eC
235.18   in length . . . breadth]   1EC, 3AC; long . . . broad
                 MS1eC
235.24   having gone]   3AC; having been gone MS1eC
235.35   twenty four]   T; ~-~ 1EC; 24 MS1eC
235.36   ammunition]   3AC; ammunitions MS1eC
235.41   Edit.]   3AC; Edit MS1eC

235.41	Vespucci] 3AC; Vespuchi MS1eC
236.5–6	"My . . . Diego] 3AC; ∧~ MS1eC
235.12	ascertain] 1EC, 2EC, 3AC; know MS1eC
236.10–11	goes on] 1EC, 3AC; goes for MS1eC
236.13	serviceable] 3AC; serviable MS1eC
236.14	with . . . determination] 1EC, 2EC, 3AC; determined MS1eC
236.15–16	co-operate with] 1EC, 3AC; work for MS1eC
236.16	his plans] 1EC, 3AC; it MS1eC
236.17	secretly] 3AC; secretely MS1eC
236.21	Vicente] 3AC; Vicenti MS1eC
236.23–24	Toro, 11th April 1507,] 3AC; Toro 11 April 1505 MS1eC
236.24	for] 3AC; as MS1eC
236.24–25	Americo de Vespuche] 3AC; Amerigo de Vespuche 1EC; Amerigo de Espeche MS1eC
236.27	1506] 3AC; 1505 MS1eC
236.30	were sold] 3AC; sold MS1eC
236.32	March] 3AC; march MS1eC
236.33	70,000] 3AC; 75,000 MS1eC
236.36	New World] 3AC; new world MS1eC
236.37	22d of] 1EC, 3AC; 22d May MS1eC
236.38	Corezo,] 3AC; ~∧ MS1eC
236.39	Colec. . . . tom.] 3AC; Collec . . . t. MS1eC
237.5	mariner's] 3AC; mariners MS1eC
237.16	Indies] 3AC; Indias MS1eC
237.17	Vespucci;] 3AC; ~, MS1eC
237.19	Lisbon,] 3AC; ~∧ MS1eC
237.19	4th of] 3AC; 4th MS1eC
237.20	1504,] 3AC; ~∧ MS1eC
237.22	relates to the] 3AC; relates the MS1eC
237.24–25	René . . . Jerusalem] 1EC, 3AC; Renato, King of Sicily and Jerusalem, and Duke of Lorraine MS1eC, 1AC
237.26–27	Latin . . . Lorraine.] 3AC; latin in 1507 in the city of St. Diez or San Deodato, in the district of Vosges, in the province of Lorraine. (*Footnote:*) *The title of the work in which it was inserted is as follows. Cosmographiæ Introductio cum qui quibusdam Geometriæ ac Astronomiæ principiis ad eam rem necessarius. In super quattuor Americi Vespucij navigationes &c. Finitu iiij Kl Setembris MS1eC; latin . . . Septembris Anno supra sesquimillerium vij. 1AC
237.30	Orbis] 3AC; orbis MS1eC

237.30	Basle] 1AC, MS2eC, MS3AC, 3AC; Bath MS1eC, 1EC
237.31	narrative] 1EC, 2EC, 3AC; digest MS1eC
237.32	New World] 3AC; new world MS1eC
237.33	René] 1EC, 3AC; Renato MS1eC
237.36	narrative] 3AC; narratives MS1eC
237.37–38	"that . . . triflings."] 3AC; that . . . triflings MS1eC
237.39	René] 1EC, 2EC, MS2eC, 3AC; Renato MS1eC
237.41	Peter Martyr, . . . lib.] 3AC; P. Martyr . . . l. MS1eC
237.41	Eden's] 3AC; Edens MS1eC
238.3	He therefore purposed] 3AC; he disposed himself MS1eC
238.3–4	the . . . contains] 1EC, 3AC; the various wonderful things MS1eC
238.8	20, 1497,] 3AC; 20 1497 MS1eC
238.9–10	employed eighteen] 1EC, 2EC, 3AC; consumed 18 MS1eC
238.16	nuovamente] 3AC; nuevemente MS1eC
238.20	René] 1EC, 2EC, 3AC; Renato MS1eC
238.22	Soderini] 3AC; ~, MS1eC
238.24	Latin] 3AC; latin MS1eC
238.25	majesty] 3AC; magesty MS1eC
238.26	employed.] 1EC, 2EC, 3AC; employed which could not have been suited to Soderini. MS1eC
238.26	René] 1EC, 2EC, 3AC; Renato MS1eC
238.29	René] 1EC, 2EC, 3AC; Renato MS1eC
238.29	Piere] 1EC, 2EC, 3AC; Piero MS1eC
238.39	Indies] 3AC; Indias MS1eC
238.41	relating] 3AC; that relate MS1eC
239.1	till] 3AC; until MS1eC
239.5	1497,] 3AC; ~₍ₐ₎ MS1eC
239.5	alleged] 3AC; alledged MS1eC
239.11	antedating] 3AC; antedates MS1eC
239.15–16	are with] 1EC, 2EC, MS2eC, 3AC; are in MS1eC
239.24	Pearl Islands] 3AC; pearl islands MS1eC
239.32	Indies] 3AC; Indias MS1eC
239.33–35	in a packet . . . 1564."] 3AC; amongst the papers belonging to the admiral Don Luis Colon, and forming part of the proceedings relating to the preservation of his privileges, from 1515 to 1564. 1EC in a pacquet . . . Colon, about the conservation of his privileges, from ann. 1515 to 1564. MS1eC
239.38	Indies] 3AC; Indias MS1eC

239.41	record] 1EC, 3AC; process MS1eC
240.1	Morego] 3AC; Morigo MS1eC
240.5	René] 1EC, 2EC, MS2eC, 3AC; Renato MS1eC
240.11	dissensions] 1EC, 2EC, 3AC; difficulties and dissensions MS1eC
240.32	Morego] 3AC; Morigo MS1eC
240.33	necessitá] 3AC; necessita MS1eC
240.33	(Hispaniola] 3AC; (hispaniola MS1eC
240.33	mantenimento] 3AC; mantenimiento MS1eC
240.34	che é] 3AC; che a MS1eC
240.34	descoperse] 3AC; discoperse MS1eC
240.34	Cristoval] 3AC; Cristobal MS1eC
240.34	piú] 3AC; piu MS1eC
240.34	fa] 3AC; fà MS1eC
240.34	molto] 3AC; multo MS1eC
240.36	christiani] 3AC; Cristiani MS1eC
240.36	questa] 3AC; questo MS1eC
240.38	vió] 3AC; vio MS1eC
240.39	embrió á] 3AC; embrio a MS1eC
240.40	descubierto] 3AC; discubierto MS1eC, 1EC
240.40	á] 3AC; a MS1eC
240.40	halló] 3AC; hallo MS1eC
240.41	descubrió] 3AC; discubrio MS1eC
241.2	and that Pedro] 1EC, 2EC, MS2eC, 3AC; and by this had sailed Pedro MS1eC
241.3	countries . . . same.*] 1EC, 3AC; parts. MS1eC
241.4	Morales,] 3AC; ~∧ MS1eC
241.6	it.] 1EC, 2EC, 3AC; it. + + . . . Idem preguntada 10 MS1eC
241.7	Numerous . . . process] 3AC; A cloud of witnesses examined in this process MS1eC; Numerous witnesses examined in this suit 1EC
241.9–10	eye-witnesses . . .ear-witnesses] 3AC; eye witnesses . . . ear witnesses MS1eC
241.11	west of] 3AC; west to MS1eC
241.18	course . . . down] 1EC, MS2eC, 3AC; route he had demonstrated MS1eC
241.20	reputation] 1EC, 3AC; standing MS1eC
241.21	if] 1EC, 3AC; that MS1eC
241.23	coast.] 1EC; strange coast MS1eC
241.24	previously. If] 3AC; previously, if MS1eC
241.27	four] 3AC; 4 MS1eC

241.31	guide] 1EC, 2EC, MS2eC, 3AC; govern MS1eC
241.32	escrivió úna.] 3AC; escribo una MS1eC
241.32	Almirante] 3AC; almirante MS1eC
241.32	Reyna] 3AC; Reina MS1eC
241.33	embió] 3AC; embio MS1eC
241.34	carta,] 3AC; ∼ₐ MS1eC
241.34	rumbos y] 3AC; rumbos e MS1eC
241.34	por] 3AC; pr. MS1eC
241.35	á la] 3AC; a la MS1eC
241.35	oyó] 3AC; oyo MS1eC
241.35	habian] 3AC; havian MS1eC
241.36	habian] 3AC; havian MS1eC
241.36	otras e por] 3AC; otras ó pr. MS1eC
241.37	ido á] 3AC; ido a MS1eC
241.38	descubriendo] 3AC; discubriendo MS1eC
241.38–39	tierra ivan personas que] 3AC; tierra que MS1eC
241.39	mostró] 3AC; mostro MS1eC
241.42	Firma] 3AC; Firme MS1eC
241.42	Process, Pregunta] 3AC; Process. preguntada MS1eC
242.2	observations] 3AC; observation MS1eC
242.4	navigator] 1EC, 2EC, 3AC; voyager MS1eC
242.5	even] 3AC; ever MS1eC
242.7	reality] 1EC, 2EC, 3AC; verity MS1eC
242.10	Ferdinand;] 3AC; ∼, MS1eC
242.11	avowed] 1EC, 2EC, 3AC; open MS1eC
242.12	suit] 1EC, 2EC, 3AC; process MS1eC
242.13	afterward] 3AC; afterwards MS1eC
242.26	Paria,] 3AC; ∼ₐ MS1eC
242.28	ho] 3AC; he MS1eC
242.28	á] 3AC; a MS1eC
242.28	magnifizenza] 3AC; magnificenza MS1eC
242.29	altra] 3AC; altro MS1eC
242.29	cosa ne] 3AC; cosa MS1eC
242.29	occorso] 3AC; accorso MS1eC
242.42	The question] 3AC; *No paragraph in MS1eC*
243.2	but that] 3AC; that MS1eC
243.12	voyages.*] 3AC; voyages. MS1eC
243.13	Fernando,] 3AC; ∼ₐ MS1eC
243.16	Indies] 3AC; Indias MS1eC
243.17	much . . . consequence] 1EC, 3AC; roughly assailed therefor MS1eC
243.18	assertion] 1EC, 2EC, 3AC; dictum MS1eC

243.20	proceedings] 1EC, 2EC, 3AC; process MS1eC
243.25	Spain; and that] 3AC; Spain. That MS1eC; Spain; that 1EC
243.26	Latin] 3AC; latin MS1eC
243.27	cited,] 3AC; ~∧ MS1eC
243.27	1507,] 3AC; ~∧ MS1eC
243.28	René] 1EC, 2EC, MS2eC, 3AC; Renato MS1eC
243.28	author,] 3AC; ~∧ MS1eC
243.30	discoverer.] 1EC, 2EC, MS2eC, MS3AC, 3AC; discoverer. Nunc vero et hos partes sunt latins lustratae, et alia quarta pare per Americum Vespucium (ut in sequentibus audietur) inventa est quam non video cum quis jure vetet ab Americo inventore, sagacis ingenii viro, Amerigen quasi Americi Terram, sive Americam dicendam. MS1eC, 1AC, 2AC
243.31–44	*Note . . .* Waldseemüller] 3AC; *missing in MS1eC*
244.6	the] 1EC, 2EC, 3AC; of the MS1eC
244.13	been corrected] 3AC; been judiciously corrected MS1eC
244.18	so] 1EC, 3AC; to MS1eC
244.20	character] 1EC, 2EC, 3AC; standing MS1eC
244.21	all,] 3AC; ~∧ MS1eC
244.33	René] 1EC, 2EC, 3AC; Renato MS1eC
244.33	Orbis] 3AC; orbis MS1eC
244.34	Cadiz, May 20,] 3AC; ~∧ ~∧ MS1eC
244.35	Cadiz, October 15, . . . (1499),] 3AC; Cadiz Octr 15th . . . (1499) MS1eC
244.35	eighteen] 3AC; 18 MS1eC
244.35	absent,] 3AC; ~∧ MS1eC
244.36	twenty nine] T; 29 MS1eC; ~∧~ 1EC
244.37	Sunday, May 11, . . . (1489),] 3AC; Sunday May 11th . . . (1489 MS1eC
244.38	eight] 3AC; 8 MS1eC
244.41	eighteen] 3AC; 18 MS1eC
245.1	liberality; it] 3AC; liberality, It MS1eC
245.5–6	of . . . world] 1EC, 2EC, 3AC; of all the world MS1eC
245.12	New World] 3AC; new world MS1eC
245.15	yet . . . never set] 3AC; yet neither the Venetians nor the English have set MS1eC
245.16–25	The glory . . . discovered] 3AC; The glory of Colum-

bus embraces the discovery of the whole western world; others may subdivide it; with respect to him, Vespucci is as Iañez Pinzon, Bastides, Ojeda, Cabot, and the crowd of secondary discoverers that followed in his track. When Columbus first touched the shore of the western hemisphere, he had achieved his enterprise, he had accomplished all that was necessary to his fame: the great problem was solved, the New World was discovered. 1EC; The glory . . . subdivide it and become illustrious upon portions. With . . . discovered MS1eC; His glory . . . When Columbus first touched a shore of the new world, even though a frontier island, he had achieved his enterprise, he had accomplished all that was necessary for his fame: the great problem of the ocean was solved; the world that lay beyond its western waters was discovered. 1AC

245.26–248.18   No . . . Columbus]   3AC. *This appendix was so extensively rewritten that collation by line is impossible. The reader may compare texts from the MS1eC version printed here.*

No. X.
MARTIN ALONZO PINZON.

In the course of the trial in the fiscal court between Don Diego and the crown, a feeble attempt was made to depreciate the merit of Columbus, and to ascribe the success of the great enterprise of discovery to the intelligence and spirit of Martin Alonzo Pinzon.

Arias Perez Pinzon, son of Martin Alonzo, declared, that "being once in Rome with his father on affairs of commerce before the time of the discovery, they had frequent conversations with a person learned in cosmography, who was in the service of pope Innocent VIII., and that, being in the library of the pope, this person showed them many manuscripts, from one of which his father gathered intimation of these new lands; for it is cited in the writing by an historian as old as the time of Solomon, which said, 'Navigate the Mediterranean Sea to the end of Spain, and thence towards the setting of the sun in a direction between north and south, until ninety-five degrees of distance, and you will find the land of Cipango, fertile and abundant, and in greatness equal to Africa and Europe.' This writing, he added, his father brought from Rome, with an intention of going in search of that land, and frequently expressed such determination; and that, when Columbus came to Palos with his project of discovery, Martin Alonzo Pinzon showed him the manuscript, which encouraged him greatly in his enterprise; and moreover he furnished him with money to go to court to make his propositions." It is probable that this manuscript, of which Arias Perez gives so vague an account from recollection, may have been the work of Marco Polo, which Columbus had already seen, with accompanying speculations concerning Ophir and Tarshish, and the voyages made by the ships of Solomon; and it is also questionable whether this visit of Martin Alonzo Pinzon to Rome was not after his mind had been heated by conversations with Columbus in the convent of La Rabida: Arias Perez always mentions the manuscript as imparted to Columbus after he had come to Palos, with an intention of proceeding on the discovery.

Several witnesses concur in declaring that Martin Alonzo Pinzon was all efficient in procuring ships and mariners for Columbus. Among others, Francisco Garcia Valleja testified, that, had it not been for Martin Alonzo Pinzon, who aided him in the enterprize, together with his relations and friends, the admiral could never have gone to discover, for nobody would have gone with him; but that, through the great desire which Martin Alonzo had to serve the sovereigns, he entreated his brother and this witness, and other persons, to go with him, and that therefore this witness engaged in the voyage.

The son of Pinzon, and his friend and adherent, this same Francisco Garcia, went so far as to intimate, that had it not been for Martin Alonzo, the admiral would have turned back in the course of his voyage, when he had ran seven or eight hundred leagues without finding land, and was threatened with mutiny and open rebellion on board of his ship. The characteristic fortitude and perseverance of Columbus, as well as the daily minutes of his journal,

furnish sufficient refutation of this charge, which the
partisans of Pinzon would have been much gratified
to establish.

It appears beyond a doubt, however, that Martin
Alonzo Pinzon was an able and enterprising navigator;
that he entered with zeal into the great idea of Columbus, and was of essential service in fitting out the
armament. In the whole course of the voyage out he
acted with spirit and fidelity, seconding and encouraging the admiral when harassed by the murmurs and
menaces of his crew. It was only after land had been
discovered, and when the prospect of immediate
treasures were held out, that the cupidity of Pinzon
became aroused, that he forgot the subordination so
indispensable to the success of every enterprise, and of
such vital importance in an expedition of this extraordinary and critical nature. MS1eC, 1AC. *Readers will
note that this MS1eC text differs in a few particulars
from 1EC. In the following cases, the reading to the
left of the brackets represents the MS1eC text; to the
right may be found the 1EC reading.* affairs of com-
merce] MS1eC;   commercial affairs 1EC;   for there
was a passage] MS1eC;   it is cited in the writing 1EC;
This writing] MS1eC;   A copy of this writing 1EC;
Vallejo] MS1eC;   Vallego 1EC;   could never have
gone to discover] MS1eC;   could never have sailed
on his voyage 1EC;   he had ran] MS1eC;   he had
run 1EC

248.19	No. XII.] 3AC; No. XI. MS1eC
248.29	Oviedo,] 3AC; ∼_∧ MS1eC
248.30	Indies] 3AC; Indias MS1eC
248.30	History] 3AC; history MS1eC
248.30	1535. He] 3AC; 1535, he MS1eC
248.31	foundation] 3AC; foundations MS1eC
248.33	History] 3AC; history MS1eC
248.33	Indies] 3AC; Indias MS1eC
249.10–11	Sabellicus . . . commonly] 3AC; Sabillicus, Peter Mar- tyr, Gustiniani, Bernaldez commonly MS1eC; Sabel- licus . . . Bernaldes commonly MS2eC; Bernaldos 1EC
249.13	Latin] 3AC; latin MS1eC
249.13	Madrignano] 3AC; Madreguna 1EC; Madriguno MS1eC

249.15	New World] 3AC; new world MS1eC
249.16	Gomara,] 3AC; ~∧ MS1eC
249.16–17	decidedly expresses] 1EC; 3AC; expresses peremptor-ily MS1eC
249.19	any] 1EC, 3AC; any any MS1eC
249.21–22	Natural and Moral History] 1EC; history Natural and Moral MS1eC
249.26	Herrera,] 3AC; ~∧ MS1eC
249.26	Indies in 1601,] 3AC; Indias ~∧ MS1eC
249.27	In not] 3AC; By not 1EC; On not MS1eC
249.27–28	as rejecting it] 1EC, 2EC, 3AC; to reject it MS1eC
249.28	and was] 3AC; and he was MS1eC
249.31	Garcilaso] 3AC; Garcilasso MS1eC
249.32	Commentaries] 3AC; commentaries MS1eC
249.33	it smoothly] 1EC, 2EC, 3AC; it roundly and smoothly MS1eC
249.33	circumstantially;] 3AC; ~, MS1eC
249.34	Gomara,] 3AC; ~∧ MS1eC
249.34	cap.] 3AC; c. MS1eC
249.35	Madrignano] 3AC; Madrugnano MS1eC
249.36	called Novus] 3AC; ~, ~ MS1eC
249.36	edition] 3AC; Edition MS1eC
249.37	Italian,] 3AC; ~∧ MS1eC
249.37	Francanzano] 3AC; Francanzana MS1eC
249.38	Vicenza,] 3AC; ~∧ MS1eC
249.38	Nuovo Mondo] MS2eC; Nuevo Mundo MS1eC
249.40	lib. . . . cap.] 3AC; l. . . . c. MS1eC
249.41	lib. . . . cap.] 3AC; l. . . . c. MS1eC
249.42	lib. . . . cap.] 3AC; l. . . . c. MS1eC
249.42	Hererra,] 3AC; ~∧ MS1eC
250.1	occurrence,] 3AC; ~∧ MS1eC
250.4	pilot] 3AC; Pilot MS1eC
250.8	seventeen,] 3AC; ~∧ MS1eC
250.9	Tercera,] 3AC; ~∧ MS1eC
250.11	hardships they] 3AC; hardships which they MS1eC
250.11	house . . . sustained] 1EC, 3AC; of their fatigues MS1eC
250.12	pilot . . . died] 3AC; pilot last MS1eC
250.14	New World] 3AC; new world MS1eC
250.16	Garcilaso] 3AC; Garcilasso MS1eC
250.16	Vega,] 3AC; ~∧ MS1eC
250.19	Indies] 3AC; Indias MS1eC

250.26	Garcilaso] 3AC; Garcilasso MS1eC
250.31	cap.] 3AC; c. MS1eC
250.34	lib. . . . cap. . . . p.] 3AC; l. . . . c. . . . p. MS1eC
250.36	Solorzano,] 3AC; ~. MS1eC
250.36	lib. . . . cap.] 3AC; l. . . . c. MS1eC
250.37	Varones Illust. . . . cap.] 3AC; Varones, Illus. . . . c. MS1eC
250.38	Annal.] 3AC; annual MS1eC
250.39	Mariz] 3AC; Maliz MS1eC
250.40	García,] 3AC; ~∧ MS1eC
250.41	Torquemada,] 3AC; ~∧ MS1eC
250.42	Riccioli,] 3AC; ~∧ MS1eC
250.42	Geograf. . . . lib.] 3AC; Geograph. . . . l. MS1eC
251.1	accusers. The] 3AC; *New paragraph in MS1eC* . .
251.2	Gomara,] 3AC; ~∧ MS1eC
251.3	contradiction] 3AC; contradictions MS1eC
251.9	clear] 1EC, 3AC; established MS1eC
251.11	Garcilaso] 3AC; Garcilasso MS1eC
251.12	No. XIII] 3AC; No. XII. MS1eC
251.16–17	Bohemia;] 3AC; ~, MS1eC
250.20–21	Regiomantanus;] 3AC; ~, MS1eC
251.21	De Murr] 3AC; Demurr MS1eC
251.23	De Murr] 3AC; Demurr MS1eC
251.24–35	*Francisco . . . 18] 3AC; "Hijos de Sevilla. No. 2. p. 42. let. F. The same is stated in Bibliotheca Hispaña Nova, l. i. f. 437. Bernal Diaz de Castillo, Hist. de la Conquist de la Nueva España, de cap. 18. Juan Bautista Munos, Hist. N. Mundo, Prologo xviii. MS1eC
252.4	Behem,] 3AC; ~∧ MS1eC
252.19	River] 3AC; river MS1eC
252.24	*Eques*] 3AC; *Equis* MS1eC
252.30	circulating] 3AC; current MS1eC
252.31	indications] 3AC; the productions MS1eC
252.34	days,] 3AC; ~∧ MS1eC
252.37	II,] 3AC; ~∧ MS1eC
252.38	the . . . heir of] 1EC, 3AC; to whom he had the intention of MS1eC
252.39	was captured] 3AC; was again captured MS1eC
252.40	*Vasconcelos. lib. 4] 3AC; *Missing in MS1eC*
253.4–5	is known] 1EC, 2EC, 3AC; is heard MS1eC
253.7	Lisbon,] 3AC; ~∧ MS1eC
253.8	Western World] 3AC; western world MS1eC

253.12	voyagers] 3AC; navigators MS1eC
253.14	looked towards] 1EC, 2EC, 3AC; looked the MS1eC
253.18	"Hii] 3AC; $_\wedge\sim$ MS1eC
253.18	duo,] 3AC; $\sim_\wedge$ MS1eC
253.18	auspicio,] 3AC; $\sim_\wedge$ MS1eC
253.18	sulcantes,] 3AC; $\sim_\wedge$ MS1eC
253.19	evagantes,] 3AC; $\sim_\wedge$ MS1eC
253.19	equinoctiali] 3AC; equinocciale MS1eC
253.20	versus,] 3AC; $\sim_\wedge$ MS1eC
253.21	projiciebatur] 3AC; procciebatur MS1eC
253.21	Aperuêre] 3AC; Apervere MS1eC
253.22	annis,] 3AC; $\sim_\wedge$ MS1eC
253.22	Januensibus,] 3AC; $\sim_\wedge$ MS1eC
253.26	De Murr] 3AC; Demurr MS1eC
253.27	of the] 3AC; of this MS1eC
253.27	5th of October 1493] 3AC; 5 October 1493 MS1eC
253.28	relate merely] 3AC; merely relate MS1eC
253.32	Bartholomeo] 3AC; Bartholomew MS1eC
253.34	for some] 1EC, 2EC, 3AC; on some MS1eC
253.34–35	with . . . two caravels] 1EC, 3AC; with two caravels and his before mentioned relatives MS1eC
253.36	Jago,] 3AC; $\sim_\wedge$ MS1eC
253.37	inserted in] 2EC, MS2eC, 3AC; foisted into MS1eC; inserted into 1EC
253.38	Silvius,] 3AC; $\sim_\wedge$ MS1eC
253.38	II,] 3AC; $\sim_\wedge$ MS1eC
253.39	who died] 1EC, 2EC, 3AC; who in fact died MS1eC
253.41	Barros,] 3AC; $\sim_\wedge$ MS1eC
253.41	lib. . . . cap.] 3AC; l. . . . c. MS1eC
254.1	New World] 3AC; new world MS1eC
254.2	Behem's] 3AC; Behems MS1eC
254.3	and without the] 1EC, 2EC, 3AC; and the MS1eC
254.9	character, of] 1EC, 2EC, 3AC; standing, by MS1eC
254.10	Franklin] 3AC; Franklen MS1eC
254.11	Philosophical Society] 3AC; philosophical society MS1eC
254.13	New World] 3AC; new world MS1eC
254.14	Philosophical Society] 3AC; philosophical society MS1eC
254.21	Nuremberg] T; Nuremburg MS1eC, 1EC, 3AC
254.23	Nuremberg] T; Nuremburg MS1eC, 1EC, 3AC
254.25	Brazil] 3AC; Brasil MS1eC

254.26	supported,] 3AC; ∼∧ MS1eC
254.28	globe,] 3AC; ∼∧ MS1eC
254.29	Nuremberg] T; Nuremburg MS1eC, 1EC, 3AC
254.30	Schoener,] 3AC; ∼∧ MS1eC
254.30	mathematics] 3AC; Mathematics MS1eC
254.33	New World] 3AC; new world MS1eC
254.34	Behem's] 3AC; Behems MS1eC
254.34	Cladera,] 3AC; ∼∧ MS1eC
254.36	Historicas,] 3AC; historicas MS1eC
255.7	Norwegians] 1EC, 2EC, MS2eC, 3AC; Normans MS1eC
255.8	Iceland] 1EC, 3AC; Ireland MS1eC
255.9	Iceland] 1EC, 3AC; Ireland MS1eC
255.10	Sturleson] 1EC, 2EC, 3AC; Sturleson or Sturlonis MS1eC
255.19	alone] 3AC; together MS1eC
255.39	book . . . chap.] 3AC; b. . . . c. MS1eC
256.11	formed long] 1EC, 3AC; formed two centuries MS1eC
256.13	Torfæus] 1EC; Thormond Torfæus MS1eC
256.15	1705."] 3AC; ∼.∧ MS1eC
256.18	New World] 3AC; new world MS1eC
256.22	comments . . . editors] 1EC, 3AC; and scientific dressing of commentators MS1eC
256.28	America,] 3AC; ∼∧ MS1eC
256.39	of the] 1EC, 3AC; by the MS1eC
256.41	Venetian,] 3AC; ∼∧ MS1eC
257.4	Ferroe] 3AC; Feroe MS1eC
257.5	Zichmni,] 3AC; ∼∧ MS1eC
257.5–6	the islands] 1EC, 2EC, 3AC; the Portland islands MS1eC
257.6	another district] 1EC, 3AC; Sorani MS1eC
257.17	island] 3AC; Island MS1eC
257.22	Latin] 3AC; latin MS1eC
257.28	Latin] 3AC; latin MS1eC
257.28	King's] 3AC; Kings MS1eC
257.39	Hackluyt,] 3AC; ∼∧ MS1eC
257.40	tom.] 3AC; t. MS1eC
258.10	them,] 3AC; ∼∧ MS1eC
258.10	went] 1EC, 2EC, MS2eC, 3AC; got MS1eC
258.11	interpreter,] 3AC; ∼; MS1eC
258.12	rich; then] 3AC ∼, ∼ MS1eC
258.20	Zichmni;] 3AC; ∼, MS1eC

258.30	Latin] 3AC; latin MS1eC
259.4	me," . . . editor,] 3AC; ~‸" ~‸ MS1eC
259.5	matters] 1EC, 2EC, 3AC; purposes MS1eC
259.7	pieces,] 3AC; ~‸ MS1eC
259.10	geographer,] 3AC; ~‸ MS1eC
259.12	Orbis] 3AC; orbis MS1eC
259.12	Mr.] 3AC; M. MS1eC
259.14	Carlo,] 3AC; ~‸ MS1eC
259.18	house,] 3AC; ~‸ MS1eC
259.23	him,] 3AC; ~‸ MS1eC
259.29	Malte-Brun] 3AC; ~‸~ MS1eC
259.30–31	North Sea] 3AC; north sea MS1eC
259.31	Zeno,] 3AC; ~‸ MS1eC
259.34	examined the] 1EC, 2EC, 3AC; examined with his usual accuracy the MS1eC
259.35	Columbus . . . accuracy,] 1EC, 2EC, 3AC; Columbus, MS1eC
259.36	correspondence] 3AC; correspondance MS1eC
259.36	Paulo] 3AC; Paolo MS1eC
259.39	Hackluyt,] 3AC; ~‸ MS1eC
259.40	Malte-Brun] 3AC; ~‸~ MS1eC
259.40	tom. . . . lib.] 3AC; t. . . . l. MS1eC
259.41	tom.] 3AC; l. MS1eC
260.8–9	Cipango] 3AC; Cepango MS1eC
260.11	No. XV.] 3AC; No. XIV. MS1eC
260.19	assertion] 3AC; dictum MS1eC
260.20	Posidonius] 3AC; Possidonius MS1eC
260.24	Hannonis] 3AC; ~, MS1eC
260.31	Horn, supposed] 3AC; Horn, and which was supposed MS1eC
260.34	Memoirs] 3AC; Mémoirs MS1eC
260.34	tom.] 3AC; t. MS1eC
261.1	parallel] 3AC; parraled MS1eC
261.3	Tome] 3AC; t. MS1eC
261.4	Periplus] 3AC; periplus MS1eC
261.20	ocean] 3AC; Ocean MS1eC
261.21	Straits] 3AC; straits MS1eC
261.23	geography] 3AC; Geography MS1eC
261.24	Phœnicians] 3AC; Phenicians MS1eC
261.27	ocean] 3AC; Ocean MS1eC
261.30	Africa] 3AC; africa MS1eC
261.33	ocean] 3AC; Ocean MS1eC

261.35	Cleomedes] 3AC; Cleomede MS1eC
262.1	continents at a greater distance] 1EC, 3AC; continents more remote MS1eC
262.1	Marinus] 3AC; Marinius MS1eC
262.2	Tyre] 3AC; ∼, MS1eC
262.6	geographers] 3AC; Geographers MS1eC
262.14	No. XVI] 3AC; No. XV. MS1eC
262.19	coast,] 3AC; ∼∧ MS1eC
262.20–21	fifteenth] 3AC; 15th MS1eC
262.23	IV,] 3AC; 4 MS1eC
262.25	quintals] 3AC; Quintals MS1eC
262.27	horses,] 3AC; ∼∧ MS1eC
262.28	carrying] 3AC; of which carried MS1eC
262.30	ship of 700 tons] 3AC; ship MS1eC
262.31	wheat.] 3AC; wheat and being of 700 tons burthen. MS1eC
262.32	there being of] 3AC; there of MS1eC
262.32	12,000 quintals] 3AC; 12000 Quintals MS1eC
262.33	others] 1EC, 2EC, 3AC; other MS1eC
263.1	Indeed,] 3AC; ∼∧ MS1eC
263.2	Bermeo] 3AC; Borneo MS1eC
263.4	convoy] 3AC; convey MS1eC
263.4	Boabdil,] 3AC; ∼∧ MS1eC
263.5	Granada,] 3AC; ∼∧ MS1eC
263.12	service;] 3AC; ∼∧ MS1eC
263.23	ship] 3AC; ∼, MS1eC
263.23	caravel] 3AC; Caravel MS1eC
263.25	Chevalier] 3AC; chevalier MS1eC
263.25	Dissertations] 3AC; dissertations MS1eC
263.30	Glossary] 3AC; glossary MS1eC
263.33	Oration] 3AC; oration MS1eC
263.33–34	considers . . . given] 1EC, 3AC; considers the true origin of the word given MS1eC
263.35	Lat. Carabus] 1EC, 3AC; Carabus MS1eC
263.35	Κάραβος] 1EC, 2EC, 3AC; Karabʋs MS1eC; Karabrod." The primitive meaning of which Greek and Latin words is crab. 1AC
263.36	caravel] 3AC; Caravel MS1eC
263.38	thirteenth] 3AC; 13 MS1eC
263.40	Capmany,] 3AC; Capomani MS1eC
264.2	*Carabelas*] 3AC; Carabelas MS1eC
264.9	caravels] 3AC; Caravels MS1eC

264.11	benches] 1EC, 3AC; banks MS1eC
264.12	galley] 3AC; Galley MS1eC
264.14–15	Amsterdam,] 3AC; ~ᴧ MS1eC
264.16	e] 3AC; & MS1eC
264.19	latine] 3AC; Latine MS1eC
264.22	fact,] 3AC; ~ᴧ MS1eC
264.31	Capmany] 3AC; Capomani MS1eC
264.35	source] 3AC; Source MS1eC
265.1	New World] 3AC; new world MS1eC
265.1	Navarrete] 3AC; Don Martin Navarrete MS1eC; Don Martin Fernandez de Navarrete MS2eC
265.2	Discoveries] 3AC; Discoverys MS1eC
265.3	Turk's Island,] 3AC; Turks-Island MS1eC
265.6	Navarrete] 1EC, 3AC; Mr. Navarrete MS1eC, 1AC
265.8	article,] 3AC; ~ᴧ MS1eC
265.10	Guanahani.] 3AC; ~ᴧ MS1eC
265.11	Salvador,] 3AC; ~ᴧ MS1eC
265.11	island] 3AC; Island MS1eC
265.12	forests,] 3AC; ~ᴧ MS1eC
265.13	fruit;] 3AC; ~, MS1eC
265.14	population;] 3AC; ~, MS1eC
265.16	shore,] 3AC; ~ᴧ MS1eC
265.16	N. N. E.,] 3AC; N.N.E. MS1eC
265.19	Turk's Island] 3AC; Turks-Island MS1eC
265.19	lying] 1EC, 2EC, 3AC; laying MS1eC, 1AC
265.20	extent.] 3AC; extant MS1eC
265.24	Turk's Island] 3AC; Turks-Island MS1eC
265.25	east] 3AC; East MS1eC
265.25	north-east] 3AC; N. E MS1eC
265.27	west] 3AC; West MS1eC
265.34	Hawk's Nest] 3AC; Hawks-Nest MS1eC
265.35	which . . . of] 1EC, 2EC, 3AC; refuses itself to MS1eC
265.36	subsistence] 3AC; subsistance MS1eC
265.38	turtle,] 3AC; ~ᴧ MS1eC
265.38	abundance,] 3AC; ~ᴧ MS1eC
265.41–42	Turk's Island] 3AC; Turks-Island MS1eC
265.42	therefore,] 3AC; therefor, MS1eC
266.2	subsistence] 3AC; subsistance MS1eC
266.3	at a loss] 1EC, 2EC, 3AC; at loss MS1eC
266.5	Turk's Island] 3AC; Turks-Island MS1eC
266.6	Turk's Islands] 3AC; Turks-Islands MS1eC
266.10	Turk's Island] 3AC; Turks-Island MS1eC

266.10   Gran]   3AC; Grand MS1eC
266.11   Navarrete]   1EC, 2EC, 3AC; Mr. Navarrete MS1eC
266.11   Columbus,]   3AC; ~∧ MS1eC
266.13   Turk's Island]   3AC; Turks-Island MS1eC
266.16   nine]   3AC; 9 MS1eC
266.17   Fernandina. This Navarrete]   3AC;   Fernandina;   this
                    Mr. Navarrete MS1eC
266.18   twenty two]   T; 22 MS1eC; ~-~ 1EC
266.18   Besides,]   3AC; ~∧ MS1eC
266.19   islands,]   3AC; ~∧ MS1eC
266.19   Turk's Island]   3AC; Turks-island MS1eC
266.21   twenty eight]   T; 28 MS1eC; ~-~ 1EC
266.22   N.W.:]   3AC; N.W. MS1eC
266.22   four]   3AC; 4 MS1eC
266.23   word,]   3AC; ~∧ MS1eC
266.24   Little Inagua]   3AC; little-Inagua MS1eC
266.25   Navarrete]   1EC, 2EC, 3AC; Mr. Navarrete MS1eC
266.26   Little]   3AC; little MS1eC
266.27   Columbus. Again]   3AC; *New paragraph in MS1eC*
266.28   eight]   3AC; 8 MS1eC
266.29   thirty five]   T; 35 MS1eC
266.29–30   Inagua. Leaving]   3AC; *No paragraph in MS1eC*
266.30   Isabella,]   3AC; ~∧ MS1eC
266.32   Navarrete]   1EC, 2EC, 3AC; Mr. Navarrete MS1eC
266.33   south]   3AC; South MS1eC
266.36–37   14th of November]   3AC; 14. Nov MS1eC
266.37   Señora]   3AC; Seniora MS1eC
266.38   Navarrete]   1EC, 2EC, 3AC; Mr. Navarrete MS1eC
266.40   fifty]   3AC; 50 MS1eC
267.1   forty five]   T; 45 MS1eC; ~-~ 1EC
267.1   Turk's]   3AC; Turks MS1eC
267.1   point,]   3AC; ~∧ MS1eC
267.3   Cuba,]   3AC; ~∧ MS1eC
267.4   extent]   3AC; extant MS1eC
267.4   twenty]   3AC; 20 MS1eC
267.5   remain]   1EC, 2EC, 3AC; remains MS1eC
267.5   Now, Navarrete]   1EC, 3AC; Whereas Mr. Navarrete
                    MS1eC, 1AC
267.6   extent]   3AC; extant MS1eC
267.6   seventy]   3AC; 70 MS1eC
267.8–9   Navarrete]   3AC; Mr. Navarrete MS1eC
267.13   11th of]   3AC; 11. MS1eC

267.14   sunset,]   1EC, 2EC, 3AC; sundown MS1eC, 1AC
267.15   west, the]   3AC; West. The MS1eC
267.15–16   three . . . hour. At ten]   3AC; 3 . . . hour at 10 MS1eC
267.16   o'clock]   3AC; oclock MS1eC
267.16   light,]   3AC; ~∧ MS1eC
267.17   four]   3AC; 4 MS1eC
267.18   twelve]   3AC; 12 MS1eC
267.19   two]   3AC; 2 MS1eC
267.19   ahead]   3AC; a-head MS1eC
267.20   twelve]   3AC; 12 MS1eC
267.20   which they ran since]   1EC, 2EC, 3AC; ran since
                MS1eC
267.20   o'clock]   3AC; oclock MS1eC
267.21   two]   3AC; 2 MS1eC
267.21   land,]   3AC; ~∧ MS1eC
267.22   Watling's Island]   3AC; Watlings-island MS1eC
267.24   Watling's Island]   3AC; Watlings-island MS1eC
267.25   ahead]   3AC; a-head MS1eC
267.25   four]   3AC; 4 MS1eC
267.26   three]   3AC; 3 MS1eC
267.28   light,]   3AC; ~∧ MS1eC
267.28   Watling's Island]   3AC; Watlings-island MS1eC
267.31   12th of October;]   3AC; 12. Oct, MS1eC
267.31   beauty,]   3AC; ~∧ MS1eC
267.37   Cat Island]   3AC; Cat-island MS1eC
267.37   east and west]   3AC; East and West MS1eC
267.40   12th,]   3AC; 12 MS1eC
268.6   sight,]   3AC; ~∧ MS1eC
268.8   Concepcion]   3AC; Conception MS1eC
268.9   La Cadena]   3AC; la cadena MS1eC
268.10   San]   3AC; S. MS1eC
268.10   S.E. and]   3AC; S.E. by MS1eC
268.11   Concepcion]   3AC; Conception MS1eC
268.13   14th]   3AC; 14 MS1eC
268.18   it. We]   1EC, 2EC, 3AC; it.; But we MS1eC
268.22   westward]   3AC; Westward MS1eC
268.23   Concepcion]   3AC; Conception MS1eC
268.25   west]   3AC; West MS1eC
268.25   westward]   3AC; Westward MS1eC
268.28   Now,]   3AC; ~∧ MS1eC
268.30   five]   3AC; 5 MS1eC
268.31   16th October,]   3AC; 16 Oct. MS1eC

268.32	westward nine] 3AC; Westward 9 MS1eC
268.33	twenty eight] T; 29 MS1eC
268.35	morning, 17th October] 3AC; morning 16. Oct. MS1eC
268.37	S.,] 3AC; S. MS1eC
268.39	therefore] 3AC; therefor MS1eC
268.40	two] 3AC; 2 MS1eC
269.2	east and west] 3AC; East and west MS1eC
269.6	steering;] 3AC; ~∧ MS1eC
269.7	storm,] 3AC; ~∧ MS1eC
269.8	18th October,] 3AC; 18. Oct. MS1eC
269.11	Exuma,] 3AC; ~∧ MS1eC
269.11	south] 3AC; South MS1eC
269.13	twenty eight] T; 28 MS1eC
269.14	extent] 3AC; extant MS1eC
269.18	are] 3AC; is MS1eC
269.18–19	westerly as well as south-westerly.] 3AC; westerly as well as S. Westerly MS1eC
269.20	extent] 3AC; extant MS1eC
269.21	twenty] 3AC; 20 MS1eC
269.22	twenty eight] T; 28 MS1eC
269.24	southerly] 3AC; Southerly MS1eC
269.30	19th October] 3AC; 19. Oct. MS1eC
269.31	north] 3AC; North MS1eC
269.31	three] 3AC; 3 MS1eC
269.32	east] 3AC; East MS1eC
269.32	it,] 3AC; ~∧ MS1eC
269.32	north] 3AC; North MS1eC
269.36	Cabo] 3AC; cabo MS1eC
269.37	Cabo] 3AC; cabo MS1eC
269.38–39	Isabella] 3AC; Isabela MS1eC
269.39	east and west] 3AC; East and West MS1eC
269.39	westerly twelve] 3AC; Westerly 12 MS1eC
269.40	Fermosa] 3AC; Fermoso MS1eC
269.41	Isabella] 3AC; Isabela MS1eC
269.42	Laguna,] 3AC; ~∧ MS1eC
270.1	20th October] 3AC; 20 Oct, MS1eC
270.3	Isabella] 3AC; Isabela MS1eC
270.5	Isabella] 3AC; Isabela MS1eC
270.6	Larga,] 3AC; ~∧ MS1eC
270.6	east] 3AC; East MS1eC
270.6	Exuma,] 3AC; ~∧ MS1eC
270.9	Isabella,] 3AC; Isabela MS1eC

270.9	Cabo] 3AC; cabo MS1eC
270.10	midnight,] 3AC; ~$_\wedge$ MS1eC
270.10	24th October] 3AC; 24. Oct. MS1eC
270.11–12	light, with rain,] 3AC; ~$_\wedge$ ~$_\wedge$ MS1eC
270.12	noon,] 3AC; ~$_\wedge$ MS1eC
270.13	seven] 3AC; 7 MS1eC
270.14	Fernandina,] 3AC; ~$_\wedge$ MS1eC
270.14	morning,] 3AC; ~$_\wedge$ MS1eC
270.15	reckoning two] 3AC; reckoning only 2 MS1eC
270.16	25th] 3AC; 25 MS1eC
270.16–17	nine o'clock,] 3AC; 9 oclock MS1eC
270.17	five] 3AC; 5 MS1eC
270.17	three] 3AC; 3 MS1eC
270.18	eleven] 3AC; 11 MS1eC
270.18	discovered,] 3AC; ~$_\wedge$ MS1eC
270.19	seven or eight] 3AC; 7 or 8 MS1eC
270.19	north and south] 3AC; North and South MS1eC
270.19	five] 3AC; 5 MS1eC
270.20	day, south] 3AC; ~$_\wedge$ ~ MS1eC
270.21	islands,] 3AC; ~$_\wedge$ MS1eC
270.21	five or six] 3AC; 5 or 6 MS1eC
270.22	extent] 3AC; extant MS1eC
270.23	Columbus,] 3AC; ~$_\wedge$ MS1eC
270.25	thirty] 3AC; 30 MS1eC
270.25	thirty] 3AC; 30 MS1eC
270.28	east] 3AC; East MS1eC
270.30	three] 3AC; 3 MS1eC
270.30	reckoning,] 3AC; ~$_\wedge$ MS1eC
270.31	conjecture,] 3AC; ~$_\wedge$ MS1eC
270.32	two] 3AC; 2 MS1eC
270.35	Isabella] 3AC; Isabela MS1eC
270.36	west,] 3AC; West, MS1eC
270.38	lying] 1EC, 2EC, 3AC; laying MS1eC
270.38	southward] 3AC; Southward MS1eC
270.39	Oct. 27.–] 3AC; Oct. 27. MS1eC
270.40	Cuba,] 3AC; ~$_\wedge$ MS1eC
270.41	seventeen] 3AC; 17 MS1eC
270.42–271.4	morning. On the . . . obscure.] 3AC; morning *New paragraph* In this part of the journal, Columbus does not describe the localities with that accuracy with which he had hirtherto noted every thing; the text also is in several places obscure. *New paragraph* The

ships having remained hove to until morning, they made sail on the 28th, at S.S.W. entering a beautiful river with a fine harbour, which they named San Salvador. MS1eC

271.5	port] 3AC; part MS1eC
271.6	Nuevitas] MS3AC, 3AC; Nuevitao MS1eC, 1EC; Muritas 1AC
271.6	eight ... west] 3AC; 8 ... West MS1eC
271.8	agrees] 3AC; coincides MS1eC
271.9	charts,] 3AC; ~∧ MS1eC
271.10	Oct. 29–] 3AC; Oct. 29. MS1eC
271.10	west] 3AC; West MS1eC
271.11	six] 3AC; 6 MS1eC
271.11	N.W.,] 3AC; N.W. MS1eC
271.12	ten] 3AC; 10 MS1eC
271.13	easterly,] 3AC; Easterly MS1eC
271.13	One] 3AC; 1 MS1eC
271.14	one,] 3AC; ~∧ MS1eC
271.15	Mares] 3AC; Maus MS1eC
271.16	lake, and having] 3AC; lake, having MS1eC
271.16	resembling] 3AC; in the form of MS1eC; formed like 1AC
271.17–18	promontory, . . . fortification,] 3AC; ~∧ . . . ~∧ MS1eC
271.19	west] 3AC; West MS1eC
271.21	Grandes,] 3AC; ~∧ MS1eC
271.21	Port San] 3AC; the port of San MS1eC
271.22	30th of October,] 3AC; 30. Oct. MS1eC
271.22	Mares] 3AC; Maus MS1eC
271.23	fifteen] 3AC; 15 MS1eC
271.23	cape,] 3AC; ~∧ MS1eC
271.24	Cabo] 3AC; cabo MS1eC
271.24	This, we believe, is the] 3AC; This we believe the MS1eC
271.25–26	river, distant, according] 3AC; ~∧ ~∧ ~ MS1eC
271.26	natives, four days'] 3AC; natives 4 days MS1eC
271.27	therefore] 3AC; therefor MS1eC
271.28	31st of October] 3AC; 31. Oct. MS1eC
271.29	shallow] 1EC, 2EC, 3AC; shoal MS1eC
271.34	Cape] 3AC; cape MS1eC
271.37	of,] 3AC; ~∧ MS1eC
271.39	combination,] 3AC; ~∧ MS1eC

271.40	Further,] 3AC; ~∧ MS1eC
271.41	west] 3AC; West MS1eC
271.41	seventeen] 3AC; 17 MS1eC
271.41	Mares] 3AC; Maus MS1eC
271.42	Mares] 3AC; Maus MS1eC
271.42	extended] 1EC, 2EC, 3AC; lain MS1eC
271.42	fifteen] 3AC; 15 MS1eC
272.1	Cabo] 3AC; cabo MS1eC
272.2	supposed.] 3AC; ~— MS1eC
272.2	north, which] 3AC; North which MS1eC
272.3	steering,] 3AC; ~; MS1eC
272.4	Mares] 3AC; Maus MS1eC
272.5	12th of November the] 3AC; 12. Nov. The MS1eC
272.5	Mares] 3AC; Maus MS1eC
272.7	lie] 1EC, 2EC, 3AC; lay MS1eC
272.7	eight] 3AC; 8 MS1eC
272.9	west] 3AC; West MS1eC
272.9	another,] 3AC; ~∧ MS1eC
272.10	Rio del Sol. It] 3AC; rio-del-Sol it MS1eC
272.10–11	to examine it] 1EC, 2EC, 3AC; to examine it to examine it MS1eC
272.13	twelve] 3AC; 12 MS1eC
272.13	Mares] 3AC; Maus MS1eC
272.13	west] 3AC; West MS1eC
272.14	Mares] 3AC; Maus MS1eC
272.14	seventeen leagues. San] 3AC; 17 ~,~ MS1eC
272.15	therefore] 3AC; therefor MS1eC
272.15	five . . . east] 3AC; 5 . . . East MS1eC
272.18	six] 3AC; 6 MS1eC
272.18	eighteen] 3AC; 18 MS1eC
272.19	Rio] 3AC; rio MS1eC
272.19	Mares,] T; Maus MS1eC
272.20	Cabo] 3AC; cabo MS1eC
272.22	Guajava,] 3AC; ~∧ MS1eC
272.26	passage, . . . two] 3AC; passage . . . 2 MS1eC
272.27	wide,] 3AC; ~∧ MS1eC
272.27	lying] 1EC, 2AC, 3AC; laying MS1eC
272.29	13th of November, having] 3AC; 13. No. Having MS1eC
272.29	night,] 3AC; ~∧ MS1eC
272.30	two . . . extent] 3AC; 2 . . . extant MS1eC
272.30	into] 1EC, 2EC, 3AC; in MS1eC

272.34	north] 3AC; North MS1eC
272.36	Guajava,] 3AC; ~∧ MS1eC
272.36	Cuba,] 3AC; ~∧ MS1eC
272.37	hours'] 3AC; hours MS1eC
272.42	seven] 3AC; 7 MS1eC
272.42	west] 3AC; West MS1eC
272.42	north,] 3AC; at North MS1eC
273.3	Little] 3AC; little MS1eC
273.6	twenty] 3AC; 20 MS1eC
273.7	14th November,] 3AC; 14. Nov. having MS1eC
273.7	wind,] 3AC; ~∧ MS1eC
273.10	Little] MS2eC; little 3AC; *Missing in MS1eC*
273.11	six] 3AC; 6 MS1eC
273.13	eighteen] 3AC; 18 MS1eC
273.14	port,] 3AC; ~∧ MS1eC
273.15	S. E.,] 3AC; S. E. MS1eC
273.18	Señora] 3AC; Seniora MS1eC
273.23	lying] 1EC, 2EC, 3AC; laying MS1eC
273.26	up, therefore,] 3AC; ~∧ therefor MS1eC
273.27	Cuba,] 3AC; ~∧ MS1eC
273.30	westward] 3AC; Westward MS1eC
273.32	thirty] 3AC; 30 MS1eC
273.36	harbors,] 3AC; ~∧ MS1eC
273.38	recesses] 1EC, 2EC, 3AC; windings MS1eC
274.6	18th November] 3AC; 18. Nov. MS1eC
274.8	east] 3AC; East MS1eC
274.8	13th of November] 3AC; 13. Nov. MS1eC
274.10	Columbus, . . . appears,] 3AC; Columbus appears MS1eC
274.12	19th November] 3AC; 19. Nov. MS1eC
274.13	sunset] 1EC, 2EC, 3AC; sundown MS1eC
274.13	seven] 3AC; 7 MS1eC
274.14	ten o'clock] 3AC; 10 oclock MS1eC
274.15	November)] 3AC; Nov.) MS1eC
274.15	fifteen] 3AC; 15 MS1eC
274.16	E.S.E.,] 3AC; E.S.E. MS1eC
274.17	lie,] 1EC, 2EC, 3AC; lay MS1eC
274.18–19	twenty five leagues] T; 25 ligues MS1eC
274.19	Isabella,] 3AC; Isabela MS1eC
274.19–20	twelve leagues,] 3AC; 12 leagues MS1eC
274.20	whom] 1EC, 2EC, 3AC; which MS1eC
274.21	which] 1EC, 2EC, 3AC; that MS1eC

274.21	eight] 3AC; 8 MS1eC
274.21	Isabella,] 3AC; Isabela MS1eC
274.23	Isabella] 3AC; Isabela MS1eC
274.24	thirty seven] T; 37 MS1eC
274.25	forty five] T; 45 MS1eC
274.26	eight] 3AC; 8 MS1eC
274.26	nine;] 3AC; 9. MS1eC
274.27	Again,] 3AC; ~∧ MS1eC
274.28–29	Isabella] 3AC; Isabela MS1eC
274.29	W.S.W.,] 3AC; W.S.W. MS1eC
274.29	west] 3AC; West MS1eC
274.29–30	S.S.W. Having] 3AC; S.S.W. having MS1eC
274.32	Isabella] 3AC; Isabela MS1eC
274.34	Isabella,] 3AC; Isabela MS1eC
274.35	west] 3AC; West MS1eC
274.37	ten o'clock] 3AC; 10 oclock MS1eC
274.38	20th November] 3AC; 20 Nov. MS1eC
274.38	west] 3AC; West MS1eC
274.39	Principe,] 3AC; ~∧ MS1eC
274.40	westward] 3AC; Westward MS1eC
275.1	four] 3AC; 4 MS1eC
275.1–2	24th November,] 3AC; 24. Nov. MS1eC
275.2	currents,] 3AC; ~∧ MS1eC
275.7	west] 3AC; West MS1eC
275.9	upon them] 1EC, 2EC, 3AC; there MS1eC
275.10	W.] 3AC; West MS1eC
275.11	north] 3AC; North MS1eC
275.12	navy] 1EC, 2EC, 3AC; navies MS1eC
275.18	26th of November] 3AC; 26. Nov. MS1eC
275.20	Cabo] 3AC; cabo MS1eC
275.22	fifteen] 3AC; 15 MS1eC
275.23	it,] 3AC; ~∧ MS1eC
275.23	Cabo] 3AC; cabo MS1eC
275.24	known] 1EC, 2EC, 3AC; know MS1eC
275.27	headlands] 3AC; head lands MS1eC
275.29	passed] 1EC, 2EC, 3AC; past MS1eC
275.29	27th,] 3AC; 27 MS1eC
275.31	headland] 3AC; head land MS1eC
275.34	time,] 3AC; ~∧ MS1eC
275.35	27th at Baracoa,] 3AC; 27. at Baracoa MS1eC
275.36	Santo,] 3AC; ~∧ MS1eC
275.36	sixty] 3AC; 60 MS1eC

275.36	leagues,] 3AC; ~∧ MS1eC
275.37	nine] 3AC; 9 MS1eC
275.37	five] 3AC; 5 MS1eC
275.37	Cape] 3AC; cape MS1eC
275.38	eight] 3AC; 8 MS1eC
275.39	port; all] 3AC; port. All MS1eC
275.42	4th of December,] 3AC; 4. Dec. MS1eC
276.2	N.E.,] 3AC; N. E. MS1eC
276.3	Bohio,] 3AC; ~∧ MS1eC
276.3	Hispaniola] 3AC; Espaniola MS1eC
276.5	twenty] 3AC; 20 MS1eC
276.6	coast,] 3AC; ~∧ MS1eC
276.8	western] 3AC; Western MS1eC
276.12–13	discovery, Guanahani,] 3AC; ~∧ ~∧ MS1eC
276.13	latitude of Ferro,] 3AC; Lat. ~∧ MS1eC
276.14	north] 3AC; N. MS1eC
276.14	Turk's] 3AC; Turks MS1eC
276.16	three . . . six] 3AC; 3 . . . 6 MS1eC
276.17	demonstration,] 3AC; ~∧ MS1eC
276.20	New World] 3AC; new world MS1eC
276.24	Rico,] 3AC; ~∧ MS1eC
276.25	five] 3AC; 5 MS1eC
276.25	El Viejo] 3AC; el viejo MS1eC
276.25–26	latitude . . . north] 3AC; Lat . . . N. MS1eC
276.27	eighth] 3AC; 8th MS1eC
276.29	eleventh] 3AC; 11th MS1eC
276.30	north] 3AC; N. MS1eC
276.34	latitudes, . . . true,] 3AC; Latitudes . . . true MS1eC
276.36	Islands,] 3AC; ~∧ MS1eC
276.37	seventy] 3AC; 70 MS1eC
276.38	forty five] T; 45 MS1eC
277.2	time] 3AC; ~, MS1eC
277.3	present] 1EC, 2EC, 3AC; present day MS1eC
277.4	north-western] 3AC; N. Western MS1eC
277.5	Caycos;] 3AC; ~, MS1eC
277.5	one, then, . . . El Viejo,] 3AC; ~∧ ~∧ . . . el Viejo MS1eC
277.6	Turk's Island,] 3AC; Turks island MS1eC
277.9	Turk's Island, where] 3AC; Turks ~∧ ~ MS1eC
277.11	laid] 1EC, 2EC, 3AC; lain MS1eC
277.15	thought,] T; ~∧ MS1eC
277.20	dealings,] 3AC; ~∧ MS1eC

277.22	Herrera's] 3AC; Herreras MS1eC
277.24	N.W., . . . S.E.] 3AC; Northwest, . . . South east MS1eC
277.26–44, 278.37–39	*Note . . . science.*] 3AC; *Missing in all previous texts.*
278.5	eight . . . fifty] 3AC; 8 . . . 50 MS1eC
278.5	castellanos,] 3AC; Castillanas MS1eC
278.5	sixty five] 3AC; 65 MS1eC
278.6	thirty four] T; 34 MS1eC
278.7	2,210] 3AC; 2210 MS1eC
278.8	eight,] 3AC; 8, MS1eC
278.8	eight reals,] 3AC; 8 ~_∧ MS1eC
278.10	castellano] 3AC; Castillano MS1eC
278.11	maravedies] T; maravedis MS1eC
278.11	383] 3AC; 393 MS1eC
278.11	maravedies] T; maravedis MS1eC
278.17	had] 3AC; have MS1eC
278.18	*real*] 3AC; real MS1eC
278.19	*real*] 3AC; real MS1eC
278.19	maravedi] 3AC; Maravedi MS1eC
278.20	eight] 3AC; 8 MS1eC
278.22	Indeed,] 3AC; ~_∧ MS1eC
278.22	dollar,] 3AC; ~_∧ MS1eC
278.23	twenty] 3AC; 20 MS1eC
278.24	eight parts,] 3AC; 8 ~_∧ MS1eC
278.26	maravedies;] T; ~, MS1eC
278.27	maravedies] T; maravedis MS1eC
278.34	New World] 3AC; new world MS1eC
278.35	three] 3AC; 3 MS1eC
279.2	four] 3AC; 4 MS1eC
279.5	New World] 3AC; new world MS1eC
279.7	fifteenth] 3AC; 15 MS1eC
279.8	sixteen] 3AC; 16 MS1eC
279.13	North] 3AC; north MS1eC
279.13–14	sixpence] 3AC; six pence MS1eC
279.34	Caballero,] 3AC; caballero. MS1eC
279.34	Say, . . . Politique] 3AC; ~_∧ . . . ~ MS1eC
281.21	No. XX] 3AC; No. XVIII. MS1eC
281.22	Polo *] 3AC; ~._∧ MS1eC
281.24	Columbus,] 3AC; ~_∧ MS1eC
281.24	would] 1EC, 2EC, 3AC; will MS1eC
281.28	East] 3AC; east MS1eC
281.28	Christendom] 3AC; christendom MS1eC

281.29–35   *In preparing . . . Polo.]   3AC; *Missing in MS1eC*
282.2   Maffeo]   3AC; Matteo MS1eC
282.3   about]   3AC; in MS1eC
282.3   1255]   3AC; 1250* MS1eC
282.4–5   Mediterranean . . . Bosphorus,]   1EC, 2EC, 3AC; mediterranean and the Strait of Bosphorus, MS1eC
282.5–33   Constantinople . . . East]   3AC; Constantinople. From hence they proceeded by the Euxine to Armenia, where they remained for a year, entertained with great favour at the court of a Tartar prince. A war breaking out between their patron and a neighbouring potentate, and the former being defeated, they were embarrassed how to extricate themselves from the country, and return home in safety. After various wanderings, they at length reached Bochara, in the gulf of Persia, where they resided for three years. While here, there arrived an ambassador from one of the inferior Tartar powers on his way to the court of the great khan. Finding that the two brothers were well acquainted with the Tartar tongue, he prevailed upon them to accompany him. MS1eC, 1EC
282.33   snow-storms]   3AC; snows MS1eC
282.35   Great Khan]   3AC; great ∼ MS1eC
282.38   West,]   3AC; west MS1eC
282.39   Latin]   3AC; latin MS1eC
282.40   Christian]   3AC; christian MS1eC
283.35   Great Khan]   3AC; great ∼ MS1eC
283.40   Christian]   3AC; christian MS1eC
283.2   Christian]   3AC; christian MS1eC
283.5–13   It has . . . Saracens]   3AC; *Missing in MS1eC*
283.14   written]   3AC; given them MS1eC
283.14–15   he delivered . . . appointed]   3AC; he appointed MS1eC
283.18   passport,]   3AC; ∼∧ MS1eC
283.21   Great Khan]   3AC; great khan MS1eC
283.25   Great Khan]   3AC; great ∼ MS1eC
283.27   Clement IV,]   3AC; Clement the 4th, MS1eC
283.29   chair,]   3AC; ∼∧ MS1eC
283.29   Vesconti]   3AC; Visconti MS1eC
283.33   mission]   3AC; Mission MS1eC
283.33–34   They . . . accordingly]   3AC; *New paragraph*: They accordingly MS1eC
283.37   pregnant,]   3AC; ∼∧ MS1eC

283.37–38	a son . . . Marco] 3AC; his son Marco, who was now nineteen years of age. MS1eC
283.40	were] 3AC; began to be MS1eC
284.2	Grand Khan] 3AC; ∧ Khan MS1eC
284.6	mission] 3AC; Mission MS1eC
284.7	Christian] 3AC; christian MS1eC
284.9	18 September 1271] 3AC; Septr 1471 MS1eC
284.11	missives] 3AC; missions MS1eC
284.14	regulation,] 3AC; ∼∧ MS1eC
284.20	friars also,] 3AC; ∼, ∼ MS1eC
284.20	Tripoli,] 3AC; ∼∧ MS1eC
284.22	crystal] 3AC; chrystal MS1eC
284.23	Grand Khan] 3AC; grand khan MS1eC
284.27	monastery. Here] T; temple. MS1eC; ∼: here 1EC
284.28	fathers,] 3AC; ∼∧ MS1eC
284.29	enterprize,] T; enterprize MS1eC
284.33	That potentate sent] 3AC; When that potentate heard of their approach, he MS1eC
284.33	days'] 3AC; ∼∧ MS1eC
284.37	Ramusio,] 3AC; Ramasio. MS1eC
284.37	tom.] 3AC; t. MS1eC
284.38	Bergeron,] 3AC; ∼∧ MS1eC
284.38	Latin] 3AC; latin MS1eC
284.39	Khan] 3AC; khan MS1eC
284.40	monstrous] 3AC; monstruous MS1eC
285.4	Khan] 3AC; khan MS1eC
285.6	four principal] 3AC; various MS1eC
285.8	in missions] 3AC; in various missions MS1eC; in various distant missions 1AC
285.14	years'] T; ∼∧ MS1eC
285.8–287.8	services . . . afterwards] 3AC; and in important affairs. In this way he gathered all kinds of information respecting that vast empire.

After residing many years in Tartary, the Venetians at length longed to return to their native country. It was with great difficulty that the khan could be prevailed on to part with them. They set out on their return in the suite of certain envoys of the king of the Indies, who were conveying home a princess of Tartary to be espoused to their monarch. They were again provided by the munificent khan with tablets of gold, to serve, not merely as passports, but as orders

upon all commanders in his territories for all necessary accommodations and supplies. They embarked in
a fleet of fourteen sail, and coasted the shores of Asia
to an island which they called Jana; from thence
they traversed the Indian sea, and arrived at the
court of the monarch of the Indies. After passing
some time here, they had fresh tablets of gold given
them by that sovereign to carry them in safety and
honour through his kingdom. They had a long and
difficult journey to Constantinople; from whence they
set sail for Venice, and arrived there in 1295, in good
health, and literally laden with riches.

Ramusio, in his preface to the narrative of Marco
Polo, gives a variety of particulars concerning their
arrival, which he compares to that of Ulysses. They
were poorly clad, in coarse clothes made after the
fashion of the Tartars. When they arrived at Venice,
they were known by nobody. So many years had
elapsed since their departure without any tidings
of them, that they were either forgotten or considered
dead. Beside their foreign garb, the influence of
southern suns, and the similitude which men acquire
to those among whom they reside for any length of
time, had given them the look of Tartars rather than
Italians.

They repaired to their own house, which was a
noble palace and was afterwards MS1eC

287.11–12	them, . . . poor] 3AC; $\sim_\wedge \sim$ MS1eC
287.15–18	When . . . and the] 3AC; When the MS1eC
287.23	After . . . retired] 3AC; After they had tasted of the viands, they again retired MS1eC
287.24	damask] 3AC; second MS1eC
287.30	them] 3AC; these MS1eC
287.32	diamonds . . . whole] 3AC; diamonds. The whole MS1eC
287.33	wealth acquired] 3AC; wealth which they had acquired MS1eC
287.34	Grand Khan] 3AC; grand $\sim$ MS1eC
287.34	and conveyed . . . through] 3AC; and which they had thus secretly conveyed through MS1eC
287.36	out of their wits] 3AC; filled MS1eC

287.40	given by Ramusio, on] 3AC; from Ramusio, who gives it on MS1eC
288.1–2	senator, . . . who] 3AC; senator, who MS1eC
288.4–5	banquet . . . came] 3AC; banquet came MS1eC
288.5	Venice, all] 3AC; Venice, and the wealth also of the travellers, all MS1eC
288.6–7	to do . . . eldest,] 3AC; to see the Polos, to caress and honour them. Matteo who was the eldest, MS1eC
288.10	Grand Khan] 3AC; grand ~ MS1eC
288.11	giving] 3AC; and gave MS1eC
288.11	courtesy,] 3AC; ~∧ MS1eC
288.13	Grand Khan] 3AC; grand khan MS1eC
288.15	Doria,] 3AC; ~∧ MS1eC
288.16	navy,] 3AC; ~∧ MS1eC
288.16	Curzola] 3AC; Cuzzola MS1eC
288.17	Dandolo,] 3AC; ~∧ MS1eC
288.26	Ramusio,] 3AC; ~∧ MS1eC
288.34–35	friend, . . . produced] 3AC; friends, produced MS1eC; friends produced 1EC
288.36	such a] 1EC, 2EC, 3AC; such MS1eC
288.38	Venice,] 3AC; ~∧ MS1eC
288.39	man's] 3AC; mans MS1eC
288.40–289.10	Fantina. The date . . . extinguished] 3AC; Fantina. The three sons of his father by the second marriage died without male issue, and the family of Polo was extinguished in 1417. MS1eC
289.16–17	Grand Khan] 3AC; grand ~ MS1eC
289.21–22	had . . . madding about] 3AC; excited so many speculations about MS1eC
289.22	East, the] 3AC; east, ~, MS1eC
290.1	No. XXI] 3AC; No XIX. MS1eC
290.4	Latin] 3AC; latin MS1eC
290.4–5	written . . . Italian] 3AC; written in Italian MS1eC
290.8	Europe. In] 3AC; *New paragraph in MS1eC*
290.9	Purchas] 3AC; Parchas MS1eC
290.14–21	and Vossius . . . world] 3AC; but Vossius assures us that it was at one time highly esteemed among the learned MS1eC
290.22	learned. Francis] 3AC; *New paragraph in MS1eC*
290.23	piety] 3AC; devoutness MS1eC
290.23	commendable] 1EC, 2EC, 3AC; recommendable MS1eC

290.25   kingdoms]   3AC; Kingdoms MS1eC
290.25–26   remote East]   3AC; remote parts of the East MS1eC
290.26   men of past times]   3AC; men MS1eC
290.29–291.11   travellers. The most . . . others.]   3AC; travellers. It is
                  manifest, however, that he dealt much in exaggera-
                  tion. The historical part of his work is full of errors
                  and fables. He confuses the names of places, is very
                  inexact as to distances, and gives no latitudes of the
                  places he visited.
                      It has been strongly doubted whether he really
                  visited all the countries he described, and whether
                  his account of Tartary and Cathay, and of different
                  parts of India and the African coasts, were not taken
                  from Mahometan narrations.
                      Ramusio thinks that a great part of the third book
                  was collected by him from narrations of mariners of
                  the Indian seas. Athanasius Kircher is at a loss to
                  know· why he makes no mention of the great wall
                  of China, which he must have passed, unless he vis-
                  ited that country by water.
                      The most probable opinion given concerning him
                  is, that he really visited part of the countries which
                  he describes, and collected information from various
                  sources concerning the others; that he kept no regu-
                  lar journal, but after his return home composed his
                  work from various memorandums, and from memory.
                  Thus what he had seen and what he had heard be-
                  came mixed up in his mind; and floating fables of the
                  East were noted down with as much gravity and
                  authority as well as ascertained facts.   MS1eC
290.38   Prevost,]   3AC; ∼∧ MS1eC
290.38   tom. . . . lib. . . . cap.]   3AC; t. . . . l. . . . c. MS1eC
291.12   Polo,]   3AC; ∼∧ MS1eC
291.13   Michale]   3AC; Michael MS1eC
291.15   countries]   3AC; Countries MS1eC
291.18   this]   3AC; the MS1eC
291.20   Prior,]   3AC; prior of it, MS1eC
291.22   others']   T; others MS1eC; other 1EC
291.23–24   on comparing it]   3AC; in company with MS1eC
291.25   Cape]   3AC; cape MS1eE
291.26   additions]   3AC; alterations MS1eC
291.33   fifteenth]   3AC; 15th MS1eC

291.35   Comte]   3AC; conte MS1eC
291.36   Ramusio,]   3AC; ~∧ MS1eC
291.36   vol.]   3AC; v. MS1eC
291.37–41   +Mr. Marsden . . . xliii]   3AC; *Missing in MS1eC*.
292.6   him. He]   3AC; him. He is supposed to have had a
                 manuscript copy by him. He MS1eC
292.15   winter]   3AC; principal MS1eC
292.15   Great Khan]   3AC; great ~ MS1eC
292.16   Cambalu, or Kanbalu,]   3AC; Cambalu MS1eC
292.15   Polo,]   3AC; ~∧ MS1eC
292.16   Pekin), 3AC; ~∧ MS1eC
292.22   "Here]   3AC; ∧~ MS1eC
292.23   silks,]   3AC; silk, MS1eC
292.25   city."]   3AC; ~.∧ MS1eC
292.26   The]   3AC; "The MS1eC
292.27   group]   3AC; groupe MS1eC
292.27   resplendent]   3AC; resplendant MS1eC
292.34   contained,]   3AC; ~∧ MS1eC
292.40   Voyages,]   3AC; Voyages. MS1eC
292.40   lib. . . . 4.]   3AC; l. . . . 3. MS1eC
293.3   literally, for he]   3AC; for truth. He MS1eC
293.4–12   circuit . . . built]   3AC; circuit*; that it is built MS1eC;
                 Canceled footnote reads: *Mandeville, speaking of
                 Cambalu, says it is ten miles of Lombardy in circuit,
                 which makes eight miles.
293.12   as built . . . has]   MS3AC; 3AC; as being built and
                 having MS2eC
293.15   has . . . three]   3AC; has three MS1eC
293.15   baths, and six]   3AC; baths. It has six MS1eC
293.17   walls,]   3AC; ~∧ MS1eC
293.18   rank.†]   3AC; rank. MS1eC
293.21   artisans,]   3AC; artizans MS1eC
293.26   Zipangu, Zipangri]   3AC; Zipangri, Zipangu 1AC
293.27   Mangi . . . Marco]   3AC; Mangi, in the ocean, lay the
                 great island of Zipangu, or is Columbus writes it,
                 Cipango, and which is supposed to be Japan. Marco
                 MS1eC
293.30   Hornius,]   3AC; ~∧ MS1eC
293.30   Origin]   3AC; origin MS1eC
293.30   "Who . . . example,]   3AC; ∧~ . . . ~∧ MS1eC
293.31   bridges.]   3AC; ~, on each of which is a tower. MS1eC
293.32   high!"]   3AC; high! MS1eC

293.33–34   Mandeville, . . . city,]   3AC; ∼_∧ . . . ∼_∧ MS1eC
293.34   Cansai,]   3AC; ∼_∧ MS1eC
293.36–39   †Sir . . . palace]   3AC; *Missing in MS1eC*
294.1   Polo]   3AC; ∼, MS1eC
294.4   the palaces]   3AC; the roofs of the palaces MS1eC
294.9   stones,]   3AC; ∼_∧ MS1eC
294.9   Great Khan]   3AC; great ∼ MS1eC
294.12–13   virtue . . . which]   3AC; virtue tied to their arms,
              which MS1eC
294.14   island was]   3AC; island of Zipango MS1eC
294.16   Zipangu]   3AC; Zipangri MS1eC
294.18   forty,]   3AC; 48 MS1eC
294.24   visit]   3AC; ∼, MS1eC
294.25   Great Khan]   3AC; great khan MS1eC, 1EC
294.30   anticipations . . . Columbus]   3AC; anticipations of
              Columbus MS1eC
294.34–41   *Supposed . . . former]   3AC; *Missing in MS1eC*
295.1   those]   1EC, 2EC, 3AC; these MS1eC
295.4   No. XXII]   3AC; No. XX. MS1eC
295.7   Great Khan]   3AC; great ∼ MS1eC
295.9   city]   3AC; town MS1eC
295.12   Asia]   3AC; asia MS1eC
295.15   Upper and Lower]   3AC; upper and lower MS1eC
295.16   Indies]   3AC; Indias MS1eC
295.18   Land]   3AC; land MS1eC
295.19   minuteness]   1EC, 2EC, MS2eC, 3AC; exactitude MS1eC
295.23   Latin]   3AC; latin MS1eC
295.31   Ortelius]   3AC; Orteleus MS1eC
296.2   calling, viz.]   3AC; calling (viz.) MS1eC
296.5   housings]   3AC; housing MS1eC
296.8   no less splendid]   3AC; scarcely less extravagant MS1eC
296.10   hall]   3AC; Hall MS1eC
296.13   care . . . and of]   3AC; care of the Elephants, of which
              there were ten thousand, and of MS1eC
296.16   Khan,]   3AC; ∼_∧ MS1eC
296.17   exalted]   1EC, 2EC, 3AC; high MS1eC
296.20   Mandeville]   3AC; ∼, MS1eC
296.30   sun,]   3AC; ∼_∧ MS1eC
297.12   Strabo,]   3AC; ∼_∧ MS1eC
297.17–18   Capricorn . . . Cape . . . Hope]   3AC; capricorn . . .
              cape . . . hope MS1eC
297.23   zones. "The]   3AC; zones, "the MS1eC

279.23–24	earth," . . . "where] 3AC; earth, . . . where MS1eC
297.26	region."] 3AC; region. MS1eC
297.27	(lib. xi] 3AC; (Lib. ii MS1eC
297.33	Portuguese, . . . true.] 3AC; Portuguese . . . true MS1eC
297.40	Aristotle,] 3AC; Aristot. MS1eC
297.41	cap.] 3AC; c. MS1eC
297.41	Pliny, lib.] 3AC; ~. Lib. MS1eC
298.4	No. XXIV] 3AC; No. XXII. MS1eC
298.7	Solon,] 3AC; ~‸ MS1eC
298.9	Nile] 3AC; nile MS1eC
298.15	continent] 3AC; Continent MS1eC
298.16	island,] 3AC; ~‸ MS1eC
298.19	Libya] 3AC; Lybia MS1eC
298.20	and all] 1EC, 2EC, 3AC; and MS1eC
298.21	resisted, however,] 3AC; ~‸ ~‸ MS1eC
298.23	earthquake] 3AC; Earthquake MS1eC
298.23	overflowing] 3AC; over flowing MS1eC
298.23	sea,] 3AC; ~‸ MS1eC
298.27	time, however,] 3AC; ~‸ ~‸ MS1eC
298.28	mud and] 3AC; mud & MS1eC
298.31	had] 1EC, 2EC, 3AC; has MS1eC
298.32	Islands,] 3AC; islands, MS1eC
299.2	continent] 3AC; Continent MS1eC
299.7	New World] 3AC; Newworld MS1eC
299.9	is] 1EC, 2EC, 3AC; are MS1eC
299.15	Typhisque] 3AC; typhisque MS1eC, 1EC
299.16	orbes] 3AC; Orbes MS1eC, 1EC
299.30	it,] 3AC; ~‸ MS1eC
299.31	nowhere] 3AC; no where MS1eC
299.31–32	eye-witnesses] 3AC; persons MS1eC
299.33	Critico,] 3AC; ~. MS1eC
300.4	1492,] 3AC; ~‸ MS1eC
300.4	M. De Murr] 3AC; M. Murr MS1eC
300.7	Columbus] 3AC; ~, MS1eC
300.9	do] 3AC; di MS1eC
300.13	Terra Firma] 3AC; terra firma MS1eC
300.13–14	Island of the Seven Cities;] T; island of the seven cities; MS1eC
300.18	caravels] 3AC; Caravels MS1eC
300.20	Borondon] 3AC; Borondan MS1eC
300.20	island] 3AC; Island MS1eC
300.22	sixth century] 3AC; 6th Century MS1eC

300.24   martyrology]   3AC; Martyrology MS1eC
300.25   patriarch]   1EC, 2EC, MS3AC, 3AC; father or superior
                    MS1eC
300.25   3,000]   1EC, 2EC, 3AC; three thousand MS1eC
300.28   ocean]   3AC; Ocean MS1eC
300.29   These]   3AC; After these MS1eC
300.30   and at]   3AC; they at MS1eC
300.30   ocean]   3AC; Ocean MS1eC
300.34   a gratifying account]   3AC; an account MS1eC
300.35   pagans]   3AC; Pagans MS1eC
300.40   Tombo,]   3AC; ∼∧ MS1eC
300.40   do]   3AC; di MS1eC
301.4   ocean]   3AC; Ocean MS1eC
301.5   crystal]   3AC; christal MS1eC
301.8   rose]   3AC; a rose MS1eC
301.10   Easter]   3AC; easter MS1eC
301.12   appears,]   3AC; ∼∧ MS1eC
301.15   monstrous]   3AC; monstruous MS1eC
301.19   Latin]   3AC; latin MS1eC
301.20–21   in which . . . recorded]   1EC, 2EC, 3AC; in which was
                    recorded the adventures of these saints MS1eC
301.23–24   Fortunate . . . Islands]   3AC; fortunate islands MS1eC
301.24   names]   3AC; name MS1eC
301.24   or the Inaccessible]   3AC; a Greek word signifying the
                    inaccessible MS1eC
301.25–26   Incarnation]   3AC; incarnation MS1eC
301.32   nor]   3AC; or MS1eC
301.35   Garcia,]   3AC; ∼∧ MS1eC
301.36   Sigeberto,]   3AC; Sigiberto. MS1eC
301.36   Tietmar]   3AC; Teitmar MS1eC
301.37   Pena,]   3AC; ∼. MS1eC
301.38   Ptolemy,]   3AC; ∼∧ MS1eC
301.38   lib. . . . to.]   3AC; l. . . . t. MS1eC
301.39   Philipo,]   3AC; ∼∧ MS1eC
301.39   lib. . . . cap.]   3AC; l. . . . c. MS1eC
302.5   and of the]   3AC; and the MS1eC
302.8   "The phantasm]   3AC; the fantasm MS1eC
302.9   however," . . . "had]   3AC; ∼,∧ . . . ∧∼ MS1eC
302.11   senses."]   3AC; ∼.∧ MS1eC
302.20   respectability]   1EC, 2EC, MS2eC, 3AC;   standing
                    MS1eC
302.22   calmness]   1EC, 3AC; quiet MS1eC

302.26–27	Borondon] 3AC; Barandon MS1eC
302.27	Vello,] 3AC; $\sim_\wedge$ MS1eC
302.27	asserted] 1EC, 2EC, MS2eC, 3AC; affirmed MS1eC
302.28	bay] 3AC; Bay MS1eC
302.28	in] 1EC, 2EC, 3AC; on MS1eC
303.5	Grand] 3AC; grand MS1eC
303.8	parts.] 3AC; $\sim$: MS1eC
303.15	It . . . the] 3AC; "It was now," he said, "the MS1eC
303.19	approaching,] 3AC; $\sim_\wedge$ MS1eC
303.19	signal] 3AC; signals MS1eC
303.25	island.] 3AC; island." MS1eC
303.26	in manuscript] 3AC; in a manuscript MS1eC, 1EC
303.33–34	island, however,] 3AC; $\sim_\wedge$ $\sim_\wedge$ MS1eC
303.40	Pena, . . . Viera,] 3AC; Pena. . . . Viera. MS1eC
303.40	lib. . . . cap.] 3AC; l. . . . c. MS1eC
303.40	tom. . . . cap.] 3AC; t. . . . c. MS1eC
303.41	Nuñez,] 3AC; $\sim_\wedge$ MS1eC
303.41	Viera.] 3AC; $\sim_\wedge$ MS1eC
303.41	Conquista] 3AC; Conquist. MS1eC
304.1	another] 1EC, 2EC, MS2eC, 3AC; another quixotic MS1eC
304.5	paradise] 3AC; Paradize MS1eC
304.11	St.] 3AC; San MS1eC
304.11	however,] 3AC; $\sim_\wedge$ MS1eC
304.14	thing] 3AC; think MS1eC
304.20	Gomera] 3AC; Gomara MS1eC
304.21	St.] 3AC; San MS1eC
304.23	Dominguez,] 3AC; $\sim_\wedge$ MS1eC
304.26	October] 3AC; october MS1eC
304.27	curiosity] 1EC, 2EC, MS2eC, 3AC; curiosity mingled with superstition MS1eC
304.28	predecessors] 3AC; predessors MS1eC
304.32	Gomera, 1759,] 3AC; $\sim_\wedge$ $\sim_\wedge$ MS1eC
304.36	telescope] 3AC; Telescope MS1eC
304.38	persons,] 3AC; $\sim_\wedge$ MS1eC
304.41	Viera,] 3AC; $\sim$. MS1eC
304.41	tom. . . . cap.] 3AC; t. . . . c. MS1eC
305.3	Observations on Natural History] 3AC; observations on natural history MS1eC
305.26	St.] 3AC; San MS1eC
305.38	tom. . . . cap.] 3AC; t. . . . c. MS1eC
306.7	No. XXVI] 3AC; No. XXIV. MS1eC

306.9	ocean] 3AC; Ocean MS1eC
306.16	island] 3AC; Island MS1eC
306.16	ocean] 3AC; Ocean MS1eC
306.19	island] 3AC; Island MS1eC
307.2	prince expressed] 3AC; prince, it is said, expressed MS1eC
307.10	Spain, reports] 3AC; Spain, extravagant reports MS1eC
307.12	clothing;] 3AC; ∼, MS1eC
307.18	New] 3AC; new MS1eC
307.20	No. XXVIII] 3AC; No. XXV MS1eC
307.23	Alcaforado,] 3AC; Alcaforada MS1eC
307.27	Juan] 3AC; Joam MS1eC
307.27	Gonzalez] 3AC; Gonsalez MS1eC
307.27	Tristram] 3AC; Tristam MS1eC, 1EC
307.29	abbé] 3AC; abbe MS1eC
307.29	General History of Voyages] 3AC; general history of voyages MS1eC
307.31	cap.] 3AC; c. MS1eC
307.32	Torquemada,] 3AC; ∼∧ MS1eC
307.32	lib. . . . cap.] 3AC; l. . . . c. MS1eC
307.33	Garcia,] 3AC; ∼∧ MS1eC
307.33	lib. . . . cap.] 3AC; l. . . . c. MS1eC
307.34	Barros,] 3AC; ∼∧ MS1eC
307.34	lib.] 3AC; l. MS1eC
308.4	participated in] 1EC, 2EC, 3AC; asissted at MS1eC
308.4	discovery."] 3AC; ∼.∧ MS1eC
308.8	story, however,] 3AC; ∼∧ ∼∧ MS1eC
308.12	III] 3AC; the third MS1eC
308.26	obtained an introduction] 1EC, 2EC, 3AC; got introduced MS1eC
308.30	France,] 3AC; france MS1eC
308.34	galloped] 3AC; gallopped MS1eC
308.37	a-trip] 3AC; a trip MS1eC
309.2	land;] 3AC; ∼, MS1eC
309.4	traverse] 1EC, 2EC, 3AC; voyage upon MS1eC
309.5	ocean] 3AC; Ocean MS1eC
309.26	met] 3AC; ∼, MS1eC
309.29	a sheltered] 3AC; a beautiful sheltered MS1eC
309.42	ocean] 3AC; Ocean MS1eC
310.10–11	broken-hearted] 3AC; broken hearted MS1eC
310.23	Morocco] 3AC; Marocco MS1eC
310.28	Morocco] 3AC; Marocco MS1eC

310.33	circumstances, . . . said,] 3AC; ~_∧ . . . ~_∧ MS1eC
310.37	III,] T; ~_∧ MS1eC
310.41	forty] 3AC; 40 MS1eC
310.42	Hakluyt] 3AC; Hacluyt MS1eC
311.1	It . . . in] 3AC; "It happened," he says, "in MS1eC
311.2	IV] T; 4 MS1eC
311.8	country,] 3AC; ~_∧ MS1eC
311.10	island] 3AC; Island." MS1eC
311.11	No. XXVIII] 3AC; No. XXVI. MS1eC
311.14	New World] 3AC; new world MS1eC
311.14	French] 3AC; french MS1eC
311.17	Moors] 3AC; moors MS1eC
311.18	Moors] 3AC; moors MS1eC
311.22	Antonio, . . . Bartholomew,] 3AC; ~_∧ . . . ~_∧ MS1eC
311.24	biographers] 3AC; Biographers MS1eC
311.26	This, however,] 3AC; ~_∧ ~_∧ MS1eC
311.26	incorrect. He] 3AC; ~, he MS1eC
311.27	dialectics] 1EC, 2EC, MS2eC, MS3AC, 3AC; the Dialectics of the peripatetic philosophers MS1eC
311.29	system] 3AC; principles MS1eC
311.33	Navarrete, Colec.] 3AC; ~. Collec. MS1eC
311.33	tom.] 3AC; t. MS1eC
311.34	T. A.] 3AC; J. A. MS1eC
311.34	Llorente,] 3AC; ~. MS1eC
312.9	meliorate] 3AC; ameliorate MS1eC
312.10	New World] 3AC; new world MS1eC
312.16	Atocha,] 3AC; ~_∧ MS1eC
312.25	Valladolid,] 3AC; ~_∧ MS1eC
312.29	colonies] 3AC; Colonies MS1eC
312.31	Indies] 3AC; Indias MS1eC
312.34	Selvagio] 3AC; Salvagio MS1eC
312.35	became . . . with] 1EC, MS2eC, 3AC; got on intimate terms with MS1eC
312.40	Selvagio] 3AC; Salvaggio MS1eC
312.41	clearly states] 3AC; states MS1eC
312.41	when others] 3AC; when all others MS1eC
313.4–5	chancellor, . . . man,] 3AC; ~_∧ . . . ~_∧ MS1eC
313.6	could] 3AC; would MS1eC
313.9	might, moreover,] 3AC; ~_∧ ~_∧ MS1eC
313.11–12	New World] 3AC; new world MS1eC
313.16	than] 1EC, 2EC, 3AC; that MS1eC
313.32–33	New World."] 3AC; new world. MS1eC

313.33	grievous] 3AC; grevious MS1eC
313.35	decree] 3AC; decrees MS1eC
313.38	havia] 3AC; habia MS1eC
313.39	Canciller] 3AC; conciller MS1eC
313.39	*expedientes*] 3AC; expedientes MS1eC
313.39	efecto,] 3AC; ~∧ MS1eC
313.40	lib. . . . cap.] 3AC; l. . . . c. MS1eC
313.41	Herrera, . . . lib. . . . cap] 3AC; ~∧ l. . . . c. MS1eC
313.42	Idem,] 3AC; ~∧ MS1eC
313.42	lib. . . . cap.] 3AC; l. . . . c. MS1eC
314.1	New World] 3AC; new world MS1eC
314.3–4	written by] 1EC, 2EC, 3AC; of MS1eC
314.8	with] 3AC; amongst MS1eC
314.8	Moors] 3AC; moors MS1eC
314.9	Christian] 3AC; christian MS1eC
314.16	V] 1EC, 2EC, 3AC; I (and V) MS1eC
314.19	with the] 2EC, MS2eC, 3AC; with a MS1eC, 1EC
314.21–22	Jeronimite] 3AC; Geronimite MS1eC
314.24	evil] 1EC, 2EC, MS2EC, 3AC; a wrong MS1eC
314.25	abuses] 1EC, 2EC, 3AC; evils MS1eC
314.30	permitted;] 3AC; ~, MS1eC
314.35	that of Las] 1EC, 2EC, 3AC; that Las MS1eC
314.38	D.] 3AC; Decad MS1eC
314.38	Herrera,] 3AC; ~∧ MS1eC
314.38	lib. . . . cap.] 3AC; l. . . . c. MS1eC
314.39	lib. . . . cap.] 3AC; l. . . . c. MS1eC
314.41	lib. . . . cap.] 3AC; l. . . . c. MS1eC
315.11	sunk] 1EC, 2EC, MS2eC, 3AC; sank MS1eC
315.13	throve] 1EC, 2EC, 3AC; thrived MS1eC
315.33	wear] 3AC; bear MS1eC
315.34	facts,] 3AC; ~∧ MS1eC
315.38	i se] 3AC; y se MS1eC
315.40	á] 3AC; a MS1eC
315.42	lib.] 3AC; l. MS1eC
316.8	Moors] 3AC; moors MS1eC
316.9	Caribbee] 3AC; Carribee MS1eC, 1EC
316.10	Islands] 3AC; islands MS1eC
316.12–13	Inquisition . . . New World] 3AC; inquisition . . . new world MS1eC
316.14	Ximenes,] 3AC; ~∧ MS1eC
316.19	General History of the Indies,] 3AC; general history of the Indias MS1eC

316.20   the discovery]   3AC; their discovery MS1eC
316.20   1520,]   3AC; ~∧ MS1eC
316.22   New World]   3AC; new world MS1eC
316.28   1559,]   3AC; ~∧ MS1eC
317.1   eyes"]   3AC; ~," MS1eC
317.9   energy]   1EC, 2EC, 3AC; pith and character MS1eC
317.27   Predicadores]   3AC; predicadores MS1eC
317.27   Gregorio,]   3AC; ~∧ MS1eC
317.30   Indies]   3AC; Indians MS1eC
317.30–31   and of Spain]   1EC, 2EC, MS2eC, 3AC; and Spain
                   MS1eC
317.38   Mons.]   3AC; Mon. MS1eC
317.38   T. A.]   T; J. A. MS1eC, 3AC
317.39   History]   3AC; history MS1eC
317.41   Navarrete, Colec.]   3AC; Navarrete Collec. MS1eC
317.41   Colec. . . . tom.]   3AC; Collec. . . . t. MS1eC
318.2   Indies]   3AC; Indias MS1eC
318.3   age,]   3AC; ~∧ MS1eC
318.10   discovery,]   3AC; ~∧ MS1eC
318.11   countrymen: men]   3AC; ~. Men MS1eC
318.14   meliorate]   3AC; ameliorate MS1eC
318.14   condition]   1EC, 2EC, MS2eC, 3AC; conditions MS1eC
318.19   No. XXIX]   3AC; No. XXVII MS1eC
318.23   on the second of February]   3AC; on February 2ᵈ
                   MS1eC
318.24   Latin]   3AC; latin MS1eC
318.26   Being at]   3AC; Being born at MS1eC
318.26   1487,]   3AC; ~∧ MS1eC
318.34   Talavera,]   3AC; ~∧ MS1eC
319.11   Moors]   3AC; moors MS1eC
319.13   extraordinary]   3AC; Extraordinary MS1eC
319.29   Indies]   3AC; Indias MS1eC
319.30   New World]   3AC; new world MS1eC
319.32   New World]   3AC; new world MS1eC
319.33   Latin,]   3AC; ~∧ MS1eC
319.39   153,]   3AC; ~∧ MS1eC
320.2   Indies]   3AC; Indias MS1eC
320.2   Muñoz]   3AC; Munoz MS1eC
320.2   allows]   3AC; allowed MS1eC
320.4   entire]   1EC, 2EC, MS2eC, 3AC; well known MS1eC
320.6   related]   1EC, 2EC, 3AC; gave MS1eC
320.7   that]   3AC; That MS1eC

320.17   May 1st, 1493,]   3AC; May 1 1493 MS1eC
320.18   Borromeo, he says,]   3AC ;~ₐ ~ₐ MS1eC
320.27   diocess]   3AC; Diocess MS1eC
321.23   thing]   3AC; event MS1eC
321.24   Columbus,]   3AC; ~ₐ MS1eC
321.27   sky]   3AC; land MS1eC
321.31   beguiled perchance by]   1EC, 2EC, 3AC; beguiled by
                MS1eC
321.31   scene]   1EC, 2EC, 3AC; event MS1eC
321.37   succeed,"]   3AC; ~ₐ" MS1eC
321.38   Farewell."†]   3AC; farewell.* MS1eC
321.39   Valladolid, February 1st, 1494,]   3AC; ~ₐ ~1ₐ ~ₐ
                MS1eC
322.1   observes,]   3AC; ~; MS1eC
322.10   9th,]   3AC; 9th MS1eC
322.20–21   weight ... mention]   3AC; that one is afraid to mention;
                MS1eC; almost passing belief. 1EC
322.21   weigh]   1EC, 2EC, 3AC; have been found weighing
                MS1eC
322.21   discover]   1EC, 2EC, 3AC; find MS1eC
322.23   or]   3AC; nor MS1eC
322.23   Polyphemi,]   3AC; ~ₐ MS1eC
322.26   Islands,]   3AC; islands MS1eC
322.29   Caribbees]   3AC; carribbees MS1eC, 1EC
322.39   Idem,]   3AC; ~ₐ MS1eC
322.40   Idem,]   3AC; ~ₐ MS1eC
323.6   Decades]   3AC; decades MS1eC
323.10   misrepresentation]   3AC; misreprensation MS1eC
323.16   No. XXX] 3AC; No. XXVIII MS1eC
323.19   Madrid,]   3AC; ~ₐ MS1eC
323.20   Asturian]   3AC; asturian MS1eC
323.28   New World]   3AC; new world MS1eC
323.29   foundries]   3AC; founderies MS1eC
323.30   grandson]   3AC; grand son MS1eC
323.31   alcayde]   T; Alcaydee MS1eC
323.32–33   historiographer . . . Indies]   3AC; Historiographer . . .
                Indias MS1eC
323.35   ocean]   3AC; Ocean MS1eC
324.1   works:]   3AC; ~, MS1eC
324.2   Chronicle . . . Indies]   3AC; chronicle . . . Indias
                MS1eC
324.3   nineteen]   3AC; 19 MS1eC

324.14	caution, and often] 1EC, 2EC, 3AC; caution, often MS1eC
324.17	Hernan] 3AC; Herman MS1eC
324.17	Matteo,] 3AC; Matheo MS1eC
324.20	New World] 3AC; new world MS1eC
324.23	New World] 3AC; new world MS1eC
324.27	No. XXXI] 3AC; No. XXIX MS1eC
324.29	Andres Bernaldes] 3AC; Andrez Bernaldez MS1eC
324.32	Deza,] 3AC; ~∧ MS1eC
324.33	Bernaldes] 3AC; Bernaldez MS1eC
325.1	history] 3AC; History MS1eC
325.6–39	Nothing . . . Deza."] 3AC; *Missing in MS1eC*
325.40	In] 3AC; *No paragraph in MS1eC*
325.40	Rich, esq.] 3AC; Rich Esq. MS1eC
326.1	chronicle . . . already] 3AC; chronicle, already MS1eC
326.3	times,] 3AC; ~∧ MS1eC
326.7	to be] 3AC; to have been MS1eC
326.8	No. XXXII] 3AC; No. XXX MS1eC
326.9	delle] 3AC; dele MS1eC
326.10	*Nuovamente Ritrovate*] 3AC; Nuevamente Retrovate MS1eC
326.17–18	voyages] 3AC; Voyages MS1eC
326.18	Mondo Novo, e Paese] 3AC; mondo novo, e paese MS1eC
326.18	Nuovamente Ritrovate] 3AC; nuevamente retrovati MS1eC
326.20	in a Latin] 1EC, 2EC, 3AC; in latin, MS1eC
326.25	Latin] 1EC; latin MS1eC
326.26	Novus Orbis Regionum, &c.] 3AC; novus orbis regionum +c. MS1eC
326.26	Basle, 1555] 3AC; ~∧ ~ MS1eC
326.30	Latin] 3AC; latin MS1eC
326.30	Portugallensium,] 3AC; ~∧ MS1eC
326.32	Decade] 3AC; decade MS1eC
327.2–3	Martyr's] 3AC; Martyrs MS1eC
327.3–4	1516, . . . Seville] 3AC; 1516. MS1eC
327.6	Historical Memoir] 3AC; historical memoir MS1eC
327.12	oblong] 3AC; lengthened MS1eC
327.13	historian] 3AC; Historian MS1eC
327.19	Sabellicus] 3AC; Sabillicus MS1eC
327.20	Martyr's] 3AC; Martyrs MS1eC
327.21	No. XXXIII] 3AC; No. XXXI MS1eC

327.23	Tordesillas,] 3AC; ∼∧ MS1eC
327.25	Herrera,] 3AC; ∼∧ MS1eC
327.26	brother] 3AC; Brother MS1eC
327.26	Gonzago] 3AC; Gonzaga MS1eC
327.29	Indies] 3AC; Indias MS1eC
327.29	II,] 3AC; 2 MS1eC
327.31	General] 3AC; general MS1eC
327.31	Indies] 3AC; Indias MS1eC
328.6	Indies] 3AC; Indias MS1eC
328.11	Herrera,] 3AC; ∼∧ MS1eC
328.14	"that] 3AC; ∧∼ MS1eC
328.16	a writer] 1EC, 2EC, MS2eC, 3AC; one MS1eC
328.16–17	intends to compose] 1EC, 2EC, 3AC; to write MS1eC
328.25	serious] 1EC, 2EC, 3AC; grave MS1eC
328.29	error,] 3AC; ∼∧ MS1eC
328.32	described] 1EC, 2EC, MS2eC, 3AC; observed MS1eC
328.33	positions] 3AC; postion MS1eC
328.33	capes . . . islands] 3AC; Capes . . . Islands MS1eC
328.34	lakes,] 3AC; ∼; MS1eC
328.40	histories,] 3AC; ∼∧ MS1eC
329.1	eulogiums] 3AC; Eulogiums MS1eC
329.2	Indies] 3AC; Indias MS1eC
329.3	Still,] 3AC; ∼∧ MS1eC
329.7	sixty] 3AC; 60 MS1eC
329.8	IV] 3AC; 4 MS1eC
329.10	No. XXXIV] 3AC; No. XXXII MS1eC
329.16	1493,] 3AC; ∼∧ MS1eC
329.24	unhealthy] 3AC; unwholesome MS1eC; ungracious 1EC
330.3	superintendence] 3AC; superintendance MS1eC
330.11	retaining] 1EC, 2EC, 3AC; holding MS1eC
330.13	colonies.] 3AC; Colonies. MS1eC
330.16	Cortez] 3AC; Cortes MS1eC
330.20	Cortez] 3AC; Cortes MS1eC
330.21	Cuba,] 3AC; ∼∧ MS1eC
330.22	Fonseca,] 3AC; ∼∧ MS1eC
330.27	Cortez] 3AC; Cortes MS1eC
330.29	Cortez] 3AC; Cortes MS1eC
330.33	talent or character] 1ES, 2EC, 3AC; talent or weight of character MS1eC
330.35	Bobadilla,] 3AC; ∼∧ MS1eC
330.36	Cortez] 3AC; Cortes MS1eC

330.39   Herrera,]   3AC; ∼∧ MS1eC
330.39   lib. . . . cap.]   3AC; l. . . . c. MS1eC
330.40   lib. . . . cap.]   3AC; l. . . . c. MS1eC
331.3   governor]   3AC; Governor MS1eC
331.4   disloyal.]   3AC; disloyal*. MS1eC. *The canceled MS1eC
                footnote reads:* *Herrera, Hist. Ind. D. III. l. iii. c. 16
331.4   Cortez]   3AC; Cortes MS1eC
331.5   Cortez]   3AC; Cortes MS1eC
*331.6–332.9   and he. . . . perfidious]   MS2eC, 3AC; *Paragraph*: When
                the disputes between Cortez and Velazquez came to
                be examined and decided upon in Spain, the father
                of Cortez and his lawyers objected to Fonseca's being
                one of the arbitrators, alleging his enmity to Cortez,
                his patronage of Velazquez, and his being on the
                point of giving his sister in marriage to the latter.
                Cardinal Adrien examined the matter thoroughly, and
                decided that their request ought to be granted. Fon-
                seca was ordered, therefore, not to preside in these
                affairs; "it being likewise alleged," says Herrera, "that
                he had publicly called Cortez a traitor; that he had
                prevented his representations from being attended
                to in the council of the Indies; and had declared that
                they should never come there while he lived; that
                he had not given the king complete information in
                matters relative to these points of service; and that
                he had ordered the India house at Seville not to
                permit arms, merchandise, or people to go to New
                Spain*." Cortez himself subsequently declared, "that
                he had experienced more trouble and difficulty from
                the menaces and affronts of the ministers of the
                king, than it had cost him to earn his victory†."
                A charge of a still darker nature against Fonseca
                may be found lurking in the pages of Herrera, though
                so obscure as to have escaped the notice of succeed-
                ing historians. He points to the bishop as the insti-
                gator of a desperate and perfidious / * Herrera, Hist.
                Ind. D. III. l. iv. c. 13. / † Idem, D. III. l. i. c. I.
                MS1eC, 1EC, 2EC
332.12   Verdujo]   3AC; Verdugo MS1eC
332.14   Cortez]   3AC; Cortes MS1eC
332.14   relenting, apprized]   3AC; ∼∧ ∼ MS1eC
332.20   Cortez]   3AC; Cortes MS1eC

332.21	Cortez] 3AC; Cortes MS1eC
332.21	Velazquez, this] 3AC; Velazquez, which took place in 1522 before a special tribunal, composed of the grand chancellor and other persons of note, this MS1eC
332.23	Cortez] 3AC; Cortes MS1eC
332.25	Fonseca,] 3AC; ~!MS1eC
332.32	lib. . . . cap.] 3AC; l. . . . c. MS1eC
332.33	lib. . . . cap.] 3AC; l. . . . c. MS1eC
333.1	No. XXXV] 3AC; No. XXXIII MS1eC
333.2	On] 3AC; Of MS1eC
333.8–9	The abode . . . indeed,] 1EC, 2EC, 3AC; The world has ever been inquisitive as to the abode of our first parents, described in such engaging colours in holy writ; and indeed MS1eC
333.9–10	some place of] 1EC, 2EC, 3AC; some such place of MS1eC
333.15	Greeks] 1EC, 2EC, 3AC; greeks MS1eC
333.16	on] 1EC, 2EC, 3AC; in MS1eC
333.20	travellers,] 3AC; ~∧ MS1eC
333.24	its] 1EC, 3AC; its its MS1eC
333.25	Island . . . Blessed] 3AC; island . . . blessed MS1eC
333.28	Syrtis,] 3AC; Syrte MS1eC
333.28	Mount] 3AC; mount MS1eC
333.28	Here,] 3AC; ~∧ MS1eC
333.29–30	a fair . . . country] 1EC, 2EC, 3AC; an embowered country MS1eC
333.31	where] 1EC, 2EC, 3AC; when MS1eC
333.32	Athenians] 3AC; athenians MS1eC
333.35	place, still] 3AC; place, but still MS1eC
333.36	exist in] 3AC; visit MS1eC; to be placed in 1AC
333.36	Canaries] 3AC; Canarys MS1eC
333.37	Fortunate . . . Islands] 3AC; fortunate . . . islands MS1eC
334.4–5	subject . . . occupied] 3AC; subject of curious disputation, among zealous Christians, and occupied MS1eC
334.6	Holy Land] 3AC; holy land MS1eC
334.14	Fortunate . . . Islands] 3AC; fortunate . . . islands MS1eC
334.20	Gihon] 3AC; Gehon MS1eC
334.21	Hiddekel. Those] 1EC, 2EC, 3AC; Heddekel. To sup-

	ply these streams the pious disputants have done little less than effect miracles. Those MS1eC
334.21–22	Holy Land] 3AC; holy land MS1eC
334.23	Gihon] 3AC; Gehon MS1eC
334.25	supplied; that] 3AC; ~. That MS1eC
334.25	Deserta] 3AC; deserta MS1eC
334.27	Gihon] 3AC; Gehon MS1eC
334.27	Stony] 3AC; Stoney MS1eC
334.28	Red Sea] 3AC; red sea MS1eC
334.29	Chaldea] 3AC; chaldea MS1eC
334.29–30	Persian] 3AC; persian MS1eC
334.31	Gihon] 3AC; Gehon MS1eC
334.33	from . . . Tigris] 1EC, 2EC, 3AC; from those of the Tigris MS1eC
334.33	Euphrates arose] 1EC, 2EC, 3AC; Eurhrates. MS1eC, 1AC
334.40	Gosselin, Recherches . . . tom.] 3AC; Gosselyn, Recherch . . . t. MS1eC
335.4	earth] 3AC; Earth MS1eC
335.8	Some contended] 1EC, 2EC, 3AC; Some, to sweep away all difficulties, contended MS1eC, 1AC
335.11–12	Augustine, . . . Genesis,] 3AC; Augustine, who in his commentary upon the Book of Genesis 1EC; Augustine, a host within himself, maintained MS1eC
335.17	deluge.] 1EC, 2EC, 3AC; deluge.*/*St Augustin L,9, c.2. Sup Genesis MS1eC
335.25	hemisphere;] 3AC; ~, MS1eC
335.33	Now,] 3AC; ~∧ MS1eC
335.41	Virgil,] 3AC; Virgil MS1eC
335.41	Mela,] 3AC; ~∧ MS1eC
335.41	lib. . . . lib. . . . cap.] 3AC; l. . . . l. . . . c. MS1eC
336.2	ancients, . . . Ptolemy] 3AC; ancients, as well as the Bramins of Ethiopia, and more especially that of Ptolemy MS1eC; ancients, and more especially of Ptolemy 1EC, MS1eC
336.20	amount*.] 3AC; amount. MS1eC
336.28	Still,] 3AC; ~∧ MS1eC
336.37	regaled with] 1EC, 2EC, 3AC; regaled by MS1eC
336.39	St. Basilius] 3AC; Appendix Operum St. Basilii Magni. Oratio. Sec. 2. Parisiis, MDCCXXI MS1eC
336.40	world,] 3AC; ~∧ MS1eC
337.2	manner] 1EC, 2EC, 3AC; manners MS1eC

337.2–3	enjoyments. There] 1EC, 2EC, 3AC; enjoyments. There reigns a temperate concordance of the seasons, wherein are united the fruitfulness of summer, the joyful abundance of autumn and the sweet freshness and quietude of spring. There MS1eC
337.5	quietude] 3AC; tranquillity MS1eC
337.6	flowers are ever] 3AC; flowers ever MS1eC
337.6	delicate] 3AC; pure MS1eC
337.7	crystal] 3AC; chrystal MS1eC
337.20	by Glanville . . . Bartholomeus] 1EC, 3AC; by Bartholomeus MS1eC
337.20–22	his . . . encyclopedia of] 1EC, 2EC, 3AC; his work de genuinis rerum, which Columbus evidently had in hand. It was a portable work of MS1eC
337.28	proceed] 3AC; proceeds MS1eC
337.30	Hexameron] 3AC; Hexaemeron MS1eC
337.31	quoted;] 3AC; ~, MS1eC
337.31–32	Oration] 3AC; oration MS1eC
337.32	former,] 3AC; ~$_\wedge$ MS1eC
337.33	Sabinus] 3AC; Sabino MS1eC
337.33–34	misquotation by Glanville.] 3AC; misquotation. MS1eC
337.36	"Paradisus] 3AC; $_\wedge$~ MS1eC
337.36	monte,] 3AC; ~$_\wedge$ MS1eC
337.37	lacum, que in] 3AC; lacum. In MS1eC
337.38	fragorem,] 3AC; ~$_\wedge$ MS1eC
337.38	lacum, nascuntur] 3AC; lacun nascuntur MS1eC
337.39	in parvulis] 3AC; imparvules MS1eC
337.39	*dicit*] 3AC; dixit MS1eC
337.40	*Hexameron, similiter*] 3AC; hexameron. Similitur MS1eC
337.40	lacu,] 3AC; ~$_\wedge$ MS1eC
337.40	fonte,] 3AC; ~$_\wedge$ MS1eC
337.41	quatuor,] 3AC; ~$_\wedge$ MS1eC
337.41	qui et] 3AC; qui & MS1eC
337.41	dicitur,] 3AC; ~$_\wedge$ MS1eC
337.42	Euphrates."] 3AC; ~$_{\wedge\wedge}$ MS1eC
337.42	Bart. Angl.] 3AC; Bartholomæi Anglici (real name Glanville de Genuinis rerum. L. 15. c.112. Francofurti, 1540. MS1eC
337.42	lib. . . . cap.] 3AC; l. . . . c. MS1eC
338.1	opinion] 3AC; opinion* MS1eC
338.2	La] 3AC; la MS1eC

338.8	names] 3AC; name MS1eC
338.10–11	and, . . . said too] 1EC, 2EC, 3AC; and may perhaps be considered to have already said too MS1eC
338.12	subject;] 3AC; ~, MS1eC
338.14	phenomena] 3AC; Phenomena MS1eC
338.19	disspelled] 3AC; dispelled MS1eC
338.23	However] 3AC; ~, MS1eC
338.28	No. XXXVI] 3AC; No. XXXIV. MS1eC
338.32	ocean] 3AC; Ocean MS1eC
339.1	ocean] 3AC; Ocean MS1eC
339.2	a] 1EC, 2EC, 3AC; an MS1eC
339.2	Cape] 3AC; cape MS1eC
339.3	and] 3AC; & MS1eC
339.14	ninety two] T; 92 MS1eC
339.15	islands] 3AC; Islands MS1eC
339.16	Monicongos,] 3AC; ~∧ MS1eC
339.21	cannibals] 3AC; Cannibals MS1eC
339.25	islands] 3AC; Islands MS1eC
339.25	letters,] 3AC; ~∧ MS1eC
339.27	islands] 3AC; Islands MS1eC
339.33	mayorazgo] 3AC; Mayorazgo MS1eC
339.36	son,] 3AC; ~∧ MS1eC
339.38	Ferdinand;] 3AC; ~, MS1eC
339.39	Don] 3AC; don MS1eC
340.10	lineage] 3AC; linage MS1eC
340.16	them, . . . them;] 1EC, 2EC, 3AC; them to be fulfilled by them MS1eC
340.27–28	justice. And] 3AC; Justice; and MS1eC
340.29	holy] 3AC; Holy MS1eC
340.30	its] 1EC, 2EC, 3AC; it MS1eC
340.32	disfigured. And] 3AC; disfigured; and MS1eC; blemished. And 1EC
340.34	lord,] 3AC; Lord MS1eC
340.42	islands] 3AC; Islands MS1eC
341.3	grandees] 3AC; Grandees MS1eC
341.4	lords] 3AC; Lords MS1eC
341.5	justice] 3AC; Justice MS1eC
341.7	noble] 1EC, 2EC, 3AC; person of titles MS1eC
341.12	bear] 1EC, 2EC, 3AC; wear MS1eC
341.14	withal] 1EC, 3AC; with MS1eC
341.22	Admiral] 3AC; admiral MS1eC
341.25	agreeable;] 3AC; agreable, MS1eC

341.30	Verde] T; Verd MS1eC, 1EC, 3AC
341.30	their] 3AC; his MS1eC
341.31	preeminences held] 3AC; privileges enjoyed MS1eC
341.35	treaty] 1EC, MS2eC, 3AC; capitulation MS1eC
341.39	First,] 3AC; ~– MS1eC
341.41	Columbus,] 3AC; ~∧ MS1eC
342.1	maravedies] T; Maravedies MS1eC
342.8	much;] 3AC; ~, MS1eC
342.8	the] 1EC, 2EC, 3AC; this MS1eC
342.9	maravedies] T; maravedises MS1eC
342.20	whoever] 3AC; who MS1eC
342.21	Item,–From] 3AC; Item–from MS1eC
342.27	Item,–] 3AC; Item– MS1eC
342.37	distrusted by] 1EC, 2AC, 3AC; suspicious to MS1eC
342.38	Item,–All] 3AC; Item–all MS1eC
343.3	estate;] 3AC; ~, MS1eC
343.6	Item,–As] 3AC; Item–as MS1eC
343.11	New World] 3AC; new world MS1eC
343.12	tithe] 3AC; tythe MS1eC
343.13	First,–] 3AC; First– MS1eC
343.22–23	from the] 1EC, 2EC, 3AC; from MS1eC
343.23–24	maravedies;] T; maravedises MS1eC
344.1	until] 3AC; untill MS1eC
344.3	Item,–] 3AC; Item– MS1eC
344.7–8	necessitous] 1EC, 2EC, 3AC; necessitated MS1eC
344.12	income;] 3AC; ~, MS1eC
344.16	tithe] 3AC; tythe MS1eC
344.18	Item,–] 3AC; Item– MS1eC
344.26	benefit] 3AC; Benefit MS1eC
344.28	Item,–] 3AC; ~∧∧ MS1eC
344.33	accrue] 3AC; accure MS1eC
344.35	Item,–] 3AC; Item– MS1eC
344.38	heirs, . . . George] 1EC, 2EC, 3AC; heirs, in what is called "Logos," a stock in the order of St. George MS1eC
344.39	six per cent.] 3AC; 6 pr 100 MS1eC
344.41	Item,–] 3AC; Item– MS1eC
345.1	personally] 3AC; personnally MS1eC
345.7	well:] 3AC; ~, MS1eC
345.8	succeed . . . trust] 1EC, 2EC, 3AC; inherit him for this purpose MS1eC
345.10	Lord] 3AC; lord MS1eC

345.21	Item,—] 3AC; Item— MS1eC
345.21–22	whoever may inherit] 1EC, 2EC, 3AC; whoever in-herit MS1eC
345.26	cent.,—I] 3AC; cent. I MS1eC
345.38	Item,—] 3AC; Item— MS1eC
345.38	whosoever] T; whomsoever MS1eC, 3AC
346.1	forbid!)] 3AC; ~∧) MS1eC
346.5	Item,—] 3AC; Item— MS1eC
346.6	honour,] 3AC; ~∧ MS1eC
346.11	Item,—] 3AC; Item MS1eC
346.15	relations,] 3AC; ~; MS1eC
346.16	the said] 3AC; said MS1eC
346.16	daughters] 1EC, 2EC, 3AC; girls MS1eC
346.18	Item,—] 3AC; Item— MS1eC
346.22	chapel is to be] 1EC, 2EC, 3AC; chapel be MS1eC
346.26	Item,—] 3AC; Item— MS1eC
346.26	whosoever] T; whomsoever MS1eC, 3AC
346.28	theology] 3AC; Theology MS1eC
346.35	La] 3AC; la MS1eC
346.36	serve] 3AC; service, MS1eC
346.39	Item,—] 3AC; Item—MS1eC
346.39	whosoever] T; whomsoever MS1eC, 3AC
347.1–2	fulfillment] 3AC; fulfilment MS1eC
347.7	No. XXXVII] 3AC; No. XXXV. MS1eC
347.13	correspondent] 3AC; correspondant MS1eC
347.14	signature] 3AC; ~, MS1eC
347.19	CHRISTO),] 3AC; CHRO) MS1eC
347.19	Greek] 3AC; greek MS1eC
347.20	second,] 3AC; ~∧ MS1eC
347.20	FERENS, . . . Latin] 3AC; FERENS . . . latin MS1eC
347.21	Greek] 3AC; greek MS1eC
347.26	Christus),] 3AC; ~∧ MS1eC
347.27	me, Xristus, Maria,] 3AC; ~. ~. ~. MS1eC
347.27–28	North-American Review] 3AC; north american review MS1eC
347.28	April] 3AC; april MS1eC
347.28–30	Josephus, . . . José."] 3AC; Josephus, which appears an improvement on the suggestion of Spotorno MS1eC
348.1	Christian] 3AC; christian MS1eC
348.2	Mahometans] 3AC; mahometans MS1eC
348.3	proscribed] 1EC, 2EC, 3AC; prohibited MS1eC
348.4	father,] 3AC; ~∧ MS1eC

348.5	"Jesus] 3AC; _∧~ MS1eC
348.12	No. XXXVIII] ARE; *Mising in MS*
349.9	calesero] T; calasero 1E, 1A, 1F, ARE
350.20	indispensable] 1A, 1F, ARE; indispensible 1E
352.2	gentleman] 1A, 1F, ARE; gentlemen 1E
353.7	whitewashed] T; white-washed 1E, 1A, 1F, ARE
353.30	with] ARE; by 1E, 1A, 1F
353.37	shores] ARE; shore 1E, 1A, 1F
354.8	is extinct] ARE; are extinct 1E, 1A, 1F
354.23	about] ARE; which is about 1E, 1A, 1F
354.24	calesero] T; calasero 1E, 1A, 1F, ARE
354.41	vineyard] 1A, ARE; vine-yard 1E, 1F
355.1	pines ... mentioned,] ARE; pines which I have mentioned 1E, 1A, 1F
355.6	Moors, has not] ARE; Moors, it has not 1E, 1A, 1F
355.20	fig-tree] 1A, 1F, ARE; ~_∧~ 1E
356.35	physician] 1A, ARE; Physician 1E, 1F
357.20	Perez,] 1F, ARE; ~_∧ 1E, 1A
358.26	Don Rafael] T; Don Gabriel 1E, 1A, 1F, ARE
360.4–5	fulfill] ARE; fulfil 1A, 1F
361.3	interwoven] 1A, ARE; inter-woven 1E, 1F
361.10	V,] 1F, ARE; ~. 1E, 1A
361.40	calesero] T; calasero 1E, 1A, 1F, ARE
362.6	No. XXXIX] ARE; *Missing in MS*
363.12	if you desire] 1A, 1F, ARE; if desire 1E
363.30	Terra Firma] 1A; terra firma 1E, 1F, ARE
363.30	of said] ARE; of the said 1E, 1A, 1F

LIST OF REJECTED SUBSTANTIVES

This list provides a historical record of substantive variants in the manuscripts and the authorized texts that appeared during Irving's lifetime, but that were not adopted for the Twayne text. Symbols used to designate the source of the readings are those found in the List of Abbreviations, p. 367.

Not included in the Twayne edition are six illustrations found in the first English edition: Convent of La Rabida at Palos, where Columbus asked bread and water for his child; arms of the Pinzon family; town of Palos, with the Church of St. George; country seat of the Pinzons; old house belonging to the Pinzon family; map.

3.8	to secure] 1E; and to secure 1A
4.9	empire over] 1E; empire in 1A
4.29–30	the heroes of these remoter adventures] 1E; the discoverers 1A
5.16	romance] 1E; tale 1A
5.25	that author] 1E; he 1A
5.33	government] 1E, ARE; Spanish Government 1A
5.34	the intelligent keeper] 1E, ARE; the keeper 1A
5.35	Herrera, . . . Gomara,] 1E, ARE; Las Casas, Herrera Gomera 1A
6.1	his own arrangement] 1E, ARE; his arrangement 1A
6.2	was] 1E, ARE; were 1A
10.27	natives] MS, ARE; Nations 1E, 1A
*11.4	From hence] MS, 1E, 1A; Hence ARE
12.22	From hence] MS, 1E, 1A, Hence ARE
*12.32	entirely] MS; certainly 1E, 1A, ARE
*15.29	prisoner] MS; prisoners 1E, 1A, 1F
*16.22	that] MS, 1E, 1A; which ARE
17.23	that] MS, 1E, 1A; which ARE
17.27	from whence] MS, 1E, 1A; Whence ARE
25.32	from whence] MS, 1E, 1A; Whence ARE
29.33	that] MS, 1E, 1A; which ARE
32.13	Hernando] MS, 1E, 1A; Hernan ARE

36.18	from whence] MS, 1E, 1A; whence ARE
38.29	from whence] MS, 1E, 1A; whence ARE
*43.39	or] MS; nor ARE
*45.36	was] MS, 1E, 1A; were ARE
54.6	which] MS, 1E, ARE; that 1A
*57.28	villages] MS; villagers 1E, 1A, ARE
58.15	water] MS, 1E, 1F, ARE; waters 1A
63.35	that] MS, 1E, 1A; which ARE
*64.15	entreated that] MS; entreated 1E, 1A, ARE
*69.24	cargoes] MS; cargo 1E, 1A, ARE
*70.15	a] MS; the 1E, 1A, ARE
73.24	in] MS; at 1E, 1A, ARE
*73.29	sallied] MS, 1E, 1A; sailed ARE
*78.25	compunction] MS, 1E, 1A; compunctions ARE
*96.29	further] MS, 1E, 1A; farther ARE
97.15	that] MS, 1E, 1A; which ARE
99.12	force,] MS, ARE; forces 1E, 1A
103.27	entrusted, abandoned] MS, 1E; intrusted, ∼ ARE; ∼, might have abandoned 1A
112.22	from whence] MS, 1E, 1A; whence ARE
114.8	Don] MS, 1E, 1A, 1F; Bon ARE
114.22	that] MS, 1E, 1A; which ARE
*116.10	quantity] MS; quantities ARE
119.22	*Further*] MS; Farther 1E, 1A, ARE
122.14	from whence] MS, 1E, 1A; whence ARE
124.9	while] MS, 1E, ARE; when 1A
125.7	from whence] MS, 1E, 1A; whence ARE
138.14	from whence] MS, 1E, 1A; whence ARE
*139.20	huge] MS; large 1E, 1A, 1F, ARE
*140.26	previous] MS; perilous 1E, 1A, ARE
141.18	that] MS, 1E, 1A; which ARE
*146.29	retired] MS; returned 1E, 1A, 1F, ARE
148.17	from whence] MS, 1E, 1A; whence ARE
151.11	from whence] MS, 1E, 1A; whence ARE
152.26	from whence] 1E, 1A; whence ARE
153.9	that] 1E, 1A; which ARE
163.1	from whence] 1E, 1A; whence ARE
165.33	from whence] 1E, 1A; whence ARE
*167.34	when intelligence] 1E, 1F, ARE; when, in 1517, intelligence 1A
*168.23	concealed in] 1E, 1F, ARE; concealed it in 1A
*170.5–6	a hooting rabble] 1E, ARE; the rabble 1A

183.16–17	from whence] 1E, 1A; whence ARE
*188.7	have drank] 1E, 1A, ARE; have drunk 1F
*189.4	to which] 1E, 1A; to whom ARE
*192.10	requiescunt] 1E, 1F, ARE; requiescat 1A

APPENDIXES

194.16	translation of the ashes] MS1eC, MS2eC, 3AC; removal of the mortal remains 1EC, 2EC
194.20–21	by a . . . remains] MS1eC, MS2eC, 3AC; by carelessness or negligence 1EC, 2EC
195.40	convocation] MS1eC, MS2eC, 3AC; commemoration 1EC, 2EC
197.6	notice is digested] MS1eC, MS2eC, 3AC; account is taken 1EC, 2EC
198.31	it] MS1eC, 2EC, 1AC, 2AC, 3AC; is 1EC
200.2	attained] MS1eC, 2EC, 3AC; obtained 1EC
202.14	father] MS1eC, 1AC, 2AC, MS2eC, 3AC; admiral 1EC, 2EC
204.38	or] MS1eC, 1EC, 2EC, 1AC, 2AC, MS2eC; nor 3AC
208.21	1525] MS1eC, MS2eC, 3AC; 1825 1EC
211.12	from whence] MS1eC; whence 3AC
211.41	477] MS1eC, 2EC, MS2eC, 3AC; 479 1EC
217.23	process brought] MS1eC, MS2eC, 1AC, 2AC, 3AC; suit, instituted 1EC
220.14	Savona] MS1eC, 1EC, 2EC, MS2eC; Saona 3AC
222.26	testament] MS1eC, 1AC, 2AC, MS2eC, 3AC; will 1EC
222.34	who . . . there,] MS1eC, MS2eC, 1AC, 2AC, 3AC; (who shall be domiciled there with his wife), 1EC, 2EC
224.19	favours] MS1eC, MS2eC; favors 1AC, 2AC, 3AC; patronage 1EC, 2EC
225.32	From thence] MS1eC; Thence 3AC
226.16	as is known] MS1eC, MS2eC, 3AC; as is well known 1EC, 2EC
227.28–34	The brilliant . . . relations.] MS1eC, 1EC, 2EC; There were many private adventurers also who engaged under the banner of the Duke of Calabria. MS2eC; The brilliant . . . enterprise . . . adventurer or . . . duke . . . historians, that . . . Genoa, . . . relations. 3AC
229.15	son] MS1eC, 1EC, 2EC, 1AC, 2AC, 3AC; nephew MS2eC

230.42   swayed]   MS1eC, 1AC, 2AC, MS2eC, 3AC; influenced
                1EC, 2EC
231.9   voyagers]   MS1eC, 1AC, 2AC, 3AC, MS2eC; navigators
                1EC, 2EC
233.12   India]   MS1eC, 1AC, 2AC, MS2eC, 3AC; Indian 1EC,
                2EC
234.15   title]   MS1eC, 1AC, 2AC, MS2eC, 3AC; title of 1EC,
                2EC
235.2   Vicente Yañez Pinzon]   MS1eC, MS2eC, 3AC; Pinzon
                1EC; Vincente Yañez Pinzon 1AC, 2AC
236.6   from hence]   MS1eC; hence 3AC
237.23   is presumed]   MS1eC, 1AC, 2AC, MS2eC, 3AC; appears
                1EC, 2EC
238.9   great gulph of ocean]   MS1eC; great ocean 1EC, 2EC;
                great gulf of ocean 3AC
238.10–11   chiefly ... mention."]   MS1eC, 1AC, 2AC, 3AC; chiefly
                inhabited, unknown to antiquity 1EC, 2EC
238.38   books]   MS1eC, MS2eC, 3AC; log-books 1EC, 2EC
238.39   armadas]   MS1eC, MS2eC, 1AC, 2AC, 3AC; armada
                1EC, 2EC
239.31   interrogatories]   MS1eC, 1AC, 2AC, MS2eC, 3AC;
                depositions 1EC, 2EC
239.31–32   witnesses ... are]   MS1eC, 1AC, 2AC, 3AC; witnesses
                are 1EC, 2EC
239.37   Jose]   MS1eC, 3AC; Tote 1EC; Josef MS2eC
240.1–2   Secondly, . . . of]   MS1eC, 1AC, 2AC, 3AC; Another
                argument is drawn from the coincidence of 1EC, 2EC
240.27   de Haro]   MS1eC, 1EC, 2EC, 3AC; de Ybarro 1AC, 2AC
240.29–30   sea chart, . . . by]   MS1eC; chart, the track by 1EC,
                2EC; the courses and steerings by MS2eC
242.28   che]   MS1eC, MS2eC, 3AC; die 1EC, 2EC
245.12   European]   MS1eC, 1EC, 2EC, 3AC; person 1AC, 2AC
251.15   were]   MS1eC, MS2eC, 3AC; came 1EC, 2EC
253.35   from whence]   MS1eC; whence 3AC
254.16   M. Otto]   3AC; Mr. Otto MS1eC
260.32   from whence]   MS1eC; whence 3AC
264.26–277.44   No. XVII]   MS1eC, 1EC, 2EC;
278.37–39

         It has hitherto been supposed that one of the
     Bahama islands, at present called San Salvador and
     also known as Cat-island, was the first point where
     Columbus came in contact with the new world. Don

Martin Navarrete, director of the hydrographical depot at Madrid and a distinguished officer of the
Spanish navy, in his introduction to the recently published 'Collection of Spanish Voyages and Discoveries', has endeavored to shew that it must have been
Turk's Island, one of the same group situated about
one hundred leagues or three hundred sea miles S.E.
from San Salvador. Let us carefully and candidly
examine this opinion of Mr. Navarrete, comparing it
with the journal of Columbus and observing if they
coincide; if they do not, let us next discover what
evidence there may be to confirm our hereditary belief that San Salvador is the spot whence Columbus
first set foot upon the new world. We shall feel the
less reluctance to approach so interesting a subject
of inquiry from having navigated extensively among
these islands.

Columbus described Guanahani where he first
landed, and to which he gave the name of San Salvador, as being a very large and beautiful island,
covered with forests, many of which bore fruit; and
as having abundance of fresh water, and a large
lake in the centre. It was inhabited by a numerous
population, and he proceeded a considerable distance in his boats along the shore to the N.N.E.,
being visited as he passed by the inhabitants of several villages. How does Turks Island answer to this
description?

Turks Island is a low key composed of sand and
rocks, extending less than two leagues in a N. and S.
direction; it is utterly destitute of wood; it has no
fresh water, the inhabitants depending entirely for a
supply on casks and cisterns in which they preserve
the rain; nor is there any lake, but only a few salt
ponds, which furnish the sole production of the island.
Turks Island can not be approached on the E. and
N. E. sides in consequence of its dangerous reef;
the only anchoring places being the open roadstead
to the W. and another less frequented at the S., called
the Hawk's-nest. This island is incapable of cultivation; the inhabitants draw all their supplies from
abroad, except fish and turtle, which are taken in

abundance and afford the chief food of the slaves employed in the salt works. The whole resources of this island consist in the produce of those works, and in the salvage and plunder of the many wrecks which occur in the neighborhood. Hence Turks Island would never be inhabited in a primitive state of society, when commerce does not exist, and men are obliged to draw their subsistence from the spot which they people.

When about to leave Guanahani, Columbus was at a loss to choose from the great number of islands in sight; which next to visit; now there is no land whatever visible from Turks Island, except the two salt keys, which lie S. He does not state what course he steered in going from Guanahani to Conception, but merely that it was five leagues off, and the current was against him; whereas the distance from Turks Island to Gran Caico, supposed by Mr Navarrete to be the Conception of Columbus, is nearly double.

From Conception Columbus went next to an island which he saw nine leagues off in a westerly direction, and which he named Fernandina. This Mr Navarrete supposed Little Inagua, though no less than twenty leagues from Gran Caico. Moreover Columbus describes Fernandina as stretching N.W. and S.E. twenty eight leagues, whereas Little Inagua has its greatest length of only four leagues in a N. E. and S. W. direction. In short the description of Fernandina has nothing in common with Little Inagua.

From Fernandina Columbus sailed S.E. to Isabella, which Mr. Navarrete takes to be Great Inagua, although it bears S.W. from Little Inagua, a course differing ninety degrees from the one followed by Columbus. Again; on the 20th November Columbus takes occasion to say that Guanahani was eight leagues distant from Isabella; now Turks Island is no less than thirty five leagues from Great Inagua.

Leaving Isabella Columbus stood W.S.W. for the island of Cuba, and fell in with the Islas Arenas; the course drawn from Great Inagua would meet the coast of Cuba about Port Nipe; whereas Mr Navar-

rete supposed that Columbus next discovered the keys
S of Iumentos, and which bear W.N.W. from Inagua,
a course differing forty-five degrees from the one
steered by the ships.

After sailing for some time in the neighborhood of
Cuba, Columbus finds himself on the 14th November,
in the sea of Nuestra Señora, surrounded by so many
islands that it was impossible to count them; on the
same day Mr. Navarrete placed him off Cape Moa,
where there is but one small island, and more than
fifty leagues from any group that can possibly answer
the description. At about the same period Columbus
gives us to understand that Guanahani was forty five
leagues from Port Principe; now Turks Island is
eighty leagues from the neighborhood, in which Mr
Navarrete supposes that point to be.

On taking leave of the island of Cuba, Columbus
remarks that he had coasted it for an extent of one
hundred and twenty leagues; if we deduct twenty
leagues for his having followed the windings of
the coast, there will still remain one hundred; whereas
Mr Navarrete only supposes him to have explored
an extent of seventy leagues.

Such are the most important difficulties offered by
the theory of Mr Navarrete, and which even if balanced—as they were in no single particular—by much
concurring evidence, might well be set down as
insurmountable. Let us now take up the route of
Columbus as described in his journal, and with the
chart before us examine how it agrees with the popular and traditional opinion, that he first landed on
the island of San Salvador.

We learn from the journal of Columbus that on
11th October, 1492, he continued steering W.S.W.
until sunset, when he returned to his old course of
W. The vessels were running at the rate of three
leagues an hour, when at ten o'clock in the night, he
and several of his crew saw a light which seemed a
torch carried about on the land. They ran on four
hours longer, and had made twelve leagues farther
west, when at 2 in the morning land was discovered
ahead, distant two leagues. The twelve leagues ran

since 10 oclock, with these two of distance from the land form a total corresponding essentially with the distance and direction of Watlings Island from San Salvador. Hence it results that if it was upon San Salvador that Columbus the next day launched, the light seen the night before must have been on Watlings Island. And since the Admiral himself received the royal reward for having seen this light, as the first discovery of land, it would follow that Watling's Island is the point for which that reward was granted.

On making the land the vessels were hove to until daylight on the 12th October, they were anchored off an island of great beauty, covered with forests and extremely populous. It was called Guanahani by the natives, and Columbus added the name of San Salvador. Exploring its coasts to the N.N.E. he found a harbor capable of sheltering any number of ships. This corresponds minutely with the S.E. part of the island now known as San Salvador, which lies E. and W. bending at its eastern extremity to the N.E., and has the same verdant appearance. The vessels had probably drifted into this bay at the S.E. side of San Salvador while lying to for daylight; nor did Columbus during his short stay at the island, or when sailing from it, open the land so as to discover what he had taken for its whole length was but a bend at one end of it, and that the main body of the island lay behind to the N.W.

From Guanahani Columbus saw so many islands, that he was embarrassed in choosing which next to visit; the indians signified, indeed, that they were innumerable, and mentioned the names of more than a hundred. He determined to go to the largest in sight which appeared to be about five leagues off; some of the others were nearer, and others more distant. The island thus selected and which he named Santa Maria de la Concepcion, is presumed to be the present island of Conception, and that the others were that singular belt of small islands called La Cadena or Chain; which stretches past San Salvador in a S.E. and N.W. direction, the nearest of the group being nearer than San Salvador, while the rest are more remote.

This opinion is sustained by the strongest evidence. Columbus tells that having left San Salvador in the afternoon he did not reach Conception until the next day, notwithstanding the short distance, having been greatly retarded by adverse currents. Now although he does not mention its bearings from San Salvador, nor the course which he steered in going to it, yet since we know that in this neighborhood the current sets strongly and uniformly to the W.N.W., and since he tells us that he sailed against it, it follows clearly that he must have sailed towards the E.S.E.; besides when near Conception, Columbus remarks another island to the westward the largest he had yet seen; but he expressly tells us that he anchored off Conception, and did not go to this large island as he wished to do, because he could not sail to the W. Hence then it is certain that Columbus did not sail westward in going from San Salvador to Conception; for from the opposition of the wind, as there would be no other course, he could not sail towards that quarter. Now on reference to the chart, we find the present island of Conception situated E.S.E. from San Salvador, and at the same distance of five leagues.

Leaving Conception on the 16th October, Columbus steered for a very large island seen to the westward, nine leagues off, and which extended itself twenty eight leagues in a S.E. and N.W. direction. He was becalmed the whole day, and did not reach the island until the next day, when he named it Fernandina. He wished to have sailed around it to another island called Samoet by the natives, and which they represented as larger; but the wind being at S.E. by S., the course he wished to steer, they signified to him that it would be easier to sail round by running to the W.N.W. with a fair wind. Accordingly, he bore up and having run two leagues to the N.W. found a marvellous port, with a narrow entrance, or rather with two entrances, for there was an island which shut it up completely, forming a noble basin

within it. It had now become calm; but shortly after
there was a breeze from W.N.W.; so they sailed out
by the opposite entrance, steering E.S.E. in order to
get an offing for the weather looked threatening. The
next day the ships anchored off the eastern extremity
of Fernandina. The whole of this description answers
most accurately to the present island of Exuma, which
lies S. from San Salvador and S.W. from Conception.
The only inconsistency is that Columbus at first states
that Fernandina bore nearly W. from Conception,
and was twenty eight leagues long; this may proceed
from his having taken the long chain of keys called
Cadena for part of the same Exuma, which continuous appearance they would naturally assume when
seen from Conception, for they run in the same N.W.
and S.E. direction; their bearings from the same point
are likewise W. as well as S.W. As proof that such
was the fact, we find that after having approached
Fernandina, instead of its extent increasing to his
eyes, as is usual, he remarks that it was twenty
leagues long, whereas before he had estimated it at
twenty eight; he now discovered probably that instead
of one there were many islands and bent his course
more southerly to reach the most conspicuous. The
identity of the island thus described with Exuma is
irresistibly forced upon the mind; the distance from
Conception, the remarkable port with an island at
the mouth, and further on its coast turning to the
W. are all so accurately delineated, that the chart
would almost seem to have been drawn up from the
description of Columbus.

On the 19th October the ships left Fernandina
steering S.E. with the wind at N.; this course brought
them in a few hours to Samoet. At its N. point they
found a little island surrounded by rocks; to Samoet
Columbus gave the name of Isabella, and to its point
off the little island that of Cabo del Isleo. This little
island lay in the direction of Isabella from Fernandina E. and W.; the coast of Isabella extended westerly from the small island twelve leagues to a cape,
which for its beauty he named Fermosa. This last
he believed to be a distinct island from Isabella. To

the cape at the S.W. part of Isabella he gave the name of Cabo de Laguna, from the lake at which he watered his ships. The whole description of Samoet or Isabella agrees so accurately with the present Long Island that it is only necessary to read it with the chart unfolded, to become convinced of their identity.

Having resolved to visit a great island, described by the natives as bearing W.S.W. from Isabella and which they called Cuba, Columbus left Isabella at midnight on the 24th October, and shaped his course to the W.S.W. The wind continued light until noon, when it freshened, and in the evening Cape Verde, as he named the S.W. point of Fernandina, bore N.W. distant seven leagues. In the night it became tempestuous, and he lay to until morning, drifting by his reckoning two leagues. The following morning, sail was again made to the W.S.W. until 9 o'Clock; when he had run nine leagues, he then steered W. until 3 oclock running eleven leagues, at which hour land was discovered consisting of seven or eight keys, distant five leagues from the ships; they were low, five or six leagues in extent; he anchored near them, calling them Islas de Arena.

The distances run by Columbus, added to the departure taken from Fernandina, and the distance from these keys at the time of discovering them, give a sum total of thirty leagues; this is about three less than the distance from Exuma, whence we suppose Columbus to have taken his departure, to the group of Mucaras, lying E. of Bayo Lobo on the Grand Bank, and which exactly correspond with the description of Columbus. If it was necessary to account for a difference of three leagues in a reckoning where so much is given on conjecture, it would readily occur to the seaman that an allowance of three leagues for drift during a long night of blowy weather, would be but a small one. The course from Exuma to the Mucaras is about S.W. by W; that followed by Columbus differs a little from it; but as it was his intention in setting sail from Isabella to steer W.S.W. and since he afterwards altered the course to W., we may conclude that he did so in consequence of having been driven to the S. while lying to the night previous.

At sunrise on the 29th October Columbus set sail from the Islas Arenas, of Mucaros as we suppose them, for the island of Cuba, steering S.S.W.; having made seventeen leagues on this course he saw the land at dark and hove his ships to. At dawn of day he made sail again, and entered a fine harbor which he called San Salvador. This we suppose the place now known as Caravelos Grandes; its bearings and distance from the Mucaras coincide readily with the run of Columbus, and its description answers to the port he visited.

Henceforth every thing becomes obvious, and there is no difficulty in tracing the course of Columbus westward until arrested by shallows at Key Cabrion; thence back to Nuevitas del Principe, and along the outer edge of lofty keys of which Cayo Romano is the chief, and finally coastwise to the eastern extremity of Cuba, where he took leave of that island of Espaniola. The distance at which Columbus estimates Port Principe to have lain from the islands of Isabella and San Salvador, with their respective bearings, the extent of the coast of Cuba which he reconnoitred, and many minute facts—small in themselves, but vastly essential as evidence—combine to corroborate this elucidation of his course, which has been undertaken and pursued with a single view to the discovery of truth. Nor is it opposed by a single objection of any force; for surely the astronomical observations of Columbus can not be so esteemed; since he tells us that the instrument he made use of to measure the altitudes of the heavenly bodies was out of order and not to be depended on. He places Guanahani or San Salvador in the latitude of Ferro, or about 27° 30′ N; San Salvador we find in 24° 30′, and Turks Island in 91° 30′; both are very wide of the truth; but it is certainly easier to conceive as we do an error of three, than as Mr Navarrete does one of six degrees.

Laying aside geographical demonstration, let us now examine how far history sustains the opinion here supported, that the island of San Salvador is the point where Columbus first landed upon the new world. Herrera, who is considered the most faithful and authentic of Spanish historians, wrote his history of the Indias towards the year 1600. In describing the voyage of Juan Ponce de Leon to Florida in 1512, he remarks to the following effect: "Leaving Aguada in Porto Rico, they steered N.W. by N. and in five days arrived at an island called El Viejo in latitude 22° 30′ N. The next day they reached an island of Lucayos called Caycos. On the eighth day they anchored at another island called Laguna in 24°. Thence they passed to the island of Manuega in 24° 30′, and on the eleventh day they reached Guanahani, which is in 25° 40′ N. This island of Guanahani was discovered by Columbus in his first voyage, and called by him San Salvador."

These remarks by Herrera are entirely conclusive as to the location of Guanahani or San Salvador. The latitudes it is true are placed higher than we now know them to be; that of San Salvador being such as to correspond with no other land than the dangerous clusters of the Berry Islands, which are seventy leagues from the nearest port of Cuba, nearly double the distance cited by Columbus in passing from island to island. But these latitudes are of little insight; for in those infant days of navigation, the instruments for measuring the meridian altitudes of the heavenly bodies, and the tables of their destinations, by means of which the latitude was thence deduced, were so imperfect as to place the most scientific navigation of the time below the most mechanical one of our day—Columbus who more than concentrated all the nautical wisdom of his age below the skipper who now directs his course across the trackless deep, and determines his position with unerring accuracy, by the aid of instruments and tables of whose principles and construction he is profoundly ignorant.—To return: the second island touched at by Ponce de Leon in his N.W. course was one of the Cayos; hence the first one called El Viejo must have lain to the S.E. and could only be Turks Island. The third island he came to was probably Mariguana; the fourth Crooked

Island, and the fifth Long Island; lastly, he came to
Guanahani, the San Salvador of Columbus and of the
present day. If this he supposed identical with Turks
Island, what has become of the succession of intervening islands touched at by Ponce de Leon on his
way from Porto Rico to San Salvador?*

No stress has been lain in these remarks on the
identity of distance between some of the points
visited by Columbus, and those which continue to
bear the same names at the present day; as San Salvador, Conception, and Port Principe; though traditional usage must ever be of most insight in such
matters. Geographical proof of a conclusive kind it
is thought has been advanced to enable the world to
remain in its old hereditary belief that the present
island of San Salvador is the point where Columbus
first set foot upon the new world. Established and
long established opinions of the kind should not be
lightly molested; and it is a good old rule that should
be kept in mind in curious research as well as territorial dealings, 'do not disturb the ancient land marks'.

*In the first chapter of Herrera's description of the
Indias, appended to his history, is another scale of
the Bahamas, which corroborates the above. MS2eC

264.32	able examination] MS1eC, 1EC, 2EC, 3AC; examina-tion 1AC, 2AC
265.10	on which] MS1eC, 1EC, 2EC, 3AC; in which 1AC, 2AC
266.42–267.2	Columbus . . . leagues] MS1eC, 2EC, 3AC; At about the same period Columbus gives us to understand that the island of Guanahani was distant by his reckoning forty-five leagues from Port Principe; now Turk's island is distant eighty leagues from the neighbour-hood in which Mr. Navarrete places Port Principe. 1AC, 2AC
267.6	island an] MS1eC, 1EC, 2EC, 3AC; island for an 1AC, 2AC
267.16	At] MS1eC, 2EC, 3AC; And at 1AC, 2AC
267.20	leagues which they] MS1eC, 1EC, 3AC; leagues they 1AC, 2AC
267.23	and it] MS1eC, 1EC, 2EC, 3AC; it 1AC, 2AC
267.30–31	the same 12th] MS1eC, 1EC, 2EC, 3AC; the 12th 1AC, 2AC

267.36–37	island . . . which] MS1eC, 2EC, 3AC; island now known as San Salvador, which 1AC, 2AC
268.39–40	bore . . .found] MS1eC, 1EC, 2EC, 3AC; bore up, and having run two leagues to the N.W., found 1AC, 2AC
269.5	sprung] MS1eC, 1EC, 3AC; sprang 1AC, 2AC
270.6	Isla Larga] MS1eC, 1EC, 3AC; Long Island 1AC, 2AC
270.7	the identity] MS1eC, 1EC, 2EC, 3AC; their identity 1AC, 2AC
270.38	previous.] MS1eC, 1EC, 2EC, 3AC; ∼, October 27. 1AC, 2AC
270.39	isles] MS1eC, 1EC, 2EC, 3AC; Islas 1AC, 2AC
270.39–40	Mucaras for] MS1eC, 1EC, 2EC, 3AC; ∼, as we suppose them to be, ∼ 1AC, 2AC
271.3	hitherto been noted] MS1eC, 1EC, 2EC, 3AC; been noted hitherto 1AC, 2AC
271.6	Nuevitas] MS1eC, 3AC; Nuevitao 1EC; Muritas 1AC
271.6	del] 3AC; el MS1eC
271.7–8	those run by] MS1eC, 1EC, 2EC, 3AC; the run of 1AC, 2AC
271.9	visited.] MS1eC, 2EC, 3AC; visited. The vessels in running in for this harbour must have passed east of the island of Guajava, of which no mention is made in the journal. Either Columbus does not notice it from his attention having been engrossed by the magnificent island before him, or the vessels may have been drifted through the passage, which is two leagues wide, while lying to in the night. 1AC
271.10	Oct. 29.–Leaving . . . port] MS1eC, 1EC, 2EC, 3AC; Leaving San Salvador 1AC
271.11	running] MS1eC, 1EC, 3AC; which ran 1AC
271.11	which] MS1eC, 1EC, 2EC, 3AC; This 1AC, 2AC
271.12	and ten] MS1eC, 1EC, 3AC; ten 1AC
271.13	will be] MS1eC, 1EC, 2EC, 3AC; agrees with 1AC
271.16	resembling] MS1eC, 1EC, 2EC, 3AC; formed like 1AC, 2AC
271.18	for a] MS1eC, 1EC, 2EC, 3AC; for erecting a 1AC, 2AC
271.18	which] MS1eC, 1EC, 2EC, 3AC; one which 1AC
271.24	we believe] MS1eC, 1EC, 2EC, 3AC; is believed to be 1AC
271.31	projected] MS1eC, 1EC, 2EC, 3AC; projecting 1AC
271.35	described] MS1eC, 1EC, 3AC; seen 1AC

271.36   entrance with] MS1eC, 1EC, 2EC, 3AC; entrance to
                this river with 1AC
271.38   bay between] MS1eC, 1EC, 2EC, 3AC; bay making
                in between 1AC
272.8   they] MS1eC, 1EC, 2EC, 3AC; he 1AC
272.9   just west of] MS1eC, 1EC, 2EC, 3AC; near 1AC
272.9   they] MS1eC, 1ES, 2EC, 3AC; he 1AC
272.10   they] MS1eC, 1EC, 2EC, 3AC; he 1AC
272.10   they] MS1eC, 1EC, 2EC, 3AC; he 1AC
272.11   we take] MS1eC, 1EC, 2EC, 3AC; is believed 1AC
272.16–17   situated . . . distance] MS1eC, 1EC, 2EC, 3AC; corre-
                spondingly situated 1AC
272.21   Curiana] MS1eC, MS2eC, 3AC; Casiana 1EC, 2EC
272.24–28   Salvador . . . Salvador.] MS1eC, 1EC, 2EC, 3AC; Sal-
                vador. 1AC
272.29   hove] MS1eC, 1EC, 2EC, 3AC; lain 1AC
272.37   sail] MS1eC, 2EC, 3AC; run 1AC
272.38   Salvador . . . and so] MS1eC, 1EC, 2EC, 3AC; Sal-
                vador, and so 1AC
272.40   on both sides] MS1eC, 1EC, 2EC, 3AC; one on each
                side 1AC
272.40–41   principal one] MS1eC, 1EC, 2EC, 3AC; principal 1AC
272.41   peak called] MS1eC, 1EC, 2EC, 3AC; peak now
                called 1AC
272.42   de Maternillos] MS1eC, 1EC, 2EC, 3AC; Maternillos
                1AC
273.1–2   which . . . Guajava] MS1eC, 1EC, 2EC, 3AC; supposed
                here to be the lesser Guajava 1AC
273.2   here] MS1eC, 1EC, 2EC, 3AC; now 1AC
273.2   sure] MS1eC, 1EC, 2EC, 3AC; certain 1AC
273.2–4   that . . . for] MS1eC, 1EC, 2EC, 3AC; that Cape Cuba
                was believed by Columbus to be the extremity of the
                island of that name; for 1AC
273.4   land mentioned as] MS1eC, 1EC, 2EC, 3AC; land as
                1AC
273.21   This . . . journal] MS1eC, 1EC, 2EC, 3AC; The jour-
                nal in this part 1AC
273.22   also] MS1eC, 1EC, 2EC, 3AC; several 1AC
273.22   if] MS1eC, 1EC, 2EC, 3AC; though 1AC
273.31   easterly] MS1eC, 2EC, 3AC; eastward 1AC
273.37   found] MS1eC, 1EC, 2EC, 3AC; find 1AC

273.40	and sailing] MS1eC, 1EC, 2EC, 3AC; and then sailing 1AC
273.41	reached in another day] MS1eC, 1EC, 2EC, 3AC; at length reached 1AC
273.42	lesser] MS1eC, 1EC, 2EC, 3AC; Little 1AC
274.3	return from] MS1eC, 2EC, 3AC; return some time after 1AC
274.3–4	clear . . . that] MS1eC, 1EC, 2EC, 3AC; clear that 1AC
274.6	went . . . to place] MS1eC, 2EC, 3AC; went on the 18th November in his boats to place 1AC
274.7	He] MS1eC, 1EC, 3AC; Columbus 1AC
274.8	Guajava] MS1eC, 1EC, 2EC, 3AC; Little Guajava 1AC
274.9	this port] MS1eC, 1EC, 2EC, 3AC; Puerto del Principe 1AC
274.10–11	Columbus . . . visit] MS1eC, 1EC, 2EC, 3AC; It does not appear that he ever visited 1AC
274.17	Babeque . . . lie] MS1eC, 1EC, 2EC, 3AC; Babeque lay or was supposed to lay 1AC
274.27	Isla Larga] MS1eC, 1EC, 2EC, 3AC; Long Island 1AC
274.27	Again, let] MS1eC, 1EC, 2EC, 3AC; Let 1AC
274.30	Having] MS1eC, 1EC, 2EC, 3AC; These different courses, with 1AC
274.30–31	These yield] MS1eC, 1EC, 2EC, 3AC; yield 1AC
274.31	course . . . S.W.] MS1eC, 1EC, 2EC, 3AC; one of S. W. nearly 1AC
274.35	Salvador . . . west] MS1eC, 1EC, 2EC, 3AC; Salvador, on the coast of Cuba, lay a short distance west 1AC
274.36–37	bound . . . established] MS1eC, 1EC, 2EC, 3AC; connected and bound together 1AC
274.38	some] MS1eC, 1EC, 2EC, 3AC; two 1AC
275.1	contending . . . until] MS1eC, 1EC, 2EC, 3AC; connected and bound together 1AC
275.5	whence] MS1eC; which 3AC
275.6–7	island . . . lesser] MS1eC, 1EC, 2EC, 3AC; Little Guajava 1AC
275.7	Further] MS1eC, 1EC, 2EC, 3AC; Farther 1AC
275.13	which . . . to be] MS1eC, 1EC, 2EC, 3AC; shown to be identical with 1AC
275.14	identical] MS1eC, 1EC, 2EC, 3AC; the same 1AC
275.16–17	appeared to] MS1eC, 2EC, 3AC; appeared at first to Columbus 1AC

275.17	Bohio.] MS1eC, 1EC, 2EC, 3AC; Bohio. He named this harbor Santa Catalina. 1AC
275.18–19	Catalina . . . described] MS1eC, 1EC, 2EC, 3AC; Catalina at 1AC
275.22–23	and . . . which] MS1eC, 1EC, 2EC, 3AC; and five leagues beyond it still another, which 1AC
275.24	be . . . as] MS1eC, 1EC, 2EC, 3AC; have been 1AC
275.29	on . . . Columbus] MS1eC, 1EC, 2EC, 3AC; on the next day (the 27th November), Columbus 1AC
275.32	supposed it to be an arm] MS1eC, 1EC, 2EC, 3AC; supposed at first that it was an arm 1AC
275.34	landed . . . Columbus] MS1eC, 1EC, 2EC, 3AC; touched at Taco, Columbus 1AC
275.36–37	Santo, he] MS1eC, 1EC, 2EC, 3AC; ~, a distance of sixty leagues, he 1AC
275.39	all of which] MS1eC, 1EC, 2EC, 3AC; These 1AC
275.42	4th of] MS1eC, 1EC, 2EC, 3AC; 4th 1AC
276.4	On taking] MS1eC, 1EC, 2EC, 3AC; On thus taking 1AC
276.6–7	the . . . measured] MS1eC, 1EC, 2EC, 3AC; there remain 100 which measured 1AC
276.12–13	He . . . in] MS1eC, 1EC, 2EC, 3AC; He places Guanahani, his first discovery, in 1AC
276.23	Leon made to] MS1eC, 1EC, 2EC ,3AC; Leon to 1AC
276.23	the . . . remarks.] MS1eC, 1EC, 2EC, 3AC; the remarks of which the following is the substance. 1AC
276.28	24°, . . . Rico] MS1eC, 1EC, 2EC, 3AC; 24°. 1AC
276.32–33	This . . . entirely] MS1eC, 1EC, 2EC, 3AC; These remarks of Herrera are entirely 1AC
276.34	latitudes] MS1eC, 2EC, 3AC, 1EC; altitudes 1AC
276.35	that . . . as] MS1eC, 1EC, 2EC, 3AC; than the dangerous cluster of 1AC
276.37	coast] MS1eC, 1EC, 2EC, 3AC; part 1AC
276.37–39	Cuba, . . . Principe] MS1eC, 1EC, 2EC, 3AC; Cuba. 1AC
276.39	But in] MS1eC, 1EC, 2EC, 3AC; But these latitudes are of no weight, for in 1AC
276.40	altitudes] MS1eC, 1EC, 2EC, 3AC; latitudes 1AC
277.4	The second] MS1eC, 1EC, 2EC, 3AC; To return, the second 1AC
277.8	Isla Larga] MS1eC, 1EC, 2EC, 3AC; Long Island 1AC

277.9	Columbus.] MS1eC, 1EC, 2EC, 3AC; Columbus and of the present day. 1AC
277.10	of islands] MS1eC, 1EC, 2EC, 3AC; of intervening islands 1AC
277.12–13	name . . . San] MS1eC, 1EC, 3AC; name between some of the points visited by Columbus, and those which continue to bear the same names at the present day, as San 1AC
277.13–14	Principe, . . . though] MS1eC, 1EC, 2EC, 3AC; Principe, though 1AC
277.18	should not] MS1eC, 1EC, 2EC, 3AC; ought not to 1AC
277.19	ought to] MS1eC, 1EC, 2EC, 3AC; should 1AC
281.29–35	*In . . . Polo.] 3AC; Ramusio, *tom. ii.* p. 17, ed. Venet. 1606 MS1eC, 1EC, 2EC
281.31–32	principally] 3AC; chiefly MS2eC
282.4	traversed] MS1eC, MS2EC, 3AC; sailed up 1EC, 2EC
282.41–42	entreated] MS1eC, 1EC, 2EC, 3AC; requested MS2eC
283.3	entreated] MS1eC, 1EC, 2EC, 3AC; desired MS2eC
283.35	from thence] MS1eC; thence 3AC
285.4	courtiers] MS1eC, 1EC, 2EC, 3AC; countries 1AC
289.19	many . . . who] MS1eC, MS2eC, 3AC; many who 1EC, 2EC
290.5	Italian.] 3AC; Italian. + / + Mardsen, Travels of M. Polo. Introduction p. XXXII MS2eC
290.38	Prevost, Hist.] MS1eC, 1EC, 2EC; Hist., 1AC, 2AC, 3AC
291.13	conserved] MS1eC, 1AC, 3AC; preserved 1EC, 2EC
291.18	from whence] MS1eC; whence 3AC
292.1–2	to have . . . lights] MS1eC, MS2eC, 3AC; to have afforded the information 1EC, 2EC
292.31–32	Province] MS1eC; province 1EC, 2EC; provinces 1AC, 2AC, 3AC
294.11	if . . . that] MS1eC, 1AC, 3AC; if what Marco Polo relates to be true, that 1EC, 2EC
294.27	can bear] MS1eC, 3AC; bears 1EC, 2EC
296.6	in his] MS1eC, 3AC; on ∼ 1EC, 2EC
299.7	further] MS1eC; farther 3AC
299.27	but] MS1eC, 1AC, 3AC; though 1EC, 2EC
299.33	Feyjoo] MS1eC, MS2eC, 3AC; Teyjoo 1EC
303.17	voyagers] MS1eC, MS2eC, 3AC; navigators 1EC, 2EC
305.35	from thence] MS1eC; thence 3AC

307.8	put down] MS1eC, 3AC; inserted 1EC, 2EC
312.5	Ovando] MS1eC, 3AC; Orando 1EC
312.30	animated] MS1eC, MS2eC, 3AC; energetic 1EC, 2EC
315.9	nor] MS1eC, 3AC; or 1EC, 2EC
315.19	would result profit] MS1eC, 3AC; profit would result 1EC, 2EC
316.33	caution and discrimination] MS1eC, MS2eC, 3AC; caution 1EC, 2EC
316.41–42	on . . . side] MS1eC, 3AC; in a generous and righteous cause 1EC, 2EC
318.17	with] MS1eC, 3AC; excited by 1EC, 2EC
319.42	in regard] MS1eC, 3AC; with respect 1EC, 2EC
320.2–3	as an . . . grave] MS1eC, 3AC; as a contemporary author, grave 1EC, 2EC,
320.39	Gades] MS1eC, 1EC, 2EC, 3AC; Gades (Cadiz) five 1AC, 2AC
321.37	succeed] MS1eC, 3AC; take place 1EC, 2EC
324.14	took] MS1eC, 3AC; collected 1EC, 2EC
329.8	charge] MS1eC, 3AC; place 1EC, 2EC
330.17	came forward] MS1eC, 3AC; appeared 1EC, 2EC
330.25	sister] MS1eC, 1EC, 2EC, 3AC; niece MS2eC
333.20	traversing] MS1eC, 3AC; crossing 1EC, 2EC
333.35	the remote] MS1eC, 3AC; the most remote 1EC, 2EC
333.38	further] MS1eC; farther 3AC
334.26	from whence] MS1eC; whence 3AC
334.29	from whence] MS1eC; whence 3AC
334.41	Feyjoo] MS1eC, 3AC; Teyjoo 1EC
335.35	from whence] MS1eC; whence 3AC
336.32	Basilius] MS1eC, 3AC; Basil 1EC
336.39	Basilius] MS1eC, MS2eC, 3AC; Basil 1EC, 2EC
337.1	smell with] MS1eC, 3AC; the sense of smelling with 1EC, 2EC
337.10	nor] MS1eC, 1EC, 2EC, 3AC; or MS2eC
337.11	nor] MS1eC, 1EC, 2EC, 3AC; or MS2eC
337.12	nor] MS1eC, 1EC, 2EC, 3AC; or MS2eC
338.18	that] MS1eC; which 3AC
339.21	hundred to] MS1eC, 3AC; hundred leagues to 1EC, 2EC
339.26	and maritime charts] MS1eC, 3AC; and charts 1EC
339.38	leaving] MS1eC, 3AC; having 1EC
340.32	disfigured] MS1eC, 3AC; blemished 1EC, 2EC
341.15	his] MS1eC, 2EC, 3AC; this 1EC

343.3	further] MS1eC; farther 3AC
343.30	Bartholomew have] MS1eC, 3AC; Bartholomew shall have 1EC, 2EC
344.25–26	other, . . . for] MS1eC, 3AC; other, for 1EC, 2EC
344.39	is secure] MS1eC, 1EC, MS2eC, 2EC; in secure 3AC
349.16	that] 1E; which ARE
349.39	from whence] 1E; whence ARE
351.30	appeared] ARE; appeared to be 1E
353.20	from thence] 1E; thence ARE
355.14	From thence] 1E; Thence ARE
363.40	forcibly] 1EC, ARE; powerfully 1AC

LIST OF COMPOUND WORDS
HYPHENATED AT END OF LINE

List I includes all compound and possible compound words that are hyphenated at the end of the line in the copy-text. In deciding whether to retain the hyphen or to print the word as a single-word compound (without the hyphen), the editor has made his decision first on the use of each compound word elsewhere in the copy-text; or second, when the word does not appear elsewhere in the copy-text, on Irving's practice in other writings of the period); or finally, if the word does not appear in Irving's other writings of the period, on contemporary American usage. Each word is listed in its editorially accepted form after the page and line number of its appearance in the T text.

List II presents all compounds, or possible compounds, that are hyphenated or separated as two words at the end of the line in the T text. They are listed in the form in which they would have appeared in the T text had they come in midline.

LIST I

4.36	seaman	227.13	meantime
7.25	household	247.26	seaman
8.5	extraordinary	251.4	ear-witness
39.15	anthropophagi	257.13	fisherman
52.4	supernatural	257.15	overtaken
57.28	likewise	267.41	daylight
68.18	without	280.19	something
74.7	ill-starred	294.40	somewhat
91.36	likewise	298.7	law-giver
120.19	undertaken	299.31	eye-witnesses
150.9	undermined	300.29	saints-errant
152.40	redoubled	305.9	supernatural
166.38	overcome	349.9	long-legged
166.42	self-denial	349.10	round-crowned
170.20	hogshead	350.13	bed-room
173.25	hereabout	350.15	pack-saddles

184.30	withdrew	350.17	out-of-the-way
185.33	death-blow	353.7	whitewashed
191.32	undertaking	353.8	bed-rooms
204.24	undertaken	353.41	landing-place
204.27	upright	354.41	vineyard
207.4	outcries	361.3	interwoven
218.29	grandfather	361.18	throughout

LIST II

5.7	high-bred	241.9	eye-witnesses
9.30	undertaken	247.18	foregoing
13.36	themselves	256.8	Malte-Brun
19.4	undertake	257.2	Friseland
56.13	overpowered	257.30	Greenland
76.13	warlike	257.32	Friseland
80.2	subsequent	258.11	Estotiland
88.18	household	259.30	North Sea
91.36	likewise	259.34	Malte-Brun
109.36	bloodhounds	269.18	southwesterly
112.19	sixty seven	274.18	twenty five
112.22	likewise	279.13	sixpence
114.28	twenty six	292.35	Hang-cheu
115.41	likewise	305.9	supernatural
144.22	overwhelmed	307.27	Porto Santo
169.36	offspring	310.10	broken-hearted
170.33	restored	323.19	seventy nine
176.21	step-father	323.28	superintend
178.8	Porto Rico	336.6	hemisphere
179.8	subaltern	340.31	excommunication
180.7	themselves	349.11	spatterdashes
188.24	gulf-stream	350.35	coadjutors
188.39	likewise	352.8	undervalue
199.25	redressed	352.20	vineyards
201.22	Viceroyalty	354.3	warehouses
204.22	Vice Queen	354.38	overlooking
212.28	household	363.31	foregoing